Chinese Creeds
and Customs

Chinese Creeds and Customs

by V. R. Burkhardt

A compilation of the best-selling trilogy

A  Publication

Copyright © 1982 South China Morning Post Ltd
Designed and published by the Publications Division,
South China Morning Post Ltd, Tong Chong Street,
Quarry Bay, Hongkong

Printed by Yee Tin Tong Printing Press Ltd,
Tong Chong Street, Quarry Bay, Hongkong

CONTENTS

Dates of festivals in the Lunar Calendar 1
New Year 7
The Budding or Second Moon 12
The Third Moon 18
The Fourth Moon 30
The Fifth Moon 36
The Lotus Moon 39
The Seventh Moon 41
The Eighth Moon 62
The Ninth Moon 69
The Tenth Moon 72
The Eleventh Moon 74
The Bitter Moon 75
Betrothal, Marriage, & the Status of Women 80
Funerals, Requiem Masses & the Path to Purgatory 96
Feng Shui, Spiritualism, Metamorphoses, Fox Fairies 111
Taoism, Buddhism, Ancestor Worship, Earth Gods & Tree Worship 140
The Eight Immortals 163
A Chinese Bestiary 186
Charms & Talismans 203
The Measurement of Time 219
The Creation 226
Family Lore 229
Societies & Martial Arts 244
Agriculture 251
Some Hong Kong Temples & Monasteries 253
Some Local Lore 277

COLOUR PLATES

Ch'ing Ming Festival: corresponds roughly with Easter 2
Dragon Boat Festival: the big crowd puller 3
Chung Yeung Festival: dissatisfied spirits may be malignant 6
Ch'ing Ming: women and children have to wear the willow catkin 15
An obligatory visit to ancestral spirits 17
Pak Tai Temple in Cheung Chau 19
Bun Festival, Cheung Chau: sacrifice for the spirits of the slain 24
Dragon Boat race: it has everything to recommend it 36
Yu Lan Festival: assuaging the spirit's hunger 43
Mass for the dead: a great faith in the power of the priests 46
'The ghosts have to be satisfied with two services' 49
Seeking the spirits' blessing—Taoist style 54
Appeasing the dead through prayers and offerings 56
Colour and pageantry for 'Hungry Ghosts' 58
Only New Year holidays surpass the Festival of Hungry Ghosts in popularity 60
A fisherman weds: the preliminaries occupy months 90
Food and gifts at a boat people's wedding 93
Funeral rites 97
Mourners at a funeral 99
The coffin is always carried out head first 102
A funeral procession 107
Signs outside a restaurant, one wishing prosperity, and the other greeting a new-born child 115
The One Thousand Buddhas monastery: a revolution through religion 141
Kwan Kung Temple, Cheung Chau: a Taoist sanctuary 144
Taoism's greatest appeal lies in ceremonies connected with the dead 145
Pak Tai Temple, Cheung Chau 147
The shrine at Tang Ancestral Hall at Ha Tsuen Shi 148
Wong Tai Sin Temple 151
A Taoist ceremony: old beliefs 154
Taoist priest: diminishing importance 156
An aspiring monk has his head shaved 159
Initiation ceremony of a Buddhist monk: a challenging religion once,
    . . . forced to accept popular beliefs 161–162
A martial arts class: a mental stimulant as well 246
A strenuous course in self-defence 248
Po Lin Monastery 254
Blessings from a thousand Buddhas 256
Tin Hau Temple, Stanley 258
Taoist Temple on Cheung Chau 261
Ngong Ping Monastery, Lantau 263
Shing Wong Temple (Buddhist) 265
Buddhist monks at prayer 271
Initiation ceremonies at the Buddhist monastery on Lantau 273
Sign of the times: Wong Tai Sin Temple with a high rise building in the background 275

Foreword

The culture and civilisation of China have been a source of constant bafflement to outsiders. Colonel Rudolphe Burkhardt's *Chinese Creeds and Customs*, first published in 1953, was a bold and scholarly attempt to delve into a complex subject. It proved to be a runaway best-seller provoking a second volume in 1955 and a third and final one in 1958.

Fourteen years after this distinguished civil servant's death and 28 years after the publication of the first volume, interest in China and everything Chinese is on the increase. Other books have been written about Chinese creeds and customs but few have rivalled Colonel Burkhardt's contribution. His trilogy remains one of the most definitive on the subject and this compilation, it is hoped, will help laymen and scholars alike.

A word of caution: the reader would do well to remember that all the material here was written in the early '50s and reflects the attitudes and concepts of a bygone era. Utmost care has been taken to preserve Col Burkhardt's observations and comments and to retain the flavour of the times in which he wrote. Even the spellings of places, rites and various gods and spirits have largely been left intact.

The Publishers

DATES OF FESTIVALS IN THE LUNAR CALENDAR

The fact that all Chinese religious festivals follow the lunar calendar, which changes from year to year, is most confusing for foreigners who are interested in these observances. Once the day of the Moon is known, however, the corresponding date can be deduced in a variety of ways. Many of the compradors supply their regular customers with a calendar giving both the foreign and Chinese date, and a knowledge of the numeral characters will supply all the information needed. The day of the moon is also always published in the morning newspaper in the column headed "Coming events". One cannot, however, work far ahead with this without knowing whether there are twenty-nine or thirty days in the particular lunar month.

First Moon

Chinese New Year covers the first three days, which are spent as a family reunion in the home, and then for visits to friends. The 2nd is usually set apart for worshipping the God of Wealth, to pray for his continued patronage in the coming season.

The first ten days of the year are the birthdays of animals and grain.

Li Ch'un (立春), the beginning of spring, may fall on either side of the lunar New Year as it is reckoned by the solar calendar to be six weeks before the vernal equinox, in the western calendar the 4th February. On this day eggs can be stood upright, and in some parts of the country there is a procession with the Spring Ox and his attendant, whose dress gives the farmer an indication of the prospects of the season.

In the North the official holiday ends on the 15th with the Feast of Lanterns, but in the southern provinces the display of them occurs on the Moon Festival in the Eighth month.

On the 18th the Star Gods are worshipped, and on the 19th the Rats' Wedding Day is celebrated, to induce the King of the rodents to divert the depredations of his subjects to those less mindful of their religious obligations.

The "Hundred Gods" are propitiated on the same day, on the principle of ensuring that no Fairy Godmother can take offense at being slighted. Though many of the worshippers are Taoists the divinities of Buddhism are included, to avoid giving offense, and national heroes, who have been canonised, such as Kuan Kung, Yueh Fei and Lu Pan, the master builder.

The Second Moon

Known also as the "Budding Moon"; Imperial sacrifices were offered to the sun, promoter of all growth, and the agricultural population propitiated the farm gods. It is usually the time when insects arouse from hibernation and, as the Chinese say, "the dragon raises his head". The date is fixed as the 6th March in the western calendar and, in the South, women worship the White Tiger. They may be seen carrying paper images of the beast which, when introduced into the house, keep off rats and snakes and prevent quarrels.

On the 19th is celebrated the birthday of Kuan Yin (觀音), the Buddhist Goddess of Mercy. This is a great occasion in all monasteries and temples of the faith, but the Saint enjoys such popularity that her shrine is found in practically all Taoist temples, and numerous devotees bring their offerings to her altar in the rival establishment.

It is always appropriate to worship Monkey, the Great Sage equal to Heaven (齊天大聖), but his official birthday is on the 23rd. Like Kuan Yin, he is common to both religions, though he was instrumental in bringing the true Buddhist scriptures from India, and his exploits before his conversion were anything but saintly.

The Third Moon

The anniversary of the Spirit of the North, Pei Ti (北帝), is kept on the 3rd. Half a dozen temples are dedicated to this saint in Hong Kong, and his image is to be found in many more. As most of his miracles in life were connected with the southern provinces, his reputation is somewhat local.

Ch'ing Ming (清明) on 5th April corresponds roughly with Easter. It is practically universally observed for ancestral worship, and thousands of Chinese visit their family graves on the mainland to worship and sacrifice.

The great festival of the month is the birthday of the Queen of Heaven (天后) on the 23rd. Being the patron saint of fishermen, the Boat People make a pilgrimage in decorated junks to Tai Miao (大廟), her great temple in Joss House Bay. Hourly ferries are run for the convenience of other worshippers. So great is her popularity that twenty-four temples in Hong Kong are dedicated to her, and her birthday is observed as the annual village holiday. There are processions, lion dancers and crackers galore, the proceedings ending with the shooting for the luck of the year.

The Cheung Chau festival to propitiate the souls of all animals and fish killed for human consumption during the past year may take place at the end of the Third, or beginning of the Fourth Moon. The date is indeterminate, as it is fixed by casting lots in the temple to secure a time approved by the island's patron Saint. The outstanding features of this religious observance, which spreads over four days, are the mountains of buns which form the sacrifice, and the procession of the Gods on the final day. The cortège accompanying the divinities

Ch'ing Ming Festival . . . corresponds roughly with Easter

Dragon Boat Festival . . . the big crowd puller

is interspersed with bands, lion dancers, and tableaux of various legendary and historical scenes enacted by young children carried on floats. Their arrangement is a marvel of ingenuity, and the effect is spectacular.

The Fourth Moon

On the 8th, exactly a fortnight after the Queen of Heaven's feast, is the birthday of Tam Kung (譚公) the secondary patron of the Boat People. The decorated junks are again put into commission, and a pilgrimage is made to the temple on the quayside at Shaukiwan. Usually about twenty of the lightermen's craft from Yaumati attend, whilst those from Causeway Bay bring their sacrifices by lorry. The worship and offerings are exactly the same as those for the Queen of Heaven at Joss House Bay, and the temple is much more accessible. The only disadvantage is that the date sometimes clashes with that of the Cheung Chau Bun festival and it is impossible to be present at both.

The same day is kept by the Buddhists as the birthday of Gautama, or Sakyamuni, the founder of their religion, and before it a night service for the annual washing of the images is held.

Two of the most popular of the Eight Immortals (八仙), Lu T'ung-pin (呂洞賓) and Han Chung-li (漢鍾離), have their birthdays on the 14th and 15th.

The Fifth Moon

The "Double Fifth" is the Chinese summer holiday and is marked by the Dragon Boat Races, which are a great feature of Hong Kong. The main contests take place just inside the western limits of the harbour, off the swimming club at Kennedy Town, where eight or nine boats compete. There is also a large crowd at Aberdeen, to see the two local dragons fight it out with visitors from Stanley and Lamma island. The races commemorate the death of a virtuous official Ch'ü Yuan (屈原), whose body was never found when he drowned himself in the T'ung T'ing lake to lend force to his unheeded protests about the decadence of the court, and the consequent collapse of government.

Though his official birthday is in the Third Moon, Yao Wang (藥王), the Celestial doctor, receives the bulk of his offerings at this time, his services being in most demand on the "Dangerous Fifth" when summer epidemics are most prevalent. Dealers in protective talismans also find a ready market for their wares.

On the 13th is the birthday of Kuan Ti (關帝), the Chinese Bayard, who is worshipped by high and low alike as the symbol of loyalty and devotion to duty. His image is not only in every temple, but often in private houses, and he is the patron of innumerable trades and societies.

The Sixth Moon

In this moon the monsoons should reach the North, bringing the rain to promote the growth of the crops. Should it be retarded, prayers are offered to Lung Wang (龍王) the Dragon King and, if he fails to respond, his image is exposed to the sun, to bring home to him the results of his negligence.

The "Double Sixth" is purely a Buddhist observance known as Airing the Classics, in commemoration of a disaster which overtook the scriptures on their journey from India.

Lu Pan (魯班), the canonised architect, and patron of the building trade, is commemorated by a big feast on the 13th of the Sixth Moon.

The Fire God, whose birthday is on the 22nd, is more honoured in the South than in the North. The divinity Huo Sheng (火聖) is also worshipped during and after a conflagration, as his red crow is supposed to be flying about, endangering adjacent buildings.

Ma Wang (馬王) patron of horses is worshipped on the 23rd, in those parts of the country where the animals are used for transport.

The 24th is the birthday of the Lotus and an occasion for making up parties to view the blooms.

The Seventh Moon

Two striking festivals fall in the Seventh Moon, which should be of interest to foreigners as most of the ritual is performed in the open, and the worshippers are complimented by their patronage. The first, held on the eve of the "Double Seventh", is the unmarried women's worship of the two star Gods, the Celestial Weaver and her lover the Cowherd. Only on this night of the year are they allowed to meet, and the girls make every preparation to facilitate their reunion and provide for their entertainment. Stalls are erected with offerings of fruit, samples of embroidery, and often miniature bedroom furniture. The gifts include paper clothing for the Weaver and her six sisters as well as her lover, and trays containing sets of toilet accessories and personal ornaments which are displayed on the walls above the altar. Various trades, like the newspaper sellers and hawkers, combine together and compete to mount the most elaborate show in honour of their patron. The streets in the residential quarters are thronged with sight-seers, and the maidens wear all their jewellery. A short service is held at midnight when the paper sacrifices are burned and the donors sit down to their annual feast.

The festival of the Hungry Ghosts dates from the introduction of Buddhism in which religion it is known as the Magnolia Festival (孟蘭) The Chinese believe that the spirits of those bereft of the consolations of ancestral worship are malignant, and may claim living substitutes, unless they are pacified by food. Universal sacrifices are accordingly offered on the 15th of the Seventh Moon to assuage their hunger, and gain their gratitude.

Almost every household burns paper clothing and incense outside their doors as a protective measure. Community celebrations of this charitable almsgiving may take place at any time between the full moon and the end of the month, when the spirits are supposed to end their long vacation from purgatory. The Boat People club together by families and friends, and select a day when they have no contract to fulfil. Three junks are used. On one of these a puppet show to entertain the ghosts runs a continuous performance. On a second a religious service is held, before the third vessel makes a round of the harbour, scattering paper clothing and money as it goes, and heaving to at seven stations to launch paper boats and distribute vegetarian food. The junk on this mission of mercy for the souls of the drowned is beflagged, and carries an immense paper image of Yen Lo (閻羅), King of the Underworld, lashed to the mast on the fo'cstle. Five priests chant the office for the dead accompanied by a band. A final service ending just before midnight is held at the anchorage, ending with the burning of the paper images.

The Water Folk complete the festival in a single day but, in the various villages and wards, four nights and three days are allotted. The last two are the most spectacular as a night service is held on each, the first for the benefit of the fishermen, and the second for the villagers. The children serve eighteen or twenty-seven altars for the burning of paper clothing and money for the dead; whilst the priests conduct a service of dedication. In the afternoon of the last day there is a procession through the streets, with a service and the symbolic release of a bird and a fish. The proceedings end on the last night with a gigantic bonfire of the paper images, and a resounding burst of crackers.

On the 15th the confectioners start selling Moon Cakes for which the Chinese have a veritable passion. They are available only for a month up to the mid-autumn festival, after which the moulds are put away for the year.

The Eighth Moon

This corresponds to the Harvest Moon, when the crops are in and heavy work in the fields is over, affording time for relaxation. The Paper Shops are full of lanterns of every shape and colour, which are bought to decorate the house for the worship of the full moon on the night of the 15th. Women only can perform the sacrifices to the planet, and her altar is erected in the courtyard, or on a flat roof. Outsiders consequently see little of the ceremony, which is performed by the younger members supervised by an elder relative.

In country districts, however, over the period of the full moon, spiritualistic séances and ritualistic dances are performed, and there is usually a large audience of both sexes.

The Ninth Moon

The first nine days of this moon are considered the most favourable for communications with the dead, as restrictions in the underworld are lifted. Wise women, who act as mediums between descendants and ancestors, are consequently in great demand to interpret the advice or wishes of departed relatives.

On the "Double Ninth", the equivalent of All Souls' Day is celebrated, when the graves are visited, and cleared of the summer growth. Sacrifices of money and winter clothing against the cold season are offered, after which the worshippers picnic in the open. It coincides with the festival known as "Mounting the Heights" (登高) when it is considered lucky to climb to a high place to commemorate a Chinese Lot, who escaped a plague on this anniversary by taking to the mountains with his family. Every hill top in Hong Kong is crowded with picnickers on this day, and long queues wait their turn for the Peak tram.

The 25th is the birthday of the City Gods (城隍) whose duty is to care for the souls of their dead parishioners, and to ward off epidemics which might add to their responsibilities. They are all historical characters, canonised for their virtuous lives and incorruptibility.

The Tenth Moon

In the North the final visit of the year to the family tombs is carried out on the 1st of the Tenth Moon instead of on the "Double Ninth".

The Buddhists observe the 5th as the birthday of Bodidharma, or Ta Mo the first Chinese patriarch, who reached Canton about A.D. 526.

The 6th is observed as the Festival of the Five Rulers, identified with the Five Sacred Mountains. They are intimately connected with Canton, which owes its name of the "City of Rams" to their visit riding on these animals. After promising immunity from famine, they left their petrified mounts as an earnest of good faith.

The Eleventh Moon

The chief event of the Eleventh Moon is the winter solstice which must fall within its limits. It is observed on 22nd December by the worship of the Nature Gods, such as sacred trees and rocks, which are to be found in every village. The small shrines of the Earth Gods and divinities of the soil and fertility also receive their meed of incense and offerings.

The Twelfth Moon

A preliminary feast before the New Year is held on the 8th of the Twelfth Moon, for which housewives prepare a dish of various forms of grains and dried fruits, flavoured with radish. In Hong Kong there is no rigid adherence to the date, and it is made in vast quantities throughout the month, to be consumed at home or exchanged with friends and relatives.

On the 20th house cleaning begins, and supplies are laid in for the New Year feast.

The Kitchen God is seen off to make his annual report on the family's behaviour on the night of the 23rd, with plenty of crackers to speed him on his celestial journey. Preparations continue during the final seven days, known as "Little New Year", free from his supervision of the

behaviour of the household. The month's extra salary, paid according to the Chinese custom of reckoning thirteen moons to the year, comes in handy for settling debts, and buying presents and food for the holiday. During this period a fair is held, both on the Hong Kong and Kowloon sides of the harbour, with over three hundred stalls in each, mainly for the sale of floral decorations which are regarded as an essential part of the festivities. This is most crowded on New Year's eve, when the customers hope that the salesmen will reduce their prices rather than be faced with a dead loss. The stationers do a brisk trade in red envelopes stamped with gold designs, which are in great demand for the distribution of "Lucky Money". All children, and unmarried girls are entitled to this, when they pay their New Year calls with their parents, and "Lucky Money" is also presented to tradesmens' boys and the performers of daily serices. Servants of friends bringing presents are likewise rewarded, so the red covers are stocked in quantities by every prudent housewife.

Chung Yeung Festival . . . dissatisfied spirits may be malignant

NEW YEAR

The advent of the Republic (1911) ushered in the Western calendar for official use, and January 1st was recognised as New Year's Day but, for the great bulk of the population, the festivities and rites connected with Chinese New Year are observed with undiminished enthusiasm. No foreigner can fail to note the complete dislocation of all normal activities and, should he be a householder, his monthly wage bill will remind him of the festive season. The full lunar year in China is one of thirteen months, and custom has dictated that salaries should be paid on a thirteen- instead of a twelve-month basis, the double issue falling at the most convenient moment for the recipient, who has his debts to pay, and numerous outgoings in the shape of seasonal presents. The outward and visible signs of the passing year are the closing of the shops, the appearance of new red door papers, and the almost continuous detonation of crackers. The actual ceremonies take place in the home, behind closed doors and, though much more interesting, they are far less obtrusive.

No one goes to bed on the night of the 30th of the twelfth moon, but all sit up to welcome in the New Year (Shou Sui 守歲). Friends and relations in ceremonial garments greet each other, and take leave of the Old Year (Tze Sui 辭歲). After dinner, attended by all generations, the children bow to their parents who give them lucky money to guarantee another year of life. Then the courtyard is strewn with branches of sesame, fir and cypress. This is first trampled, and then set on fire to mark the passing of the year. The origin of this custom appears to be to ensure that no evil spirit is lurking to enter with the New Year. There is always the chance of a visit from the Skin Tiger (皮虎), who steals the cakes of the poor to carry them to the rich on the assumption that, as they have lived on the wealthy during the year, it is equitable to make some return for favours.

Crackers are let off as an additional precaution, and the lamp is lit at the shrine of the Kitchen God who is due back from his Celestial visit. The doors of the house are locked and sealed. At dawn anyone who has gone to bed gets up, and the master of the house unlocks the doors, and removes the seals, uttering a few words of good omen for prosperity in the coming year. This ceremony is called "Opening the gate of Fortune" (K'ai Ts'ai Men 開財門).

The first thing the master does on the opening is to worship Heaven and Earth. Sticks of incense are ignited on a high candlestick facing the entrance, and the head of the family arms himself with a large branch of sesame, paper representations of the gods and an inscription of thanks for the beneficence of the two estates. This is burned amid a burst of crackers.

Accompanied by the male members of the family, the master then makes three deep bows before the family gods and the ancestral tablets. The altar is garnished with the usual Wu Kung (五供), an incense burner flanked with two candles, and two vases of flowers. The ceremony is named Pai Chia T'ang (拜家堂), or saluting the Family Hall. The Kitchen God, who has returned overnight, is also entitled to three bows, two candles, and his ration of incense. Women are excluded from the ceremony and if any, from excess of devotion, bow down before these deities, it does not count to them for righteousness. The master of the house, as the head of the family, is the sole representative qualified to offer the sacrifices as he is responsible to the gods for all his clan. In the South, a wooden receptacle, filled to the top with rice, is placed on the altar, surrounded with flowers, branches of cypress (the emblem of longevity) and ten pairs of chopsticks. The service is called "Presenting the New Year's rice", and is a thanksgiving for the mercies of the past year, which is repeated in the hope of continued favours when the dawn of the coming season is saluted.

No outsiders are invited to these family feasts for seeing the Old Year out, which is known as the "making up feast for the New Year". All quarrels are supposed to be forgotten, and it is an occasion for general reconciliation. Outlying members of the family make a point of attending, and it is seldom that less than twelve sit down to table.

The God of Wealth

For a few thousand years, prior to the levelling of incomes under the new dispensation, there were no more ardent worshippers of Mammon than all classes of Chinese society. Rich and poor alike cultivated his favours, for no one could have too much money. The poor needed it to raise themselves above the level of starvation, and with the rich it created a vicious circle, in that wealth tended to increase the family and the number of dependants for whom provision had to be made in accordance with the laws of Confucius. The shrine of Ts'ai Shen Yeh (財神爺) was to be found in nearly every home, and his temples were very numerous as were the forms under which he was worshipped. Under the name of Lu Hsing (祿星), the Star God of Affluence, he is worshipped on the 20th day of the Seventh Moon, but normally a visit is paid to his temple very early in the New Year, when the Essential Family Gods have been propitiated.

In the South there is a belief that one god of wealth is responsible for one's earnings, or fixed income, whilst a totally different entity brings windfalls, cash sweeps, and gambling increment. The former was a deified hermit from O Mei Shan in Szechuan, named Marshal Ch'ao Kung-ming, to whom all Chinese Emperors rendered homage on the Second day of the First Moon. His history is reminiscent of the Norse legend of Balder, and the medieval waxen images for the destruction of an enemy. Summoned to fight for the High Priest of Taoism, he had achieved considerable success; but his enemy made a straw image of his person and, after forty-nine days of incantations, shot it through the heart and eyes with peach-wood arrows. In life he could, and did, ride a black tiger, and he used pearls with devastating effect as hand-grenades. These accomplishments ensured him a posthumous divinity, and he obtained release from the underworld. His image holding a silver ingot is almost as universal as that of the Kitchen God.

Ch'ao Kung-ming's (趙公明) predilection for his peculiar charger evidently persisted after death, for he is always depicted astride his tiger, brandishing a steel whip. It is as much his attribute as the Dragon with which the Patron Saint of England is perpetually engaged. The explanation of his black face is more difficult but, south of the Yangtze at any rate, he is identified or connected with one of the Five Rulers, who visited Canton leaving their ram steeds behind them. The Jade Ruler is believed to have appointed Marshal Ch'ao as Hsuan T'an (玄壇), Ruler of the North and associated with black as a colour. The Taoists in consequence always place his effigy on the north side of their shrines.

Very often he is accompanied on the cartoon by two supporters, Chen Chia-kung and Yao Hsiao-ssu, generals who fell in action under his command. Two boys, Hsiao Shen and Ts'ao Pao, are attached to his staff as distributors of his blessings.

There are various explanations of the connection of the number five with this universal deity. Some consider that the essential Gods of the Household, Kitchen, Door and Gate Guardians were banded together to produce him, each contributing something to the result. One of the Door Gods, Yu Ch'ih Ching Te, certainly has a black face which lends colour to the theory. Chinese religion is remarkably free from eroticism, but their primitive faith did recognise Five Spirits, known as the Wu Sheng who were worshipped to keep off disease in the farmers' poultry-yards and pig-sties. They were sometimes identified with the spirits of badgers, weasels and small deer, and were highly popular under the Mings. The prudish Manchu Dynasty, however, took exception to them as indecent little gods, as they claimed brides who already had husbands, and were a disturbing influence in marital life. The throne prohibited their veneration, but was powerless to root them out of people's memories.

The South, being furthest from Imperial control, took little or no notice of the ban, and even near Peking their shrines, somewhat resembling dog-kennels, may be seen on the outskirts of many villages. Sometimes their temples were dedicated to other gods, notably Kuan Kung, the Patron Saint of the Manchus, and in one case near Peking they were deliberately kept in being under the guise of the God of Wealth, who is thus multiplied into a fivefold personality. These are the gods generally addressed by gamblers, as they are more concerned with the casual acquisition of riches than with settled incomes. As the spirits of hedgehogs and weasels are less commendable to the Chinese than those of human origin, they have been furnished with a plausible biography to justify their inclusion in the pantheon. Originally five notorious bandit brothers, they finally paid their debt to society by the executioner's sword. Their redeeming quality was that, like Robin Hood, they robbed the rich to give to the poor. Consequently their shades are more likely to answer the petitions of the indigent than of those who exacted the penalty for their depredations.

A candidate for the mantle of the God of Wealth, dating from the legendary era, is Pi Kan (比干), a sage of the twelfth century B.C. related to the infamous Emperor Chou Hsin, last ruler of the Shang Dynasty. Pi Kan took him to task for his wickedness, whereupon the tyrant caused an operation to be performed on his heart to discover whether it had seven orifices. This proved fatal, but his virtues were recognised by his subsequent deification as the Civil God of Wealth. Ch'ao Kung-ming, from a similarity of profession, has more appeal to the Military. It is to be suspected, however, that they are more concerned with courting the favours of those deities who cater for casual windfalls, as payment of a regular salary to soldiers in China was ever regarded as a superfluous extravagance, and they were driven to live on the country whether it were hostile or friendly.

The image of the God of Wealth, like that of the Kitchen Prince, was usually kept in the home, and was ceremoniously burned, and replaced by a new one. On New Year's afternoon poor children went from door to door with these gaudy posters crying, "We have brought you a new Ts'ai Shen (財神)! Here he is under his money tree, whose fruits are gold, and its branches are bowed down with coins." Men gave freely, as they hoped to receive abundantly. Those who visited the temple usually consulted the omens, after making their obeisance and leaving their offerings. An old priest had charge of a hollow bamboo, in which he rattled numbered tally slips. The tube was shaken till a stick dropped out, and a book was consulted for the motto which corresponded to the number. In the South, a platform was sometimes erected before Ts'ai Shen's shrine, and a wooden mortar was loaded with a small charge of powder for the propulsion of a hollow rattan ball. This was fired into the air above the crowd of worshippers, and the lucky man who caught it as it fell was presented, in the name of the god, with an ornament for his ancestral altar. The same method is used in Hong Kong among the Boat People at the Festivals of T'ien Hou and Tam Kung, to determine the Luck of the Year.

New Year Customs

During the New Year Festival no cutting implement, such as knife or scissors, may be used in the house, so all food is prepared and made ready for the table on the preceding days. Gifts are exchanged between all friends and relatives. In the North, the customary presents for relations consist of clothing, but food is the universal manifestation of goodwill. As a rule, politeness demands that not all the contents of the basket shall be accepted, and a portion should be returned as an indication that the gift is too generous. A duck will be divided in half, and the original donor is then at liberty to send the remnant to some less important acquaintance. In all cases, the messenger must be rewarded, and "Lucky Money" placed in the receptacle which contained the gift. "Lucky Money" is enclosed in special red envelopes with a design in gold. This usually carries the double Hsi (囍) for marital bliss, the characters Ta Chi (大吉) "great luck", and Ta Li (大利) "great advantage". The pictorial design includes the peach and pine of longevity, and the carp, symbol of success through endeavour. The carp was the stimulant to students to pass their examinations, for through his persistence he forced his way upstream against the rapids, and was rewarded by achieving the status of a dragon. The pine, being evergreen, conveys a wish for a vigorous old age. In the South, the cypress is often used as a substitute.

The first day of the New Year, or at any rate the morning, is spent within doors, and is sacred as a family reunion. All members who are within reach make every endeavour to attend, unless positively bedridden. The individual is so dependent on the family that one wonders at the fate of the student, returned from overseas study, whose outlook on life has been changed by his associations, and who can have little in common with the old traditions. As a rule he has not substituted a new code of ethics for those he has discarded from materialistic enlightenment, and he runs the risk of using his education more for personal aggrandisement than for the common weal. The Chinese have been accustomed to shoulder obligations without rights, whereas the Western world is going to the other extreme, and demands rights without obligations.

For the first five days of the New Year women are not supposed to go out, though the men pay calls on relatives and friends to wish them the compliments of the season. On the evening of the first day there is a great traffic in the sale of pictures of the God of Wealth, whose birthday is celebrated on the morrow. On the morning of the second day, the old paper god is taken down, and burned in the courtyard or street, and a fresh effigy is installed with incense and firecrackers. Sacrifice is also offered, according to the means of the family. When the offering is placed on the table before the picture, a cup of fiery wine is ignited, and the head of the family makes the threefold kow-tow.

To many people food is a subject of absorbing interest. Even Alice, in "Through the Looking-glass", when introduced to the Bread and Butter, and Rocking-horse Fly, demanded what they lived on. Chinese festivals, like their Western counterparts of Shrove Tuesday, Christmas, and Thanksgiving Day, are usually accompanied by some characteristic dish which varies in different districts according to the raw material available. Poverty is so widespread, and incomes among the labouring classes are so low, that meat is rarely on the bill of fare, but every family will endeavour to raise a dish of pork dumplings to celebrate New Year.

Among the more wealthy the feast is varied by the presents of food contributed by friends and relations, and a whole roast pig takes the place of our Christmas turkey, whilst chickens and ducks form the side dishes. All must be prepared before midnight on New Year's eve. The head and tail of the pig, wings and legs of the chicken are removed, and stored in the family rice bin for consumption on the second day.

The traditional feast to celebrate the departure of the Kitchen God consists of doughnuts composed of sticky rice with a filling of some sort of sweet preserve, to induce a favourable report on the behaviour of the family. For New Year itself, large fried balls of sweetmeats, some plain and some stuffed, are baked to tell the future. Their shape is symbolic of the complete round of the year so, if they turn out fluffy and spherical, luck will be assured, whereas a mis-shapen, heavy batch portends ill fortune.

The banquet takes place on the vigil, New Year itself being observed as a fast day on which no meat is eaten. Theoretically only vegetables and bean-curd cooked in oil, and not lard, should appear on the table. In sending food presents certain vegetarian dishes are included to conform with this observance. Some families are not as strict as others in the abstention from meat, and include it in the evening meal, but breakfast, the first meal of the year, is usually vegetarian. Children are deliberately kept awake all night as this ensures their parents' longevity.

On the second day a rooster, not a capon, should figure as the principal dish. This is probably a relic of sun worship, as the herald of the dawn has his abode in the sun whose appearance he daily salutes. At any other time the Chinese consider the flesh of the cock to be rank poison, but its toxic properties are neutralised on this occasion. In Kwangtung Province the other concomitants of the meal are dace, fresh-water mussels and oysters, as their names in combination produce an auspicious motto for the coming season.

The well must also be reopened on this day, with a special prayer to the spirit which guards it, for a continued supply of pure water. When the first bucketful is raised candles are lit, incense is burned and the usual salute of firecrackers is accorded. Before closing the well-head on New Year's eve, decorations consisting of sacred pictures, red streamers, and an inscription requesting the continuance of past favours, are arranged against a rock overlooking the orifice.

The red papers with auspicious inscriptions are usually obtained from the shops devoted to the sale of religious accessories, but occasionally a decayed scholar, whose savings have vanished in opium dreams, sets up a table and stool in the village street, and augments the earnings of his wife by capitalising his dexterity with the brush. Some of his stock-in-trade consists of the usual stereotyped desires for health, wealth and happiness, but he has on hand a supply of blanks which he is prepared to inscribe at the dictation of his client. An inscription which enjoys considerable local popularity is an invocation to the T'ien Kuan to descend and bestow happiness. The Taoist Trinity of the T'ien Kuan (天官), Heaven, Ti Kuan (地官), Earth, and Shui Kuan (水官), Water, represents happiness, forgiveness of sins, and delivery from evil, respectively. Their cult is particularly prevalent in Fukien Province for averting calamity and disease. They also act as recording angels of the virtues and crimes of mortals, so that on their birthdays no capital punishments were inflicted.

The calligraphist, in addition to producing lucky invocations, also provides certain of the Household Gods for, in the South, these divinities are more often represented by the inscriptions denoting them than by their portraits. The Kitchen God is almost invariably indicated by the two characters for Stove King (竈王), or Prince. Even the squatters' huts at this time of the year sport red paper to mark the abode of the Earth God's Happy Spirit just outside the ramshackle door.

In the village T'u Ti (土地) shrines, constructed of brick, the deity is often represented by a pointed stone, a relic of a much more primitive worship, though occasionally a clay image of the Earth God shares a corner of the altar. A gilt talisman is pasted at New Year on the stone, with three more on the lintel of the door. Red scrolls are hung on the side posts, proclaiming that yellow gold is bestowed upon the lucky man, a reassuring statement in these days of shortage of hard currency.

No worship is performed on New Year's day itself, but at midnight all the junks come in illuminated with the pressure lamps normally used to attract the fish, and burning masses of paper in honour of their Patron Saints. The second day is heralded with a roar of crackers to attract the attention of the Queen of Heaven, Tam Kung, and Hung Hsing, who hold the fishermen's fortunes in their hands.

As China depends so largely on agriculture, the fortunes of domestic animals are of considerable concern to their owners, and the first ten days of the year are devoted to their birthdays. Should the weather be fine, with an absence of wind or rain, it will be a good year for the beast commemorated. Thus, the first day of the year is dedicated to chickens, the second to dogs, the third to pigs, and the fourth to ducks. Cattle have their birthdays on the fifth, horses on the sixth. The year will be good or bad for human beings according to the outlook on the seventh. Rice and cereals take the eighth, whilst fruits and vegetables know their fate on the ninth. Corn and barley prospects are determined by the weather on the tenth day.

There is a belief that on the Li Ch'un (立春), or first day of Spring, it is possible to stand an egg on end upright on the ground. Anyone interested in the phenomenon can try the experiment for himself, and will probably discover that it can be performed on any other day as well, the chief desiderata being a mat surface such as a table-cloth, and a steady hand. A certain amount of friction is essential, and the egg is unlikely to remain upright on a porcelain plate, unless the expedient devised by Columbus is adopted. Anyway it worked with an abnormally long egg on the rough cover of an album on an off-day as far as the opening of Spring was concerned.

Very early in the morning of the sixth day all merchants and shopkeepers rise early to worship all the gods, a sort of vicarious exercise to ensure that no evilly-disposed fairy godmother is omitted. They are represented as gilt figures on yellow paper, and the picture is bought on the last day of the Old Year, and worshipped during the first five days of the New. On the morning of the sixth, it is taken out into the street and burned to the accompaniment of incense and crackers. When the last cracker has spent itself, the shutters are taken down, and business is resumed in the shops.

This old custom is not so rigorously adhered to in modern times and most shops do not stay shut for the full period of five days, though some of the prosperous businesses can afford the full holiday.

The stars are supposed to exert such an influence on Chinese lives that it is not surprising that they are honoured early in the year. During the third watch (11 pm–1 am) an altar is set in the courtyard, facing north, with two coloured prints representing the Star Gods, and the cyclical signs. The Master of the House first worships the group, and then the particular god who presides over his own birthday. Three to five bowls of rice balls, cooked in sugar and flour, form the offering, but a hundred and eight little lamps with red and yellow paper wicks are ignited whilst the head of the household performs his prostrations. These burn out in a matter of minutes, and then the boys of the family take their turn

in lighting three before their own special star, their prospects being determined by the length of time the flame flickers.

The womenfolk are debarred from the actual worship, but join in the consumption of the offerings.

In the North the official holiday ends on the 15th with the Feast of Lanterns, but in the southern provinces the display of them occurs on the Moon Festival in the Eighth month.

The Beginning of Spring

The great majority of Chinese festivals are observed according to the Lunar calendar, and consequently vary every year of the Gregorian mode of reckoning time, which is based on the time taken by the earth to circumnavigate the sun. The Chinese system, if followed exclusively, would make the seasons for sowing and reaping vary by as much as a lunar month, so they have divided the solar year into twenty-four fortnightly periods of fifteen days each. The climate is so regular that the appellation of each period invariably denotes the kind of weather to be expected, and the change is nearly always noticeable on the exact day fixed by the calendar. Foreigners in North China were often surprised by their servant making preparations to paste up windows on a blazing day in October but, on going out after lunch, they would find a drop of twenty degrees in the thermometer, and admit his sagacity in following the calendar rather than the evidence of his senses.

Li Ch'un (立春) (Establishment of Spring) falls every year about 4th February, fairly near to that movable feast, Chinese New Year's Day, which is reckoned to fall on the day of the first new moon after the sun enters the constellation Aquarius. It so happened that in 1952 Chinese New Year was early, 25th January, but Li Ch'un, keeping its place in the solar calendar, came after, and not before, New Year's Day. The effect of this was that 1951 was a "blind" year, and had no Establishment of Spring. This was perfectly disastrous for the superstitious element of the population, for it is considered most unlucky for a child to start its education in a year which has no Li Ch'un. It means missing a whole year of education, and some of the primary schools are likely to have a lean intake.

In the North, where the calendar was compiled, Li Ch'un marked an abrupt transition from the Ta Han or Great Cold fortnight which preceded it. It was a definite end to the skating, and coolies set to work dismantling the matshed which protected the ice from the sun's rays.

The festival is entirely bound up with agriculture, and no peasant was supposed to plough his land until certain appropriate sacrifices had been performed by the Head of the State, and, in the Provinces, by the local magistrates. The rites were originally connected with the worship of the Soil Gods, and included the slaughter of an ox. This, as enlightenment and an urge for economy dictated, eventually was replaced by a clay effigy, much as human sacrifice gave place to the substitution of a domestic animal. In recent days, the value of the sacrifice has degenerated like the currency, and the gods have to be satisfied with a paper ox or water-buffalo. Fukien Province held out the longest against Chinese civilisation, and persisted until quite recently in butchering a buffalo, whose carcass was divided among the officials.

A procession, in which the Spring Ox (春牛) was the principal feature, was organised to celebrate the occasion. Very occasionally a real ox was used for the purpose, led by a child, who probably in unenlightened days formed part of the sacrifice. Now both are made of stiff paper. As the new calendar was available at the time, the ox and various traditional figures were painted according to its predictions. The crowd of holiday makers, many of whom were totally illiterate and could derive no benefit from the perusal of the document itself, were thus enabled to absorb a certain number of warnings from the conventional colours employed. If the head of the ox were painted yellow, great heat would be experienced in the summer. Green betokened sickness in the spring, whilst red foretold a drought. Black stood for an overabundance of rain, and white a warning of high winds and storms. The Meng Shen, or Spirit Driver (夢神), also acted as a tipster for, if he had some form of head-dress, the year would be dry. No hat meant rain, whilst shoes indicated torrential downfalls. A barefooted driver meant drought, whilst great heat was portrayed by heavy clothing, and cold by light. The Meng Shen, being a spirit, reacts to the vagaries of the elements in exactly the opposite way to a normal man, so he puts on a fur coat in July, and wallows naked in December snows. If he wore a red belt, usually a sign of rejoicing, it consequently meant much sickness and mortality, whilst the white cincture of mourning betokened a light casualty list.

The Spring procession was brought three times to a halt by a cavalier, who dismounted in front of the magistrate, and promised him promotion, for which he received a luck penny in cash. On arrival at an open space on the east side of the city, the magistrate and his yamen staff went through the motions of beating and prodding the buffalo to stimulate it to work as an example to the farmers. This had to be done with bamboo poles decorated with strips of coloured paper at the exact hour when spring began. This auspicious moment was determined by placing a large hollow bamboo upright in the ground, with chicken feathers in it. As the feathers fly upward from the first breeze, which is supposed to arise the moment the ox is beaten, the onlookers are appraised that spring has really arrived. The ceremony ends by burning the effigies, while the crowd scrambles for the charred embers as talismans of luck. The officials then go home and change their fur robes for spring clothing.

In some provinces, the sacrifice of the Spring Ox took place at an altar erected to the God of Agriculture which would connect the rites with some bygone notion of promoting the fertility of the crops. The beating of the animal probably represents an effort to stimulate the spring and accelerate the fruitfulness of the soil, though this meaning has been lost, and the popular belief is that it drives off diseases which usually assume epidemic form with the passing of the frost.

Occasionally the flails, instead of being of bamboo, are willow branches and the vital energy of the tree, which symbolises the Sun, is transmitted to the Ox to carry out his task of driving away the winter. According to the Book of Rites, "The Clay Ox at Li Ch'un escorts the cold away."

On the 18th the Star Gods are worshipped, and on the 19th the Rats Wedding Day is celebrated, to induce the King of the rodents to divert the depredations of his subjects to those less mindful of their religious obligations.

The "Hundred Gods" are propitiated on the same day, on the principle of ensuring that no Fairy Godmother can take offense at being slighted. These include some of the oldest divinities of the Chinese Nature Cult, figures of Heaven and Earth, the Dragon Kings, Household, and City Gods, Confucius and his disciples, the Star divinities and Saints of the Seasons. There are also the dispensers of Luck and Longevity, of Medicine and of various diseases, ministers of thunder, lightning and of water. Though many of the worshippers are Taoists the divinities of Buddhism are included, to avoid giving offense, and national heroes, who have been canonised, such as Kuan Kung, Yueh Fei and Lu Pan, the master builder.

THE BUDDING OR SECOND MOON

By the second month the Sun has appreciably gained in strength, and the "plants on the mountain are changed to jade". In other words, every small leaf and bud is preparing to greet the giver of life. It is consequently appropriate that the human race, which owes its sustenance to the beneficence of that heavenly body, should worship him in the early days of the Second Moon. In Peking, the Temple of the Sun is outside the eastern wall of the Tartar City, whilst the altar of the Moon occupies a corresponding position on the west. The Emperor, as Sovereign Intercessor between Heaven and Earth, performed the sacrifices in the capital on the second day of the Second Moon, whilst his subjects observed the Festival by preparing Sun Cakes. These resembled our griddle cakes, but were thinner, and varied in size. They were skewered together on a sliver of bamboo decorated with a cock made of dough, and coloured red.

In most homes, five saucers filled with these cakes were placed in the courtyard facing the sun, shortly before midday. An outdoor service was held, beginning with prostrations to the Sun, and ending with the usual bonfire of paper money. Women were admitted to the ceremony to afford them the chance of placating this male deity, and craving his indulgence. Knowing that, in the next world, they will be forced to drink all the water they have wasted upon earth, and that the sun's all-seeing eye is a recorder of their prodigality, it is considered only fair to afford them the chance of petitioning him to overlook at least some of their misdeeds. As all water had to be drawn up, and transported by hand, its waste entailed extra work for some member of the family, so the legend was invented to obviate unnecessary journeys to the well. Propaganda for the revival of the belief might alleviate the water restrictions in Hong Kong.

One of the early stories of the Chinese Genesis credited P'an Ku (盤古) with bringing order out of chaos, and regulating the Cosmos. He forgot, however, to give any orders to the Sun and Moon, who retired to the Han Sea leaving the world in darkness. This state of affairs proved so inconvenient that the Terrestrial Emperor despatched an officer known as Terrestrial Time with orders that the Heavenly Lanterns should emerge and take their places in the sky. Faced with their refusal to co-operate, P'an Ku's services were again requisitioned. At the direction of the Lord Buddha he wrote the character for 'sun' in the palm of his left hand, and that for 'moon' in his right. He then visited the Han Sea and stretched out his left hand to the sun. Repeating an incantation seven times, he called the moon and set both orbs in the places they have since occupied, for the warmth and lighting of the world. In matters religious, the Chinese are completely uncritical and accept the dogma without worrying whether the evidence is conflicting or not. The two organised religions, Taoism and Buddhism, were for centuries bitter rivals, but in this case Buddha is discovered giving orders to P'an Ku, who is purely a Taoist conception.

Similarly Monkey, whose birthday occurs on the 23rd of the Second Moon, gained his original notoriety in the Taoist Heaven where he stole the peaches of longevity from the garden of the queen. As he had already acquired immortality, the question of dealing with him presented almost insurmountable difficulties. Finally recourse to Buddha's intervention had to be invoked, and he was imprisoned until, by Kuan Yin's intervention, he was enabled to purge his fault. By accompanying Hsuan Tsang to India to fetch a copy of the Scriptures, he attained sanctity and was canonised in the Chinese pantheon as the "Great Sage equal to Heaven". His image may be found in Taoist and Buddhist Temples and, though his official birthday falls in the Second Moon, it is always appropriate to sacrifice to Monkey, and the paper shops keep his outfit of new clothing perpetually in stock. This consists of a golden fillet, a scarlet embroidered jacket, and a pair of "cloud-stepping" shoes, with a carrying pole from which dangle a pair of buckets.

On the 3rd day of the Budding Moon a character associated with Monkey is also worshipped. This is none other than Erh Lang (二郎), nephew to the Heavenly King, with his dog who howls towards the sky. He and his hound were instrumental in capturing Monkey after he had made heaven too hot to hold him, so the dog shares the altar in his temple in Peking. Pet lovers sacrifice at it when their dogs are out of health and, in cases of recovery, contribute china or fur-covered animals as tokens of their gratitude. The cure is effected by burning incense and carrying the ashes home for the dog to swallow with his next meal. In this particular shrine the dog is really the senior partner, for Erh Lang's image is barely visible, whereas there is no doubt about the dog-kennel and the clay image of its occupant. According to the legend, a butcher's shop was situated next to the temple, which did a thriving business. Every night, however, a dog used to crawl in and help himself to a ration of pork, until the enraged proprietor stabbed it with a carving-knife. Following the trail of blood to the temple, he was horrified to discover that it disappeared on crossing the threshold. This convinced him that he had committed sacrilege, an assumption which was confirmed in the eyes of his neighbours by the fact that the dog was never seen again, and that the butcher's business was ruined.

After the Sun had been congratulated on his restored vitality, it was the natural corollary for an agricultural people to propitiate the earth on which their livelihood depended. Though worshipped at the New Year, the Gods of the Locality celebrated their official birthday on the "Double Second". Under the Mings some sort of attempt was made to give them uniform responsibilities and a fixed establishment. Each T'u Ti was allotted a parish of one hundred families. Under their successors the Cult of the God seems to have spread, and he may serve a village or a single compound. In Hong Kong a dozen shrines may be seen in one street and, where gold and silver shops are concerned, he appears to be an essential part of the business. In the country districts he is known as T'ien Kung (田公), the Old Man of the Fields, and in the Sung Dynasty the appropriate offerings were either pork, mutton, or beef, laid under a tree, and afterwards consumed by the contributors. In later days special dumplings of millet meal, flavoured with dates, were substituted in North China, whilst in the South a sort of bean cake formed the sacrifice.

T'u Kung (土公) and T'u Mu (土母), God and Goddess of the Soil, must not be offended by digging in the ground on inauspicious days, nor neglected when the plough turns the first furrow of the year. A thanksgiving service is held for them when the harvest is gathered, in token of benefits received. Their good offices are also sought by the wrestling fraternity in hopes of falling softly in their contests.

Several other divinities connected with agriculture were called to remembrance on this day, for there was a special God of Harvests, and practically every crop had its particular deity. In a negative way the God of Locusts was also propitiated, in order that he might transfer his attentions to others who had been less free-handed. He was identified with Marshal Liu Men (劉猛), either a T'ang or Yuan General and, as former Chinese soldiers were dreaded even more than the insects, on much the same grounds, it is not unnatural that a military man should have been selected to represent the predators. For some mysterious reason the beggars have chosen him as their patron, though in the North he is often revered as a scholarly graduate of the Sung Dynasty. Some insects have no king to regulate their migrations, and the people of Weihaiwei consider them greater pests than the locusts, as they no chief to appeal to.

Ranking with, but after, the Farm Gods, is the Taoist Trinity known as the San Kuan (三官), three Primordial sovereigns who exert a general superintendence over Heaven, Earth, and Water. They only date from the 5th Century A.D. and represent the sources of happiness, forgiveness of sins, and deliverance from evil. They are occasionally invoked in Hong Kong, by means of inscriptions, to bestow blessings. In addition to averting calamity and curing sickness, the "Three Beginnings," as they are sometimes termed, record the good and bad deeds of mortals, so no punishments can be inflicted on their birthdays.

The Feast of Excited Insects

About the 5th March, in the Western Calendar, falls the Ching Chë (驚蟄), or "Arousing from hibernation", when the insects who have lain torpid all the winter resume their activities with remarkable punctuality. In the North, even the most unobservant will have his attention attracted to creeping creatures on that anniversary, as their movement cannot fail to catch the eye. The date is about a fortnight in advance of the time when the hibernating butterflies in England may be seen regularly on the wing. Though a warm, windless day in February may bring out the Small Tortoiseshell and Peacock, and even the striking sulphur of the Brimstone in a leafless copse, there will be no vestige of life for many days after unless the conditions are re-peated. Butterflies must eat to survive once the winter torpidity is cast off and, unless the yellow blossom of the sallow, or pussy willow, is available, they will perish of starvation. An old entomologist was in the habit of collecting Commas for breeding purposes in the autumn, and one year amassed a hundred. He placed the lot in a large wire-netted cage to protect them from spiders and wrens and stowed them all in an unheated loft. Only one survived when he took the breeding-cage down in mid-March, as the unnatural warmth had aroused them from torpidity before any food was available to sustain life. In a state of nature the Comma clings to the rough bark of a tree, where its indented wings and underside colouring simulate a dried leaf. In Hong Kong there are a few blooms of lantana open all the year round, so a premature butterfly, tempted out by abnormally warm weather, has a good chance of accumulating enough energy to reproduce its species.

This is the time when, as the Chinese say, "the dragon raises his head". The lordly Dragon goes into hibernation in September in the form of a tiny creature, and thus remains unobserved till he calls the insects to life. On the day of the "Excited Insects" certain fetishes are displayed to placate them. In North China, a block of ice is often laid on the dung heap in the farm-yard, possibly to delay their depredations, or a paper pennant is mounted on a reed. In Shantung, people awake before sunrise and cook a sort of dumpling guaranteed to assist Nature in her work of stirring the dormant vitality in the vegetable and animal kingdoms. Water-jars have to be scoured, and the clay sleeping platform must be fumigated before its torpid inhabitants wake up and get to work. Women are debarred from needlework lest their implement prick the Dragon, and he retaliate by afflicting them with boils.

In the South, women worship the White Tiger. They may be seen carrying paper images of the beast which, when introduced into the house, keep out rats and snakes and prevent quarrels.

The Birthday of Kuan Yin

When the two essentials for keeping body and soul together, Sun and the Soil, have been propitiated men, or rather women, worship the divinity who has the power to solve their mundane difficulties. One drawback to the acceptance of Buddhism in China was the lack of a female divinity to whom the distaff side of the congregation could pour out their sorrows, and confide their pressing necessities. The Chinese solved this problem in accordance with the doctrine of reincarnation, by selecting the compassionate Bodhisatva, Avalokitsvara and canonising him in female form. Up till the twelfth century he was portrayed as a man, stoutly built and well furnished with whiskers. As a male divinity he is depicted in one of the Kwangtung monasteries, Hoi T'ung. His Indian name is usually taken to signify the "Lord who looks down upon, or hears the cries of the world", which is shortly translated in Kuan Yin's title "Observing, or taking note of sounds." Her image, enthroned on a lotus and holding a vase, is to be found in every Buddhist, and a large number of Taoist temples. Sometimes there is what corresponds to a Lady Chapel

The birthday of Kuan Yin

dedicated to her, but often she forms the right hand figure of a trinity behind the main altar.

The first reference to her Chinese naturalisation is to be found in the works of a Buddhist Abbot, P'u Ch'an who lived in the Sung Dynasty (A.D. 960–1279) and records that her father was a petty prince of a nebulous country called Hsin Lin, located near the modern Cambodia. In any case it was east of Burma and south of Thailand, which in those days lay between Kunning and Lashio. His personal name was P'o Chia, but he was civilised enough to adopt the Chinese system of reign titles, and selected Miao Chung to indicate the era of his rule. He shared the obsession of Henry VIII for a male successor to perpetuate the dynasty with even less result, though there is no record of how he disposed of his un-cooperative partners. His offspring consisted of three daughters, Miao Ssu, Miao Yin, and Miao Shan, born on the 19th of the Second Moon. As the production of an heir male was beyond his powers, he issued a decree to legalise the succession through the female line, and set about seeking eligible consorts for his daughters. Only the youngest proved recalcitrant, preferring to embrace religion to submission to the dictates of an alien spouse. The legend gives no account of the fate of her elder sisters, who were presumably prior to her in the line of descent, but her father evidently was infuriated by her disobedience. She was confined to a garden court in the palace but, on the pleading of her mother, was allowed to join the convent of the "White Sparrow" as a novice. It is more probable that her mother connived at her escape, for the monarch sent his bodyguard to set fire to the establishment, and the

flames were only extinguished by an effusion of her blood. She was stabbed, but recovered. According to one version of the story, her father ordered her execution, but she was carried off by a tiger. In another she strangled herself with a bowstring, preferring death to her father's hatred. In both cases she descended into hell, but her sweetness converted it from a place of punishment to a paradise, and Yen Lo, King of the Underworld was forced to petition the Jade Emperor to order her removal. She was accordingly returned to earth where she sojourned in a cave, known as Hsuan Ai, in Hwei Chou county. There, for nine years, she devoted herself to religious exercises and attained Buddhahood.

Her act of filial disobedience might have alienated her from the Confucian element, so a sequel is recorded to rehabilitate her in the eyes of the literati. After her death, her father was struck by a mortal illness and was advised that the only cure was to obtain the hand and eye of the Pu T'ien jen (never angry one), who dwelt in the cave which was her retreat. She freely despatched the healing parts of her body, which effected the King's recovery and he sent a minister to express his gratitude. It was than discovered that he owed his cure to the daughter he had murdered. Miao Chung was so smitten with remorse that he abandoned the campaign of religious persecution he had initiated, and became a convert to Buddhism.

The reincarnation of Kuan Yin as a female divinity was not entirely satisfactory to scholarly Chinese of a philosophic turn of mind for, in the Ming Dynasty, one Hu Yin-lin, who wrote the Chuang Yu Wei T'an, analysed the question saying:—"Nowadays, all the

Ch'ing Ming Festival . . . women and children have to wear the willow catkin

15

images of Kuan Yin are in female form, because all Buddhists wish to endow their divinity with the most exquisite characteristics, and not only Kuan Yin, but **Wen Shu Pusa, and P'u Hsien.** Yet, to have them portrayed in women's attire is something never seen before. According to a book of paintings of the Sung dynasty (Hsuan Ho Hua P'u), Kuan Yin's pictures by famous artists in the T'ang and Sung dynasties were not so dressed, and the superscription gave no indication that she was a woman. It is only because of late Kuan Yin was idolised by the female element, and her popularity was capitalised by ignorant monks in the Yuan (Mongol) dynasty."

As might be expected in the early stories of Kuan Yin's miraculous appearances on earth, the male form is assumed. Like the angel who delivered St. Peter from his chains Kuan Yin, in the habit of a monk, caused fetters to fall off and prison doors to open in the Chin and Sung dynasties. The guise of a Taoist priest was adopted in rescuing an officer whose army had been routed. It is typical of the tolerance displayed by the Chinese in religious matters to credit a Buddhist Saint with a miracle performed in the habit of the rival sect. As emperors favoured one, or the other, fierce persecutions took place. Yet, in the final result, tradition has so interwoven the two beliefs that their ritual is often indistinguishable, and their objects of worship are common to both. It has already been remarked that Kuan Yin was released from the underworld at the order of the Jade Emperor, the Supreme Taoist divinity, but in the story of the White Monkey's expulsion from paradise, only an appeal to the Lord Buddha could disembarrass the Gods of this intolerable pest. Later, he entered the service of Kuan Yin and became a reformed character, achieving canonisation as the "Great Sage equal to Heaven". His act of expiation restored him to the Taoist pantheon, although during his pilgrimage he was anything but favourably disposed to their beliefs, and today his favours are indiscriminately sought by both congregations.

The history of the Six Kingdoms, which preceded the T'ang Dynasty, makes several mentions of visions of Kuan Yin as a woman, but the question of her sex remained contentious till after the Sung Dynasty, when she was definitely awarded female status.

Extremely devout women observe a period of preparation before her festival, starting their worship on the 1st of the Second Moon. On the morning of her birthday, the 19th, **Buddhist and Taoist temples are** besieged with the bearers of offerings. Well-to-do women are accompanied by servants carrying the sacrifices, food, paper clothing and money, whilst the richer members of the congregation employ a whole retinue to bear the roast pig and chickens. Worship is performed before noon, and the deafening explosion of crackers in the temple court marks the termination of each individual service.

The Ch'ing Ming Festival
(清明)

The Chinese Festival of Ch'ing Ming (Clear and Bright) takes place at the end of the Second, or beginning of the Third Moon, and has many similarities with the western Easter. The winter is definitely past, and trees are in bud, giving a firm impression of resurgence of the year. Being the eighth division of the Solar year, its incidence varies with the Lunar calendar, just as Easter, based on the moon, falls on a different date according to western ideas of time-keeping. One of the first trees to put forth its buds in England is the sallow, or pussy-willow, whose yellow blossom is the first flower to attract the bees and hibernating butterflies. Under the name of "Palm" it is used in the religious observance of the Easter Festival. On the day of Ch'ing Ming, all Chinese women and children must wear the willow catkin. If they neglect this precaution, they risk being reborn as dogs in the transmigration of souls. The custom of sporting the willow dates from the Emperor Kao Tsung, of the T'ang Dynasty, who reigned from 650 to 683 A.D. On the third day of the third moon, after bathing in the waters of Wei Yang, he plucked some willow branches, and distributed them to his retinue, with orders to wear them in their caps. He explained that this was a sovereign remedy against the stings of scorpions, which leads one to wonder if the distribution of shamrock by the Sovereign to the Irish Guards immunises them from adders in a country from which St. Patrick omitted to banish them.

Both festivals are connected with the afterlife for, whereas Easter emphasizes the belief in resurrection, Ch'ing Ming entails an obligatory visit to those ancestral spirits who hover around the tombs. Cemeteries being in the midst of a farmer's fields, it was natural at the beginning of the agricultural year to invoke the ghosts of the forefathers to promote a bountiful harvest. The Chinese leave no stone unturned, and even the Christian communities in Hong Kong take their offerings of flowers, and tidy up the graves like their compatriots.

On the eve of the festival everybody used to observe the Han Shih, when nothing hot was eaten and no fires were lit for twenty-four hours, a relic of the rekindling of the sacred fire. As late as the Han Dynasty this latter was effected by rubbing two willow sticks together; and the children of the courtiers performed the ceremony in front of the Imperial Palace. The winner of the competition received a golden cup, but the scarcity of the metal, and the advent of the Mongol barbarians, put a stop to this hoary tradition. It is, however, a third explanation of the connection of willow with the feast.

Ch'ing Ming was, originally, a sort of Saturnalia, when the Spring fret caused youths and maidens to dance together, garlanded with flowers, to celebrate the obsequies of the dead season. Its alternative name is Chih Shu Chieh (植樹節) (Tree Planting Festival), which exactly corresponds to Arbor Day. The Emperor, or his delegate, on that day planted trees in the palace grounds, and the custom was preserved by the President of the Republic, or some high official.

The connection with the dead, at the moment of the celebration of the revival of life, was undoubtedly the desire to invoke their aid, or at any rate ensure that they did nothing inimical in the production of the annual crop. Tombs were repaired, and a feast was set out for the comfort of the spirits. Richer families placed the Wu Kung (five vessels) on the altar, incense burner, candlesticks and flower vases. This ceremony was called Sao Mu Ch'a Liu (掃墓插秧), sweep the tombs and adorn them with willow. The meal and three goblets of wine

An obligatory visit to ancestral spirits

THE THIRD MOON

A T'ien Hou Festival
(天后)

For the Boat People, the birthday of the Queen of Heaven, celebrated on the 23rd day of the Third Moon, is the most important of their religious festivals. To her, the Holy Mother, they make their supplication for fair weather and good fishing, and to her they take their tributes for success in the past twelve months. Her shrine is in every junk cabin, and her temples are in every village which fronts on the sea.

Her origins are obscure, as she is also called the "Matron of the Measure" (斗姥), whilst she has some affinity to the Buddhist Goddess Maritchi, and is certainly the Taoist equivalent of the ever popular Kuan Yin. In many temples, Kuan Yin's image is incorporated in her shrine, so that the worshippers can take their choice in making their appeals. Of course the Taoists fitted her out with a biography, as they invariably do to make their saints more convincing. According to the legend, she hailed from Fukien, where she was the daughter of a fisherman. One day, whilst her parents were engaged in earning their bread, she fell into a trance, and dreamed that they were in imminent danger of being overwhelmed by the elements. Running to the beach, she pointed fixedly at their boat which, alone of all the fleet, safely reached the shore. Since her deification, she is credited with curing an Emperor of a disease which defied all the court physicians. Her attendants, "Thousand Mile Eyes" (千里眼), and "Fair Wind Ears" (順風耳), are supposed to possess abnormal powers of sight and hearing.

The most important celebration of her birthday in Hong Kong is the pilgrimage to Tai Miao (the Great Temple) in Joss House Bay. It is probable that the derivation of this extraordinary word is a corruption of the Portuguese "Dios" for God. This race was the earliest to have commercial contacts with China and, as some form of the Divinity was worshipped in these edifices, it was natural to term them generally as "God" houses.

Joss House Bay is a tiny cove near the eastern approaches to the harbour. The distance from the vehicular ferry is about nine miles, and, to cope with the crowd of pilgrims, half-hourly services are run all day. The Boat People usually club together in Societies, and one family finds the junk to carry the party. As the wind cannot be depended on, the junks are always towed by a launch, and sometimes as many as four are lashed together with one tug in the centre. In front of the mast is erected an ogival screen, with the name of the Society in large characters, and "A Happy Birthday to T'ien Hou" in a horizontal line below them. Each ship is dressed with a hoist of signal flags, and two to four large triangular banners are stepped just behind the mast and on the poop. The latter also carries two big lanterns. The banners are shaped like the traditional Chinese flag of Imperial days, with a wavy edge, and characters taking the place of the Dragon. Two long pennants surmount each banner. The most popular colours are yellow, green, and petunia. Two shrines to the Queen of Heaven are placed in the well-deck at the aft end, up against the rise of the high poop. These are carried up to the Temple before anything else is done, and are ranged against the front wall, some of them reaching to the eaves.

Taking a ferry, with two of the Boat People in the party, it was discovered that every seat was full, and the lower deck was equally crammed. The Chinese, however, are a gregarious race, and there is always room for half a dozen more, so no objections were raised on either side. The lower deck was a seething mass of humanity, and among the men, women and children, who crowded every available corner, wriggled purveyors of food and drink. A bar had been established near the bows, consisting of an unplaned cupboard and an erection of squared timber above, with shelves piled with cakes and sweetmeats. There was some method of heating tea, whilst crates of soft drinks, in which orange and lemon vied for predominance, were stacked handy to the servers.

Most of the passengers had furnished themselves with baskets for their picnic lunch, and offerings of paper clothing and gold sycee money for the Divinity they were honouring. In case any had omitted this necessary precaution, one or two hawkers had established stalls amidships to remedy the deficiency.

In five minutes under the hour the ferry entered Joss House Bay, and dropped anchor about three hundred yards offshore. The whole hillside was wreathed in smoke, not only from the incense and burned offerings from the Temple platform, but on account of two grass fires higher up the slope, one of which appeared to have taken a good hold. A number of large, three-masted fishing junks, with hoists of bunting between their masts, were lying well offshore, but the harbour lighters were drawn up fifteen yards off the beach, with ingenious double gangplanks from their bows from which the passengers could disembark dry-shod.

Launches of all sizes and descriptions were anchored outside the row of lighters, and sampans, invariably managed by women, picked up their complement for the shore. A swarm approached the ferry before she had lost way, and crashed their bows into her side with a rattling of oars. Passengers climbed down the sides as if they were abandoning ship for their lives although, had a little patience been exercised, the approach to the temple would have been more easy. The Chinese prefer their muddle to the foreigner's order, and are ever in a hurry to get anywhere. The beach consisted of a strip of firm sand, only a couple of yards wide, leading to a narrow belt of shingle and boulders. Above that, the ground, covered with rough grass and scrub, rose steeply. Access to the temple was by a fairly broad stairway of granite slabs, and on either side were booths for the sale of the usual talismans.

Some stalls had racks of metal medals, commemorating the Goddess, others, stands of toy halberds, as the word signifies "something auspicious". Cartoons of the

Pak Tai Temple on Cheung Chau

Queen of Heaven and her two attendants in colour were displayed everywhere, and almost every child had a paper windmill in gaudy colours. A new line in plastic was selling like hot cakes. The whole passenger list of the ferry seemed to be assaulting the stairway simultaneously, and their anxiety to mount was only surpassed by the enthusiasm of the returning pilgrims to reach the vessel that had just been emptied. At one point, near the summit of the steps, there was a complete block, as the contending parties insisted on walking four abreast, and neither seemed inclined to give way. The temple platform was thronged with worshippers. Biers, laden with roast pig, chickens, pink dumplings, and the inevitable red eggs, stood awaiting their turn to be offered to the Divinity. Women came down the steps from the main entrance with bundles of flaming paper in their hands, which they disposed of either in a large metal brazier, or a square concrete incinerator. Almost every worshipper who came out bore a smouldering stick of incense. By paying a fee to the attendant, one can test one's luck in the coming year, by drawing a slip from a container and reading the inscription thereon.

It is always lucky to mount to high places, and a path leads upwards from the southern end of the temple to a col between two peaks. Every self-respecting pilgrim must climb this slope. A short distance up a spring has been tapped in a little basin of squared granite, and here two or three Hakka women have established a place of refreshment for the weary. They furnish any pilgrim with a wooden basin of water, soap, and a towel. As they come all the way from Shaukiwan for a single harvest in the year, their charge is not excessive. It is a pleasant resting-place anyway, as it is overhung by two well-grown trees, whose shade is grateful and comforting on a hot day; our party made it their lunch headquarters.

Later, the young men of the Guilds began to carry their Society banners up to the crest of the col for the annual scramble for luck. This carries on from year to year, and the Head of the River, or last year's No. 1 Luck, has to provide the most magnificent shrine. No. 2 provides a slightly less ornate abode for the Goddess, and so on. The contesting teams formed a mob on the col and, from the side, a bamboo projectile was shot into the air, so as to fall into the scrum. This contained a number, and the team which secured it took that luck for the current year. The shrine went with the luck, and was carried back in triumph lashed to the mast of the junk which won it. As it must often happen that one team secures two numbers, and another fails to acquire any luck at all, everybody takes a duplicate shrine, as it would be too humiliating to return without any effigy of the Goddess.

There is something extremely friendly about a Chinese religious festival. All classes attend, but there is not the slightest distinction between them apart from dress. Ladies in silks sit next to Boat People in their customary black, or amahs, hawkers and shop girls, conversing as if they had known them all their lives. It must be remembered that there is no weekly Sunday break for the Chinese, and that the pilgrimages, like the Medieval festivals in Europe, described in the Canterbury tales, correspond to the modern Bank Holiday. 'Arry and 'Arriet monopolise Hampstead Heath, but religion brings together the Wife of Bath and the publican, and they derive as much entertainment from casual conversation as the party which lightened its way to Becket's shrine.

Village T'ien Hou Festival

Though the Boat People celebrate the birthday of their Patron Saint by a pilgrimage to T'ai Miao (大廟), the Queen of Heaven receives the homage of at least twenty-three other localities in Hong Kong where her temples are the most popular in the Taoist pantheon. Her birthday is observed as the annual village holiday. The Residents' Association is responsible for the arrangements, and starts collecting funds for a theatrical performance about a month before the 23rd of the Third Moon. They are assisted in money-raising by the local Lion dancers, who practise in the morning before the temple, parading the streets during the forenoon to relax the purse-strings of the shopkeeper and householder. The Lion is stimulated to greater activity by the display of a banknote and a lettuce, sufficiently out of reach to cause the man working the head to mount on another's shoulders to secure the prize. Sheng ts'ai (生菜), the lettuce, is symbolic of life and, when used for ritual purposes, must always have the roots attached.

About three weeks before the day, a contractor's lorries are busy bringing material for an immense matshed, whose bamboo framework covers an area of ninety feet by one hundred and fifty. The whole structure is lashed by strips of rattan, and holds together, if judged by Western engineering standards, by habit and the Grace of God. The theatricals do not necessarily take place on the actual day of the feast, for during this season actors are in short supply, and there are not enough troupes to give simultaneous performances for all the places who indent for their services. Some have to wait their turn till nearly a fortnight after the festival.

Early on in the great day, worshippers begin arranging the sacrifices in the streets outside their houses. The food offerings are laid out on tables covered with red paper to serve as a cloth, and consist of red eggs, cakes or dumplings of a different shape and colour to those presented by the Boat People, roast chickens or ducks and oranges, though the latter are expensive at this time of year. The roast pigs are supplied by caterers in Hong Kong and are unloaded from a lorry to the number of about thirty. These are duly claimed by the various guilds or associations who have clubbed together to provide the more lavish displays. The burnt offerings consist of a red paper trunk to pack the clothing for the Queen of Heaven, which is surmounted by a round cardboard box for her jewellery and toilet accessories and a headdress in the style of the Chou Dynasty.

No festival would be complete without its complement of beggars, and the blind, halt and maimed have found their way out of town, and are busy with their bowls among the crowds of spectators. A greater attraction is a juggler, who moves from shop to shop, picking up an article at random and balancing it on his nose or in his teeth. Possibly his best feat is to poise one chopstick on another at right angles, then to place an egg on the tip of the second and, throwing back his head, to straighten the whole lot into one vertical line. In the next shop he seizes on a step-ladder which he balances on his chin by one leg, repeating the feat with a huge glass jar of sweets at his next port of call. A bicycle, shop shutter, and a forked log weighing about thirty catties follow in quick succession. In each case he mulcts the shop-owner of a few cents, not an excessive fee for the performance and the advertisement given to the gaping crowd.

The paper shrines dedicated to T'ien Hou are practically all red, in contradistinction to those taken by the Boat People, in which white predominates. The first procession, headed by a Lion dancer and his band, proceeds along the waterfront to the temple in a continuous *feu de joie* of crackers. On arrival the Lion performs a dance before entering the sacred edifice, and the shrine, after being exhibited before the altar, is placed on some vacant shelf.

In the ante-chapel is a large square granite tank in the centre of which stands a brazier for the burning of the more elaborate sets of clothing for the Goddess. Individual small offerings are set alight by the women who bring them at the oil-lamp before the high altar, after which they are consigned to an old kerosene-tin in the sanctuary itself. The food offerings are brought before the altar, where they are dedicated before being taken back to the village for distribution. The temple manager, with several assistants, receives monetary offerings whilst a woman sells incense and candles. As each society brings its shrine, he reads out the names of the subscribers and throws two divining blocks to test their luck. Individual worshippers can avail themselves of the bamboo slips to tell their fortunes, and can get the written interpretation from the girl who dispenses the incense. The red paper shrines bear inscriptions which are a clue to their proprietors' mutual interest. One is "luck in fishing", an obvious connection with the waterborne side of the population, whilst another is "the lucky baby" in whom the hopes of the family repose. The mahjong addicts contribute to luck in gambling and horse-racing, though the connection of a Sea Goddess with the latter seems somewhat obscure.

The Lion dancers work overtime for they escort each of the main processions both to and from the temple, and perform solo when not so engaged. There are three or four of them, each with its own band. One, whose colours are red, white and blue, is evidently a patriotic relic of the Coronation. The general colour scheme of the others was red, the body and tail being composed of pink and white striped material. Each beast is preceded by a lad carrying a long bamboo, in leaf at the top and with a scarlet lantern attached. The band consists of cymbals, gong, clarinet and drums, and a continuous supply of crackers. The food offerings are traditionally carried by women whose race is recognisable by their clothing: Hoklos, Hakkas, Cantonese, and Boat People may all be recognized. The shrines are the responsibility of their menfolk. Children in swarms accompany each procession, but it is impossible to determine whether their presence is due to ritual observance or the natural curiosity which besets the young. The Lion exercises a powerful fascination and he is invariably attended by a crowd of unattached urchins. On the other hand, individual worshippers may be seen with a baby on the back, accompanied by a toddler carrying a miniature outfit for the Queen of Heaven and thus acquiring merit in the eyes of the goddess.

Half an hour after midday the last shrine has been housed in the temple, and the food offerings, bereft of the essence which is the perquisite of the divinity, have been apportioned to the subscribers. The streets of the village are full of children sucking the last juicy fragments from the pork bones, or with their faces pink with the crumbs of the doughy buns. The crackers are silent, and a great peace descends during the digestion of the Gargantuan feast.

The crowd then reassembles for the shooting for luck, which determines the new ownership of the shrines, and carries a monetary prize into the bargain. At the top of the beach in front of the temple is placed a table covered with a red cloth. In the centre is a large incense-burner with red candles, three thick sticks of incense, and two triangular scarlet silk banners. Offerings in the shape of a plate of oranges and a dish of cakes testify to the religious aspect of the ceremony. The practical side consists of a battery of scarlet trench-mortar bombs, ingeniously contrived to be self-propellant. The actual missile is about six inches high, and consists of a paper grenade bound into four slips of bamboo which project about half its length above it. A fuse runs down the centre alongside a stick to which is attached a metal tag, inscribed with the number of the shrine and its corresponding luck. Another table serves as a rostrum for the Master of Ceremonies who announces each shot, and the monetary prize which it carries. There is a descending scale, with a few consolation prizes and one or two scrambles for luck alone.

Before the actual contest, an inconspicuous Taoist priest standing behind the improvised altar suddenly unfolds a bundle which he takes from under his arm and vests himself in a very worn scarlet robe adorned with trigrams. Assuming his cap he strikes on a gong and presumably gives his blessing to the proceedings. The competitors form a large circle on the beach, in the centre of which is placed an unpainted board supported by two trestles which acts as a launching site.

The starter, a powerfully built man in a white vest and black trousers, arms himself with one of the sticks of incense and a scarlet banner from the altar, and places the first grenade upright in the centre of the table. The Taoist priest moves behind him to associate himself with the proceedings, and the Master of Ceremonies makes his announcement. A second official gives the signal to start by letting off a bunch of crackers, whereupon the fuse is lit with the stick of incense, and the operator encourages the missile to rise by violent upward jerks of the scarlet banner. There is tremendous suspense as the fuse slowly smoulders followed by a rush as the explosion fills the air with scraps of paper and detonating crackers. All eyes follow the stick which rises about fifty feet before falling like a plummet through the floating ashes. Its speed of descent is such that it usually evades the outstretched hands, and strikes the sand amid a wild scramble of humanity. A couple of policemen stand by to see fair play, and that the man who has fallen on the prize is not bereft by some more powerful snatcher. The tally is taken to the Master of Ceremonies who records the winner, and the next shot is prepared. If there is a tendency for the fall to favour one side of the ring more than another, the launching site is moved to even up the chances. About twenty grenades are discharged, and as each team is rewarded with a prize it retires from the contest to give a chance to the less successful.

The winners of shrines then assemble at the temple, and the processions home start as soon as their Lion escorts are available. Each party is played back with the appropriate honours and is followed by an admiring crowd of relatives and supporters. By sundown there is an eerie silence after a day of continuous detonations, and the streets are comparatively deserted. Towards the end the Lions may be showing signs of wear and tear, and their antics may be less exuberant, but they stay the course and deserve well of the community.

Occasionally some old woman on returning from the temple with her food offerings, may be noticed laying them on the ground before the shrine of her local Earth God and lighting a stick of incense on his behalf. As the principal divinity has theoretically absorbed the essence of the sacrifice, it may be wondered what is left for the lesser fry. The Chinese, however, credit their gods with the same virtues and failings as they themselves possess, and it is not good manners to accept the whole of a present. Some is invariably returned to the **donor**, who can pass it on to a third party. Thus after the satisfaction of the Queen of Heaven there is always something left for the T'u Ti (土帝).

The Spirit of the North

Pei Ti, or to give him his Cantonese pronunciation Pak Tai (北帝), is an extremely popular divinity in Hong Kong, where six temples are dedicated to him, and many more Taoist shrines include his image on their altars. His alternative names are Hsuan T'ien Shang Ti (玄天上帝) or Chen Wu (真武), Superior divinity of the deep, dark Heaven, or the True Soldier. He received enlightenment, and practised perfection, on the lovely mountain known as Tzu Hsiao (紫霄) whose name, on account of the connection, was later changed to Wu T'ang Shan (武當山). His reputation was not confined to earth, and his merit was so outstanding that the Yuan Shih T'ien (元始天尊) or Taoist Primeval Deity decided to invite him to join the Company of Immortals. He accordingly despatched five dignitaries from among the Heroes of the Second Heaven, and a host of Immortals from the First Heaven, to summon him to the Golden Palace. He was canonised under the title of Pei Fang Chen Wu Hsuan T'ien Shang Ti (北方真武玄天上帝).

A fantastic series of legends have been woven around the period of the fall of the Shang (商) Dynasty, when the Demon Kings (鬼王) and their armies were ravaging the universe. Mankind on both sides evoked the aid of the Gods, who descended and fought with every kind of unorthodox weapon. Even gas warfare was anticipated by a generation singularly devoid of chemical knowledge, whose imagination far outdistanced its scientific attainments. The Taoist Primeval Deity himself engaged in the struggle, and ordered the Jade Emperor (玉皇) to appoint the Spirit of the North, as Commander-in-Chief of the twelve generals of the heavenly legions, to intervene on earth. Pei Ti fought bare-footed, with his hair flowing over his shoulders, dressed in a black robe over which there was a golden breastplate. Amid the lowering clouds he raised his black standard. Mo Wang (魔王),

for such was the title of the Demon King, conjured out of the atmosphere a grey tortoise and a gigantic serpent as his allies, but these adventitious aids failed miserably to gain him the advantage. Pei Ti emerged from the struggle victorious, with a complete rout of his enemies, who were destroyed and flung in chains into the maw of Hell at Feng Tu (酆都). This chasm in the mountains is believed to exist in Szechuan, and to be the gate of the infernal regions.

On his return to the skies Pei Ti was awarded the title of Yuan T'ien Shang Ti (元天上帝) or First Lord of Heaven.

This legend explains the presence of the tortoise and the snake under his feet in the images of the God manufactured locally, for their position is a tribute to his victory over the servants of evil.

This is by no means the only biography of the divinity, for practically every temple dedicated to him has a different story of his origin, or some embellishment to graft on the version accepted by others. According to one account he lived in the Hsia (夏) Dynasty, which covered a period of four hundred years, about 2,000 B.C. He may be remembered as an historical character who introduced flood control by drainage and the erection of dykes. These benefits to mankind earned him canonisation as the Spirit of the North. He is worshipped by all classes for the protection he offers to men and women, young and old, at home or abroad.

A homely legend of his origin casts him in the part of an orphan who was brought up by an aunt. Like many small boys he had an aversion to water when used for ablutionary purposes, so the old lady was extremely surprised and gratified when he suddenly demanded a bath. She hastened to comply with his wishes, and soon had the water heated. When the lad had thoroughly scrubbed himself, and the greyness of the liquid bore evidence to the desirability of the cleansing process, there was a further shock in store for his guardian, for he forbade her to throw away the dirty water. Being a proud housewife, and an enemy to any speck of dust, she ignored his warning, believing that his mind had become unhinged. She firmly emptied the bath into the street, but the following morning the rumour reached her that all the neighbours were scrambling for gold outside her dwelling. Emerging to investigate she was able to pick a few pieces, but the bulk of the treasure had already been dissipated. When she re-entered the house and went to rouse her nephew she discovered that he had been translated to paradise during the night. It then dawned upon her that he had had a premonition of death, and wished to requite her solicitude by solving her financial problems. When the villagers heard of the miracle, they adopted the spirit of the boy as a patron, and found that their petitions to him were fulfilled. The effigies of Pei Ti are always barefoot, as he was translated whilst in night attire.

The above narrative would indicate that the Spirit of the North is regarded as one of the numerous Gods of Wealth, and there is considerable confirmation for this theory in another of his biographies in which he is assigned to the Chou (周) Dynasty, 1122–255 B.C., and given the name of Li. Again he is connected with Wu T'ang Shan, for it was there that he was summoned to paradise whilst washing his feet. All the stories agree on the point that he was unshod. Li also subdued two monsters, a tortoise and a serpent, who were ravaging the northern districts.

Among his other conquests were the two magicians: Ch'ao Kung Ming (趙公明) and the Peach Blossom Girl (桃花女) the former being a well-recognised God of Wealth. In temples dedicated to Pei Ti, this pair are often displayed on his left and right. They may be seen in front of his altar in the Temple of Jade Vacuity (玉虛宮) in Cheung Chau. There is a considerable discrepancy here with the authorised version of the story of Ch'ao Kung Ming, whose downfall was attributed to the witchcraft of the Peach Maiden, without any assistance from the Spirit of the North. As she encompassed his death by confectioning his image in straw, worshipping it for twenty days, and then piercing its heart with a peach wood arrow, his subsequent subjugation would appear superfluous.

Pei Ti certainly receives more honour in the south than in the north of China, and the conflicting stories of his origin reflect the unorthodox attitude of the local priesthood. Though there is no official hierarchy in the Taoist church, the Master of Heaven is usually recognised as its head and in the Yangtze Valley two deputies superintend religious organisation. Priests wear a distinctive dress, and their hair in a topknot. In Hong Kong the clergy are not affiliated to any temple, and their religious duties do not provide full time employment. They are mostly shop assistants, though they specialise in those establishments which provide the necessities for worship. The Taoist Pope is not recognised, and there is a considerable diversity in the ritual.

A Pei Ti Birthday Festival

In spite of the fact that the merchant ranked almost lowest in the order of society in ancient China, taking his place below the farmer and the artisan, his enterprise and industry have been rewarded overseas. No longer subject to arbitrary taxation by envious officials, who resented the accumulation of wealth by any means other than the tortuous path through the Examination Hall, the emigrant who left his country's shores as an indented labourer soon set up in business, leaving a fortune to his descendants. In South East Asia practically all the trading vitality is in the hands of these immigrants, from the shopkeepers to the owners of large rubber estates. They are shrewed bargainers, and indefatigable workers.

As they treat their divinities in the same way that they would their fellow men, it was not surprising that when the temple of the Spirit of the North at Stanley was reconditioned, the God was put on probation. The official birthday of this rather local divinity is on the 3rd of the Third Moon, but it was decided that he should have no birthday celebration till the following year when he had, so to speak, proved himself. If he brought luck to the village, the honours paid to him would be commensurate with the prosperity he engendered.

The village elders shoulder a considerable responsibility in religious matters, as they are the organisers of all those festivals which are on a community scale. If an epidemic breaks out, or the fish change their grounds, charges will be levelled at them that the propitiation of the God concerned was inadequate. To raise the funds they have to resort to a house to house collection, the results depending a good deal on what sort of a year the villagers have experienced. Every contribution is entered in a book, not only as a guarantee of good faith, but to ensure that the divinity is aware of his indebtedness.

At an appropriate time before the festival the following year, the village was visited by the priests which it habitually employed. Not that their services were required as intercessories, for only mortal sickness or death will induce the Chinese to employ them in their religious capacity. Their far more lucrative side-line is the provision of paper shrines, incense and firecrackers, and it was to take orders for these that they made their rounds. They also supplied the band whose members, when not performing, were also architects in paper. The programme of music was arranged with the village elders, with certain injunctions, which were later circulated to the congregation. On the eve of his birthday, the God was serenaded for half an hour by the musicians alone. There was no human audience as it was considered that to be present at this service would cut luck and destroy hopes of longevity. At midnight, the worshippers assembled to wish the God a happy birthday.

The bearing of presents was reserved for the following day, and the processions started before noon.

Though the Chinese loathe regimentation, and have little or no regard for time, a certain amount of organisation was necessary in this case to avoid complete confusion. The temple itself was minute, and there was no space for forming groups, whilst the path leading to the shrine permitted only one-way traffic. The pilgrims had to cross a stretch of sand and scale the rocks, whose ascent had been slightly ameliorated by a few rough-hewn steps. The path contoured the hillside for half a mile, with minor obstructions in the form of squatters' huts forcing the wayfarer to the crumbling edge which descended precipitously onto the beach. There were occasional additional hazards in the form of sleeping sows suckling their young.

Each group of worshippers was preceded by two members carrying a large red paper shrine, followed by two women with a litter on which lay a decorated roast pig. Two more bearers were in charge of a square table with dishes of pink cakes and boiled eggs. The providers of the feast followed with bundles of paper clothing for the God and sticks of incense. Attendants strewed the path with crackers to ward off the depredations of unfriendly spirits.

The greater sacrifices were provided by the guilds of tradesmen who had had a satisfactory balance sheet over the year. Among them, resplendent in his best blue clothes, marched the wood-carver who had not only obtained the contract for the temple's decoration, but had had a further wind-fall when the elders decided to rebuild the small shrine on the promontory. This was dedicated to the "Nation-defending old Water God, Protector of the People", but the tablet had become almost illegible.

The craftsman had been commissioned to remedy this, and had produced an elaborate design surmounted by dragons and smothered in gilt. The tablet also bore the inscription of the God of Wealth and, though he had no mention, the Earth God T'u Ti (土地) shared the

Bun Festival, Cheung Chau . . . sacrifice for the spirits of the slain

altar. He undoubtedly resided in the pointed stones, emblems of fertility, on either side of the tablet for some pieces of ginger were hung up to acquaint the divinity of the answer to prayer. This is the alternative to pasting up red cut-outs of babies on the walls of the Earth God's temple; fresh ginger in a shrine always indicates an increase in the population.

The Guild processions were interspersed by private individuals, who had no objection to waiting their turn. Plates of roast pork, or a chicken and a few pink buns, constituted the food offerings. Occasionally there was a small red shrine carried in one hand, whilst a bundle of paper clothing and incense sticks occupied the other. After concluding the worship, the pilgrims went home to dissect the roast pigs for distribution among the subscribers for the evening feast.

Later in the afternoon the village elders repaired to the beach to superintend the shooting for luck. One of them was delegated to ignite the fuse of the self-propelled missile, and urge it upwards with the wave of flag. After the first half dozen discharges there was little competition for the rain had increased, and those who had obtained the lucky numbers drifted away, leaving the field to swarms of children. Their size normally debarred them from taking part in the scramble but, when there was no adult competition, they rolled and tussled in the sand like a pack of puppies.

The Bun Festival of Cheung Chau

The island of Cheung Chau (長州), with its sheltered harbour, must have been a natural fishing base from prehistoric times. Stone and bronze implements have been discovered on the adjacent island of Lamma, and probably richer finds await the archaeologist, should modernisation disturb the primitive houses raised on piles in the villages of Stanley and Cheung Chau.

The population is about thirty thousand, of whom a third are Boat People. Normally fishermen flock to the temple of T'ien Hou on her birthday, the 23rd of the Second Moon, which marks the beginning of the fishing season. To her they pray for full nets in the opening year, and render thanks for her favours in the past. In Cheung Chau, however, although the Queen of Heaven's temple is adjacent to the main shrine, Pei Ti (北帝), the Spirit of the North, in the Palace of Jade Vacuity (玉虛宮), overshadows her in the esteem of the local inhabitants.

The main annual religious festival is one of expiation and, though Pei Ti extends his patronage to the proceedings, the objects of worship are the spirits of all those animals and fish whose lives have been sacrified in the past years, in order that man may live. The festival last four days, during which time no pig or chicken is killed on land and the fishing junks lie at their moorings, without casting a net or dropping a line. All meals are vegetarian, though an exception is made in the case of oysters, who are not credited with the possession of a soul.

The actual date of the festival is literally in the lap of the Gods, for the organising committee cast lots before the image of the Spirit of the North to determine its incidence. The limits appear to be the last days of the

Bun Mountains, Cheung Chau

25

Like birds let us fly and mate in the sky

The village elder and the lion dancer

third and the tenth day of the fourth moon. There is always an elaborate theatrical performance daily and nightly throughout the proceedings, so the date depends to a large extent on the availability of a troupe of actors. It is their busy time of the year, for the temples to the Queen of Heaven are by far the most numerous in Hong Kong and theatrical companies are booked up for her birthday in the last week of the third moon. In their connection with religion, they resemble the performers of the mystery plays in medieval times in western Europe. The plays performed by the "Brothers of the Pear Orchard," as these Thespians are known, are called Canton Opera, and bear little resemblance to the more classic drama of Peking. The theatre is a huge matshed, affording protection from the rain and the sun to an audience of perhaps a couple of thousand, who pack themselves in tightly and come and go as they please. No nails are used in the construction, but the bamboos forming the frame are tied together with strips of rattan. The work of erection is incredibly fast, as every workman is a specialist. The dismantling is even faster, as the lashings are cut away with a sharp hooked knife, being the only part of the structure for which there is no further use.

The real feature of the festival is the erection of three pyramidal towers surrounded by scaffolding to accommodate the cakes which form the sacrifice for the spirits of the slain. These are known as the "Bun Mountains" and, when the framework is completed, large round pink

Fisherman's tableau

Instrument makers' guild

Taoist priest

and white cakes are affixed in tiers. The most desirable bun, crowning the edifice, is about sixty feet above ground level. In the making of the confectionery, over a thousand sacks of flour and a hundred and thirty pounds of sugar are consumed. As at this time of year the weather is uncertain, the towers are protected with tarpaulins, once the edifice is completed, until the final service and distribution.

It is well worth while exploring the odd corners of the village in the forenoon of the great day, when the guilds will be discovered preparing the tableaux to represent them. The children are being bandaged to the supports, and the artifice is completely concealed as soon as they are robed.

In front of the Lion Temple the bannermen form three large rings with their triangular silk standards of every colour of the spectrum. There are probably at least a hundred in each circle, some with spear heads, and others with halberds on their staves. Inside, the crowd is three or four deep, watching acrobats, clowns, or in some cases highly skilled exponents of shadow boxing. In the centre ring a troupe of amateur actors depict the adventures of Hsuan Tsang during his pilgrimage to India in search of the true Buddhist scriptures. A man with a pig's head represents "Pigsy", and there is Monkey and the Marine Monster "Sandy". Most Chinese artists recording their adventures portray the four robed as if for an audience at Court, instead of in the rags engendered by contact with the craggy passes of the Pamirs, but the local talent

Boys leading unicorns

has the travel-stained appearance consistent with the accounts of the original expedition.

In the village, floral arches are erected at all road junctions, and the various guilds tax their ingenuity to mount tableaux to represent them in the procession which takes place on the last day. These are most ingeniously contrived, and are very convincing. The actors are usually children between the ages of five and eight, as they have to be carried shoulder high on platforms instead of a wheeled float. A concealed framework enables a child, for instance, to appear to be standing on a fan, held below by a companion, or to be mounted on a fiddle, arranged so as to give the impression of dancing. There are numerous legendary and mythological subjects, such as the battle between the kingfisher and the oyster, which points out a moral like the fables of Aesop. The kingfisher found the oyster open, and attacked him, whilst the bivalve closed his shell imprisoning the beak of his assailant. Neither was willing to cry quits and call the battle off so, whilst they were still locked in useless combat, a fisherman put the pair into his bag. Children are thus admonished that it is better to agree than plunge in strife, from which only a third party benefits.

The girl representing the oyster is of maturer years, as are the couples symbolic of fecundity who display the unicorn as the emblem of large families. The girl is mounted on the mythical beast as a hobby-horse, whose reins are held by her male companion. In contrast a tiny child holding a fan impersonates a Taoist priest in full canonicals.

On the two final days of the festival the participants in the procession form up in the square before the Temple of Jade Vacuity. Chinese lanterns lead the cortège, with a band preceding the members of the organising committee. The religious element is furnished by portable images of the chief divinities of the island, with the Spirit of the North in the place of honour. Hung Hsing, worshipped by the Water Folk for his influence over wind and wave, is followed by no less than four representations of the Queen of Heaven, guardian angel of the sailor. The Buddhist Goddess of Mercy, who ranks just after T'ien Hou in the estimation of the Taoists, forms part of her retinue. Finally, there is a second image of the patron of Cheung Chau, Pei Ti (北帝), under his title Hsian T'ien Ta Ti (至天大褅), the Supreme God of Profound Heaven.

Soon the whole street is filled with a mass of colour and animation, for the gaily decorated floats are interspersed with forests of waving banners. Three or four troupes of Lion dancers and clowns entertain the crowd with their antics. Inhabitants of the various streets erect their own decorations and, at the junctions, elaborate the floral arches with tableaux of their own contriving some of which exhibit a keen sense of humour. The Chinese are far more censorious than westerners of mixed marriages and demonstrate their disapproval with a sort of Rake's Progress depicting the "Girl who wed a Foreign Devil".

An allegorical display is entitled "The girl who won a husband after three fights with him". The White Monkey, to whose ingenuity Hsuan Tsang was indebted during his search for the Buddhist scriptures, is always a prime favourite, and he figures in his journey to the Eastern Seas.

Great consideration is shown for the children acting

Two fair princesses shut up in the palace

Lamp-makers' guild

in the tableaux, and if the sun is fierce they are protected by umbrellas carried by attendants. The procession halts frequently while the infants are refreshed by soft drinks absorbed through straws. The pilgrimage through the village lasts an hour and a half and, by tradition, is completed at a run to the temple door. The ceremony is known as "Running the God," and its performance is credited with inducing luck in the coming season.

The mass for the souls of the creatures whose lives have been sacrified for food begins before midnight on the last day, when the hungry spirits surround the Bun Mountains to take their fill. The whole populace gathers round, to see them get their deserts, and profit by their leavings. The priests conduct a service in every way similar to that performed at the Magnolia Festival in the Seventh Moon. The invitation to the ghosts to assemble and partake of the feast is issued, and the sacred elements are consecrated and symbolically distributed. The congregation consists of the whole population of the island, anxiously awaiting the moment for the officiating priest to give the signal for the assault.

As far as the dead are concerned, only he can determine when their appetites are satisfied. From time to time the celebrant raises an amber monocle to his eye and peers around, to detect any belated spirit whose tardy arrival has handicapped its complete satisfaction. At last he announces that the last has departed, and that the coast is clear. This is the supreme moment for the congregation, which loses no time in the scramble for the luck of the year. The higher the cake, the greater the honour conferred by its acquisition, so the youth of the island swarm up the scaffolding in a wild race to reach the summit and detach the crowning bun. As there are thirty thousand more, there are plenty of consolation prizes for the less active, and the organisers are not without their compensation, for they sit down to a banquet of thirty-six tables to break their fast.

THE FOURTH MOON

As an offset to the Taoist Festival of the local Saint, Tam Kung (譚公), the Buddhists celebrate the eighth day of the Fourth Moon by a ceremony known as "Washing the Buddha". This is obviously an importation from India, from which country the religion was introduced into China about the beginning of the Christian era. The occasion chosen is the birthday of Sakyamuni, though there is some controversy about the exact date, as the orthodox Indians favour the eighth of the Second, whilst the Chinese Buddhists aver that the bulk of the written evidence on the subject confirms the correctness of the fourth month.

The water for laving the image is scented with various aromatic substances such as sandalwood, musk, ambergris, garu wood, turmeric, and aloes. These are boiled, and the liquid is strained off into a large basin. When all is ready, candles are lighted, and incense is burned whilst the image is immersed and washed. A large congregation is always present as the residue is credited with curative properties, and it is drunk by the faithful. Any which remains is dispensed by the monks to subsequent visitors to their monastery.

In private shrines the Buddhas are not removed from their places but, for the sake of decency, strips of paper are pasted over their eyes, so that they may not watch each other's ablutions. They are also blindfolded whenever the sanctuary is dusted. In some Northern temples the congregation takes part in the washing, for the image is placed in a large jar, and everyone empties a spoonful of water on its head, as they pass in single file. Before the days of currency depreciation, it was the custom to empty a handful of coppers as well on the head of the statue, the value being later expended in incense. The ceremony always took place at night, and was extremely impressive with the illumination of the candles, the smoke and scent of the incense, and the chant of the choir.

The Tam Kung Festival

Tam Kung (譚公) is the second of the Patron Saints of the Boat People, ranking in their affections just after the Queen of Heaven. He appears to be the particular patron of the Hong Kong lightermen, who load and unload ships in the harbour. His name does not appear in the list of Black Letter divinities, for he is a local worthy who attained enlightenment in Kowloon. His amazing powers over the weather determined his popularity, for he can fling up a handful of peas, and call down rain upon the parched crop, or abate the most violent tempest. His placation is, therefore, of the greatest interest to those who have their business upon the waters, for presumably he can call off, as easily as he can create, precipitation, and fine weather for unloading is just as important to a lighterman as a favourable breeze. By throwing up a cup of water he can act as a fire-extinguisher, so he should be cultivated by the

Tam Kung Festival, Shaukiwan

squatters' settlements, were his existence and powers more widely known among the refugees in Hong Kong. Originally a native of Wei Yang, a Hakka District in Kwangtung Province, his power derives from the Nine Dragons, whose petrified remains protect the harbour from the evil influences of the North. His main shrine, on the Kowloon side, was demolished by the Japanese during the Occupation, to make way for the extension of the aerodrome. On the Eighth day of the Fourth Moon his rather dingy temple at Shaukiwan was the centre of attraction, not only of the floating population who arrived in their decorated junks, but of a vast concourse of devotees who packed the buses and the tramway system. The temple is situated on the quay, north of the fishing village, where the foreshore makes a crescent-shaped convex curve. The decorated junks, each with a paper screen on the fo'c'stle with birthday greetings to the divinity, thus formed the arc of a circle of which his shrine was the focal point. The main door of the temple was not fifteen yards from the water's edge. On its north side was a rough shed of unplaned deal planks, knocked up for the occasion to shelter the inevitable puppet-show, and between the entrance and the quay was a large brazier for burning the paper clothing offered to Tam Kung as his summer outfit.

Junks appeared to arrive at any time of the day to suit their working hours but, as a general rule, the day was observed as a holiday. The numbers who proceeded by water were strictly limited to the life-saving equipment carried but, before the 'non-passengers ashore' bell rang, the decks were swarming with friends and relatives, and professional "see-ers off". All the signal flags in the locker were used to dress ship, and the fo'c'stle was adorned with a huge screen in silver and pink, rose, petunia, or green, with the name of the Guild, and birthday greetings to the divinity. Nine lanterns, covered with paper flowers, were hung under the awning over the well-deck, one in the centre, and four on each side. The centre lamp was connected with the corner ones by garlands of fresh frangipani blossoms, and these flowers were also interwoven with the paper decorations of the lanterns. Aft, against the poop, were two huge paper shrines, each containing a sacred picture, almost concealed by floral decoration and cardboard images of the Eight Immortals. A papier mache monster with wings like a butterfly topped the whole structure, which was set off by a strip of scarlet silk, draped across the top with its ends hanging free on either side. The name of the Guild, "Amassing Righteousness Youth Society", was in black lettering on gold below the guardian demon. The shrine on the port side was the real one, and the other was carried in case of misfortune at the scramble to take place after the presentation of offerings. Should the crew be unlucky enough to fail to snatch their ticket, the shrine would be forfeit to the junk crew who were nimbler in the scrummage. In front of these sacred trophies were three huge incense sticks, five feet high and of three inches calibre. These burned for about six hours, and about eighteen inches remained when the vessel returned to her Yaumati anchorage. For'ard of the shrines was a table with the roast pig decorated fore and aft with red rosettes, and between his ears the red trade card of the supplying firm. He was flanked with a dish of pink dumplings, and another of circular serrated brown biscuits. A few token red eggs, for children born and

vows requited, were displayed with the offerings, but the bulk of the chickens' produce was stored in three huge baskets. There must have been a couple of thousand for the twenty-five families contributing to the feast, whose lanterns, later to be blessed by the divinity, were stacked behind the mast. Each child, born during the year, was commemorated by a piece of ginger, affixed to the No. 1 shrine with a red thread, the boys on one side, and the girls on the other. The band, consisting of clarinet, gong and drum, and loud cymbals, was accommodated in the waist on the starboard side, and obliged with a tune during the warping out from the Praya, to the accompaniment of a volley of crackers. The owner having recently acquired a smart green motor launch, this picked up the tow as soon as the junk was over her anchor, and she bowled away at six knots down the harbour. The band settled down to mahjong, and the "Old Lady" took over the tiller. Off North Point other dressed junks were seen converging on Shaukiwan.

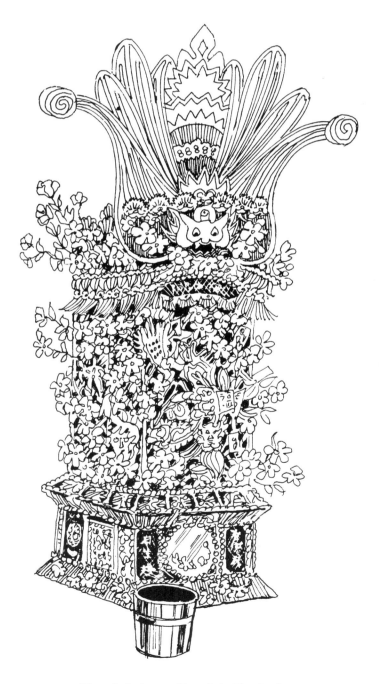

Floral shrine at People's Festival

31

Crossing the bay, the launch made for the left of the line, and cleverly slipped the tow so as to let the lighter nose her way into the quay, pulled up by her stern anchor without a jar. The band played her in, and a volley of crackers saluted the temple as she came to rest. After putting down the gangplank, the procession was organised with the shrines in front, then the band, and finally the roast pig and offerings on a bier. Lastly came the womenfolk with sticks of incense, and bundles of paper clothing for the god. The banner of the Guild was set up with the shrines, facing the temple door, to await a vacancy before the altar. The recent rains and the high humidity of the morning had turned the foreshore into a sea of liquid mud, and the boatwomen all took a reef in their baggy trousers, displaying their calves. They argue that the lining is easier to wash than the material, and their legs are nothing to be ashamed of. All wore their best clothes, and displayed their jewellery to the best advantage. Some had thick gold necklaces, of the dimensions of an "Albert" in Victoria's day. Others had signet rings which would have been massive on a man's hand. Gold and jade bracklets were universal, and the small children were as lavishly bedecked as their elders. The junks made a brave sight with their huge triangular Guild banners of every hue. None of the colours, though striking, are discordant. Like a bunch of sweet peas, no two seem to clash in spite of their diversity. A triangular flag was at every mast, and at least three bore the seven-starred emblem of the Sword of Tzu Ko-liang, who employed it to dissipate evil. Two were white on a cobalt blue ground, and the other was on black.

Two of the biggest cargo junks staged a Lion Dance on the fo'c'stle for the benefit of an admiring crowd, and then the lion was played ashore to be blessed. Its human operators stood on the shoulders of a couple of stout boatmen, who steadied them by the ankles, and high above the throng the lion performed his antics. After he had made his obeisance to Tam Kung, he was piped aboard in similar state. Another Lion, lorry-borne this time, was contributed by a shore-based Guild. In fact it was a great day for lions. A most convincing fur replica, mounted on a green stand with purple wheels, with a movable head and pink tongue in a highly coloured mask, was being retailed at a dollar. It sold like hot cakes, and every junk acquired a pride of lions for the homeward voyage. Just north of the temple, and possibly one of its discarded guardians, was a small stone beast who had seen better days. The right side of his face, and one of his popping eyes, had disappeared but he had not lost his status as the King of Beasts. Between his paws stuck upright in the mud, was a small forest of red incense sticks. Some of his admirers had remembered him though, before they were burned out, the heedless crowd had trampled the sticks into the mire.

The crowd was far denser than the previous year, and the Fair was better. Racks of charms did not seem to be doing a brisk business, but every child had a windmill for "turning luck", or a halberd, the synonym for anything auspicious. A very demure little girl with a briefcase was offering fans, with really well-made bamboo sticks, bearing an attractive design on one side with a Chinese poem on the other. As her price was very low her little store was soon exhausted, and one wondered what profit she made on each. Endless processions seemed to be arriving at the temple door, and there was a constant stream of emerging women with incense, or flaming bundles of burning paper clothing in their hands. The explosion of crackers was continuous, and some of the larger junks ran up set pieces to their yards. Clouds of incense and black powder smoke marked the immediate vicinity of the temple, and a continuous stream of pedestrians like columns of ants choked the lane which led to the tram terminus. Half way down this street was the temple of the Queen of Heaven, whose festival took place about a fortnight previously, and whose shrine was temporarily deserted. A side show, almost opposite, advertising 21-year-old triplets, was doing a languid business. Occasionally a car tried to force its way through the good-natured mob, which was either bent on its devotions, or was in search of refreshment in one of the restaurants in the main street.

For the climax of the festival, the crews of each junk made their way with their Guild banner to a quarry just north of the temple. The crowd followed and took up vantage points on the slopes of rotten granite, whilst the level space below was left for the contestants. All around were ranged openwork cylinders of iron, for discharging maroons into the air. Each contained a shower of crackers, and a wooden sphere with a stick as a tail. Each of these contained the number of one of the Guilds, and it was the object of the team to whom it belonged to secure it in the mêlée. The junk men acquire the luck of whatever number they capture, and in this case the "Amassers of Righteousness" succeeded in collecting the luck of the largest and most opulent junk. This meant that they inherited the most splendid shrine to display in their port cabin for the year, though it carried the obligation of being the biggest contributor to the feast on the next anniversary. To determine which member of the Society would be the guardian of the shrine during the year, lots were cast during the voyage home. A representative of each junk burnt incense before the shrine and had ten throws with a couple of wooden objects, round on one side and flat on the other. If they fell the same way up when dropped on the deck, one point was scored, with nothing if a round and a flat was obtained. Ten throws were allowed to each competitor, and the man with the highest score became custodian. The scramble was a serious affair, as the contestants were smothered in burning debris and exploding crackers, and half-blinded by the acrid smoke. As a rule they took the precaution of tying a handkerchief around their heads to keep the smouldering particles out of their hair. When the luck of the year had been decided, the shrines were re-embarked and lashed in triumph to the mast facing the prow. The junk warped out by hauling on the anchor chain, which pulled her straight astern. The launch then passed the tow rope and either circled or made a figure of eight with her lighter. Each time the junk came head-on to the temple she saluted with bunches of crackers flung into the air, while the band played a rousing tune with a predominance of percussion instruments. In the case of the "Amassers of Righteousness" the capture of the luck so went to their heads that they continued to make tight circles until the supply of crackers ran out, when they set their homeward course.

The band settled down to mahjong, and the crew then started the share out of the feast. The firm which had supplied the roast pig had also contributed twenty-five brown paper carriers, and into these went the eggs, dumplings, and biscuits in equal proportions. Though a family may contribute little to the offerings and thereby earn a reputation for stinginess, yet all share alike in the feast. It is not considered good form, but allowances are made, and there is no discrimination.

The rivals of the Buddhists have two festivals on the 14th and 15th of the Fourth Moon, when two of the most popular of the Eight Immortals receive their birthday congratulations. Except perhaps for Li T'ieh-kuai, the crippled beggar, Lü Tung-pin and Han Chung-li are the most popular of these Chinese worthies. The foreigner is apt to translate the word "Hsien" (仙) as fairies, but it really represents a superior class of human beings who, having been deified, dwell in mountains and hills remote from the habitation of man. They have no temples, and are not of very remote antiquity. However, considerable power is attributed to them, as they can raise the dead, and are possessors of the philosopher's stone, by which not only base metal but any substance can be transmuted into gold. In this respect they are more fortunate than most modern Finance Ministers, who are becoming acutely aware of the paper shortage. The same term Hsien is applied to heaven, gods, earth, water, and the human soul, as the five genii by way of eminence.

Lü Tung-pin (呂洞賓) is the patron saint of barbers, and is also worshipped by the sick, which leads one to suppose that the hairdresser, as in England, combined blood-letting with his tonsorial activities. In his representations he is depicted with a Taoist fly-switch in one hand, and his emblem, a sword, is usually slung across his back. Like Saint Anthony, he was exposed to numerous temptations and, having overcome them, was rewarded with a supernatural sword with which he traversed the earth, ridding it of evil, for over four hundred years. There seems plenty of scope for his services at the present day.

He is still active in Hong Kong. His tablet is on the central altar of a private Taoist Temple at Fanling, and its attendant will assure the visitor that a huge honorific board, which is the show-piece of the establishment, was written by the Immortal himself, with quite a small brush. The characters betoken the scholar, and the size of the brush to execute them is convincing proof of his magical powers. Before the Imperial examinations were abolished, Lü Tung-pin was in great vogue with the candidates, for all they had to do to ensure success was to burn a few bundles of incense sticks before his image, and they were rewarded with a dream, revealing the subject of the theme which would be set. This afforded time to prepare the answers beforehand.

Han Chung-li (漢鍾離), or Chung Li-ch'uan, is the chief of the famous band, and was the teacher and companion of Lü Tung-pin. He is said to have lived some thousand years B.C. and to have obtained the secrets of the elixir of life, and the alchemist's stone, or powder of transmutation. He is usually depicted as a fat man, with a bare midriff, and he sometimes holds a peach in his hand. His emblem of identity is, however, his fan, with which he is believed to revive the souls of the dead. In his biography he sometimes figures as a warrior, sometimes as a Taoist priest, and again as a beggar receiving the Pill of Immortality. His military prowess is not apparent from his dress, as he is invariably depicted in plain clothes, with no weapon to identify him as a soldier.

The Fourth moon is known as the "Peony Moon" for it is in this month that the blossoms come to maturity, and the 19th is the birthday of Wei Shen, their protectress. People gather in their gardens to celebrate the anniversary.

The Tree Peony (Paeonia arborea) is known as the Hua Wang, or King of Flowers (花王), and has the alternative name of Flower of Riches and Honour, which accounts for its popularity among the Chinese. It is regarded as the blossom of the Yang, or Male principle, of brightness and masculinity. As the petals do not vary, the names chosen depend upon the colour. The deep red are known as "Ink", the white as "Jade", and the cream as "Bright" Mou Tan. Those esteemed most highly are the "Ink", and a variety with a yellow mark at the edge of the petal, known as the "Golden Border". More than thirty kinds are cultivated, usually on terraces, and the blooms are protected from the sun, when at its fiercest, by mat awnings. Up till the outbreak of the War with Japan, the President used to issue invitations for Peony viewing, when the flowers were at their best, and the beds in the Central Park in Peking were illuminated by night.

The flower is an emblem of love and affection, and a symbol of feminine beauty. It is one of the seasonal flowers, representing spring. The lotus follows it for summer, whilst the chrysanthemum and prunus symbolise autumn and winter. The peony acts as a kind of barometer of the fortunes of the family. If it is in good leaf, and bears abundant flowers, it is a sign of good fortune. Should the leaves suddenly dry up, and the flowers fade, or turn a sickly shade, poverty stares the owner in the face, or the household is threatened with some overwhelming disaster.

A Peking Pilgrimage

One of the features of Peking was the annual pilgrimage to Miao Feng Shan (妙峯山), a Taoist temple on a peak 4,000 feet high, about thirty miles from the old Chinese capital. The city lies in the flat plain which gave rise to the new, or rather revived, name of Pei P'ing (北平), adopted by the Nationalists when they moved their metropolis back to Nanking. To the south the ground extends level to the sea, but to the east, north and west lies a horseshoe of barren hills stretching from Mongolia to the province of Shansi.

The Western Hills are the most accessible, and are studded with the relics of magnificent temples, on which successive emperors have lavished fortunes. The decay of the dynasty and the waning interest in religion deprived the monks of the means of maintenance, and disintegration would have been complete had not well-to-do foreigners adopted them for their summer quarters. This at any rate kept the roofs sound, and the heavy July rains from destroying the carvings and gilded images in the buildings dedicated to worship. It also prevented the destruction of the magnificent old trees, for, in a country where firing is scarce, temples are the only places of refuge for sizable timber. The Japanese "incident" probably dealt the death blow to the "Eight Great Places" (八大處) and other monasteries of the Western Hills. Ideal as a hideout for guerillas they were burned in punitive expeditions, or fell to pieces from neglect.

The Festival at Miao Feng Shan (the "Marvellous Peak") took place from the first to the eighteenth of the Fourth, or "Peony", Moon, and was attended by all classes of society. The Western Hills facing Peking were of their winter steely blue, and had not yet assumed the greenish mantle which clothes them after the July rains. The two most popular routes to the summit are from the railway which connects the anthracite mines at Men T'ou Kou with the West Gate of the city, the walk beginning at San Chia Tien, or by the motor road past the Summer Palace to the Black Dragon Pool, and the Temple of Ta Chueh Ssu, at the foot of a steeper trail.

The devotees usually organise themselves in parties, like Chaucer's Canterbury Pilgrims, and the whole performance is a strange mixture of the holiday spirit combined with real religious sentiment. Along the path mat-sheds are erected for the refreshment of the worshippers, often by philanthropic societies, where there is no charge for the hot tea supplied to wealthy patrons and donkey boys alike. Small shrines dot the roadside and, as every pilgrim passes, even a dog, the attendant registers his presence with a stroke on a low-toned gong to inform the gods of another worshipper on the way to acquire merit. The crowd is a complete cross-section of the population, from wealthy officials to beggars in an advanced stage of leprosy. Those in urgent need of the assistance of one or all of the three goddesses, in whose honour the pilgrimage is performed, will go to any length to ensure a favourable response to their petitions. Some compass the twenty-nine miles wearing chains hired from a temple. Others are under a vow to prostrate themselves with a triple kow-tow, at every so many paces. A childless woman will make the nine full-length prostrations and, stretching out her fingers, will repeat the process on the spot their tips have reached. One middle-aged gentleman was observed sitting, wearing the cangue, by the side of one of the shrines, with a strong sun beating on his bald head.

Leaving the railway at San Chia Tien, the first two miles are across the flat bed of the turbulent Hun River which, lower down, is spanned by the famous Marco Polo Bridge. A ferry takes the party and animals across one of its tributaries and, passing through a village on its banks, they engage on the path which leads to the summit sixteen miles away.

The ascent at first is very gradual, and the path is sometimes flagged and bounded by rough stone walls. Suddenly it rises steeply to cross a divide, crowned with a watch tower and shrine, to drop into one of the loveliest valleys in the Western Hills. The eight-mile climb up the glen was sheer delight. The motley crowd was of never-ending interest. The members of the Mountebanks Guild carrying their professional paraphernalia on poles, their loads decorated with bells and yellow flags, were much in evidence, and one troupe gave their time-honoured performance on the conclusion of their religious exercises. Descending pilgrims, with souvenir staves carved with dragons' heads, passed the time of day with those who had yet to qualify for this distinctive favour. The usual Chinese greeting is "Shang na'rh" (Where are you going?). It might have been applicable to the returning host, but was too obvious to apply to the hill climbers. Anyway the answer is the same as the question, much like the English "How do you do?" where no one expects a catalogue of one's acquaintance's symptoms.

The pilgrims are supplied with a sort of Baedecker for their guidance, in which they learn exactly which shrines they must patronise, and what solatiums are expected. Beside the aids to worship, a secular guide for comportment towards superiors, equals and inferiors is included.

At the bottom the glen is broad, and the track leads over the stony bed of the stream which is only flooded in the summer rains. Higher up the gorge deepens, and the rocky path contours the hills some fifty feet above the brook. Occasionally a crystal spring pours over a stone conduit and spills across the roadway, forming some village water supply.

At night the whole glen seems full of moving fireflies, as the torchlight procession mounts slowly upward. The air is throbbing with the boom of gongs, the tinkle of bells, and the cries of bearers overtaking the slower-moving traffic. The villagers offer fans and ornaments of plaited straw, and "Lucky flags" in red chenille, as fairings, and do a roaring trade as some souvenir must always be brought home to bring luck and register the accomplished vow.

After passing the last village the valley peters out, and the hills become wilder. The last five hundred feet to the peak is a stiff climb. Jagged limestone rocks, interspersed with coarse grass, and a few weather-stunted stone pines compose the scenery. Beggars line the track, smitten with every form of loathsome disease. They stand singly a few yards apart, so as not to cramp one another's style, but each hoping for patronage on account of his special infirmities. The expenditure of 165 coins, distributed to each, without favour or certainly affection, only exhausted about two-thirds of the tally.

The actual buildings which crown the Peak are insignificant after the magnificent temples in the Western Hills. Legend attributes their construction to a Taoist monk, a Buddhist, and a pious layman in 1622, and who are we to dispute it? The three goddesses are not good examples of graven images, but they have enormous appeal to Chinese mentality, just as some disreputable rag-doll may find a warmer spot in a child's heart than a waxen creation of real artistic merit. The main divinity is one of the most attractive of the Taoist pantheon—the Jade Lady (玉女). She was invented under the Sung Dynasty, as a parallel to the Buddhist Kuan Yin, who was exciting altogether too much interest to please the rival sect. Her success was instantaneous, as the devotees of Taoism were badly in need of a female divinity to take an interest in their requirements. She was at the height of her popularity under the Ming Dynasty, and is still a best-seller, though under different names in the various provinces. In Fukien she is simply "Mother" (母). Her local name at Miao Feng Shan is the "T'ien Hsien (Heaven Fairy) Niang Niang" (天仙娘娘), and she is sometimes identified with the Granddaughter of the Spirit of the Sacred Mountain T'ai Shan (泰山).

The Yen Kuan Niang Niang (眼光娘娘) cures ophthalmia, and is therefore much in request, as the disease is a positive scourge in North China. She is represented as an old woman in a blue peasant's coat, and was unofficially canonised.

The third of the Trinity is the Tzu **Sun Niang Niang** (子孫娘娘), who attends to the family part of the business, with an emphasis on sons. She is sometimes represented masked, with a sack over her shoulders in which she carries infants for distribution. Thanks-offerings of red eggs and children's shoes are placed on her altar, and childless women will often purloin the latter in the hopes that they may bring them the same luck, in which case they provide the altar with a new pair.

The temples of these three goddess are on three sides of a square court-yard, on the fourth side of which is an immense brick platform, walled around, to contain the bundles of incense sticks and prevent their dissemination by the wind. The whole mountain top smokes like a volcano, with continuous stoking throughout the twenty-four hours. Endless prayers are offered, for none of the shrines are neglected, and the copper coins contributed fill several deep pits. At the actual worship the crowd is intent on nothing else, and it was interesting to see how two women members of the Japanese Legation Staff remained absolutely unnoticed. As the Kwangtung Army had just overrun Jehol at this time, and were increasing their demands on Peking itself, their presence might have been embarrassing but, neither in their holiday mood, nor in their religious fervour, did the crowd show the least sign of resentment.

There is always merit to be gained in China by ascending high places, as foreigners in Hong Kong will have noted by the crowding of the Peak Tram at the autumn festival of the "Double Ninth", when such an act of piety is positively *de rigueur*. Accordingly, their religious observances concluded, the pilgrims crowd on the terrace overlooking the valley of the Hun, before embarking on the descent. The "Tea-Burden Procession" (採茶隊) is over for the year, and they step out with lengthened pace, full of jokes and good humour, to the dispersal point in the Northern Plain.

Dragon Boat race . . . it has everything to recommend it

THE FIFTH MOON

The Dragon Boat Festival
(端午節)

The celebration, known to foreigners as the "Dragon Boat Festival", is always referred to by the Chinese as the Wu Yueh Chieh (五月節) Fifth Month Festival or the Double Fifth, as it falls on the Fifth Day of the Fifth Lunar Month. The boat race is by no means a universal accompaniment, and is not practised in the North. According to de Groot these contests represent fighting dragons, in order to stimulate a real dragon fight in the heavens, which is always accompanied by heavy rain.

The day is one of the three settlement days for accounts, and also marks the turn of the year, as far as agriculture is concerned, and all over the world it has been celebrated from time immemorial as the Summer Solstice. Primitive peoples, in this month of plenty, had time to propitiate the gods in whom they put their faith for success in hunting, fishing, or clan warfare. As China, south of the Yangtze, abounds in rivers and lakes, it is to be presumed that these rites have survived in the cult of water-gods, upon whom their livelihood depended for an adequate supply of fish. The first water divinities included the ghosts of the drowned who, for want of a comfortable sepulchre, were liable to become wandering, and therefore malevolent, spirits. The offerings of rice cast upon the waters, and lanterns set adrift to guide the spirits to the feast, were intended to placate these hungry ghosts, and divert their attention from those who gained their living in ships. The dragon is the controller of the waters, and the dispenser of rain, which is due in China

in the last week of the month. His propitiation is therefore to be sought to ensure an adequate supply for the crops which are now ripening.

The legend of Ch'u Yuan (屈原), the virtuous Minister of the State of Ch'u, who lived in the feudal period of the Fourth Century B.C., is exactly the sort of semi-historical basis which the Chinese love to attribute to far more distant myths. The races are said to commemorate the death of Ch'u Yuan, whose body was never found when he drowned himself in the T'ung T'ing lake to lend force to his unheeded protests about the decadence of the court, and the consequent collapse of government.

There is little wonder that the Midsummer Festival is the most popular of the Chinese religious observances among foreigners. It has everything to recommend it, as the scene is packed with interest, and the races take place at such short intervals that an hour seems like ten minutes. For the Chinese, the races are but part of the celebrations, and represent the holidaying mood, the religious festival being observed in the home, with sacrifices and offerings to the ancestors; also the religious significance of the contests is never lost sight of by the participants.

For the greater part of the year the craft lie on chocks, covered with rattan matting, adjacent to the shrine of one of the sea divinities. Sometimes there is a boat house, as at Cheung Chau, which accommodates three, or at Shaukiwan which has a pair alongside the Tam Kung Temple. At Aberdeen two craft winter in the open on either side of Island Road, and at Stanley the 90-foot boat lies on the edge of a small creek thirty yards from

Dragon Boat races

T'ien Hou's Lucky Altar. The head and tail of the dragon are kept within the sacred precincts, as are the drums and banners of the crew. The Stanley percussion instruments are painted royal blue, with the name of the guild, Ho Ch'ing Tang (和慶堂) (the Harmonious Lucky Society), in white characters.

The general rule in Hong Kong is to start training on the day of the Tam Kung Festival, the 8th of the Fourth Moon but, trusting to the magic of their name and divine assistance, the Stanley crew only launched their craft five days before the contest. As soon as the boat took the water, she was dressed overall with six banners, each tipped with a sprig of evergreen, and the dragon's head was decorated with boughs of cypress. The stern ensign was triangular with a wavy border like the old dragon standard of the empire but, instead of the Royal emblem, the field carried the cypher of the guild.

As soon as the crew was in place the drummer beat the stroke, and the craft was paddled seaward for about three hundred yards. The bow was then turned directly towards the T'ien Hou Temple and three runs were made to the edge of the beach, a burst of crackers accompanying the roll of the drum which gave the signal to backwater. Having obtained the blessing of the church, training began in earnest, and spurts of increasing distance were made on a course ending opposite the centre of the village. Owing to its length the dragon boat has a big turning circle, but it is so constructed that it travels with equal facility in either direction, and the rowers have only to reverse in their seats to propel it stern first to the mark boat. As training progressed, it was paced by a motorised junk on each side. These vessels act as mother ships to the dragon, towing it round to the races, and accommodating the crew at night.

The contests at Aberdeen are held in the harbour between the quay and Apleichau, the finishing line being just opposite the fish restaurants. The course is lined on either side by junks, launches and sampans. A very good view may be obtained by hiring one of the latter, as the old boatwomen who manage these craft are quite unscrupulous at worming their way into the front row to give their passengers a seat in the stalls. In spite of the shortness of practice, the Stanley boat returned at noon on the following morning with three more banners than it set out with, in high fettle undampened by torrents of rain. It was towed round the headland into the West Bay, where it was manned to return to base. With drums beating and nine banners waving, it made three runs in towards the temple, announced on each occasion by a volley of crackers. The boat was then stripped of its decorations, and was carried up to its winter quarters. The drummer ensconced himself in a sampan pulled up on the beach and, sheltered by an umbrella, continued his accompaniment till all was snug. The whole crew then entered the temple to give thanks for their success to the Queen of Heaven, presenting before the altar the trays containing the feast they had earned. Finally the drums and banners were brought in with the dragon's head and tail ornaments, for storage till next season.

The basis of the feast is roast pork, but the essential concomitant has a religious significance as the recipe is alleged to have been furnished by none other than the Patron Saint. When the spirit of the virtuous Ch'u Yuan (屈原) appeared to the villagers who had been casting their bread upon the waters for his sustenance, it complained that a monster intercepted the gifts, and suggested a remedy. The sacrifices were to be wrapped in pointed leaves, resembling the demon-dispelling sword, to ensure their safe delivery. In Hong Kong specially selected leaves of bamboo are sold to wrap the Ch'ün Tze (粽子), as the cakes are called. The foundation is glutinous rice, with green beans, pork, lotus seeds and the yolk of a salted egg as ingredients. Each portion is wrapped in five leaves, and is then boiled for four hours. Ch'u Yuan prescribed that the bundles should be tied with silk threads of the five colours, red, yellow, blue, black and white, but this practice has fallen into disuse, and a sort of raffia is used to keep the packet from falling apart. Confectioners make these cakes in all sizes, to suit every purse, and they are eaten all over the country, often by people who are ignorant of the origin of the custom but who expect them, as agnostics accept hot cross buns, at the appropriate season. In Peking, the Ch'un Tsu, as they are called, are triangular in shape, but in the South the square form is adopted.

Another year, the Boat People issued an invitation to witness the main regatta from their No. 2 Junk, but poor liaison resulted in an unloading contract being accepted for the day by one of the family who had not been consulted. The "Old Man", however, worked all night to clear the cargo, and was at the rendezvous well before zero hour. As the junk warped out and made fast her hawser to the launch, a dragon boat, with drum beating and colours flying, swept past in a cloud of spray. Seen so close it is a most impressive craft, eighty to a hundred and twenty feet in length, with a beam of five and a half feet, and a depth of two feet six inches. There is very little freeboard and, with the splash of the paddles, the crew have a pretty damp time. The bow is ornamented with a carved dragon's head, and the stern with his tail, and also a triangular banner on a long pole. The drum for keeping time in this case was amidships, with a gong just behind it. Other competitors had the band in the stern or bows. Before the launch and junk were settled on their westerly course, the dragon boat was several hundred yards ahead, skirting the inshore shipping. Just astern, the thump of other drums attracted the attention, and two more dragons were seen coming up in tow of fast launches. They did not seem, however, to be lessening the lead of the craft proceeding under its own power.

Making for Green Island at the western limit of the harbour, the junk cast anchor at the east end of the bay. The maritime audience at that time consisted of about thirty launches, and a couple of representatives of the Hong Kong Yacht Club. Boats continued to arrive until there must have been well over sixty, from wallah-wallahs to sea-going cruisers. The shore was crowded with spectators, many in bathing-dress, and the junk, which lay only fifty yards offshore, was boarded once or twice by boys who imagined they could get a better view of the race from the fo'c'stle than the water-level.

The first three dragon boats, with their drums going hard, paddled out together to the starting-point. Their return was so level that it would have needed a photo finish to determine the winner, and it was the general opinion that it was merely the parade, and not the actual contest, which was being witnessed. They were hardly home before two fresh crews took their place. There was no doubt about a race this time. The drums seemed to have increased their tempo, and the standing men gesticulated wildly to encourage their crews. There is far more excitement in the circular motion of the small paddles, whipping upon the foam, than in the leisurely stroke of English university oarsmen. On the Thames the cox's encouragements may be heard, but not seen, and the audience provides the noise. Chinese spectators are by no means behind-hand in their vociferous appreciation of the efforts of the rival Tongs, and the silent inscrutability, erroneously attributed by Europeans to the nation, was conspicuous by its absence. As a spectacle, the sprint races of the dragons are unrivalled, and one contest was hardly over before the next two boats were on their way to the starting-mark.

Next, the chief event of the day took place. The four boats left the shore amid a burst of crackers which lasted until they had reached the three-quarter-mile limit. They came in at a tremendous pace, and were neck-and-neck about a hundred yards from the finish. Seen against the sun, there was a haze of spray as they drove along. The drummers were working overtime, and the standing bowmen wildly waving to encourage the crews, rather than to distribute the Ch'ün Tze (粽子) to appease the hungry spirit of the virtuous Ch'u Yuan, their ostensible function. One boat seemed to be about a third of a length behind the others but, in racing parlance, a handkerchief would have covered the lot. The last hundred yards was a frenzied flurry, as Wo Ho Tong short-headed Hop Yee Tong for the winning pennant. Excitement among the supporters ashore was intense, and the applause greeting the victors was wholehearted. A Chinese holiday crowd is always appreciative, and it is a tonic to see how they enjoy themselves. They have certainly solved the problem of employing their leisure to the best advantage.

After a couple more matches, five dragons went out for the final, before drawing up parallel to the beach to receive their prizes. The spectator launches began to slip away one by one, and the junk weighed anchor to take advantage of a favourable wind to run for home. China tea and a feast of ch'ün tze and dumplings commemorated the sad fate of the upright official. The junk ghosted before the slight breeze, with scarcely a ripple at the stem. The cheering died away, and one was left with a sense of physical lassitude engendered by strong mental excitement. The glare on the water, the riot of colour of the decorations, and the violence of the struggle between the contesting dragons, all combined to tire the eye, and overtax the brain with impressions. Sitting under an awning in a cool breeze, with an ever ready teapot within reach, is hardly a strenuous occupation, compared to the bustle and struggle of a race course, but unless a fortune hangs on the result, the mental strain is infinitely greater.

From the spectator's point of view there is no doubt that the launch is the solution to the problem. The dragons are seen on the beam, instead of bow on, and the action is infinitely more vivid. They really give the effect of some sea monster tearing through the water at incredible speed and with singleness of purpose. When moving out to practice they are more majestic, and give the impression of benevolence, as their paddles rotate in perfect rhythm but, pitted against one another, there is something terrifying in their dash, suggestive of a beast of prey in its final spring upon the quarry.

All over Kwangtung Province boys go round on the Double Fifth with a model of the Dragon Boat on a stick, making house-to-house calls to collect money. A special Boat Song is peculiar to this visitation and, after their vocal contribution, the model is nailed to the gate post to ward off disaster and bad luck, for which service the singers are rewarded. In some families the offspring are made godchildren of the Dragon Boat, and are thus placed under its protection.

About a hundred and fifty years ago, during the Napoleonic wars, an English merchant residing in the Canton factories gave an order for a book of water-colours, executed by a Chinese artist, depicting all phases of native life from the artisan to the official. One of the drawings represented the boy with the Dragon Boat. He is poorly dressed in a pale blue jacket over a rather ragged gown, and slung round his neck are a gong and a drum. The boat is an extremely elaborate model with a blue hull given a scaly effect with white lines. The head is decorated with a red beard and the tail consists of green feathers. The rowers all wear conical red hats, and three officials are on the upper deck, the leader sheltered by a red umbrella. There is a pencil note by the owner of the album who was under the impression that the boy was an ordinary beggar but, though he expected some return for his talismanic model, he could no more be classed as a mendicant than the carol singers at Christmas.

THE LOTUS MOON

The Sixth Moon of the Chinese calendar is known to poets as the Lotus Moon, for on the 24th is the birthday of the flower associated with the Lord Buddha, which coincides with the real breaking of the summer rains. The Lung Wang, or Dragon Prince, who is responsible for an adequate water supply, celebrates his anniversary on the 13th, and dragon processions are organised throughout the fifth and sixth moons to ensure a favourable response to prayers for rain. The Chinese leave no stone unturned to provoke the moisture essential for their crops and, in 1926, there is a record of the inhabitants of Ch'ang Ch'un (Manchuria) invoking the aid of the Greek Orthodox priest to hold a service for rain, as their own divinities had proved unresponsive.

A good many liberties were taken with the Dragon Prince, if he was sluggish in granting the requests of the populace. A favourite way of getting action was to make him uncomfortable by exposing his image to the burning rays of the sun. This expedient is attributed to a Ch'ing emperor who made a pilgrimage to the Black Dragon Pool, near Peking, to pray for rain, without result. He retaliated by issuing a mandate banishing the Dragon to the frozen steppes of Hei Lung Chiang, the northern province of Manchuria. A start was actually made in the Dog Days, or period of greatest heat, and the farther the dragon's tablet went, the hotter and thirstier he grew. After a few miles the dragon could stand it no longer, and rain began to fall. Kao Tsung therefore rescinded his order, and he was brought back, the bearers splashing through empty villages. It is considered unlucky to be out of doors when rain falls, particularly in the neighbourhood of Peking, for it is unbecoming to witness this mystery of nature by which the earth is revitalised.

The only animal who knows when it is going to rain is the tortoise, and he is held in such low esteem that speculations on rainfall are taboo lest the implication should involve comparison with a creature who has forgotten the eight laws of politeness.

As the dragon, or for that matter the clerk of the weather all the world over, can never be depended on not to overegg the pudding, dispensing more water than is required, the Chinese hold in reserve one of the Star divinities, the Sao Ch'ing Niang Niang. This daughter of San Shou, the Broom, has a besom with which she can sweep away the clouds when an excess of rain is liable to rot the crops. To invoke her services it is necessary to cut out a paper figure of the goddess, and hang it up behind the door, which precaution, sooner or later, causes the sun to reappear.

One of the Fire Gods, for there is a whole ministry to deal with conflagrations, is commemorated on the 22nd, particularly in South China. Canton used to hold celebrations in his honour, with elaborate puppet-shows which lasted most of the month. The main divinity, who is worshipped on the 17th of the Eighth Moon, is Chu Jung (祝融), once a Minister of the Yellow Emperor.

There is, however, considerable diversity of opinion about his origin, as he is also identified with Ch'ung Li (鍾黎), the deified son of the legendary Emperor Chuan Hsu (顓頊), who was given control over wood and fire, whilst another pedigree traces him to the era of Fu Hsi (伏羲), (B.C. 2593). He governs the South, and is sometimes known as Nan Fang Chun (南方君) (Prince of the Southern House). Another of his names is Hui Lu (回祿), when he is represented as an animal with a human face, with a brace of dragons as chargers. As becomes his occupation, his face is flushed and he has an extra eye in the centre of his forehead to enable him to see all round. His temple attendants hold various emblems as omens of fire. A pair of birds, a fiery serpent, a fire wheel, and a note-book to record the places of visitation constitute his stage properties. Conflagrations are spread by his red crow, which flies from place to place fanning the flames. One of his characteristics is an extreme sense of propriety, so housewives take out an insurance against his visitation by hanging indecent pictures in the kitchen. His importance in a country where organised precautions against fire are practically unknown can hardly be overestimated.

The birthday of Lu Pan, Patron Saint of Builders, is celebrated throughout the country on varying days during the month. He was a contemporary of Confucius, being born in 606 B.C. and was a skilful carpenter, until he forsook trade for the life of a recluse. In his mountain retreat he studied magic, and built a palace for Hsi Wang Mu, besides repairing the pillars of heaven, and dabbling in aeronautics.

The locals, attributing his supernatural powers to the evil one, finally murdered him, but the incidence of a prolonged drought convinced them of their mistake and, like the Maid of Orleans, he was finally canonised. In his disembodied state he returned to the Li Shan Mountains in Shantung, where he completed his mastery of magic before mounting on high leaving a legacy of his axe and saw. Numerous stories are recounted of his assistance to craftsmen faced with difficulties in design, and the double set of eaves on the Mongol Temple in Peking is due to his inspiration. When a house is built, a feast is spread for him on a day chosen by the diviner, with the accompaniment of incense, crackers, and the burning of spirit money. With the orgy of construction in Hong Kong he must be working overtime, and violating all the laws of a self-respecting trades-union.

The "Double Sixth" is purely a Buddhist observance known as Airing the Classics, in commemoration of a disaster which overtook the scriptures on their journey from India. The boat carrying the pilgrims upset at a river crossing, and the books had to be spread out to dry after their immersion. In all monasteries the library books are taken from their shelves and examined, to prevent mould and the ravages of noxious insects. In the days of the Empire this day was also chosen for going through the Imperial archives. Women wash their hair, and give baths to their pets.

The Birthday of the Lotus

The birthday of flowers in general is celebrated on the twelfth, or in some provinces the fifteenth, of the Second Moon, and their protectress, Wei Shen, is honoured on the 19th of the Fourth, the day being known as the "washing of the blossoms" (洗花). The Lotus, however, having a special sanctity, on account of its connection with Buddhism, enjoys an anniversary of its own on the 24th of the Sixth Moon when the summer rains are expected to break in the North. Its blooming in the ponds and moats around Peking, particularly in the once Royal enclosures, is a sign that the prayers to the Dragon Prince have borne fruit, and that the moisture necessary for an abundant harvest has been showered on the parched earth. Viewing the lotus is to the inhabitants of the capital what the cherry blossom is to the Japanese, and crowds invade the lakes of the Winter Palace to enjoy the pink blossom through which lanes are cut to facilitate the passage of rowing boats.

Confucius, in his teachings, never speculated on the after-life, laying all his stress on behaviour in this world and leaving the future to take care of itself. The essence of Buddhism was the doctrine of universal redemption, of which the lotus, nurtured in the foulest mud, yet rising immaculate, is the symbol. Buddha, himself, is imagined at the apex of all things, seated on a lotus contemplating with compassion the sorrows of mankind. In his temples the main manifestations of the divinity are always depicted on a lotus throne.

The red lotus, *Nelumbium speciosum*, occurs throughout China, but its cultivation seems somewhat neglected in Hong Kong. A good pond, however, lies at the foot of the hillside on which the Hsi Lin Monastery (西林寺) is built, a couple of hundred yards from the north-east end of Shatin railway station. It is crossed by a zig-zag bridge leading to a restaurant from which the blossoms can be seen to great advantage. The little nunnery at Fanling, another old ladies' contemplative retreat, has a circular tank with a stone parapet for the sacred flower in the centre of the court outside its main temple, and a nursey garden between Tai Po and Fanling always has a good show.

The lotus is classed as one of the Eight Treasures, or auspicious signs of the sole of Buddha's foot, and sometimes symbolically represents the liver of the divinity.

The blossom itself is regarded as the flower of summer and fruitfulness. Chinese artists are very fond of painting a series of pictures denoting the four seasons, winter being represented by the prunus, spring the peony, and autumn the chrysanthemum. The lotus appears also in the designs for carpets, architecture and embroidery often being highly conventionalised. The jewel in the lotus flower, so often used in Lamaistic Buddhism as the Sanskrit invocation "Om Mani Padme Hum", is the drop of dew collected by the leaf which flashes in the morning sun like a diamond.

The idea, like so much else in Lamaism, is borrowed from the Indian worship of Brahma, who is sometimes represented seated upon a lotus flower which issues from the navel of Vishnu, who floats upon his back in the ocean. The prayer expresses the hope that the soul of the supplicant may be like the gemmous dewdrop, before it falls into the peaceful obscurity of the lake, and merges with the infinite, thus losing its identity.

Every part of the lotus has a name and function. It may be cultivated in earthenware or porcelain tubs containing goldfish, purely for ornamental purposes, or in large ponds and lakes for commercial use. Peking is the place par excellence to admire it, for not only are the moats of the Forbidden City choked with its jade green, leathery leaves, but the great lakes of the Winter and Summer Palaces are pink with its blossom. White lotus is rare in the neighbourhood of the old Capital, though small patches exist near the western barracks, between the Yen Ching University and Wan Shou Shan, the favourite residence of the Empress Dowager. The beds are particularly beautiful after a shower, as great drops of water collect at the base of the leaves, shining like diamonds in the sudden sun.

Roots, fruit, and leaves are used for food, and the seeds make one of the best sweetmeats of a Chinese feast. The flowers are rarely gathered, as their beauty is enhanced by natural surroundings. The dried stamens are used as a cosmetic, and as an astringent remedy. The seeds also have a medicinal value. The kernels are boiled in soup, roasted, or eaten raw. The roots, when cut transversely, exhibit the structure of a tubular boiler. When sliced, they are used as an article of diet, or they can be ground into paste to form a species of arrowroot. The leaves are mainly used for wrapping, and the seed-pod, which resembles the rose of a watering-can, finds a market with the druggist.

When Buddha attained enlightenment under the bodhi tree, compassion for his fellow-men took possession of him, and he envisaged them like lotus buds in a lake, springing from the oozy mud, and striving to attain the surface to blossom. The lotus became the symbol of purity, as it grew in mud and was not defiled. Its constant use as an emblem appears to result from its wheel-like form, the petals representing the spokes of the Wheel of Life. Buddha is usually represented seated on a lotus throne, and he surmounts the heaven of his creed seated on the same flower.

The Taoists also have a great admiration for the blossom, which is the emblem of Ho Hsien-ku, the Lady Immortal, who holds the stem and seed-pod in which occasionally flowers or peaches are represented. Like the pomegranate, the number of seeds in the pod makes the lotus a symbol of numerous offspring.

THE SEVENTH MOON

The Double Seventh

The most picturesque and popular legend connected with the Star Gods is celebrated on the Seventh Day of the Seventh Moon by unmarried women who, on that night, make their offerings to the patroness of needlework. For weeks before, the maidens embroider shoes and garments for the Heavenly Weaver, whose seat is in the star Vega. There she fabricates the garments of the celestial host, awaiting the one night of the year when she may rejoin her husband across the Milky Way.

Though one of the daughters of the Kitchen God, she was once a mortal, and therefore has a sympathetic understanding for lovers, who do not appeal in vain for her assistance. Her husband is the Cowherd, now immortalised on the star Altair in the constellation Aquila. He was a younger brother of a farmer named Niu, whose possessions included a supernatural ox and a very disagreeable wife. The lady in question took an unreasoning dislike to her brother-in-law and drove him from the farmstead, with the buffalo as his sole stock-in-trade. The ox soon became the senior partner in the firm and, on his advice, the young man rapidly became prosperous and acquired a house of his own. This naturally entailed the quest of a wife to look after the domestic affairs, whom the ox undertook to provide. Taking his master to the Bridge of Fair Maidens (Chih Nu Ch'iao), they surprised the seven daughters of the Kitchen God in the act of bathing, and ran off with the clothes of the prettiest, who chanced to be the Weaving Maid. She was forced to present herself in a state of nature at the Cowherd's home where, to end her embarrassment, she consented to become his bride. The marriage was a complete success and, during the three years it lasted, she bore her husband a son and a daughter. Unfortunately, the gods' wardrobes had suffered grievously by the absence of their dressmaker, and they were beginning to look shabby. The meeting of the lovers was therefore restricted to one night a year, when Chih Nu could see her husband and children across the river which had been their first meeting-place. This state of affairs continued till the Cowman's death, when he became an Immortal, and was translated to the heavens. The Queen of Heaven, who was a dressy lady, determined not to be deprived a second time of the services of her couturière so, with a sweep of her hairpin, she drew the Milky Way across the sky to separate the two stars in which the lovers dwelt. Though they can always see one another, they may only meet on the Double Seventh, when all the magpies in the world take compassion on the pair, and form the Great Bird Bridge with their wings. Oddly enough, on that particular day magpies do seem to disappear but, should the sky be overcast, the bridge cannot be thrown, and the rain, in the shape of the lovers' tears, bears witness to the fact that they must endure another year of separation. After the Weaving Maid has recrossed to her own star, the birds disperse, leaving behind only those whose time has come to die. The sound of the lovers' weeping at the parting can be heard by anyone sitting under a grapevine between midnight and dawn. The twin children are the small stars near Vega in the constellation of Lyra.

The festival is essentially one for women and, in the North, usually takes place within the compound, with only small boys still under their mother's wing being present. Formerly the ladies of the house held an exhibition of needlework with prizes for the best embroidery.

Needle-threading competitions were also popular, and difficulties were introduced by only permitting the fitful light of the first quarter moon, or the glow of a stick of incense, to illuminate the procedure. At midnight, the young girls and their amahs visited the well and drew water in large containers, after invoking the Goddess and her sisters to bestow on it medicinal properties. The jars were then sealed and were placed in a special bin for the use of the family in case of sickness. The Weaver is also invoked as the symbol of married happiness to ensure a good husband and the children which set the seal on the union. She is particularly indulgent to orphan girls and extends her protection and sympathy for the loss of their home life.

On the evening of one such festival, the skies had cleared after a three-hour thunderstorm and, by nightfall, all the side-streets were thronged with sight-seers. The chief offering to the Seven Sisters was a circular tray whose centrepiece depicted the meeting of the Cowherd and the Weaving Lady, who stood on a bridge spanning a stream in which waded the Magic Buffalo led by the Cowherd. In the background were the six sisters. Round the tray were the ornaments and toilet requisites for all seven; a fan, mirror, powder puff, bracelets and cosmetics, sometimes a flute, and always paper flowers for the hair, and a comb for dressing it. The trays varied from the cheapest variety in paper, on which the emblems were printed in colour, to huge electrically illuminated discs, hung on shop frontages, with mechanical tableaux in the centre. Some were fifteen to twenty feet across. Hanging at the side were elaborately painted paper dresses of Ming period style for the sisters, and a black and gold costume for the Cowherd. The altar, set just outside, or immediately within the doorway, was furnished with the usual five vessels, and three thick sticks of incense smouldered in the burner. In front were piles of fruit and nuts. Oranges lent a bright spot of colour. Green melons, bananas, dragons' eyes, and carambolas, regardless of price, formed part of the offerings. On one altar a white porcelain bowl filled with pure water, on which floated two pummelo leaves, symbolised the ritual bath for the bride. That Chinese religious ideas move with the times is demonstrated by the fact that an aeroplane is occasionally provided to ensure the meeting of the Celestial Lovers in the case when the weather is cloudy, and the magpies cannot form the bridge. Similarly at funerals a cardboard motorcar has replaced the old Peking cart for those Chinese whose affluence enabled them to enjoy the comfort of a limousine during their lifetime.

Cheapest form of paper tray with toilet articles for the "Seven Sisters".

Perhaps the prettiest display consisted of a huge illuminated tray hung above an altar which was set on a balcony in front of the ground entrance to an building. As there was no house opposite, the effect of the lighting was enhanced, and crowds of sight-seers stood below, or on the steep staircase. An enormous roast pig was the centrepiece of the table, which groaned with its load of fruit. Nothing for the comfort of the seven sisters had been omitted, for they were even provided with a cigarette and a lipstick apiece. The outlay for all this magnificence was considerable, and had been contributed by six girls, none of whom belonged to any guild. As a rule the maidens form clubs, according to their trade, and contribute a small monthly sum from their earnings. Should a girl marry after she has agreed to subscribe, she must continue her payments till the next festival, in which she takes part as an unmarried woman. Should a child be born during the period, a fine is levied, in eggs for a girl baby, with a chicken in addition for a boy.

The fish and vegetable hawkers are great supporters of the seven sisters, and form numerous clubs to celebrate their anniversary. Should a contributor die during the year, all her associates must buy a suit of white mourning, and attend her obsequies. These girls run their own business, often very efficiently, in spite of their size and tender years, and can usually well afford their annual celebration. It is an occasion for the display of all their jewellery, into which their savings are put instead of the bank. Bracelets weighing a couple of ounces, and massive gold necklaces are openly flaunted in the dark streets for, on that night, they have perfect immunity from the bag snatcher. Public opinion in China is rarely on the side of the police, but on this night of nights every soul

becomes a special constable in the protection of the worshippers of the two Star Gods. Everyone is out for a good time, and there is not a chance of a girl being molested.

Nearby was an enclosure which, from the street, appeared to house merely an Economy Canteen whose neon sign explained the brightly illuminated diners at the tables. On entering, the place appeared to be a veritable rabbit-warren of small booths, in many of which a fortune-teller was plying his trade. The Double Seventh is a peculiarly propitious day to look into the future, and many of the celebrants are anxious to discover if it is the last time they will be taking part in the festival as a maiden. A number of the inhabitants of this queer community had dragged their beds into the open. Children wandered about everywhere in the cool of the evening, and occasionally flames flared from the burning of a tray and its accompanying vestments. These sacrifices would end with a burst of firecrackers.

The Festival of the Hungry Ghosts

The festival of the Hungry Ghosts dates from the introduction of Buddhism in which religion it is known as the Magnolia Festival (盂蘭), The Chinese believe that the spirits of those bereft of the consolations of ancestral worship are malignant, and may claim living substitutes, unless they are pacified by food. Universal sacrifices are accordingly offered on the 15th of the Seventh Moon to assuage their hunger, and gain their gratitude.

Boat People's Festivities

The ceremonies among the Boat People for the Festival of the Dead are somewhat different, and tend to be more costly and elaborate than those provided in the villages.

For one such celebration in 1950, two junks were moored at the praya, with a small cargo lighter between them. In front of each was a bamboo pole with twelve lanterns bearing Chinese characters alternately in red and black. The inscription read 大中天二品赦罪地官清虛大帝 (The Most Heavenly Great God, Ch'ing Hsu, who is second in rank, is a lenient magistrate). Ch'ing Hsu is the divinity who deals with mortals in the nether world. The staff was surmounted with a scarlet acorn-shaped ornament, enclosed in a frame of flat metal, with a fringed ring below. A straw hat topped the string of lanterns which were hung singly, one above the other.

The westernmost junk was dressed overall with signal flags of the international code, and a continuous puppet-play was running from an early hour on the well-deck, with the audience accommodated on the poop and fo'c'stle.

On the fo'c'stle of the easternmost vessel was the ghostly crew, with Yen Lo Wang (閻羅王) on the port side, and the magistrate with his attendants, plus the Wu Ch'ang-kuei (無常鬼), to starboard. A small paper shrine, like a dog-kennel, with a penthouse roof in green and yellow with a scarlet lining, stood just for'ard of

Yu Lan Festival . . . assuaging the spirits' hunger

Yen Lo, Ruler of the Underworld

built up of red and white sweetmeats in balls, and the hand has the index and third finger closed on the palm holding a red talisman. The right-hand cone is white with a pattern and open hand, whilst the left is of dark green spinach, though the hand is white. On the table in front of them is a pyramid of four oranges and some crystallised fruit.

Five is a sacred number with the Chinese and recurs in many of their beliefs. There are five quarters of the earth—north, south, east, west and centre; five colours which were combined in the first Republican flag—yellow, white, blue, red and black; five heavenly kings, who visited Canton and left their ram steeds behind; and five sacred mountain peaks. The human hand, with fingers outstretched, symbolises these mountains. When placed palm outwards, it signifies the outside world of men or spirits, palm inwards being for the family. The first finger is not true, therefore it is folded down; the second raised means the "Protector". To hold up the first finger means that the guarding power is absent, and gifts are always handed and received between the thumb and middle finger.

Before the main altar was a table with the offerings, at the back of which stood the usual five vessels in tinsel paper. These appeared to be present only for form, for the three huge incense sticks were directly before the altar, and the burner was in front of a seated image, with right hand raised, and the candlesticks and flower-vases were unfurnished. The offerings comprised an immense roast pig, a dish of pink dumplings, and the usual lavish display of fruit.

There was virtually no congregation at this service, apart from casual idlers who peeped in from time to time to see that they had got their money's worth, before transferring their attention to the puppet-play. The priests continued their intoning on a time basis, and certainly gave full value, though their picturesque vestments and elaborate ritual gestures were wasted as far as a human audience was concerned. They welcome curiosity from outsiders, and have not the slightest objection to sketching or photography during the performance of their office. In fact they are most anxious to see the results and, in the short intervals, passed round the sketches and furnished their address, complete with telephone number, with a request for prints. Having witnessed them so often at work they have become quite old friends. It is always a matter of speculation what vestments will be produced. In England we have the "Sarum use" as well as the orthodox seasonal colours, but the "Kowloon use" defies description, and appears to be the arbitrary taste of the leader of the troupe. Last year, the morning dress was crimson with blue and gold embroidered patches on back, shoulders, and skirt. The centre of the back piece was the T'ai Chi (light and darkness symbol), surrounded by the eight Buddhist emblems, whilst the side patches carried the Taoist trigrams. In evening-dress the officiating priest wore crimson, whilst his assistants donned the yellow robe of the Lama, with black stoles and Taoist cap.

On this occasion the company had been entirely re-dressed. The chief priest wore an orange robe with blue and gold patches and a white biretta somewhat similar to the Tibetan Sakya k'ri z'ya, with gold embroidery and an ornament on top in the stylised form of a lotus. His supporters were dressed in lime green, plain robes

the group, with two wine cups on the deck before it. On the back of the shrine inside was the character "Shen" (Spirit 神) which endowed it with an occupant worthy of worship.

The well-deck was screened off fore and aft, and had been converted into a complete chapel. The side walls were hung with four good, ancient scrolls on either side, and the sanctuary next the poop was divided from the nave by a screen through which could be seen pictures of the "Three Pure Ones", the deities of the Taoist Trinity.

On either side of the rood-screen was a large cartoon of two of the Eight Immortals, in front of which were tables bearing white plaques on blackwood stands, painted with sacred pictures. At these tables sat the supporting priests, chanting the responses and accompanying themselves on their peculiar instruments.

The objects of veneration at all festivals for the dead are three cones, each surmounted by a hand made of some sweetened glutinous rice. The centre pyramid is

and an equal number of sailing junks but, like the officiating clergy, the colour scheme had been altered. The steamers had pink, patterned smokestacks instead of blue, and the awning curtains were yellow. The hulls were white with green upperworks. The junks had red hulls with yellow and green bulwarks, and white sails on which was inscribed "Take advantage of a following wind".

At midday the ghostly crew was transhipped from the large junk, and Yen Lo was lashed to the mast. The string of lanterns was run up on a halyard, and the ship was dressed with three hoists of signal flags. Closing down the service on the large junks, the priests came aboard, and two altars were rigged amidships by utilising a couple of square tables supported on gate-legged trestles. On the altar abaft the mast were placed the three hands, a pyramid of oranges, and a dish of sugared fruit. As the wind was fresh, one of the hatches was removed and the sticks of incense, having been ignited, were placed below decks, their fumes spiralling up behind the objects of veneration. On the quarter-deck the second table was spread with a red paper-cloth, and on it the priests laid out their musical instruments, of which each was responsible for one or two. The starboard watch had two treble gongs, whilst the port side ran the drums. One of these was a hollow wooden block, shaped like a plum-pudding, and its musician could ring the changes on an oblong wooden box. His companion had a drum stretched on a metal frame of almost spherical shape, and the gong chimes which emitted a tinkling note when struck by a rod. In shape it was like a small frying-pan raised from the table on three metal legs. The usual wooden fish-head drum was absent. The lay orchestra consisted of two clarinet players, one of whom was also responsible for the bass gong slung in a nest of cordage from an awning slat. The other contrived to play his wind instrument, and keep a cigarette alight in a manner almost miraculous, for he never missed a note. The loud cymbals seem to be common property, and are passed from hand to hand round the troupe. A wealth of expression and attitudinising can be put into

Hungry Ghosts Festival—"The Three Hands"

with black stoles.

When the service of invocation, and initiation to the feast was ended, the chief priest, before disrobing, knelt in front of the altar and read through a list of the subscribers, written on red paper. As he repeated each family name aloud, he cast on the deck two wooden objects, to determine their fortune for the year. These are shaped like a split walnut, one side being round, and the other flat. Should both fall the same way, the luck is good, but a round and a flat cancel each other and no good luck can be expected.

The small centre junk was deputed to carry out the actual ceremony of bringing comfort to the needy spirits and, up till noon, bore no distinctive marks of festivity. The well-deck contained some skips full of paper of various colours, and the boats to be launched at various points in the harbour. Women were busy making them seaworthy, by cradling the hulls with straw-matting floats. As in last year's service, there were seven steamers,

Preparing the ships for launching

Mass for the dead . . . a great faith in the power of the priests

the proper wielding of these discs, and no one seems willing to forgo his share of the entertainment. Even the high priest, in the intervals of his chanting, rose from his seat to stretch his legs and postured before bringing the instruments together in a rapturous clash.

Once everything was ready for the start, the junk warped out on her stern anchor. A tug lashed itself alongside, and brought the tow round in a circle with three bursts of crackers before starting to beat the bounds of the harbour. Course was then set for Sulphur Channel and the wake was blazed with paper clothing and money. An iron cresset had to be rigged over the stern, instead of the bows, on account of the fresh wind, and a continuous stream of stokers kept the furnace roaring. The children either assisted in bringing up the clothing and money in baskets or distributed it over-board piece by piece on their own account. The notes were printed to the value of $100,000 on the BANK OF HELL, giving rise to the supposition that, with the arrival of some of the late Nationalist Treasury officials, inflation has spread to the infernal regions. Prior to the War a ten-dollar tip was considered adequate for the needy spirit. The notes had a constant serial number and were printed in red and primrose in front, and blue at the back. The signatures of C. P. Sing Kuang and YUKWANG, before and behind, were in foreign script. A two-storeyed Chinese building, like one of the audience halls in the Forbidden City, formed the back design, and represented the issuing bank. The notes were valid in Heaven or in Hell.

Other scraps of paper in lavender, blue, yellow and green were cut in the form of a Chinese jacket, as was the clothing to replenish the wardrobes of the drowned. Off the bathing beaches in Belcher's Bay the first stop was made, and a steamer and junk were launched from the tug, which had a lower freeboard. The priests intoned the dedication, and two women in the bows ladled over the offering of bean curd, rice and fresh vegetables. The two craft were provisioned for their journey with a few leaves of tea, a drop of oil and token rice ration, whilst the steamer, for motive power, was fuelled with a drop of petrol from a flask of lighter fluid. Everyone joined in littering the sea with paper money and clothing, and clouds of smoke rose from the brazier at the stern. Cymbals and gong called the ghosts to the feast, and a burst of crackers concluded the ceremony. The second launching took place just south of the centre of Stone-cutters under similar circumstances, and the junk turned westwards to circle the wireless station before repeating the distribution a cable's length south of Laichikok. The Yaumati typhoon shelter, being the permanent anchor-age of the Society contributing to the festival, received special attention. Skirting the breakwater, the junk launched a steamer just inside the south entrance. Proceeding up the Kowloon side of the shelter and leaving a broad wake of paper of every colour spangling the smooth surface, the red junk with its white sail took to the water at the western approach, and the mission turned southwards inside the protecting wall. A complete circle of paper offerings surrounded the two lanes of anchored lighters before the junk left the shelter by the southern exit. Passing the "Star" Ferry and Holt's wharves, a halt was made in the centre of Kowloon Bay, before proceeding to the eastern limit off Quarry Point. A tremendous distribution of paper was made as the vessel turned, but there was no launching to warn the spirits of the charitable bequest. Two boats had been prepared by the women and were stowed on the upper deck of the tug ready for putting into the water. As the junk turned into the fresh south-west wind on her homeward journey, a gust caught the steamer, which was propped against the funnel, and effected an im-promptu, and entirely disastrous, side launching. The gay paper vessel, on her beam ends, and devoid of fuel, drifted rapidly astern at the mercy of the waves. This meant that Causeway Bay, an important port of call, had to be put off with a single sailing-ship, but the crew made amends by an outstandingly lavish distribution of clothing and bank-notes. Every child on board dealt out the paper but, as a storm was brewing, the awnings on the lee side were rigged, and most of the ghostly provender whirled up and, coming inboard, plastered the poop.

The last two boats were then provisioned for a final launching at the starting-point. Approaching the quay the dedication was read, and priests and laymen brought every instrument into play. The gong and clarinet vied with the loud cymbals, now in the hands of the disrobed officiating priest. Crackers added to the din, as the launch cast off her tow about three fathoms from the sterns of the parent junks. It seemed impossible to squeeze between them, but the little vessel, with fenders out, shouldered its way to its berth till checked by the stern anchor. The priests packed their musical instruments in boxes, and folded up their vestments, whilst the laity made tracks for the gangplank. Boatwomen had their babies strapped to their backs and, as they passed before the three pyramids which all day had been the object of veneration, the white hands which crowned them mysteriously disappeared into capacious pockets. The pilgrimage had taken four hours. The priests had been chanting continuously since early morning, and were due for another four-hour service at Yaumati, after the feast in which the roast pig formed the pièce de resistance. As midnight approached they could hardly be grudged a glance at the wrist-watch after a twelve-hour day.

At the typhoon anchorage the junks were moored in two lanes, with the festival vessels at the north end, where a knot of lighters had collected with their bows inwards, pointing in all directions. Climbing from fo'c'stle to fo'c'stle, the junk on which the service was being held was reached after crossing three others. The morning's decorations had been stripped and an entirely new scene met the eye. At the front end of the well-deck was a small square altar on which was erected the three handless cones. Behind were paper banners, and in front a pyramid of oranges, a dish of dried sugared fruit, and wine cups with libations. Three thick sticks of incense burned before the altar. Aft of it were two tables arranged like the letter T, with the cross piece for'ard. On this were two lamps with green shades, and a variety of curios on folding wooden stands with little silk fringed mats. One of these was a "Buddha's hand" carved in white jade, and there was a well-shaped bowl in the same material. A very rich red frontal, covered with a white gold embroidery, concealed the legs of the table. At the second table sat four assistant priests, robed in sky-blue vestments with dark blue and gold patches. In front of them was a gilt image, facing the main altar and with an

Mass for the dead, 15th of the 7th Moon

and altar. This dedication lasted for half an hour, and during it women placed three large incense sticks before the three cones surmounted by the symbolical hands. The centre one, which was composed of small dumplings in rings, was by now completely deprived of food value as it formed part of the sacrifice at each stopping place whilst beating the bounds of the harbour. Its lowest tier was brought to the priest just before disembarkation, and when he had blessed the food he threw it by handfuls to the congregation to scramble for. To catch one of these small lumps of dough insures good luck for the year.

Next the senior assistant priest brought the robes in which the most solemn part of the service must be celebrated. These were scarlet with white facings, and a white embroidered stole. The officiant first presented them to the lotus throne and the gilt image of Buddha on the table. The biretta worn at this juncture was a four-pointed affair topped with a gilt lotus, and not the special lama headdress only used for the eucharist. As soon as the officiant had donned his vestments, a procession was formed, and the whole party, played off by the band, mounted the fo'c'stle, to intercede for the Souls with the King of Hell. The chief priest was then assisted to mount the throne and, before seating himself, stood with his face screened from the altar with a square of red embroidered material, whilst he made his dedicatory prayer. Still standing, he gestured with his hands, while his assistants lit incense before the altar. This part of the service lasted ten minutes, and the officiant then seated himself, and spent a similar period in manual gesture with a vase. He then assumed the five-pointed biretta for the final act.

The celebrant himself wore the five-pointed headdress in which a lama priest performs the eucharist. The general colour scheme of the vestments was scarlet, with blue and gold embroidery. From the sides suspended two broad, white, embroidered streamers reaching to the knee. There was evidently a white silk wide-sleeved undergarment below the scarlet mantle, worn over a pale blue silk skirt. Sitting cross-legged on the throne the celebrant had an ethereal appearance, enhanced by the exceedingly graceful ritual movements of the hands. A server handed him a vase, which he manipulated with slow, rhythmic motions, making as if to sprinkle its contents over the world. On being handed a goblet, he circled the two together, first clockwise, and then in the reverse direction. They were then revolved in a figure of eight, and finally the mystic fluid of the Kuan Yin vase was poured into the goblet. The vase was then returned to the acolyte, and the same procedure of manipulation and sprinkling was repeated. Two bells succeeded the goblet with which the sacrificing priest accompanies the chant. Lit from the pressure gas lamps suspended from the awning, the shadows on the priests' faces and the whole setting was most impressive. There was virtually no congregation, though a passer-by might look in for a few minutes. The children swarmed to see a foreigner with a sketch book making studies, but the gestures of the priest and the rhythmic music of the orchestra had less appeal than the noisy puppet-show whose deafening cymbals threatened to drown the soft chanting.

After an hour a man produced a nest of red paper receptacles shaped like lotuses, and proceeded to fill each

incense burner before it. The lotus throne of the officiating priest was very elaborate, with heart-shaped and oblong mirrors behind the celebrant, and a square base, fringed with white lotus petals. Before the priest were two artificial pink lotuses in bud, flower, and seed.

The evening service started as darkness fell. Each junk taking part had a string of oil-paper lanterns surmounted by the acorn-shaped insignia lashed to the prow as a jackstaff. If one of the lanterns caught fire, nobody seemed to mind; they had to be burned some time, anyway.

Prior to the service proper, the officiating priest must dedicate himself before taking his place on the lotus throne, and he appeared at the end of the table accommodating his assistants, garbed in white, with the black Taoist cap, and white shoes. Facing the throne, with his back to the altar, he prostrated himself, touching the deck with his forehead. He then took an incense burner with a gilt dragon as a handle, and censed both throne

'The ghosts have to be satisfied with two services'

Taoist services on a junk for the Hungry Ghosts Festival

of them with a few drops from an oil-can. These little lamps were then handed to women on small junks, and were carried out to the fairway. The women stood in the bows, ignited each lamp in turn and, after bowing three times with the blazing object in their hands, they launched it on the tide. Any woman who can capture one still alight, will also "catchee baby" according to the tradition. The sampan women who serve the junks were active in the pursuit, and it was reported that one at least "catchee twins!"

Later, a tremendous bonfire was made of Yen Lo and his ghostly companions. A cresset was hung in the narrow space between the junks' bows, and every scrap of decoration was burned. Men with buckets of water stood by to keep the intense fire from spreading. First the magistrate and his victims went on to the pyre, followed by the "abnegation of normality", who had been intruding into the audience owing to the rising gusts which heralded a violent rain storm. The lanterns and their red-capped pole were just about to join the conflagration caused by the return of the Prince of Darkness to his satrapy, when the rain descended in torrents. Side awnings were hastily rigged, and the coming and going between the various junks ceased. Those who found themselves at home called it a day, and retired to their sleeping quarters. The men stood by, however, waiting for the drenching storm to abate and, as soon as it showed signs of letting up, completed the destruction of the representatives of the Hungry Ghosts.

Cantonese Hungry Ghost Festival

Whereas the Boat People organise their religious observances on a family basis, the villages in Hong Kong adhere to the Chinese tradition of delegating such matters to the Elders, or the elected committee known as the K'ai Fong or Residents' Association. Representatives of this body make a house-to-house collection and, according to the funds received, decide on the scale of the celebration. For the Hungry Ghosts, generous donors are entitled to a complimentary lantern to hang at the front door, smaller lamps being awarded for lesser contributions.

Individual sacrifices to the Hungry Ghosts are made on the eve of the full moon in the seventh month. Outside every shop on the main street a small bank of sand acts as an incense burner and as soon as dusk falls the women of the house emerge and light about a dozen sticks. A few short prayers are said before this improvised altar, and then a bundle of paper clothing and ingots, representing gold and silver, is burned for the comfort of the neglected spirits. The more opulent families add to the sacrifices a tray illuminated by two candles, on which are set out cups of tea, three pairs of chopsticks and some small bowls containing a vegetarian diet and local wine.

The communal religious ceremonies should take place towards the end of the Moon, as a solace to the ghosts about to be re-incarcerated after their holiday. Four nights and three days are devoted to the services in Stanley, the dates being fixed by casting lots before the shrine of the Queen of Heaven, on whose temple the proceedings are based.

On the afternoon of the vigil a gigantic effigy of Yen Lo (閻羅王), King of the Underworld, is placed on the west side of the antechapel. His apron is adorned with the Chinese characters for longevity interspersed with butterflies. Perched on his gilt paper stomacher, surmounting a pink lotus, are three doll-like figures representing two of the released souls on either hand of the Goddess of Mercy. Facing Yen Lo against the opposite wall is a group consisting of the "lenient magistrate" Ch'ing Hsu (清虛), flanked by four ticket-of-leave ghosts who are subject to him for the rest of the year. Broken chains hang from their wrists to indicate their release. The party wall separating the ante-chapel from the open-air central court has been removed revealing a long altar in front of the sanctuary on which a reredos with the images of the Taoist "Three Pure Ones" (三清教主) has been erected. These are the Jade Emperor (玉帝), in the centre, supported by Tao Chun (道君), who controls the relations of the Yin and the Yang, and Lao Tze (老子), founder of the religion. Each of these groups is furnished with a table covered with red paper as an altar, with incense, candles, and the usual sacrifices. In the sanctuary itself incense burns before every divinity, with a swelling flare of candles at the main shrine of the Queen of Heaven. The "dark altar", dedicated to the nine gods who protect mortals from devils and the calamities attributed to them, is furnished with a miniature set of the fiends from Hell, including two red horsemen. The landsmen seem to dispense with the Wu Ch'ang-kuei (無常鬼), or Unpredictable Ghost, who is always among the guests at the Boat People's parties.

Outside the temple, against the male guardian lion, is a small red box-like shrine below the bamboo staff headed with a red paper acornshaped ornament. This should carry a string of thirteen lanterns eulogising the lenient magistrate, but the full complement has been divided up among the numerous minor shrines dedicated to the local spirits. The lion's share is four of these lanterns, but some of the tree and rock spirits have to be content with a pair. A Cantonese coolie-hat is attached to the staff below the apical ornament. These red shrines are labelled outside with two characters meaning "Beckoning the Spirit" (招魂) and within is the inscription "The shrine of the child guarding the banner".

As darkness falls, the steps in front of the temple become crowded with children, who penetrate the ante-chapel to watch the preparations. An elder boy on the grass between the lions starts clanging a gong, and its notes bring reinforcements of the younger generation from all points of the compass. Some of the girls carry babies on their backs and, if there is no other way of ensuring that the toddlers can be present at the ceremony, an elder brother undertakes their transportation. Proceedings are opened with an overture from the band, performed entirely on percussion instruments. Three Taoist priests, robed in red, start the service with the invocation to all neglected spirits to present themselves from all directions and partake in the charitable feast.

Gungry Ghosts Festival

The officiant wears a high biretta, consisting of a black skull cap surmounted by a superstructure of coloured silk pompoms, which can be illuminated by battery from within at specially impressive passages in the ritual. At the end of the service the lay helpers marshal the children in procession. This is led by the boy with the gong, followed by welldressed children with banners bearing the characters Ch'ing (清道) (The Pure Way) or paintings of Tigers, to clear the path of evilly-disposed demons. The band consists of two men with clarinets, who precede the priests. The officiant is followed by a small boy bearing a blue and silver shrine containing five books with the names of the subscribers. Two male assistants carry incense and food offerings on trays or in buckets. Over a hundred unattached children swell the crowd and add to the din by vocal imitations of the gong. The procession stops at each of the tree and rock shrines where incense is ignited, libations are poured out, and the officiant offers prayers for the enjoyment of the feast. As a benediction the priest sprays the tree with liquid from his mouth. On returning to the temple the service is continued, but there is no lotus throne for the officiant, and the ritual is less akin to the Buddhist ritual than that performed at the Boat People's festivals.

The proceedings on the second day are not spectacular, and the Ghosts have to be satisfied with two services, followed by a procession round the outlying shrines. On the third day there are three services, and the hands made of dough surmounting a pyramid of dumplings, which are such a feature in the Boat People's ritual, make their first appearance. In the Boat festival there are three hands, two on cones of paste and spinach, and the central emblem above concentric and detachable rings of small balls of dough, which are distributed at each launching of the mercy junks. The villagers substitute for this a pig's head in ground-rice dough with black button-like eyes.

The evening service starts with a band overture in the ante-chapel of the temple. Later an adjournment is made to the beach of Chik Chu Wan. The bay is probably more prolific in unattended spirits than any other place in Hong Kong, for it was there that the blessings of Japanese "Co-prosperity" were brought home to superfluous mouths by wholesale liquidation.

On the foreshore in front of the temple two square gate-legged tables are placed together, the one nearest high water mark being furnished with an incense burner and two thick red candles in square glass lanterns to protect them if the wind is gusty. The two hands form part of the sacrifice, and there is also a plate of fruit and some sweetmeats. Facing this improvised altar, with his back to the sea, is the portable image of the King of Hell, and at his feet is the pig's head with two candles and some incense sticks stuck upright in its skull. Behind His Satanic Majesty the children have been busy constructing a range of nine sand-castles, for burning the paper money and clothing dedicated to the ghosts. In each there is a central keep, consisting of a round hole with a wall of sand, then a smooth space for the cups of tea, wine and food offerings, and finally an outer vallum, in which are planted candles in pairs and sticks of incense. Each brazier, representing a table set for a feast, is about six feet in diameter, and when all are illuminated the effect is very striking. The second altar

Priest with illuminated biretta

table is entirely for the use of the officiant and his two supporting priests, and accommodates the sacred books and the instruments: fish-head drum, chimes, and treble cymbals used to accompany the chants.

The chief priest sits under an arch formed by two uprights and a transom, covered with red-and-white patterned cloth. When everything is lit up by lay helpers, the priests take their seats, with appropriate music from the band which is established behind them. The officiant intones the invocation and then dedicates the sacrifices. This part of the service lasts half an hour, after which the officiant stands and, accompanied by the music of his assistants, performs a number of rhythmic movements of the hands, every one ending with a different gesture of benediction. As each exercise is performed, one of the supporting priests tears off a numbered red slip from a sheaf, hanging from the right-hand upright of the arch. The movements of the hands are fascinating to watch, for they are performed with a fluid grace which leaves the impression that the members are boneless. Endless practice must be necessary to acquire the dexterity displayed, and to keep the wrists and fingers in the condition of suppleness exacted by the performance. Before beginning each number the priest separates his hands and snaps his fingers as if to discard the previous movement before embarking on the next. Lay helpers then fill up the tea and wine cups in the sand-castles from pots on the altar, and the small boys start burning clothing and paper money in the pits. When the sacrifices are consumed, the candles and incense surrounding the pits are also consigned to the flames, the wax causing them to burn fiercely.

The officiant then takes a rest, and one of his assistants stands up to read the list of names of those who have contributed to the entertainment of the ghosts. It takes some time as few of the villagers care to neglect this form of insurance against haunting by disappointed spirits. A lay helper then places a stick of incense in each of the hands of rice-dough and propitiates Yen Lo by similarly decorating the pig's head in front of his image. A plate of uncooked rice with a number of coins is then handed to the officiant who arranges the money in a pattern. Having dedicated this offering he picks up a pinch at a time and casts it towards the sea, across the altar, for the children to scramble for luck. Not too many of the coins accompany the rice, and the priest becomes residuary legatee of a good handful which remain at the bottom of the dish, and disappear by sleight of hand into the wide sleeve, and later a capacious pocket. The dumplings below the hands are next distributed, each having a burning stick of incense affixed before it is cast away. Bunches of crackers flung into the smouldering pits scatter the ashes in all directions and contribute to the enjoyment of the finale. The congregation consists predominantly of children, either assisting with the burnt sacrifice, or merely as onlookers. Among the Boat People the younger generation takes little interest in the services, being wholly absorbed with the Puppet Play which is mounted for the benefit of the departed. The villagers, however, attend in force at every stage of the proceedings, from the temple worship to the long processions in the burning sun.

The dates for the ceremonies of one particular seventh moon had been fixed after consultation with the Goddess T'ien Hou (天后), who opted for the 26th of the Moon. This would have completed the rites by the 29th, or final day. As the priests were not available, an alternative starting point had to be selected with the deity's permission. This meant that the final two celebrations took place after the spirits had returned to Hades from their summer vacation.

Like the sycophantic courtiers of King Canute, the villagers have a pathetic faith in the power of the priests, backed by the Queen of Heaven, over the elements. It was thought that the approaching typhoon could be restrained long enough to complete the ceremonies and, on the final day, the usual procession round the local Stanley shrines was performed though, in view of the impending storm, the officiants armed themselves with furled umbrellas. Two hours later the wind reached gale force, and safety precautions took precedence over everything else. The temple doors were closed, and boats were hauled up on to dry land. Even vegetables recently planted on low-lying ground were pulled out and placed in baskets. The village elders consulted with the priests who, in consideration of a "refresher", the amount entailing some hard bargaining, consented to perform the final ceremonies as soon as the weather abated.

On the last day, the sound of the drum and gong announced the approach of the Lion dancers, who presented themselves before the shrine of the Queen of Heaven before taking part in the proceedings, and made their prostrations before the altar. In front of the temple small boys had been busy digging holes in the grass, on the same pattern as the sand-castles on the beach. Their previous efforts had been wiped out by the typhoon, so they drew a double fee. Some of the properties were already arranged in front of the temple steps, and lay helpers were busy marshalling the procession. The two square tables furnished as altars, with incense burners, candles and plates of fruit and sweetmeats, had carrying poles lashed to the sides and behind them stood the portable shrine of the Queen of Heaven. This was a red-and-gold wooden sedan with a pointed roof ending in a ball decorated with a scarlet silk knot. The ordinary official chair in green paper was occupied by the effigy of the "Lenient Magistrate", and his bearers were boys with faces painted as black-and-white tiger masks. They sported a uniform of black jackets with white facings, and on their heads were open wicker-work tall red headdresses, like upturned waste-paper baskets, which imparted a tolerably hellish demeanour. A blue, red and silver pagoda occupied a table to itself and in this was placed a cage with two live rice-birds, destined to be released as part of the service. Buddhists can acquire merit at any time by releasing birds, purchased in the market for that purpose. The original idea had its points, but the law of supply and demand soon intervened, and a new occupation was found for small boys in trapping hitherto neglected wild fowl for ransom and immediate release. In the present case the act was symbolic of the release of souls from purgatory through the intercession of the living.

The procession was led by a number of urchins in red-and-white jackets, carrying banners or staves surmounted by the Eight Taoist and Buddhist Symbols, well jumbled together. The coins and the vase, mystic knot and gourd, umbrella and rhinoceros cup were paired off. Then came the magistrate in his green chair, which gradually distintegrated under a stiff breeze and rough usage by the demon porters. The Lion, dancing furiously to the strains of his personal band, was an attraction in himself. He certainly worked his passage, for his antics never ceased from the moment he left his lair to report at the temple till he finally divested himself of his make-up on his return to the den. The bird pagoda followed the Lion, and then came the officiating priest with two of the senior village elders in attendance. Women carried the altars in front of the shrine of the Queen of Heaven. Like the King of Hell she has two manifestations, one permanent and only unveiled on her birthday, and one for everyday use, which is portable. In addition to her carriers, four attendants bore red-and-gold fans, whilst a fifth was in charge of an embroidered ceremonial umbrella. One of the senior members of the Residents' Association followed with the small blue and silver shrine, which had been carried in all the processions, as it contain the books with the names of those contributing to the festival, and it was desirable that the spirits should be constantly aware of their benefactors.

A motley crew under the command of the portable King of Hell brought up the rear. There was a red three-master fishing junk, with its stern inscribed "May a following wind bring advantage", for launching on behalf of the Boat People. In the harbour the Mercy junks are always single masted like the lighters for unloading cargo, but the Stanley Water Folk earn their living by fishing, so their own type of craft is simulated, that the spirits may be under no misapprehension as to the identity of the donors. Another member of the rearguard was a red horse mounted by a yellow jockey with a white face, and known as the Water Horse (白馬).

The procession moved fairly fast along the main street of the village, halting to salute any of the outlying shrines on the route before each of which the Lion performed his antics, and the priest said a short prayer. Nearly every shop had put out a table dressed as an altar with incense, candles and sacrifices, whilst a most explosive burst of crackers made the swarms of non-official children skip like little rams.

The service was held in front of a row of single-storeyed houses near the centre of the south beach. A fairly wide space in front of the buildings was bounded by a belt of large-leaved trees whose welcome shade sheltered the Lion dancers. The principal performer was glad enough to shed his skin, as the day was uncommonly hot, but the band continued to play, and formed a rival attraction to the main ceremony. The congregation split into three groups, for a launching party had taken the paper junk to the water's edge, and was provisioning it with tea, wine and oil before consigning it to the waves. On the terrace the shrine of the Queen of Heaven was deposited in the shade of the trees, and the two altars were set up before it. The magistrate and his four clients with the King of the Underworld formed a group on T'ien Hou's right hand. The pagoda with the birds was level with the front altar at the right of the officiant priest, whilst the church orchestra took up position slightly behind him on the left. The drum and gong were on a covered litter, the former hanging from the roof, and the latter sunk in a socket in the bed. The two clarinet men were free to move about. The officiant, facing the Queen of Heaven's shrine across the altars, opened the service with an exhortation, standing. He was supported by seven of the village elders, one holding a patched umbrella to shade him from the sun, and another vigorously fanning him. For the greater part of the service he sat cross-legged in the Buddhistic attitude, and great hilarity was caused when he signaled to his supporting village elders to prostrate themselves at the more solemn moments. His devotions lasted about twenty-five minutes, and then he rose. After receiving his blessing, one of the lay attendants took a bundle of paper clothing and the Water Horse, and made for the beach, followed by a crowd of children. Discarding his burden he ran off at full speed like a fox before a pack of hounds. The winner in the race was rewarded, and at any rate acquired merit and, what is more important, luck. On returning at a walk a match was set to the paper and the Water Horse, and bunches of particularly violent crackers dispersed the crowd.

The cage with the two rice-birds was then handed to the priest by one of the elders, and the inmates were blessed. The bars were then removed, and the elder caught one bird in his hand and delivered it to the priest. The officiant poured a drop of wine on to its head, and then opened his hand to let it fly away. The process was then repeated with its companion. Originally pigeons were used but, as they were domesticated fowl, they simply flew back to their original owner who capitalised on the transaction by effecting a double sale, once for the liberation, and again for their consignment to the pot. The birds therefore derived little benefit from their temporary freedom, and it was felt more consistent with the teachings of Buddha to substitute captives who resumed their wild life. The benediction was then given, and the service ended with a chant during which the priest moved over to the orchestra and took his place

Seeking the spirits' blessings, Taoist style

as the drummer.

The procession then re-formed and marched back to the temple, its trail being blazed with scraps of green paper from the magistrate's disintegrating sedan. When a contract is made with the priests they become responsible for procuring the furnishings, whose magnificence depends on the amount subscribed and the honesty of the clergy. Each band has its connections with one of the paper shops, from which it naturally expects a commission for its patronage. In this case, the liaison was evidently very close for, in the afternoon, one of the supporting priests was discovered executing repairs and making fresh trunks to hold the paper clothing for the evening sacrifice.

The final service was held on a semi-circular grass patch before the temple. The fifteen-foot paper statue of the King of Hell was carried from the temple to the centre of the parapet facing T'ien Hou's temple door, the image being illuminated by a pressure lamp slung to a tripod. The industrious children had dug eighteen burning pits and, as soon as it was quite dark, each was lit up by a circle of candles and incense sticks. A ration of eight cigarettes to a pit was part of the reward of the juvenile attendants, but when it came to the distribution it was discovered that the brats had got at the magazine, and a fresh supply had to be produced. Two large skips, full of buns, biscuits and dumplings, were contributed through door-to-door collection from resident families for ghostly refreshment, but they were not supposed to be consumed till the end of the service. Rations for the ghosts, of rice, tea and vegetables, were handed out by committee members, the saucers and cups being placed on the flat space between the burning pit and the vallum for the incense. Paper money and clothing were taken round as required, and the children stoked their fires leaf by leaf.

The furnishing of the two tables which acted as altars was much the same as for the beach ceremony but, at the appropriate moment, three instead of two pyramids of dumplings surmounted by paste hands were set out. A stick of burning incense was then placed in each hand, and then the dumplings were similarly furnished, till they looked like porcupines.

On the priests' table were the musical instruments, a bowl of tea, and a rectangular wooden shrine inscribed with characters, which represented the personal Patron Saint of the officiant.

The band appeared, and played a short overture, before joining the priests at their self-dedication in the temple before the altar of the Three Pure Ones. The village elders, representative patrons of the charity, had also to take an active part in this worship, including the nine prostrations. After about ten minutes the officiant made his appearance, carrying an incense burner with a straight stem, with which he censed first the King of Hell, and then the altar with the hands. The priests then took their places for the service, the assistants seated, whilst the officiant stood to cense the congregation, and performed a short ritual dance with rhythmic movements of his long-sleeved hands. On taking his seat he placed the incense burner on the table and, opening the sacred books, intoned a short prayer. From the depths of his robe, he produced from his pocket-book a white paper charm, sealed with red and, folding it, set it alight. The ashes were dropped into the bowl of tea which he drew

towards him, imparting to the liquid hallowed and magical properties.

He then vested himself for the Mass, by laying before him the biretta used by Tibetan Lamas for the Eucharist and a string of beads. This form of headdress is five-pointed, each of the central panels being embroidered with pictures of the Three Pure Ones, and the outer with the guardians mounted on the dragon and the tiger. After being sprinkled with holy water it is tied on over the black cap with the silk pompoms.

Standing up, and accompanied by the band, reinforced by the instruments of the supporting priests, he performed the thirteen mystic movements of the hands evoking and distributing power. The prayers of invocation and dedication followed and the members of the committee distributed fresh paper for the burning pits. Meanwhile, a rising wind was causing trouble with the Demon King. He subsided backwards, and had to be reinstated, whilst the magistrate was positively fractious. No amount of adjustment would induce him to remain upright and, in his wrestle with the attendants, fragments of his green chair and clothing were fluttering in all directions in the breeze. The focus of all attention was the King of Hell and, when the pressure lamp suspended operations, one of the elders directed a torch as a spotlight on his face. An improved footlight was provided by stoking one of the burning holes directly in front of him with inflammable material, which cast a ruddy glow reminiscent of the accepted idea of the infernal regions. A freshening breeze, however, proved his undoing, and he disappeared backwards over the parapet into the pig wallow. Helping hands were not wanting to reinstate him, but their very numbers militated against his rescue. His back was broken, and even the professional image-making priest abandoned the repair work after a brief inspection.

While the list of contributors was being publicised for the last time, His Satanic Majesty was laid out for cremation, and the magistrate was hustled off to the temple for the removal of the papier-maché head, which is apparently not an expendable article. Souvenir hunters set to work among the ruins, and one of the elders got busy with a long bamboo, chasing the more daring among the children. Great luck, and probably pecuniary advantage, may be derived from the acquisition of the image of Kuan Yin mounted on the pink lotus and, when it was discovered that a man had run off with her, a pursuit was organised. When finally recovered, she was reverently placed on the altar, but an argument as to ownership proved of more absorbing interest than the conclusion of the service, and drew off four-fifths of the congregation. The officiant then performed the coin trick, and duly scattered the sacrificial rice. The children, however, were apathetic, as their sharp eyes had detected the manoeuvre on the previous occasion, and made no attempt to scramble for what was not forthcoming. Seeing the lack of competition the priest accommodated himself to the circumstances, and not a single ten-cent piece escaped his fingers.

After the symbolic distribution of food and money came the benediction. The officiant replaced the incense in his portable burner with a candle with which he made mystic passes in the four directions, and over the consecrated tea-bowl. During this ritual all motions were made counter-clockwise for the first time in the cere-

Appeasing the dead through prayers and offerings

mony. Finally he set aside the incense burner, and uttered the benediction, dipping his fingers between each phrase in the bowl, and sprinkling its contents over the assembly. The bowl was then delivered to the senior elder, who performed the same office for the ghostly crew about to start on their return journey to the Underworld.

Prior to the opening of the service, all the subsidiary shrines had been collected, and were added to the group of paper images. The typhoon had dealt hardly with them, and only the bamboo flag-poles, with an odd battered lantern, remained as trophies. Yen Lo was evidently of most inflammable material, as the moment a blazing rag was applied he burst into brilliant flame, and clouds of choking smoke soon dispersed the congregation and hid from view the altar and the priests. The canopy over the officiant was quickly whipped away by a temple attendant, responsible for its safe custody. The bonfire attracted all attention but, when last seen, the priests were sticking to their guns, and fulfilling their part of the contract. It is only what is expected of them for, should any unusual sickness or calamity affect the community, it is attributed to the inadequate propitiation of the ghosts. A certain amount of criticism was heard because only three, instead of the normal five, priests were employed, and because only tea and not their full meals was awarded to the lay helpers. The total money expended for the whole festival, less voluntary contributions in kind, was relatively little compared with the expenditure *per capita* of the Boat People.

The Magnolia Festival

The nunnery at Fanling, about a quarter of a mile short of the railway station, is really a retreat for unattached women who enjoy a community life. The only qualification is to practise the Buddhist faith, and to observe its rule in the matter of vegetarianism. Retired amahs can compound to be kept for the rest of their days, and have the privacy of a room to themselves in which they are surrounded by their own furniture and intimate souvenirs, for a large donation. A reduced scale is available for those of slender means, by which rooms are shared, and the member takes part in the work of the establishment. There are no professed nuns, who have taken the vows, but the vestments of the long black gown and sandals are worn by those assisting in religious services. These are performed by a priest from Shatin, who officiates whenever required in the imposing temple which forms the centre of the compound.

The notion of providing for the spirits of the dead originated with Buddhism, and is celebrated by Buddhists as the Magnolia festival. Thus, at this time, the principal shrine's main altar was draped with curtains of scarlet and gold for the Festival, and it stood before three gilded representations of the manifestations of Buddha. The usual Chinese arrangement is for Amitabha to occupy the central position, with Kuan Yin supporting him on the left, and T'ai Shih-chih (太勢至), Mahasthama, on the right. There was a considerable space in the centre of the hall in which was placed a footstool for a worshipper or the officiant, and behind it was a long table on which were laid out the instruments of music used at the service. These consisted of chimes, small gongs and the wooden fish-head drum. A larger drum was placed on a pedestal to the right in front of one of the wooden columns which supported the roof.

The origin of the fish-head drum is attributed to Hsüan Tsang, or Tripitaka, who made the famous pilgrimage to India in search of the Buddhist scriptures. He suffered untold hardships, which daunted his original companions, but he persisted in his mission. Once he nearly perished from hunger but, coming upon a stream, he found a large fish stranded on the bank which sustained him for days, until he reached human habitation. To remind him of the miraculous aid which had been vouchsafed to him, and to strengthen his resolution to persist to the end, he kept the head and tapped it with a stick to hearten him on the march.

Against the wall to the left of the main altar was a shrine to Wei T'o, guardian of the inmates, who is also warden of the sacred books, preserving them from loss and damage. The corresponding chapel on the right had an image of the beloved Ti Tsang Pusa whose gracious function is to unbar the gates of Hell, and rescue tortured souls. He carries over his shoulder a sack, and an alarm-staff with jingling rings to warn small creatures of his approach and avert traffic accidents. On the left wall was pasted a large picture of a red pagoda covered with black characters and before it a small image of the Healing Buddha.

Outside the main building is a court-yard with a circular lotus-pool surrounded by a parapet about three feet high. This bears an inscription but is so covered with vegetation as to render the characters indecipherable. Two doorways on the far side flank a shrine to Wei T'o (韋陀). As a rule this divinity faces inwards, as the guardian of the personnel of the religious house, and at his back is an image of Mi Lei Fo looking out of the doorway. He is, at present, neither Buddha nor Pusa, but will be a Bodhisatva when he appears on earth, and is in fact the expected Messiah. Here Wei T'o faces outward, and there is no "Laughing Buddha". The shrine gave onto a passageway, on the far side of which were two altars. One of these had a rack as reredos on which stood rows of green Spirit tablets with gilt lettering. There were about three and a half ranks of twenty, some with a double inscription to denote man and wife. Two pathetic little gaps were filled by photographs of children, one a small girl of about four in a foreign bridesmaid's dress, which would eventually be replaced by a tablet. People with no settled homes where they can take proper care of their ancestral tablets, entrust them to the pensioners who provide them with the comforts to which they are entitled.

These are permanent responsibilities, but the altar on the other side of Wei T'o's statue is for special requests. Relatives furnish yellow papers with the details of their dead, which are pasted on the wall, and a private service is held for the repose of their souls. Paper trunks or parcels of clothing and paper money for their use in the underworld are delivered at the temple, addressed to the departed.

It was unfortunate that both hostesses should have been incapacitated by an accident, but the honours were done by the nephew of the Mistress, a schoolboy of about 17 with an excellent command of English. Quite a number of children were present, as one of the functions

Colour and pageantry for 'Hungry Ghosts'

of the establishment is the care of orphans and those separated from their families. There is no obligation for them to embrace a religious life, and the girls marry when of age, whilst the boys are educated at good schools in Kowloon to fit them for some profession.

A very lavish meal was served, entirely vegetarian but the dishes so presented as to create the illusion of a normal Chinese feast. Brinjals not only looked but tasted like oysters, and there was even mock fat pork, so beloved of the Cantonese. Fresh fungi, and the dry kind, Tung Ku, were reinforced by English button mushrooms, which might have come from Fortnum and Mason. Half a dozen children sat round, forming an audience, and two little girls of about fourteen, with pigtails tied with pink ribbon, assisted in the service. Buddhist monasteries are bound by their rule to entertain and feed strangers, the only stipulation being that the food should be immune from adverse criticism. Travelling monks carry with them a circular letter from their own parent house, which acts as an introduction to all monastic establishments. The length of their visit is never questioned and they are free to come and go as they choose. No fixed charge is made for food from visitors to whose conscience it is left as to what donation they leave for the general use of the temple.

The celebration of the Magnolia Festival began with with the officiating priest standing before the high altar to the three manifestations of Buddha. He wore a black, long-sleeved cassock, over which was a blood-red surplice draped so as to leave the right shoulder free. In that hand was a black scarf about four inches wide, held so that the index and little finger were visible, whilst the middle and third were concealed. Behind the long table with the musical instruments chanted four priests in brown robes, and on their left three of the members of the community in black cassocks. The two little pig-tailed girls had robed themselves similarly, and one stood to the right of the assistant clergy whilst the other derived evident satisfaction from beating the big drum. All, whilst they chanted and played their instruments, kept a black fan in continual motion with the left hand.

The opening service lasted for fifteen minutes, and culminated with a deafening detonation of crackers in the court-yard.

A move was then made to the shrine in front of the picture of the red pagoda, the characters on which represented the names of the invalids who desired the prayers of the congregation. The officiant stood, silent and motionless, before the image of Yo Shih Fo (藥師佛), the Healing Buddha, whilst the choir formed two ranks at right angles to the wall. The service lasted about ten minutes, and then the pagoda was detached and carried into the court, where it was burned to the accompaniment of a fusillade of fireworks. This ended the preliminary service, as the Mass for the Dead and great holocaust of paper was deferred till darkness fell.

The women of the establishment returned to the preparation of the money and garments to be sacrificed, on which they had been busy for days. Every spare room was stacked with black paper trunks with gilt fittings, and families whose ancestral tablets were cared for in the temple had sent their individual contributions suitably addressed to their dead. In some cases the paper clothing was enclosed in bags the size of an oat-sack decorated with talismanic pictures and inscriptions to insure them

from highway robbery by forgotten, and thereby malignant, spirits.

In popular worship there is no hard and fast line between Buddhism and Taoism so it was not surprising to find the inscription on the sacks referring purely to the latter faith. On the flap of the paper envelope was printed "Lucky place for Dragon-Tiger Mountain road to Hell". Now the Dragon-Tiger Mountain is the palace of the Taoist Pope, the hereditary head of that religion for sixty-three generations. Chang Tao-ling, or the First Master of Heaven as he is called, was a great magician, and a remarkable scientist to boot. His image, astride of a tiger, is stamped on the bag as the divinity who "safely keeps the dead". With his demon-dispelling sword, and striped mount, the terror of malignants, he escorts the souls to their shadowy destination. An inventory is enclosed to assure the recipient that no pilferage has occurred on the way. It is regarded as the greatest sacrilege to deprive the Hungry Ghosts of anything intended for them, and foreigners should be warned never to let a passion for souvenirs tempt them to abstract a Hell bank-note or a single article of paper clothing.

Billions of dollars, undedicated, can be obtained at any paper shop for a few cents, but the idea of depriving some forlorn spirit of the means to alleviate his misery is wholly repugnant to the Chinese. The Buddhists, of course, sacrifice no life, either for their own or the dead's benefit, but part of the Taoist offering is nearly always a chicken. At the feast of the Ghosts, however, a duck is substituted, as a hen is always pecking and scratching. On the road to the underworld, therefore, its spirit may set to work with beak and claws on the clothing for the dead, and the souls may be forced to dress like beggars for the next twelve months. The duck's flat bill and webbed feet are wholly innocuous, so it is admirably fitted to accompany the material gifts to the Land of Shades.

The nunnery is sufficiently well off to employ a gardener, and the grounds are full of citrus trees, whilst every court-yard and corner has orchids and other flowers in pots. Orange, lemon and pummelo serve as good plants for the larvae of most of our spectacular Swallowtail butterflies, which are safe from molestation here because of the tenets of the religion. They add life to the shady walks as they flash between the trees, and well deserve the name of flowers of the air.

The Hungry Ghosts of Fukien

The festival of the Hungry Ghosts ranks high in the order of popularity among the religious celebrations in China, and its universal observance is probably only surpassed by the New Year holidays. Even the modern worship of the State has not dimmed the sense of responsibility towards the unfortunate spirits who, deprived of the services of their descendants, are dependent on vicarious charity. The city of Ch'uan Chow, on the Fukien coast, has tenaciously clung to the old customs in the memory of its nameless dead, the ghosts of those who resisted the Manchu invasion, and refused to shave their heads in token of submission.

Republican China rarely had a good word to say for

Only New Year holidays surpass the Festival of Hungry Ghosts in popularity

60

the fallen rulers, despite the fact that under their reign the Empire achieved its greatest territorial and artistic glory. "The evil that men do lives after them, the good is oft interred with their bones" is strikingly true in this instance. There was, however, some justification for the severity of the conquerors in this case, as the coast was the base of the famous pirate, Ch'eng Kung (成功), known to Europeans as Koxinga, whose father, for a price, threw in his lot with the Ming Pretender. The Manchus were not a maritime race, and overran the country with their cavalry, so they were at a disadvantage against a sea power.

Early in the seventeeth century a Fukienese fisherman named Chen (鄭), who was of a roving disposition, went overseas to better himself, and tried his luck in Macao, the Philippines, and finally Japan, where he married a native. His son, Ch'eng Kung (成功), was born in 1624. The father acquired capital for his piratical enterprises through an act of barratry, selling in Amoy the cargo with which he was entrusted, and investing the proceeds in a fleet of armed junks.

The coast, with its numerous creeks, and dearth of interior communications, was admirably adapted to his piratical tactics, and he soon became the terror of the South Seas. The Mings were in decline, and the ruling emperor, unable to check his depredations on trade, tried the old Chinese expedient of conciliation, and made him an admiral. This appointment set the seal on his respectability, for he was entitled to live openly and in great splendour in Amoy, from where he hunted his own ships without ever bringing them to book. His imperial commission entitled him to impress crews, and he extended his trading operations to all the adjacent seas. He sent for his son Ch'eng Kung and gave him a classical education, which enabled him to take a brilliant degree at the examinations.

On the Manchu invasion of the North, the successor to the Ming title established himself in the isolated province of Fukien, and fostered an idea of a return to power with the aid of the pirate fleet. He was much impressed with Ch'eng Kung's personality and scholarship and, to win over the support of the wealthy father, gave the youth his own surname and appointed him Controller of the Imperial Clan Court. The title, Lord of the Country's families (國姓爺), in the Amoy dialect Kox Sing-ia, accounts for the appelation known to Europeans. The admiral, however, was ambitious and, before committing his fleet to the weaker party, he demanded that his son should be recognised as the Heir Apparent. This was too much for the proud Mings to swallow, and the condition was refused. Old Chen then deserted their cause, and made overtures to the Manchus, but they did not trust him and, when he was rash enough to accept their invitation to Peking, they threw him into prison, lest he should change his mind again.

Though his father had betrayed him in a minor skirmish, Ch'eng Kung was infuriated at the double-dealing of the new conquerors and threw himself whole-heartedly into the Ming cause. As the armies of the Manchus penetrated the mountainous area in the interior, the ports of Fukien were threatened, so he assembled his fleet and sailed off to a secure base in the Pescadores. From the Formosa Straits he harried all the coastal traffic, and even made inroads on to the mainland. He acquired an army at Amoy by murdering his

cousin who commanded it, and established himself in that area for some time. The petty successes achieved by guerilla operations were not however commensurate with his ambitions, and he formed a plan with the objective of the capture of Nanking. He was obsessed with the idea that a blow at the old Ming capital would provoke a general insurrection, and the grateful people would hail him as the new emperor. He assembled the most powerful fleet ever seen in Chinese waters, consisting of upwards of three thousand junks, and picked up smaller contingents from his outpost islands, on his journey north. Fortunately for the Manchus, he hesitated to land before Nanking, and they were afforded time to collect enough river craft to attack him at his anchorage. The pirates were carousing when the Tartars fell upon them, setting fire to their ships, and slaughtering the crews in the confusion. At least three thousand perished and Ch'eng Kung was forced to relinquish his design and return with the remnants to Amoy. There he was in his own waters, and he successfully beat off all attacks by the pursuing forces.

Thus, he remained the master of the southern seas but the Manchus, to deny him a foothold ashore, ordered the withdrawal inland of all the inhabitants, and built forts at intervals of three miles to enforce the scorched earth policy. It was probably this measure, rather than the wearing of the queue, which caused them to be execrated by farmers and fishermen alike. With so long a tradition of "free trade", it is doubtful if there were any who could claim immunity from the taint of piracy, and conquerors were unlikely to give them the benefit of the doubt. The souls of those executed are still believed to haunt the coast, and their propitiation devolves on those who wish to lead a quiet life.

In the main, Taoist priests are engaged to celebrate the rites and, to make the borrowing of their rival's ritual less obvious, they have combined the worship with that of the Ti Kuan (地官), the member of their Heavenly Trinity who ensures the forgiveness of sins. Ch'uan Chow has a temple, named the Chin Hsien Kung where only these three divinities are worshipped, and there is a day for each. The T'ien Kuan is feted at the Feast of Lanterns in the First Moon, the Ti Kuan on the 15th of the Seventh Moon, and the Shui Kuan on the 15th of the first winter moon. Food for the Hungry Ghosts is offered on their altars, the drowned being commemorated on the birthday of the last, as he is in charge of the waters.

As everybody wishes to render himself immune from the importunities of unsatisfied ghouls the crowds at the temple used to beggar description and, until the authorities decreed that the days of worship should be staggered, brawls and disturbances were not uncommon. It became recognised that offerings could be presented from the Double Seventh till the first of the Eighth Moon. Rich people, however, either from the motive of segregating themselves from the common herd, or because they feared that the ghosts might be insufficiently aware of their benefactions, extended the time limit by presenting themselves on the 29th of the Sixth Moon or the 3rd of the Eighth. The Guilds held their celebration when everyone else was done, on the 4th of the Eighth Moon.

THE EIGHTH MOON

This corresponds to the Harvest Moon, when the crops are in and heavy work in the fields is over, affording time for relaxation. The Paper Shops are full of lanterns of every shape and colour, which are bought to decorate the house for the worship of the full moon on the night of the 15th. Women only can perform the sacrifices to the planet, and her altar is erected in the courtyard, or on a flat roof. Outsiders consequently see little of the ceremony, which is performed by the younger members supervised by an elder relative.

In country districts, however, over the period of the full moon spiritualistic séances, and ritualistic dances are performed, and there is usually a large audience of both sexes.

The Moon Festival

Cloudy weather ruins enjoyment of the Moon festival, and an eclipse is a positive disaster. Though Chinese astronomers were able to predict eclipses as far back as the 8th century B.C., popular belief maintained a totally different cause for the phenomenon than that generally accepted in the rest of the world. In the North, an ill-disposed celestial dog makes periodic attempts to swallow the moon, but is always obliged to disgorge at the sound of a band, whose varied instruments rival those enumerated in the Book of Daniel. The moment the shadow creeps over the moon's surface, every villager, old and young, sallies forth with pots, pans, and fire-irons, and the resulting uproar has never failed to achieve its object. To quote Calverley, they "rattle the bones, hit a tin-bottomed tray hard with a fire-shovel, hammer away". In the South, where the marauding dog is replaced by a frog in some districts, the people seem to have stumbled on a garbled version of the Moon Lady, Heng O, who was changed into a three-legged toad, after swallowing her husband's pill of immortality. The fact that she dislikes loud noises throws grave doubt upon her Chinese nationality, but the racket of pots and pans apparently drives her to distraction elsewhere than in the destruction of her own home. A few years ago the Chinese might have been criticised for the illogicality of imagining that anyone would wish to annihilate the planet on which she lived, but recent efforts of the scientists in the frenzied search for a bigger and better atom bomb shake one's faith in the sanity of mankind. In Chekiang province, the explanation of an eclipse is a nearer approximation to the truth, for the people have envisaged a dark double to the planet, which circles round and, at certain periods, tries to exclude it. The false moon is as susceptible to noise as the frog and the dog, so the same treatment is applied to frustrate its object.

The festival is made an occasion for giving parties and, as every guest contributes to the feast, boxes of four moon cakes are abundant in every household. It is the time for showing curios, and the children, having less valuable possessions, display their toys to their small friends. The decorations play a great part in the brightness of the scene. The contributors make their selection coincide with the recipient's tastes or aspirations. A scholar will get the carp which swam up the Yellow River through the T'ung Kuan rapids, and became a dragon, to stimulate him with the need for effort in passing his examinations. The butterfly conveys a wish for longevity, and the red lobster, whose local name is Ha, brings mirth, and hence contentment with one's condition. The carambola, which the Chinese misguidedly call a "foreign peach", is an essential at this time of year, when round fruit is in demand for the moon offering. It is rather early for the fruit, so it is expensive, but the fabrication of lanterns in its shape costs no more than the flower pots and butterflies. Those with a slender purse can deck the feast with a paper representation, which will be just as pleasing to the deity as the genuine article. The spirits have no more difficulty in cashing notes on the Bank of Hell than they would on any of the financial establishments sponsored by the late government, so the Moon is unlikely to cavil at the offering of a paper carambola. The intention is everything and, if this exotic fruit is part of the ritual, it matters not what

Clothing and shrine for Moon Festival with watercalthrop

Lanterns and Moon Rabbits

form it takes.

In China, autumn begins about the 6th of August and, by the fifteenth of the eighth month, the powers of darkness begin definitely to exert their superiority over the light. The "Yin", or female principle, personified by the moon, is in the ascendant, and it is the moment to propitiate her. This is essentially a feminine festival and compensates for the fact that the ladies may not worship the Kitchen God, though much of their life is spent in his domain. The Emperor was the only exception to the rule, as the moon was his celestial sister.

Moon Cakes

Coming events cast their shadows before them, and this is certainly the case in the eighth month, when the appearance of moon cakes on the market heralds the approach of the planet's festival when she arrives at the full. About a month before the Harvest Moon, every confectioner starts baking the cakes which are the symbol of the feast. On the fifteenth of the moon not one is to be seen in the shops. Their popularity is immense, and the bakers count on making all the overheads of the year on their sale alone. In Hong Kong, as well as in many parts of China, women join a sort of slate club with certain confectioners and, the moment the Moon

Festival is over, start paying in a small monthly contribution which accumulates in their names till the following season. For the interest on their money they get a better rate than the ordinary customer, and can fulfil their obligations to their friends without having to raise a considerable sum of money at a possibly inconvenient moment.

Foreigners tend not to like moon cakes, and excuse themselves of partaking by alleging that they are indigestible. It is a moot-point whether this reply springs from a lack of a spirit of adventure, for the English are more conservative about their food than anything else. It is freely admitted that, in the North, Chinese confectionery is uninteresting, and is inclined to turn to ashes in the mouth but, in the regions where sugar is plentiful, the Chinese display much ingenuity in this branch of the culinary art. The cakes are enclosed in golden brown pastry, shaped like a small pork-pie, and stamped on top with the emblem of the deity. There are fillings to suit all purses and tastes. The basic filling of the moon cake is a sort of paste composed of sugared beans, lotus seeds, or sesame, ground fine to impart the flavour. In this are embedded ducks' eggs, nuts, or occasionally meat according to the individual taste. As food is the primary idea of a present in China, an enormous trade is done in this form of comestible, and it is not unusual for a household to have a couple of hundred catties on hand if a wedding occurs during the month. They are not all for home consumption, but are distributed to friends and relatives who have sent gifts to the young couple.

The Chinese, in spite of Marco Polo's encomiums, were peculiarly averse to the domination of their Mongol conquerors who, for internal security, elected to billet one of their own men on every household. These spies, as the Chinese considered them, were particularly obnoxious, and arrogated to themselves the right to issue orders to their unwilling hosts, "taking to themselves the powers of rulers in the homes, and causing all to bow to their wills". The women, especially, were slaves under their yoke. Great indignation was caused by their overbearing manner and, at length, a Sicilian Vespers was planned. To co-ordinate the plot, and fix the zero hour, the Chinese passed their directives on scraps of paper stuck in the moon cakes. When sent, as they still are, from friend to friend, and neighbour to neighbour, the pastry contained an order for a midnight rising. Arming themselves with kitchen choppers, they made short work of the dispersed garrison, and the revolt thus started led to the overthrow of the alien dynasty. Some women bake the cakes themselves as an act of piety, in gratefulness for the delivery of their ancestors, and are lavish in their extravagance in the filling. Lard, spices, eggs, orange-peel, almonds and sugar are ground into a paste, and the ingredients of the contents are varied and wonderful. "Even to dream of a moon cake spells riches" is one of their sayings. In some villages moon cake societies are formed, the baker acting as treasurer, and all members contribute a small amount monthly. When the festival arrives, every family is presented with its quota of Yueh Ping, stamped with the image of the Moon Hare, or the Three-legged Toad.

The Chinese have never traced the features of the Man in the Moon, which are familiar to every English child, but in the lights and shadows of her extinct volcanoes they saw the image of the toad Ch'an (蟾). The myth is of Indian origin, but was readily adopted by the Chinese, who had already established a connection between the moon and the tides, and considered it natural for the planet to be inhabited by amphibious creatures. Heng O, the Moon Lady, was not transformed into the common or garden frog, but took the shape of the miraculous three-legged toad, who wears on his throat the characters for "8" signifying that he belongs to that month of the year. He secretes water in his pads, thus identifying himself with water, and his scaly armour is proof against arrows. From Heng O's (恒娥) point of view this latter attribute was a consummation devoutly to be wished, as her husband was a noted archer, and his first instinct was to string his bow when he discovered her treachery.

Heng O and her spouse Hou Yih lived in the reign of the Perfect Emperor, about 2000 B.C. Like most of these legendary characters, the husband was something of a wizard who trod the side-paths of air, and fed on the nectar of flowers. He was also an officer of the Imperial Bodyguard, and a sort of Robin Hood in his management of his enchanted bow. On one occasion the day broke unbearably bright, and it was noticed that there were ten suns in the sky. The Emperor, mindful of the people's distress, ordered Hou Yih to shoot nine of them out of the sky, a feat he accomplished to the great admiration of Hsi Wang Mu, who commissioned him to build her a palace of multi-coloured jade in the Western Heavens. As a reward for turning into a successful architect, she presented him with the pill of immortality, but cautioned him not to swallow it until he had undergone a year's preparation of prayer and fasting. On reaching home, he hid his treasure under a roof rafter, before starting his course of self-discipline.

Unfortunately his services were in so much demand that, before the time was up, he was called away to pursue some now unidentifiable criminal named "Chisel Tooth". During his absence, his wife, Heng O, noticed a beam of white light streaming from a cranny in the roof-tree, and was drawn to the spot by an exquisite perfume. Curiosity conquered prudence and the moment she had swallowed the pill, the force of gravity ceased to exert itself, and she experienced the novelty of being air-borne for the first time. Realising that her husband had unexpectedly returned, and would demand an explanation for her unwarrantable misappropriation of his property, she made haste to take advantage of her new accomplishment and flew through the window. As Hou Yih was as much at home in the skies as on the ground, he pursued her with his bow, half-way across the heavens, but got caught in a typhoon and was turned back to earth. Heng O was so breathless when she reached the moon that in a fit of coughing she ejected the capsule containing the pill, which took the form of the Jade Rabbit, whilst she herself assumed the shape of the three-legged toad. This she has made her habitation ever since, whilst her husband was translated into the sun, and as Yin and Yang they rule the universe. They meet but once a month, on the 15th, when the moon is at the full, and that is why she is most beautiful at that phase. How her husband achieved his delayed immortality is not recorded but, as it was granted in the end, he has presumably forgiven his spouse for sharing it with him.

Observance of the Moon Festival

In most religions women are more devout than men and in China particularly, where the necessity for a male heir is paramount and their status so largely depends on fulfilling this primary mission, they are more ready to seek divine assistance. The mid-Autumn festival is purely a feminine affair and the date is chosen in the Eighth month, the season when the female principle in nature is definitely in the ascendant. Summer heat has given way to autumn coolness, and the brightness is becoming eclipsed by the dark. The fifteenth night is the moon's apogee and at no other time is the planet so brilliant. The Chinese declare that it is only then that she is completely round.

Men may not worship the moon, nor may women propitiate what should be their guardian angel, the Kitchen God. For the birthday of the planet, who represents the female influence now beginning to dominate the sky at the turn of the year, all offerings must be round.

The altar for the Moon Festival must be arranged by the younger female members of the family, under the supervision of the "Old Lady". It is set in the open air, and on it are placed five dishes of round fruits, such as apples, peaches, and pomegranates, whose seeds betoken many sons, grapes and small melons. The shape not only symbolises the moon, but betokens family unity. The moon cakes are an essential part of the feast. Baked of a greyish (moon-coloured) flour, they are piled thirteen in a pyramid, for in a full year there are thirteen lunar months. Odd numbers are always lucky, and they represent a complete circle of happiness.

One of the offerings at the festival in Hong Kong is a brown seed, called Ling Ke (菱角), or water calthrops, about two and a half inches across the tips of what resemble buffalo's horns. It is exactly like the conventionalised Chinese bat, a lucky emblem, which probably accounts for its presence. It is sometimes employed in art, carved in jade or modelled, as the knob on the top of a tea-pot lid, the sides being decorated with snails and water chestnuts. At this time of year it also forms a child's toy, pierced with a hole, and having a string run through to whirl it.

Three cups of tea form the liquid refreshment, and in the centre of the table which serves as altar is a sand-filled receptacle for candles and sticks of incense. The Moon's consort is honoured at the same time by the provision of a cardboard effigy combining the characters for sun and moon in complementary colours of red and green. Suits of paper clothes are offered to the divinity and her consort. These have a gilt and red crown, mounted on bamboo, a red apron with gold embroidery, and a sort of square-necked bodice. On the left breast is the Chinese character for the sun, and on the right that for the moon. Below are the representations of two attendant maidens, each holding a lotus. No particular reverence is shown to these offerings, and a certain amount of horse-play often takes place whilst the preparations are being made with one girl putting the crown on the head of another during the folding of the gold and silver paper to represent ingots of metal.

The actual ceremony is very short. The women go forward one after the other, and make their three bows, offering two lighted candles, whilst bundles of ignited incense sticks are planted in the family burner. The portrait of the Moon Rabbit is pasted on the wall, sitting under his cassia tree and compounding the elixir of life on the head of the famous toad. After he has received his salutations, he is taken down and burned, so that he may return to his usual habitation. Someone sets fire to a cardboard bowl containing the clothing and money sacrifices and, as the flames die down, bundles of crackers are thrown in the blaze, whose explosion scatters the ashes to the four winds of heaven. The remainder of the evening is spent in consuming the fruit and moon-cakes which are an essential part of the feast, as are poultry and roast pigs, and Chinese bacon, cured with sugar, and packed in long strips.

In wealthier houses moon-viewing parties are arranged with a banquet at midnight, when the planet is high in the sky, accompanied by blind musicians singing the famous poems of Li T'ai Po. These moon-viewing parties date from the reign of the Emperor Wu Ti, a hundred years before the Christian era. This Sovereign is reputed to have ordered the construction of a special Toad Terrace on which he gave banquets with an uninterrupted view of the object of worship. The ladies, whose festival it was, were segregated to a special verandah, or terrace of their own, where they carried out the rites incumbent on their sex, and blind musicians were hired for their entertainment, who played and sang the odes of Li T'ai Po (李太白). He, perhaps the most famous of Chinese poets, divided his allegiance between wine and the celestial lady, and is reputed to have lost his life trying to grasp her reflection in the water when he had toasted her too freely in the flowing bowl.

The Moon's birthday is an occasion to consult the future and, as she influences matrimonial prospects, young ladies are naturally curious about their fate. They slip away one by one and burn their sticks of incense, whispering their question. Hiding behind the gate they listen to the chance conversation of the passers-by, the answer, lucky or unlucky, being deduced from the first phrase they let fall. Most of the requests have some bearing on matrimonial prospects, and are addressed to the Yueh Lao-yeh (月老爺), an old man in the Moon, who shares the tenancy with the Rabbit and Three-legged Toad. Chinese maidens burn their candles to the old matchmaker, hoping he will reveal the house to which the red chair will eventually carry them.

The blind musicians, whose presence adds greatly to the charm of any party on the night of the Moon Festival, number about a hundred, and have formed a sort of colony near West Point and Kennedy Town. It is not a closed shop, for their wives are in many cases in full possession of their vision, and the daughters who accompany them on their engagements do not necessarily marry into the profession. Their normal avocation is playing at restaurants. When engaged for private parties they pick up about five times their normal wages.

One usually plays the recorder, an obsolete form of flute, whilst his companion is equipped with a lute, whose sounding board is constructed of a coconut shell. This performer punctuates his music with an ivory clapper. The airs are all traditional tunes, common to the whole of China, and the songs are taken from Cantonese drama. The effect is very soothing and admirably adapted to the occasion when all the guests are intent on watching the object of worship riding high in the Heavens. As some lady put it, "It blends perfectly with the conversation, without in the least interrupting it." The whole atmosphere is peaceful, and entirely divorced from the clash of cymbals and boom of gongs, which dominate the ordinary Chinese orchestra. Broadcasts of Elizabethan music give the modern listener some idea of an evening with the recorder and theorbo, enjoyed by Samuel Pepys, as an alternative to hot jazz and swing, and the contrast between ancient and modern Chinese music must be very similar.

It is essentially an open air entertainment, with the verandah facing the moon, and the lawn glowing with the soft light of the decorative lanterns. Candles should be used for illumination, as some of the more elaborate lamps depend for the movement of their silhouettes on the draught created by the flame, and neons are harsh competitors with the September moonlight.

The Mister Rabbit

A glance at the paper shops for a fortnight before the Moon Festival will reveal that their stock-in-trade, always appropriate to coming events, consists almost entirely of lanterns and rabbits. As a matter of fact, the latter often perform the functions of the former, and play a dual part in the celebrations. Although the official ending of the New Year festivities is marked by the Feast of Lanterns, in the South their display is far more evident in the worship of the moon on the fifteenth of the eighth month. Some of the specimens are very elaborate, and are adorned with tassels of silk, or paper strips, whilst a ring of silhouetted figures throws its shadows on the panes set in an octagonal frame. Others are in the form of butterflies, conveying to the recipient the wish that he may live for seventy or eighty years. Huge red lobsters, with their feelers looped back, are most effective when illuminated from within. The origin of the Feast of Lanterns, when householders put up lamps over their doors, and hung branches of evergreen as a symbol of longevity, is supposed to date from the Han Dynasty, two thousand years ago. It began as a ceremonial worship at the Temple of the First Cause, from the 13th to the 16th of New Year Moon, marking the end of the holiday with a religious service, though the lantern display was not adopted till eight hundred years later, when all religious significance had been lost.

The rabbits commemorate the most popular of the moon's inhabitants and bring the children into the picture, for Mr. Rabbit is their especial toy. In the North he is always constructed of clay, and is dressed either as a civil or a military official. Oddly enough he is the only rabbit who exists in China, for the word is only used in polite society with the prefix of Mister. The Chinese have a hare, in fact two species, one living north, and the other south of the Yangtze, the former being a true lepus, and the latter a caprolagus. The only similarity to the habits of the rabbit is that both shelter in holes, instead of forms, but neither takes the trouble to dig them, preferring to be tenants in other peoples' houses. Other races have connected the hare with the moon, and Pausanias recorded its aversion to honest toil, for he states that the Goddess of the Moon, having been consulted by some soothsayers as to where to build a city, replied "Where a hare makes its burrow."

The hare owes its elevation to the satellite for an act of supreme self-sacrifice, and it entered Chinese mythology with the Buddhist religion. In the days of the Master there was a forest glade where holy men came to meditate. In this earthly paradise the air was scented with flowers, and the gurgling brooks made music for the ear, whilst the eye was rested by the deep shade of the heavy foliage which caused the fierce sun to disperse in dappled markings on the moist ground. The spirit of holiness which pervaded the spot even affected its normal inhabitants, who elected the hare, on account of his inoffensiveness, their expounder of the scriptures. As teaching is an honourable, rather than a lucrative profession and, as in any case the hare gave his services for nothing, he lived in dire poverty. One evening Buddha came to this other Eden, with a following of his disciples, and sat down to expound the law. All night long he discoursed till the sun was high in the heavens. As noon approached he assumed the likeness of a Brahmin, and cried out as one who had lost the road, and was consumed by weariness and sorrow, "Alone, and astray, having lost my companions, I am hungry

and thirsty. Help me ye pious." All the forest dwellers heard his cry of distress, and all begged him to accept their hospitality. The otter brought fish, and the jackal his kill, but, when it came to the turn of the hare, he presented himself empty-handed, and humbly said, "Master! I, who have grown up in the forest, fed by grass and herbs, have nothing to offer you but my body. Grant us the boon of resting thy Holiness among us, and vouchsafe to me the favour of feeding thee with mine own flesh, since I have nothing else to offer." As he ended the sentence he perceived a mound of magic charcoal, glowing without smoke, hard by. He was about to leap on the pyre, when he paused, and gently combed his fur with a chip to dislodge the livestock which battened on his charity. "My body I may sacrifice for the Holy One," he murmured, "but your lives I have no right to take." Placing the insects in security, he threw himself on the blazing fire. Resuming his own form, Buddha praised the sublimity of the sacrifice, saying, "He who forgets self, be he the humblest of earthly creatures, will reach the Ocean of Eternal Peace." To reward the hare, the Master decreed that his image should adorn the face of the moon, as a shining example to all eternity, and, since that day the Buddhists have known the planet as hare-marked.

The Taoists could not neglect a story with so powerful an appeal, so they adopted him into their pantheon as the Gemmous hare and, to fit in with the legend of Heng O, and the pill of immortality, picture him as compounding the elixir of life, using the head of a toad as a mortar. He sits under the sacred cassia tree, as its bark is one of the ingredients, and it is always in flower about the time of the moon festival. In an old medical treatise dating from the 4th Century A.D. there is a prescription, "Thoroughly mix cassia bark with bamboo juice, and the brains of a frog. This potion if drunk will cause you to walk upon the waters after seven years"—in other words attain immortality. It is probable that the Taoists had this recipe in mind in accounting for the hare's occupation, rather than that Heng O, in the guise of the Three-legged Toad, was undergoing this punishment to fit the crime of purloining her husband's pill.

The Moon Hare has a companion in the shape of the Woodcutter, condemned like Sisyphus to an interminable task. His punishment was to fell all the cassia groves on the moon's surface and, as it is an alleged property of the tree that it renews itself as fast as it is chipped, his occupation, to say the least, is unprofitable. Beyond the fact that he was a poor scholar, little is known of the Woodcutter's biography. The cassia tree is, however, the emblem of forgiveness for, though the celestial scholar seeks to destroy it, it remains friendly to the seekers after learning. Those who took the second literary degree were said to have "plucked a flower from the topmost branch of the Pavilions of the Moon".

Hong Kong's Moon Rabbits are much less like the rodents they are supposed to represent than those sold on the stalls at a Peking fair. They have a rather ovine appearance and profile, and only the ears betray the intention. They are usually mounted on wheels, and are dragged about with a string. The coat is also like a woolly fleece with a "perm" instead of the straight fur of a hare.

The Harvest Moon

Man's first demonstration of gratitude towards the divinity he worshipped appears to have taken the form of a Harvest Thanksgiving, at which selected specimens of the fruits of his cultivation were laid before the altar. The custom dates back to time immemorial and, if the chronology of the Old Testament is to be accepted, the first harvest thanksgiving, in which Abel lost his life, was only one generation after the Creation.

The Harvest Moon is a time of relaxation, for the heavy work of garnering the crop is over, and the peasants again worship the Soil Gods to whose benevolence they look for their living. A special hymn of praise is quoted in the Book of Odes, dating from the 8th Century B.C., "With offerings of millet, and of sheep, we sacrifice to the Gods of the Soil. Our fields have been reaped, and the people rejoice. Let us play upon the lute, and the lyre, and beat the drums to invoke the Father of Husbandry. Let us humbly beg of him the blessing of the soft, warm rain that our grain may multiply during the coming year, and the land be blessed with abundance."

Crops, in a country with so varied a climate as China, are gathered throughout the summer. Kwangtung and Fukien run to a double harvest of rice, which is the staple food up to the Yangtze Valley. North of the great river, particularly in Honan, is the wheat belt and, above that again, the peasantry depend on kaoliang for the bulk of their diet. This giant millet grows to a height of eight to ten feet, forming concealment for a mounted man, and only when it is down can the shape of the countryside be determined. No plant is more useful, with the possible exception of the bamboo, for its seeds form nourishment for man and beast, whilst the stalks are woven into screens to protect the vegetables from the bitter north-west wind. Finally the roots are used as fuel to stoke the kitchen fire and the stove during the winter cold

In the countryside the peasants again worship their T'u Ti, or Earth Gods, and, in addition to the thanksgiving for their harvest, proffer prayers for rain to stimulate the growth of the spring wheat. It is a time of general relaxation, and roving theatrical companies reap their annual harvest by catering to the distraction of those members of the community who should be in funds. Lion dancers and stilt walkers compete with acrobats and mountebanks to amuse the rural population, and in Kansu small girls are carried on a raised board by men performing a ritualistic dance. The custom is known as the "Yang Ko" (秧歌), yang meaning to raise. It is usually employed in the sense of rearing, but the dance is a survival of the old "No" procession for the expulsion of pestilential diseases. It is a moot point if the Communists picked it up in their wanderings in the Western wilderness, and adapted it to modern uses. It certainly is not an importation from behind the Iron Curtain, for the Russians never had anything to correspond to it. The head-coverings of the participants, resembling the Mohammedan turban, must originate in the western provinces, for they are the last thing a self-respecting Russian would wear. There is a legend that Confucius himself put on his court robes, and attended one of these performances in order to identify himself with the country folk, so the Communists have tradition on their side.

The Gods of the Measure

In addition to the great Moon Festival, which takes place in the middle of the month, several other divinities' birthdays are celebrated during this lunar period. The worship of the "Measure", Northern or Southern according to the season, is widespread, especially in South China. This takes place on an auspicious day in the eighth moon, which sometimes coincides with the main festival itself. The Northern Measure, a group of stars in our Great Bear, is the celestial residence of the God of Wealth, Lu Hsing (祿星), whilst the Southern, Canopus in the constellation Argo, houses the God of Longevity. This delightful old figure, easily recognisable by his domed head, and the peach he invariably carries, enjoys an enormous popularity in Chinese art. Ch'in Shih Huang Ti, after he had unified China, was induced by the Taoists to build a temple in his honour, and the T'ang Dynasty introduced sacrifices to the Star God at the autumn equinox. The purely Chinese Ming Dynasty neglected him, and there is every sign of his falling into disrepute under the present regime. His long beard and staff denote his old age, and the P'an T'ao (蟠桃) or peach, which he holds, is culled from that miraculous tree, which blossoms every three thousand years and only fruits three thousand after. He is sometimes depicted surrounded by mushrooms (Ling Chih) which confer immortality, and so far he has survived political change. Whilst the Old Man of the Northern Measure has power over death, the Longevity Star can prolong life as the following story bears witness. Once upon a time a bright lad met a famous fortune-teller, who deplored the fact that such a promising boy should have so little life before him. On pressing to know the number of years allotted to him, he learned with dismay that he must die at nineteen. In great distress he asked if there were any remedy, and was told to seek out two elderly gentlemen who were playing chess. His instructions were to furnish them with a lunch of venison and a jug of wine, and to remain silent until he was addressed. The game was on no account to be interrupted, and the youth was counselled as to the request he was to make. The old men were duly found, sitting on the top of a hill, absorbed in their game, so the young man laid down the lunch, and waited till they had finished. The old gentlemen set to work on the food, and then inquired how they might repay the donor. The boy besought them to avert the early death with which he was threatened, so they referred to their ledgers, and altered the one into a nine, making the entry read ninety-nine instead of nineteen. However, they warned the young man that it must not be made a precedent, and that he must convey a reproof to the fortune-teller, who had no business upsetting people with information which no mortal should acquire. On his return home, the boy's mother was overjoyed, and realised that the ancients were none other than the Gods of the Measure. She accordingly instituted the sacrifices in their honour, which have been perpetuated whenever there is sickness among the juveniles of the family. Incense is burned to ensure longevity and honours.

In the ceremony for the worship of the Star Gods, a bushel half filled with rice is placed in a perpendicular position, with various implements at the corners. These consist of a pair of scales, a foot measure, a pair of shears, and a mirror. An oil-lamp stands in the centre of the rice, and the container is decorated with stars. The altar is also furnished with the Wu Kung, or five vessels, incense burner, candlesticks and flower vases. Taoist priests are called in to officiate, who walk round the table chanting, to the accompaniment of bells and music. Various dishes of food are offered on the altar. According to a Chinese saying, "Rice is the staff of life, so the rice bushel is its measure." The word for measure has the same sound as that for constellation, which probably accounts for the connection. The "Mother of the Measure" is an alternative name for the Queen of Heaven, the chief divinity of the Boat People of Hong Kong, and she has her seat among the stars which form the Great Bear. When represented as the Tou Mu she is accompanied by two attendants Yu Pi and Tso Fu, and she is enthroned on a lotus supported by the stars of the Dipper. Her Indian origin is manifest by her multitudinous arms, and a caste mark on her forehead. In her Chinese guise as Queen of Heaven her attendants are the female "Thousand Mile Eyes" and "Fair Wind Ears". Though her birthday is celebrated on the 23rd day of the third moon, she receives a share of attention with the other two Star Gods at the Festival of the Measure.

A widely different character from the Gods of Longevity and Affluence celebrates his birthday about the 17th of the month. This is the God of the Thieves, who finds plenty of mischief for his idle adherents at the moment of the year when everyone should be in funds after the harvest. Not only do his followers appeal to him for assistance in their nefarious enterprises, but their victims propitiate him in the hopes that he will divert the attention of his adherents to those who have omitted to take the precaution. Like Mahommed's coffin he occupies a position midway between heaven and earth from which he derives the title "Midway in the Heavens". Men make no images of him, and their prayers for his protection are offered in the open air. To the Chinese he occupies the position of our Robin Hood, not that he robbed the rich like a socialist for the benefit of his voters, but because he stole from filial piety to ameliorate the lot of his parents. He thieved to support his mother, and she a widow, so he has everybody's sympathy, except perhaps that of the gods, who are taking no chances of admitting him to their celestial society.

In Kiangsu the Festival of the Measure is more elaborately celebrated than in some other provinces. A paper moon palace is placed on the measure, which is partly filled with sticks of sandalwood. In it is a bundle of incense sticks which are ignited early in the morning, and smoulder all day until the structure is consumed. A figure of the Patron Saint of Literature is placed in the palace, as he is one of the divinities who has his residence in the Northern Measure. Originally the constellation K'uei was regarded as the abode of Wen Ch'ang, who is worshipped in the third moon, as well as on an auspicious day in the eighth. The star Kuei was later substituted, and was designated as the abode of the deformed scholar, who was refused the prize of honour by the Emperor, who was revolted at his appearance. His image is always placed before that of the chief God of Literature, Wen Ch'ang, though he is not regarded as his attendant. The former is always shown as a handsome man in a sitting posture, whereas Kuei Hsing's deformities are only too obvious in his representations. Wen Ch'ang is the Taoist Patron Saint of Scholars, and is said to have originated in Szechuan during the T'ang Dynasty; reincarnated several times, he was finally deified by the Mongols in A.D. 1314.

THE NINTH MOON

The first nine days of this moon are considered the most favourable for communications with the dead, as restrictions in the underworld are lifted. Wise women, who act as mediums between descendants and ancestors are consequently in great demand, to interpret the advice or wishes of departed relatives.

The Double Ninth

On the "Double Ninth", the equivalent of All Souls' Day is celebrated, when the graves are visited, and cleared of the summer growth. Sacrifices of money and winter clothing against the cold season are offered, after which the worshippers picnic in the open.

Also, on the Ninth Day of the Ninth Month all good Chinese must visit high places. It is a day of picnics, and an auspicious occasion to be photographed. As the eighth month was dedicated to the Yin, or Female principle, as personified by the moon, so the ninth reflects the Yang, and the Double Ninth, being an odd and lucky number, is selected for the "mounting the heights" Teng Kao (登高), or Chung Yang Chieh, which is connected with the male.

The accepted legend connected with the holiday goes no further back than the Han Dynasty, when a primitive custom was codified by inventing a story about a single individual. The parable in the Old Testament is the warning received by Lot, who escaped the destruction of Sodom and Gomorrah by taking to the hills in consequence of a Divine warning. The Chinese Lot was a virtuous scholar who was advised by a soothsayer of an impending disaster. He was told to hasten with all his family to the shelter of the mountains, till there was nothing between them and the sky, and to carry provisions with him. As his liquor consisted of chrysanthemum wine, the season is fixed fairly accurately to be some time in the autumn. When he returned home at the end of the day, he discovered that his cattle and poultry had died violent deaths, and counted himself lucky to have escaped their fate.

Chrysanthemum wine is connected with sun-worship on account of the shape of the flower, which resembles its flaming disc. One of its attributes is the promotion of longevity. Special cakes are carried for the picnic, called "Teng Kao", on account of the pun on the word for cake, which also means promotion. Hence the popularity of the exercise with the official class, to whom the mounting of physical heights was symbolical of the climbing of the ladder of promotion.

In the days when scholarship was the only road to rank and power, the Double Ninth was essentially the festival of the literati, and the Court of Peking held chrysanthemum parties to view the autumn-coloured blooms in the palace grounds. Poetic competitions were held in the pavilions overlooking the lakes, and efforts were stimulated by sipping the wine of longevity.

To search for the origin of the festival it is probably necessary to revert to the most primitive ages. In England fortified hill-tops were the refuges of neolithic man. In times of peace he grazed his flocks in the valleys, where the proximity of the streams assured the water supply. Clearings in the forest were probably few and far between, and the threat of war, or a mere raid, imposed concentration. To meet attacks in force, the villages or communities clubbed together, and constructed a refuge on a bare hill-top, with ditches and ramparts of earth and chalk, sufficient to accommodate their families and the flocks which were their means of subsistence. The entrances were always most cunningly designed, to baffle a stranger and facilitate the defence. Some of these entrenched camps are monumental, like Maiden Castle, near Dorchester, or Hod Hill, a few miles from Blandford.

In China, the campaigning season is the autumn, when the ground is bare of the high crops such as kaoliang. The harvest is also in the granaries instead of on the stalk, a great convenience and temptation to a raiding force. It may be taken that the fall was the dangerous time of the year, until the frosts of winter terminated the campaigning season. It is reasonable to suppose that, before snugging down for the winter, the hills around were picketed to give early warning of

Sweeping the graves at Ching Ming and on the Double Ninth

impending attack, and that the refuges were manned and provisioned.

The fact that the superstition lingers that the earlier the hill is climbed the better the luck, lends colour to the theory of the refuge, as the laggards risked the chance of being cut off.

In the North the month for flying kites is March, but in Fukien the Double Ninth is consecrated to this diversion. Given fine weather, huge crowds congregate on the hill-tops round Foochow to witness the contests, and special police are mobilised to prevent clan fights, which are liable to result from disputes among the competitors. The Festival kites are enormous, needing several hands to manipulate, and are the property of guilds, and private clubs formed by the gentry. It is part of the game to bring down a rival kite, and knives are sometimes attached to sever the strings. On a favourable day the sky is full of butterflies, dragons, frogs and centipedes, fluttering and wriggling as they dip and mount in the breeze. As the Chinese like noise, a musical accompaniment is provided by the attachment of Aeolian harps, called Yao ch'in, gourd-shaped frames of bamboo, with slivers of the same plant stretched across to form the strings. The Chinese are loath to admit that the musical accompaniment is merely a refinement which adds to the pleasure of the sport, so they have been obliged to invent a legend to account for its origin. During the reign of the first Han Emperor, a general on the losing side found himself surrounded, and threatened with annihilation. Like Gideon with the pots and candles, he devised a ruse to scare his enemies, and broke his way through by attaching Aeolian harps to kites, whose eerie whistlings from the skies deluded the hosts of Han into the belief that they were being attacked by supernatural powers. A somewhat similar origin is attributed to the whistles carried by the pigeons who circle the roofs of Peking. A besieged general established a carrier-pigeon post with the main armies, and his adversary countered by flying hawks at his messengers. The screaming whistle was too much for the falcon's nerve, and the encircled army was eventually relieved.

There is almost certainly a religious connection between the kite-flying exercises and ascending the heights, as the most famous of the former takes place at Black Rock Hill, near Foochow, which is crowned with a multitude of spectators. The Chinese are a happy race, and have the knack of making light of their sorrows, so there is nothing incongruous in their celebrating by a picnic the disaster which overtook the virtuous scholar's cattle and poultry. The soothsayer's name is given as Pei Chang-fang, and the scholar, who was also one of his disciples, was Wang Chin or Huan Ching. Both are probably forgotten by the majority of those who ascend the Peak to enjoy the view and picnic in the clear air, lazily watching the kites wheeling above the harbour.

The 25th is the birthday of the City Gods (城隍) whose duty is to care for the souls of their parishioners, and to ward off epidemics which might add to their responsibilities. They are all historical characters, canonised for their virtuous lives and incorruptibility.

Cheung Yeung

In the North the final visit of the year to the family

tombs is carried out on the 1st of the Tenth Moon instead of on the "Double Ninth". This is the last of the three great festivals of the dead, which are spread throughout the time when men labour in the fields. The most important is the Spring Festival of Ch'ing Ming, a survival of the celebration of the renewal of life, whilst mid-summer is marked by the Feast of the Hungry Ghosts, who are relieved by the charity of the benevolent.

The Chinese belief that one of the three souls of the departed takes up its residence in the cemetery is responsible for the care they bestow on tending the resting-places of their defunct relatives. In the more leisurely days of the Empire, the son who was responsible for the ancestral worship was obliged to reside at the family graveyard, dressed in coarse white mourning, for three years, whilst he attended to the sacrifices in honour of his forebear. The house erected for his accommodation was then turned over to a retainer, whose duty it was to protect the cemetery from grave robbers and woodcutters, and generally attend to its maintenance. On the occasions when the family visited the tombs, the house was available for the night, should they come from a distance. The belief in the presence of the soul was shared by all classes, and stories are current of mysterious footsteps to the door during the night, and knocks for admittance which, when answered, proved that the visitant was no mortal.

The disposal of the dead deprived agriculture of an immense amount of valuable land for, in the immediate environs of the capital, wealthy families often bought up several acres which produced nothing but coarse grass and cypresses. Immense mounds, shaped like a pepper pot for the Manchu, and a cone for the Son of Han, interfere with the ploughing in almost every field in China. Around Shanghai oblong brick graves are the custom, and these are placed above ground, owing to the water in the soil. In the early days of Hong Kong, those who were too poor to acquire a site for a grave simply deposited the coffin on any waste piece of ground, from which the law forbade its removal. Foreigners were often exploited in this way, and it was not unusual to find a coffin on the tennis-lawn, which unwelcome presence could not be conjured away till the landlord had parted with sufficient cash to purchase a permanent resting-place. In Hong Kong the problem of disposing of corpses is acute. The very poor solve it by dumping, leaving their responsibilities to the authorities, but those who have not lost all sense of their duties to their relatives rent a grave for a period of three years, after which the bones are handed over to the next-of-kin.

Chinese coffins are larger than those in use in the West, and the importance of the deceased is demonstrated by the size of his sarcophagus. Even in quite humble households, these are too bulky to negotiate the stairs of the rabbit-warrens in which the family resides, and it is not unusual to see a ramp of bamboo built outside to the appropriate window. By knocking out some bricks, an orifice is produced of sufficient dimensions to permit egress, and it is brought down the ramp, either for interment or for temporary disposal. It may be several months between the date of decease and the funeral, which cannot take place until the astrologer has decided on a lucky day. During the interval, the coffin is lodged in a repository, whose proprietor is in the funeral furnishing business. It is quite usual in the case of sickness which may end fatally to order the coffin in advance, and one old gentleman, who had a narrow escape at fifty, kept his with the maker for forty years, before he finally needed it. As prices were considerably cheaper in those days, it was found that he had been too generous to himself, and pounds of wood had to be chipped away before it would fit into the grave. Coffins above ground are always a source of anxiety to the relatives, particularly in thundery weather. They are convinced that Lei Kung, the Thunder God, may strike the deceased as a punishment for his sins, and presumably wreck any chance he has of attaining immortality. Consequently, if a storm is threatening, the coffin is covered with hastily torn up grass to give it the appearance of a haystack, in which case it will be overlooked by the Goddess of Lightning, who flashes her mirror to assist her partner in directing his bolt.

A special association, known as the "Society of Neglected Bones", inspects isolated graveyards at this season, and advises relatives of the need for essential repairs. It also provides coffins and grave sites for the poor. Each member makes a certain monetary contribution, besides giving his personal services in tidying up neglected cemeteries.

Apart from the actual visit to the cemetery, All Souls Day is observed in the home by the ceremony of the "Burning of the Clothes". Winter has now set in, and the dead are in need of warmer garments and other household necessaries. Imitations of wadded garments, and notes on the Bank of Hell for current expenses, are addressed to the spirits for whom they are intended. A sort of Bill of Lading is drawn up and signed in the presence of witnesses, stipulating that on its arrival in Hades, it shall be handed over to the addressee. The Deed contains a list of everything included, money, clothing, paper servants, etc., and it is burned along with them, so that the contributors have every confidence that their gifts will reach the proper destination. An extra parcel is often made up to propitiate any hungry spirits who may be infesting the route like footpads, partly from a sense of charity towards these neglected souls, and partly as an insurance against pilferage on the journey.

The exaggerated reverence for the spirits of the dead fell into disuse with the advent of the Republic (1911), and a foreign-trained class of official who had substituted materialistic Mammon for the cult of Confucius. The Fourth Article of the Treaty of Abdication of the Manchu Dynasty provided that the temples and mausolea of the Imperial family, with their appropriate rites, should be maintained in perpetuity. The Republic of China was to be responsible for the provision of guards for their adequate protection. This, like every other clause of the only "Equal" Treaty that China has ever signed, was violated by one of the many warlords, and no punitive action was taken by the government. Practically all the tombs of the nobility in the vicinity of Peking were desecrated in the search for the treasures and ritual objects which had been inteered at the time of the funeral. The jades found their way into the curio market, and can usually be recognised by the staining from their contact with the salts in the soil, and the loss of patina on their surface.

Although a married woman adopts the ancestors of her husband's family, in one Province at least, Fukien, she is expected at this time of year to honour a deceased parent. To this effect she provides a cardboard trunk with straps, fitted with a variety of miniature household utensils, which is burned at her old home. In addition, she must take a food present to her family, including a duck, half of which is returned to her by the local tradition of "dividing the duck". Both Kwangtung and Fukien Provinces have customs differing widely from those observed in other parts of China, for they were comparatively recently absorbed, having drawn their original culture from the Man Empire whose predominant influence was derived from Indo-China. Their habit of carrying the baby on the back is quite foreign to the Chinese race, who originated on the banks of the Upper Yellow River, and finally spread their language and culture to the whole seaboard of the vast Empire. The bulk of the overseas Chinese come from these two provinces and thus do not share the prejudices of a continental race about crossing the water. Though annexed two hundred years before Christ, the Cantonese did not completely absorb Chinese civilisation till a thousand years later, and still call themselves the men of T'ang, whereas the Northerner styles himself a son of Han. Political rivalries still survive, and neither tamely submits to the domination of the other. The two great revolts against the Manchu rule, the T'aip'ing Rebellion and the Revolution, both had their origin in the South, whilst Peking was never wholly comfortable under the sway of the Kuomintang. The Cantonese, as a unit of the Empire, somewhat resembled the Irish in the British Commonwealth, as rebels against any form of Central Government. To illustrate the point, though they had been largely instrumental in the abdication of the Manchus, the fallen monarchy drew its greatest support from Cantonese subcriptions, and K'ang Yu-wei, who had been atrociously treated by the Empress Dowager, was the leader of the Restoration Movement under the guise of a Confucianist revival.

The differences of customs are so strong that Northern refugees who have flocked to Hong Kong feel as if they were arriving in a foreign country, and they are inclined to be critical of ways which they stigmatize as non-Chinese. Although tolerance of religious belief is a marked characteristic of the whole race, divergencies of customs and manners are not so readily excused.

Communism places utility before everything, and it is to be anticipated that the plough will level many of the mounds dotted about the countryside, whilst the worship of the State will be substituted for that of dead and gone ancestors, who contribute nothing to its welfare, and occupy an inconvenient amount of space. Still, old customs die hard, and a century of foreign rule has had hardly any effect on the customs of the Chinese in Hong Kong. Overseas Chinese still wish to enjoy their long sleep in the ancestral graveyard, so it would be a pity to deprive them of the comforts to which their religion entitles them, and their descendants of the peace of mind deriving from the fulfilment of their duties.

THE TENTH MOON

The Kindly Moon

The Tenth Moon in the Chinese Calendar is known as the Kindly Moon. "Helpful", and "Benevolent" are also terms applied to it by the farmers, who expect the first sprinkling of light snow to moisten and establish their sowings of winter wheat.

On the Fifth of the Tenth Moon, after the Chinese have commemorated the last great festival of the dead, and have made their ancestors comfortable for the winter, they celebrate the anniversary of Ta Mo (達摩), the first patriarch of the Buddhist church, who reached Canton after a three years' journey from India. Wu Ti, of the Liang Dynasty (A.D. 502–577), then occupied the throne. Son of an Indian Prince, Bodhidarma took holy orders and, as a monk, rose to be the twenty-eighth patriarch of his religion in India, before the urge to spread his gospel fired his missionary zeal. This decision may have been influenced by his unpopularity at home, as he had aroused the enmity of his fellow Buddhists as a sectarian, who invented, or at any rate founded, the "Ch'an", or Contemplative School. The doctrine was peculiar as it depended on thought transmitted by thought, without the aid of the spoken or written word, and its adepts claimed to be able to read the mind of the founder of their religion by simple meditation. It was alleged that this power of thought-transference was transmitted from patriarch to patriarch, and that Bodidharma communicated it to his Chinese successor. The date of his arrival in the country is fairly authentic, A.D. 526, but his identification with the Christian St. Thomas probably only rests on the deceptive similarity of sound, as the "doubter" must, by that time, have been buried for nearly five centuries. His chief claim to fame in China is as the discoverer of the tea-plant, for it is recorded that, having fallen asleep during one of his meditations, he cut off his eyelids to prevent a recurrence of the interruption, and they fell to the earth and sprouted. The shrub is therefore regarded in China as the symbol of eternal wakefulness.

The Blue-eyed Brahmin's miraculous crossing of the Yangtze on a reed is a favourite subject with artists. This was after a distinctly unsuccessful interview with the Emperor Wu Ti, who loved the trappings of religion, and extended little sympathy to a sage, who despised them and preached simplicity as opposed to form. As the "Emperor remained unenlightened", to put it in the words of the Chinese chronicler, Ta Mo left the Court, and founded a monastery in the Kingdom of Wei, called Shao Lin, near Loyang in Honan. One of the greatest treasures of the now ruinous establishment is the stone in front of which the patriarch is said to have sat in silent meditation. During one of his vigils it is alleged that his legs dropped off, so, in Japan, his images are still made legless, but with a counterpoise so that, if knocked down, the figurine bobs up to resume its sitting posture. His doctrines probably were accountable for the decay of learning in Buddhist monasteries, and for a tendency to somnolence, but they saved the religion from a slavish worship of images and relics which constricted thought in Ceylon and Indo-China.

The Sixth of the Tenth Moon is the usual anniversary of the Five Rulers, whose birthday is as popular in Canton as that of the City's Patron Saints. They are identified with the Five Sacred Mountains, cardinal points, colours, and elements. China even has five seasons, mid-summer being the fifth, and the rulers are the spirits who hold sway over time and space. The Yellow Emperor, who presides over the Centre, is incarnate in Sung Shan (嵩山), a peak in Honan, and is the ruler over the waterways and forests. The Red Emperor of the South, Spirit of Heng Shan (衡山), presides over the stars and creatures of the deep. The White, or Western Emperor, looks after the minerals and birds, and is incarnate in Hua Shan (華山), in Shensi. Another Heng Shan (恒山), in Hopei, houses the Black Emperor who has dominion over the Four Great Rivers and the animal kingdom, while the Green Emperor of the East resides in T'ai Shan (泰山), and governs the destinies of mankind. The Chinese are delightfully vague about the interpretation of the character Ch'ing, which may mean green, blue (azure), black, or clear. In the five-coloured flag of the original Republic it was certainly blue, and the symbolic guardian of the East is generally referred to as the Azure Dragon. This lack of precision is very confusing to a foreigner, when dealing with a race which has a perfectly good word for blue, and another equally distinctive for green. As a matter of fact there is even an obscure character defining the particular shade of bronze green on a beetle's wing! But the Chinese prefer approximation above all things, particularly as regards time and space. The distance between two fixed points varies according as the road is up or down hill, simply because it takes longer to go one way than the other. The fact that only one word exists for he, she or it, renders it impossible for a newcomer to understand what the conversation is about, if he missed the beginning of it.

The worship of the Five Rulers, whose origin is lost in the mists of antiquity, is particularly popular in the South, and one of their largest temples is in Canton. According to the legend, the gods rode into the town mounted on rams, which gave it the name of the City of Rams. They were dressed in white, yellow, azure, black and red respectively, and each bore in his hand an ear of corn in earnest of a promise that famine should never visit the district. As they passed the Market Place, the rams were turned into stone, and have remained ever since as evidence of the visitation. The gods are invoked in time of pestilence, especially during a cholera epidemic, which recurs fairly regularly each summer. On these occasions, their effigies are removed from their shrines and paraded in procession through the streets. Each god is carried in his own sedan-chair by voluntary bearers, and the scene is brilliant with waving banners. Paper models of junks, known as "disease boats", are taken along to carry away the pestilence, if the divinities so approve. They are taken to the foreshore and are set afloat, the omens being taken as to whether they drift out to sea with their fearsome burden, or are stranded further down. To obviate such a disaster, an alternative method is adopted, and they may be consumed by fire in the presence of the Five Rulers.

Prior to the "Liberation", the Mountain cult, associated with these divinities, was very strong and the various sacred hills were the object of many pilgrimages. Probably the best known was that of T'ai Shan, in Shantung, close to the home of Confucius, and on which a temple was erected to his memory as late as 1714. To the Taoists belongs the guardianship of the mountains connected with the Rulers, and the pilgrimages furnished them with a handsome source of revenue. The rival sect was consequently obliged to follow suit, and they adopted Four Sacred Mountains to correspond with the Four Earthly Elements—Air (Wu Tai 五台), Fire (O Mei 峨嵋), Water (P'u T'o 普陀) and Earth (Chiu Hua 九華). O Mei, in far west Szechuan, has fallen on evil times, for the Communists, in the belief that cats who are not mousers are not worth keeping, have taxed it out of existence. According to recent reports, the monks are dispersed, and the abbot is seeking a living by hawking vegetables. Of minor peaks, the Dragon Tiger Mountain in Kiangsi was famous as the home of the Chang T'ien Shih, the Taoist Pope, but he too, finding the tenets of Communism incompatible with the exercise of his priestly functions, has left his palace until the return of a less materialistic regime.

THE ELEVENTH MOON

The eleventh month in the Chinese calendar is known as the White Moon, when real precautions against the bitter days to follow are taken in North China. Ventilation is entirely dispensed with and, according to the Imperial calendar, officials with the right to wear martin skins appeared with them on the 1st. The Chinese, in the heyday of the Empire, discouraged individuality, and held that tradition was invariably wiser than the mediocre intelligence. The eleventh moon always included the winter solstice, which put a term to the agricultural and astronomical year, as the sun had run his course, and was about to usher in a new season of productivity. The passing of the shortest day has been celebrated by every primitive nation on earth with the kindling of the Yule-log and the renewal of the Sacred Fire, symbolic of the rebirth of the sun, on whose warmth depended every agricultural process. The event was of supreme importance to the Chinese, whose economy was based almost entirely on the products of the soil.

The solstice is observed by the worship of the Nature Gods, such as sacred trees and rocks, which are to be found in every village. The small shrines of the Earth Gods and divinities of the soil and fertility also receive their meed of incense and offerings. The Chinese period of Tung Chih, which begins at the winter solstice and lasts twelve days, corresponds exactly with the Teutonic Yuletide which, according to the Rig Veda, was the period of the sun's holiday. During its retirement, a lesser deity took charge, corresponding to the God of the Hearth of the Lapps who, on the adoption of Christianity, became St. Nicholas or Santa Claus. In China, under the Empire, the sovereign himself performed the ceremonies to mark the turning point of the year, and the event assumed such importance that it was prophetically averred that "When no winter sacrifices are offered, the State has lost its independence." Having blundered into the Bear Pit, the Chinese are in a fair way to see the fulfilment of the prediction.

Though, under the Republic, ritual sacrifices failed to fit in with modern ideas of democracy, certain public offices were closed to mark the festival, whilst the people continued uninterruptedly to celebrate the occasion in their own homes. Dough cakes named Hun Tun are baked for the family feast, rice and vermicelli being the attributes for the observance of the summer solstice. In some provinces a very old custom prevails, the cakes being confectioned by any new bride who has married into the family during the year. Her right to the red skirt, and asking blessings for the first time, is calculated to ensure abundance to eat and wear for her relations. When she has kneaded the dough, each member of the family detaches a small bit and rolls it into a ball to be boiled separately as an offering to the Door Gods. Some households limit the number to twelve to ensure prosperity in every month of the year, but the number is not fixed, and extra cakes are occasionally affixed to outer gate-posts and window-sills to prevent the entry of malignant spirits. Farmers' wives extend the protec-tion to their livestock by placing rude images of swine and chickens on the family altar.

The dying year evokes remembrance of the departed, and the best fare the family can muster is laid before the ancestral tables. One of the three souls is the guardian of the home, and is appealed to for advice in all domestic crises, and this one is honoured at the family feast. Chairs for the spirits are set at the north side of the altar, whilst the head of the household stands on the south, facing his forebears. In perfect silence the family stand whilst he invites the ancestors to share the Winter Feast, and past and present then sit down to an annual reunion.

The Chinese believe that the spirits partake of the essence of the sacrifice, and that the nourishment has gone out of the remains, which are consumed by the survivors. The Boat People aver that, when carrying back the roast pigs which have been offered to T'ien Hou, or Tam Kung, their burdens are actually lighter, but the fact that the return journey is usually downhill may be a partial explanation.

The winter sacrifices to the dead are traceable back to the commemoration of military heroes who, in primitive times, earned their reputation in the autumn of the year. In all countries, peoples settled their differences after the harvest had been gathered and the ring was clear for campaigning. Plunder was at its best with the crops in the granary, and the frozen soil, or absence of rain, was favourable to transportation. There was also a super-fluity of labour at the dead season, so the Book of Rites ordained that the Ministers of State should inspect weapons, train recruits and strengthen city defences. Patriotism was stimulated by offering sacrifices to keep green the memory of fallen heroes, much as Remem-brance Day is observed in Western countries. The pellets of dough offered to the Door Gods were the contribution of the common people, for these guardians of the gate were distinguished generals who protected an Emperor from the incursions of Evil Spirits.

Winter was also the fashionable season for celebrating marriages, as the winter solstice symbolised the cessation of the struggle between the male and female elements, then in abeyance before the rebirth of life. It was the moment of the reunion of Heaven and Earth prior to the latter's refertilisation in Spring. The legend of the mystical marriage of the Celestial Weaver and the human cowherd, celebrated by maidens on the "Double Seventh", is traceable to this reproductive instinct. According to de Groot, in ancient times the two stars in Lyra and Aquila, the heavenly homes of the patrons of marriage, were simultaneously at their zenith in the eleventh month. The herdsman brought in the flocks before the bitterly cold weather which follows the winter solstice, and the weaver occupied the days, when it was impossible to go out of doors, in making and repairing the family clothing. With the procession of the equinoxes in the course of millenniums, the two stars are now highest in the heavens during the seventh, and not the eleventh month, so the observation of their festival takes place in the summer. Conservative families, how-ever, cling to the old date.

THE BITTER MOON

The Twelfth, or Bitter Moon, invariably lives up to its reputation in the North, as it embraces the three coldest periods of the year, when the average temperature is half a dozen degrees below freezing point with occasional descents below Fahrenheit zero. It contains the two fortnightly periods, the "Hsiao Han" and "Ta Han", the Small and Great Cold, the culmination of winter, which last from about 5th January to the early days of February, when the weather becomes comparatively mild at the beginning of Spring. In Peking, the Christmas period ushers in the skating season, which lasts through the "Small" and "Great" cold, ending as suddenly as it began, in the first week of February.

After the Tung Chih, or Winter Solstice, the cold weather is divided into nine periods, each of nine days, of which the third is the most bitter, driving the Northerners into enforced hibernation, every cranny in the houses being blocked up and the paper windows only admitting a dim, religious light. Time passes slowly before the frost-bound earth will yield to the plough. The peasant has no distraction in reading, so it is not surprising that he feels the urge to mark off the days of his imprisonment. Accordingly, he constructs a chart of the lessening of the cold. This consists of nine lines, on each of which are inscribed nine circles, each divided into four sectors with a small circle in the centre. The upper sector serves to record cloudy weather, the lower a fair day, and the left wind. The right is reserved for rain, and the centre for snow. One circle is cancelled each day after the weather has been recorded. The more highly educated, with some skill with the brush, trace a decorative design of a branch of prunus with eighty-one five-petalled blossoms. One of these is tinted each day in imitation of a tablet at Si An, once the old capital of Chinese under the name of Ch'ang An. This shows an engraved vase holding a nine-branched tree of plum, each bearing nine flowers.

This home-made almanac is an accurate indication to the farmer of the date to start his spring sowing for, in China, he is never likely to be caught by the late frosts which are the bane of our English climate. When the last blossom has been filled in, the farmer can attend to his fields with the certainty that the Yang principle has gained the mastery, and that spring is so firmly established that he has nothing to fear. As the proverb runs, "After the eighty-one days the last icicle has melted, and the ox stands fetlock deep in new grass."

This transition is known as Li Ch'un (立春), the beginning of spring, when winter is definitely broken, and the earth awakens from her long sleep. It has appropriately been chosen for the Chinese New Year, which falls on the day of the first new moon after the sun enters Aquarius. This brackets the date of the festival between 21st January and 19th February. In Western countries for centuries the beginning of a new year was reckoned from 1st April, which is still the financial year in England. With a climate so uncertain, it was not till the vernal equinox that the countryman could be assured that his fields would not be frost-bound, and even so there was a chance of being made an April Fool by the Clerk of the Weather.

The Eighth day of the Twelfth Moon is kept as a preliminary festival of very ancient origin, and early in the morning the women of the household set to work preparing a thick porridge, which corresponds to our Christmas pudding as a national dish. Its composition is almost as diverse as its English counterpart, for the ingredients include whole grains of several kinds, but never meal or flour, special old rice, beans, nuts and fruit, and four different kinds of sugar. When cooked, the pudding is first offered to the Ancestral Tablets, and then every member of the family receives a share. The surplus is sent to relatives and friends, and custom decrees that it must be delivered before the first stroke of noon.

In Hong Kong the pudding is strongly flavoured with radish, giving rise to the suspicion that, when the Cantonese adopted Chinese customs under the T'ang Dynasty, the La Pa (臘八), or sacrifice of the eighth day, was corrupted into Lo Po (蘿蔔) or radish, and Radish Pudding it remains to this day. Tradition attributes its origin to a poor mother, driven from home by an unfilial son, who went the round of her neighbours begging a meal. One contributed a handful of beans, another a dish of dried fruit, and a third some miscellaneous grains.

The Buddhists improved on this with their own version of the story, pinning it on their most popular Goddess, Kuan Yin. The feast is observed in commemoration of her last day before leaving her father's home to become a nun, when she gathered grains and fruits for her final meal. As the ingredients are entirely of vegetable origin, Buddhist monks are adepts at preparing the dish, especially in the great temples of Peking. It is first offered to the Divinity to obtain the seal of sanctity, and is then sent round to wealthy parishioners, who return alms for the honour conferred upon them.

In Hong Kong, the Buddhistic significance of the sacrifice has either been lost, or was never recognised, for dried shrimp and chopped Chinese sausage are added for flavouring. The basis is old rice, ground with the radish from which the dish is named.

Green vegetables are short at this time of year in the North, so a similar distribution takes place among friends of a broth made of white cabbages which have been exposed to the frost buried in shallow pits. They are laid in rows with a thin blanket of earth between each, the whole clamp being roofed with thick dried mud. Under these conditions, the vegetables not only keep fresh, but put forth tender sprouts which make delicious eating. They foretell, by their sweetness or acidity, the good or evil fortunes of the recipients.

The Chinese calendar, by which all self-respecting people regulate their lives and actions, allots the twentieth day of the Bitter Moon to the sweeping of the house, which corresponds in its thoroughness to the spring cleaning of the conscientious British matron. It is an uncomfortable time for the menfolk and domestic animals, for every large piece of furtniture is displaced, and the accumulated flume of the past year is abolished. Grandmas, too old to take part in the exercise, admonish the younger generation to be thorough, lest the slightest speck of neglected dust fly into their eyes and blind them.

Rich people re-lacquer their front gates with the cinnabar red beloved by the Chinese as the colour of rejoicing, whitewash outer walls, and repaper the windows. All these activities are symbolic of the re-birth of the year, and the desire to start with a clean slate. In England, for climatic reasons, the renovation is deferred till Easter, but the underlying principle is identical.

As soon as the house is swept and garnished, the mistress starts laying in provisions for the New Year Feast, and the alleys are thronged with pedlars hawking every kind of food and seasoning. All this must be procured well in advance, for tradition forbids cooking on New Year's Day, lest a sharp implement be used which might cut luck. In any case, once the date-line is crossed all business ceases, so it is impossible to procure any ingredient which has been overlooked. Shops rarely open before the third day, and pedlars have their own rites to attend to. The family takes precedence over everything, and no one has time to attend to the wants of improvident outsiders. At New Year it is everyone for himself, for the family reunion is distinctly a closed shop which welcomes no intrusion into its affairs.

New Year Preliminaries

Chinese New Year is the most important of the three financial settling days, as everybody desires earnestly to start again with a clean sheet. Not only have debts to be liquidated, but a residue has to be set aside for the celebrations, and food has to be laid in for several days during which all business is at a standstill. Everybody goes round collecting debts in order to clear up his own liabilities, and money is everywhere scarce. There is usually a shortage of small change at this season, as the ten cent pieces and notes are hoarded to put in red envelopes, stamped with gold designs, for the children's "Lucky Money", and tips for the errand boys bringing gifts of food between neighbour and neighbour. The annual bonus to servants should be paid out well before the dawn of the New Year, as they have numerous commitments for which the extra money already is earmarked. The period, known as "Little New Year", which opens with the departure of the Kitchen God to render his annual report, is one of tremendous activity. The streets are thronged with shoppers, crowding round the pedlars' booths in search of sesame and pine branches as talismans against the powers of evil. Some buy flowers and flowering shrubs, which have been forced in paper hot-houses so as to be in bud or fruit at the psychological moment. In Hong Kong the weather is more tricky than in the North, and a spell of muggy weather may accelerate the flowering which, to ensure good luck for the year, should occur in the house after the plant has been installed. Purchasers choose their plants in pairs, and carefully watch the packing of their gifts. Convention, ages ago, limited their choice, which simplifies matters for all concerned and no one is worried to remember if Aunt Maria had a tea-cosy or a

pincushion on the last occasion. Members of the family are limited to silks, ornaments, or even jewels. Distant relatives and friends may expect growing flowers (never the cut variety), fine tea, rare fruits and food, for which a use can always be found at this season of the year. Food gifts have their own symbolism, as they indicate that the donor has a superfluity of the good things of life, which he is anxious to pass on to others. Chickens are usually delivered alive, as a guarantee of good faith, and are accompanied, if the people are well-to-do, with one or two prepared dishes in round lacquered boxes. It is bad form to accept everything that is sent. The recipient makes a choice and tips the messenger according to the value of what he retains, returning the rest with a message to the effect that his friend is too generous. The system is not without its merits, for what is rejected by one person can be sent on to another of lesser degree.

As soon as the shopping rush is over, tradesmen close their accounts for the year. Between the three settling days, New Year, the Dragon Boat Festival, and the Harvest Thanksgiving, people live mostly on credit, even for household necessities. This system results in a terrific last-minute scramble for cash. Custom, which sometimes overrides the law, requires an individual to pay up if it is humanly possible, and a man may steal to satisfy his creditors, thereby saving his reputation! Curio dealers often sell at a sacrifice at this time of year to meet their obligations and, among foreigners, it was a favourite time for bargain hunting in Peking. The squaring up process is apparently conducted as a game, with a fixed set of rules ordained by tradition. Even honest people, who have no intention of evading their liabilities, will not pay up until dunned. A creditor will stalk his quarry through the streets and, if this loss of face does not produce the desired effect, will establish squatter's rights on his doorstep. The poor are assailed with bad language, not altogether unaccompanied by violence.

If all hopes of settlement are extinguished, a man goes into hiding. Old Shanghai residents were familiar with the inevitable response to enquiries for an absconding debtor, "I think he go Ningpo more far!" A native creditor would not be satisfied with so simple a solution, for he would know that his victim would almost certainly be within doors for the New Year reunion, and would conduct a personal search. Theoretically the man had to be found before the sun rose, but it was one of the rules of the game to carry a lighted lantern to extend the hours of darkness, and it was a disgrace, hardly to be borne, to be hag-ridden by this ill-omened Will o' the Wisp. As in the Middle Ages, sanctuary could be found in the Church from pursuit by the Law, so the Temple of the City God is the refuge for the insolvent debtor. At this time of year, all Comedians in the town are morally bound to give free performances in honour of the patron deity. These theatricals begin at Little New Year, and last out the Twelfth Moon. No creditor detecting his victim in the crowd dare accost him to dun him for his bill, lest he suffer violence from the audience distracted from its enjoyment. The courtyard of the god is a convenient Alsatia for debtors wishing to combine business with pleasure, and find entertainment to while away the critical hours. Once the deadline is past, no further claim can be made till the Dragon Boat Festival in the Fifth Moon, which gives several months' respite for finances to right themselves.

Not all families, however, are in such straits and, after the normal settlements are made, houses and junks are decorated with "Luck bringing inscriptions". This is the moment to see how the most primitive forms of worship still linger in Hong Kong. The Earth Gods, whose shrine may, for eleven months in the year, have been mistaken for a boot-scraper, will now be decorated with a piece of red paper and, in the New Territories, almost every village will have a Sacred Tree and Well marked with honorific inscriptions. The junk will very likely carry "May the boat bring advantage", whilst the merchant will display "Successful in Affairs", "Acquisition of Treasure", or simply "Great Prosperity". Farmers invoke bountiful harvest, and innkeepers a full house.

In private dwellings the inscriptions usually refer to wealth, longevity, and a full quiver of sons, the Chinese ideal of terrestrial bliss. Favourite mottoes are "Accomplishment of wishes" which, in nine cases out of ten, are limited to their version of Health, Wealth and Happiness. "Ten thousand generations, and long duration" exemplifies their ardent desire for continuity which is at the root of the conservatism of the race. "May your entering and departure be peaceful" is a favourite door motto in Hong Kong, and the characters are often embroidered on the baby-carriers on mothers' backs. A subtle way of attracting the favour of the gods is to post on a neighbour's wall "Prosperity to those facing me", in the hope that more attention will be paid to the invocations of a third, and presumably disinterested party.

Luck papers, except in the case of recent mourning, are always red. Blue is used to denote a death in the family, and temples affect yellow. Talismans may be large or small, simple or elaborate. A common form is a piece of stiff paper with a silver tinsel seal. There are also cut-outs in lacy paper called "Five Lucky Happinesses which knock at the door", being Felicity, Honours, Longevity, Joy and Riches. Sometimes they simply take the form of a single character "Fu" (福) for Luck, whose popularity dates from the Ming Dynasty. One of its Sovereigns took offence at a cartoon, which was displayed at this time of year, which he considered to be a slight on his Empress. He therefore ordered the character Fu to be pasted on houses which did not carry the objectionable picture, and his guards liquidated all families deprived of its protection. Its Imperial connection survived till recent times, for one of the most valued gifts to officials at New Year was the character written by the hand of the Son of Heaven and, under the Republic, the President honoured his ministers in the same fashion. The character used to be attested by the superimposition of the Dynastic seal.

On the 24th of the Twelfth Moon comes the sacrifice to the Tsao Wang (竈王) or Kitchen God, who is one of the oldest of the household deities. He may even be identified with some anonymous ancestor, which would enhance the reverence in which he is held. He is usually represented by one of the highly coloured pictures, which can be obtained at any "paper shop" for a few cents, though in South China the characters for his name often replace his image in poorer families. It would appear that his present form of worship dates from Wu Ti, great patron of Taoism in 133 B.C. In the household he plays a dual role, for he not only looks after the hearth, but has constituted himself the censor of morals of the family. He is the connecting link between God and Man and, seven days before the New Year, he is despatched to make his annual report. Where officials are concerned it is axiomatic in China that every man has got his price, and the Kitchen God is no exception to the rule. The family, whose record is about to be laid before the All Highest, makes every effort to ensure that a favourable report shall be rendered. As a rule, the effigy of the Tsao Wang occupies a small bamboo or wooden shrine, and he is depicted with his horse beside him. On the night of his departure incense is burned, and some straw, or in the North, kao-liang, is ignited by the stove as forage for the steed's journey. A bowl of water is also poured out by the stove. A special sticky sweetmeat, named T'ang Kua, is part of the sacrifice, and a portion is burned with the picture of the god. This is to ensure that he will only say sweet things, but it is not unusual to make certain of his silence by smearing his mouth with opium, or steeping the effigy in wine, to render him drowsy or fuddled when he reaches the end of his journey. He then risks expulsion for drunkenness before he can get a word in with the Jade Emperor and, as the family is free from his surveillance for seven days, they are indifferent as to how he spends his time.

Though it would be logical to suppose that the Kitchen God is the familiar of the ladies of the household, this

The Kitchen God

is not the case, and they are debarred from his worship, just as men are excluded from the rites accompanying the Moon Festival.

During the last week of the month, the effigies of the tutelary deities of the household must be renewed. The burned cartoon of the Kitchen God, now on his seven days' holiday, is due for replacement on New Year's Eve. The doors of the house must be protected, not only by the Spirit Screen, which forces evil influences to deviate from a straight line, their only mode of progression, but by a pair of Gate Gods who guard means of ingress. These brilliantly coloured warriors are pasted on the double panels of the front door, with the edges of their halberds turned towards the direction of danger. They are among the most ancient of Chinese deities, and the Taoists invented a legend of their origin as an excuse for including in their pantheon objects of prior worship which their adherents were reluctant to abandon. According to ecclesiastical tradition they were two brothers, who lived under a peach tree of such vast dimensions that five thousand men, with arms outstretched, could not encircle it. Assuming the role of protectors of mankind, they captured demons, and threw them to tigers, a feat commemorated in the Magistrate's Court by a peach-wood image of the Twain over the door and a tiger on the Yamen Gates. Tigers thus came to be sworn enemies of evil spirits, particularly those noxious to the dead. They are therefore carved on tombs and monuments and, in the T'ang Dynasty, the sleeves of the burial robes of important officials were weighted down with small bronze tigers.

A later story accounts for the Gate Gods and makes them date from the middle of the 7th Century. The great Emperor T'ai Tsung (A.D. 627–650) met a disaster in Korea comparable to recent history and, overcome with rage and mortification, suffered from insomnia. His hallucination took the form of imps, rather than pink elephants, so he may be acquitted of overaddiction to strong liquor, but the court physicians were unable to conjure them. Finally, to soothe him, two of his favourite generals offered to mount guard on the gates, and deal with any evil spirits who attempted to intrude. Fully accoutred they took their posts, and the Emperor, whose malady appears to have responded to suggestion, had a comfortable night's rest. As soon as he recovered, he informed his faithful servants that, as they were losing their sleep, he would order the court painter to execute their portraits in full armour that the evil spirits might be deceived, and his nights might remain undisturbed. The two generals were Ch'in Shu-pao (秦叔寶), who propounded the scheme, and Yu Ch'ih Ching-te (尉遲敬德), his companion in arms. The former is portrayed with a white face, and the latter has a black face. Each is shown in full armour, grasping a gemmed halberd, and having a whip, chain, bow and arrows at his belt. Should the family be too poor to afford the few cents which command these gaudy effigies, a couple of characters, specifying the civil or military Gate Gods, are just as efficacious, if less decorative. In Hong Kong, it is the rule, rather than the exception, to indicate the Kitchen God in this manner.

Some of the Earth Gods' shrines also have no image, but as New Year fresh red paper, with an inscription honouring the T'u Ti's Happy Spirits, directs attention to a small hole in the wall, and charred sticks of incense indicate that this friend and counsellor of the family has been duly honoured.

After the debt settling period is over, thanks should be given to the three Gods of Wealth. These are Kuan Ti, also the God of War (關帝), Hsuan T'an Shang Ti (玄壇上帝), a sort of infernal Pluto, who presides over the altars of the Shades in the Taoist after-world, and Ts'ai Shen, the God of Riches (財神).

Secondary deities are also placated with offerings of pork, chickens and fish, and some of these are peculiar to the Mahommedan population. The Guilds also have their special Patron Saints (Tzu She 祖師). These sacrifices cannot be carried out until all debts are acquitted, and the creditor also does not ignite his crackers till all his outstanding accounts are gathered in.

On the last day of the year there is a general clean up all round, in the shape of baths and hairdressing.

The New Year Fair

The celebrations connected with Chinese New Year are largely of a domestic order, conducted within doors, and consequently unnoted by the foreigner. There are, however, numerous outward and visible manifestations of the general rejoicing. No outsider, except the stone-deaf, can be unaware that something unusual is taking place in the Chinese world, for every child is armed with a supply of crackers, in addition to the regulation display which renders the nights memorable. On New Year's Eve, and for the next two days, the waterfront from Shaukiwan to West Point reverberates with an almost continuous roar, whilst by daylight urchins career about the residential areas, letting off what they have salvaged from the household stock.

A feature of the festivities is the Fair which takes place annually during the last ten days of the old year. This used to correspond to the Mediaeval Fairs in England, usually connected with some ecclesiastical festival such as that of St. Etheldrida at Ely. All sorts of trifles were brought by pedlars to the cathedral town, and disposed of to yokels in search of a fairing as a present for sweethearts, or to please their children. Ely was notorious for the rubbish unloaded on the public on these occasions, and St. Audrey, as Etheldreda was popularly known, was responsible for introducing the word "Tawdry" into the English language. Prior to the War, the Wanchai fair in Hong Kong was the grand occasion of the year for the hawkers to make a killing, and they deserted their pitches in the alleys to seek a good-natured market of easy spenders, keyed up with the holiday spirit. Nothing was organised about it, and the Chinese loathe regimentation. So they voted it great fun, and preferred the casual confusion to the greater convenience enjoyed in a more orderly display. Nowadays, the stalls, set out in straight rows with an ample aisle between them, are mostly rented by shops, who have an uninspiring display of their everyday stock-in-trade. A relic of old times is the flower trade, for at New Year gifts of growing plants are only next in popularity to donations of food. It is a chancy speculation, for the buyers insist on the purchases being in bud, so that their lasting properties may be prolonged. A few days of mild, warm weather will cause the blossom to open, and lose its attractiveness. All sorts of subterfuges are resorted to in order to retard the growth, such as dipping stems in sea-water. This, sooner or later, kills the plant and, even if the stems of the Bell Flower are cut short, and the salinity is washed out, there is always a chance of the buds dropping off, instead of opening. When trade with Canton was normal, enormous quantities of flowers came in from the hinterland, but the facilities for cheap water transport have recently been much restricted.

The Bell Flower, and certain budding fruit branches, such as prunus and peach, are exceptions to the rule that cut flowers are unwelcome in the house. The Bell, however, is subject to a special ban, and may not be sent as a gift, for the expression "Sung Chung" has a most inauspicious implication. It is used for seeing off a dying man's soul to the Nether World, and the Chinese do not like to be reminded of death. For a similar reason, any family whose surname is Bell must forego this type of decoration. The shrub, whose classical name is *Enkianthus Quinqueflora*, is a member of the heather tribe, and is an erect bush growing to the height of fifteen feet or more. The flower, which resembles a gigantic bell-heather blossom, is pink, and wax-like at the base. Its opening in the house portends a prosperous year, so the sea-water treatment, which makes it buds fall off before maturing, causes acute disappointment to the purchaser. It is protected by law in Hong Kong to prevent its complete extinction for, not only do the branches fetch high prices at the Fair, but its woody stem burns magnificently, and it is much in demand by the Hakka fuel collectors. The cutting does not kill the shrub, but checks its flowering capacity for several seasons. Masses of it are on sale as, if it behaves properly, it is regarded as an omen of good fortune.

The display in 1950 was a tribute to Chinese ingenuity in overcoming difficulties. In the season just after the Pearl River traffic had been interrupted by the Communist occupation of the delta, shops greatly outnumbered the flower stalls. On the next occasion the proportion was reversed, and the florists dominated the fair. Prices were also more reasonable as the supply much exceeded the demand, and there was an infinite variety of choice. Huge fascines of bell flower, peach blossom varied with almond, and an occasional "Pussy" willow, were stacked on most of the booths. Some stalls were arranged with tiers of oranges, or loquats in pots reaching to the matting roof. Sheaves of gladioli and dahlias of all shades were a good selling line, but very high prices were asked for orchids and tree peonies. Huges pots of hollyhocks had an attractive look, until the buyer considered the transport problem. Coolies are available, but saloon cars are not ideal receptacles for high growing plants, covered with buds and flowers, and the average fair-frequenter lacks a lorry.

On entering the Fair from the western end the crowd was deceptive, for it had not yet had time to be coagulated by the loitering stall gazers and would-be purchasers. As these took effect, a central stream was borne irresistibly along in both directions, with a bias in favour of the eastbound throng. It took a determined effort to get more than a fleeting glance at the displays, and Londoners would have been reminded of the "Hi' along please" efforts of the female tube attendants to stimulate their activity. Purchases were apt to be delayed, partly from indolence at the thought of the effort necessary to detach oneself from the human torrent which bears one along, and partly from the disinclination to load up with something fragile so early in the proceedings. The last night was the most crowded, particularly by the flower buyers in search of a bargain. There was a very wide choice, and a great range of prices. A favourite decoration with the Chinese is the "Water Fairy", a jonquil of the narcissus family, which is grown upright, or in flat bunches resembling a crab. Two or three stalls had attractive pots of cacti and dwarf trees. The fish merchants were here with their goldfish, and the curio dealers had a much better display than usual. Porcelain shops were full of modern blanc de chine effigies of Kuan Yin on shelves, and vase-like spittoons on the floor. Stationers had trays of the red and gold envelopes for the "Lucky Money". About three-quarters of the way down the seaward aisle, the crowd diverged to the right, and it was practically impossible to stem the tide of humanity surging up from the east. The stalls at the back were easier of access. Many dealt in children's toys and paper imitation flowers. The shop fronts under the protective colonnade were hung with a display of scrolls, but the attractive ones were very highly priced. A painting of the Lao Sou Hsing (老壽星), with a comical expression of distress at the filching of his peach by a child, was the most amusing, but its owner set too exaggerated a value on its merits. In many cases the alleged authorship of these works of art were the most entertaining things about them.

There was no regimentation about the crowd, which milled indiscriminately in every direction, but it was full of good humour and, as is usually the case in China, everyone eventually achieved his desire without anything more than bodily friction.

The Fair was better patronised by Europeans this year than last and, in spite of it being nearly midnight, plenty of Chinese children were in evidence, mounted on their fathers' shoulders for their greater edification and as an insurance against the risk of loss. By half-past eleven, the crowd began to thin and drift away towards their homes, presumably to prepare for the roar of crackers which, with the trumpeting of the harbour craft, heralded in the New Year.

BETROTHAL, MARRIAGE & THE STATUS OF WOMEN

The Moon and Marriage

Many races attribute to the moon an influence over marriage. In the British Isles, maidens bow to the planet, and turn their silver in their pockets but, whether the connection is that the metal was associated with the pallid sphere, or that they utter a silent prayer that she will reveal the names of their future husbands in a dream, is a moot point. In Holland, as in China, lovers sighed for the moon twenty-five centuries ago, and from India to the Hebrides her influence over marriages was acknowledged. The Chinese believe in a Yueh Lao Yeh (月老爺), or Old Man of the Moon, who is envisaged as a greybeard, who presides over all marriages made on earth. He provides and knots the red cord which binds the betrothed together for life, and there is a saying that marriages are made in heaven, but prepared in the moon. Yueh Lao's decisions are irrevocable, and the Chinese recognise that to dispute them is unavailing.

A legend of the T'ang Dynasty supports this supposition, for at that remote period of history a certain youth, named Wei Ku, during a journey observed an ancient seated in the moonlight consulting a book. In passing the time of night, he inquired what the volume contained, for he was of a literary turn of mind. The Sage replied that it was a register of the marriages of all on earth and, to support his contention, produced a red cord from his sleeve. With this, he said, he bound the feet of men and maidens whom fate decreed should be joined together, and there was no escaping the bond, no matter whether their clans were at enmity, or that their ancestral homes were separated by the width of the country. He then volunteered to show Wei Ku his future bride, and pointed out a repulsive old vegetable hawker as his father-in-law. The child was then a mere infant of no pedigree, and the youth was looking for something far higher to advance his career. As female children of that age were of little account, and one more or less never would be missed, Wei Ku went into conference with one of those bandits who were ready to "kill a little baby for the coral on its neck". The man employed collected the cash, but bungled the job, though the maiden bore the scar of his attentions to her dying day. Fourteen years later, Wei, a prominent official in a distant province, contracted a marriage, through the usual go-between, with an eligible consort but, when the veil was raised, he recognised her by the scar over her eyebrow. Inquiries proved, beyond a shadow of a doubt, that she was the bride originally destined for him and pointed out by the greybeard. As, in Imperial China, the interested parties had no choice whatsover in the selection of a mate, one suspects that this story was invented to silence all criticism of the parents' choice. Though the current Yueh Lao Yeh myth probably only dates from the popularisation of Taoism by Chang Tao-ling, the mystical union of the sun and the moon must have

been a belief which goes back to the earliest history of the race. Workers in the fields noted the full disc of the pale planet illuminated once a month, and attributed its radiance to a visit from its more powerful consort.

The Old Man of the Moon is by no means the only Chinese divinity who occupies himself with the matrimonial affairs of mortals. One of the host who interests himself in these matters is known as Hsi Shen, the Spirit of Joy. The title must have been awarded to him in derision, for his claims to canonisation have little foundation. During his earthly sojourn, nothing could be advanced in his favour, for he was the reincarnation of the infamous Chou Wang, last ruler of the Shang Dynasty, who left a reputation of which Nero himself might have been ashamed. His cruelties finally brought about his destruction, with the assistance of the gods, by one of his vassals who, on founding a new dynasty, raised the fallen monster to an object of veneration. In life, his uxoriousness rivalled that of Henry VIII, and even the goddesses were not immune from his attentions. He was smitten with the beauty of Nu Kua, sister of the Perfect Emperor Fu Hsi, whilst worshipping at her temple, and inscribed on the wall a wish to take to wife a lady as lovely as herself. As she had a female head and serpent body, few of his subjects fulfilled the requirements, so Nu Kua furnished him with, not only one, but three fairy monstrosities. The first of these was a pheasant into lady, omitting the feet. The second was a stone guitar, and the third a fox fairy with nine tails. She eventually became empress, and rivalled her husband's reputation for cunning and cruelty. Nobody has attempted to explain how the head of this extraordinary menage was elected as patron of connubial bliss. In any case the Chinese draw the line at erecting temples to him, and he is entitled to no sacrifices. He is enshrined in the planet Venus, and the only acknowledgment of his power is a shy glance in that direction by the bride, who is forbidden, by Chinese prudery, even to utter a silent prayer.

The **Tzu Sun Niang Niang, a very popular** female divinity, seems out of place in the retinue of this Spirit of Joy, for she was the blameless wife of a virtuous official, and committed suicide rather than yield to the attentions of a too ardent sovereign. Prior to her untimely end she had provided her husband with the classical family of five boys and two girls, so was canonised as a model of chastity. Her presence at the marriage feast is commemorated by the eating of special cakes, Tzu Sun Po Po, by the bride and bridegroom, as they sit side by side on the couch after the ceremony.

Antagonistic Animals

With a country so vast as China, whose population is composed of so many races, only bound together by a common culture, it is not surprising to find that the customs relating to the marriage ceremony differ slightly from province to province. The wonder is that there is so much uniformity, for tribes recently absorbed, like the Manchus, would tend to preserve their primeval practice. Apart from local variation, however, the framework remains constant throughout the country, and the Chinese notion of what corresponds to our table of consanguinity is universally accepted. Inbreeding is effectually prevented by the custom that no union shall take place between two bearers of the same clan name, though there is no more blood relationship between them than would exist between a Mr. Smith of Stepney and a girl whose ancestors followed the same profession in Stuttgart.

The preliminary arrangements for a bethrothal are still usually undertaken by "Mei jen" (媒人) or go-betweens. Some are professionals, but quite often they are friends or relatives of the parties concerned. When the principals are in general agreement as to the suitability of the match, Men Hu Tieh (門戶帖), or lists setting forth particulars of each family's status, are exchanged. In the event of these being mutually accepted, the all-important "Eight Character" certificates are submitted. These furnish the hour, day, month, and year of birth of the interested parties. An astrologer is called in to determine whether the horoscopes are compatible. The year of birth is all important, for certain years in the Chinese calendar are unharmonious, and if the bride and bride-groom's elements and animals are mutually incompatible the engagement must be broken off. Each year, in the cycle of sixty, is denoted by the combination of one of the five elements and a beast from the twelve animals of the zodiac. As far as the elements are concerned, a "Fire" girl will consume a "Wood" husband, whereas one born under the "Water" sign will nourish her mate. The animals are similarly sociable, or antagonistic, and the Chinese have a formula for each of the pairs whose dispositions preclude a happy union.

"The white horse will not share a stall with the black cow" (白馬不配青牛)

"The boar and the monkey are soon parted" (豬猴不到頭).

"The sheep and the rat soon separate" (羊鼠一旦休).

"The dragon takes to the clouds at the sight of the hare" (龍見玉兔雲端去).

"The golden cock dissolves in tears at the sight of the dog" (金鷄見犬淚姣流).

"If the snake catches a glimpse of the tiger, it is as if it were wounded with a knife" (蛇見猛虎如刀斷).

As soon as the astrologer's verdict assures the parents of the bride-groom of an auspicious union, Ting Li (定禮) or engagement gifts are despatched to the girl's home. They consist mainly of clothing and ornaments, the number and value depending on the financial status of the family concerned. The bridegroom's family determines the date of the wedding by means of a Tung Shu (通書) written on red paper. This allows about a month's warning, though in country districts it is often despatched far earlier.

The next step is the exchange of marriage contracts, called Lung Feng T'u (龍鳳圖), setting forth full particulars of the ages and dates of birth of the betrothal. The prospective bridegroom's is on red paper, decorated

with a dragon, whilst the bride's reply is on green, embellished with a phoenix. The bridegroom's letter is accompanied by gifts of food, clothing, ornaments and furniture and, in Peking, must always include a goose and an earthenware jar of wine. The Pekingese do not eat geese, and though the wine might enhance the conviviality of the proceedings, the inclusion of the bird is purely symbolic. Family life in the city is very secluded, as each compound is screened from public gaze by a high mud wall shutting it off from the street, so an outsider rarely gets a glimpse of the domestic scene. In the villages, however, where privacy is of secondary importance, or of no moment at all, pink geese may often by seen waddling round in search of sustenance. The scarlet dye, which served them as a wedding garment, soon fades under the influence of rain and, as the moult takes place, the birds present a ludicrous appearance.

The origin of this singular gift is traced to a legend of the Chin (晋) dynasty, when a noteworthy official Hsi Chieh was in search of a suitable husband for his daughter. In the course of his quest he inspected a school, where his reputation as an outstanding statesman insured a most ceremonious reception. The pupils, coached by the headmaster, were models of propriety, save for one unchin, who not only failed to rise with the others but sat cross-legged, contorting himself in a most unseemly manner. The pedagogue was aghast, fearing a reprimand from the minister on the absence of discipline, but the great man was amused at the boy's independence of spirit and thought he would make his way in the world. He accordingly entered into negotiations with the Wang family to arrange a marriage with his daughter. The Wangs were desperately poor, so the offer was refused, but Hsi Chieh had set his heart on the match and, being a man accustomed to getting his own way, it was eventually arranged. When the moment for sending wedding presents arrived, the boy was at his wits ends, for his father was a sot, who had sold every family possession to gratify his vice. All the movable property remaining consisted of a goose and half a jar of wine reserved for the evening debauch. In desperation the boy despatched these derisory gifts, which received the same commendation as the widow's mite. He gave all he had, or rather all he could lay hands on, for a veil had better be drawn over the father's reactions to the empty bottle, and his action has been approved by tradition throughout the ages. Presumably the marriage was a success as in Chinese art the goose is a symbol of marital happiness.

The selection of a bridegroom of humble birth for a family immeasurably above him in social status was by no means unique in Imperial China, which was a happy combination of feudal tradition with the best elements of democracy. Brains, initiative and tact could raise the peasant to the prince, and the lack of such qualities degraded his descendants to their original level. The local squire took an interest in the village school and, if his attention were drawn to a particularly brilliant scholar, he acquired merit by acting as his patron. Should the lad be successful in passing the competitive examination and be appointed to an official post, he could easily contract a marriage, where his wife's wealth and influence furthered his career. The titles, however, were personal and not hereditary, and a duke's grandson, if he won no honour in the service of the country, reverted to a commoner.

Betrothal and Wedding Customs

Betrothal and wedding customs vary slightly all over China, but descriptions in foreign languages have usually been written from the angle of the bridegroom as, from the time of the marriage ceremony, the bride quits her clan, and is an integral part of her husband's family. Most accounts put little stress on the woman's side and, though from the photographs in the weekly paper it would appear that marriages in Hong Kong differ little from those in Western lands, enough old customs remain to show the grain of the wood beneath the veneer.

In one particular case, the bride's parents were cook and amah, whilst the bridegroom's family was better off, but stipulated to the go-between a girl of the same clan name as its own female line. The engagement preceded the wedding by about six weeks, and took the form of a procession of gifts on a day declared by the soothsayer as propitious. Only the immediate family of the bride is invited to this function. Four red boxes containing cakes, one of pork and one of wine, with two coconuts accompany a gold lacquer box containing the bridegroom's pedigree and the marriage contract. This box also holds a gift of "Big Money", and can only be opened by the senior male member of the fiancée's family.

The girl returns two large steamed rice cakes with four characters on them, two roots of lotus, and material for a pair of trousers. On her arrival in her new home, she is expected to be able to cut out and make up the garment under the criticism of her mother-in-law. She now sets to work to make and embroider shoes for her bridegroom's female relatives, to prove her skill at needlework.

Ten days before the date fixed for the wedding is the formal betrothal, when the bridegroom sends presents of gold, accompanied by pork, chickens, wine and coconuts. The "Dragon and Phoenix" cakes symbolising a happy married life are part of the ceremonial, and in this case two hundred catties were contributed. These serve as notifications of the wedding, and are sent round to relatives and friends as an intimation of the date, in lieu of an invitation card.

The bride-to-be is now taken charge of by her unmarried girl friends chosen as bridesmaids, who attend her constantly until she finally leaves her parents' home. When friends or relations call to inspect the presents, she is produced weeping, or at any rate simulating distress at parting from her family. On the day before the wedding, her furniture is removed to her new home and, should any new article be purchased, it must be sent from the shop first to her parents, and not direct to her future residence. A procession is formed for the removal and, though both parties may enjoy the blessings of modern plumbing, the thunder box has pride of place, and leads the van. As no article may be sent empty, the convenience is filled with eggs or pomegranates.

During her seclusion, the bride is provided with light literature in the form of a confidential book to prepare her for her married responsibilities. This is passed on to the next bride of her acquaintance.

On the morning of the day, the girl takes a ceremonial bath, with an infusion of pummelo leaves, which should be gathered by her sister, or a near female relative. She then sits in the tray used for drying the family rice, while her hair is dressed in the married women's style.

Before leaving her home, the girl performs ceremonial prostrations to the ancestral tablets, and her parents, and thanks them for their care. The bridesmaids give her "lucky money", as pocket money, and she leaves the door surrounded by them. The motor-car has largely superseded the red chair which a woman may only use once in her life, and where it is used the bridegroom presents himself to claim his spouse. Before he can lead her to the carriage, he must pay ransom to the bridesmaids, who demand their fee; following the universal rule of the country, a bargain has to be struck. This custom is worldwide, and is strictly observed in Russia. In England traces of it remain in the present to each bridesmaid, which is the bridegroom's responsibility.

The bride's parents do not attend the wedding, and remain in their work-a-day clothes, only marking the occasion by giving a dinner party to their intimate friends and relatives. The go-between alone accompanies the bride in loco parentis, together with her girl friends as moral support.

On the third day after the ceremony, she returns to visit her own family, dressed in the red skirt indicating her new status, and a black jacket decked with all her jewellery: rings, bracelets, and lockets in gold. Before leaving her husband's house, she bows before the family gods, and performs the same ceremony before saluting her parents. In the North, this visit is performed on the fourth, sixth, eighth, or tenth day after the wedding. The bridegroom sends presents of food, the *pièce de résistance* consisting of two roast pigs. They are carved in ceremonial fashion by removing the face, rump with tail, and four trotters. A small portion of the internal anatomy is also cut off, and the extremities of the pig are arranged on a tray. The face and two feet are backed up against the tail and hind feet. Two oranges and three kinds of vegetables for "luck" are added to the garnishings, and the tray is sent back as a return present. An acknowledgement must invariably be made of a gift, even if it be a token, and in this case the substance is retained, and the shadow returned.

Slices of the meat are sent round to all relatives and friends who have sent wedding presents to the bride. The significance of the two oranges and three vegetables is a wish for three generations. The importance of posterity is so paramount that most of the ceremonies connected with the bride are designed to ensure it, just as rice, flung over the newly married couple in England, is emblematic of fecundity. The wreath of orange-blossom worn by the bride has the same symbolical signification.

Should the red sedan be employed, the prospective husband awaits the bride's arrival at his home. The chair is provided by the bridegroom's family, and is thoroughly purged of evil spirits before despatch. In Peking a mirror is placed on the seat to discourage their return, but in Hong Kong the bride protects herself by hanging one round her neck. Should she die, it must on no account be buried with her, lest she should return to life, with a fresh, and presumably noxious, spirit which has animated the body.

The bride's brothers provide a length of red silk or cotton, which is twisted into a decoration for the sedan, and a red silk head-covering which acts as a veil. On her arrival at her new home, her future husband taps her on the head with his fan, and then raises the veil with it. Fire-crackers signal the departure from her old home, and arrival at that of her new family.

Wedding Walk

Almost every village in England has its Lovers' Lane, where the rustic swain and his sweetheart seek the seclusion of a leafy path to whisper their declarations in each other's ear, but Hong Kong must be unique among the possessions of the British Empire in its owner-ship of a "Marriage Road". This is the path which forms the eastward extension of Bowen Road, beyond the Military Hospital, which contours the steep hill-side on a dead level till it debouches on the west slope of Wong Nei Chong valley near the filter beds and reservoir. Engaged couples, adhering to the customs of their remotest ancestors, come here in all earnestness to pray for a fruitful union, and a posterity to keep their memory green. The existence of the "Amah Rock" is well known to the older inhabitants of Hong Kong, but few seem

The Amah Rock, Bowen Road

able to describe it, and fewer still have climbed from the path to its level, and can say whether the shrine comprises an altar, or whether the rock itself bears an inscription. The whole length of the path, from the Military Hospital to the main road from Mount Parish to the Wong Nei Chong Gap, is two and a half miles. A quarter of a mile after taking the track the path crosses a bridge over a ravine, on either side of which is a rough path leading to the junction of two torrents which descend from Magazine Gap. The westerly stream falls sheer over a rock in a single spout of white water to which attention is called by a marble tablet bearing two large characters "The Living Water". At the side is an in-scription to the effect that its musical sound is a constant companion. It is evidently a favourite place for picnics and, before the war, a benevolent Government had supplied many amenities. Concrete benches still stand, but railings have been torn away. On the far side of the stream is a blackened oval fireplace, beside which stands a large brick and concrete cupboard. Opposite this is a cement dresser, and sink for washing up. The latter has been broken on one side, but the plug hole for draining clearly identifies it.

After another three-quarters of a mile, the path crosses a deeper ravine and a steep track running from town up to Wanchai Gap. The gulley bites deep into the hill-side, and, for the last three hundred yards, the continuing path on the other side of the gorge is almost parallel to that on which the approach is made. The distant spur carries a massive granite outcrop, and, as a track led up the hill-side, it was explored in the hope of identifying the Amah. The approach was flattering as it consisted of a cement causeway, which rapidly degenerated into a series of steps of decomposed granite and clay. Recent rains had converted these into a series of greasy potholes, only negotiable by a hand-hold on the overhanging shrubs. The only compensation was the wealth of butterflies. Papilio sarpedon was tame enough to be picked off a twig with the fingers, for examination, before release to sail away and resettle a few feet higher up. Though many butterflies will not fly without the sun, they can have too much of a good thing, and the majority take a siesta in the hottest part of the day. The yellow terias hecabe seems an exception, for it lit up the landscape like the male brimstone in England, which takes advantage of the first warm day in February to brighten the leafless copses. On arrival at the clump of granite it was found that the path led onwards up the hill. It did not even hesitate, and the rocks were obviously not its objective. Ascending a few yards further, the ridge of the knoll was reached, and on the next spur to the east stood the "Amah", crowning a great jumble of grey rocks. The climb had achieved something, though revelation would have come less arduously by keeping to the broad and level road.

She is far more impressive from below, for her pedestal of sheer cliff rises a hundred feet above the path. A wall of granite, gently rounded at the top, has been blasted on the north side to form the road, and rises almost perpendicularly. The object of worship resembles a wooden soldier with a busby, with one shoulder higher than the other, and a distinct list to starboard, or port, according to the angle of view. From the west she leans to starboard, with the shoulder on that side the lower.

A flight of undressed granite steps give access to the

shrine from the west. They are fairly continuous, with a couple of breaks, where the ground is apt to be slippery and treacherous. The "Amah" is approached from the side away from the path, that is to say the south. Some huge boulders surround a small open space which forms the sanctuary. A long rounded rock, slightly undercut, forms a shelter for a couple of rough earthenware teapots and two libation bowls. In front of this improvised altar lie three thick incense sticks, with the stumps of many of the thinner kind planted in the ground. Among them are small banners of thin native paper, perhaps half a dozen, stuck upright in the ground. These are "Chao Hun Fan" (招魂旛) or "call the Spirit flags", though none of them had any inscription or invocation to the Spirit. Plenty of burned paper, some with references to the stone shrine still legible, were lying under the rock.

Behind the altar, and immediately at the foot of the "Amah", is a well-squared oblong block of granite, its surface worn smooth by the friction of the seats of many couples, who have made their vows, and take a well-earned rest before returning to the bustling world below. The "Amah" stands a gaunt sentry over the stone sanctuary. She bears no inscription, but it is hard to believe that she is a freak of nature, and that man had no hand in shaping her. On the northern side, her pedestal is formed by a gigantic mass of granite forming a level platform six feet wide to a convex curve, which then falls perpendicularly to the Wedding Way.

The trilithons of Stonehenge are pigmies compared with the erectiles of Hong Kong, shafts of pure granite laid bare by the weathering of the decomposed rock which forms the soil. In any case, the Chinese are convinced that "There's a divinity that shapes their ends", and that his propitiation will ensure that children bless the union.

From the debris littering the floor of the sanctuary, it is not difficult to reconstruct the ceremony. The couple plant their incense sticks in front of the altar, light them, and kneel side by side to make their silent prayer with clasped hands. A libation is then poured out on the ground, and a written request for protection is burned. This takes the form of a square red talisman, with three-inch sides, enclosed in a printed envelope with a printed design of the goddess. The only four legible characters of a partly consumed cover read "Nine Heavenly dark ladies . . . ." On the right is the personal prayer of the engaged couple. "May the Spirit of the goddess protect the Stone shrine, and . . . ." Then the full names of the betrothed. It seems quite possible that the envelope bears the characters for the seventh of the Nine Niang Niangs, all of whom are protecting divinities. Her name is the Tzu Sun Niang Niang, and it is she who grants posterity. Not enough of the paper was left unconsumed to confirm this, but the theory is plausible, and, as the journey is undertaken with this object in view, her connection with the ceremony would seem obvious.

This mixture of Taoist ritual and primitive worship is typical of the Chinese thoroughness in their religious observances, and it may be truly said that they leave no stone unturned to ensure that their petitions have a chance to reach at least one competent authority.

The phallic implications of the shrine are obvious from its Chinese designation, the Yin Yang Shih, or Female and Male Principle Stone. This early conception of the balance of the two powers which rule the Universe is extended to light and darkness, positive and negative, active and passive. It is a constant motif in Chinese symbolism, and is the central decoration on the patches worn by Taoist priests. It was even used as the watermark on the Imperial postage-stamps in the form known as the T'ai Chi. The Amah Rock's virtues are not only confined to engaged couples, but it is also a place of pilgrimage for married women, who wish to retain the waning affections of their husbands.

The Chicken's Bride

The Chinese have a rooted objection to a man standing as proxy at a wedding and, in one district of Kwangtung, the Shun Teh area, a cock is used as a substitute for an absent bridegroom. The bride is transferred in the usual red chair to the home of her husband's family, of which henceforth she is a member, and on arrival in the countryard a live cock is thrown over the chair, to be scrambled for by her attendant relatives. Its capture brings luck to the successful contestant. Her husband may be abroad, and may never see her but, none the less, the marriage is valid in Chinese law, and she is entitled to her share of the property on his decease.

In a case in 1940, a "Chicken's Bride" married an overseas Chinese, resident in New York, and her two children, by a previous marriage, were legally adopted into his clan. The only other claimant was a grand-nephew of the deceased. The Court ruled that the property should be shared by the four claimants in equal parts, and that costs should be similarly apportioned. According to the journal, the tradition is not really valid in law, but as the custom is so long established there is no intervention, except if a dispute arises, when an impartial judgment is given after investigation. The present case entailed a journey abroad to claim property, and the validity of the marriage had to be established to obtain the necessary visa.

The question of succession presents a problem in these proxy marriages. The business activities of the bridegroom may preclude his return to his native village, and he may never see his bride. It is essential that there should be a male heir to carry on the ancestral worship, and circumstances may interfere with the begetting of the desired son. It is probable, in the case cited above, that only two of the widow's sons were adopted, and that a third existed to satisfy the ancestral claims of the clan she had entered on her first marriage. Should the husband fail to acquire an heir, recourse is had to adoption or purchase. Four districts in the Province of Kwangtung, Toi Shan, Sam Ling, Hoi P'ing and Yan Ling, provide the bulk of the emigrants. Children are purchased through a go-between, who evidently runs some form of Registry Office, marking down the poor families with a super-abundance of olive branches. These part with a child for a cash consideration, but the purchase money must be accompanied by the gift of a kitten or a puppy. This satisfies the principle of a life for a life. It is permissible, in some cases, where the vendor is allergic to livestock, or has parted with a child on account of his inability to feed it, to substitute a mug or vase, symbolic of a mouth for a mouth.

Some clans object to keeping unmarried women, with no ancestral duties to perform. These are also wedded by proxy to one of the ancestral tablets, and become, by the ceremony, responsible for attending to the grave, and comforting the spirit which resides in the homestead. If an unmarried son dies before reaching adult age, the parents seek the services of the Registry Office go-between to discover a family who has lost a daughter of corresponding age. An alliance is then contracted, and the betrothal and wedding ceremonies are enacted, the tablets taking the place of the principals. The girl's coffin is then exhumed, and is reburied in the boy's ancestral cemetery, beside his own.

The go-between is an essential of Chinese family life, for without her services no union can be contracted, according to conservative Chinese ideas. Marriages were arranged by her, and the bridegroom never saw the face of his future wife till he raised the veil on her emergence from the red sedan-chair. She is usually a woman of the status of elderly servant who has free entrée into the houses of those desirous of contracting matrimonial alliances. In actual fact, such women are marriage brokers. Sometimes they are specially invited by the parties desirous to avail themselves of their services, and sometimes they arrive unsolicited, acting on "information received" by their intelligence organisation. Once the initial steps are taken, they are responsible for the stage-management of the whole affair. Their duties begin by obtaining the girl's name, year, day and hour of birth, and submitting it to the fortune-teller, who casts her horoscope to ensure that nothing conflicts with that of the prospective bridegroom. The go-between then returns with the offer of marriage. The assent in writing is then demanded, after which presents are sent to the fiancée's parents. She then requests the principals to select a lucky day for the wedding.

If one of a betrothed couple dies before the wedding, the marriage may still take place, with the tablet representing the deceased person.

Though old maids were unpopular in China, in some districts feminism asserted itself, and the young ladies resented the prospect of submitting to the whims of a tyrannical mother-in-law. Sororities were formed, who vowed themselves to celibacy, and to drastic action in case of compulsion. Oddly enough, the district of Shun Teh (Shun Tak) celebrated for the "Chicken Marriage" had such a society and, if a girl was forced into marriage, she returned home on the third day, and refused to rejoin her husband. Some, if sufficiently wealthy, offered money to purchase a substitute, whilst others made away with themselves if pressure was exerted to enforce their return.

The "Golden Orchid Society" was perhaps the most notorious of these secret guilds who bound themselves never to marry. Apparently the custom had some religious origin, for in an old brochure on the subject nuns are mentioned as disseminating the doctrine, one of whose tenets held that celibacy was a purer form of life. Those belonging to such an association were taught by these ladies to disembarrass themselves of their spouses by charms and incantations, taking hairs from their queues for unrevealed purposes, and procuring bones of dead children to obtain material which was buried under the bed, fireplace, or family rice jar. Failing this, four ounces of white arsenic was recommended to obtain quicker results. The nuns, however, made a heavier charge for this, and the more unscrupulous were not above substituting the ashes from a furnace, at ten dollars a dose. Later on opium was carried on the person for suicide use in case of an enforced marriage. The Manchus, who were sticklers for the sanctity of family life, strongly disapproved of these tendencies, and the girls themselves mostly lapsed into a conventional union.

With modern education, and freer relations between the sexes than obtained under the Empire, these old customs are dying out, and the young people have far more chance of becoming acquainted before they unite as partners for life. Still, the case of the "Chicken's Bride" goes to show that traces of the old order still exist, and must be recognised to enable the laws of inheritance to hold good.

Marriages Made in Heaven

The Chinese are firm believers in the saying that Marriages are made in Heaven, and as far as they are concerned there is some truth in the assertion. A case has recently occurred in Kowloon where a wedding between two deceased persons has been celebrated, and the families concerned have been left with no shadow of doubt as to the supernatural influences which brought it about. A certain man married and had two children by his first wife, a boy and a girl, of whom only the latter survived. The wife also died, and there were several further children of the second marriage. When the eldest girl approached marriageable age there was the usual family council about her prospects. One of the younger children, speaking in the accents of his deceased stepbrother, registered an objection, and declared that it was impossible for his step-sister to marry until his elder brother had a wife. On being asked how a wife was to be found for him, he said that he had found a suitable maiden among the Shades, and that an intimation would arrive to determine his choice. Almost simultaneously a similar council was being held in another family, whose eldest daughter had not survived, and in this case the address of the boy's family was divulged. A visit was accordingly made to the dead boy's home, where the parents of the girl inquired if indeed such a person had been a member of the family. Both parties were now convinced that the marriage had been predestined, and the usual exchange of the Eight Characters followed. As all seemed to be in order, the families concerned discussed the amount of the dowry (payable in notes on the Bank of Hell) and the clothing and furniture to accompany the bride. As this was all in paper, the outlay was considerably less than that normally required for a wedding of the living, but the boy who had initiated the whole proceedings again made an amendment which was accepted. Part of the bridal furnishings must be real, including a gold ring, and skirt for the bride. These were to be kept, and bestowed on the offspring of the girl whose marriage was first in question, and he (the younger brother) must be adopted into the deceased boy's clan, to carry out the Ancestral worship for him and his Heavenly bride. As both families agreed to this proposal, the wedding of the ghostly spirits was duly celebrated. The cakes and chickens, at any rate, were real, so the ceremony was made the occasion for a feast to which both families, and friends, were invited. The red bridal chair was not used, but the green sedan, also employed for funerals, was decked with a strip of red paper, and an incense burner was placed on the seat, before either the tablet or a sheet of red paper on which the bride's name was inscribed.

This seems an exceptional case, but it occurred quite recently, and the facts are as related by one of the guests. It is not unusual in Kwangtung, when a son dies before marriage, for the parents to employ a go-between to seek out a family, whose daughter of approximately the same age has died prematurely, and at about the same time. The betrothal and wedding ceremonies are then performed as if the parties were alive, the tablets taking the place of the principals. The girl's coffin is then exhumed, and buried beside the boy's in the graveyard of his clan.

Swatow has its own marriage customs, for the bride does not ride in the traditional red chair, nor is she laced in. A larger chair is used for her journey to the bridegroom's home, approximating in size to that affected by the old time official. Red cloth hangings are festooned over it, and a couple of catties of raw pork are hung by a string outside the door. On her arrival at the bridegroom's house, she steps over a fire of dry grass, to purify her from any devils who may have beset her during the journey. She does not return to visit her old home on the third day after marriage, as is the case with the Cantonese, but must allow four months to elapse. On the third day, however, the Swatow bride receives a visit from her younger brother, or from some boy from the neighbourhood of her parents' house, if they have not provided her with a closer relative.

This lad, or the younger brother, as the case may be, brings a little peanut oil for the lamps. The Swatow bride also goes to worship at the Ancestral Hall on the 15th of the First Moon on the first three years of her marriage. Men, as well as women, strangers, or acquaintances have the right to go and look at her. She is expected to provide loose skinned oranges for the children, and must offer tea to the adults. Married people in return present her with cash in red "Lucky-money" envelopes.

These envelopes play a tremendous part in the lives of the Chinese, and are much in evidence at New Year, and family festivals; they are stocked at all the paper shops. Various designs in gold are printed on a bright red ground, the Longevity character, and the Five Bats being a favourite motive. Others, particularly appropriate for weddings, bear the double Hsi for Married Happiness, with designs of Lotus, and the characters for Great Luck. It is a graceful way of bestowing a tip, and the recipient is always left in joyful anticipation of the amount of money thus tantalisingly concealed. New Year tips, corresponding to Christmas boxes, are dealt out in this way to errand boys, and such constant callers at the door.

The Hakkas, of whom there is a large community in Hong Kong, particularly in the New Territories, have slightly different customs from the Cantonese though, by twenty generations of sojourn amongst them, they have adopted many of their habits. In the Third Century B.C. they lived in a belt of country which is now traversed by the Lung-Hai Railway, on the southern borders of Shantung, and the northern edge of Anhwei and Honan. Dislodged by a persecution in the Ch'in Dynasty, they began their southward migration, and further attacks on them caused them to settle in southern Kiangsi and

Kwangtung Provinces. Their language is nearer to Mandarin than Cantonese, and the women never bound their feet, and had a much freer time of it altogether. The dress of the peasant women is notably different from the Cantonese, as they wear a much longer jacket, reaching nearly to the knees, and their broad crownless hats have a valance of cloth round them. The word Hakka means 'strangers' (K'o chia) indicating that they come from afar. The ordinary red chair is used for the bride at a wedding, and the Lion Dance should form part of the ceremony. The girl does not return to her home on the third day, but her relatives come to the husband's house to visit her.

The traditional cakes supplied for the wedding feast differ from those used at a Cantonese marriage, one in particular being a huge beignet, fried in deep fat, and hollow, without any filling.

The Hakkas are rather prone to take a small girl into the family, and bring her up with the other children as a bride for one of the sons. This, at any rate, has the advantage of getting her familiar with the ways of her future mother-in-law, who will play a great part in her married life.

The Status of Women

The position of women in Chinese society differed considerably from that obtaining in other oriental countries. The birth of a boy was welcomed, as a male heir will ensure the survival of the family name and comfort the souls of his ancestors in the afterworld, whereas a girl must eventually impoverish the family by the expenses of her wedding and the abstraction of a dowry. So little of an asset were girls regarded that a Chinese, if asked the size of his family, would only mention the number of sons. If nature had been so unkind as to deny him an heir, he would reluctantly admit that he only had one daughter. This obvious cause of embarrassment debarred such a query from polite conversation, and only a foreigner would have been guilty of such an indiscretion.

Discrimination started from the cradle for, whereas the male child was provided with silver mascots, such as an abacus or a chicken's leg to determine his career, the girl was awarded a tile as her only plaything. According to ancient tradition, from the age of seven boys and girls did not occupy the same mat, or eat together. Women's clothes should not hang on the same peg as a man's, nor should the same place be used for bathing by both sexes. Strictly speaking a wife should not eat with her husband, but among the lower classes such nice points of etiquette were honoured more in the breach than the observance.

The only person who had a soft place in her heart for a daughter was her mother, who secretly welcomed the child as an unpaid baby-sitter to keep the rest of her brood out of mischief whilst she attended to her household duties. In the great majority of cases in old China a girl was not taught to read and write. Embroidery, plain sewing, and the manufacture of shoes constituted practically her whole education. Her up-bringing was designed to stifle any will of her own and to ensure submissiveness whatever befell her. Marriage was arranged by the parents, and she had absolutely no choice in the matter. The suppression at home was a valuable training for wedded life, when she became the slave of her mother-in-law. To her she owed filial obedience, a breach of which formed grounds for divorce.

Mothers-in-law are the subjects of perennial jests on the Western stage, but in China they are no joke to the blushing bride, rather an affliction from which there is no escape. They are not in the house for a temporary visit, but are a permanent establishment. In a dispute the husband dare not take the part of his wife, so she is defenceless. Her only consolation is that one day the tables will be turned, and she will have a daughter-in-law to bully. As the rule of nature allows a longer span of life to the woman than to the man, the old grandmother is often the head of the household, which has to submit to her desires, by virtue of her seniority, and she holds the purse strings. A case of this occurred in the country just outside Peking in 1914, when the widow Liu, who owned considerable property, was approached by her sons to hand over control. She replied that as long as she was living she knew they would be adequately provided for, but if she abdicated she had no guarantee that her interests would be respected. She was somewhat of an eccentric for she resented the fact that she would not be conscious of the supreme moment of her life, her funeral. Accordingly, she had a rehearsal, having thoughtfully invested in a magnificent coffin in advance. She watched the procession and interment from a royal box and derived the utmost satisfaction from the rueful countenances of the chief mourners who saw their fortune melting away to gratify her extravagance.

The law of seniority was so rigid that even the Emperor was obliged to defer to the wishes of his aunts, and rescind decisions which were distasteful to them.

According to the "Sayings of Confucius" a man may divorce his wife for seven different reasons: barrenness, lasciviousness, jealousy, talkativeness, thieving, disobedience to his parents, and leprosy. This would seem to afford a wide choice of offences under which to indict an uncongenial companion but, in practice, there were many deterrents to taking action. The reaction of the wife's parents had to be carefully considered and, if they were no longer living, she could not be repudiated, as she had no home to receive her. She could not be divorced if either of them was in mourning for a parent.

If no son be born of the marriage, it causes much less unpleasantness all round to ensure the succession by taking a concubine, continuing the process till the desired result is obtained. Neither will a divorce stand if the husband was in poor circumstances when he married but, by the turn of fortune's wheel, he became rich and wished to contract a more advantageous alliance. All these restrictions nullified what would appear to be an easy dissolution of matrimonial ties, and resulted in making divorce in China no more frequent than in countries where the grounds for separation are more narrowly defined.

A married couple could agree to separate, and Chinese law punished a husband whose wife was guilty of misconduct if he did not put her away.

Though the husband's powers in the matter were considerable, the wife had little redress if the cause of complaint was on her side. If she suffered from broken bones in the course of chastisement, the husband was amenable to law, but otherwise she could only reply on the sympathy of a somewhat tepid public opinion, or by appealing to her own clan to ameliorate her condition by threats of intervention.

The situation was entirely different in the case of secondary wives, the "Minor Stars" of the household. They were not wives in the sight of the law, and did not stand on a footing of equality with the one legitimate spouse. A man was perfectly free to dismiss them from hearth and board when he felt so inclined, but this treatment was modified by the fear of reprisals from their relatives, and their social position. If they lacked this support their plight was lamentable, and they often drifted into prostitution unless they found some protector to take them into his family under conditions similar to those they had previously enjoyed.

The degree of seclusion of women varied in different provinces. In Peking, the town dwellers were rarely seen in the streets. In the residential area the narrow lanes run between high mud walls, pierced with doors, but windowless. Hawkers pass down the street daily, crying their wares and signalling their approach by the noise of some distinctive instrument such as a drum or trumpet. The housewife comes to the front door to make her purchase, and it is only on these occasions that a glimpse of the courtyard may be had by a passer-by. Women rarely earned their living in domestic service, so amahs were scarce, and commanded wages equivalent of those paid to the No. 1 Boy. Women of the better class could not go out unattended, and they were usually laced in their sedan chairs screened from the public gaze.

The lower classes had more freedom of action, as they were not confined to the compound, but went about to perform such duties as were necessary towards contributing to the household budget. Seamstresses sat at street corners repairing clothes, and farmers' wives helped in the operations in the fields. Goat-footed women ravaged the hillsides for sticks for fuel, or cut grass for fodder. In Hong Kong the Boat girls did all the sampan rowing, their menfolk being employed on junks for the heavy work of cargo handling. It is impossible, however, to generalise on the subject of female employment in tasks usually performed by men for, whilst in the Canton delta women were everywhere to be seen, in the neighbourhood of Swatow they were conspicuous by their absence from the fields.

Much more liberty has been granted in recent years, for girls go to school unattended, are not ashamed to be seen in the theatre or cinema, and even have some latitude in the choice of a husband. To a sensitive girl, marriage in the old days must have been a nightmare, for she severed all ties with the home where she was nurtured, and was projected with awful suddenness as a stranger into a society which might prove most uncongenial. She was the target of criticism of a host of unknown relatives, debarred from speaking in her own defence and, until she produced a son, was worse off than a hired servant. The separation from her own family was carried to such an extent that, should her fiancé die during the engagement it was considered an act of virtue for the girl to leave her own home, and enter that of her betrothed to live in subjection to the deceased's mother till death dissolved the tie.

Though public opinion did not demand such a sacrifice, as was the case in India, the suicide of a widow was regarded as a virtuous deed. On the other hand, remarriage was distinctly frowned upon, and a woman who took a second partner had no rights to the red chair, or to be considered anything better than a concubine.

A Boat People's Wedding

Although the marriage customs of the Chinese have formed the subject of innumerable articles, little appears to have been published on the peculiar rites observed by the Tan-gar, or aborigines of the West River delta. The Egg family, as they are called in derision by the Cantonese, are extremely conservative and, whereas among the land population of Hong Kong, foreign marriage ritual is becoming more and more popular, the ceremonies performed afloat have remained unchanged for centuries. Few foreigners are invited as wedding guests, and fewer still seem to have felt the urge of recording their experiences. An invitation is not lightly given or lightly accepted, for the celebrations last for the best part of the twenty-four hours, the culminating events taking place during the darkness.

Many sentimentalists have inveighed against the Mui Tsai system and the purchase of children but, on balance, there is much to recommend the practice. The child, if a boy, is enrolled in the clan and enjoys the same rights in succession to property as a natural son. A girl must be suitably married at the age of eighteen and, as she was originally acquired from a family in very poor circumstances, she has enjoyed a higher standard of living than could have been expected in her natural surroundings. The wedding about to be described is that of the eldest adopted daughter of No. 3 Boat Lady who, being childless, was obliged to resort to purchase to maintain her dignity as a married woman. The scale of entertainment was so lavish that there was a certain amount of family comment on the endowment of a junior member compared with similar occasions affecting natural daughters by senior consorts. For all practical purposes, however, the phenomenon may be explained by the enhanced prosperity of the business, though that was not what the ladies said.

The preliminaries occupied months, as the prospective mother-in-law was a hard business woman, the widowed mistress of a junk in her own right. The bridegroom, being an only son, was an extremely eligible party, as all property rights were vested in him. The go-between certainly earned her fee in striking a mean between two such experts in the art of bargaining. Sometimes the marriage was on, sometimes off. Sometimes the matter was dropped for weeks together. Finally the fortune-teller had to select a lucky day and draw up a document with the warnings necessary to avert any possible misfortunes during the ceremony itself.

For the convenience of the guests and the reception of the wedding presents, the junks of the bride's family left the anchorage in the centre of the typhoon shelter, and were moored at the quayside, head on, with gang planks ashore at the bows. A tablet honouring the ancestors is placed on the shelf outside the port cabin which always contains the shrine of T'ien Hou, the Patron Saint, as well as the family gods. Before it burned incense, and food offerings of cakes and roast chickens were laid out on the improvised altar. Every guest boarding the junk bowed to this family shrine, as an officer salutes the quarter-deck of a warship, before offering his congratulations. The mast of a lighter is stepped just abaft the fo'c'stle at the extreme for'ard end of the well-deck, and here was arranged a red tablet, surmounted by a white rosette surrounding a gold talisman, representing the bridegroom's clan. Behind it was pasted the red certificate, the gift of the fortune-teller. Part and parcel of the tablet was a red incense bowl in which two pairs of candles burned upright, among a forest of incense sticks. The main display of food, in the shape of whole roast pigs, was laid out before this shrine. In the starboard corner of the well-deck, level with the mast, were four large decorated jars of oil and wine with an incense burner before them—a gift of the bridegroom, symbolic of his future responsibility of providing for the maintenance of his family. As no one was likely to sleep that night, the whole of the main cabin accommodation was handed over to the bride who was housed with her attendants in the owner's stateroom. Over the door was an inscription in gold, on red paper: "May every corner of the Universe extend its blessing." On either side of the sliding hatch were pasted square red papers. That to port wished 10,000 years of good luck, adherence to the laws and tradition to the clan. On the starboard side, the gold characters proclaimed a similar period of prosperity and offspring to promote the family affairs.

During the forenoon, a small gaily-decorated junk with two red lanterns on the poop, and a red silk streamer at the peak of the yard, came alongside, bearing the bridegroom's gifts. With it arrived the match-maker, resplendently dressed as mistress of the ceremonies. A casket, containing the marriage contract and an inventory of the presents, including personal gifts to the bride, was by far the most important item of the cargo. This was placed in front of the bridegroom's tablet, and could only be opened by the senior male member of the bride's family. The whole of the well-deck was quickly spread with food offerings—two roast pigs, two crates each containing a pair of live geese, live ducks, chickens, peanuts and oranges. There was a basket with two very long lotus roots and two huge coconuts. On the tables were placed the boxes of cakes. The amount was specified in the contract, and even the name of the confectioner who was to supply them, lest a second-rate article be substituted. The mother-in-law, being a notorious screw, in this case was suspected of exercising economy, and not without cause for, though the goods were up to sample, she sent short weight, a fact which did not escape censure. The gifts must all be handled by a senior married woman representing each family. In the box containing the contract was a specified sum of money, which goes to the bride's father to offset his expenditure on the trousseau, consisting in this case of forty-two dresses, exclusive of underwear and shoes. The dower chest and trousseau are on exhibition to the guests prior to the arrival of the contract. On the table was an opened box containing funeral clothes, made by the bride, later to be burned at the husband's ancestral shrine, before serving ceremonial tea to her mother-in-law. In the North the bride presents the old lady with slippers worked by herself to demonstrate her skill at embroidery. In return for her homage she is presented with a piece of family jewellery. A large tray containing rice, wine, oil, a sample of all the gifts, and even two large pieces of firewood, is the perquisite of the match-maker.

There is an element of "touch and remit" in the sharing out of the gifts, which is carried out by the married women of the bride's family. Only the seniors take part, expectant mothers and those with infants on their backs are barred. Each box handed back contains part of the original gift and a red envelope of lucky money as acknowledgment. In addition to the remnants of the feast, the married women must send back a contribution of their own, consisting of a slice of roast pork, oranges and sweets for tea. The funeral clothing made by the bride is sent back along with the return presents, in charge of the match-maker. The go-between junk, which later fulfils the role of the red sedan-chair in normal weddings, departed to the beating of saucepans instead of gongs, and a subdued volley of crackers, that is, as many as it was judged would not attract the undesirable attentions of the police, whose permission had not been solicited.

During the preliminaries, nothing was seen of the bride, who remained in the stateroom, consoled by her nine attendants. Unmarried Chinese girls have a passion for forming clubs, the monthly contributions being pooled and expended on some festival like the Seven Sisters, or reserved for occasions such as a marriage or a funeral. At these happy, or lamentable events, the members are to the fore as bridesmaids, or mourners, and nine of them were sustaining the bride for her final ordeal. At a Western wedding the bride is the centre of attraction, and is waited on hand and foot, every effort being made to spare her undue fatigue. Her Chinese counterpart never knows a moment free from embarrassment, until the last guest has departed and she starts her married existence. She has to sit motionless for hours under the fire of criticism of her female relatives, and her whole is one of self-effacement, with the prospect of the tyranny of a mother-in-law darkening the horizon.

In the evening the guests sat down to a feast sent in by one of the best restaurants in Kowloon. Both junks were needed to accommodate the nineteen round tables, each seating twelve. The bride and her nine hand-maidens made up one party, whilst the "Old Man" and his two elder sons honoured the foreigners with his presence. Shark's fin soup was in the lead, followed by innumerable dishes consisting of prawns, with and without shells, chicken, pork, roast duck, mushrooms, fish and finally a huge tureen of Tung Ku soup. Chinese wine, beer, and orangeade for the ladies, circulated freely.

When the well-deck of the big junk was swept and garnished, nothing remained but the husband's family shrine, the four gift jars of wine and oil, and the bride's household gods in the port cabin. The long gang planks, specially stiffened for sliding heavy weights, were so arranged along the sides of the deck as to afford two tiers of seats, one on the gunwale, and the other on the prow. An immense audience gathered, consisting entirely of women, who packed not only the seating accommodation thus provided, but the whole of the poop above the living quarters. Four of the bridesmaids, with yellow bows in their hair, emerged from the stateroom and, in a thin chant, serenaded the bride whilst the stage was being set. Two of the most senior women, one, the "Old Man's" sister, and a lady of similar degree from the bridegroom's family, then took charge of affairs. A table was set up in the centre of the well-deck covered with a red paper-cloth, and on it were placed food offerings, two candle-sticks, and six white wine and tea cups, three large and three small. On the port side of the deck another square table was rigged by the bridesmaids, on which they set out their personal presents. These consisted of the bride's intimate property—a charcoal iron, thermos flask, scent bottles and cosmetics and sewing accessories. When all was laid out, and candles and incense had been ignited before the various shrines, the "Old Man", in a battered straw hat set at a rakish angle, made his final appearance and, having consulted the fortune-teller's instructional red paper, announced that all spectators of the ages of 21, 45 and 69 must avert their eyes during the ceremony. He then withdrew to mahjong, as the sequel was purely a women's affair.

On his departure, the bride was brought out bare-footed, dressed in clean, dark-blue working clothes, with a black sash edged with red. Over her head was a black cloth, serving as a veil and preventing her from seeing anything that was going on. As all the side awnings were down and the auditorium was packed with humanity, she must have been half stifled for the five hours during which the ceremonies were continuous. The two matrons of honours took up their station at the for'ard end of the table facing the bride, each holding a thick wax candle horizontally before them with both hands. The bride's veil was then raised by an attendant to let her see what she was doing, and enable her to pick up and place on her end of the table a huge pot with a growing orange tree. The veil was lowered again and the matrons of honour bowed three times to the bride. The candles were then lighted on either side of the shrub and covered with red paper shades about three feet high standing flush with the table.

Then came the libations. The two matrons filled the six cups with wine, oil and tea, and one of them carried the sacrifice on a pink enamel tray to the bride, who raised it three times in the direction of her husband's shrine. One of the wise women relieved her of her burden, and, taking the tray to the foot of the mast, offered it to the family gods before pouring out the contents into a receptacle at the side. The ceremony was repeated before the bride's ancestral deities, in the direction of her new home, and before the four jars of wine and oil in the starboard fore corner of the well-deck. Whilst the bride's veil was raised for the performance of this act of devotion, a red and white sheet was held up at arm's length by her young brother and another boy, masking the sky which might otherwise be visible under the awning. There is some grave objection to the stars intruding at this stage of the proceedings, and, though the night was overcast with a fine drizzle descending, no chances were taken.

The ceremony ended by a small child taking her stance at the far side of the table and waving a red veil to the bride, before coming round to offer the tray three times. This gesture was acknowledged by the bride raising her veil.

The bridesmaids next retired to change from working dress into bright silks, and a professional, also veiled, recited a long incantation of advice as to how a married woman should conduct her life. This is a traditional admonition, and is exceedingly ancient. The woman

A fisherman weds . . . the preliminaries occupy months.

intoned in a strong clear voice, very different from the bridemaids' piping chant. As she finished, the bride's bedding was carried out from her stateroom which she was never to re-enter.

The nine bridesmaids, resplendent in their silk dresses and each with a feather fan, were marshalled by the matrons of honour in line facing the bride, with the table separating them. The girls were shown how to hold their fans open by the outer sticks covering their faces. They then saluted the bride by bowing twice, and an extraordinary dialogue followed. As a rule, the subject of death is strictly avoided by the Chinese, so the leave-taking of the old life and home must have been framed before the Boat People absorbed their civilisation. The bride initiates each sentence, addressing her hand-maidens in turn, bewailing her sad fate, only to be answered by a reassuring sentence. The whole conver-sation is impromptu, misery from the bride, and cheer-fulness from her companions. She says she is dying, and the first had better go to the coffin-maker. The latter counters that she has just given her a thermos flask, and they'll all go for a picnic in the hills. A demand for the second to buy grave clothes is countered with a reminder of the iron for freshening up her party clothes. So it goes on till they open a box containing a long red scarf with gold tassels and the name of their Society blazoned in the centre, which finally goes to the mother-in-law as decoration for the bridal chamber. With this extended full length, they move counter-clockwise, the bride moving in the opposite direction so as to face the centre.

During the final stages of the bride's farewell to her family, she has two assistants to support and prompt her. They are either professionals, or women of the clan well versed in the ritual. Both are veiled, and one is usually at her elbow, whilst the other sits near the family shrine. The leave-taking seems interminable, and the strain on all concerned is reflected in their voices. Towards the end they become incoherent, and the bride is reduced to making inarticulate sounds which evoke hysterical responses. The whole scene is reminiscent of the "Death of Poor Cock Robin", though the libretto probably antedates the nursery rhyme by many centuries.

The comforting of the bride, which lasts over two hours, is succeeded by her attendants' homage to her mother. In this case there were three to be honoured for, though her adopted parent would seem to be the only one concerned, by Chinese law the Senior Lady is the real *mater familias*. Thus a childless wife may urge her husband to take a concubine to provide her with a son to carry on her ancestral worship. In this case, No. 1 Lady took her place seated in the starboard centre of the well-deck with No. 2 in the place of honour on her left, and the girl's real mother by purchase at her right hand.

The bridesmaids lined up in front of the matrons and bowed in salutation. They then knelt and performed the triple kow-tow to No. 1 Lady, touching the deck three times with their foreheads. Rising from their salutations, they presented her with sweet soup containing an egg, and a tray with two boxes of cakes.

No. 2 Lady is a roley-poley slattern, whose good nature and fecklessness endear her to the family. Her sense of fitness is blunted by absent-mindedness of a mirth-provoking nature, which adds considerably to the gaiety of life. On this occasion, she suddenly remem-bered that she had mislaid a hundred-dollar note, and

left her seat to secure it just as her turn to be served arrived. An unavoidable hitch in the timing occurred, as it was impossible to serve No. 3 Lady before her Senior. The quest for the missing note appears to have involved the removal of No. 2's voluminous trousers and, flustered with the clamour for her presence, she omitted to restore them, and made her appearance in short underpants and bare legs, amid roars of laughter and ribald jokes from the feminine audience. Not a whit perturbed, she resumed her seat, and received her homage with the immobility of a Buddha. In China no acknowledgement is required for the ceremonial pro-strations.

The bridesmaids then retired to change to clean work-ing-dress whilst the bride sat on the floor and wailed, smothered in her black veil. By this time she was com-pletely inarticulate, and simply gave vent to muffled babbling in an effort to sustain her part.

At 2 a.m. the bridal chair, in the shape of the small junk, came to fetch her. Two large red lanterns glowed on the poop as it glided alongside. As soon as it was made fast, two gangplanks were lashed parallel to each other about three feet apart, while a brace of married sisters-in-law attended to the dressing of the bride.

In a Chinese wedding, the ceremonial bath with pummelo leaves is part and parcel of the ritual, and the bride leaves her home dressed in review order. The Boat People, however, despatch the girl in a most summary fashion, and the wedding-dress is only donned on arrival at her new home. Normally the decks are kept scrupul-ously clean, as nearly all work is done barefoot, but, with guests coming from the shore and rain falling, there was no opportunity to wash down before the farewell ritual. The soles of the bride's feet were as black as the ace of spades when she was seized by the elder women, and a pair of white socks were forced on her. She was then bundled into a green skirt, over her working-dress, and a red cloak was thrown round her. This was ab-solutely stuffed with paper inscribed with incantations and talismanic signs of a devil-defying potency. Her veil was then raised from the back, to hang in her hair a number of cash paired together with red silk cord. As the old copper coins with the square hole in the centre were unobtainable, Hong Kong five-cent pieces had been drilled for the purpose. The number of these is commen-surate with the affection in which the bride is held in her family, who load her with riches on the final parting. On arrival at her new home, the mother-in-law lifts her veil and judges by the decoration her popularity in her old family. Lucky money is made up in red envelopes for her to hand the children who have taken part in the ceremony.

As soon as the dressing was complete, the officiating matrons seized their victim under the knees and shoul-ders and ran her down the double gangplank like a sack of potatoes, dumping her in a sitting position on a mat under the starboard gunwale of the small junk. There she was left wailing, but surrounded by comforting bridesmaids, whilst her effects were put on board. These were treated with far more ceremony than their owner. The red bundle of bedding occupied the place of honour in the centre of the well-deck, and alongside it was the dower chest containing the forty-two changes of raiment. The presents were then carefully arranged so as to pro-duce the best effect on arrival. Finally the bridegroom's family gods were shipped together with the fortune-teller's red paper, which is ceremoniously burned three days after the wedding. With the departure of her companions, the little bride is left alone, a disconsolate bundle of misery, for all the world a departing spirit committed to the last dread passage of the Styx. As the boat glides silently away, the bridesmaids line up, their heads covered with handkerchiefs, for a final wail, as a muffled burst of crackers dispels any lingering malignant spirits. A few minutes later, a much louder discharge announces the arrival of the bride for the actual ceremony of marriage.

The audience crowding the deck of the girl's old home, however, does not disperse, for there is one more ritual to be observed. After a Chinese wedding the bride does not revisit her old home till the third day, but with Boat People she is back at dawn resplendent in her scarlet dress. There was plenty of food for conversation to beguile the waiting hours. The parsimony of the mother-in-law for sending short measure evoked general censure, for it was everybody's business. The wedding-cakes provided by the bridegroom are shared out among the guests in proportion to the value of their presents to the bride. The "Old Man", however, after giving vent to his emotions in no uncertain terms, more than made up the deficit with an order to the confectioner, and everybody must have been eating cakes for days afterwards. It was generally conceded that the mother-in-law was a blot, but the girl's disposition was so admirable that she would probably get along with her better than anybody else. The bridegroom was unexceptionable and a friend of the family. The great point in favour of the match was its material aspect. As an only son, at the old lady's death the whole inheritance would not suffer division. With no death duties to worry about, capital and goodwill would remain intact. The Old Lady could not live for ever, so the girl had the certainty of becoming a junk mistress in her own right, without working up to that exalted position through a partnership.

The "Old Man" was in his element, for he had gained enormous prestige among the Boat People for the lavishness of his display. He went round rallying the guests and teasing the bridesmaids, alleging that their pretence of weeping only concealed their laughter. Strictly speaking, the men are off stage during the bride's farewell to her family, and retire to beguile the time at mahjong in the consort junk. The Master, however, exercises a general supervision and solicitude for the comfort of his guests. The women, who form by far the bulk of the congregation, formed a symphony of black and gold, for all jewellery is worn for such occasions. The Boat People put all their saving into gold or material which is their capital. Nearly every woman had a thick gold necklace, bangles and a ring. Not all is visible, for some find it undesirable to advertise their wealth, in which case the thick gold chains are buttoned under the collar, but it is there for all that. Even the adopted daughter took three ounces in raw metal to her new family, proving that it is not always a misfortune to be a "Bartered Bride".

Domestic Difficulties

In Old China one of the Seven Deadly Sins was splitting the family. As the household grew, fresh buildings were added to the compound which spread in a most uneconomical way from the point of view of utilisation of the land. When the patriarch died, the heir assumed the headship of the family, but his brothers stayed on with their families, often in spite of mutual antipathies. Should tension become unbearable all the relations and neighbours stepped in with advice to prevent a rupture, which might entail a younger brother setting up a separate establishment.

In Hong Kong, a strong adherent of this tradition was a Hoklo farmer, well past middle age, who made a home for his sister in spite of her disruptive influence on his family relations. History does not relate if the bridal chair ever stopped at his door, for he seems to have had a bias for contracting common-law alliances with widows with encumbrances in the shape of a ready-made family. The first of these was a compatriot who failed to appreciate his feckless ways, and resented the interference of her sister-in-law, who arrogated to herself the ordering of the house and proved a veritable termagant. She accordingly decided that domestic service was preferable to domestic brawls and, for ten years, supported herself as an amah. Her place was taken by a Hakka woman, also a widow with a daughter, who was not afraid of hard work, and could stand up for herself. This second investment paid dividends, for the lady was an expert pig-breeder and all-round farmer. An uncle leased a few acres of hillside and she soon made the farm into a flourishing concern.

By the time she had been a partner for nine years, the Hoklo was a comparatively wealthy man. Not only had he a good stock of Berkshire pigs and a considerable vegetable garden, but he had been able to erect a stone-built four-room house with a terrace and chicken run, and owned a herbalist's shop in the village. Here he could sit at ease and gossip, while his wife managed the estate doing a labourer's work into the bargain. The house was ideally situated on a knoll formed by a loop in a mountain stream which provided water for the crops. A flight of granite steps led down its steep banks to a plank crossing the brook which turned into a raging torrent in the summer rains. All might have gone well had not his first wife discovered his affluence and decided to exercise her marital rights.

After a desertion of ten years she returned to the household, and teamed up with the sister to make life unbearable for the cause of all the prosperity. The first dispute arose over the disposal of the Hakka's daughter by her previous marriage who was then over twenty-one. Having modern ideas, the young woman wanted a husband in her own walk of life, whereas the sister and head of the household had other plans for her future. He adopted the attitude of a Roman father with the powers of life and death over his family, and decreed that the girl should wed a rich man. A normal wedding takes money out of the family, but he was determined that this one should be the reverse as he intended to demand a large sum in the sale of a concubine. The Hakka woman and her daughter, however, took legal advice, and the girl was told that the laws of Hong Kong permitted her to dispose of her person without her step-father's interference. The wedding was paid for by the sale of a pig, the property of the mother, and not belonging to the family stock. The pig market in Hong Kong has many ramifications, and people who have

Food and gifts at a boatpeople's wedding

nothing to do with breeding or feeding can have a gamble in the trade. Anyone can buy a sucking pig cheap, and get someone to feed it on a percentage basis of the return when it is converted into pork. The only risk is that the piglet may not survive to maturity. The husband, with sister and first wife to support him, disputed the ownership and denied the validity of the Married Women's Property Act, as applicable to the situation.

The Hakka woman, however, like many of her race, was a fighter and had the best of the first two rounds. The loss of the price of the pig, coupled with that of the girl, decided the two old hags to work upon the husband to evict her. Being of thoroughly uncharitable dispositions the occasion they selected was the night of a typhoon when, after a beating, she and her six-year-old daughter were driven from the home. As she reached the top of the slope after crossing the gully, she fired a parthian shot at her husband. "You have beaten me, may Gods beat you." The divinity addressed was evidently powerful enough to influence the direction of the wind, for later in the night a terrific gust took the roof off the house, wrecked the sheds on the terrace, and left every room exposed to the driving downpour. Nothing but the pigsties were left for shelter for the night, whilst the Hakka woman and her offspring found a haven and a good meal with a compatriot amah.

The discarded wife, realising that a breach was inevitable, consulted her prosperous uncle and took out a judicial separation by which she was entitled to her personal effects, six chickens, two sows, and a litter of six small pigs. Her relative also presented her with a plot of land, which she sowed, and by her industry was able again to enter the vegetable market within six weeks.

The husband, however, was in no hurry to fulfil his part of the bargain and, as long as he withheld the property, she considered herself entitled to draw rations as a member of the family. Her visits for this purpose occasioned endless strife, for she rightly suspected the female elements of the household of stealing her effects, or of concealing them to spite her. Still she persisted, for the bonds of family are so strong that she felt that if she did not exercise her rights she would forfeit her status and claim upon her share. The climax came during her husband's absence, when the two old harridans, aided by the Hoklo's daughter-in-law, set upon her and tried to beat her up. A homeric contest ensued which ended with all parties in the police station.

The Hakka woman seems to have accepted her husband's beatings as part of her wifely obligations, but with the ladies of the family she arrogated to herself the right of defence. As the victim of a triple assault she felt she had the choice of weapons, and selected bottles. The station was full of broken glass and wounded women, with the Hakka in the cage yearning to continue the fray. None of her adversaries were in hard condition, working with their tongues rather than their hands, whilst she could lift a two-hundred-and-forty-pound pig on to her shoulder and carry it to the top of a mountain. The Law took a lenient view of her conduct, the provocation she had received being taken into consideration in mitigation of the offence, and she was released with a caution. By this time she had already built accommodation for her pigs, and had started on a house for

herself and daughter. The incident had the advantage of hastening the splitting of the home, which by now had lost much of its desirability. Shorn of her masterful influence weeds choked the bean field in front of the house, and the temporary repairs to the roof did nothing to render it waterproof. In fact it still looked as if it had been shattered by bomb blast, with odd pieces of tin plate crookedly nailed to rafters laid askew. Her solicitor had made two unsuccessful journeys to supervise the share-out, but on each occasion the husband had absented himself and had gone into hiding. Now, the Law undertook to prevent further evasion and to produce him when required.

Almost two months to a day after the deed of separation had been signed, a small procession climbed the hill to the farm—uncle and solicitor in the lead with the representative of the law, the defendant trailing behind in a dog-robberish tweed overcoat in spite of the warmth of the sun. A small crowd of neighbours, mostly with babies on their backs, had gathered to see the Hakka woman, with whom they had every sympathy, receive her rights. Everybody collected on the field about ten feet below the terrace on which the house and outbuilding stood. As the crowd grew the Hakka woman made her appearance, in working dress and bare feet, but to mark the importance of the occasion her black apron was supported by silver chains, and a new woven ribbon secured it at the back.

Her uncle having assured her that nothing she said would be held as evidence against her, she proceeded to take the centre of the stage and address her audience in the style of Mark Antony whipping up the Roman mob to avenge the murder of Caesar. In this case Brutus and Company were the visible objects of her attack and she did not spare them. The hag-like sister was soon laughed out of court and slunk away to hide her shame, but the Hoklo wife and her fifteen-year-old daughter-in-law were forced to stand their ground, as they were accused of purloining clothing and household effects whose production was in the contract. When all their sins had been laid bare to the multitude, the discarded wife entered the outhouse and pulled out the rubbish which had been set aside as her portion. She flung a tattered cloth waistcoat at the husband, which bonneted him and raised a roar of laughter. A ragged quilt was held up for inspection, as a cheap-jack advertises his wares, and was thrown into the mire. Every article of clothing only fit for the ragman, which was to have been foisted on her, was scattered in the farm-yard filth. She then proceeded to help herself to the bedding and furniture she wanted with no one daring to gainsay her.

The same procedure was adopted with the livestock. Six undersized cocks were exchanged for the same number of laying hens, without much opposition, but the pigs proved a greater obstacle. The husband had intended to substitute a new litter for those agreed on in the deed of separation, but had to retreat from his position when she pointed out that they were not even born on the date he entered into the agreement. The piglets she claimed were all fine Berkshires, and so well grown that only three instead of the usual four could be crammed into the carrying basket. With one of the farm labourers to help her, she carried off her bacon, and installed the piglets in their new sty. The "Large White" sow gave more trouble, as no basket was large enough to take her bulk, neither could two men lift her weight. With her rump sticking out, held by a sort of breeching of cord, two of the bed stretchers were lashed to the sides, enabling four bearers to effect the transfer. At least another half-hour was needed to clear up matters to everybody's satisfaction. The sour-faced daughter was despatched to her home to surrender a battered enamel basin which she had secreted, and a note was made of two bedposts and a blanket which had to be produced or replaced.

As night was closing in, the woman, in spite of her husband's protests, produced a bundle of incense sticks and approached the Earth God's shrine. This divinity having, in the man's opinion, already brought disaster upon the roof tree, he was terrified that a further appeal would complete the ruin of the home, and beseeched the woman not to curse him, enlisting the services of the uncle and lawyer on his behalf. They saw no reason to intervene, and he was much relieved when she merely informed the god of the locality of her departure from the family and notified him of her change of address. The loss of face for the man was devastating, whilst the Hakka woman's enhanced prestige was the talk of the whole village. His pecuniary loss was considerable but this was only the beginning of his decline. He had to take on two extra labourers to replace his wife, and the farm soon had a down-at-heel appearance. Fields were unweeded, and stagnant water lay everywhere, whilst the extra labour consumed the vegetables which previously found their way to the market. The splitting of the house foreshadowed its decay.

FUNERALS, REQUIEM MASSES & THE PATH TO PURGATORY

Burial Customs

In a land where such reverence is displayed to the departed it is only natural to assume that the rites connected with the dead are of primary importance. Indeed, the Chinese have a saying that the most important thing in life is to be buried properly, and sometimes the whole of the deceased's estate is swallowed up in his obsequies. The actual customs vary all over the country, and, in the Old Treaty Ports as well as in Hong Kong, the final procession has been speeded up to keep pace with the times. Paper motor-cars are burned instead of the traditional Peking cart, and bands of musicians, dressed in Western uniforms, have supplemented the gongs and clarinets of the Taoist orchestra. A motor-hearse has replaced the gigantic catafalque with its ragged bearers, and the mourning women bring up the rear in sleek limousines. Much of the barbaric splendour has passed, as the bands are more familiar with a quick-step than the Dead March, and they may even hustle the corpse to its final resting place to the strains of "Polly-olly oodle all the Day".

The first intimation the outside world receives of a death is the placing of blue and white, or yellow and blue, lanterns at the front door of the house of mourning. The red "Good Luck" strips are pasted over with white paper.

As soon as death occurs the astrologer is called in, who reckons out the day and hour on which the spirit will leave the body as a visible vapour. The family is informed of the colour and height of the manifestation, and the direction it will take. This is to ensure that it finds no obstacle in its path, and it is considered an omen of death should anyone witness its passage. Notices are consequently posted to warn off friends, and strangers, and the family withdraws to another room as the hour approaches.

Immediately after death the body is washed an uneven number of times, as odd numbers are always fortunate. For the ablutions special water is procured from a well which is dignified with the possession of a Guardian Spirit, and a lucky penny is left in exchange. This is known as "Buying the water", and is accompanied by the burning of incense, and explosion of firecrackers. After the body is bathed, the limbs, body and head are all swathed in wadding before the clothing is put on. In wealthy families the outer covering is silk, but cotton is the more usual material. No buttons are used, but the garments are fastened with ties of the same fabric. The clothing in most parts of China resembles the vestments worn by Buddhist priests, with a similar headdress, and the women are decked with a seven-cornered "Lotus Flower Hat". This head-dress is often seen on statues of Kuan Yin in Buddhist temples. The woman's hair is dressed on the top of the head, and is ornamented with gold, or jade, whilst a jade snuff bottle is often enclosed in a man's coffin. Gold leaf, or a pearl, is often placed in a man's mouth, and a twist of red paper containing the ashes of incense. The custom of putting jade in proximity with the body is very old, as cicadas fashioned of the stone, and emblematic of the resurrection, are constantly found in early tombs.

After the body is clothed, and furnished with socks and shoes, the feet are bound with a hempen cord, to prevent it leaping about should it be tormented with evil spirits. The corpse is then laid out on the bed for the inspection of friends and relatives. In Peking, in order that the family may be discovered in suitable attitudes of grief when these visitations occur, a drummer is stationed outside the front door. If the deceased is a man, the drum is placed on the left, and in the case of a woman, on the right of the entrance. On the approach of the sympathisers he announces the arrivals with a tattoo, which gives the relatives time to drop their household chores, and assume a becoming attitude indicative of their sense of bereavement. The face and body of the corpse are covered with a veil of silk or cotton, five feet long. This is turned down from the face when the remains are en-coffined. The coffin is usually on the spot at the moment of death, for it is bought as soon as it becomes obvious that recovery is unlikely. Filial sons will often procure them for their parents when they are perfectly hale and hearty, thus easing their minds on the question of their treatment after death. The action pleases and comforts them, as it ensures that proper respect will be paid to their remains, and the maker is always prepared to give storage room to his wares until they can be put to their predestined use. The Irish, also, like to be ready for emergencies, and may buy their shells thirty or forty years before they need them, if the price is attractive.

All over China a thunderstorm is dreaded whilst an occupied coffin remains in the house. In Hong Kong, if a storm is brewing, the coffin is covered with grass in the hopes that the God of Thunder (Lei Kung) will mistake it for a haystack. The coffin is placed on two stools, with the head pointing to the door, and a table, acting as an altar, is arranged with the five vessels. In the vases are blue and white paper flowers, and the two candlesticks are illuminated at night. They are re-enforced with a pagoda-shaped lampstand containing a bowl of sesame oil in which floats a wick of twisted cotton which burns during the whole lying in state. The spirit tablet, which bears the name of the deceased, and into which one of his souls has passed, is in the centre of the side of the altar next to the coffin. On the table, food is offered at each meal of which the family partakes, and a banquet is spread on those occasions when relatives are invited to pay their respects. In the case of the guests offering the feast, the food provided by the family is temporarily removed, and that brought in by the guests is substituted. The altar furniture is all rented from the funeral undertakers. On the arrival of a guest, the whole family takes up its appropriate positions around the

Funeral rites

deceased. At the left shoulder kneels the eldest son, with his wife opposite him on the right. Next follow the other sons, and then paternal nephews. Below them in rank are the grandsons and their wives, and then any unmarried daughters of the house. The guest kneels at the head of the coffin, and is served with a brass wine-cup on a tray. This is filled with wine by a serving maid, and the guest pours out a libation into a bowl set on the floor for the purpose. Three prostrations follow in which the whole family join. The guest then laments, and the family join in the chorus.

On guest days a meal is laid in the courtyard, and the strangers sit down six to a table, the sexes being separated. When all have taken their place, one of the sons, or failing a son a nephew, goes to each of the men's tables, and prostrates himself. The women are similarly saluted by one of the wives. Gifts are always taken by the visitors in the shape of money in a yellow envelope, with a strip of blue paper to indicate mourning. Other gifts in the form of banners, or scrolls, may be presented to the deceased. These carry inscriptions such as "May the soul return to the Western Heaven", and are intended to be carried in the funeral procession, where they are burned after the committal service. Other gifts are gold and silver paper money, paper carts and horses, and all those concomitants which lend to the splendour of the final cortège.

Before there can be any thought of burial, several specialists have to be consulted. The religious authorities determine, according to the means of the family, the number of masses which must be sung to ensure an easy entrance into the Western Heaven. Normally the virtues of the deceased are extolled but, should he have been a notorious evil-liver, the services of the priests are devoted to putting up a plea in mitigation, and they implore the bad spirits to release the soul of their client, and show leniency in their punishments.

The Feng Shui adept determines, from the horoscope of the departed, the most favourable site for interment. Her stars being propitious, a secondary wife may thus be allotted the luckiest plot in the family cemetery, to the mortification of the First Lady, and the delights of the local gossips. The Diviner is also called in to consult the spirits of the tenants of the graveyard, and obtain their acquiescence to the proposed arrangements. As there is always a certain amount of circumlocution in the transaction of Chinese business, and it is essential to preserve the usual forms of politeness, inquiries as to the comfort of the ancestors precede the request for their permission. In the case of the burial of the second wife of a pre-deceased Hakka, the spirit of his original spouse declared that she was delighted with her hillside tomb overlooking Aberdeen, and that her legs were so strengthened that she found no difficulty in making the ascent. Her husband, however, was rather peevish, as the photograph which identified his grave had yellowed with exposure. He requested that two palm trees be planted to shade the grave, and complained bitterly that it had not been swept at the Ch'ing Ming Festival. He said that he realised that it was the Hakka custom to defer this annual ceremony until the Moon Festival, but that he felt neglected when all the surrounding graves had their visitors in the spring, and that he had lost face. As he raised no objection to his reunion with his second wife, there was no necessity for an alteration in procedure.

When the days set apart for the masses for the soul are ended, the family prepares the paper offerings representing the objects with which the deceased was familiar in life. Servants, with names attached, carts or motor-cars, horses and rickshaws are got ready for his use in the after-world. Friends and relatives also contribute to the increase of his comfort, and the enhancement of his importance in nether world society. Before sun-down, on the eve of the funeral, these objects are taken into the street, or to an open space, and are burned. An attendant beats them with a long pole to prevent the intrusion of wandering spirits who might misappropriate property which was not intended for their use. In Hong Kong, special incinerators are provided by the authorities to prevent risks of fire from flying sparks. Boiled rice and water is often scattered on the bonfire to distract the attention of the Hungry Ghosts from the belongings of the deceased.

Chinese coffins are very large, and in some of the tenement houses in Hong Kong the staircases are too narrow to allow them being manoeuvred down to street level. In this case, a bamboo ramp is erected outside the building giving access to the room in which the body lies, and the window is enlarged to permit the exit of the coffin. On the morning of the funeral the priests, both Buddhist and Taoist, chant the offices for the dead whilst the relatives kou t'ou and weep. The coffin is carried out, always head first, and is placed in the catafalque, or hearse in the case of Hong Kong. This custom of proceeding head first accounts for the extraordinary loop of railway at Tang Ku, the Port of Tientsin. A Manchu Prince's coffin was being sent by rail from Peking to the ancestral burial ground at Mukden. Normally, the train, on reaching Tang Ku, took a fresh locomotive on the rear end, and proceeded on its journey tail first. As the coffin could not be taken out and turned round, a special loop had to be constructed to conform with Chinese custom.

When the coffin reaches the door, the youngest son breaks an earthenware saucer at its head, to provide the occupant with a drinking utensil in the other world. These saucers are part of the funeral furnishings, and have a hole in them. As all water wasted during life has to be drunk after death, the hole ensures that a certain amount of it will run away, and that the deceased will escape part of the penalty for his thriftlessness.

The bearers of the coffin are always in multiples of eight when the catafalque is used, the smallest number being thirty-two, and the largest eighty. The sedan-chair of the deceased is carried in front of the coffin, and his car, or carriage, also precedes it. The soul is supposed to ride in this, and is nowadays represented by a photograph. In the North, a white wand contained the spirit, except in the case of a Honan man, where a white cock was carried in the procession. It had no sacred significance after the interment of the body, when the soul took up its residence in the cemetery, and usually became a perquisite of the bearers, or rather the man who directed their motions by clapping together two slabs of wood.

In the procession are men and boys carrying banners with eulogies of the deceased, umbrellas, lanterns, paper flowers, and sometimes animals made of cypress twigs for burning at the grave. A noted general may even have a whole squadron of life-sized paper cavalry to

Mourners at a funeral

escort him to the tomb. At intervals along the route, particularly at cross-roads, paper cash is flung into the air to distract the attention of malignant wandering spirits.

The men mourners walk immediately in front of the coffin, the eldest son being held under the arms by two of the other mourners to sustain him in his grief. Sometimes a white screen hems him in, and conceals him from the vulgar gaze. He carries in his hand a three-pronged banner bearing the name of the deceased. If there be a second son, he carries a small shrine with a paper tablet also inscribed with his father's name. These objects are burned at the graveside with the other articles borne in the procession.

The women mourners follow the coffin in cars or carts, in strict order of precedence. The wife comes first, and then the eldest son's wife followed by the other daughters-in-law. Then the wives of paternal nephews, and finally the wives of the grandchildren. All the carts of the close relatives are white covered, but those of the grandsons' wives are enlivened with a red pomegranate flower, pinned on the left side for a grandfather, and on the right if a grandmother is being mourned. Married daughters ride in carts with blue covers, with a band of white calico round them as a mourning emblem.

On arrival at the cemetery, the coffin is lowered into the grave, and the diviner invites the relatives to satisfy themselves of its suitability. The leader of the bearers gives the signal for the mourners to group themselves around the grave, where they prostrate themselves, while the band obliges with a dirge. Each member of the family contributes a handful of earth which is scattered on the coffin, and relatives and friends join in this last tribute to the dead. All weep and wail in taking leave of the deceased, while a bonfire of the paper articles is made at the graveside. As the flames die down, the mourners turn, and the ceremony is ended.

Requiem Masses

The reverence of the Chinese for the dead is exemplified by the elaborate ceremonies held on certain fixed days after the decease, for the comfort of the soul on its journey to its final destination. No expense is spared to ensure its salvation, and both Buddhist and Taoist priests are engaged to bestow the advantages of their religions. As regards the former, nuns are considered more efficacious than priests and command increased emoluments. Most foreigners must have heard their low chants accompanied by tinkling music, through the open windows on a summer night, and have found sleep, regardless of the fact that the service continued till daybreak. It is impossible to describe the ceremonies in detail, for it is a twenty-four-hour affair and each incident has its own significance. The Chinese know them all, and are quick to comment if any particular ceremony is omitted. Guests are welcome, as they do honour to the bereaved family, and give face to the departed.

One day in October the matriarch of a well-to-do pig-jobber family in T'ai Tam departed this life, and the astrologer pronounced that the hour of her death was most auspicious. Seven is a lucky number, so that dates for the commemoration services were fixed for the 21st,

35th and 49th days after the demise. The eldest son was to pay all expenses for the first and third celebration and the women of the family for the second. In their case everything must come from their private purse. Rice, for instance, is common to the household, but that used for this occasion must be bought outside. Similarly the water for cooking must not go through the family meter, for the head of the household pays the bill.

The ceremonies of the three-times-seven began at daybreak. An annexe of bamboo scaffolding had been erected in the yard against the front door, and protected from the weather by a tarpaulin roof. The walls were formed of blue cloth hangings with gold characters interspersed with ornaments. Against the north wall was an altar with sacrifices laid out, and a sacred picture as a reredos. In addition to the lavish offerings of duck, chicken and pork, were the two hands surmounting a pile of dumplings, and a real pig's head, instead of the dough facsimile used at the festival of the Hungry Ghosts. Along the south wall of the annexe was an ordinary barrack-room table on trestles to accommodate five Buddhist nuns with shaven heads, dressed in the sober robes of their order. Various properties from the paper shop occupied most of the rest of the space, to which finishing touches were later put by the Taoist priest when not occupied in his religious exercises. Two round lanterns flanked the doorway to the main reception room of the house and, in the place of honour on their left, the deceased's personal lantern with the characters P'an Mother (潘母孝金) in blue. The leader of the nuns sat at the end of the table and, propped against the wall behind her, were two staves, like bishop's croziers, from which depended paper crowns ornamented with longevity emblems and bats for happiness. From the centre of each hung a silk scroll with the deceased's posthumous name and titles. These staves represent the soul, the white one that of the dead, and the red its re-birth. In the North, only the white wand is carried at the funeral and, in the case of a Honan man buried outside his own province, a white cock accompanies the coffin to the grave.

In the reception room there were two altars with paper shrines, one enclosing the tablet of the deceased and the other that of the House Gods. A yellow-robed Taoist priest stood at the left of the main altar, whilst in front of it knelt the family ranged in degree of relationship. The immediate descendants wore coarse, white cloth robes with pointed cowls concealing the face to the chin. The grandchildren simply had a broad band of the same material round the forehead, knotted behind; the mourning of the boys being relieved by a small oblong flash of red in the centre. Seventeen people in all were in mourning, including a small baby.

As soon as this service ended the family removed their mourning robes, and the eldest son went the round of the guests to welcome them, providing tea, fruit, sweet cakes and cigarettes, and thanking them for their sympathy in coming to support him. The Taoist priest, having folded up his robes, became the expert paper-shop man, and set to work making black and gold trunks for the clothing, and the construction of the gold and silver mines. These are two pillar-like structures of flowered paper with a projecting framework on top, in which crumpled gold and silver paper is arranged to represent a rock. When wired paper flowers are inserted, the whole is surmounted by a flag with the inscription "The P'an family Gold (or Silver) Mine" (潘府金礦). In the North their use is usually confined to women's funerals, but here they are common to both sexes.

One elaborate edifice, four feet six inches high, represents the gate in a city wall. It is painted to give the appearance of being constructed of red brick with white pointing and has two black doors with gilt bosses, and lion-head knockers. On a balcony above is the figure of a black-faced demon, dressed in a white nightshirt with kimono sleeves, stretching out his arms to welcome in the spirit of the dead. On the lintel is a plaque identifying the entrance to the "City of Hell", and at the right side the inscription "Through the gate of the Immortal palace to Hades" (仙府門通渺冥).

In addition to paper clothing an actual dress of the old lady was burned that something intimate might accompany her. It was not her best nor her working attire, but a suit which she wore on less formal occasions.

Later in the evening, the nuns took over, and the Buddhist service began. They came from Shanghai, and their Order is evidently not very strict. They smoked endless cigarettes, which are forbidden in religious establishments here, and had not abandoned all feminine frivolities. The officiant recited from a red-cover manual

Chief mourner accompanying the spirit of the deceased

entitled the "Pure Buddha's Scriptures", and her four supporters responded in a chant, accompanied by a man with a drum and another with a clarinet. This short service was the preparation of the soul for the journey to purgatory, and the officiant finally held up the staves over the table, the white first, and then the red, whilst the dedicatory words were pronounced over them.

Meanwhile, outside in the yard, the road to purgatory was being prepared. A long strip of white cloth is laid on a table, the broadest part being the middle whilst sloping planks at either end form ramps up and down which the soul must pass. At intervals all along this way banknotes are pinned for the spirit's travelling expenses, and a large bowl with candles and incense is placed under the table for illumination. The Hakka onlookers were critical of the arrangements as, according to their custom, the strip of cloth should be much longer, and a sand-castle with candles and incense surrounded with ducks' eggs should be provided for light refreshments of the travelling soul. In a corner of the yard stood a paper model of a house two storeys high with a walled garden in front of the porch planted with red rosebushes. The building was an imposing modern-style family mansion, with flat roof and penthouse, whose plans would certainly have been approved by the Public Works Department. Beside it was a green carrying-chair with two life-sized bearers in yellow uniform edged with scarlet and old-fashioned mandarin official hats.

Whilst the dedication of the soul was proceeding the family resumed its mourning, and formed a procession headed by the eldest grandchild who placed himself with the deceased's personal lantern at the far end of the Spirit Road to light the way. The younger generation grouped themselves behind the link bearer, whilst the immediate descendants, including one adopted son, formed a close escort to the soul. The shrine containing the spirit tablet was placed on the ascending end of the ramp with the second son on the right, holding the white staff, and the heir on the left, with the red. The whole procession chanted in unison accompanied by the band, and moved slowly forward by stages with halts in between. According to the Hakka tradition this was a jerky procedure, which spoiled the effect and the whole motion should be performed at a uniform creep. As it was, the journey occupied a quarter of an hour before the end of the descending ramp was reached, and the shrine was carried back to its altar.

As soon as the shrine with the ancestral tablet had been restored to its place in what had been the bedroom of the deceased, lay helpers started to prepare the nuns' table for the Mass which continues till daybreak. A white cloth was laid, with a frontal of red satin embroidered with a phoenix on a rock surrounded by peonies, facing the door of the mortuary chapel. A small statuette of Kuan Yin occupied a position near the centre of the table facing the shrine of the deceased. In front of the Goddess were arranged small stands, each covered with a fringed cloth on which were placed eight valuable objects. These are not the conventional "Eight precious things" of Buddhism, but are curios mostly of quite good quality. Two bits of jade, a carving in agate, a Ming porcelain cup, a snuff-bottle and a bronze incense-burner were in impeccable taste, but the set was spoiled by the inclusion of a wretched Japanese liqueur glass with a green stem.

The coffin is always carried out head first

Self-dedication of the officiating nun

In front of the officiating nun were placed two bowls of uncooked rice and a silver vase in addition to her breviary bound in red paper. Before robing herself in the vestments appropriate to celebrating the Eucharist, the officiant performed a short service of self-dedication at the side of the table, where a clean bamboo mat had been spread on the earth floor. The statuette of Kuan Yin had been turned a quarter circle so as to face her. Removing her ordinary habit and shoes, she stood facing the divinity in a flowing white robe with long sleeves, and well-fitting nylon stockings of an expensive brand. Two nuns supported her on either side, making the responses as she intoned the preliminary prayers of the ante-Communion. When kneeling to perform the prostrations the officiant laid in front of her a Parma-violet coloured stole on which she placed her forehead. She was then furnished with a scarlet robe, worn so as to leave the right arm free, though covered with the long white sleeve of the undergarment. A chant in unison ensued, the officiant holding the Dragon incense-burner at first, and then making the nine-fold prostrations. Before taking her seat at the head of the table a procession was formed, and the altar in the annexe with the dough hands and pig's face was censed. Prior to this ceremony a scroll depicting a dancing figure holding aloft the "Wheel of the Law" was hung behind the altar. This is known as the "Dispenser of clothing, and distributor of nourishment" (分衣施食). The officiant then put on the embroidered biretta which concealed her shaven head and greatly enhanced the attractiveness of her appearance. Whilst the nun on her right led the chant, holding the incense burner, she made the responses. The five-pointed biretta, reserved for the Eucharist, was

then produced from a plastic bag and placed before the officiant, whilst she rose to her feet and covered her face with her left sleeve. On folding this back into place she took the incense burner and led a chant accompanied by her four supporters.

Still standing she performed the gestures of the hands, used at the feast of the Hungry Ghosts, poured liquid from a flagon into the chalice, and consecrated the rice by tracing characters over it with her middle finger. The choir of nuns accompanied the consecration with a low chant. They were apt servers, and always had the right article to hand at the appropriate moment. One of them now produced a small looking-glass in an ornate plastic frame, which was passed up as soon as the officiant had blessed the Eucharistic biretta and had tried it to her forehead. She was taking no risks that her headdress was not on straight.

Now in full canonicals, which are exceedingly becoming, the officiant issues the "invitation to the feast". This is a personal appeal to the departed to partake of the pure contents of the vessels before her, and her invitation is reinforced by the wailing of the bereaved family in front of the Spirit tablet. The women of the party implore the soul to return, tempting her by a recital of the favourite foods prepared especially on her account, and telling her that she cannot possibly disappoint the guests gathered together in her honour. Every inducement to appear is proffered, and the old lady would be stony-hearted indeed to withhold her presence from the party. The rest of the proceedings till dawn resemble an Irish wake, with the continual keening of the women, and the soft chant of the nuns accompanied by their tinkling music. One taps on the fish-head drum, another plays the chimes, whilst the officiant punctuates her

Officiating nun

intoning with two bells surmounted by the thunderbolt emblem. No one sleeps a wink but, as the sky shows the first signs of the false dawn, the old lady's household effects for her after-life follow her in a gigantic conflagration. Her mansion and sedan chair, the gold and silver mine, and the gate to the palace of the Immortals are transmuted into smoke and ashes. The trunks containing her clothing and personal effects, plus her celestial bank balance, follow by the same ascending path.

As the sun rises the family set about the distribution of the funeral baked meats, part of which were consumed in a communal feast, and part were dispatched to the houses of guests who honoured the ceremony with their presence. The latter were accompanied by a white envelope with a design in red roughly stamped, and consisting of a Manchurian crane, emblem of longevity, holding a string of coins in its claws. Below were two peaches, inscribed "Long Life" and "Money", whilst the sides were decorated with the pine symbol of a vigorous old age. These gifts must not be acknowledged by "lucky money", neither is any portion returned as is usual with a gift of food.

The family had a very short respite after its night of exertion, for it was now the 21st day and the Old Lady's spirit was receiving callers. The Village Elders arrived to pay their respects to her tablet, and compliment her with an honorific banner, which had be hung in a place of honour. After much heart-searching it was finally placed on the outside wall of the house on the left of the personal lantern. All friends of the family and acquaintances who attended the requiem were escorted before the shrine containing the Spirit tablet, where they bowed three times, before withdrawing to refreshments of tea and fruit in the annexe. Each was presented with "lucky money" wrapped in white paper. The latter was to be discarded and thrown away immediately after leaving the house of sorrow, to shake off the signs of mourning, and the money to be spent on sweets before returning home.

The attitude of Chinese Christians to this Devil worship, as they call it, is inconsistent. Devil, in the Western sense, is not the word to apply to a spirit. Confucius can by no tolerant religion be classified as a demon, which implies malignancy, yet he is a "Kuei" (鬼), but neither a Hsien (仙), Immortal, nor a Ti (帝), God. To stand aloof in times of sorrow or rejoicing is disruptive of family unity, the basis of Chinese society. With their genius for compromise a *modus vivendi* has been worked out which makes for harmony all round. Though they may not buy the sacrificial offerings, it is no concern of theirs how their monetary contribution is expended. They refrain from burning the clothing, but holding the blazing pile down with a stick to prevent a general conflagration is a meritorious act. They draw the line, however, in joining the feast, for they are as certain as any pagan, as they crudely put it, the Old Lady has licked over all the offerings and abstracted their nutritive value.

Only the most fanatical keep away, for the party spirit is very strong, and the Chinese are essentially gregarious. The festivals make a break in the dull monotony of the daily task, and an extra picnic like a wedding or a funeral is always a windfall.

They even believe that if the night is very still, crunching and nibbling are distinctly audible; the simpler explanation of rats and mice being responsible for the attentions to the unguarded food is not entertained. Should any participant be taken ill, as might easily happen from fly contamination, it is believed that the victim has aroused the animosity of the deceased, either through incompatibility of the Eight Characters, under which they were born, or from some breach of respect at the funeral ceremonies. In this case the offender must put him or herself right with the deceased by paying a special visit to burn incense and perform the prostrations before the tablet. Should the defunct person have passed away at a ripe old age, after a hale and hearty life, the consumption of sacrifices of which its spirit has partaken is believed to confer similar qualities on those who attend the service.

The second requiem, paid for by the women of the family, was not nearly so lavishly mounted as that provided by the heir. It was celebrated on the thirty-fifth day after the decease (7 × 5), according to the astrologer's prescription. The same bamboo annexe had been erected but its roof and walls were bare tarpaulins, with no inside hangings to conceal their nakedness. At the

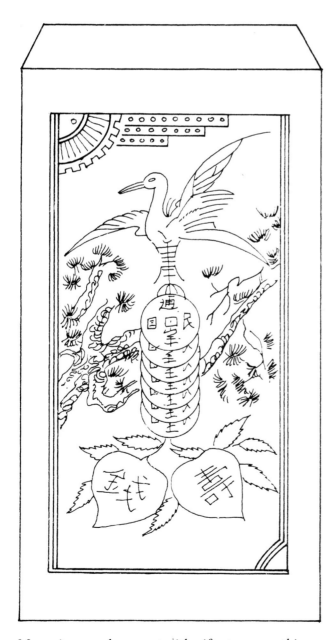

Mourning envelope sent with gifts to sympathisers

entrance was mounted an effigy of the Manchurian crane with its scarlet crest, symbolising longevity, and from its beak depended three concentric rings of bamboo, each fringed with strips of green, yellow and red paper. The central ring was the largest and carried four paper banners, while from the lower circle hung a scarlet paper bucket.

This is an elaborate version of the "Spirit calling banner" (Chao Hun Fan 招魂旛), a feature of all communications with the spirit world.

Just behind, and slightly concealed by this ornament, stood a green patterned paper replica of the Gate to Hell, its flags made of Christmas wrapping-paper decorated with poinsettia. Two paper sedan-chairs, each with a pair of bearers, were parked on the other side of the entrance.

Against the north wall of the annexe was an ordinary square table, acting as altar, with candles and incense, and a teapot for the refreshment of the clergy and guests. Behind it, hung on the wall, was a scroll depicting the fierce-looking dancer, holding aloft in his right hand the Wheel of the Law. His presence is evidently essential to the ritual for, on the previous occasion, the service was delayed until the scroll could be found and installed in its proper place. The degree of tolerance of the Chinese was manifested by the fact that, whilst the Buddhist nuns chanted their liturgy, a Taoist priest was comforting the stricken relatives in the inner sanctuary. The five nuns occupied a long table on the south side of the annexe, arranged as for the previous service. Only, a better wine-glass had been substituted for that which figured in the previous service.

The mourners, all of them women, had mostly discarded the full garments of woe, and were without the coarse white hoods, substituting at the most solemn moments a square of cloth of the same material. The only men taking part were the Taoist priest, and the band, who were reinforced by a flautist in addition to the usual drum and clarinet. The nuns, considering that they had given a practically continuous performance since early morning, were remarkably alert when they started the celebration of the Mass with the self-dedication of the officiant. The Chinese are not the least impressed by the solemnity of a religious service. As long as the prescribed prayers are said with their accompanying ritual, they betray little sign of reverence. This attitude was exemplified by an incident which took place during the service. The production of a sketch-book always attracts an audience. First the children shyly peer over the artist's shoulder, and, if they recognise a likeness, the fact goes round like wildfire. Soon the elders join in, and forget all about the rival entertainment. The contagion spreads to the priests, or nuns, and a request is made to examine their own portraits, for their comparative immobility singles them out as natural models. The passing of the pencil studies round the table, accompanied by a mob of chattering women and children, practically disrupted the devotions. The nuns were all giggling, and the officiant who had had the lion's share of the artist's attentions performed superhuman efforts in keeping up the chant, manipulating two bells, and examining her portraits with every outward sign of appreciation. Appearances evidently are never neglected with this lady, all of whose vestments are of the finest quality, her red robe being secured by a handsome green jade ring.

During a recess in the services in the afternoon she made use of the occasion to lead her troop to the T'ien Hou Temple to strengthen their spiritual powers by a visit to the shrine of Kuan Yin, who, in most Taoist temples, ranks with, but after, the Queen of Heaven. The shaven-headed nuns made this pilgrimage in ordinary everybody dress, with wide black trousers, those of their leader being of the best-quality patterned silk.

After the consecration of the sacred elements, by the tracing of characters with the third finger dipped in the chalice over the rice and wine, the officiant intoned the invitation of the spirit to the feast. The chant was echoed by the mourners in the inner chamber, kneeling, or seated, before the main shrine containing the ancestral tablet. Candles sweated on the altar which was well stocked with offerings of fruit, roast pork, and the special chicken with the head left on and the neck forming a curve like a swan. The mourners took it in turns to commune with the spirit, wearing different degrees of mourning according to the closeness of relationship. The nearest had the full white coat, without the hood, but others contented themselves with a white cloth on the head, and some keened in their ordinary best clothes with appropriately placed white or blue knots in their hair. Rarely more than two at a time knelt before the altar. The rest circulated in the annexe with the chanting nuns attending to guests or putting sleepy babies to bed.

Proceedings were cut short by the approach of a typhoon. The rising wind first blew over the white crane, which hung head downwards, whilst the red bucket depending from its beak performed a fantastic dance. As the rain started well before dawn, a consultation was held in which it was decided to advance the time for the burning of the properties as, once soaked, incomplete combustion was certain to deprive the deceased of a portion of her dues. The chair-bearers seemed likely to prove particularly intractable, and great loss of face would have accrued to the old lady were she to be reduced to pedestrian status.

The guests dispersed after the bonfire, but the family feast was deferred, as usual, till daybreak. By the time that the period for digestion and rest had elapsed the wind had increased to gale force, with promise of more to come. Fine rain, driving in horizontal sheets, blotted out all visibility, and villagers not under the necessity of feeding pigs secured their houses against the typhoon. The customary visit to pay respects to the deceased had to be abandoned, and the complimentary distribution of portions of the feast to contributors was deferred until the weather abated. Very strict rules govern this return of courtesies. Gifts in kind, of paper money and clothing and food, are accepted in their entirety, but a portion of the latter is returned with the white envelope and "lucky money" on the day of the feast. If a monetary contribution for general expenses is sent, the full half must be returned, together with a proportionate share of the sacrifices.

There is an element of mystery about the nuns who are practically always employed for these requiem masses. In South China, at any rate, it is hard to say where Buddhism and Taoism begin or end, as each religion has borrowed so much from the other. It is

Memorial services

doubtful, however, if any orthodox Buddhist community would recognise the sisters who hold these services for they are not strict vegetarians, neither have they submitted to one of the inevitable features of the consecration where seven pastilles are burned on the shaven head, leaving lifelong scars. Kuan Yin, however, is their patroness, and the canon they follow is entitled the Pure Buddhist Scriptures. Their efficacy is unquestioned by the layman, who regards them as far more potent than the priests, and they consequently command a higher tariff. All that can be said is that they satisfy a legitimate need, in accordance with the law of supply and demand.

Chinese families are often on the ragged edge of bankruptcy in ensuring that their dead are well disposed, partly from a desire to omit no ceremony that might foster their security in the after-life, and partly to impress their neighbours. It was not surprising that, when the day for the celebration of the "Seven times seven" farewell arrived, the heir had to take stock of his outgoing and, finding he was considerably in debt, he decided to reduce expenditure to the minimum consistent with decency. The nuns were dispensed with as their fee is always high, and the entertainment for five over a period of twenty-four hours entails a considerable outlay. A single Taoist priest was engaged to conduct the last rites, which are performed on the vigil of the Feast to celebrate the attainment of the rank of worshipful ancestor by the defunct.

The annexe was not rigged up, but the main doorway was illuminated by the same large lanterns, with the Old Lady's personal lamp on the left. Her shrine of red and gold paper remained in the same place, in what had been her bedroom, but the offerings on the altar before it were reduced in number. A little before midnight, the priest robed and the whole family assumed full mourning clothes, except for the smaller children who wore the usual white band around the forehead. A small table was placed in the yard, immediately outside the front door, with candles, incense, three wine-cups and pairs of chopsticks, whilst the offerings consisted of a plate of apples, persimmons and round cakes. The priest, tinkling

a bell, started his chant behind the altar, the eldest son acted as server, pouring out the wine, whilst the family supported him on the threshold or within the room. This short service lasted about ten minutes after which the whole congregation adjourned to the death chamber and knelt before the altar in order of seniority. The priest recited his office on the right of the altar, the family making the responses. The children are first divested of their mourning, then the women, and finally the men, the son being the last to remove his hood and coarse white robe. Under the altar was placed a red-and-gold paper trunk containing clothing for the deceased, and addressed to her in the underworld. This was now carried out into the yard together with several skips of paper ingots. The priests, bearing a flaming piece of paper lighted from the oil-lamp on the altar, set fire to the pile, intoning the prayers for its safe delivery. The death chamber now had to be cleared and swept of everything connected with the departed woman, and it is evident that in former days all her utensils went into the fire. The extravagance of this gesture is now generally recognised, so the table used as the altar, with her chair and stool, were simply passed over the blaze and then carried back to the house. Her shoes, however, were consigned to the flames, as was the earthenware pot in which her daily ration of sacrificial rice was cooked.

When the flames showed signs of flagging all the candles and incense were thrown in to revive them along with the three lanterns whose inflammable nature created a most satisfactory blaze.

The last object consigned to the fire was the paper shrine in which the spirit tablet had been ensconced throughout the proceedings. This was flung in by the officiating priest himself, who departed at a run to catch the last bus, after a hasty assurance to the family that the Old Lady would have good luck. As he was ignorant of the Hakka language, he failed to appreciate the roar of laughter at his expense when an onlooker called after him, "May her spirit pursue you".

A general cleansing then takes place in the house, and the death chamber is meticulously scrubbed out and

A funeral procession

swept. The women wash their hair, and the heads of their children. Dishevelled hair is a fairly general sign of mourning throughout the Orient. The Chinese do not assist nature by the addition of ashes, but seven weeks' abstention from the attentions of the barber produces a sufficiently unkempt appearance among the men.

The morrow of this final parting is a day of rejoicing, for the deceased is about to join the ancestors and will be partaker of a huge feast held in honour of that event.

The priest for this occasion must not be the same as the officiant in the days of mourning.

As the dinner of six tables was to take place at noon, the service to elevate the deceased to the gods began half an hour earlier. Her bedroom was swept and garnished, and filled mainly with paper envelopes containing clothing and skips full of ingots of gold and silver foil. The altar was erected just opposite the front door with a shelf above for the spirit tablet. The offerings consisted of roast pork, a chicken, green onions, pink cakes, and, as it was near the Old Lady's birthday, a special pile of cakes in the form of the peach, emblem of long life.

The Spirit tablet, framed in red cloth with gold ornaments at the top, was placed on a black-and-gold lacquer tray with a scarlet interior. This contained a lump of yeast, dried lichees, unhusked rice, green and red beans, and split lotus-seeds. The priest proceeded to decorate the ornaments on the tablet with small sprigs of cypress as symbols of longevity. About twenty envelopes containing paper clothing were then addressed by him to the deceased, the names of the senders being endorsed on the yellow forwarding slip, a custom much the same as the Western habit of attaching a visiting card to a wreath sent to a funeral. One of the packets was embellished by a number of prints of jewellery and personal ornaments pinned on to the envelope, from some well-wisher who desired her old acquaintance to present an opulent appearance in purgatory.

The senior members of the family then started preparing the altar by lighting the candles, and igniting thick sticks of incense at the oil-lamp upon it. All the household gods were appraised of the ceremony by candles and sticks of incense before their shrines. Under the altar itself was the home of the House God, whilst the T'ien Kuan (天官), Source of Happiness, had his niche on the left door-post. The Earth God's incense burner was just to the left of the door, below the spot where the old lady's lantern had been suspended.

The priest, robed in crimson with blue and gold patches embroidered with the Trigrams, after a short prayer, took the Spirit tablet from the lacquer tray and carried it into the sunlit yard. This is the supreme moment of the service, when the spirit is elevated from mortality to immortality by the addition of a dot to the character Wang (王), Prince, which changes it into Chu (主), Lord. A chicken, with its legs tied, had been placed in readiness under the altar to commune with the House Gods until its services were required. It was now brought out by the heir who pricked the comb enough to draw blood. The priest, dipping his brush in the scarlet fluid, transformed the character, and carried the tablet back to the altar. The eldest son then took it from his hands and placed it reverently upon the shelf above, to receive the homage of the family. He was the first to kneel and salute his ancestor with the full prostrations, and the family followed in order of senior-

ity. All women wearing silver earrings removed them and substituted gold, which entailed a certain amount of borrowing, for every honour must be accorded to the newly created divinity.

The new mistress of the house donned a black silk skirt obviously made for the occasion, for the only pretence at fitting the figure was a draw-string round the waist. It is an old Hakka custom that a skirt must be worn when the ceremonial tea is served to the matriarch so, as the deceased's birthday was advanced to coincide with the end of the period of mourning, her spirit tablet was honoured exactly as if she had still been alive. There being no point in permanently sacrificing good material, the garment had simply been tacked together, so that it could be unpicked without damage for conversion into trousers or a jacket. After the tea ceremony, the senior lady stationed herself by a tray containing "lucky money" in red paper wrappings and handed a packet to each of the worshippers as they rose from their prostrations. Only the intimate members of the family received the dole from her hands, more distant relatives taking their package from the tray.

The deceased had not been forgotten in this distribution, for the red paper framing her tablet had been lined with eleven ten-cent pieces.

As soon as the homage is completed the priest performs the final ceremonies of purification of the premises after death. A glass of pure water is placed on the altar and consecrated. After the appropriate prayers, paper is burned in all the corners of the room, and the officiant dips his third finger in the holy water, sprinkling the altar, sacrifices and the floor. Among the offerings to the House Gods below the altar are five old coins with the square hole in the centre, lying on top of the rice. These are sprinkled and picked out to be thrown on the floor to bring back money to the house. Finally a list of the contributors is read that their merits may be brought to the notice of the departed.

It only remains to despatch the clothing, money and gifts by burning in the court-yard. With the priest chanting an invocation for safe delivery each packet is placed in the brazier and the fire is started by the officiant. The ceremony takes a considerable time for, not only have the deceased's wants to be satisfied, but a despatch must be made to other dead members of the family lest their feelings be hurt by being neglected. In this case there was an argument about the existence of some misty grandfather who was finally propitiated by the hasty purchase of a packet in the village, very inferior in quality to the town-made products addressed to his relatives. It is most important that every scrap of paper should be consumed, so every bit scattered by the wind is retrieved and returned to the bonfire. When the last flame has died down the eldest son brings out a bunch of fire-crackers whose explosion scares off marauding devils and marks the end of the ceremony.

Urn Burial

Apart from the Monastic orders the Chinese do not practise urn burial. Where it is possible everyone has more than his six feet of earth, and much valuable agricultural land has cheated the plough until the family died out and the cemetery, for want of a claimant, was absorbed by a neighbouring farmer. Hong Kong has its special problem, for the configuration of the ground militates against building and the raising of sufficient crops to support the teeming population. A vast proportion of the area consists of granite hills, which centuries of deforestation before the British rule have stripped of every cultivable patch of earth, through erosion. The living must be considered before the dead so, in the public cemeteries, it is only possible to grant a lease, and not a freehold. Every six years there is an exhumation, and the bones are handed over to the relatives, who make their own arrangements for their disposal. Ancestral worship dictates that the graves must be tended, and it is essential to know their exact location, not only for this purpose, but for communication with the spirit of the deceased through a medium. The bones, received from the authorities, are placed in an earthenware urn, usually with a brown or green glaze, and are transported to some waste spot on a hillside. Judging by their usual location a Feng Shui man is employed to select a favourable spot, for they are nearly always sheltered from the north by a steep slope, whilst they face the sea, or other moving water such as a stream.

They are tended twice a year, at Ch'ing Ming in the spring, and on the 9th of the Ninth Moon in the autumn. Candles are lit and incense burned after which a sacrifice is presented and a bonfire is made of paper clothing and money for expenses in the underworld. If the site is visited shortly after one of these ceremonies it will be observed that on top of the urn is a bundle of paper, weighted down by a stone. This paper money is intended to distract the attention of Hungry Ghosts and malignant spirits who are liable to intercept gifts despatched to the underworld for more fortunate souls.

If a good coffin has been provided it takes six years for the corpse to disintegrate, and even seven for a superior article. In this case the coffin may be returned to the undertaker at a discount and, after reconditioning, it serves for another client. The eldest son holds the burial certificate, and it is his duty to take it to the Registry to apply for an exhumation order. When the permit has been received the whole family, accompanied by the coffin-maker, repairs to the cemetery, not so much out of respect to the deceased as to ensure there is no

possible error in identification. Someone is certain to recognise the exact locality of the grave, and to remember the articles of jewellery and jade which were interred with the body. It would be disastrous to transfer the solicitation for the comfort of the dead to an alien set of bones. The valuables contained in the coffin are first removed and revert to the family. If there is a grandson available the skull is handed to him to hold in a fold of his gown whilst the bones are being removed. Otherwise the heir is responsible for this duty. Great care is taken in assembling the skeleton. The large bones are easily identifiable, but the small ones in the hands and feet might get mixed, so they are separated out and, after cleaning, are wrapped in paper and labelled. The cleansing is now done with sandpaper, though originally probably sand alone was used as an abrasive. It is enjoined that the greatest reverence should be shown during this operation, as the spirit will pursue anyone who plays with the bones. A case is cited of an uncle who, fortified for the ordeal of an exhumation with strong liquor, stirred up the urn with a stick, and was smitten shortly afterwards with a paralytic stroke. Though probably attributable to his alcoholic content, the family firmly believes that the bones were taking their revenge for the sacrilege, and that his physical disability stems from his drunken indiscretion.

The packing of the urn is entrusted to the undertaker, who arranges its contents in the natural order with the skull on top. His fee, which covers the provision of the receptacle, consists of a sum of money, plus a tip in the form of "tea money" and a share of the refreshments. Before Hong Kong suffered from overpopulation, people selected the final resting place of their deceased relatives for their own convenience as well as that of the departed, but sites are now allotted by Government. The coffin shop arranges transportation, the cost varying with the distance, and the bones are accompanied to their final resting place by a small deputation of the family, which performs the usual ritual with candles and incense, and offers sacrifices after the installation. The urns are called Chin T'a (金塔), or "Golden pagodas", and serve the same purpose as the more imposing structures, save that they house the relics of sinners as well as saints.

The Path to Purgatory

"Facilis decensus Averno" is probably the best-known quotation from Vergil, and is generally taken to mean that the turnpike to perdition on the road through life, is easier to follow than the craggy goat path leading to the Golden Gates. Before burial the Romans placed a coin in the mouth of the corpse to pay its toll across the River of Death, and left the dread ferryman to do the rest. The Chinese, however, regard the journey as a most serious affair, in which the departed soul is in need of every human and divine aid which can be afforded. The solicitude for its welfare must be generally attributed to affection for the deceased on his journey to Purgatory, which caters for the just and the unjust alike, though in the case of the poorer classes there is a manifest desire to do the right thing lest the spirit return and plague them. If the rites are not fully observed there is always the chance that the soul may become a hungry ghost,

Burial urn

and haunt the homestead in search of a substitute, so it is highly desirable to ensure that it is safely bestowed in the custody of those who will be responsible for its maintenance.

The journey of the departed spirit is divided into seven periods of seven days, which correspond to its wanderings in the infernal regions. In the first week, when the traveller reaches the Kuei Men Kuan (鬼門關), or Demon Barrier Gate, he is beset by footpads demanding money, alleged to have been borrowed from the treasury of Hell during his previous occupancy. If he has spirit money to pay, he is allowed to pass, but if his scrip is empty, he is stripped, beaten, and heaped with indignity. Hence the burning of paper money to safeguard him against being caught without cash.

In the second week he reaches the Weigh bridge, where he is placed on the scales. The good man proves to be as light as air, but the sinner is borne down by his evil deeds, and pays for it by being sawn asunder, or ground to powder. This, however, is only a temporary expedient and a foretaste of what is to come, for he is restored, to continue his way, by a wave of the fan.

In the third week he reaches the Bad Dogs Village (惡狗村) where, if a virtuous man, he is welcomed with wagging tails, but if evil, he is set upon and torn till the blood flows in rivers.

In the fourth week he finds the Mirror of Retribution (業鏡), giving him a glimpse into what the future holds in store for him. Good is reflected in all the beauty of innocence, but the sinner sees his reincarnation portrayed as a beast. Possibly he sees a grunting swine wallowing in the mire, under the shadow of the butcher's knife, or a serpent slithering through the grass, with the hand of every man against it.

So horrified is the spirit with the vision of what is in store that in the fifth week it begs to be allowed to return to life, but the escorting God replies that it is no longer fit to mix with uncorrupted mortals. A great longing for family life then assails the unfortunate ghost, and it begs for one glimpse of the homestead it has lost. It is allowed to mount a high platform where it gets a vision of the old scene with all going about their familiar tasks, and its heart is rent at the realisation that it has irrevocably lost its place.

In the sixth week the wanderer reaches the bridge across the Inevitable River (奈河橋) which is high above the flood, filled with rapids and whirlpools. Enormous snakes raise their heads from the water searching for human flesh. At the approaches stand lictors, armed with flails and iron maces, who force travellers up the ramp to embark on the perilous crossing. Those who essay it are aware that they are doomed to inevitable destruction, for it is merely a single rope, a hundred thousand feet high and only an inch and three-tenths in width. The crossing can only be made astraddle. The good are not forced to attempt the passage, but are conducted by the "Golden Lad" and his companions on to the Fairy Bridges of gold and silver which span the river on either side of the Devil's crossing.

In the seventh week the spirit enters the realm of the Prince of the Wheel (轉輪王), to whom a petition must be presented to expedite the process of transmigration. The traveller is placed in charge of a runner, who accompanies him to the place of the Wheel. A rest house, presided over by old Mrs Meng (孟婆), is a stopping place on the journey, and passers-by are supplied with free tea. The virtuous enjoy a comfortable sensation, and are refreshed as by a cool draught, but for the evil-doers the liquid induces a state of oblivion and the past, good and bad, is wiped from their memories.

On reaching the Wheel of the Law (法輪) the subject finds himself between the revolving spokes and is whirled around. If he is permitted to escape at the top right hand corner, he discovers himself, on re-incarnation, a member of the nobility. If the exit is at the top left-hand angle, his status will be that of a widower, widow, orphan or childless. Or, he may be reborn with some physical disability such as lameness, or lack of sight. Still, he is better off than those cast off at the right hand lower corner, where he will be classed among the viviparous animals, or the lower left, where he will be hatched from an egg.

There are, however, even lower depths to which he can sink, for the bottom on the right is reserved for the reincarnation of creatures who have scales or inhabit shells, whilst the insect world is reborn from the lower left.

The spirits the Chinese call kuei (鬼), or demons, are the 'Pretas' of Indian mythology, inhabitants of the subterranean and other prisons called Ti Yu (地獄) or hell, as opposed to purgatory. Many of them formerly belonged to the world of mortals, and these haunt the places where their bodies perished. They hunger for food as, their graves being unknown, they are bereft of family care and worship at the ancestral altar. They are for ever seeking a substitute to regularise their position, but will not molest those who feed them. As they are released from hell for the whole of the Seventh Moon and return to earth, they are capable of infinite mischief if their wants remain unsatisfied. Hence, the feeding of the Hungry Ghosts by all sections of the population, and the religious services to alleviate their condition, which are the feature of the month. The sacrifices begin at the full moon but may be performed on any day until the thirtieth when all the spirits are mustered and returned to purgatory.

FENG SHUI, SPIRITUALISM, METAMORPHOSES, FOX FAIRIES

Feng Shui
(風水)

Prior to the advent of football pools, the average Englishman did not concern himself much with luck. A few superstitions lingered on. Before the motor drove the horse off the roads, it was lucky to pick up a horse-shoe, but nobody would burden himself with a discarded tyre. One avoided walking under ladders, for the good reason that there might be a careless individual with a paint-pot at a higher level. The new moon was greeted with a bow, and silver was turned in the pocket. The English have little folklore, but the Celtic element of the population preserves many more taboos. The Chinese, however, have brought them to a fine art, and have developed a science which absolutely rules their lives. Its name is Feng Shui, or the influence of wind and water.

Just over eighty years ago Dr. Ernest Eitel, of the London Mission, published a study of Feng Shui (Wind Water), or the Rudiments of Natural Science in China. The Celestial Empire, surrounded by primitive tribes, and cut off from intercourse with Western nations till the art of navigation was far advanced, evolved a system totally unlike that practised in other lands where the study of nature was pursued by practical tests and experiment. They invented no instruments to bring the heavenly bodies within the range of the human eye, abhorred collections of dried flowers and insects, and neglected the chemical analysis of inorganic substances, but evolved out of their inner consciousness a complete system of natural science, which governed their every action. Though largely empiric, and incapable of proof by Western standards, this theory preserved in Chinese Feng Shui a spirit of sacred reverence for the divine powers of nature. According to Eitel, the Chinese "see a golden thread of spiritual life running through every form of existence, and binding together, as in a living body, everything that subsists in heaven above, and on the earth below".

Though the rudiments of the science may be found in the ancient classics, the codification of the system is of comparatively recent origin. Its methods and practical application are based on the teachings of Chu Hsi (朱熹), who lived under the Sung Dynasty in the 12th and 13th centuries A.D. He traces the Creation from one abstract principle, called the "Absolute Nothing", which evolved out of itself the "Great Absolute". When this was in motion its breath and vital energy congealed to produce the male element and, when it rested, the female principle was born. As the Supreme Cause thus divided, that which was above became Heaven, and that which was below, Earth. As motion and pause succeeded one another, men and animals, vegetation and minerals took their place in nature. The perpetual energy produced by these two contending principles is the Ch'i (氣), or breath of nature. This, however, did not work spasmodi-cally, but according to certain set laws, known as Li (例), which could be traced mathematically and illustrated by diagrams exhibiting the numerical proportions of the universe, Shu (数). The form and appearance of nature, recognisable to the human eye, was called Ying (陰), and these four manifestations constitute the system of Feng Shui (風水).

Feng Shui is the art of adapting the residences of the living, and the dead, so as to co-operate and harmonise with the local currents of the cosmic breath. The shape and form of hills and watercourses are potent factors, but, in addition, the height and form of buildings and the direction of roads must be taken into consideration. From instant to instant, the force and direction of the spiritual currents are modified by the movements of the sun and moon, so that at any particular time the direction of the celestial bodies from the point considered is of importance. The professor of Feng Shui employs a Lo-pan (graduated astrolabe and compass) (羅盤) to observe directions and astrological harmonies, while simultaneously he notes the forms which the spiritual forces of nature have produced.

By talismans (dragons, and other symbols on roofs or walls, pagodas on hills, or bridges) and charms (pictures of spirits, or "words of power" inscribed on paper scrolls, or stone tablets) the unpropitious character of any particular topography may be amended.

The rudiments of the magic art are to be found in ancient China, being manifestations of the Yin and Yang, representing the dark and the light, or female and male principles. After the twelfth century it was elaborated into a science destined to play a large part in the ancestral worship, particularly the disposal of the dead. All possible reverence is due to the corpse, so it is natural that the descendants should desire to see it bestowed in the most comfortable fashion. The site for the burial has to be selected to combine all that is good for the children and grandchildren, as well as for the peaceful repose of their ancestor. As this may require considerable time, and, as a propitious day for the funeral has also to be chosen, the coffin may have to wait for months for interment. Even when the eldest son has discovered such a site, and is confident that it will bring happiness and prosperity to his descendants, it may be that the location will have the very opposite effect on the prospects of a younger brother, necessitating a fresh reconnaissance, until a compromise is reached which is favourable to all parties. So many elements are involved in determining lucky sites that the services of a professional are essential to reconcile the claims of all parties.

Although the disposal of the dead is the chief attribute of the Feng Shui man, he must also be consulted in the selection of the site for a house, or an ancestral hall, or the building of a temple. He may even be called in to modify the arrangement of an existing dwelling, whose inhabitants have experienced some inconvenience. A bedroom may be changed to a sitting-room to suit the psyche of its occupant, or a partition may be erected to counteract some adverse influence. If the expert cannot find the ideal site or if circumstances, such as built up areas, dictate the adoption of an unfavourable location, he must produce the necessary antidote. Hong Kong is full of houses with mirrors facing some line of approach of malevolent spirits to deflect their path and protect the inhabitants from their evil designs. Most of them are re-enforced with the Eight Trigrams, which are disliked by the evil spirits to the same extent as Holy Water is abjured by the Prince of Darkness. The forms of hills, direction of watercourses, forms and heights of buildings, direction of roads and bridges, are all supposed to modify the Ch'i, or spiritual breath of the universe, and Feng Shui is the art of adapting the residences of the living and the dead to conform, as far as possible, with the local currents.

The expert works with the Geomantic compass, which is on sale in most Chinese towns. Those taken home as curios are invariably mistaken for the Celestial form of mariner's compass, which they are not.

The instrument of navigation is rarely seen in the shops. The "reticulated plate" (盤古), or astrological compass, consists of a wooden or baked clay disc, six or more inches in diameter, with a magnetic compass about an inch in diameter in the centre. The disc is coated with yellow lacquer, and is inscribed with concentric circles. The centre is the limitless circle of the Yin and the Yang, and the whole arrangement synthesises the Chinese conception of the harmonies between the forces of nature, the time relations as indicated by the sun and moon, and the directions in space from any point on the earth. As many as sixteen concentric circles may surround the compass, but the local practitioners work with considerably fewer. According to the explanation given by one of them, the Pa Kua or Eight Trigrams form the innermost circle. These denote figuratively the evolution of nature and its cyclic changes. The eight represent respectively Heaven, Water as in a lake, Fire, Thunder, Wind, Water in rain, Hills and the Earth. They also stand for eight animals. Horse, Goat, Pheasant, Dragon, Fowl, Swine, Dog and Ox, and the points of the compass.

In the next circle are the twenty-four hills, each divided into three parts, from which derive the fortnightly climatic periods of the solar cycle, and the 24 characters, including four of the Pa Kua, eight of the Ten Celestial Stems and the Twelve Terrestrial Branches. This is colloquially called Trench Hill over the Land Line.

Next come 72 lines, each divided into five parts (metal, water, wood, earth and fire) making 360 combinations, named Over Sky Lines.

Outside are the twenty-eight constellations.

The seasons correspond with four of the elements, summer being fire, autumn metal, winter water, and spring wood.

In choosing a burial-site, the Azure Dragon must guard the body's left, and the White Tiger the right side. The left is the weaker, and the right the stronger of the two, so the former should be higher. A small hillock or table should be in front, with flowing water, and mounds should flank the coffin. The Line is chosen in accordance with the time of birth of the deceased, summer being fire, etc.

The height of the hill is material, as it may exert a good or bad influence. If the birthday is unpropitious, an excellent site may have to be discarded. Sometimes a counteracting feature may be discovered. A big tree, pollarded so that it has lost its leader, makes little difference to its virtue, but a mutilated sapling is a hopeless proposition. Water and fire can never combine, but wood and water are propitious, as the former nourishes the latter.

It is not a simple matter to find a Feng Shui expert in Hong Kong, as advertising is against etiquette, and no shop-sign marks his presence. The Chinese, however, always know how to lay their hands on one, and an introduction is not difficult. His business card announces that he is an expert of Yin Yang, and is well versed in geomantic knowledge, picking lucky days, and telling fortunes by the Eight Trigrams. He is equally proficient in all other methods of foreseeing the future, including the Eight Characters (date, hour of birth, etc.).

In the early days of foreign intercourse with China, Feng Shui proved a formidable obstacle to modernisation, and the first proposal to erect a telegraph line between Hong Kong and Canton was opposed on the following grounds. The capital of Kwangtung is the City of Rams, which is suitably guarded by the Tiger's mouth and the Nine Dragons of Kowloon. Nothing could be more unpropitious than to lead the Ram by a string into such dangerous company.

Sites for foreign houses also caused infinite friction for, if the Tiger were higher than the Dragon, death or bad luck would result. A two-storied European residence could not therefore be erected next to, and on the right-hand side of, an existing Chinese house.

Every hill and tree in China influences the Feng Shui of the locality, and foreigners, ignorant of its mystery, were soon in conflict with the inhabitants. When laying out Hong Kong for trade, the leading merchants endeavoured to make Happy Valley the business quarter of the town, but failed ignominiously on account of Feng Shui. The locality was malarious, and when some of the engineers contracted the disease, and the foreign houses already built had to be abandoned, the natives triumphantly declared it was a just retribution. Senor Amaral, Governor of Macao, who combined a passion for road construction with an unlimited contempt for local tradition, was waylaid and decapitated by his Chinese subjects, for interference with the situation and aspect of certain tombs of their ancestors.

Occasionally the foreigner gained enormous prestige with the Chinese for unwittingly improving the Feng Shui of the locality. The mortality of the garrison of Murray Barracks was alarming until the Colonial Surgeon proposed planting a bamboo grove on the hillside above the buildings, strictly in accordance with the rules of the system. When it was found that the disease was checked, probably by a weekly dose of quinine, Feng Shui was given the credit for the victory.

It was taken for granted that the British knew a great deal more about the science than they cared to admit, for foreign residents started building their villas on Pokfulam Road, which Feng Shui declares to be the best site on the island. The establishment of a reservoir there, and of filter beds on the north side of the island, were also master strokes. The policy of planting trees, and forbidding the removal of earth from places where there is much decomposed rock, were strictly in accordance with Chinese tradition, and the Surveyor-General acquired the reputation of being a profound expert in Feng Shui. The site selected for Government House was the most propitious on the north side of Victoria Island. It is screened at the back by the tall trees and gently sloping terraces of the Botanical Gardens, and is skirted by roads with graceful curves, safeguarding it from the attention of evil spirits which can only move in straight lines.

One of the principal duties of the adept in Feng Shui is the location of sites for tombs, as the belief is universal that one of the souls of the deceased inhabits the grave and, unless it is comfortably disposed, it will be unco-operative towards the petitions of its descendants. In the early days of Hong Kong this belief was so firmly enshrined that Chinese employees of British firms actually made pilgrimages to Happy Valley and worshipped at the graves of foreigners that their influence might be exerted in their favour with the reigning T'aipan.

The worst possible location for a settlement is on featureless ground, a flat plain with no undulations. For this reason such terrain was always offered to foreigners as a Concession when their importunities could no longer be resisted. Shanghai, Tientsin and Hankow Concessions were all mud flats liable to floods, and the Shameen in Canton was a sandbank regarded as habitable only for white ants. Human agencies can, however, counteract the disadvantages of nature, and the addition of a cairn can alter the unpropitious outline of a mountain, so, in time, the Concessions became a political bone of contention.

Western contacts have done little to wean the Chinese from their beliefs in the influence of Wind and Water on their material welfare in life and death. No house is built, nor grave site selected, without reference to the Feng Shui man, and "enterprises of great pith and moment their currents turn away" at his unfavourable verdict. It would be thought a matter of ordinary prudence were the practitioner consulted before an irrevocable step is taken, as a veterinary surgeon might be called in to give a certificate of soundness prior to the purchase of a horse, but, in many cases, property is acquired and abandoned on account of an unfavourable report. Thus, in what was formerly the old West Park an individual bought the site for a house, and even dumped a pile of granite blocks, but threw up the whole project when told that if he built he would die within the year. The Feng Shui man in this case seems to have had a gift for diagnosis, for his client only lived a few months after becoming a landed proprietor though not a house owner. In another case where a large block of flats was in course of erection the foundations were actually put down before the services of the geomancer were requested. He condemned the project out of hand on the grounds that the building exactly faced Government House. He hastened to explain that the objection was not to the seat of Government, or those who administered it, but that the former Japanese fort on top would have a disastrous influence on the fortunes of his employer. To soften the blow he predicted that if the foundations were slewed round, and moved twenty feet, the owner would enjoy forty, instead of twenty, years' good luck.

In another case a foreigner, who had just concluded a deal for his house, feared that the transaction might be revoked when the new owner appeared one afternoon with a Feng Shui man and the implements of his trade. The cheque was safely lodged in the bank, but he felt a moral responsibility should the location prove a death trap to its purchaser. The verdict mercifully was favourable. A hill sheltered the back, and there was running water in front. A nearby hill might have proved an unfavourable feature, but for a building which neutralised its dangerous influence. Another house was said to have the best Feng Shui on the island with the hill behind and the harbour before. Two groups of rocks, representing the Dragon and the Tiger, protected the left and right approaches, whilst it looked directly towards Kellett Island, the luminous Pearl which is the absorbing passion of the Nine Dragons of Kowloon.

The British, in their ignorance, have done many things to the landscape which violate its sacred principles. Victoria Peak is known as T'ai P'ing Shan (太平山), the Hill of Great Peace, but has an alias as the "Man who brings longevity" (老壽星). When a path was engineered round the mount, the Chinese said that a halter had been placed on the neck of the Old Man, and that Hong Kong would not long remain in British hands. This prophecy seemed in a fair way of fulfilment but, with the expulsion of the Japanese, the word went round that the halter had been placed too low and that, though the Old Man was inconvenienced by his girdle, he had escaped strangulation.

Though Kowloon boasts of nine dragons it has by no means a monopoly of the monsters. Early Chinese settlers on the island were much distressed when the engineers of the Public Works Department severed the spine of one of these creatures to drive the road through the Wongneichong gap. Hong Kong has deposits of both red and yellow ochre and, when the road was made through Wanchai, the colour of the subsoil led the inhabitants to believe that the dragon had been bleeding and mortally wounded. A stone as a memorial to this, "The broken Dragon" (掘斷龍), exists to this day, and magical properties are attributed to it. A rival lover who wishes to cause dissension between his inamorata and her fiancé visits the rock and, after making his petition for a separation, lays a sheaf of flowers upon the monument.

Evidence of the Feng Shui man's activities may be seen at many corner houses, particularly if a straight road gives access to the building. Evil spirits can only move directly forward, and can be deflected by being forced to make a right-angled turn. Hence the Spirit screens which guard the main entrance in North China. In Hong Kong a mirror, often reinforced by the eight trigrams, is fixed to the wall of a house facing such a route, to turn back the malignants.

A similar potent devil-discourager is the seal of one of the Star Gods, bearing the assurance that he has his eye on them. This is carved into a stone, or block of concrete set in the wall which faces the threatened direction. When the divinity is depicted on a scroll for indoor use he is represented as a pop-eyed individual, mounted on a Pekingese dog, and carrying his talismanic emblem in his right hand with the inscription plainly legible: "Tze Wei Cheng Chao" (紫微正照), the Purple Planet looks straight.

The purple plant has his eye on you

2 and 4 in the morning, "One-armed" Sutton, who was no early riser, tried the effect of a case of tinned peaches to retard the hour of departure to 10 a.m. If there is anything in Feng Shui, Chang's untimely end may be attributed to the triumph of peaches over the astrolabe.

Birds and animals are often regarded as emblems of good or bad luck. A white cock is said to be a protection against baneful astral influences, and to be the only capable guide of transient spirits. Hence he is always carried on the coffin in the funeral of a native of Honan. The picture of a red cock is often pasted on the wall of a house in the belief that it acts as a fire insurance. A fowl getting on the roof of a house is a bad omen, and it is very unlucky if it thunders while a hen is sitting.

The coming of a strange cat to a household is an omen of approaching poverty. It is supposed to foresee where it will find plenty of rats and mice in consequence of approaching dilapidation, following the ruin or poverty of its inhabitants. It is also considered very unlucky when a cat is stolen from a house.

The fortuitous arrival of a dog, however, indicates coming prosperity. The Chinese has none of the aversion felt by many Europeans for the bat. The character representing the creature has a similar sound to that indicative of happiness; hence the bat is taken as its emblem, and the "five bats" are a common form of symbolical decoration.

It is unlucky to meet a bald-headed man on the way to a mahjong party. On the other hand, bad luck can be shed if the road is crossed in front of a fast-moving vehicle which cuts off, and inherits, the evil influences pursuing the individual who has performed the feat. Foreigners glare in fury at some Chinese urchin who has made it by the skin of his teeth, and to the detriment of screeching back tyres, when he is picked up by an adoring parent, and petted instead of spanked for risking his life.

A lucky day must be awaited before embarking on any great enterprise. Coffins are kept for months before the day indicated by the necromancer arrives for their interment. Outside Peking, three miles from one of the city's western gates, stands the lovely pagoda of Pa Li Chuang. The slightest breeze evokes a musical tinkling from the thousand bronze harebells which are hung round its thirteen storeys. Incised on each is the inscription: "Presented by the Palace Ladies, in the 4th Year of the Great Ming Emperor Wan Li (1576) the 8th Month, a Lucky Day".

A Taboo is a Polynesian term for a system, or act of setting apart a person, or thing, as accursed, or sacred. Its definition has been widened into embracing everything in a society that is "not done". To pour one's tea into the saucer at a Victorian party would have been distinctly taboo, and John Burn's red tie when he took his seat as Member of Parliament failed to set a fashion even among the ranks of the Radicals. China, in her long isolation, built up a system of taboos unfamiliar to the foreigner who established trade relations, and his non-observance of her system must have confirmed the Celestials in their conviction that they were dealing with barbarians.

The Emperor's personal name was taboo in the Polynesian sense, and was too sacred to be mentioned, just as the Israelites never uttered the name of Jehovah. No one was permitted to say or even write it so long as

Feng Shui is essentially a personal doctrine, and sites which may be propitious for one individual may be inimical to another. In congested areas like Hong Kong, where there is little choice in the siting of a new building, the professor must be called in to neutralise the adverse influences, as the power to determine the initial layout is in other hands.

The necromancer is ubiquitous, and inquiry may elicit the fact that baby-amah's uncle is a practitioner. Should a foreign resident be in need of his assistance, he will be produced before there is time to smoke a cigarette. He is on the staff of all high officials, and probably dictates the zero hour for the military operations. He certainly did in the case of Chang Tso-lin, the Manchurian warlord. Every time a move was planned he was called in to decide the propitious hour. As his selections for displacements were between the hours of

Signs outside a restaurant, one wishing prosperity and the other greeting a new-born child

the family remained on the throne. On the accession of a new monarch, a "Year style" to designate his reign was chosen, and dates were reckoned according to the year of this period. To say that Chien Lung received the embassy of Lord Macartney is equivalent to referring to Cromwell's excesses in Ireland as the visitation of the Commonwealth. On his death the Emperor was given a temple or posthumous name, known as a Miao Hao, such as the Great, or Martial Ancestor. The title of Lord Macartney's host is Kao Tsung, the Lofty Ancestor, and by this he is always designated when a Chinese refers to one of his personal acts. In the Abdication Treaty the first article was to the effect that the title and dignity of the Ta Ching Emperor was to be maintained, and not abolished, and that he was to be treated by the Republic of China with the courtesies which it is accustomed to accord to foreign monarchs. This clause, as well as the other seven constituting the first "Equal Treaty" the Republic signed, was consistently violated, as the other party had not the physical force to maintain its rights.

It is not proper for a son to use his father's personal name which is taboo, as is a husband's name to a wife. There are four hundred and eight single, and thirty double surnames, which form the Po Chia Hsing, or "All the family names", and it is taboo for a marriage to take place between two members bearing the same patronymic. This must be an exceedingly ancient ban, corresponding to the table of consanguinity in the Prayer Book for, by no stretch of the imagination, could a Cantonese Wang be related to a Pekingese of the same name. If the four hundred and thirty-eight names were evenly distributed, as they are not, about a million individuals in the country would be entitled to each. The seriousness with which this relationship is still regarded was typified at the last Dragon Boat Festival, when it was announced that the descendants of the virtuous official, Ch'u Yuan (332-295 B.C.), were meeting in Hong Kong to observe the anniversary of his suicide.

The Chinese numerals, like the Roman, do not adapt themselves to calculation, so the abacus is invariably used for the most simple accounts which the ordinary salesman would solve by mental arithmetic. The calculating board lying on the counter has an irresistible attraction for the European shopper who, though he does not understand the principle on which it is worked, cannot restrain his fingers from fiddling with the beads. This is taboo, and justifiably so, for the instrument may register a complicated calculation which the merchant is ready to transfer to his ledger.

Many taboos are connected with eating and drinking. When a party sits down to tea the spout of the pot should never be left pointing at one of them. This position is supposed to engender a quarrel, and probably has the same origin as the upsetting of the salt-cellar in the days when that condiment was a highly-taxed commodity.

The fishermen, like those of a similar profession in the West, are highly sensitive to actions which may spoil their luck. In toasting a friend, "no heel-taps" are customary at every dinner-party on land, but at sea an empty glass foreshadows empty nets, and the practice is strictly forbidden. When laying down the chopsticks after the completion of a meal, they should never be placed across the bowl, or the vessel will run aground.

Anything dropped or broken on a feast day brings bad luck, but it may be conjured by saying Sui-sui p'ing-an (歲歲平安), which means "peace for many years". The Sui (歲) for "ages" has the same sound as the word for broken (碎), just as the p'ing means peace, or a vase or bowl. With so few sounds in the language, the Chinese have endless opportunities for punning, and take every advantage of the fact.

Children may not open an umbrella indoors, or they risk being stunted. Putting on two hats will also retard their growth. On every festival day each family holds its party, and extra places are laid for absent friends. Taking into consideration the ramifications of the usual Chinese household, this seems a very reasonable precaution.

If left to arrange the furniture of a room, Chinese servants will always place the beds north and south to correspond with the direction of the magnetic currents. They are shifted slightly according to the calendar.

Dogs are never kept in a litter if they have white tips to their tails, as it indicates mourning. Other white markings have not the same significance, and are immaterial. The animals are discouraged from digging, as it is supposed to foreshadow the preparation of a grave.

In the North, the Chinese object to being photographed, as it is regarded as a harbinger of sorrow. The Cantonese and Boat People regard it as lucky, particularly on certain festivals, such as the "Double Ninth", when mounting heights and having a pictorial record of the achievement is almost obligatory. Rainbows are treated with the utmost respect and should never be pointed at, or a broken finger may be exacted as a penalty.

The superstition of the broken mirror is common to the East as well as the West, but does not incur as much as seven years' bad luck. It can be only of comparatively recent origin, as the bronze and steel looking-glasses which preceded the mercury-coated glass must have been indestructible.

Exorcists

Before medicine became an exact science evil spirits usually shouldered the blame for rheumatic pains and mental disturbances in the human race, and the ministers of religion were appealed to for treatment rather than the general practitioner. But, whereas the Mohammedans classified the maniac as "afflicted of God", most other creeds diagnosed the unfortunate as "possessed of devils".

The Chinese believe that animals as well as human beings may harbour evil spirits and, if a Christian amah introduces infection among her poultry by the temptation to purchase a diseased bird for next-to-nothing, she may disinfect her depleted chicken run, but will complete the cleansing process with three rounds of jumping crackers. Microbes mean nothing to her, but devils are lurking everywhere. They are at their worst at Chinese New Year, when respectable spirits rally to their homes, and rejoin the family circle for the annual feast. This is eaten in the presence of the Ancestral tablets, to whom it is offered before being placed on the festive board. Hungry ghosts, who have no descendants to care for them, are wandering everywhere in search of sustenance, but are barred out from all homes by sealed doors. The services of exorcists are in great demand at this season, and processions of priests in bright robes move through the streets to the discouragement of the demons. In houses which have been dogged by ill-fortune throughout the year, special services are held, usually by a Taoist exorcist in a red robe and a black cap.

A special altar is arranged on which are burning candles and incense sticks. In many countries peachwood is believed to possess mystic qualities, such as are attributed to the mistletoe in Scandinavian lands, so the exorcist is provided with a sword of that material, or the demon-dispelling weapon formed by welding copper cash coins into a tapering line. This was also hung above the bed of a person suffering from nightmares. The priest places it upon the altar and prepares a scroll on which talismanic inscriptions are penned. The officiant reverently burns the charm and mingles the ashes with a cup of pure water from the spring. With the sword in his right hand, and the cup in his left, he prays for power: "Gods of Heaven and Earth, invest me with the healing seal that I may purge this dwelling of all evil lurking therein!" Having received his mandate, he invokes the demons: "As quick as lightning, begone." He then picks up a sprig of willow which he dips in the cup, and sprinkles first the east, then west, north and south corners of the house. To reinforce the spell he fills his mouth with the water, and spurts it against the east wall with the invocation "Slay the azure spirits of the east, spawn of unlucky stars, or let them be expelled to a distant country". The red demons of the south, the white in the west, and the yellow in the centre, are similarly banished to the accompaniment of gongs and crackers whose efficacy is commensurate with the riot of sound they create. When the pandemonium is at its height, the exorcist raises his voice to be heard above the din and screams: "Evil spirits of the East get you back to the East, of the South return thither. Let all demons seek their proper quarters and vanish forthwith". The officiant then makes his way, sword in hand, to the door and goes through the exercises to preclude all chances of return.

Exorcists are not tied down to a set form of ritual, and vary their methods to suit their clientele. Sometimes the door-posts are sprinkled with the blood and feathers of a freshly killed cock, and a single demon may be disposed of by fixing a padlock round his neck. People are very tolerant about the methods employed. The great thing is to abate the nuisance, and some will try anything within their means, being totally indifferent if Buddhists, Taoists, or both are employed.

As epidemics are attributed to the machinations of demons, the exorcists are kept busy during the "Dangerous" Fifth Moon, when the Chinese pray to the Taoist Ministry of Exorcisms to avert cholera and plague. This Medical Board has in its faculty seven chief ministers charged with expelling evil spirits from dwellings and generally counteracting their mischievous propensities.

Of the seven members the two most famous are P'an Kuan (判官), Guardian of the Living and those who have been translated to the Underworld, and Chung Kuei (鍾馗), Prince Protector against Evil Spirits. The latter, who ranks higher in popular esteem, was a Shensi physician who considered himself unjustly deprived of his rightful honours at a public examination, so called attention to his grievance by committing suicide on the steps of the Imperial palace. The Emperor, Ming Huang (A.D. 712-56), was apparently oblivious of the desecration of his doorstep till, in a bout of fever, the ghost of the disgruntled official appeared to him in a dream and relieved him of a nightmare in the shape of a Red Imp, who gave his name as "Emptiness and Devastation". In gratitude for the fever leaving him the Emperor ordered the doctor's corpse to be exhumed and reburied in the green robe reserved for the Imperial clan. A portrait was executed by the court painter from Ming Huang's description, and the physician was canonised with the title of "Great spiritual chaser of Demons for the whole Empire". Copies of the portrait are used as talismans throughout the country and are pasted on the lintels of doors during the dangerous Fifth Moon.

Chang Tao-ling, the first Master of Heaven, is credited with being the originator of the doctrine which popularised the Taoist religion, and with being no mean exorcist himself. He bequeathed his talents to his lineal descendants and successors in office, who wielded the demon-dispelling sword and immobilised their adversaries by sealing them in jars. It was generally believed that the present Master of Heaven had a whole cellar full of them at the Dragon-Tiger palace in Kianghsi, which, with the magic sword, he was compelled to leave behind on the approach of the Communists. It would be interesting to know if the contents of the jars formed part of the Liberation policy, as the tempers of the malignants cannot have been improved by their long confinement.

The first Chinese priests were dancing and chanting exorcists, attached to temples dedicated to gods who were worshipped and entitled to sacrifices, but the Adoration of Heaven could only be performed by the ruling monarch, who was the Chief Priest for all his people. Ecclesiastical and political functions overlapped, statesmen and soldiers doubling the parts of divines. This probably accounts for the lack of a hierarchy in the Taoist Church, which persists to the present day.

The belief that the Chang T'ien Shih (張天師) or Taoist Popes, laid down a cellar of bottled spirits is accounted for by the story of Grand Exorcism, though the narrator is frankly sceptical of the good faith of the participants in the ceremony. A wealthy family in Peking, of the name of Chia (賈) were disturbed by ghosts who infested the garden of their mansion. So many complains were laid before the master of the house that he had no option but to call in the Chief Exorcist. The latter, having determined a lucky day for his operations, had an altar erected in the reception hall, and hung the walls with pictures of the Three Pure Ones, the Twenty-eight Constellations, Thirty-six Heavens, and the Four Celestial Marshals. He then arranged the the band of drums and bells, with numbers of lanterns, incense burners and banners.

Forty-nine exorcists were mustered to perform the rites. After a day of abstinence and self-dedication, three acolytes performed a preliminary censing and sprinkled holy water. Then the big drum began to boom, and the exorcists robed themselves with a biretta embroidered with the seven stars of the Great Bear, and vestments ornamented with the Nine Celestial palaces and the Eight Diagrams. Their feet were shod with cloud-stepping slippers. After prostrating themselves before the sacred pictures, and invoking the Genii, they chanted the Office of the Grand Exorcism for a whole day. Then they solemnly posted the ban of the Superior on all malignant Spirits, and his invocation for assistance from the well-disposed.

At this juncture, all the inmates of the mansion, whose curiously had got the better of them, crowded in to see the capture of the demons. To begin with, the younger exorcists armed themselves with banners, and took up their positions at the five cardinal points. Three seniors acted as supporters for the Superior, one with the magic sword, another with a rod made of peachwood, and the third sprinkling holy water, whilst the officiant murmured the formulae of exorcism. Preceded by the master of the house the four made the round of every apartment, opening cupboards, and paying particular attention to dark corners. They thus drove the demons into the court, where the flag-bearers, who had broken up their groups to form a line, hemmed them in. As the circle contracted, the sword was brandished with ever increasing vigour and the peach rod flailed the air. The Superior then called for a bottle and, having gone through the motions of putting something into it, he sealed the mouth, and ordered an assistant to carry it to the cellar under the tower of their monastery. Then he addressed Chia and told him that his task was over, and that all the spirits had been confined. The old man prostrated himself, thanked the Superior, and paid his fee. The younger members of the family, however, were disappointed at such a tame ending to the spectacle, and were inclined to laugh. After such elaborate preparations the finale was an anti-climax, for no one had seen anything. Had the spirits really been captured? Old Chia told them to be silent, for the demons were maleficent influences, which only appeared when they were condensed, and in their ethereal form they could not be seen by mortal eye. It was in this state that they were bottled. Some accepted this explanation, and some did not. In any case the manifestations ceased.

Spiritualism

Though in England clairvoyance, and mediums generally, had a great vogue in the nineteenth century, so many frauds were exposed that no general credence is given to them today, in spite of converts of such distinction as the scientist, Sir Oliver Lodge, and author Conan Doyle. In China, however, communication with the dead is a very live issue, and such is public opinion that the wishes of the dead, through the mouth of a medium, have the force of law. During the Occupation, the husband of a woman of the amah class was conscripted by the Japanese, and was shipped to Hainan for forced labour. In the first year of his captivity he managed to communicate with his wife, but then all letters ceased. Application to the occupying power to trace him had no effect, nor were the efforts of the Red Cross after the expulsion of the Japanese of any more avail. As he might still be living, the clairvoyant could not be applied to, but on the death of his mother she was called in. It was quite obvious to Chinese mentality that the mother, having passed over, would know if her son had joined her or not, so the old lady's spirit was evoked. Her confirmation of the family reunion in

the Taoist paradise was as good as a death certificate, and, in the eyes of the family and neighbours, the woman is a widow.

It is probable that telepathy plays a great part in the manifestations, for, according to Hudson's Law of Psychic Phenomena, if one individual in the circle has knowledge of a question put to the medium, the correct answer can be deduced. The clairvoyant, for most of the practitioners are of the female sex, is usually tested by a question whose answer is known to her employers, and, if a correct response is given, confidence in her further utterances is established. Thus, in the case of a married couple where the husband had died in Australia, and the coffin had been shipped home, the medium declared that the husband looked as he did in life, whereas the girl's body was unrecognisable. This was not surprising, as there were members of the audience who were well aware that the man had been embalmed for shipment from the Antipodes, but the circumstantial details were enough to ensure credence for the remainder of the séance. The spirit the clairvoyant appeals to is apparently that of the Pleiades, and the science is connected with religious observances. Spiritualistic séances are often held under the auspices of priests, who are gifted with psychic powers. The lady practitioners known as Ma Chiao (馬腳), Kuo Yin (過陰) and Ling Ku (靈姑) sometimes work themselves into frenzies or fall into trances, before contact with the other world is

Spiritualist and protective talisman

118

established. Ancestral worship is so rooted in the Chinese that it is natural that they should wish to consult the dead, whose spirits are always supposed to be hovering around the homestead, keeping a watching brief on the fortunes of the family. In times of difficulty, when a decision is required, it is not unusual to call in a clair-voyant and take the course of action which she prescribes in the name of the departed.

Consulting mediums is more popular in the South than in the North of China, and there is usually a reluctance to employ the local practitioner who is certain to be informed of the family affairs. Thus, if a household living in Aberdeen is in need of ancestral advice, the odds are that a medium domiciled in Victoria or Kowloon will be approached. The clairvoyants are, as their calling suggests, temperamental, and may refuse to entertain a large crowd of relatives gathered for the performance, no matter how far they have come. Chinese invariably feel the urge to cling together as a family, and, if a member is taken to hospital for examination, he, or she, is accompanied by as many as the transport will admit, and usually more.

Though the Taoist priests who practise clairvoyance appear to prefer to work in darkness, or at any rate in a dim, religious light, the female mediums hold their séances in the day-time. A table is rigged up as an altar, with flowers, two candlesticks, and a bowl of rice. The medium takes her place before this, seated on a Chinese stool. A few grains of rice are thrown in the direction of the member of the family to whom the deceased desires to make a communication. There appears to be no crystal ball or glittering object required by the clair-voyant to induce hypnosis.

The study of religious beliefs and customs is greatly facilitated by the co-operative attitude of the Chinese, once it is understood that the interest evinced has no taint of idle curiosity. Their devotions may be described as "public worship" in every sense of the word, for no form of audience troubles them in the least. The surest way to establish good relations is to attend some of the main festivals and to make a small donation to the organiser, thereby identifying oneself with the com-munity. Once contact has been established, information of every unusual ceremony quickly filters through and, if interest is evinced, an invitation to attend is promptly despatched.

Chinese constantly consult the spirits of their ancestors when embarking on a new venture, such as opening a business or building a house. Where, however, the ancestral tablets are not available, owing for instance to absence from home, a medium is used to obtain contact. In this case it is essential to know the location of the grave of the person with whom it is desired to com-municate.

Two sisters, employed as wash-amahs in different houses in Hong Kong, wished to get in touch with the spirit of their deceased mother, who is buried in a village near Kukong, up the North River from Canton. The journey is expensive and tedious, and letters are few and far between. The Communist censorship also takes any savour out of the gossip retailed. A third sister is working in Singapore but fails to answer letters. The idea was that a talk with the mother would clear up questions of the family welfare and solve the mystery of the sister's silence.

Hong Kong has no lack of mediums, and the most unexpected women appear to be gifted in this way. A few are professionals, but the vast majority are amateurs who have no fixed fees, and give their services for "lucky money" a percentage of which is always returned. The obsolete English law concerning fortune-tellers, sturdy rogues and vagrants may be obscure in its administra-tion, but still exercises a deterrent effect. In these con-versations with the dead there is no hocus-pocus of a darkened room and soft music, but everything is done in broad daylight with the afternoon sun streaming through the windows.

In this case, the medium's only properties consisted of a cigarette tin filled with rice and covered with a scrap of red paper, which acted as an incense burner. Having lit her three sticks, she clasped her hands above her head, intoned a short prayer, and then seated herself in front of the improvised altar. Her clients sat alongside her on the sofa, and provided her with the data con-sisting of the name of the departed with whom com-munication was desired and the exact location of the grave.

The medium closed her eyes, and joined her open hands with the finger tips touching and thumbs separate. This forms the "Eight directions", in one of which every spirit in the universe is to be found. The first com-munication was startling, for the spirit replied that the mother was not available, as her father-in-law wished to speak with his grandchildren instead. Being of the senior generation he naturally had precedence, and no objec-tion could be raised to his monopolising the conversa-tion. He first identified himself by giving an account of the family, which children had died, and how the others were employed. These details are always expected to ensure that the right spirit is at the other end of the line. Having established his identity the grandfather declared that the family had decayed since his days and that, though not actually in want, his descendants were none of them prosperous. He himself was a well-to-do goldsmith and dealt in jewel jade. He attributed the reduced circumstances of his descendants to the fact that a house had been built in front of the family mansion which had broken its luck. The Chinese are firm believers in such changes in the Feng Shui of a locality, sometimes with justification. When an apartment house was erected in front of Basilea, the occupants of the old Basel Mission declared that the luck of the place was gone. Within two years the landlord pulled down the six colonial houses, and the site has been derelict ever since.

Communication with the spirits has some resemblance to the "over to you" of radio-telephony. The medium delivers the message to her clients, and then blows lightly into the tunnel of the Eight Directions to establish contact with the other world. As to the present condi-tions in the family, the grandfather stated that the Kitchen God was unhappy, the Door God disgruntled, and that even the Ancestral tablets found nothing to rejoice in. As attempts have been made to get them burned, and abolish all the old traditions in favour of pure materialism, there seems some justification in their apprehension.

As to the correspondence with the girl in Singapore the old man stated that her letters were being stolen, and that they should write by registered post with receipt to sender. To the Chinese this explanation appeared highly plausible though it sounds strange to foreign ears. The working classes, however, rarely give the address of their place of employment for their correspondence. The job may be lost, with a parting in anger, and the employer is unlikely to put himself out to oblige an unsatisfactory worker by re-addressing his mail. Accommodation addresses are therefore very fashionable, but a certain amount of risk is inevitable in selecting a trustworthy *poste restante*. An errand-boy working for a compradore is quite likely to pick one of his customers as his Postal Box and, if the arrangement is satisfactory, continues even if his clients move across the harbour, and sever all connection with the firm which employs him.

The possible explanation of these communications with departed spirits is telepathy. The Chinese are highly sensitive in this respect and it has been a subject of remark with many foreigners. In their relations with their servants their thoughts are often translated into action without a word being spoken, and often the wish is no sooner formed than the servant's footsteps are heard coming to execute the unuttered command. Distance is immaterial, and the most extraordinary example in my experience occurred to me in Shanghai over a space of five miles. I was working in the Embassy Buildings on the Bund and, just before returning to my flat at the far end of the Great Western Road, suddenly thought I would like an old Harris tweed jacket instead of my lounge suit. I had never worn it before or thought of asking for it since I had acquired my Shantung No. 1, who had previously been the Governor's servant at Wei Hai Wei. I wondered idly how I should describe it in Chinese, for I had no idea where he had put it when he originally unpacked nine months before. I need not have bothered, for I found it hanging over the back of a chair in my dressing room, as soon as I went to change out of uniform.

"Theirs not to reason why" is evidently the motto of the Chinese who employ mediums to commune with their dead. It is a cheap way of keeping abreast of family affairs, and the pronouncements are usually in accord with their own preconceived ideas. The séance, from this point of view, was eminently satisfactory, and the medium's reputation is likely to add to her circle of clients. On the termination of the conversation the old man was of course asked if he were in need of anything. He replied that he was well off for clothing but could find a use for money, and gave minute directions as to how it was to be sent. The mode of communication was through the "Third daughter-in-law" (三娘), and "Fifth Princess" (五宮主), through whom the medium carries out all her transactions with the Spirit world. As the Nationalist currency inflation has been reflected in purgatory, most of the notes on the Bank of Hell are now of $500,000 denomination. Possibly gold and silver paper sycee will surmount this difficulty.

In sending these remittances it is usual to remember other dead members of the family at the same time, lest their spirits should feel resentment at being neglected. In this case the mother, with whom communication was first sought, would certainly be propitiated by a packet. Gifts are also included in the despatch on behalf of other living members of the family, who have not had the opportunity of hearing the request of the deceased.

There are two classes of medium—one, who like the present example does not communicate directly with the dead but passes her messages through the intermediary of her familiar, or patroness; and the other, who actually communes with the departed spirit. The Chinese esteem them much more than the first order, as they actually speak in the local dialect and voice of the deceased, which lends conviction to their utterances. At a subsequent séance this medium confessed to having the power, but was reluctant to use it, as it was too exhausting and left her unfit for hard work for three days. As it was, when she came out of the trance her hands were stone cold, and she was not her normal self until hot tea had been administered. On the first occasion she objected to the presence of dogs in the room, as their movements distracted her. When she had gained confidence she admitted that she was afraid of strange animals, and raised no objection to their presence. One of the dogs, who is intensely nervous during a thunderstorm, exhibited the same symptoms, shivered all the time the medium was under control, and came for protection to his mistress.

Of course the old gentleman's modest demand was not taken at its face value and, when the time for despatch arrived, packets of notes on the Bank of Hell and quantities of white paper stamped with a golden square were purchased from the purveyor of underworld commodities. The expenditure on infernal currency is negligible, and the rate of exchange must be the best in the world. The registered envelopes are of flimsy white paper with a design of two guardian spirits stamped in green, on either side of the vertical space left for the address. They are about twenty inches by twelve, intended to take clothing as well as money. The gift is entirely personal and, in the folding of the paper ingots, no outsider's assistance may be accepted.

A lucky day, fifteenth after the conversation with the grandfather, was chosen for mailing the packet, and at noon the consigner presented herself with her parcels at the medium's hut. The woman's small business consists in selling rice soup in the morning to the fishermen returning with their night's catch. In the afternoons she is free to render what spiritual assistance may be demanded of her to those who might be described as the poor of the parish. Her hut consists of two rooms and a lean-to kitchen, scrupulously clean throughout. The bamboo table altar was backed by a watercolour of her Patron Saint, "The Third Daughter-in-law", evidently an original painting and not the usual rough wood-cut reproduced in thousands. This strengthens the theory that the Goddess is her own familiar, or at any rate is recognised only by a restricted circle. Above this portrait of a very personable peri, riding the storm in a lurid effulgence, betwixt wind and water, was a framed representation of Kuan Kung, inscribed "Heaven and Earth, the Ruling Essence" (天地正氣). Kuan Kung has a universal appeal in Hong Kong, and all sections of the population regard him as their patron. His shrine is to be found in every police station, where a red lamp burns before his image in the Detectives' room. The origin of this custom dates back to the early 1930's when the Senior Officer at Yaumati installed a shrine to this incarnation of courage, loyalty and devotion to duty, to keep these virtues perpetually stimulating the consciences of his staff. The example was followed by other stations throughout Hong Kong, and the Chinese Bayard was adopted as the Patron Saint of the C.I.D.

The money to be despatched is placed on the altar accompanied by a quantity of cheap blank paper slips with rough holes punched in two rows lengthways. These represent the insurance, and are intended to distract malignant spirits who infest the route from interference with the packets. Similar precautions are taken at funerals, where paper money is scattered at crossroads and before temples, where uncared-for ghosts are most likely to assemble. The priestess, after lighting three sticks of incense, places herself on the right of the altar and the client takes up her position on the left. After committing the packages to the safe keeping of the Saint, with a few short prayers to beseech her good offices, the money is enclosed in the pre-addressed envelopes. The officiant offers them one by one, igniting a corner of the envelope from the candles on the altar. They are then handed to the consigner who moves to the front of the altar and waves the blazing mass three times up and down, before carrying it to the door to be consumed in a brazier.

The whole ceremony only occupies about ten minutes and the participants have the same confidence in this mode of despatch as they have in the services of the General Post Office.

A fairly typical séance was the case of an old lady whose advice was required on some point of family procedure. She does not appear to have been very popular on earth, as her relatives decided the time of her demise to suit their, rather than her, convenience, and put her in her coffin somewhat prematurely. At all events she revived and only complained that the bed was very hard, and abandoned it on all fours for her own couch to expire duly a few hours later. She did not seem to bear any grudge for the indecent haste evinced in disposing of her, and declared that she was quite comfortable on the other side, but that the trunk in which her effects were packed at the funeral had arrived in a damaged condition. One of the relatives then confessed that she had dropped the cardboard receptacle at the funeral, and that one end had fallen out of it, scattering the paper clothing. This piece of circumstantial evidence fully convinced the family that they had got in touch with the right spirit, and lent weight to any advice which was proffered.

To the Chinese a consultation with the clairvoyant is of no more moment than the purchase of a new umbrella, and the ladies must do a roaring trade. No cheaper method could be devised for obtaining professional advice, which has a legal significance as far as public opinion is concerned.

The medium is by no means the only way of communicating with departed spirits, as divination has been practised for centuries by means of the Fu Chi (扶乩), or planchette, which is placed before the shrine of a god, and provides the answers to questions put to the oracle. The apparatus consists of a sand board and wooden pen. The board is a tray, twenty-six inches square and two and a quarter high. A wooden pen, nine inches long, straight at the top and slightly curved at the end, is fastened to a rod three feet long. It is manipulated by two persons, one holding the rod in his left, and the other in his right hand. When the spirit responds, pressure is felt on the rod, which impels the pen to trace Chinese characters in the sand. A third person calls out the character, and a fourth transcribes. This method has the disadvantage of getting into communication with any disengaged spirit, and is far less personal than the clairvoyant, who professes ability to put the call through like a telephone exchange. It is used extensively by the Red Swastika Society, which receives directives as regards doctrine exclusively by this means. As its use entails a knowledge of the written character, it is obviously more suited to the literati than the uneducated masses, who prefer to lay their personal difficulties before their own kith and kin, rather than disturb a powerful deity with trivial matters.

Sidelights of Moon Festival

The mid-autumn festival corresponds exactly with our Harvest Thanksgiving. The toil of the summer is over, the crop is safely gathered, and money is not so tight as during the rest of the year. It is a time for rejoicing and relaxation, and the peasantry are in search of any form of entertainment. In the old days travelling theatrical troupes toured the villages seeking engagements, and putting up a somewhat tawdry performance for an uncritical audience. Lion dancers and mountebanks with performing animals roved the countryside and, in the absence of professional talent, amateur dramatic societies formed by the farmers put on a play which they enjoyed as much as the villagers.

The Moon festival is considered the appropriate moment for excursions into the Underworld and, in Hong Kong, the spiritualistic mediums are busy organising personally conducted tours for any volunteers who express the inclination to dabble in the occult. Some discretion must be exercised in selecting a subject, as the strong-willed are resistant to hypnotic influence and fail to respond to control. The Chinese believe that the look in the eye determines the degree to which hypnosis may be induced in any individual.

There is always an interested audience for these séances, whose remarks are often as entertaining as the performance, and the proceedings form the topic of village conversation for days after the event. The propitious time for these incursions into the underworld is the four days beginning with the eve of the Moon Festival and, on the night itself, several simultaneous and varied manifestations of occult power may be staged.

In one case, on the night of the full moon, a medium announced that she had an invitation from her familiar spirit, the "Fifth Princess", to visit thirteen Halls or Palaces in the Land of Shades. (The identity of her control was later revealed as the third daughter of the Moon Goddess.) A table was carried to a flat piece of uncultivated land just below her cottage, on which were laid out an incense burner, a plate of five oranges and a dish with four Moon Cakes arranged in a pyramid. One of her grandsons placed a chair for her, facing the moon, and hung her coat over the back, in case she felt the cold, though the temperature was well over 80. The audience of about fifty arranged itself in a horseshoe, so as to leave a clear space between the medium and the Queen of the Night. Hypnosis always seems to be induced by stretching the arms above the head, accompanying the action with a short chant, but in this case the medium also held a silk handkerchief stretched between fingers and thumbs. When she took her seat, she constantly twirled the handkerchief at full length, sometimes moving it from side to side across her body. Meanwhile, she chanted her experiences in each of the localities she visited, ending each stanza by crumpling up the handkerchief with a musical laugh. Most of her visions were pleasant, but the discovery that some palaces were overcrowded with dogs and bears dimished their attractiveness as a place of permanent residence. Kuan Kung, God of War, and one of the most popular divinities on account of his power to mitigate its horrors, was discovered in the tenth Hall of Heroes, with a retinue of kindred spirits. The medium was daunted by the height of some of the mansions in her itinerary, and excused herself from attempting the ascent. Finally she reached the Palace of the Moon and described its beauties, shaded by scented cassia trees. It was, however, bitterly cold, so she asked that her coat might be thrown over her shoulders, and demanded a cordial of wine in which the ashes of incense had been infused.

The posset, she complained, was not strong enough so her grandson collected more glowing embers from the table and added them till it assumed the right degree of potency. Quite suddenly the chant ended and she stood up, clasping her hands in prayer before making the final gestures to dismiss her control.

Meanwhile the audience had been drifting away attracted by sounds of revelry higher up the valley. On a threshing-floor two women, also under the influence of hypnosis, were performing a ritualistic dance. Their arms were swinging two beats to every pace, with a violence unattainable in a normal condition. The force put into each swing was incredible, and at each forward movement the hands were brought level with the shoulders. Though the audience were perspiring profusely, dressed in shorts and singlets, the women seemed impervious to heat in their best black silks with wide trousers. As a change, the arm swinging was punctuated by slapping both things between the strokes. On the following morning one neophyte confessed that her thighs were indigo blue from one great bruise, but at the time of dancing she felt nothing.

In the corner of the arena, on the side of the full moon, stood a table with incense, candles, and a bowl of pure water. Round it were seated acolytes, busy burning the cheap paper money, punched with holes, usually reserved for the pacification of marauding spirits. This is loosely rolled and, when ignited, is held upright till it burns to the base on the altar.

Round the threshing-floor was a crowd of about eight people, men, women and children, taking the keenest interest in the proceedings, and voicing their encouragement of the performers. The neophyte finally gave in and walked fairly steadily to the table, whilst another woman took her place as partner of the medium.

The Mistress of the Ceremonies is regarded as the most powerful medium in the district. Most of these wise women specialise, one in communications with the dead, while another may practise the healing art. When consulted she makes her diagnosis and then proceeds to the temple, where she prays to her divinity to indicate the appropriate remedy.

When the first girl fell out, the medium darted into the crowd and dragged in an unwilling substitute, who broke a way after a struggle, amid roars of laughter from the audience. A volunteer almost immediately took her place, and the three women joined hands to form a circle, stepping forward and back, and bringing the arms with a swing to the centre. After about a quarter of an hour of this exercise the newcomer went into a trance and, while the other two continued to swing with joined hands, performed alone. She took a pace forward with her left foot, raised on her toes and rocked as in the Highland Reel, and then changed feet, never moving more than two steps from her original position.

Meanwhile, with unceasing industry, the assistants at the altar burned strips of paper money, each being ignited as the previous one's flame expired. It is believed that the dead spirits who possess those in a trance lose their motive power if they are deprived of travelling expenses and, to keep the séance going, they must be continuously supplied. Similarly as the candles burned out they are immediately replaced to give the necessary illumination. At midnight the medium called a halt to the proceedings. On the previous night dancing had continued till 3 a.m. and a rival practitioner, outside the district, had offered to mount a show which should last till dawn.

Ritualistic dances have been a feature of every primitive religion. In oriental countries, where conservatism is strong and new ideas have been merely grafted on the old, without discarding earlier beliefs, these exercises survive with remarkably little change. In the East Indies, the island of Bali resisted Islam which permeated the rest of the archipelago, and retained many of its animistic beliefs, on which Hinduism had been superimposed. The friezes in the ruins of Ankor vividly recall the modern dancers of Siam, so it is reasonable to suppose that the Thais, who originated in Yunnan, adopted some of the rites of the conquered Kmers before surrendering to Buddhism.

According to an ancient work describing the customs of northern China, sickness was dispelled by calling in a sorceress to perform a ritualistic dance. The ceremony was performed by a venerable witch who, beating an iron drum covered with sheepskin, trussed up her skirts and assumed various postures known as "Dancing to the Gods". It was usually associated with well-to-do families, where the younger married women assisted in the rites. The accessories included a wooden frame, on which were placed sacrifices of pork and wine, on a table in the reception hall. This altar was illuminated with large candles, giving the room almost the aspect of daylight. The officiant bound up her skirts, and bent one foot, making the figure of the "Sheep Dance". Two men supported her, one taking each arm. During the movements she talked incessantly, repeating the same sentences again and again, as if chanting or offering supplicatory forms of prayer, with different and irregular intonations. Then the drums struck up, crashing like thunder, whilst her mouth opened and shut, uttering indistinguishable words. Her head hung down, and her eyes rolled from side to side. Whilst standing she had to be supported under the arms on either side, for if the prop were removed she would fall prostrate on the ground. Suddenly she stretched out her neck and took a violent leap into the air. Immediately, all the watching women, petrified with horror, exclaimed "Our ancestor

has come to enjoy the feast". The lights were extinguished, and none of the audience dared to utter a word during the time it takes to consume a meal. Then the sorceress called out in a stern voice for illumination to be brought and the candles were relit. The medium bent forward to solve doubts and avert calamities, and showed the company that the sacrifices had disappeared. Her clients observed her countenance to see if she were smiling or sorrowful, and then propounded a series of questions, to which she replied with the accuracy of an echo. The disappearance of the sacrifices under cover of darkness leads one to presume that the two supporters are in collusion with the medium, if not indeed part of her family. The long gown affected in the old days by Chinese men was an admirable place of concealment. Inquisitive minds were discouraged by another sentence or two in the book, which made it clear that sceptics were liable to punishment by the presiding spirit for any infraction of the laws of decorum. ("When the Goddess discovered the culprit, he was immediately singled out and apostrophised in the words "You have laughed at, and ridiculed me with the greatest indignity: I will now strip you of your lower garments!" The offender, finding himself debagged looked round in the greatest amazement at his nakedness, and promptly climbed a tree outside the house.")

An ancient work on costume mentions an antique girdle made to resemble a sheep's head, which was realistically portrayed, and called the Shang Sheep belt. The Chinese character (商) is the same as that for the celebrated Shang dynasty (B.C. 1766–1122) which after ruling for 644 years was succeeded by the Chou. The sheep, when living, is the emblem of filial piety as it kneels to receive nourishment from its dam. When sacrificed it is the memorial of resignation as it dies without a sound of protest. In time of drought, with the consequent threat of famine, it is considered a felicitous animal, and is carried in processions with dancing and music.

Throughout the Manchu dynasty, which reigned nearly three hundred years till 1911, confronted with the religion of the conquered country, all the Emperors honoured Confucius and many were devout Buddhists; yet the Manchus secretly retained the Shamanistic rites brought from the dark forests where they originated. These were practised annually in the Forbidden City, presumably for the entertainment of the spirits of their forebears who had not enjoyed the enlightenment of Chinese civilisation. The hall used for the ceremonies was named the Palace of Earthly Tranquillity (K'un ning kung 博寧宮) and the utensils and musical implements employed were left in situ for many years after the fall of the monarchy. There was a large stove, with a gigantic cauldron for boiling the sacrificial meats and, on the terrace outside, a wooden pole or sacred post (Shen chu 神柱) on which strips of meat and bones were hung and around which the worshippers used to dance. The rites were very secret and were performed in the early hours of the morning, all observers but Manchus being excluded. The signal for the start was given by the "Guardian of the Nine Gates" who ordered an actor to crack a long whip three times, which was echoed by three strokes on a large drum before the T'ai Ho Tien (太和殿). The band then played while the Emperor mounted his throne. Troops of actors, from sixteen to thirty-two in

number, then performed a sort of pantomime, called Mi-hu-ma-hu (密呼媽呼) based on a legend that Nur Ha-chi, founder of the dynasty, had in his youth slain bears and tigers who devoured children. The mummers were formed up in two ranks, facing each other with a considerable interval between. One row was dressed in black sheepskins, and the other in bearskins, each wearing the mask of the animal he was supposed to represent. The leader of the troupe, in the role of Nur Ha-chi, wore a high helmet and fantastic costume. Mounted on a horse he rode between the ranks discharging arrows to the right and left. One of the actors, on whom a hit was supposed to be registered, fell down whilst his companions scattered and fled for their lives.

Another tableau was the "Yang Shang Shu" (羊上樹) or Lamb up a Tree, to commemorate an incident where the monarch suspended a lamb in a branch as bait for a marauding tiger, which he despatched with an arrow and saved the lamb's life. Another of his adventures with tigers was his meeting with the beast in a farmyard when he was unarmed. By picking up the winnowing fan, and scraping the teeth with a stick he prevailed upon the tiger to take flight.

Demonic Possession

The Chinese believe that when a person goes into a trance the soul wanders abroad, and the vacant body may be entered and possessed by an alien spirit. Unless proper precautions are taken it may become the permanent tenant, and the original spirit be condemned to wander as a hungry ghost.

On the night after the Moon Festival, the most propitious season for investigating the Underworld, one of the most powerful mediums offered her services, on condition of finding some suitable supporters and volunteers on whom to practise. A second medium was enticed away from the cinema and a subject, who expressed a desire to see dead members of her family, was induced to desert her stall in the market. She was rather apprehensive of her husband's possible discovery of the early closing act, and skulked round a back way to the rendezvous, to escape detection. The second medium was also reluctant, and had to be forcibly escorted, as she was on bad terms with her rival practitioner. A violent quarrel broke out as soon as they got face to face, about the respective merits of their controls, and its pursuit provided one of the highlights of the evening.

As soon as the performers had assembled, a table and benches were carried out of the medium's hut and placed on a flat piece of fallow ground just in front. Someone suggested making the lawn in front of the temple the site of the séance, and a general move was made in that direction. The medium, however, stopped the procession near the well, and ordered the table to be set up on a small square of beaten earth, which usually served as a distributing point for the pigs' feed supplied by the local distillery.

There had been an argument as to whether the subject should be made to dance, for which more space was desirable, but her request for an excursion into the underworld probably decided the locality selected. It was rather a sinister spot, shaded from the moon's rays by two huge banyan trees whose naked roots, writhing like a basket of snakes, formed a backdrop to a scene reminiscent of a Rembrandt. In the corner near the well the old witches took their seats at the table, their wrinkles thrown into strong relief by the flickering light of unprotected candles. On the altar stood a bowl of pure water and the smoke of incense rose from the glowing sticks in the usual improvised burner. The principal medium was a tall, commanding woman, who appropriated as of right the seat facing south, with her short rival opposite to her. On her left, at the corner near the well, a gray-haired woman occupied herself with the continual burning of ghost money, laid out in packets before her. A narrow bench, on the side of the table nearest the full moon, accommodated another assistant and the subject. This volunteer of slovenly disposition was generally known to the community as the Grubby Girl. Her clothing was none too clean, and her shortish hair had little acquaintance with the comb. Rather it had the appearance of being cut with a knife and fork, or nibbled by a goat. No fault could be found, however, with her cooperative attitude towards the séance, for she collapsed forward on the table in an attitude which is considered best calculated to induce receptivity. Both elbows were placed on the board, and her head rested on the left forearm, whilst the removal of any restraining pins she possessed caused her hair to fall over her eyes.

The officiant, as usual, opened the proceedings by putting herself into communication with her control in a standing position, and then sat down with her fingers interlaced, and the thumbs free. For fifteen minutes she chanted, with the hands constantly in motion, but the Grubby Girl remained unresponsive. The rival medium, who was seething with indignation at being denied a part in the control, but had borne her humiliation in silence, then started chanting, extolling the superior merits of her familiar spirit. This provoked the officiating priestess to fury. She ceased weaving her hands, and began drumming on the hard earth with the heels of her wooden clogs, and on the table with her crooked fingers. A violent argument started on the lines of "Anything you can do, I can do better," while the merits and demerits of the conflicting Gods were chanted. The short woman put her case without any heat, whilst her rival grew more furious and uncontrolled. Her actions increased in violence, and she began an assault upon the table which threatened its stability. The incense sticks leaped from their sockets, and the water splashed over the lip of the bowl as she beat with her hands in the intervals of drumming. The Chinese aver that although the thighs are definitely bruised during these séances the hands, though battered against a hard surface, never show any sign of injury. Apparently the Third Degree Divinity prevailed, for the tall woman suddenly stood up, clasped her hands in prayer to dismiss the control, and stalked off in a fury. During her tantrums, the spirit had moved the supporter on her left, who started an assault on the table almost equal in violence to her own. This died down on her departure and the woman relapsed into immobility.

The second medium now dominated the proceedings, and, shortly after the abdication of her rival, began to achieve results. The Grubby Girl, who had remained inert during the altercation, suddenly began rubbing the surface of the table with the tips of the fingers of the right hand. Then her shoulders began to shake, and she swayed from side to side, abrading the skins on her elbows in the process.

Never raising her head she began a conversation with the medium, describing her experiences. She found herself walking in a long narrow street, fetid with the reek of decayed fish. Suddenly she turned a corner and was brought up short by a corpse, covered with blood and in an advanced stage of dissolution. She tried to escape but everywhere she found the horror in her path. The medium spoke soothingly, and promised to lead her to a garden, where all would be forgotten in the scent of the flowers and she would see her loved ones. For a moment she caught a glimpse of a dead son, but he was snatched away, fading into mist as the gruesome body reappeared before her. The medium continued her suggestions but was powerless against the influence. By this time the audience had swelled to a hundred, and hung upon every word. They were on completely familiar ground, as if awaiting the next instalment of a thrilling serial story.

Only eight days earlier, the site had been the scene of a distressing tragedy, which had been still in everybody's mind. A young girl, married only four months, had been carrying heavy buckets of pigs' feed when she fell and sustained fatal injuries from internal haemorrhage. No assistance was at hand, and she painfully dragged herself home, crossing the very spot. She succumbed from loss of blood before medical aid could be rendered. Her spirit, not yet secure in purgatory, was wandering seeking to express itself. The indications were that the Grubby Girl had lost her identity and was henceforth the mouthpiece of one who had recently left this world.

The audience was not disappointed, for she began to keen, punctuating each sentence with a strangled wail. It was an eerie performance, and past ordinary comprehension as the intonation was that of the dead girl, and the language Hoklo, a Fukienese dialect, totally foreign to the Hakka woman who delivered the lament. She bewailed her sad lot, dying so young, just as she was married to a kind and understanding husband to whom she was devoted. She complained that no one helped her when she fell, and that she was abandoned by all to die alone. Till she married she had been unhappy at home, with a shrewish mother from whom she had escaped to enjoy life for the first time. The animadversions on the old lady were well received by the audience, for hardly one of them had escaped the lash of her tongue. She disdained no weapons in her quarrels and, on parting in anger, was wont to repair to the temple with a bunch of incense sticks, to invoke the aid of the Gods against her opponents.

When the lament died away, the spirit unfolded the reason for its return. Once purgatory was reached there would be no other opportunity of seeing the husband she adored, and she demanded that he be fetched as she had a communication to make to him. For some mysterious reason the old harridan of a mother was included in the invitation, but it was never discovered if the request for her presence was prompted by filial piety, or a desire to discredit her before the assembled multitude. The medium tried to temporise, but the spirit declared that she would stay there all night until her demands were satisfied. It seemed obvious that the Third Degree Divinity had let matters get completely

124

out of hand, and it was possible that the medium knew no formula for exorcising the ghost, and restoring the Grubby one to consciousness. In any case the short woman made a discreet and silent exit, leaving the paper-burning assistants to cope with the situation. For over half an hour the demands to see the husband were reiterated, until some of the distillery staff, which had employed the dead girl, set out in search of the husband. It was generally agreed that the production of the old crone was out of the question, as she was practically bed-ridden, and even if they got her down on her feet, she would have to be carried back.

At last the young man appeared, and took his place in the forefront of the crowd close to the hypnotised girl. She expressed the greatest pleasure in seeing him, renewed her vows of love, and then pronounced some shattering injunctions. He was not to re-marry for five years, or she would return and kill the wife who had supplanted her. If he remained single for the specified period his affairs would prosper, and he would be the father of a happy family of five. These commands never varied and were repeated over and over in spite of his arguments. Various people tried to put a stop to the séance by calling out "Enough", "Enough", and some zealous acolytes nearly set her hair on fire by burning paper before her eyes, but without avail.

As midnight approached the crowd got restive, but nobody dared to undertake the awakening. At last the tall medium was summoned, and at once took charge of the situation. She was an impressive figure as she took the stage and clasped her hands to invoke the aid of her familiar. After a short incantation the power came to her, and she seized a bundle of fresh incense sticks, which she ignited at a candle and passed over the bowl of water. Placing herself on the right of the unconscious woman she waved the smouldering incense three times with a circular motion round her head. She then dipped her hand in the holy water and, throwing back the hair, passed it over the woman's face. Practically simultaneously she brought the flat of her hand down on the table with a crack like a cannon shot. The Grubby Girl immediately sat up, and quite unconcernedly began putting the pins in her hair. Meanwhile the medium had retired to the opposite corner of the table, where she cried out a warning that she could still see the spirit. The crowd, assembled in the direction indicated, ran like rabbits to clear its path, and the medium followed it with her eyes down the land. As the audience dispersed, she uttered a warning to keep to the centre of the path, and on no account approach the bushes of lantana at the side. In view of the dramatic experiences of the evening this injunction was meticulously obeyed.

Apart from the absence of skin on her elbows the Grubby Girl experienced no ill results, but the excitement of the quarrel, and the subsequent triumphal finale, caused the tall medium to pass a sleepless night.

As is usual in dreams, the waking subject rarely has a clear idea of the visions induced by hypnosis. An impression of the street of stinking fish may persist, but the general outlines are blurred. As, however, the full details of the séance were public property in the village it was not long before the principal actor was fully appraised of her experiences. In this case it was with a feeling of frustration that she learned that she had been the mouthpiece of the dead girl, and that her relatives had never entered the picture. To remedy this omission she offered herself again on the last night of the festival, seeking the services of another medium.

On this occasion her desire to be reunited with the departed members of her family was gratified, and a series of interviews was recorded. There was a similarity about them all, however, which palled on the audience. Being a thrifty soul she never demanded if they were in want of anything, and so saved the outlay on paper money and clothing which normally forms part of the expenditure.

The only point which excited interest was the gift of tongues which the subject again displayed, as several of her dead acquaintances were using some up-country Cantonese dialect foreign to her native speech.

These spiritualistic séances are undoubtedly regarded as a form of entertainment, and attract considerable crowds whose comments are a feature of the show. They follow the proceedings keenly, and when some character appears whose foibles in life were familiar, they express their feelings with complete abandon. Every point is taken, and the general atmosphere is one of hilarity. There is always someone in the audience who recognises some peculiarity of the deceased and makes appropriate comments, which usually raise a laugh.

On the other hand, the demands of the spirit are taken quite seriously, and it would be a rash individual who neglected to comply when they are public property. The declaration by a spirit that a certain soul is in the underworld is accepted by society as valid proof of decease and remarriage, in the case of a missing husband, is perfectly in order. The young man, debarred from taking another wife for five years, must consider public opinion if he runs counter to the injunctions of his deceased wife.

Fox Fairies

From demoniac possession it is but a step to the intrusion of Fox Fairies, who figure so largely in Chinese folklore. Of all the beasts, the fox is probably the most intriguing and controversial, for almost every nation has a different view of his characteristics. The German, in "Reynard the Fox", weaves an allegory round his slyness and infinite capacity for drawing advantage from an apparently hopeless situation, whilst in the immortal tales of Uncle Remus he is so obtuse as to be victimised, time without number, by his natural prey "Brer Rabbit". In England, whilst the horse was the only means of transportation, he was virtually canonised as the provider of sport, and the man who shot the fox was ostracised as an enemy of society. Man originally hunted for food, so the survival of the pursuit of the deer by hounds was logical, but the Anglo-Saxon has always been a source of wonder to the foreigner for his passion in the pursuit of a creature whose motheaten brush represents the expenditure of so much energy.

The Chinese worship the fox from motives very different from those of the English sporting squire, for it is believed to be a beast endowed with supernatural powers of transformation, and it is always wise to be polite on meeting one, lest it should eventually become

Fox shrine in Shantung

Giles in a work entitled "Strange stories from a Chinese Studio." Most of the fox legends familiar to foreigners are derived from this work.

One of these "Lady into Fox" stories concerns a countryman called Ma T'ien-jung, who lost his wife when he was about twenty years old, and was too poor to remarry. One day, whilst hoeing the weeds among his cabbages he saw a nice-looking girl, well turned out and made up, leave the path and approach him at his work. Thinking she had lost her way he addressed her with some rustic jokes in rather poor taste. He was dumbfounded when she told him to go home, saying that she would be with him later. At midnight she duly arrived, and Ma discovered that her face and hands were covered with a down of fine hair, so he suspected that he was entertaining a fox, and she did not deny it. Ma determined to seize the opportunity of benefiting by the encounter, and said that if she were really one of those wonderful creatures she would be able to fulfil all his desires. The first consideration was money, and he pleaded his poverty as an excuse. The young lady made promises, but was slow in fulfilment, and he pestered her nightly until she withdrew two pieces of sycee from her sleeve. Each weighed five to six ounces, and both were of the finest quality. Ma was highly gratified, and stowed them away in a cupboard. When he needed some capital he took them out and carried them to a money-changer who rejected them, saying they were only pewter, and demonstrating his assertion by biting a large piece out of one of them. Ma was alarmed at being in possession of false currency, so hid them away and abused his lady roundly. She replied that it was all his bad luck, as his destiny was too inferior to merit real silver. There was a certain coolness between them and Ma did not improve matters by telling her that he had always been under the belief that Fox Fairies were of surpassing beauty, and that she did not come up the expected standard. She replied that they adapted themselves to their surroundings, and that with his means and manners he could hardly expect a princess. Among big-footed, hump-backed rustics she was, however, outstanding.

After a few months she wearied of her boorish companion and came to Ma with three ounces of silver in her hand, telling him it was a parting gift, with which to buy a wife to his liking. The man had no immediate prospects for remarriage, so asked what his new partner would be like. The fairy replied that she would surpass beauty, a statement received with a certain amount of incredulity as pretty girls get wealthy husbands, and three taels did not look like going a long way. Ma asked why she was leaving him, and she replied that it was improper only to meet by night, and he had better get a permanent wife to look after him. Next day, sure enough, a go-between called on him, and Ma at once asked what the prospective wife looked like. He was assured that she was passable enough in appearance, and that the wedding present would only amount to four or five taels. Ma agreed to the price, but demanded a peep at the lady, a highly improper suggestion which was, however, winked at in a large majority of Chinese betrothals. This was arranged, and he caught a glimpse of the girl sitting with her head bent forward, and a woman scratching her back. She was very modest in her demands when the marriage settlements were discussed,

one's sister-in-law, or even one's wife. This dread of the vulpine species arises from the fact that the animal and man are incompatible. The fox may raid the farmer's hen-roost but, unlike the Chinese, he prefers to live in solitude rather than in company. He choses his earth in a locality unlikely to be disturbed and, if he has to associate with man, prefers him dead rather than alive. Hence his predilection for cemeteries, where digging is easy and the presence of human beings is not a daily occurrence. Scared peasants, seeing a fox emerge from a grave, have endowed him with supernatural qualities, and a whole literature about his transformation has sprung up. Chinese foxes, represented as frequenters of ancient sepulchres, turn into elves of the forest, and by moonlight imbibe the ethereal essence of heaven and earth. They exhume bodies and place the skulls upon their foreheads. Then they turn to the North Star, and bow to the firmament. If the skulls do not fall down whilst they perform their prostrations, they change into lovely and fascinating females.

As regards their relations with mankind, they are usually considered dangerous, and they are revered on account of their longevity of eight hundred to a thousand years. They have a peculiar virtue in every part of their body, and can produce fire by striking the ground with the tag of their brush. A series about their transformation was collected by one Pu Sung-ling in the XVII Century, and some of these were translated by Professor H.A.

and asked for only one or two ounces of silver to buy clothes, so Ma gave the go-between a present for her services which just exhausted the money he had received from his fairy friend. An auspicious day was chosen for the wedding but, when the bride descended from the red chair, she turned out to be hump-backed and pigeon breasted, with a short neck like a turtle, and feet fully ten inches long. The significance of the Fox lady's conversation then dawned on the reluctant bridegroom.

The Chinese believe that the fox, once he succeeds in effecting the transformation into a fairy, develops a predilection for human society. He enjoys the pleasures of the table and is inordinately fond of good wine. The scent of fermented liquor attracts him, and he has as keen a nose for a drunkard as a traffic policeman. He can only retain his human form by an effort of will and, if he loses consciousness through sleep or intoxication, he reverts at once to his animal guise.

One of his attributes is the knowledge of the locality of hidden or buried treasure, which he appropriates for his own use, or reveals to his friends. He is also no mean meteorologist, a gift which evokes the admiration of the Chinese farmer. Spring rains alter the whole of the crop-planning. Buckwheat, which is an emergency harvest, can be sown late if the early rains have failed and the summer downfall has been meagre. It only takes a few weeks to mature but, as in normal years it is in no demand, seed grain is usually scarce in a bad season.

Père Leon Wieger, in Modern Chinese Folklore, collected a number of stories about the Fox Fairy, illustrating all angles of the characteristics ascribed to it. The work was published fifty years ago, with parallel columns of the original Chinese and the French translation. The Chinese authors nearly all add verisimilitude to their stories by introducing the names and addresses of their principal actors. The fox, in his relations with the human race can be benevolent or vindictive, according to the treatment meted out to him, but he is usually a friend rather than an enemy.

Thus, a certain scholar named Che combined an addiction to wine with an income which hardly warranted the expenditure. To enable him to get a good night's rest, he found it necessary to put away three tumblers. As a further precaution, on retiring to bed he placed a reserve pot of liquor on a table by his pillow. One night, on turning over in his sleep, he became conscious of a bed-fellow, and on stretching out his hand he found that it was furry, but larger than a cat. He lit the lamp and saw under the quilt a fox which was dead drunk. His wine pot also was drained to the dregs. This amused Che, for he recognised a kindred spirit. He got carefully back to bed to avoid arousing his companion, but left the lamp burning to see how he would effect his transformation. About midnight the fox yawned, and woke up. Che asked if he had slept well and drew back the quilt, whereupon a charming youth jumped out of bed, bowed to him, and thanked him for sparing his life whilst he slept. Che told him to return whenever he liked, and to entertain no suspicions of any evil intentions on his part. Then he went to sleep again and, in the morning, found that the fox had vanished. In the evening he laid in a double ration of wine, and the fox returned. He told Che that he knew that he was not rich, so he must contribute his share for the drinks. He then revealed that a passer by had dropped two taels of

silver on the path about a mile to the southeast, and told his host to collect them at dawn. With this unearned increment, Che increased the scale of entertainment, but his guest refused to be under an obligation, and disclosed the locality of some buried treasure on the property. On another occasion he told his host that a large consignment of buckwheat was coming on the market, and that it would be to his advantage to buy it all in. Che took his advice and purchased forty piculs (over two tons) to the great amusement of all the farmers. However, that year there was no rain. Buckwheat was the saving crop and, as Che had cornered the market, he sold his seed grain for ten times the price it had cost him. He was very soon owner of two hundred acres of first rate growing land. Every year he consulted his fox as to what he should sow, and in the autumn he invariably harvested a bumper crop. The fox stayed on as mascot of the family, and called Che's wife his sister-in-law, and the children his sons and daughters, but when the master of the house died he vanished.

Another story concerns one Yin T'ien-kuan (殷天官) an indigent scholar but a stout-hearted lad, who hailed from Lin Ch'eng (歷城). Near the city stood a large country house whose buildings and grounds covered many acres. It had, however, a bad reputation as there were reports of strange goings-on, which led to the belief that it was haunted. In any case it had been uninhabited for a considerable period, and even in the full light of day no one dared to approach within its precincts. The whole place was overgrown with weeds and briars, from long neglect.

One day Yin T'ien-kuan joined a drinking party with several other young scholars, and they challenged him to spend a night in the house, offering to give a grand dinner if he took the bet. Yin promptly accepted and, picking up his bedding, set off for the place accompanied by the whole band of drinking companions. When he reached the gate, one of them jokingly said that the party would remain outside and, if he shouted, they would come to his rescue. Yin refused the offer, saying he would tell them in the morning if he saw any signs of a witches' sabbath or met a fox fairy. With that parting shot he entered the grounds, but all traces of the path had been obliterated with a tangle of undergrowth.

The feeble beams of the crescent moon afforded just enough light for him to force a passage through the jungle, and discover the door of the building. He crossed several outer courts and reached the verandah of the principal hall, an imposing edifice with two storeys. The moon sank below the mountains which formed the horizon, outlining their crests against the silver sky. Yin could not take his eyes from the beauty of the scene, which seemed to banish all suspicion of dark doings. He spread his bedding in the shelter of the verandah, selected a stone for a pillow, and was just dropping off to sleep, when he heard footsteps heralding the approach of a numerous party. A man, dressed in black and carrying a lantern, came into view and, seeing Yin, halted, and informed those following that a living man was at the house. An old fellow then came forward, and looked at the scholar, who pretended to be asleep. He gave a favourable report, saying that it was merely young Yin, who would not be in the way. The party then entered the reception hall, which was soon a blaze of light. Yin then pretended to awaken, and was approached by the old gentleman, who bowed in a most respectful manner and told him that he was celebrating his daughter's wedding. It would cause him no inconvenience, but all the same he apologised for the intrusion. Yin acknowledged his salute, and said that if he had been warned in time he would have brought a wedding present. The old man said that he would be only too honoured with his presence, as his excellent reputation would banish all evil influences. He called his wife, a woman on the shady side of forty, and formally presented her to the young man. At this moment the strains of music were heard, and a servant announced the approach of the bridegroom. He was a fine young man, about eighteen years of age, and, as soon as he had been introduced, all took their seats at the wedding breakfast. Wine and food were served in gold and jade receptacles. Then the bride was invited to join the party and, after the interval dictated by modesty, she made her appearance, brilliantly robed, and took her place by her mother. The wine was circulated again in goblets. Yin could not resist slipping his cup into his sleeve, to carry back the proof of his adventure to his friends. To cloak his action he let his head fall on the table, and feigned to drop asleep.

The wedding party concluded that he was overcome with wine, and took no further notice of him. The band played, and the bride and bridegroom took their departure together. The servants cleared away the table and collected the plates and drinking cups. One of them noted that a globet was missing, and said the guest must have taken it, but the old host told him to hold his tongue. At that moment the lights went out. Yin raised his head, the place was just as deserted as when he found it, though it was pervaded with the smell of wine and food. The dawn was just breaking, as Yin left with the globet still in his sleeve. His friends were waiting at the gate, and were surprised to see him looking so fresh and composed. They had their suspicions that he had slipped out a back way, and spent the night in his bed, returning before daybreak, but were convinced when he told his tale and exhibited the proof. Knowing the state of his finances did not run to the possession of an article of such value, his story was given credence.

Later, he took his doctorate, and was appointed to an official post at Fei Chiu (肥邱). On his arrival an extremely wealthy family named Chou invited him to dine and, to do him honour, brought out the best gold service. The servant who unpacked the set seemed disturbed, and whispered something in his master's ear which upset him considerably. A moment later the drinking goblets were set on the table and Yin noticed that they were identical with the one he had appropriated. There were seven. "Just think of it" said his host. "I had a set of eight which have been packed away for ten years, and I only opened the case in your honour. Now there are only seven and my service has been ruined"! "Perhaps I can make it up for you" said Yin and, on returning to his quarters he sent the cup to Mr. Chou who compared it and found it was the missing piece. Chou came to thank him, and heard the whole story, which goes to prove that foxes borrow valuables, take them considerable distances, and eventually return them.

One of the Fox Fairy stories introduces Chang T'ien Shih (張天師) the Taoist Pope, and defines his relationship with these familiar spirits. The "Master of Heaven" was the supreme exorcist, and the Chinese credited him

with stocking a cellar of evil spirits, bottled up in jars, and corked with his seal. Had the allegation any foundation, it might have been thought that the Pope reigning during the T'aip'ing rebellion would have been tempted to release his captives when the insurgents sacked and burned his palace.

The tale recounts that a scholar, named Chou of Hangchow (杭州) was travelling with the Master of Heaven, and put up at an inn in Pao T'ing Fu (保定府). At the door of the hostelry, a pretty girl prostrated herself before the Pope as if to make a petition, but remained silent. Chou asked his illustrious companion who she was, and was told she was a fox, who desired that he should grant her the offerings of a certain temple. Chou asked why he did not exorcise her, and was told that she was as bad as she was pretty, and might get up to any sort of mischief. However, he was so struck with her beauty that he pleaded her cause. The Pope relented and said that out of consideration for his companion he would accede to her demand, with a strict time limit of three years. He ordered his secretary to make out the necessary license on yellow paper, and stamped it with his seal of office.

Three years later Chou left Peking for the South on appointment to a provincial post. On passing through Soochow (蘇州) everyone was talking of the power of the image of Kuan Yin in the shrine on Mount Shang Fang (上方). He decided to visit the temple and, at the foot of the mountain got involved in a whole caravan of pilgrims. He was told to get out of his carrying chair, as the Goddess forbade any approach to her sanctuary except on foot. As an official, he spurned the counsel of the common herd but his sedan, carried by ten stout soldiers, suddenly collapsed, and he was obliged to walk. When he reached the temple he found it thronged with pilgrims burning scented candles. He asked a priest where the Goddess was, as he failed to see the principal image, and was told that she was behind a veil, as she was so lovely that pilgrims coming to pray might be distracted from holy thoughts. Chou drew back the curtain, and revealed a remarkably handsome woman, whom he was perfectly certain of having seen before. Then he remembered the incident at Pao T'ing Fu, and recognised the fox. He determined to have his revenge for the broken litter, and to punish the fairy for her ingratitude. She owed her position to his solicitude, and had overstayed her three years of grace. He upbraided her for mischievous behaviour and, as he ended his tirade, bade her begone. The image promptly disintegrated, and fell in a shower of dust. The priest was frantic, but there was nothing to be done. Chou gave him the money to order a conventional statue of Kuan Yin, but the temple revenues fell off to a very moderate income.

A pleasant story of a fox paying a debt of gratitude is told of Yang Hsiung (楊雄) who, orphaned at an early age, was adopted by a maternal uncle Chou (周) who was stationed as a colonel in the garrison town of Ho Chow (河州), Kansu. The child ingratiated himself with the family on account of his lively intelligence. Chou had a daughter of about the same age, and they were brought up together by a governess. One night, when Yang was adolescent, he woke up owing to the stifling heat and went out into the court for a breath of air. Quite suddenly Miss Chou joined him. The two fell in love, and after that met every night. The governess, hearing laughter and whispers in Yang's room, spied on them and revealed the whole affair. The colonel upbraided his wife for not taking better care of her daughter, but the lady said the story was impossible as the girl slept in her room every night. Chou, however, was taking no risks and, seizing a pretext, flogged young Yang and turned him out of the house. After wandering about for some time, the young man finally found shelter in a ruined pagoda near Lanchow.

One day a cart pulled up in front of his refuge, and he recognised his lover, handsomely dressed and with a wealth of baggage. She declared that she had come with her uncle Chou Wu (周鋙) and that they would all live happily together. Now Chou Wu was the younger brother of the colonel, and he had just arrived in Lanchow as Town Commandant. Yang Hsiung called on him, and the visit was returned. When he introduced his wife, however, the commandant was aghast. He declared that his niece was still at Ho Chow, as he had just left the place and, if she had been coming to the provincial capital, his brother would certainly have informed him. A few days later, when he returned to Ho Chow to settle up his affairs, he told his brother. The latter asserted in the strongest possible terms that his daughter had never left the house, and immediately consulted his wife. The lady was under no illusions as to what had occurred and declared that the double was a fox fairy, who was bent on ruining the family by making it appear that there had been an elopement. There was only one way of averting scandal, and that was to summon Yang and marry him off as as possible. This seemed the solution so the lad was recalled and a hasty wedding took place.

When the bridegroom retired to the nuptial chamber he found himself confronted by two brides, who were identical in every respect. Fortunately one of them stepped forward and relieved his embarrassment, by

The Fox Tower, Peking

informing him that the other was his wife, and that she was a fox. She declared that once upon a time, when his ancestor was out hunting, she was struck by an arrow and captured. The good general tended her wound and, when she was able to take care of herself, he had released her in the forest. In gratitude for this act of kindness she had now repaid the descendant of her benefactor. Knowing that he loved Miss Chou without much prospect of obtaining her hand, she had intervened in the way he knew of, to force the issue. As her task was now accomplished, she bade them adieu.

Fox worship in China, though less universal than in Japan, is fairly prevalent, particularly in the North. The headquarters of all these spirits is T'ai Shan, the most sacred mountain in China. This probably accounts for the great number of shrines in Shantung. They are often very small and one, in that province, has an entrance so narrow that it has to be approached on hands and knees. The offerings mainly consist of tiny women's shoes as, in transformation, the vixen was supposed to have bound feet, the sign of a lady of good birth. Fir branches covered with paper flowers, stuck in a lump of clay, were left to decorate the shrine.

One of the guard houses on the south wall of the Tartar city of Peking is known as the Fox Tower, and it is believed to be the habitation of the King of all the tribe. About the beginning of the present century the watchman used to receive visits from an old man, who stayed to chat with him whilst he was on duty. On one of these occasions, which happened to be New Year's Eve, the watchman invited him to celebrate with a pot of wine. The ancient not only drank deep but presented his host with two pieces of silver, each worth ten taels. He then climbed on the table and fell into a heavy sleep. The guard threw a quilt over him, and had the shock of his life when the man's features gradually changed into the likeness of a fox and then, in the manner of the Cheshire Cat, faded away into nothingness. Next morning he returned in human guise and apologised. As the watchman was obliged to supplement his official salary by acting in the daytime as a hawker, the fox fairy promised him that his takings would be henceforth increased by fifty coppers a day, and this increment was continued for three years, though he never again set eyes on his benefactor.

Ghosts

The Chinese share the universal belief in ghosts and have adopted the ancient Roman methods of propitiating them. As long as spirits are well fed, they will do no harm to mortals, hence the wide-spread custom of providing food offerings for the hungry ghosts during the Seventh Moon when they are released from Hell. The conservative nature of the race has induced the Chinese to retain their primitive ideas that all inanimate objects of nature, such as trees and rocks, harbour a spirit which may influence the destiny of man and, as all their ancestors still retain the family connection, they are surrounded by the supernatural in every walk of life. A man's deceased relatives are literally his familiars, for he does not hesitate to call them up whenever he is in need of advice. Wide-spread illiteracy precludes the normal means of correspondence, but the dead are always within reach and, apparently, willing to communicate through the services of a medium. As long as the site of the grave is known the spirit appears to be responsive, though the best time for communication is the first nine days of the Ninth Moon, when the censorship in the underworld is lifted.

Ghostly society in Chinese folklore is composed of all the elements found in a mundane community, from the benevolent magistrate to the criminal classes. Spirits of the departed can right injustice, or take revenge for injuries suffered in their earthly existence. There are vampires and mischievous poltergeists, as well as the spirits of those who have met an unnatural death. These are greatly feared as their only means of redemption is to lure a living soul to destruction as a substitute for their own soul.

Trees on which men have hanged themselves, and wells in which there has been a suicide are avoided, particularly after nightfall, by the local inhabitants. Even highly educated Chinese share this dread. Walking through the Forbidden City in Peking with one of the Empress Dowager's former ladies-in-waiting, a party of foreigners asked their guide if they were not passing the well in which the "Old Buddha" had ordered the Pearl Concubine to be drowned. The mere suggestion was enough to cause her to take to her heels like a startled hare.

A ghostly manifestation peculiar to the Chinese is a high wall, which erects itself round the traveller at night, and follows his movements never letting him escape. The defence against the Kuei Tang Ch'iang (鬼擋牆), or Wall-building ghost, is to squat down, and look steadily in front. Having exercised the power of the human eye, the face must be covered with the hands. When they are removed it will be found that the obstruction has disappeared.

Imperial China may have discouraged foreign contacts, but the immigration laws were relaxed with the introduction of Buddhism, to admit a quota of Indian Rakshas (Yeh Ch'a 夜叉) to whom the worst atrocities are imputed. They are the inhabitants of three separate kingdoms, whose subjects are man-eating demons. Ghosts who commit acts of violence are usually identified with these aliens. The catalogue is expanded with incubi, succubi, imps, gnomes and hobgoblins, and other figments of a fertile imagination.

The popular explanation of these apparitions is that they are the souls of those who have died a violent death, earthbound until the date predestined for them in the Sheng Sau Pu (生死簿) or Book of Life and Death. Not being free-moving spirits, they remain in the neighbourhood of the tragedy, and frequently molest those brave enough to live in their vicinity. Such houses are designated as unclean, Tsang Fang (臟房) and the owners have great difficulty in letting them. The belief persists that after three years the ghostly inhabitant will try to escape by finding a substitute, and another death will take place.

The reluctance of the Chinese to rescue a drowning man is due to the belief that he is in the clutches of a soul which is seizing its chance of redemption, and that it is not for them to interfere with the designs of Providence. For this reason the greatest caution should be observed by those who find themselves under the necessity of walking on the banks of a river or sheet of water on a dark night. A comparatively recent story is told of a man, returning from a party after midnight, who shortened his journey by crossing a piece of waste ground bordering a small lake. He had his apprehensions about the place, and was much relieved to find that he was not alone, as a figure was striding along the path in front of him. He made no attempt to overtake, as these rural tracks only admit single file traffic. Suddenly, he found himself up to his knees in water, and sinking in the soft ooze of the pond. By a violent effort he recovered himself and, seizing the sedges on the bank, drew himself clear of the suction of the mud. His companion was nowhere to be seen, so he was convinced that he had been lured to his destruction by a water spirit.

In Peking many lives were lost on the bridge which crosses an arm of the Pei Hai (北海) where donkeys could be hired. It was alleged that after dark, an old man with a white ass would solicit fares, and those who stepped on the parapet, to mount, were pushed into the water by this malevolent ghost.

Hidden treasure is revealed by the apparition of Will o' the Wisps, ethereal fairies who guard the spot. They are harmless, and merely an indication that someone has hidden valuables without being able to communicate with his legitimate heirs.

Ti Mo (地魔) are black patches which move around at night, in spite of the fact that they are devoid of arms and legs. They are not dangerous to man, but a certain amount of embarrassment may be caused by a variety which emanates from a coffin lid, and follows people about, attracting undesirable attention.

Ghosts are essentially nocturnal, and fade at cockcrow which heralds the dawn. If they are surprised by daylight they liquidesce into a pool of blood. They consequently have the greatest aversion to the sight of human gore, and may be expelled by biting the tip of the middle finger and threatening to rub it on them. The Chinese consider the middle to be the master finger, and, as the blood is believed to flow to it directly from the heart, its powers of conjuration are all the more effective.

The dry atmosphere of Peking in winter is conducive to the production of electric sparks when friction is applied to fur or hair. Spirits are scared by the illumination so obtained, and can be prevailed upon to depart by a strenuous rubbing of the scalp.

The nocturnal habits of these manifestations militate against accurate reporting, and a credulous peasantry is apt to attribute supernatural phenomena to perfectly normal causes. Quite recently an Alsatian dog escaped, and roamed about the hillsides for several days, before his master reported the loss. He was seen on several occasions after nightfall among the vegetable gardens, and left anything but ghostly footprints in the soft soil. Nevertheless he was described as a "spirit" bear, eight feet high, who had placed his paws on one man's shoulders, and had run through the cabbage patch of a Hakka cultivator. A wise woman was consulted who made images of pigs and chickens in dough, and after performing a service of exorcism, scattered them among the kale, in the hope of inducing the spirit-bear to abate his appetite for their living counterparts.

It is believed that ghosts can return to earth with the permission of the judges of the underworld, to right some injustice inflicted on them during their lifetime. An example of this is to be found in a narrative concerning one Jen Chien-chih (任建之), a native of Shantung, who earned his living as a dealer in skins and felt. On a journey to Shansi to replenish his stock, he fell in with a certain Shen Chu-ting (申竹亭), and their friendship ripened to the point of taking the oath of blood brotherhood. Whilst both were attending to their affairs Jen fell grievously ill, and Shen nursed him with the utmost solicitude for about ten days, whilst he grew steadily worse. As he was sinking fast, the dying man confided his last wishes to his companion. He said that his family was in poor circumstances, and entirely dependent on his earnings. As death was overtaking him so far from home, he could only turn to his friend to protect their interests. He had two hundred taels in his wallet, and he desired that half should be set aside for his funeral expenses, and that the remainder should be remitted to his family with the injunction that his body should be brought back for burial near his ancestors.

The same evening he passed away. Shen bought the cheapest possible coffin for five or six taels, and handed it over to the priests at the nearest temple, making off with the balance of the deceased's possessions. He did not return to Shantung, and it was only a year later that the family heard by chance of the death of the bread-winner. The eldest son Jen Hsiu (任秀), a lad of nineteen, was obliged to interrupt his studies, and begged his mother to allow him to retrieve his father's body. At first the widow, fearing to lose him also, withheld consent, but she finally gave in and he set out on the journey, accompanied by a faithful old retainer. Six months later he returned safely with his father's coffin. After the funeral the family was in great distress, and had hard work to make both ends meet. As soon as the period of mourning was over, however, Jen Hsiu passed the examination, and took his degree. Unfortunately, the sustained effort was too much for him, and he took to gambling, to the great distress of his mother who was a woman of the highest principles. There was no breaking him of the habit, and he failed miserably at the triennial examinations. His mother took the disgrace very hardly, wept bitterly, and practically ceased to take any nourishment. The boy pulled himself together, shut himself up and devoted every minute to study. At the following examination he passed near the top of the list. His mother wanted him to be a schoolmaster, but his previous reputation was such that no one would trust him with a pupil. Then a maternal uncle, named Ch'ang, who was in business in Peking, offered to sponsor him in the capital, where there were more openings. Jen Hsiu accepted and made the journey with his uncle by boat on the Grand Canal. When they reached the port of Lin Ch'ing (臨清), they found the waterway blocked by a fleet of salt junks, and they were obliged to anchor for the night.

The lapping of the wavelets, and the sound of voices prevented the young man from getting a wink of sleep. As the night wore on, he detected the sound of the rattling dice in a neighbouring craft, which aroused in him all his old desires. He pulled out a string of cash from his baggage, and was just getting up when he remembered his promise. He lay back in bed, but the noise continued. At last he could hold out no longer and, taking the string, he climbed on board the vessel where the game was in progress. There were two players and the game was big. He offered to cut in, and was accepted. Then a fourth man joined in and the stakes mounted. Jen Hsiu was in a winning vein and with every throw he cleared the board. The three gamblers renewed their stakes from the master of the junk, paying each time in notes, but Jen Hsiu continued to clean them out.

His uncle Ch'ang, having awakened, discovered his absence and, hearing the noise of dice and the clink of money on the adjacent junk, soon put two and two together. He boarded the junk, determined to bring his nephew back, by force if necessary, but when he saw him seated on a heap of cash, he called his boatmen to transfer them to his own vessel. There were over ten thousand. At last, when the gamblers had run out of notes and the junkmaster had no more coin, they stopped playing, and the party broke up. The sky began to lighten with the dawn, and the fleet made preparations to continue the voyage. The junkmaster examined the notes he had accepted and found they were the money burned for the dead which, whatever their value in the under-world, were not legal tender in the Empire. He went to get an explanation from Jen Hsiu, and began by asking his name. Directly he heard it he made haste to be off. His behaviour was so odd that the young man started enquiries, and discovered that the boatman was called Shen Chu-ting. It was the man he had heard about, when he went to fetch his father's coffin in Shansi, who had absconded with the two hundred taels. Then the light dawned on him. The players on the previous night were demons, who had sold Shen false money to the amount of two hundred taels, and had restored the equivalent in good cash to the heir of his victim. He handed over his windfall to his uncle, who invested it profitably in his business, and ten years later the lad was a respected citizen, and a very wealthy man.

Vampires are generated when the P'o (魄) or animal spirit in man is powerful enough to resist the dissolution of the body, and clings to the bones, usually the skull. The following story obviously has a Buddhist origin, as Wei T'o (韋陀) the Protector, is credited with intervening to save the prospective victim. One Li Chiu (李九), a Soochow cloth pedlar, was passing on his rounds through Huo Shan (霍山), where he could find no room in an inn. He was consequently obliged to take shelter for the night in a small temple. He fell into a heavy sleep and dreamed that Wei T'o the Protector appeared, and aroused him with a tap on the back, saying "Act quickly. You are in deadly peril. Hide behind me". Li woke with a start, wondering what was wrong, when he saw a coffin, which had been deposited awaiting burial, suddenly split open, and a vampire emerge. The apparition was covered with white hair, and its eyes were hollow and glowed like coals as it leaped upon the man. He barely had time to put the statue of the Protector between him and the monster. The vampire's arms encircled the image, whilst it sank its teeth in the club with which the divinity is armed. The screams of the terrified pedlar aroused the priests, who came running with lanterns to ascertain the of the disturbance. The vampire retreated to its coffin, and the lid closed. Li gave an account of his experiences which were reported by the priests to the local official. He ordered the coffin to be burned. It was then found that the club in the statue's hand was broken in three pieces. Li, in his gratitude for his escape, ordered a new golden image for the temple.

The description of the apparition in the next narrative bears a strong family resemblance to the Wu Ch'ang Kuei (無常鬼), or Unpredictable Ghost. In the North, he is believed to be the spectre of a suicide by hanging, and his protruding tongue lends colour to the identification. In Hong Kong the priests attribute his origin to a man, who in accordance with the old tradition, spent three years in full mourning at his parent's tomb in the mountains. When he returned home he was such a pitiable object, with an unkempt beard and matted hair all over his shoulders, that his wife laughed at him, and refused to admit him to the house. In despair he returned to his hermitage, where he died of grief.

The story is recounted by one Hsu Shih-chiu (徐世球) who, in his youth, was a resident pupil with a scholar named Han. The tutor had a man-servant called Ah Lung (阿龍), a youth of twenty years, who looked after the school with great energy. One evening whilst Hsu was studying in the cockloft, he sent the lad for a cup of tea. An Lung returned gibbering with fright, and said he had met a creature in white, who gave him a nasty look, and would return no reply when addressed. Hsu simply laughed at him, but next evening Ah Lung absolutely refused to climb the stair. Hsu called another servant, Liu, but when he went to fetch the tea, he stumbled over a body stretched at the foot of the staircase. It was Ah Lung in a fainting fit, but still breathing. His throat bore the marks of fingerprints, black and blue, whilst ears, eyes nose and mouth were plastered with mud. He was brought round with ginger infusion. When he came to, he declared that he had seen the same figure dressed in white, who appeared to be a man some forty years of age. He had a straggly beard, and his face was black, with his tongue at least a foot long protruding from his mouth. When he attempted to cry for help, he was seized by the throat. Then another ghost, an old man with a tall hat and white hair, said "Spare him. He's quite young". Ah Lung was on the point of suffocation when Liu fell over him, but he remembered seeing the creature in white withdraw into the house.

Ah Lung was carried to his bed, and someone kept watch by him. All night mysterious lights like Will o' the Wisps flitted round the chamber. Next day he was rambling in his mind, and refused to take any form of nourishment. A magician was called in, who examined the patient, and diagnosed that he suffered from demoniac possession. He instructed the master to borrow the brush of the local magistrate, with which sentences were inscribed in vermilion ink. This medium was to be used to write three characters on the sufferer's body: Cheng (正), or Upright, over the heart, Tao (刀), or Sword, on the neck, and Huo (火) Fire, on the palms of both hands. He guaranteed this would effect a cure. Han followed out his instructions, and the moment he traced the second character for Fire, the demon screamed "Don't burn me. I'd sooner go away". Ah Lung immediately recovered, and lived to a ripe old age. The talisman forbade the powers of evil to harm a man who was pure in heart, under the penalty of being pursued by fire and sword.

Inanimate objects can become Mei (魅), or bewitched by a savage and homicidal spirit. A rice-merchant recounted an experience in which a broom was the habitation of a drowned ghost, bent on luring others to destruction. In the course of his business he was travelling, mounted on a water buffalo, to Chia Hsing (嘉興), in Chekiang Province, when he came to a ford with an excessively muddy bottom. When he reached mid-stream a black hand emerged from the water, and groped for his foot. He quickly drew up his leg, and it then seized the buffalo by the fetlock, bringing it to a complete standstill. The man, by this time, was scarced to death and shouted for assistance. Fortunately there were peasants within hail, and they pulled and shoved at the beast without being able to shift it an inch. Finally one set fire to its tail and, with a supreme effort it plunged through the mud, and reached the bank. It was then discovered that an old broom, black and emitting a horrible stench, was sticking to the animal's belly. It was knocked off with blows from a stick, and as it fell it groaned and started bleeding. The peasants cut it to pieces with a billhook and then made a bonfire of wood, in which it was entirely consumed. It was a month, however, before the place was clear of the disgusting effluvia which it emitted, but since that time no one has lost his life at the ford, where previously there had been numerous drowning casualties.

There is a Barber's ghost, Kuei T'i T'ou (鬼剃頭) who shaves portions of the head during people's sleep. The hair never grows again on these spots, which remain bald and shining.

Sufierers from malaria may be possessed of Nueh Chi Kuei (瘧疾鬼), and if this proves to be the case the disease is reckoned to be infectious. The point attacked is the spinal column and if on examination a swelling is found, the seat of the trouble has been located. The demon can be expelled by puncturing the spot with a needle.

A particularly troublesome ghost is responsible for the death of very young babies, and if it is successful with the first born, its successor will not live more than two or three years. If the curse continues to the third child, one of its fingers must be cut off, to conjure the spirit, which will continue to haunt the family unless the further issue is dedicated to the priesthood.

Premonitions of death are attributed to the advent of two harbingers, the Kuei Ch'ai (鬼差) who are despatched to summon the soul, by the power who controls the destiny of man. Dying people, whose perception is sharpened by their imminent dissolution, sometimes declare that they have seen them entering the room, and that the end is at hand.

Dreams

The Chinese conception of dreams differs radically from the theories of Dr. Freud, and it is extremely difficult to persuade them of the subjectivity of their visions. According to their beliefs, during the hours of sleep the superior soul, or hun (魂), escapes from the body through a hole at the summit of the cranium and wanders abroad. The adventures it encounters, and the personages met during its excursions are as real as those experienced in everyday life. There is always an element of danger in nightmares for during its absence the soul may be captured, or be so alarmed as to be unable to re-enter its integument. In this case, either the inferior soul continues to activate the body, and the subject becomes demented, or it fades away, and death ensues. Certain individuals, during the hours of sleep, are believed to possess the faculty of projecting their souls to a distance on missions of exploration, or to gain information.

A story, dating from the XIII Century, tells the disastrous results of a practical joke on a student who was a heavy sleeper. His fellow pupils, in search of distraction, entered his cubicle which was at some distance from the college buildings, and arranged the room as it would be for the funeral obsequies. Candles and incense were lighted, with flowers, fruit, paper money and the usual trappings of the mortuary chamber. The jokers then concealed themselves to see the reactions of their victim on his awakening. He finally stirred, and opened his eyes. Seeing all the paraphernalia of dis-solution around him, he said to himself "I must be dead" and with that lay down again, gasped a little, and appeared to resume his sleep. As his body remained rigid, his companions came closer and examined him, and found that he was dead indeed. They promptly removed all the incense and candles and effaced the traces of their ill-considered action, binding each other to secrecy. It was evident to them that the soul of their comrade, which had left the body in a dream, had been deceived by their pantomine into thinking that there was no return, and had dissipated itself.

Metamorphoses

In Europe beliefs in the supernatural are apt to take regional forms, the Balkans specialising in vampires, and werewolves being of Germanic origin. China seems to have found a parallel for every myth current in western history since the civilisation of the Greeks and Romans. The sorceress Circe changed her admirers into swine, whilst a Chinese witch solved her transport problems by transforming her clients into a troop of donkeys. The destruction of an enemy is achieved by making a straw, or waxen image and piercing it with pins or arrows in the best tradition of Mediaeval magic, whilst numerous animals are believed to be capable of assuming human form.

The creatures who make their homes in burrows in the ground were credited with supernatural power, as it was believed that, during the stillness of the night, they overheard the secrets of Mother Earth. This ac-counts for the cult of the Wu Sheng (五聖), or Five Seers, whose worship was proscribed by the prudish Manchus. Snakes, badgers, weasels, small deer and hedgehogs had to be treated with due reverence, and the respect for them increased with their age. They usually took up their residence in old and dilapidated buildings and, if their treatment failed to reach the standard to which they were accustomed, unpleasantness ensued. Doors opened and windows rattled, whilst servants gave notice rather than live in a haunted house. If a move was impracticable the only alternative was to seek the services of a Ch'ao Hsiang Ti (瞧香的) who was supposed to have an influence over the spirit. Unfortunately, this class of person was in limited supply and the treatment was expensive. The exorcists were generally old people, who were highly specialised. The practitioner who was good

for badgers was no herpetologist, and the weasel expert was powerless in the presence of hedgehog. This led to a great deal of abuse and charlatanry, so the police intervened to declare the practice illegal. Exorcisms, however, continued in secret. When the charmer visited a patient, incense was burned and the medium fell into a trance, during which the spirit was transferred from the victim to the practitioner. As the latter was on good terms with his familiar, burning incense to him every day, he suffered no inconvenience from the operation.

Wolves were a perfect scourge in North China and, in some parts of Shansi, medical missionaries found them accountable for the bulk of the casualties brought to them for treatment. Constituting such an ever present menace, it is quite understandable that they have found a place in the folklore of the country. A story, dating from the year 765, concerns a youth of the above men-tioned province, who fell seriously ill at the age of twenty, and worsened rapidly. Unfortunately his malady affected others as well as himself for he developed the ability to expedite his soul, in the form of a wolf which devoured children. Before he fell sick, he was an odd job man about the village. One day, as he was passing in front of a house where a child had been eaten, the owner said he had need of his services on the following day, and that he would be well fed. The boy burst out laughing and said he had no need to work, as there were plenty of plump children left. The villager cocked an ear, and asked him to repeat himself. He replied that he had been put into the world to consume the human race, and that the previous day he had made an excellent meal of a child of six years old. The unfortunate father then realised what had become of his son. He seized the lad, saw that his mouth was still blood-stained, and fell upon him with a mattock. As he expired, he changed into a wolf.

Another Shansi story concerns the mother of General Wang Han (王含) of T'ai Yuan Fu. She was a Tunguse, and a noted Amazon, whose sole distraction was gallop-ing through the forest glades bow in hand, slaughtering hares, deer, bears and foxes. When seventy years of age her strength waned, so she shut herself up in her bed-room, and refused to let anyone enter. One night, when the household was sleeping, the servants heard the door of her apartment open. They spied on her, and saw a female wolf emerge, and leave the house. She returned as dawn was breaking, regained the bedchamber, and shut the door. The maids were thoroughly scared at what they had seen, and reported the matter to Wang Han. On the following night he kept watch from a hidden position, and witnessed the same performance. The discovery that his mother was a wolf horrified him, and he soon had further proof. The old lady demanded venison for dinner so he bought a stag. When he asked how she would like it cooked, she told him to serve it raw, and disposed of the whole beast at a sitting. Wang saw no solution to his domestic problems, which were the constant topic of conversation among his retainers. One day the old lady overheard them discussing her. That night, when the wolf wanted to leave the house she found the door barred, so she crashed through the framework of the window and escaped. That was the last that was heard of her, to everyone's immense relief.

The Tiger, whose depredations cause much destruc-tion, is also credited with assuming human form after dark. A certain woodcutter in the Sung Yang (松陽) district of Chekiang who was helping himself to fuel in the mountains, found himself benighted. Cornered by two tigers, he took refuge in a tree. Unfortunately, the perch was not far above the ground but, high as the beasts leaped, they could not reach him. One of the tigers addressed the other, and said "If Chu Tou-shih (朱都事) were here, we'd soon have him down." "Go, and fetch him," replied the other, "while I stay here, and mount guard." The first beast was soon back, with a longer and lither tiger. This third made a leap, and clawed the skirts of the woodman. He disengaged his axe from his belt and, at the second bound, sliced one of his assailant's forepaws. The three tigers fled, roaring horribly. Their would-be victim took care not to put his foot to ground before it was broad daylight. When he got home, he told the whole village his experiences, and one of them recognised the name of Chu Tou-shih as a man living in the neighbourhood, to the east of the hamlet. It was decided to go and look him up, and half the village accompanied the expedition. When they asked to speak to the man, they were told that he had been out the night before, and had injured his hand. This left no doubt in their minds that he could turn into a tiger when he liked, so they sent a deputation to the magistrate. The official armed his satellites, surrounded the cottage and set fire to it. Suddenly a tiger burst through the flames, broke out of the cordon, and disappeared. That was the last that was ever seen of Chou Tou-shih.

The Chinese Circe is the heroine of a typically Taoist lengend set in the T'ang dynasty when, to the west of K'ai Feng Fu, there was a famous hostelry known as the Bridge Inn. The hostess was a woman of about thirty years of age, whose origins to say the least of it were obscure, as nobody knew the slightest thing about her. The general gossip had it that she was widowed, without children or family. She kept a magnificent stable of asses, and was most obliging, being widely known for her liberality. If a traveller presented himself with little or no money, she would accept him at a reduced rate, or put him up for nothing. As her reputation became established, her inn was always full. Between the years 806 to 820 A.D. a certain Chao Li-ho (趙李和) put up at the inn for the night, on a journey to Lo Yang, which was then the capital. There were already six or seven guests, who had taken up the beds in the common dormitory. Chao, as the last arrival, was allotted the last bed in the far corner next to the party-wall which separated the room from the mistress' chamber. The innkeeper, known as the Third Lady, served her guests with a first rate dinner. When the moment came for retiring for the night, she stood a round of wine, and drank their health. Chao alone did not partake, as he was of abstemious habits. In the second watch, when all the guests were asleep, the Third Lady entered her room, shut the door and blew out the candle. Whereas all the others were snoring, Chao could not get to sleep. When it was approaching midnight, he heard his hostess moving something about in her room. He peeped through a crack in the partition. She lit a candle, and then drew out of a box a miniature ox, a plough, and the figure of a countryman. The figures were about six or seven inches high, and she laid them out before the altar on the beaten earth of the floor. Shen then squirted a little water from her mouth on the puppets, which immediately came to life. The peasant goaded his ox, which drew the plough up and down, breaking as much ground as might be covered with a mat. When the soil was prepared, the Third Lady handed the ploughman a small packet of buckwheat seed, which he planted and it began immediately to sprout. The grain ripened, was reaped and winnowed, and seven or eight quarts were handed over to the mistress, who ground it in a small hand mill. When this operation was completed the puppets, who had again become inanimate, were restored to their box, and the lady made griddle cakes. Soon after this the cocks began to crow, and the guests arose to get ready for their departure. The hostess refused to let them go without breaking their fast, and placed on the table a dish of cakes. Chao, having seen how they were prepared, felt a loss of appetite, and made his excuses before he left the house. However, his curiosity got the better of him and, instead of resuming his journey, he hung about to watch the sequel. As soon as the guests took a bite out of the cakes, they fell to the ground and started to bray. Then they scrambled to their feet as superb donkeys, and the Third Lady drove them to the stable, appropriating their baggage. Chao said not a word about his adventure, but promised himself to turn the tables on the sorceress.

A month later, having completed his business, he passed again that way, and asked a lodging for the night, after taking the precaution to provide himself with some fresh buckwheat cakes of the same shape as those served by the landlady. That evening he was the only guest and his hostess was all the more attentive. Before going to bed she enquired if he wanted anything further, and he replied that he would like breakfast before setting off in the morning. The Third Lady assured him that his desire would be gratified, and made her preparations as on the previous night. At daybreak she appeared, put a plate of cakes on the table, and went out for a moment. Chao took one of the bewitched cakes, and substituted one of his own, and then awaited the return of his hostess. She chided him for not eating, but he said he was waiting for her to keep him company, that he had brought some cakes of his own, and would not eat hers, unless she took one from his supply. She agreed, and he passed her the enchanted cake he had abstracted from the dish. At the first mouthful she fell, started braying, and arose a most wonderful ass. He promptly bridled and saddled her, and mounted to continue his journey after confiscating the box with the puppets.

The Third Lady proved the best donkey in the world, for nothing stopped her, and she could make thirty-five miles a day. Four years after her metamorphosis Chao Li-ho was on a journey to Ch'ang Nan (昌南) when he passed near a temple on Hua Shan. In his path he saw an aged man, clapping his hands and laughing. "So it's the good lady of the Bridge Inn!" he cried "So you've come to a pretty pass". Seizing the bridle he said to Chao "She had evil intentions as far as you were concerned, but her penance has lasted long enough." He grasped her muzzle with both hands, and wrenched the jaws apart until the lips where the bit bears were torn. Immediately the Third Lady wriggled out of the donkey skin, made a profound reverence to the magician, thanked him, and vanished. She never was heard of again, and history does not relate what became of her former guests.

Compounding a Quarrel

The Chinese are a smiling race, and have the good sense to accept a compromise rather than nurse resentment for failure to achieve a complete victory. Harmony ranks high among the virtues they admire, and they dread taking an irrevocable step, whose consequences may be unpredictable. Living, as they do, in such close proximity to one another it would be a miracle if tempers were not sometimes frayed, and hasty words did not lead to temporary estrangements. Though they habitually look on the bright side of things, they have some redoubtable termagants, and a family possessed of a Ma Chieh-ti (罵街的) has no cause for congratulation. These "Curse the street" women, as they are called, bring discredit upon the house by airing their grievances to the parish at large, or washing their dirty linen in public. When their feelings get the better of them, they open the gate of the compound and treat the neighbourhood to an unending string of abuse at the top of their voices. They seem to have lungs of leather, and a vocabulary which would do credit to Billingsgate. In the old days they were disciplined at New Year, by being forced to make obeisance to their husbands, and promise amends.

When local Chinese women quarrel, and there is no chance of a reconciliation, they break a comb signifying in the language of the Lower Deck that they have parted brass rags. It is exceptionally unlucky to pick up one of the fragments, as this action transfers the dispute to the finder of this toilet accessory.

Certain women invoke the aid of their patron divinities to punish their adversaries, and make straight for the temple with a bundle of incense to lay their wrongs before the altar and to demand revenge.

Judging by the spectacular results achieved in certain cases, this method has its merits, though it hardly conforms to Christian ethics. Probably it only appeals to the Ma Chieh-ti for the more normal have recourse to religion only to dissipate the bad feeling.

Sacred Rock, Stanley

They apply to one of the spiritualistic mediums, or wise women, explain their trouble, and leave the matter in her hands. Their presence at the service for exorcising the demons responsible for the dispute is unnecessary, but they are invited to nominate a deputy, to see that the ceremony has been properly performed.

Recently a young married woman brought her case to one of these mediums, who practised well out of her district. She had difficulties with her husband who, while generous with his friends, kept too tight a hold upon the purse strings where she was concerned. The lack of trust galled her, for otherwise there was no meanness about her man. The wise woman determined a lucky day and hour, and invited her to be present but, as a friend of her husband's worked in the village, she was afraid of his reporting her presence, and left all the arrangements to the exorcist.

The village Earth God is the presiding deity for the intimate affairs of the parish, the registrar of births and deaths, and the general tutelary, so he is regarded as the arbiter of disputes even, as in this case, out of his district. As the matter was in the hands of one of his flock, the wise woman, he presumably was the competent authority.

The ritual accessories consisted of a talisman invoking the Gods of the Dark Altar (玄壇), offerings of paper clothing, a square of yellow paper, and a representation of the Five Demons at the root of the trouble.

A generous supply of the most lethal firecrackers obtainable was essential for their destruction, and an earthenware teapot to concentrate the effects of the explosion. Candles and incense are the concomitants of any form of worship, but for dealing with a dispute, fresh eggs have to be broken.

The Earth God's shrine contained a brick altar, in the centre of which was the pointed stone, representing the God of the Soil and the principle of fertility. In a corner was the clay statuette of the Divinity of the Locality. All over the walls were red cut-outs representing babies, votive offerings of clients who have been blessed with posterity.

Candles and incense were first lit on the altar, and the name of the client was communicated to the divinity. The invocation followed, whilst the exorcist waved the yellow paper in front of the image. The crackers were then inserted in the teapot, and the strip of paper with the Five Demons was placed on top of them, care being taken that they were head downwards, so that their skulls received the full impact of the blast. The offerings for the deity were next burned and the blazing mass was passed to and fro over the incense before being carried out to the brazier. The officiant had brought a supply of eggs in a saucepan together with a small metal bowl. Removing one of the eggs, she brought it down with a lighted taper at the altar candles, and then the fuse of the crackers was ignited and the congregation dispersed to await the explosion. This was eminently satisfactory, and the shards of the teapot flew in all directions.

Before the smoke had cleared away, the officiant returned and carefully examined the debris, without discovering a trace of the culprits. This was a highly favourable omen that their destruction had been encompassed, and that no further trouble was to be anticipated.

The name of the girl suppliant written on a slip of

paper was burned to reveal her identity as responsible for the sacrifices, more incense was lighted, and a prayer was intoned. This was followed by the waving of a fresh supply of paper offerings over the incense and candles accompanied by an invocation. A second egg was dashed into the bowl and shattered, and the service concluded with the burning of the remainder of the paper.

Vindictive old crones, who enjoy nothing more than cherishing a grudge, try to discover the Eight Characters of the time of birth of the individual who has offended them. These are written on a slip of paper and either placed under the image of the God, or dropped into an urn containing human bones, with a request for appropriate action. If the spirit is responsive, the nominee falls sick and turns yellow, or may be affected mentally. The latter affliction usually demonstrates itself in doing foolish things, or acting on bad advice which would normally be rejected. The only remedy for overcoming this is a quite appreciable expenditure for a special service at the Temple of Kuan Yin, if a Buddhist, or T'ien Hou, if the sufferer adheres to the Taoist religion.

Spirits of Healing

In all primitive religions, and in some modern ones for that matter, disease is regarded as a punishment by the Gods for offences committed against their divinity and the laws promulgated by their ministers on earth. Prayers are therefore offered to remove the affliction, and sacrifices are made in propitiation of the offence.

Instead of calling in a doctor to treat a case of measles, a peasant mother in China will attribute the complaint to the machinations of evil spirits, and will apply to her patron Saint to assist her in their expulsion. Even if a medical man be summoned, he is quite likely to foster her belief, and reinforce whatever treatment he prescribes by the administration of a charm, written on paper and burned, whose ashes are credited with effecting the cure.

The connection of sickness with religion is so firmly established, that even a well-educated Chinese, about to undergo treatment by a western-trained physician, will often submit himself to a service conducted by a medium, with offers of gifts to ensure divine protection, and he enters hospital with a talisman around his neck.

A favourite haunt for the spirits of healing is to be found in the sacred trees, of which each village in Hong Kong possesses at least one representative. The island of Cheung Chau regards the inhabitant of its arboreal shrine as its communal ancestor, distributor of progeny and general practitioner. The trunk of the tree is pasted over with innumerable red cut-outs of infants born in answer to petitions, and the walls of the sanctuary are decorated with inscriptions testifying to the efficacy of the spirit in restoring petitioners to health. In other parts of the country the branches are festooned with paper scrolls, inscribed by grateful worshippers or, if the purse and literary attainments are deficient, hung with gaily coloured rags in acknowledgment of answered prayer.

Worship by individuals is naturally performed as circumstances dictate, such as if there is sickness in a family, but the spirit is not neglected by those fortunate enough to enjoy a clean bill of health. Sacrifices are made at the solstices and particularly at New Year, when children are brought by their grand-dams to be introduced to the source of their existence. At the Feast of the Hungry Ghosts, a banner surmounted by a coolie hat and strung with lanterns is erected at the foot of the tree, accompanied by a paper shrine to the "Guardian Child". Three times a day this is visited by the priests in procession, and libations are poured out for the spirit.

In prefectures and county capitals part of the obligations of the City Gods is to avert and dispel epidemics. If cholera or plague break out, the image of the Magistrate of the Dead is carried in procession through the smitten wards and, if a river should run through the town, a service of intercession is held on the banks. As a culmination to the rites, a paper boat is launched to carry off the disease. If this is fairly caught by the currents and transported out of the precincts, the omens are favourable, but if a back eddy carries it ashore, the plague will return.

This expulsion of the devils causing disease is also practised privately in Hong Kong by the mothers of children whose sickness does not respond to ordinary home treatment. In one case, the petitioner took a garment belonging to the patient and knotted up a number of peanuts in the skirt. These were to act as prisons for the offending spirits and, though other receptacles would have been equally efficient, peanuts were the cheapest.

A visit to the Paper Shop furnished candles and incense, clothing, and the money consisting of gold squares printed in the centre of white sheets of paper. These were carried to the verge of the sea, where a sand altar was erected on which the incense and candles were lit. The mother knelt facing the waves, and made her intercession for removal of the cause of the disease. Lighting a bonfire of the sacrifices she took the child's garment and, still praying, passed it several times with a circular motion over the blazing paper. To dispel the demons, who were now confined, a paper boat was set adrift, to carry away those with maritime instincts, after which the frock was unknotted to remove the peanuts. One of these was thrown away to the left, one to the right, and the third over her shoulder behind the petitioner. This disposed of the land-based demons, who had thus been expelled from the garment and scattered to the four winds of heaven.

Subsequent inquiries elicited the fact that the mother had consulted a wise woman, to diagnose the cause of her offspring's affliction, which took the form of a wasting sickness. The practitioner demanded no fee, except the customary honorarium of twenty cents "lucky money", and based her treatment on the examination of the child's hand. In this case she declared that the little one had been scared of the water, which accounted for the service being held at the sea-side. Normally, to get ride of devils, rice moistened with water is the medium employed, but here water was tabooed, and peanuts prescribed. If a child has a narrow escape from being run down by a car, and suffers from a mild shock which affects the appetite, a similar sort of service must be held in front of some parked vehicle. Part of a bucket of water is thrown over the car, and the residue is taken home and the patient is bathed with the fluid, from which the demons have been expelled.

These home remedies are peculiar to the Hakkas who

inhabit the little valleys in Hong Kong, cultivating vegetables and rearing pigs. They find it cheaper than calling in a doctor and, from the class of practitioner they are likely to employ, they probably achieve equally satisfactory results. They literally believe in the "hair of the dog that bit them" for, if a child's indisposition is attributable to canine allergy, a tuft of the animal's coat must be procured. This is tied with a cord or ribbon, and is hung round the patient's neck. Children with scraps of fur, in the midst of a bunch of amulets, are commonly to be seen in the New Territories. The silver lock to bind them to life, and the chicken's leg to enable them to scratch a living, are among the charms in most general use.

Evil spirits, the world over, are most active after the shades of night have fallen, and many children dread the dark. Though they cannot banish these fears of the unseen, precautions can be and are taken to deal with the demons. The cubbyholes where the children sleep are fumigated by burning charms and sacred paper, and the explosion of crackers completes the exorcism.

Fortune Telling

A desire to see into the future seems inherent in the human race. Even in England, the Sunday papers feature "Nostradamus", and "What the Stars Foretell" and, were their predictions omitted, there would be a greater outcry than would be provoked by the disappearance of the Times crossword puzzle. China probably leads the world in ordering its life and timing its actions in accordance with the dictates of fortune. Old Moore's Almanac is popular in England, but in China every action permissible or forbidden is clearly laid down in the calendar for each day of the year. No one dreams of starting a business or repairing a house on one of the days unlucky for such an enterprise. Even a visit to the coiffeur on an unpropitious day may entail a very unpleasant penance for a relative in the other world, who is condemned to drink the dirty water for a month after her descendant has committed the indiscretion.

For those who wished to order their lives according to the Chinese calendar, its injunctions for three weeks of the 2nd moon in 1954 were as follows:

1st of Second Moon. Element: Earth. On this day it is inadvisable to prepare sauce, or paste, neither should one dress up, or attend important functions. On the other hand, it is a good day for religious devotions, and results are likely to be obtained. Generally speaking it is not a propitious day. There is an eclipse of the sun, but not visible in China.

2nd of 2nd Moon. Element: Metal. This is a bad day for altering watercourses, and opening dykes. It is also no good for asking favours of the gods. On the other hand, luck will attend weddings, and it is favourable for paying visits, making clothes, and exchanging gifts. It is good for business, annulling contracts, setting up a roof beam, taking cattle out to graze, buying livestock, and attending funerals. Taken by and large, it is a lucky day, and undertakings will prosper. From 3 p.m. till 5 p.m. are lucky hours for anyone born on this day, but they must beware of those born under the sign of the Monkey.

3rd of 2nd Moon. Element: Metal. This is a very bad day for those involved in law suits, and no occasion to choose for digging wells, or making ponds. Money should not be lent. It is propitious for starting studies, calling, or making excursions. Weddings held on this day will be blessed with luck. There is no objection to taking a bath, or consulting a doctor, dissolving contracts, or putting in a new door in a house. The storeroom should be restocked, and it is a good day to select for the assumption of official mourning. (This does not depend on the date of death. Sober clothes are immediately put on, but the mourning laid down by tradition does not begin till a fortunate day is indicated by the calendar.) It is a good day to bury people, and 5 a.m. till 7 a.m. is the lucky hour. People born on this day should avoid those born under the sign of the Cock. Various worries are declared up.

4th of Second Moon. Element: Fire. On this day the storeroom must not be opened. Giving way to tears must be avoided at all costs, as it will entail several deaths in the family. It is lucky to call on friends, make clothes, make and repair fish nets.

5th of Second Moon. Element: Fire. It is inadvisable to do any planting, or start on a long journey. It is, however, good for repairing roads against the day when such a trip is contemplated.

6th of Second Moon. Element: Water. It is most dangerous to consult a doctor on this day, or to take medicine, build the kitchen stove, or go in pursuit of game. It is a good day to take new members into the family, and all right for calling, weddings, dressmaking, exchanging presents, opening a shop, and financial transactions of all kinds. One may safely start building, erecting pillars, or setting up the roof beam. Planting, taking livestock out to graze in the fields and burying relatives are all in order. 5 p.m. till 7 p.m. is a very lucky time for those born on this day, but it is equally good for anybody else. "Rat" people are the enemies of those born on this day. All vegetation now starts new growth.

7th of Second Moon. Element: Water. This is one of the days when any sort of visit to the barber is forbidden. Hair-cutting, shaving, or permanent waving are out of the question, as is any form of medical treatment. The day is a good one for coming of age, travelling, starting studies, house moving, or paying calls. Dressmaking is recommended, and most building operations, including the repair of the storeroom. Planting, and buying livestock will bring good results. It is a good day for burying relatives, and 5 p.m. to 7 p.m. is the luckiest period. People born on this day should have nothing to do with those born under the sign of the Ox.

The 8th day of the Second Moon is dedicated to the Earth element. It is a bad day for investing in land, or making the sleeping platform on which the beds are laid. On the other hand it is good for indulging in a bath, for medical consultations, and for house-cleaning. Taken all round it is an unlucky day.

9th of Second Moon. Element: Earth. A bad day for giving entertainments, or calling on friends. It is lucky to worship the gods, for coming of age ceremonies, or opening business. Construction of houses should be begun, and it is a favourable day for funerals, but generally speaking it is not a good day.

10th of Second Moon. Element: Metal. One must refrain from eating dog's meat, but it is the day when all insects arouse from hibernation, and the first real warmth is observed in the air, so apart from this one deprivation, it is a very lucky day.

11th of Second Moon. Element: Metal. Wine should not be brewed, and food presents should not be given. It is a bad day for weddings, but good for hair-cutting and having a bath. Taken all round it is a good day. If the sinking of a well is started the water will be sweet. If, however, a death in the family occurs on this day, another will soon follow.

12th of Second Moon. Element: Wood. A bad day to have anything to do with irrigation work, or to consult a fortune-teller. It is good for taking new members into the family, for coming of age ceremonies, visits to the coiffeur, or for concluding contracts. Financial transactions will be successful, and it is a good day for undertaking repairs, or planting trees. Anything else undertaken on this day will be unsuccessful.

13th of Second Moon. Element: Wood. A bad day for anything connected with growing things, maintenance of land, and irrigation channels, disturbing the earth for foundations, or disposing of coffins. It is a lucky day to begin studies, for travelling or calling on friends, taking up a new appointment, or setting up a roof tree. Cattle may be taken into the fields to graze, but generally speaking it is a bad day.

14th of Second Moon. Element: Water. The storeroom should not be opened on this day, nor should the gods be worshipped. One should not pay out cash. It is good for starting studies, for coming of age ceremonies, for cutting out clothes, and for business transactions. It is lucky to receive cash. Repairs, or any sort of earth work will prosper. Doors may be put in, and kitchen stoves may be built. Wine may be brewed and food preserved. A good day for funerals. Much danger threatens on this day, and one is, so to speak, "in the Mouth of the Tiger".

15th of Second Moon. Element: Water. An inauspicious day for planting, digging wells, or any disturbance of the soil. Good for religious exercises, travelling, paying calls, or assuming new duties. People who reach their majority on this day will be lucky, as will those who deal in financial matters, balance their accounts, or make new clothes. On the whole, it is a propitious day for expansion of business.

16th of Second Moon. Element: Earth. A most unlucky day for repairing the kitchen stove, but a good occasion for moving house if it is past praying for. A good day to take a bath, or clean the house. It is good to make contact with the earth, either in planting, or construction work. On the whole a lucky day.

17th of Second Moon. Element: Earth. It is unlucky to visit the barber, or disturb the soil, but all right to pay friendly calls, cut out clothes, exchange gifts, open business, or any commerical transactions. One can set a roof beam with confidence, or send cattle out to graze. Generally speaking, a day on which any undertaking will prosper.

18th of Second Moon. Element: Fire. A bad occasion to invest in farm property, to make wine, soya sauce, or other preserves. A good day, however, for repairing roads, and painting or decorating the homestead. Taken all round it is a lucky day, but no undertaking will prosper.

19th of Second Moon. Element: Fire. Avoid dissolving contracts, consulting a doctor, or taking the medicine he prescribes. The gods, however, may be petitioned with good hope of success, particularly in the case of a desired male heir. It is a good day to receive new members into the clan, for travelling, calling, and receiving visits from friends. The earth may be broken for construction work of all sorts. Wine should be brewed, and preserves made. The storeroom should be repaired to receive them, and it is an excellent occasion for funerals. The luckiest hours for everyone are from 1 p.m. till 3 p.m., particularly for those whose birthday it is, but they should beware of those born under the sign of the Ox.

20th of Second Moon. Element: Wood. Unlucky for making nets, or for all transactions as a middleman. Good for house-cleaning, during which operation the male members of the family may profitably indulge in hunting or fishing. If these are beyond their means they may acquire merit by releasing captive animals, or buying their own coffins, as it is a favourable occasion for going into mourning. On the whole it is a day when unpleasantness might exceed anticipation.

21st of Second Moon. Element: Wood. Noodles, soya, or shrimp paste should not be made. It is a bad day for entertaining, so one may safely get down to repairing houses, or walls. This is a most unlucky day, as if the roof were about to collapse, and bury the family.

In many respects the Chinese calendar is more logical than ours, for their spring begins on 6th February, and not at the vernal equinox, and their summer on the 6th May. Nothing can explain why an English summer officially starts on the 21st June, with mid-summer only two days later, except Lord Byron's belief that the elusive season opened on the 31st July, and the winter began on 1st August. In China the seasons are far more clearly defined, and the Great Cold definitely ceases on the first day of spring, whilst a cool breeze dispels the sultriness of the Dog Days on the 8th of August. If their day-to-day prognostications were as well substantiated as their fortnightly weather forecasts, life would be greatly simplified.

The Chinese calendar has always been regarded with particular reverence for, as a race, they were remarkably quick at discovering the interdependence of the earth and sky. The first directives to the astronomers date back to the Perfect Emperor Yao (堯) (2254 B.C.) who issued instructions to them to ascertain the solstices and equinoxes, employ intercalary months, and fix the four seasons. The register of years was prepared by a special Board of Mathematicians, headed by a Minister of State. Their production was held in such reverence that, when copies were distributed to the highest officials of the Empire, they were carried in sedan-chairs, placed upon a pedestal on arrival, and were saluted with prostrations and a salvo of guns. They enjoyed a special copyright law, for the death sentence was inflicted for piracy or counterfeiting.

The luck, or unpropitious character, of each day of the year was determined by the compilers by taking cognizance of the five seasons, elements, colours, parts of the body, animals and tastes, which control one another and influence the life of the Chinese. Combined with the twenty-eight constellations, known as the Palaces of the Moon, they exerted their influence over the weather and the affairs of mankind to such a degree that the almanac listed the dates propitious for the observance of rites, duties and pleasures.

The Chinese constellations are far more definite in their prognostications than our stars.

The sign of the Porcupine is favourable to starting silk culture, and a man born under it will never lack servants. The sign of the Swallow forbids any man to build a house, lest he risk having a violent death in the family, suicide by hanging, and the drowning of children under the age of three.

Fortune-tellers reinforce this invaluable vade-mecum, and are always employed for the three great events in life—birth, death and marriage. A new arrival in the world is invariably submitted to a Professional, who casts his horoscope and predicts his future. A case recently occurred among the Boat People where the soothsayer gave an unfavourable verdict, and foretold that a male child would bring no credit on the family, and had better be given away. The grandfather, however, though his belief in omens is not a whit inferior to the rest of the Boat People, has many patriarchal attributes, and decided that it was a nice baby, and that the risks of its retention were well worth accepting. So it stayed.

Part of the training of a Taoist Priest is in telling fortunes, but it is rather on the hit-and-miss principle. For a fee he proffers a hollow bamboo or box, out of which a slip of paper is drawn, and he gives his client an interpretation of the characters inscribed on it. This system is in great vogue at fairs and temple festivals, when the crowd is in a holiday mood, and money circulates freely.

Horoscopes are cast from the hour, day and year of birth, and the conjunction of the stars at the time. Another method is the numeral system by which 785 is added to arbitrary numbers, and the corresponding characters are looked up in a key. These, when strung together, form a couplet which gives a clue to the fortune.

The Manual of Fortune Telling by Physiognomy, conformation of all parts of the body, and posture, was written in the reign of K'ang Hsi by one Fan Lai, to assist those interested to read their own fortunes by their features. It is studied as a text-book by the professionals but, as it enters into such intimate details as the lines on the sole of the foot, which may compensate for a bottle-nose, their opportunities for a comprehensive examination of their clients must be limited. The work is entitled the "Water Mirror, too good to be true, Fortune-teller", and it describes the effect on character and luck of every organ of the body.

The Manual begins by dividing the human race into fourteen animal types, of which the first is the Dragon. He has a long face with high-bridged nose and popping, gold-fish eyes, which scintillate. The brows are wide, and the individual above the average height. Arms and legs are well-proportioned and finely boned. He will have good manners and be extremely clever.

The Tiger has a huge head with a broad forehead and round nose. His mouth is big, and his hair and moustache are sparse. His voice is thunderous, and his gaze fixed. He is tallish, and walks with a heavy gait. Such a man is invaluable in the fighting services, but lacks commercial instinct.

The Ch'i Lin type has a domed skull sloping back-ward, ears set high, and deep-set eyes, thick brows and a broad forehead. He will rise high in the world like the Dragon and the Crane.

The Lion is another military type, with yellowish pupils in eyes which are round and large. The bridge of the nose is flat and receding, mouth large and square. Eyebrows irregular, beard and moustache thick.

The Crane has an ethereal look, with a long neck and stride. He radiates good humour, and has a clear, musical voice.

The Deer man has dark lustrous eyes, with long ears set high, prominent cheek-bones, and thick moustache. His arms and legs are hirsute, and he has a trotting gait. Altogether a harmless individual, with no positive qualities.

The Ox type is strongly built and placid, with black rolling eyes, a big head, and thick neck. A stolid, slow mover and a hard worker without much recompense.

The Snake is narrow skulled, with a long, flat forehead and narrow eye-slits. He has a wide mouth, narrow, pointed nose with a red tip, an undulating waist when walking, constantly turning the head and leaning back. Not a trustworthy individual.

The Horse has a long face with big eyes and mouth filled with huge teeth. His body is long and his walk rapid. He is a hard worker.

The Sheep, harmless and stupid, has a square head and long, flat-cheeked face with pointed chin, and narrow jaw. The pupil of the eye is turgid, with the haw showing.

The Pig has a big head and long face, with long eyelashes and big ears. He has a thick, short neck and a shapeless figure. The individual who resembles him is just plain stupid.

The Dog has a large head with yellow pupils to the eyes, a narrow face and pointed chin, a big thin-lipped mouth, and a quick temper. He compensates for this by being a hard worker.

The Phoenix, as it is connected with Royalty like the Dragon, has favourable implications. It is characterised by long, narrow, clear and beautiful eyes with well-shaped brows and an aristocratic nose. The general build is slender and not too plump, with small bones and a voice like an echo.

The Eagle is not a popular type as it betokens untrustworthiness. The head is square, and the forehead round. Naturally the nose is hooked, and the eyes with golden-red pupils resemble the bird. A hasty temper never recommends itself to the Chinese.

The Peacock has an unstable nature, and loves luxury. It is denoted by a small face with small round eyes, disproportionately large body.

The Lu Ssu bird is the harbinger of rain, and is essentially a feminine type. It has a tiny body, with narrow slit eyes and long eyebrows. The head is also narrow, but the neck is square, and the waist long, as are the legs. It walks lightly, and is volatile in nature.

These are mere generalisations, to sum up the subject at a glance, after which his character is assessed by a detailed examination of his anatomy, each item playing a part to confirm or neutralise some other characteristic. Posture and movement are of the utmost importance, and the perfect man should stand as firm as a pine, sit as well based as a mountain, and walk like flowing water.

139

TAOISM, BUDDHISM, ANCESTOR WORSHIP, EARTH GODS & TREE WORSHIP

Chinese Religion

Francis Bacon, possibly the greatest master of English prose, prefaced one of his essays with the words: "What is Truth, said jesting Pilate, and stayed not for an answer." The great bulk of the Chinese race, apart from a small minority of devout Christians, Buddhists, and Muslims, probably share the indifference of the Roman Proconsul, or consider that speculation is unprofitable.

The Chinese have a saying that Confucianism, Taoism, and Buddhism are like the three legs of a tripod supporting the whole of their ethical life, and they see no inconsistency in subscribing to them all. Confucianism tightened the links of family life and those of the community, discouraging individual selfish adventure, and preaching that co-operation and virtue alone could preserve national unity. By stressing loyalty and truth, and condemning violence and disorder such as now afflict the world, China, in spite of many invasions, never disintegrated like so many other empires.

The insistence on filial piety and respect for elders and teachers produced a disciplined youth, and formed a substitute for the system of rewards and punishments in the after life, the anticipation of which exercises a restraint on the adherents of other religions. Ancestral worship is the hard core of all Chinese belief, and though, like the primary rocks of geological formations, it has been overlaid by subsequent strata, it remains the solid foundation which bears them. The teachings of the Sage were conservative in the extreme, and he sought to preserve and enshrine in his doctrine those qualities and creeds which were estimable in the past.

Although pure Confucianism was confined to the upper classes who, in Imperial days, ruled the country thanks to their profound knowledge of its tenets, which were the key to success at the literary examinations, the common peoples' lives were deeply imbued with its doctrines. Morality was imposed by the belief that an unworthy action was an offense against the ancestors, and that a blameless life ennobled them.

Confucius had great sympathy with the peasantry, and lent his patronage to their rustic festivals such as the grain dance, or Yang Ko, where a child is raised upon a portable platform to symbolise the sprouting of the corn. It is one of the fertility rites practised since earliest times, and is still prevalent in China. The worship of rocks and trees, or the spirits which inhabit them, is practised in every village in Hong Kong. The sacred trees are regarded as the ancestors of the community, and the rocks are relics of one of the most primitive forms of religion. In the case of the more important erectiles, such as the Yin Yang Shih (陰陽石), above Bowen Road, Taoism has invested the monument with an identifiable divinity, namely the Tzu Sun Niang Niang (子孫娘娘), she who furnishes posterity.

Grafted on nature and ancestral worship are the organised religions of Taoism and Buddhism. To gain acceptance both had to admit, or tolerate the primeval beliefs. Earth Gods and the Warden of the Kitchen were added to the pantheon of the former, and Buddhism, which had already been obscured by borrowings from Hindu mythology, could easily afford to accept a few extraneous deities.

Taoism in its pure form made little progress in the land of its birth. Instead of trying to infuse harmony into practical life, its followers sought freedom from the material. Their ambition was to escape the body so as to become free and powerful spirits. Only those with means which absolved them from earning a living, or confirmed vagabonds, could afford to lead the hermit-like existence prescribed by this doctrine. It entailed the abandonment of family ties, which mean more in China than anywhere else, and isolation from the community at large. It thus had little hope of commending itself to a society so gregarious as the Celestial Empire.

It was transformed into a popular religion through the genius of Chang Tao-ling (張道陵), the first Master of Heaven (天師), an inventor of magical spells, who introduced charms and talismans to ward off evil spirits from man and beast. He is still a power in the land, and his cabalistic antidotes for averting misfortune are published annually in the calendar. He founded a school of exorcists, and introduced faith healing into medicine. This new form of insurance against any form of calamity had a great appeal for the Chinese and the religion spread like wildfire. Lineal descendants of the founder acted as Pope, but there was no religious hierarchy, such as obtains in Christian churches. Neither are the temples, in Hong Kong at least, served by a regular priest. If an individual has a petition to make he goes in person, or in exceptional cases, arranges for some wise woman to deputise for him. The clergy specialises in exorcism, and the care of the souls of the departed. In certain cases of sickness they are employed, more to conjure the spirit responsible for the malady than in the hope that their prayers will be of any avail. They also officiate at Thanksgiving services after recovery, but demands for these ministrations are insufficient to provide them with a living. Most of them are employed in the Paper Shops, which make religious furnishings for festivals and funerals.

The introduction of Buddhism produced a revolution in Chinese religious thought, with its doctrine of reincarnation and purgatory. The Chinese did not take kindly to the idea of a place of eternal punishment after death, and the hells had to be considerably modified before they could be accepted. Spirits of the departed were awarded three holidays a year, when they were freed to revisit the earth, a whole month being granted in the Seventh Moon, with a short recess at Easter and All Souls' Day. The new conception led to an extension of the obligations imposed by Ancestral worship, for the souls had to be cared for in the afterlife. Hells were

The One Thousand Buddhas monastery . . . a revolution through religion

organised on exactly the same lines as the Imperial administration of justice, with magistrates, warders, and tormentors. As all of these were credited with the same rapacity as their earthly counterparts, it was necessary to provide the dead with money to ameliorate their treatment. Special services and dispensations of food, money and clothing were arranged for the benefit of ghosts deprived of the ordinary care by the extinction of the family responsible for their maintenance, to prevent them in desperation from becoming a menace to the community.

The new religion received a tremendous impetus under Imperial patronage during the T'ang Dynasty, and threatened the status of the native Taoism by drawing away its adherents. The Taoists were obliged to invent their own hells and saints, to compete with the new attractions. The Buddhist Goddess of Mercy, Kuan Yin, entered China as the male Bodhisatva, Avalokitsvara, but assumed female attire in the XII Century. Her popularity in this guise was so great that the Taoists had to retaliate with the invention of the Queen of Heaven. Saints were created from legendary heroes with little regard for accuracy, or even the laws of probability. Indian divinities found a place in the pantheon with their attributes transferred to historical Chinese characters. Borrowings of ritual and vestments were wholesale, resulting in the sort of compromise so dear to the Chinese. They are nothing if not tolerant, and Kuan Yin frequently occupies a shrine next to the Queen of Heaven, whilst a temple to the latter has an honoured place in the island of Pu T'o Shan, the stronghold of the Goddess of Mercy.

The conception of a personal God, Lord and Creator of the Universe, never occurred to the Chinese, but if they have an overriding divinity it is Luck. In the quest for good fortune in their mundane affairs they will propitiate any divinity, from the Lord Buddha to the legendary Monkey, who has the reputation of possessing the power to grant their desires. No spirit or belief dating from the most primitive times seems to have been discarded, whilst they are always receptive to new ideas if these promise to be advantageous.

The Chinese attitude to religion has often been summed up uncharitably in the words "The Chinese are not religious, only superstitious." This word is defined in the dictionary as misdirected reverence. What is Truth? The Chinese certainly believe in faith and, from the tokens of gratitude which adorn their humble Earth God shrines, their appeals for assistance are probably just as fruitful as those to the saints of Western civilisation. Prayers for personal advantage are common to East and West, where the English liturgy includes an invocation for rain, which may benefit the farmer, and ruin the bank holiday of the factory hand. Chinese, like most primitive people, filled the rocks and trees around them with spirits, beneficent or malevolent. They deified emperors, ancestors, and all the heavenly host. As time went on, they collected divinities with the same enthusiasm and lack of discrimination as a boy philatelist. But they extended their own tolerance to their divinities, and had no manner of use for a "jealous god" who demanded their sole allegiance. They were quite prepared to accept the whole Western pantheon provided that it supplemented, and did not displace, their own cherished beliefs. Nothing is likely to wean them from

The call to prayer

ancestral worship, which has the most steadying influence on their character.

According to Gibbon: "To the common people all religions are equally true, to the philosopher all equally false; and to the magistrate, all are equally useful." The conception that an unworthy act reflects upon a beloved ancestor has a great restraining influence, and inculcates a respect for the law, while the necessity of ensuring posterity to care for the souls of the departed fosters the solidarity of the family and clan. This intimate relationship makes the acceptance of an iconoclastic creed, which forbids normal reverence to common ancestors, a virtual impossibility for the individual, and the ramifications of the clan preclude the likelihood of a mass conversion. While the convert to Christianity will discard the fables of Taoist, and popular Buddhist mythology, he will cling tenaciously to the older religion which prescribes the care of ancestral tombs, and the sacrifices to the spirit tablets.

The agnostic returned student is, in all probability, a totally different person in the presence of the senior generation. The Emperor himself had to defer to the opinion of his aunts, when it came to a question of a break with tradition such as the abolition of the palace eunuchs, so the man in the street stands little chance of defying public opinion. There is a special hell for those guilty of unfilial conduct, and the Chinese take no chances were the future is concerned. Hence the presence

Fan Ling Buddhist service

of the clergy of all denominations at their final obsequies.

This filial relationship would seem an insuperable bar to the setting up of a Police State, on the lines of Nazi Germany, where the son denounced the father, and the family was divided against itself. Parricide was always regarded as the most heinous crime in China, and it is doubtful if an offender could long escape the fury of the clan. For thousands of years the welfare of the family has taken precedence over all other issues, and public spirit is almost non-existent. The total absence of foreign relations until the last century excluded the word patriotism from the dictionary, and the only substitute was xenophobia.

The Manchu official could always divert popular discontent at his maladministration by provoking an anti-foreign riot, and the same technique has been adopted by his Republican successor. The credulity of the lower orders is incredible, and the same story of babies' eyes being sought to make camera lenses served to incite the Tientsin riots of 1870 and the anti-British crusade of 1925.

It is one thing, however, to unite the people by stirring up resentment against the foreigner, and another to include public spirit to the extent of parting with something of commercial value for the benefit of a section of the population outside the family or clan. The Japanese invaders found that the farmer would not feed the industrial worker in the town unless he got the market price for his produce. Marxism is no substitute for the doctrine of his forefathers, on which Confucius himself set the seal.

Recent evidence, however, shows that attempts have been made to suppress all organised religion by using temples as barracks, and forcing the priests into productive labour. Ancestral worship is discouraged, and children are indoctrinated to criticise, and even betray, their parents if they utter sentiments inimical to the Party rule. The present policy is to bring up the younger generation, particularly those of middle school age, to discard all previous tradition, and substitute the worship of the State as the one Supreme Being, whose prophet is the chairman of the ruling class.

The organised religions of China, Buddhism and Taoism, were obliged, not only to leave intact these primitive beliefs, but to modify their teachings to conform with the susceptibilities of their converts. The Earth Gods were reluctantly admitted into the Taoist pantheon, and popular saints became interchangeable between the two rival sects. Whilst educated Chinese and certain monastic establishments adhere to the pure teachings of the founders of these religions, the mass of worshippers maintain their temples from very mixed motives.

Patron Saints are common to the religions of both East and West, and the priests of both have endowed them with birthdays, on which it is appropriate to honour them. The reform of the calendar in Czarist Russia was indefinitely shelved to avoid offence to the worthies who would have been deprived of their annual festival. The Chinese have invented a divinity to cover almost every action of human life, and a good many for the hereafter. As spirits have always been an obsession with them, it is not the idol, but the spirit within it, which is appealed to. And, in their case, there is a spirit. When the image is delivered from the maker to its shrine, an orifice is deliberately left communicating with the hollow interior. Into this the priest inserts an insect or a fledgling, before sealing it up, and removing the paper from its eyes to give it sight. The spirit of something which once had life therefore animates the representation of the divinity. The prosperity of a temple largely depends on the popularity of the gods it houses for, though there is a trickle of individual applicants throughout the year, the main income is derived from the annual festivals.

The Chinese have no weekly holiday on a Sunday, and these festivals, of which there is about one a month, are positively essential for recreational purposes. This fact has been recognised by most Christian missions, who organise outings for their adherents to correspond with the native celebrations. They are as much a holiday as a bean-feast of the Ancient Order of Buffaloes. The Chinese are essentially gregarious, and attendance is by guilds and clubs. Even the girl vegetable and fish hawkers form their sororities, each contributing a small amount monthly. Of this a percentage goes to the temple, part is spent on paper offerings and money for the god, and the residue provides an enormous feast as the culmination of a day in the open. It also acts as a Provident Society for, should a subscriber die during the year, her funeral expenses, with her fellow contributors as mourners, are a charge on the fund.

There is nothing gloomy in this aspect of Chinese religious life, for a festival is a riot of fun from beginning to end.

The Chinese pantheon is always in a state of growth and, like the Athenians, they always have an altar to the Unknown God. The Emperor had the power of canonisation, and the last raised to divine honours was a doctor in 1911. During the First World War an army officer and a local magistrate in Shantung evolved a new religion, which has made great strides. It was called the Tao Yuan (道院) (Hall of the Way), and combined what is best in Christianity, Confucianism, Buddhism, Taoism

Kwan Kung Temple, Cheung Chau . . . a Taoist sanctuary

Taoism's greatest appeal lies in ceremonies connected with the dead

and the Mohammedan creed.

Its tenets are purely humanitarian, and its aim universal brotherhood. Its best known manifestation is the Red Swastika Society which concentrates on educational, medical, and relief work. Prior to the Sino-Japanese War it maintained five hundred branches in China proper, most of them running a school for poor children, and practically all with a medical clinic. Its extension would go far to supply that public-spirit, which has been hitherto so conspicuous by its absence in the land.

Taoist Worship

Apart from ceremonies connected with the dead, and thanksgivings for the recovery from sickness, the services of Taoist priests are not greatly in demand in the actual worship of the host of divinities included in their pantheon. Even at the greater pilgrimages on the birthdays of the Queen of Heaven and Tam Kung the clerics are conspicuous by their absence. The males in the congregation present the sacrifices of pork, eggs and chickens, whilst the women occupy themselves in burning the paper clothing and investing in sticks of incense or lighting candles before their Patron Saint. Death, of course, is a more serious matter, and it is essential to neglect no precaution to secure the benignity of the spirit in future dealings with the family. A troop of priests is engaged to sing the appropriate masses, predict the hour and direction of departure of the soul, and finally to ensure its proper bestowal in the cemetery. During the Feast of the Hungry Ghosts in the Seventh Moon, charitable people also subsidise them to beat the bounds of the harbour to comfort the spirits of the drowned who have no known place of sepulchure, or those whose descendants have died out and are left with none to observe the ancestral worship. Having no living, in the Western sense of the word, the Taoist priests are obliged to supplement their income by fortune-telling and the sale of talismans.

In general, people enter the temples to worship as the spirit moves them, avoiding those days in the calendar which declare that the exercise is unprofitable. Minor shrines, like those of the village Earth Gods, the sacred trees and rocks, are propitiated when there is a family crisis of which they should traditionally be informed, and on certain fixed days in the year. These are the solstices, New Year's Eve, and the seventh day of the First Moon which is the birthday of all mankind. They are visited daily during the festival of the Hungry Ghosts by a procession of children headed by a priest, who offers prayers and libations. The client is usually of the fair sex, and brings with her a tray of food, which will later serve as breakfast for the family. This she lays down in front of the roots of the great banyan, whilst she arranges an altar with a flat stone. On this she lights two small tapers, from which she ignites a bundle of thin sticks of incense which are placed upright in an old cigarette tin. A short prayer of dedication is then made, kneeling, and a bundle of paper clothing is set on fire. This is waved three times up and down before the divinity and is placed on the ground to be converted into smoke. A string of firecrackers to prevent ill-disposed demons intercepting the gift concludes the ceremony.

The Temple of the Queen of Heaven provides a wide choice of divinities, and there is the added inducement of the facilities for telling one's fortune. The attendant, for a suitable fee, supplies the requisites of worship, candles, incense and paper clothing, after which the supplicant is left to his own devices. The Nine Gods, including the Tiger, who ward off calamities are so popular at New Year that a special incinerator for their offerings is placed in front of their shrine. In order that none of the divinities may feel neglected the worshipper first lights a couple of candles before the Patron Saint, and two more before the gods whose good offices are desired. A bundle of incense sticks is ignited from an oil-lamp and the worshipper goes round making a distribution. Certain deities like Kuan Yin get two or three, whilst those deemed as less efficacious have to be content with one. Straw mats, for kneeling, are placed in front of the image of the Queen of Heaven and the demon-scarers, before whom the worshipper kneels and performs the nine-fold kow-tow. A yellow paper is then waved with a circular motion over the candles and incense burner, after which it is used to wipe the face, before being consigned to the flames.

This is a talisman obtained from a priest to take the place of medical treatment, for some such malady as toothache or neuralgia.

The worshipper, now assured of protection against all forms of calamity, returns to the high altar of the Patron Saint in whose incense burner three superior sticks of incense are planted. Whilst these are smouldering a suit of paper clothing is set on fire, waved above the candles, and then raised and lowered three times before the ashes are consigned to a place of safety.

The client then consults the oracle by picking up a bamboo tube full of slips, from the altar. That it may give a true decision it is waved over the incense before the Goddess a number of times, and the supplicant again performs the nine-fold prostration. Kneeling, the container is shaken up and down until it is seen that one of the slips is rising above its fellows and eventually falls to the floor. Its number is taken, but not finally accepted until confirmed by the casting of the two objects used in divination. These are usually of wood, boat shaped, and rounded on one side whilst being flat on the other. If both fall the same way, the omen is good, but no answer attends one round and one flat. If the slip is confirmed in this way, its number is entered in a notebook. The other slips are disregarded as having no significance. Mathematically it should work out that one throw in three turns up in this way as either two rounds or two flats give a favourable answer. When nine definite replies have been recorded the worship is complete, except for a final burst of firecrackers in the central court outside the sanctuary. The expansion of gas on the explosion is supposed to drive off spirits which are part of the atmosphere, but it is a moot point if the demons dislike the noise as much as the Chinese appreciate the racket. Prescriptions or fortunes are issued by the temple attendant corresponding with the numbers on the slips.

The Taoist Pope

One of the picturesque survivals of Imperial China,

146

Pak Tai Temple, Cheung Chau . . . a Buddhist bastion

The shrine at the Tang Ancestral Hall at Ha Tsuen Shi

though his importance has diminished in a materialistic age where the God of Wealth alone commands the respect of all classes, is Chang T'ien Shih (the Heavenly Leader), the Supreme head of the Taoist religion. The title is hereditary in the family of Chang, and the present incumbent is the sixty-third of his line. His Palace is in the Dragon-Tiger Mountains of Kiangsi Province, which lie to the east of the capital Nanchang, but he has a town address in Shanghai and, in search of a less disturbed atmosphere than that prevailing at the moment on the mainland, he was paying a visit of indeterminate duration to Hong Kong.

The first of the line, Chang Tao-ling, was the inventor of the written charms which are still so popular with the adherents of the Taoist faith. He arose to prominence during the rebellious days which preceded the fall of the Han Dynasty, and was largely responsible for giving the religion a form which popularised it among the masses. The Chinese, being a practical people, have never set much store by abstract mysticism, but the quest for longevity has always had its appeal, and Chang preceded the alchemists of the Western Middle Ages in the search for the Philosopher's Stone. In the same way that Moses received the Tablets of the Law, he received a mystic treatise from Lao Tze himself, by means of which he was enabled to compound the Elixir of Life, and a vision directed him to a stone hut in which were concealed the writings of the Three Perfect Emperors and an ancient book of rites. He was not only a politico-religious genius but, for his day, he was an outstanding scientist. By dint of self-discipline he is reputed to have acquired power over the elements, and could match himself successfully against the Powers of Evil. His magic sword is still one of the family heirlooms, but is reposing in the Dragon-Tiger Mountains with the remainder of the Papal Regalia. The seal of office of the Leader of Heaven, however, accompanies the holder of the Papacy and is used to authenticate talismans of good fortune, written by his own hand. These are two mystic symbols inscribed on Imperial yellow silk, and stamped with the personal seal of the Chang T'ien Shih (張天師), as well as the much larger (four and three-quarter inch square) chop of his office.

A popular talisman is a bronze medal with a picture of the original Chang Tao-ling (張道陵) riding on a tiger and brandishing the magic sword with which he vanquished the "Five Poisonous Animals". According to the legend, he captured them, and placed them in the box in which he distilled the Elixir of Life. On the fifth day of the fifth moon they yielded their venom which contributed to form the true elixir, which was named after the domicile of the magician. Paper charms with the same device are on sale in Hong Kong, and probably in every other town of the size of a magistracy on the mainland. At the age of a hundred and twenty-three, Chang Tao-ling swallowed the pill of immortality, and ascended to the heavens. The title "Master, or Leader of Heaven" was granted by Imperial decree in A.D. 424, and its holder was entitled to confer buttons and seals of office to visiting priests. This was equivalent to sharing, with a spiritual leader, an attribute which belonged to the Emperor alone.

The present incumbent, the sixty-third of his line, is a charming and cultured gentleman, who received his guests with old-world courtesy and replied to their questions in excellent Mandarin, evincing a mental alertness and interest which rendered the conversation a pleasure. He stated that there is no organised hierarchy in the Taoist Faith, in the shape of Provincial equivalents to Bishops, and that the number of practising adherents is about a fourth of the population. He had little knowledge of the Taoists in Hong Kong, as he had only arrived from Canton a fortnight previously, and had not had time to acclimatise himself. The Taoist Hostel, which had taken him in, was in too bustling a thoroughfare to permit of rest and contemplation, and he would like to find a quieter retreat. He was not making any religious or social contacts, but came here for rest from a distracted country. He was not practising magic, and had left behind his properties for its accomplishment. This included the magic sword, which is in the Dragon-Tiger Palace.

There are, however, three Metropolitans, Yen Hung-ching (嚴洪清) in Shanghai, Tseng Hsi-ching (曾習勤) in Kiangsi, and Lei Tze-tung (雷紫東) in Hangchow, who are his spiritual lieutenants.

Chang En P'u (張恩溥), the sixty-third of his line, is about five feet seven inches in height, slightly built, with a scholar's stoop. He was dressed in a dark grey, long Chinese robe, unrelieved by any ornament, save a plain gold signet ring on the left hand. For a man, his hands are exceedingly small and beautifully formed, but capable, as the firmness of his grip testifies. His clean-shaven, kindly face has all the marks of centuries of good-breeding, and his charm of manner puts his guests at their ease, and banishes all embarrassment. He gave the appearance of thoroughly enjoying the conversation, and of genuine regret when his guests took their leave on the understanding that they were keeping him from an engagement. His invitation to return bore all the marks of a genuine desire to renew the acquaintance, and the guests departed with the feeling of having made a friend.

The Chang T'ien Shih presented his guests with the official history of his lineage, of which the following is a translation:

The first T'ien Shih, Chang Tao-ling, or Chang Fu-han, was in the ninth generation from Lord Chang Liang, of the Han Dynasty. He was born on the eve of the Hsiang Yuan Festival in the year Chia Wu, of Emperor Kuan Wu of the East Hans. At the age of seven he received from the Jade Emperor the Book of Morals. As he advanced in years, he mastered all the classics and every branch of learning from geography to astronomy. His span of life was 123 years, and his posthumous honours include the titles of San T'ien Chiao Chu (三天教主) i.e. Pope of the Three Heavens, and Fu Fa Ta T'ien Shih (輔法大天師), or Law Preserving Great Master of Heaven. He used talismans and spells to exorcise devils and defeat evil spirits, and prayers to dissipate calamities and evoke blessings. Though no longer a member of the world he was granted the hereditary title of "T'ien Shih" by one of the Han Emperors, which has been recognised and honoured by his successors on the throne. The eldest son of each generation succeeds to this title in accordance with Chinese tradition, and the present T'ien Shih is the sixty-third.

Chang Tao-ling himself selected the site of the palace on one of his wandering journeys from Szechuan Province, because he was so much impressed with the scenery. Two mountains resemble a dragon and a tiger bowing to one another. It is situated about twenty-five miles south of the Kwei Hsi district of Kiangsi, and the buildings are in palatial style. It is divided into two compounds, the Hsiang Ch'ing Palace, and the T'ien Shih mansion. The former is the temple proper, and accommodates 40 Taoist priests. The latter is the official residence.

The Chinese have a proverb which, loosely translated, means that no matter what catastrophe may overtake the country Chang and K'ung (Confucius) need not worry (天下雖亂張孔無憂). Oddly enough, most people take the saying literally, and regard the displacement of the Chang T'ien Shih as portending the end of all things, whereas the originator of the proverb meant that the Taoist and Confucian religions were so deeply rooted that no political upheaval would displace them in the people's affections. For that matter, the T'aip'ings burned the Dragon-Tiger Palace in the middle of the last century in the name of Christianity, without weakening the adherence to the old faith, so there is every reason to wish the Master of Heaven a happy issue out out of the present affliction.

Ancestral Tablets

Ancestral worship is the cement which binds the Chinese into a nation, and prevents its disintegration in times of conquest and changes of Government. The deification of the spirits of the departed is probably coeval with the worship of conspicuous rocks and trees, and is the basis of all religious belief. It is in fact the bedrock on which other strata have been superimposed, and those creeds which appealed most strongly to the race, Buddhism and Taoism, were obliged to build on its foundations. Hallowed by the veneration of Confucius, who subscribed whole-heartedly to the doctrine, it permeates the everyday life of the Chinese to an extent undreamed of by foreigners. Social customs, judicial decisions, appointments to the office of prime minister, and even the succession to the throne were influenced by it. The nomination of Te Tsung (德宗), whose reign title was Kuang Hsu, to succeed the Empress Dowager's own son, was a violation of the tradition as, being of the same generation, the ancestral worship could not be performed. One of the Imperial censors, having filed his protest, hanged himself at the grave of his dead master to emphasise his disapproval. A magistrate used to pass a much lighter sentence on a criminal if he were the eldest or only son, in the case where one or both of the parents had recently died, for fear of interfering with his sacrifices for the souls of the departed.

Ancestor worship has been defined as including 'not only actual worship, but also whatever is done directly or indirectly for the comfort of the spirits of the departed.' It further includes 'precautionary measures to avert their hostility for acts of omission'. The necessity for ensuring the succession to carry on the prescribed rites is responsible for concubinage and adoption, whilst indirect consequences determine housebuilding, the institution of hospitals, laying out of streets, modes of revenge, and methods of capital punishment. A hundred years ago a Chinese condemned to exile in the north-west would gladly exchange his sentence for decapitation,

as his banishment precluded his exercise of his obligations to his forebears. The consuming desire to have sons to carry on the family name, and to care for the soul of their progenitor in the afterworld, centres in this primitive form of religion, which is the only one entitled to be regarded as the national creed of China. The dead are the objects of worship by rich and poor, young and old, throughout the length and breadth of the country. According to those who have endeavoured to propagate other forms of religious belief, the Chinese are willing to relinquish every other form of worship, but this is so interwoven into the texture and fabric of their everyday life, and has so firm a hold on them, that scarcely anything short of the miraculous would induce them to abandon it.

Believing that the spirits in the underworld stand in need of the same comforts and necessities as in their existence upon earth, it is held the bounden duty of the descendants to supply their wants. Whenever the sacrifices are forwarded by burning, provision must also be made for the beggar spirits, who lurk around to intercept the goods destined for the more privileged, as it is believed that nearly all the ills to which flesh is the heir, such as death, calamity and sickness, are inflicted by these unfortunates.

On death, the soul of the departed takes triple form. One enters into the ancestral tablet, one accompanies the body to the grave, accounting for the Chinese reverence for their cemeteries, whilst the third starts on its journey to the underworld. The ancestral tablet is generally a slip of plain wood, rounded at the top, and fixed at the base in an oblong cross socket. The title is written with an ordinary Chinese brush and is headed with the reign in which the subject lived—now the Republic. Then comes the word "deceased" and the full name of the departed. If husband and wife are commemorated, the names are inscribed in parallel columns. Below them, in a vertical line with the reign are the three characters Chih Shen Wang (之神王) "their spirit prince". On the back of the tablet are given ages, date of death, and any honorific posts they may have held. The custom is said to date from the Chou Dynasty (350 B.C.) in memory of one K'ai Tzu-chu who sacrificed himself for his sovereign. This retainer, when accompanying his lord who was fleeing before his enemies, saved him from starvation by cutting off a portion of his own thigh. Unable to keep up with the refugees, he was perforce left on a mountain side to fend for himself. When the Lord of Tsin was returned to power he wanted to reward his henchman but he rejected all honours. The soldiers, after reporting his refusal to come to court, were sent back to bring him by force and, to dislodge him, set fire to the undergrowth which concealed him. Only his charred corpse was ever found. As a memorial of his disinterestedness, His Majesty ordered his name to be inscribed on a wooden tablet which was brought to the palace, where it was enshrined and honoured with the daily burning of incense.

For forty-nine days, during which the spirit is seeking the way to purgatory, the tablet is enclosed in a paper shrine and is placed behind an altar on which sacrifices are laid out, and daily offerings of freshly cooked food and wine are presented to assist the spirit on its journey. On the seventh night services are held by Taoist priests and Buddhist nuns, and the tablet is escorted by the

Wong Tai Sin temple

151

principal mourner over a long strip of cloth which starts the soul in the right direction for the gate of the Earth Prison, or the Land of Shades.

On the morning of the forty-ninth day, when the spirit is taken to be safely bestowed in the custody of the myrmidons of the underworld, a final service is held to endow the tablet with properties entitling it to daily worship. The officiating priest, with a brush dipped in blood drawn from a cock's comb, adds a scarlet dot to the character "Wang", (王), converting it into Chu (主) or Lord. It is then placed on a shelf above the family altar with the other ancestors and becomes part of the

family. Sacrifices are usually offered on the first and fifteenth of the moon, and at the great feasts like New Year, the ancestors are served before the family sits down to their banquet. No one but the head of the household may touch the tablets and, if any query arises concerning particulars inscribed on the back of one, he alone may take it from the shelf.

The case often occurs, particularly in Hong Kong, where so many residents have their homes on the mainland, that it is impossible to carry out the prescribed ritual. It goes entirely against the grain that forebears should be deprived of the attentions due to them, so the tablets are committed to a temple where a special altar is provided, and the monks or nuns accept the responsibility for their welfare. The tablets have a green or red ground with the characters raised in gold, in Sung (宋) Dynasty style. Every Buddhist establishment has one of these private chapels for guest ancestors and, at festivals, the relatives who have installed them make a pilgrimage to offer their personal worship and sacrifices.

Wealthy clans may build and endow a temple, where the tablets for generations are stored and looked after by a resident priest. The principle is the same as that which inspired the robber barons of the Middle Ages to found a chantry chapel in expiation of their sins on earth, and in the hope that priestly prayers would alleviate the pains of purgatory. Families in China have no trouble in tracing their descent back for hundreds of years, so the problem of storage of these memorials becomes acute for the inhabitants of a peasant's hovel. The ancestors are credited with wisdom and experience far beyond that of their descendants, who never embark on any undertaking affecting the fortunes of the house without consulting them. With time, however, the spirits are supposed to lose their potency, so they vacate the home altar after three generations have elapsed. The tablets are then reverently burned, the names remaining only in the roll of the clan.

The Boat People, whose storage space is even more limited than that of the cottagers, have smaller tablets which are kept in a locker above the shrine of the Queen of Heaven in the port cabin. Immediately after death, plain tablets are used, and they are not ornamented and inscribed for three years. Images are made of the deceased relatives.

Though they have adopted the custom of the Chinese in this form of commemoration of the dead, they have deviated in one respect. Those who die before marriage are not ancestors, and thus do not qualify for a tablet, but the Water Folk keep mementos of the children they have lost among the Family Gods in the form of small wooden images, the boys mounted on horses or tigers and the girls on white cranes. These may be seen in the shops dealing in religious articles in any fishing village in Hong Kong, such as Aberdeen and Cheung Chau.

In some parts of China, in wealthier families, post-humous portraits of ancestors are ordered which are hung up as sacred heirlooms in family temples. As in all Chinese portraits, no shadows are shown on the face, though the robes are portrayed with a wealth of detail. The artists were veritable craftsmen for, by the time they were commissioned, their model was well underground, and the picture had to be painted from a description given by survivors. Part of their stock-in-trade was a book showing various numbered types of features: nose,

Ancestral tablets

eyes, lips, etc. The relatives having decided on the nearest approximation to each feature of the deceased, it was entered in a notebook, and the artist retired to work out a composite likeness from the specification. Occasionally a wealthy gentleman would leave a conundrum portrait for his descendants to solve. This ensured the effigy being kept in the family, to his greater glory as, in these degenerate days, they are marketable commodities, and there was always the chance of the hidden treasure falling into the hands of that member of the family who had the greater share of brains. The clue might be a play on words or some gesture of the subject, which would ensure his residuary estate falling into worthy hands.

On the Nature of the Soul

The Chinese are united in the belief that the human body is possessed by two souls, a superior spirit, the Hun (魂), or Shen (神), and an inferior or animal controller known as the P'o (魄). Where they differ, according to the religion they practise, is in their conception of what becomes of the former after death. Confucius refused to be drawn into argument on this subject, which he dismissed as idle speculation, so his followers dispose of the question on the assumption that the soul merely dissipates itself. The Taoists consign it to Hell, and the Buddhists adhere to the doctrine of reincarnation. In fact, this belief is fairly universally accepted, as every Chinese knows the reason that a Celestial body is born with a blue spot in the small of its back. The soul, knowing from previous experience the tribulations that life on earth has in store for it, is most unwilling to quit the security of Paradise, and needs a good kick behind to propel it into the world. The bruise is regarded such conclusive evidence that the belief is as widely held in the South as in the North.

The superior soul only takes possession of its integument at childbirth, before which the inferior P'o is in possession. At death, the Hun escapes through an orifice at the top of the cranium, but the P'o remains until decomposition sets in. According to the force and energy of this spirit this process may be delayed and, if it has unusual strength, the body may continue possessed of a Chiang Shih (僵屍), when it becomes an appalling vampire, which devours men and violates women. To guard against such an eventuality any body which refuses to respond to the ordinary process of nature should be cremated. A fleshless skeleton, a skull, or even a single human bone, may, from the fact that the inferior spirit still clings to it, commit all sorts of atrocities, so the mortal remains are feared, and are always interred as far as possible from human habitations.

When dreaming, the superior soul leaves the body by the same orifice as in death, and wanders abroad. During these excursions its adventures are regarded as real happenings, and it is extremely difficult to persuade the Chinese of the subjectivity of dreams. According to their theory, during this separation from the body the soul may be captured, or so terrified that it is unable to return. In this case the inferior soul assumes command and the man loses his reason. Alternatively, it may literally give up the ghost, and decomposition sets in. The deformity of Li T'ieh-kuai (李鐵拐), most famous

of the Eight Immortals, is attributed to the fact that during the separation of his soul from his body the latter was inadvertently destroyed, and he had to be content with that of a crippled beggar who had just rendered his last account.

The Chinese believe that under mental stress an individual can go into a trance and expedite his soul to a considerable distance, to accomplish some particular mission or gain information. The law of Psychic Phenomena, as formulated by Hudson, admits this possibility, and it is illustrated by a charming story translated by Pere Wieger from the Chinese text, in which filial piety is rewarded. A young flower-seller in Peking was the sole support of her aged father, who fell ill and became bed-ridden. She neglected nothing for his comfort, and spent sleepless nights grieving over her inability to mitigate his suffering. Hearing that a married acquaintance was preparing to join a party for the pilgrimage to Miao Feng Shan (妙峯山), she visited her friend and asked her if she could effect her father's cure by making the journey to the temple. The lady told her that all who went there to pray with a pure heart obtained their every request, so the girl inquired the distance, and was told twenty-five thousand paces.

Chinese distances are elastic, and depend largely on the time element. If a rustic is questioned his answer is variable according to whether the objective is up or down hill. Thus he may tell a traveller that it is seven miles to the top of a mountain, whereas an inquiry at the summit would elicit the reply that is was only three back to the starting point. The girl, however, memorised the figure given and, from that day onward, as soon as her father had dropped off to sleep for the night, she lit a stick of incense and went out into the court-yard. There she walked up and down, carefully counting her steps until her strength gave out, when she prostrated herself in the direction of Miao Feng Shan and prayed to be excused from making the pilgrimage in person, as she was an unattached girl, and could not leave her father. At the end of the fortnight she had completed the 25,000 paces at the exact moment when the first batch of pilgrims arrived at the top of the sacred mountain.

An enormous crowd presented itself in which nobles and peasants, rich and poor were mingled. For it was of the utmost importance who should be the first to enter the shrine after cock-crow as, according to tradition, the earliest to plant an incense-stick before the altar was certain to have his requests granted. That particular day an extremely rich eunuch from the Palace, who had many sins of extortion on his conscience and sought absolution, was blocking the way, determined not to be forestalled. The moment the door was opened he entered and was dumbfounded to find a stick of incense already smouldering in the censer. He was furious and tackled the temple guardian, who assured him that the door was closed until he had used it, and that he had no idea who had offered the incense. The eunuch announced his intention of trying again on the morrow, and charged the guardian to secure the door firmly after the last pilgrims had left in the evening. True to his word, he was at the door well before the dawn and, when it was opened, he ran forward towards the altar. A stick of incense was already burning there and, in front of the censer, was a young girl prostrate, praying

A Taoist ceremony . . . old beliefs

to the goddess. The apparition vanished at the noise made by the eunuch. "Who on earth can it be?" he asked himself. "What spirit or demon can be offering incense to this goddess?" He hurriedly left the temple to retail his experience to the crowd of pilgrims, and asked what they thought it could be. The married lady whom the florist had consulted overheard him, and provided the solution. The girl was unable to come in person, as she could not leave her father, so she had sent her soul to pray for his recovery. The eunuch was mollified and, being a good fellow at heart, he went immediately on his return to the capital to find the flower-seller. He praised her for her filial devotion, and put a generous sum at her disposal for her father's treatment, which ended in his complete recovery and enabled the two to live in comfort. The girl finally married a rich merchant.

As in this case, the superior soul when it leaves the body is practically always represented as preserving its normal appearance, costume included, though it may appear under another form such as a fly, or a cricket.

Pagodas

Foreigners usually admire the Chinese pagoda without much idea of its significance. If they speculate at all, the chances are that it is taken for a temple, until closer inspection reveals its inadequacy for the accommodation of a congregation. The tower is certainly regarded as an embellishment to the landscape, or such a disastrous version would not have been introduced to Kew Gardens where the designer completely ignored the sense of proportion which is such a feature of Chinese architecture. Most Chinese pagodas are, however, too costly to be erected merely to add to the amenities of a locality unless to counteract some evil influences in the Feng Shui for the benefit of a wealthy landowner.

The pagoda is not indigenous to China but was introduced from India with the advent of the Buddhist religion in the third century. It is in fact a reliquary to mark the spot where the bones of some saint have been interred. The Sanskrit name is Stupa, and it is sometimes called Dagob, from Dhatu Garbha, meaning a relic preserver. The monument has also occasionally been erected in commemoration of some unusual act of devotion, or as an omen of good. After the death and cremation of the Master his ashes are said to have been divided into 84,000 parts each of which was enshrined in some locality in the Orient.

Pagodas are usually either circular or octagonal and the number of storeys must be odd. A simple version has five or seven, but those erected under Imperial auspices near Peking mount up to thirteen. From recollection, the Kew version has ten, but even numbers are considered unlucky in China.

The partiality for seven or nine storeys may stem from the belief that seven Buddhas are reputed to have existed at various periods, and that the original is the ninth incarnation of Vishnu.

Small stone pagodas are occasionally set up to improve the geomantic influences of a given locality, and plutocrats are fond of this form of decoration in their pleasure gardens.

Most of the genuine reliquaries are built of brick, with double walls inside which a staircase winds round giving access to the chambers on the various storeys.

Occasionally glazed tiles are superimposed on the brickwork outside, and the structures are then known as porcelain pagodas. The most famous one was built in the reign of Yung Lo (1403–25), at Nanking, to commemorate the virtues of his mother. It took nineteen years to construct, practically the whole of his life on the throne, and cost a fortune. It was unfortunately destroyed in 1856 by the T'aip'ing rebels whose iconoclastic zeal was also responsible for the wreckage of the porcelain industry in the Yangtze Valley.

Hexagonal pagodas are rare, but square are not uncommon. In some case several shapes are combined in one tower, with the cylinder superimposed on the octagon. Some are solid being only divided into storeys by projecting cornices on the outside. The highest in China is at Ting Chou in Hopei, whose 360 feet overtops the famous Nanking tower by one hundred and ten feet. The fashion for building such monuments was at its height in the Ming and Manchu Dynasties, and few have been erected in recent years, possibly owing to a decline in virtuous people to commemorate. It is estimated that more than two thousand are scattered about the country.

Very handsome examples are to be found in the neighbourhood of Peking, where emperors delighted in honouring their relatives with such memorials. About three miles outside the western wall of the sity is the village of Pa Li Chuang (八里莊), and to the north of the road leading to the hills stands the Yung An Shou T'a (永安壽塔), Pagoda of Everlasting Peace and Old Age. The plot on which it stands was originally purchased by one of the palace eunuchs as a burial ground, but he broke the rule forbidding such palace servants to leave the capital, and his property was confiscated. The pagoda was built in 1578 with funds provided by the mother of the Emperor Shen Tsung (神宗), whose reign title was Wan Li. The octagonal tower has thirteen storeys, under each of which hang rows of little bronze harebells which tinkle as the clappers sway in the slightest breeze. One occasionally falls to the ground when it becomes a perquisite of the caretaker.

From the point of view of the Feng Shui man a pagoda not only warded off evil influences, but had a positive merit in causing the youth of the city to gain literary distinction at the Civil Service examinations. The two pagodas inside Canton are likened to the two masts of a junk, whose poop is a huge five-storey structure on the north wall of the city. A large commercial centre is thus symbolised, foretelling the prosperity of the city as an emporium, as long as this felicitous combination remains undisturbed.

There is an enormous difference in style between the pagodas in North and South China, the latter being influenced by the architectural traditions of Indo-China and Siam where the curves are greatly accentuated in all buildings. The Northern derived from the nomad tent, and is severe in outline, whereas the Cantonese tradition imitates the swelling of the cumulus cloud. The two systems may be compared with the French furniture of the Louis XIV and Louis XV periods, or the trend in Church architecture which transformed the decorated in England to the perpendicular, whilst the French more logically progressed to the flamboyant.

A Taoist priest . . . diminishing importance

The Earth Gods

Religious tolerance is a strong characteristic of the Flowery People, and exceptions which prove the rule have usually been due to political pressure on the highest level. If anything, the Chinese are overinsured, and at funerals it is not uncommon to observe representatives of several religious denominations.

A new religion may be accepted, but this does not entail an entire break with the old. The family system sees to that, for Ancestor Worship has survived all State-sponsored rites, and the ramifications of the clan preclude the shepherding of all its members into one fold. In spite of a century of foreign contact, forms of worship connected with the Neolithic Age still survive in Hong Kong. The inhabitants of Victoria continue to bow down to wood and stone, like their primitive ancestors who conceived a spirit in every work of nature. In Peking, in the Temple of Tan Che-su, is a gigantic Gingko Tree (Maidenhair Fern Tree) which has an honorific p'ai lou in front of it, with an altar for incense. This was canonised by Imperial decree. Similarly, in the T'ai Miao (太廟), the Imperial Ancestral Temple, there is a "Spirit Tree" before which the Son of Heaven invariably descended from his sedan-chair and made obeisance.

When man made God in his own image, the Chinese created the T'u Ti (Earth Gods) (土帝), a race of genii loci who looked after the immediate neighbourhood. The T'u Ti has survived all organised religions, and has persisted in spite of Imperial rescripts and persecutions from rival sects. He is usually a rough clay or stone image, in a sitting posture, about twelve to eighteen inches high. His temple is so small that it resembles a dog-kennel, and no worshipper can enter. Outside is usually a mud trough for incense and, very occasionally, a receptacle for burnt offerings is placed on the east side of the edifice. In Hong Kong, T'u Ti's temples may be even less pretentious, and consist simply of an incense-blackened niche on the left side of a door-entrance. Were it not for the fact that it is sometimes decorated with a red paper with a black inscription, it might easily be mistaken for a boot-scraper. T'u Ti may serve a whole ward, as in Peking, a village, compound, or single family. As the peasantry in England "tell the bees" of a death in the family, so the Earth God is the recipient of all local gossip, and is the Registrar of Births, Deaths, and Marriages. He is the comforter in times of sickness and distress, and votive offerings of rags attached to sticks are made to him in recognition of his services in the case of recovery or granted wishes. The worst affliction of a Chinese is to be banished beyond the range of communication of his local guardian spirit. Even so there is a remedy, for T'u Ti is credited with the ability of the transmission of messages to those at a distance, and of delivering the answer.

In the shopping-district of the town, the Earth God is as constant a custodian of the Gold and Silver Exchange shops as the Indian watchman with his shot-gun. His shrine may be at the entrance, with the inscription "Men K'ou T'u Ti Fu Shen" (The Happy Spirit of the Doorway Earth God) (門口土帝福神) or he may have a more elaborate abode, either in front of, or under, the counter. In the former case it is not unusual to see a miniature altar, complete with the "Wu Kung", or five ritual objects, consisting of two vases, two candlesticks, and a central receptacle. One T'u Ti, one shop, is the rule and, opposite one market, there are three such establishments adjacent to one another, each with its own shrine.

On account of his intimate relations with the district he serves, T'u Ti is essentially a family man, for his clientele is largely composed of the fair sex, whose line of approach is through his spouse. This lady occupies the place of honour on his left and, should he be endowed with a concubine, she is made smaller than the wife, and is placed on his right. In one of the wards in the north-west corner of Peking is a small shrine with a solitary Earth God sitting in state in "Catch Thief Lane". It appears that he shared the national addiction to gambling and, at a game with a T'u Ti in the East City, staked and lost his wife. At all events the tumble-down temple in Ta Fang Chia Hutung houses two ladies besides its tutelary deity.

The T'u Ti is earth-bound, so to speak, and only responsible for his immediate entourage. There is a Chinese saying that the God at the East end of the village is helpless at the West. Thus, in Cheung Chau there is a shrine in the courtyard in front of the big Taoist temple, and two more within a couple of hundred yards to north-east.

The Earth Gods were first mentioned in the "Li Chi" (禮記), one of the five classical books, in A.D. 200, but these embody a much older tradition. The images may represent some forgotten hero, or possibly the deified ancestors of the first settlers, just as all kinds of oddly named saints have transmitted their appellations to Brittany villages. The fact that deaths are announced to the T'u Ti's, as to the Ancestral Tablets, lends colour to the latter supposition.

As, in the Christian religion, certain days are set apart as Saints' Days, so each Chinese Divinity is celebrated on his, or her, birthday. The Earth Gods share the New Year celebrations with the Household Gods: Tsao Wang (灶王), Patron of the Hearth, the Gods of the Gates, and Doors, and Mao Ku Ku, Patroness of women, needlework, and the lavatories. A few other intimate members of the household are occasionally thrown in, such as the Warden of the Central Hall, the Spirit of the Well and the God and Goddess

Earth God's shrine, Cheung Chau, brazier for burning gold and silver paper

of the Bedchamber, whose function it is to prevent babies rolling off the k'ang (坑), a clay platform which serves the dual purpose of couch and central heating. This is the occasion to look out for their temples in Hong Kong, for they will certainly be marked with red paper, and incense sticks may be seen burning. Customs in the South vary from those in the North, and occasionally characters are put up to replace the image of a divinity. This is certainly the case in Hong Kong where the God of the Hearth, or Stove King (Lu Wang), is concerned, and the fact that some T'u Ti shrines are empty leads to the supposition that the same procedure may be adopted in this instance.

There is something primitive and simple about the Earth God which is rather attractive. His worship takes place in the open street, and no priest interposes between the deity and the suppliant. Judging by the thank-offerings, appeals to him are just as efficacious as to the more elaborately housed divinities, who are less approachable. The Chinese are most punctilious in honouring their side of the bargain and giving value for favours received. With them it is not a case of "Hope springs eternal in the human breast. Man never *is* but always to *be* blest." They often exceed the recognised tariff, as a thanksgiving offering, by several times the amount.

The Familiar Spirit's rewards involve no great outlay, and consist of scraps of rag, attached to sticks, or hung on a bough overhanging the shrine. They are merely a token that thanks for favours received have been duly acknowledged. A similar custom obtains in Tibet, and fluttering rags are always seen at the Obos in Mongolia. The offerings are made by persons cured of sickness, under the belief that the disease has been transferred to the bit of material. It is a simple faith, but then T'u Ti was invented by a primitive people, and the fact that he has survived both official persecutions and the onslaughts of rival creeds goes to show that he has not yet outlived his usefulness. Magnificent temples, both Buddhist and Taoist, on which a succession of Emperors have lavished fortunes, have fallen into heaps of shapeless ruins. Their gilded images have returned to the dust which made them; but the Earth God's hovel is usually in good repair, and he still holds the affection of his tiny parish.

Primitive Religion

Entirely apart from the organised religions of Buddhism and Taoism, a surprising volume of completely primitive worship persists in Hong Kong. This passes unnoticed by the casual visitor, as its manifestations are only apparent at certain seasons of the year, and at some distance from the main arteries of communication. Buddhist and Taoist Saints have their birthdays spread over the lunar calendar, whilst the objects connected with Ancestral Worship are commemorated only at Chinese New Year. For a month after that festival, inscriptions on red paper mark the unpretentious shrine of the Earth Gods, whilst the eye is arrested by a similar splash of colour on the north side of the communal well.

Holy or Wishing Wells were common in England in medieval days, and the name Holywich persists in the Southern counties. The anchorite, needing a constant water supply, probably sited his cell in close proximity

Well shrine, New Territories

to a spring, which after his death became an object of veneration from its connection with the ascetic. If he lived to an advanced age, its waters were credited with curative powers, and it became a centre of pilgrimage. In China, the well-spirit counts among the Household Gods, and incense is burned before it on New Year's morning after the propitiation of the Ancestors, Earth Gods, and other domestic deities. In the remoter valleys of the New Territories, most primitive shrines are arranged for its worship. These consist of three upright rocks. The centre stone is capped with red paper bearing the inscription "En Shen" (恩神), "Honour, or cherish the Spirit". Two red scrolls flank the monument, praying for an unfailing supply of liquid jade to rejoice the hearts of men, whilst the flanking stones are decorated with cheap pictures symbolising wealth, longevity and fecundity. A cylindrical receptacle of pottery, or even a cigarette tin, serves as an incense burner, and occasionally a small porcelain cup is left for libations.

"Tree worship, which like river and mountain worship flourished in every part of the world, including Europe, still survives in various sequestered corners of China. The religious rites connected with trees are just as simple and harmless as the old maypole ceremonies in England (indeed much simpler and plainer) though from the point of view of the missionary they doubtless form a breach of the Second Commandment." This was said of the aboriginal tribes of Yunnan, but it is unnecessary to go further than a mile from Tai Po, in the New Territories, to find an instance in every Hakka hamlet.

Primitive man detected spirits in rocks, trees, and rivers, and, in spite of the shortage of fuel which has led to the deforestation of large areas of China, and impoverished the country through soil erosion, a prejudice persists against felling a large tree. In southern Fukien, their spirits are regarded as dangerous to offend. Many of the trees, however, are occupied by friendly spirits,

158

An aspiring monk has his head shaved

Sacred tree, Our Radiant Common Ancestor

who grant petitions, and are especially efficacious in cases of sickness. These are garlanded with paper scrolls inscribed by grateful clients, or brightly coloured rags, accompanied by the same characters "Honour the Spirit" which crown the reredos of the well altar. In one case a semicircle of rocks formed a sort of open-air chapel, whilst a large flat stone served as altar. The incense burner bristled with half-burned red sticks, and two or three libation cups were a mute testimony to the generosity of the congregation. These decorated trees are to be found near any small grouping of dwellings, whose inhabitants are too impoverished to maintain a temple. The ownership is usually communal, and it is by no means the largest tree in the neighbourhood which is selected for the honour. The custom is not confined to the Hakkas, though the Cantonese inhabitants of Lantau Island deck out their altars in a somewhat different fashion. A conical stone is wedged in the roots, capped with red paper with the usual inscription. Sometimes a small gilt talisman is pasted on the face of the stone, between two red scrolls. A very primitive P'ai Lou, or honorific arch, is constructed of two forked boughs with a cross bar, roughly lashed with twine. Pasted on the uprights are two sets of Chinese characters. The right-hand one reads "The Four Seas admire the pure and prosperous day", and the left "A myriad homes all congratulate you on your birthday". Pasted on the reredos rock is "Bless and Honour the Spirit". The altar is a level scrap of bared earth, with the usual incense burner and cups of wine. In the small village in the centre of Tung Chung Wan on the north coast of Lantau, two of these trees were seen close together, one

more elaborately decorated than the other, and therefore probably more efficacious. A hamlet about a mile up the valley had another, on the edge of the rice cultivation, set in a little lawn cleared of granite boulders, which had been used as material for the sanctuary.

Tree worship seems to have died hard in lands penetrated by the Bible, for the Jews were always in conflict with the sacred groves of the autochthonous population of Palestine. The Druids in Wales were not rooted out until the reign of Henry VIII who, as Defender of the Faith, felt an urge to suppress the pagan rites of the Land of his Fathers.

Rock worship in Hong Kong deserves closer investigation. Composed of distintegrated granite, Victoria Island and the New Territories have many shafts of hard rock, known as erectiles, and undoubtedly some of these have a sacred significance. As the emblem of fertility, of paramount importance in a race devoted to ancestral worship, they receive their tribute from engaged couples whose duty it is to ensure the perpetuation of the clan. Incense is burned at these Amah rocks, and prayers are offered for a fruitful marriage. About a mile south of Shatin station is an elaborate altar at the foot of a bare knoll surmounted by a squat shaft of granite, almost certainly connected with the cult, as a well-worn path contours the hill to the object of veneration.

Some sacred places in Hong Kong are quite new, and derive their status from the disappearance of the original shrine. In driving a new road the Public Works Department may find it necessary to cut down an old tree, or a private individual in levelling a building site may blast some huge block of granite. Should either be an object of worship, its neighbours will hold a service and invite the spirit to move its residence to some adjacent site, which they deem suitable. One of the rocks on the beach of Chik Chu Wan being demolished to lay the foundations of a house caused its deity to be urged to move to a huge banyan tree fifty yards further inland. As its tangled mass of roots had crawled, like a basket of snakes, over another rock, it was felt that the spirit would raise no objection to its new quarters. On New Year's eve a red paper inscribed Great Luck was pasted on the tree, whose old clients brought their offerings and burned incense.

Both Buddhists and Taoists have their Sacred Mountains, and shrines to their Ruling Spirits exist in Peking, both in the Forbidden City and in the Temple of Agriculture. Neither religion was able to eradicate the belief, so each followed the line of least resistance and admitted the primitive gods to its pantheon. In this way no revenue was lost, as the Chinese thoroughly enjoy pilgrimages, which furnish the organisers with a lucrative source of income. Birthdays of the rulers are fixed to suit climatic conditions and, whereas the summer heat is preferable in the North, the Southern peaks are mostly honoured in the winter and spring. It stands to reason that these elaborate excursions are not available to all, so local rocks and hills have been endowed with their own sanctity and serve the needs of a large proportion of the population. The fact that their "birthdays" coincide with those of the Household Gods is an indication of their antiquity, and the survival of the cult demonstrates the persistence of the race in its adherence to its primitive divinities.

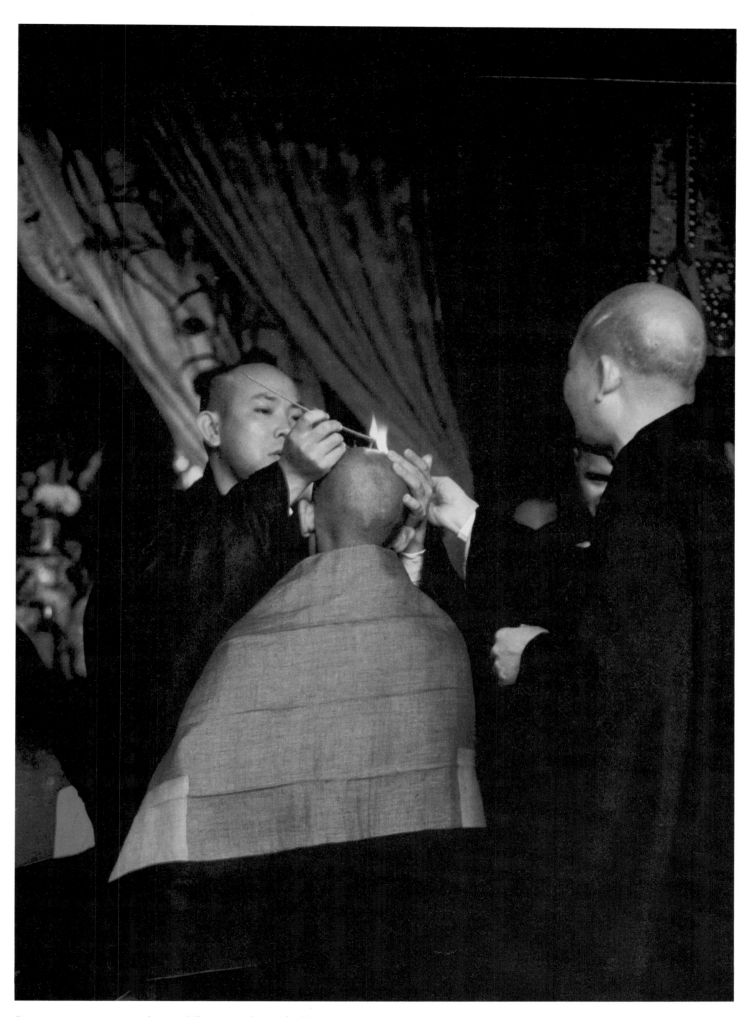

Initiation ceremony of a Buddhist monk : a challenging religion once . . .

. . . forced to accept popular beliefs

THE EIGHT IMMORTALS

The Eight Genii, known as "Hsien", or fairies, are a conception of the Taoist faith which has the strongest possible appeal to Chinese mentality. They are depicted in art from the most important jade piece to the humblest tea-pot, and their images, often beautifully carved in blackwood, decorate the table at birthday celebrations. The full set is eleven for, on these auspicious occasions, the Immortals despatch two children, mounted on water buffaloes, in search of the God of Longevity, who patronises the feast with the peach of immortality in his hand.

The Immortals represent a superior class of human beings who, after canonisation, dwell on mountain peaks, retaining their bodily form, and still very much in touch with the world. Anyone was eligible for this distinction, but its attainment was extremely difficult, for it entailed a strict bodily regime, coupled with the discipline of the soul, and the unending quest for the Elixir of Life. Various degrees could be attained, the first being the ability of the soul to leave its shell and, while retaining its human semblance, to discard the limitations of time and space, and to achieve eternal happiness without the dread of disease or death. Then came the perfect man, who could ride the clouds, like Wagner's Valkyries, and was deified as a hero. A first-class Immortal could make his transformation acts in full daylight, whereas the lower orders were restricted to the hours of darkness. Many of them live in the Palace of the Hsi Wang Mu, or Mother of the Western Heaven, but their deeds and attributes have been largely forgotten, and they are thrown completely into the shade by the famous "Eight", whose names are household words throughout the land. Their adventures are retailed by story-tellers at village fairs, and their images are to be found on the cheapest posters. Pastrycooks name their products after them, and some act as Patron Saints of trades and guilds. No temples are dedicated to them, though they are credited with the power of being able to raise the dead, and transmute any substance into gold by means of the Philosopher's Stone.

A sense of humour is a perpetual feast to the Chinese, and laughter is never far below the surface. The somewhat uncouth and roistering Immortals, full of selfish tricks designed to appeal to every section of the population, caught their fancy and won their undying affection. In the past, they have helped mortals to overcome their difficulties, so there is always the chance that an appeal to the appropriate Immortal may induce him to leave his revelry, and attend to the wants of the suppliant.

The Eight represent different conditions of life, viz. poverty, wealth, aristocracy, plebeianism, age, youth, masculinity and femininity, thus catering for every section of their worshippers. Each has his emblem, which identifies him in art, and these symbols are occasionally used separately to indicate their owners.

The Chief of the Genii is Chung Li-ch'uan (鍾離權), who discovered the secret of the Elixir of Life some thousands of years B.C., and invented the powder of transmutation. He is depicted as a stout individual with a bare midriff, sometimes holding a peach, and invariably with a fan for reviving the souls of the dead. The God of Longevity, on the other hand, clings to the peach, his other hand manipulating a long staff.

Chang Kuo Lao (張果老) belongs to the historical period, as he was a recluse in the 7th and 8th centuries A.D. who possessed supernatural powers, and could render himself invisible. In some mysterious way he became possessed of a white mule on which he covered immense distances. When not in use it could be folded up and filed. Chang preferred to ride with his face to the tail, so presumably left the destination to his mount, or exercised some form of thought transference. Like Lao Tze, he was old from birth, and claimed that he was a reincarnation of the "White Bat which succeeded the First Chaos". He stands for old age among the Immortals, but his picture offering a son is frequently the decoration of the bridal chamber of a newly-married couple. His emblem is the Yu Ku (魚鼓), a musical instrument in the form of a hollow bamboo, with two rods to beat it.

Lu T'ung-pin (呂洞賓), who lived about A.D. 750, was a scholarly recluse, who studied the secrets of Taoism under Chung Li-ch'uan, and attained immortality at the early age of 50. Originally of the family of Li, he rose to a high official position, but fell foul of the usurping

Chang-kuo-lau   *Chung-li Ch'uan*

163

Lu T'ung Pin   *Ts'ao Kuo-chiu*

integument had been somehow mislaid, and it was obliged to take over the only carcass available, that of a crippled beggar. Li expostulated frantically at this disgusting habitation for his personality, but was advised by Lao Tze, with whom he had been communing, to make the best of it, and was presented, as a consolation, with his famous iron crutch and a gold fillet for his hair. His emblem is the pilgrim's gourd, and he is sometimes pictured standing on a crab, or accompanied by a deer. He is the patron of druggists and exorcists who use their art for curative purposes.

The sixth of the series is Han Hsiang-tzu (韓湘子), nephew of Han Yu (韓愈), a famous scholar of the 9th century A.D. He could cause flowers to spring up and blossom instantly. He was a pupil of Lu T'ung-pin, who carried him to the supernatural peach tree, from which he fell and gained immortality. He is depicted with a basket of the flowers he loved and a jade flute, which entitles him to patronise all musicians.

Lan Ts'ai-ho (藍采和), whose sex is indeterminate, with a bias towards the distaff side, wears a blue gown, and has one foot shod and the other bare, as she wanders through the streets on begging expeditions.

He, or she, is a sort of natural, about whom little is known beyond the information provided by himself. As a street-singer he described himself as "A man, and not a man", and he denounced this fleeting life, and its delusive pleasures. His complete disregard for the money he earned by his jeremiads was, to the Chinese, conclusive proof of his insanity but, as he carries, like Ophelia, a basket of flowers, the florists have adopted him in spite of the superior claims of Han Hsiang-tzu.

There is no doubt about the sex of the last of the Eight. Ho Hsien-ku (何仙姑) was the daughter of a shop-keeper of Lingling, Hunan, who lived in the 7th century. She achieved immortality by eating a peach from the Tree of Life, given her by Lu T'ung-pin. Her symbol is the lotus flower of open-heartedness, and she is sometimes depicted playing on the reed organ.

The flower, however, is not her original emblem, but the first story seems to have been forgotten by Chinese artists. In early representations the maiden is shown with a ladle, and the form of the lotus sometimes recalls the shape of that homely utensil. The maiden was, in fact, a Cinderella, condemned by a cruel step-mother to a life of drudgery below stairs. She was so hungry that at times she fled to the forest, and subsisted on the meagre diet of moonbeams washed down by the evening dew. The Immortal took pity on her but, in his haste to remove her from her uncongenial surroundings, she was carried off with the kitchen ladle still in her hand. To commemorate her humility she was awarded the wooden spoon as her badge, but Buddhist influence probably substituted the lotus.

Sometimes she is represented poised on the floating petal of the lotus, with a fly-whisk in her hand. House-hold management is her province, so possibly a feather-duster would be a more appropriate symbol.

The Immortals cater for all tastes from the scholar to the lunatic, who receives a greater share of honour in the Orient than in more materialistic societies. They lead a carefree life, unstinted in drinking and festivities, and generally comport themselves with the irresponsibility of school-boys. Promoters of mirth, they banish care, and help to enliven the drab struggle for existence.

Empress Wu, and took refuge in the mountains. There, he prudently changed his name, studied alchemy, and took to ridding the world of the more obnoxious form of dragons, though his loyalty to the throne provided immunity for the worst of the evils which beset the Empire. His usual symbol is the "devil-destroying sabre", and a fly-whisk, or cloud sweeper, which indicates his mastery over space. He is the patron of the scholars and, by a confusion of sound so common in China, of a class at the opposite end of the social scale. A certain Lu Tsu Ta Hsien, a disciple of Lao Tze, was such a notorious evil-liver that he was expelled from heaven, and had to return to the world. At the Labour Exchange there was nothing to offer but a barber's pole, so he was obliged to accept the degrading profession to earn a living. This scamp is actually the Patron Saint of the profession, but the Guild has transferred its allegiance to his more reputable namesake.

Ts'ao Kuo-chiu (曹國舅) was alleged to be the son of Ts'ao Pin (曹彬), a military commander, and brother of the Empress Ts'ao Hou (曹后), of the Sung Dynasty. He is depicted in court-dress and official robes, and carries a pair of castanets. The actors have adopted him as their Patron.

Perhaps the most beloved Immortal is Li T'ieh-kuai (李鐵枴), who is represented as a lame beggar leaning on his iron crutch. He was the first to gain immortality, as he was the pupil of Hsi Wang Mu herself, who took him in hand after curing him of an ulcer in the leg. He had a hard childhood, as his parents died when he was young, and he was ill-treated by a shrewish sister-in-law. Taking refuge in the hills, his soul left his body to visit the Sacred Mountain of Hua Shan. On its return its

Tales of the Eight Immortals

The Eight Immortals are venerated by the Taoists as having absorbed the Elixir of Life, or otherwise obtained indestructibility. They are comparatively modern divinities for, although individual legends are found earlier, the full group receives no mention before the Yuan dynasty (A.D. 1206–1368). Since that time they have been an inspiration to artists, from the decorators of porcelain to the wood and ivory carvers, and have provided themes for both painters and poets.

The chief of the band is Chung Li-ch'uan (鍾離權) whose origin is dimly seen through the mists of history or legend, and only the doctrine of reincarnation can reconcile the different accounts which build up his biography. One places him under the family name of Chung-li in the Han dynasty, so he is often referred to as Han Chung-li, a source of confusion to the foreigner, who is apt to regard the reign title as his personal name.

His birth is, however, traced back by others to the cyclical year 2496 when he became Marshal of the Empire, later resigning this honourable office for a hermit's cell on Yang-chiao Shan in the Province of Shansi. His deeds in active service and retirement earned him the title of King Emperor of the True Active Principle.

Another story credits him with being a mere Vice-Marshal in the service of Duke Chou Hsiao, where his military attainments were by no means transcendent, for he was defeated in battle and escaped to Chung Nan Shan. There he met the Five Heroes, the Flowers of the East, who instructed him in the doctrines of immortality.

There are authorities who maintain that his name is not a personal but a territorial appelation, whilst others say he was a Taoist priest called Chung Li-tze. A more extravagant version of his career makes him a beggar who presented one Lao Chih with a pill of immortality, which induced dementia, causing him to leave his wife and ascend to Heaven. Chung Li then proceeded to work miracles on earth, transmuting copper and pewter into silver and distributing the proceeds among the poor, who would otherwise have starved in times of famine. One day while he was meditating, the stone wall of his cell among the mountains gaped apart, revealing a jade casket which contained a tablet imparting the secrets of immortality. With no worldly matters to distract him, and the whole day for contemplation, he set about the study of the rules, and followed the instructions. When he had completed the course, his room was filled with many-coloured clouds and divine music, to the accompaniment of which a celestial stork bore him away to the realms of immortality.

He is usually represented holding his feather-fan, Yu Mao Shan, with which he has been known to revive mortals who have breathed their last, but sometimes he carries the peach of immortality. On several occasions his return to Earth has been reported, and he has imparted the secrets of eternal life to one or two of his colleagues, notably Lu T'ung-pin. The latter was a much later creation, having been born in A.D. 798 at Yung Lo Hsien in Shansi. He was the scion of an official family, his grandfather having been President of the Board of Ceremonies, and his father, Prefect of Hai Chow. He was not a tall man, his height being only five feet two inches, and he was still unmarried at twenty, two years beyond the normal age for contracting an alliance. At this time he made a trip to Lu Shan in Kiangsi, where he encountered the Fire Dragon. The interview was entirely a friendly affair, and Lu created so good an impression that they parted with the pilgrim enriched by a magic sword which enabled him to conceal himself in the heavens.

He continued his tour to Ch'ang An, then the capital of the Empire in Shensi, where he met the Immortal Chung-li, who extended his powers by instruction in alchemy and the distillation of the elixir of life. When the Master revealed himself as a supernatural being, Lu expressed the wish to aid in converting mankind to the true doctrine. Before accepting him as a missionary, Chung insisted that he should undergo a test and withstand ten temptations. On his successfully accomplishing this feat he was invested with magic weapons and the power to employ them, after which he traversed the Empire, ridding the country of noxious reptiles and evil influences for a period of four hundred years. In A.D. 1115 the Emperor Hui Tsung conferred on him the title of Hero of Marvellous Wisdom, and later he was raised to King-Emperor and Strong Protector.

Another version of Lu T'ung-pin's elevation to immortality is known as the "Rice-wine dream". Here he met Chung-li at an inn, where the old magician was heating a jug of rice wine. Lu, tired after his journey, dropped off for a nap whilst the evening meal was being prepared, and dreamed that he was promoted to very high office, and was enjoying an exceptionally successful career. Suddenly he lapsed from grace and committed a fault which entailed his exile and the extermination of his clan. Alone in the world, in the outer darkness of the border provinces, he was bemoaning his fate, when he woke with a start. The dream was so vivid that he felt he had passed through a lifetime, and yet the wine in Chung Li's beaker was not yet hot. This convinced him of the transitory nature of life and the hollowness of worldly dignities, so he followed Han Chung-li to the Ho Ling mountains in Shensi, to be initiated by him into the divine mysteries.

Both stories stress his missionary zeal in spreading the doctrines of Taoism, for after his own enlightenment he visited Yueh Yang in the guise of an oil seller, intending to confer benefits on all those who were content with the weight he offered for a given price. For a whole year he only encountered shrewd bargainers, with one exception, an old lady who was content with his offer. He followed her to her house and threw a few grains of rice into the courtyard well. The water was miraculously transformed into wine, from the sale of which the old dame amassed a fortune.

Lu was a noteworthy swordsman, and is always represented with his magic weapon, called Chan-yao Kuei the "Devil-slaying sabre". In one hand he holds a fly whisk, Yun Chou, the "Cloud Sweeper", a common Taoist symbol showing the ability to fly and walk upon the clouds. He is often depicted with a male child in his arms, a promise of numerous progeny among whom will be found those of superior intelligence, who will graduate as scholars and noteworthy officials. For this reason he has been adopted as the patron saint of the literati.

In Hong Kong a clan temple at Fanling is dedicated

to him, and the attendant assures visitors that the title of the shrine was written by Lu himself, with "quite a small brush".

Of all the famous Eight, the one with the most universal appeal is the crippled beggar Li T'ieh-kuai (李鐵枴), or Li with the Iron crutch. He is a very ready help in adversity for, despite his physical affliction, he is always cheerful and the gourd which he carries is stocked with magic drugs to relieve pain and distress.

One biographer states that his earthly name was Li Yuan, though he was also known as K'ung Mu, and that he studied to become immortal under the Queen of the Western Heaven, after she had cured him of an ulcer on the leg. He was canonised as Rector of the East, and was a man of commanding stature and dignified appearance. Hsi Wang Mu made him a present of the iron crutch, and sent him out as a missionary of Taoism. This story is far from convincing, as there is no explanation why the crutch should be necessary after the limb had been restored to vigour by divine assistance.

The more generally accepted account is that he was originally Li Ning-yang, and such a promising subject that the Founder of Taoism, Lao Tze himself, descended from heaven to instruct him in the mysteries of the religion. Shortly after he had been perfected, his soul left his body to visit the sacred mountain of Hua Shan. He left instructions with a disciple Lang Ling that, if he failed to return within seven days, the discarded body was to be cremated. Unfortunately, before the week had elapsed, the guardian was called away hurriedly to his mother's death-bed. Fearful of leaving the corpse unattended he arranged for its cremation before his departure, and Li returned to find only an urn of ashes.

It is a common belief that the soul leaves the body during a trance and wanders abroad, and that during its absence there is a danger of intrusion by some un-authorised spirit. This accounts for Li's precaution of setting a watch at the time of his departure. He was now threatened with the fearful fate of becoming a Hungry Ghost but fortunately in a forest he came across the body of a beggar who had just succumbed to hunger. The corpse was not a desirable residence for its head was long and pointed, the face black and the beard woolly and unkempt. One of the legs was shrivelled, making locomotion impossible, so Li prayed that death might release him from this horrible predicament. Lao Tze, however, counselled patience and gave him an iron crutch, and a gold fillet to bind his unruly locks. The eyes of the revitalised corpse were enormous, which accounts for his soubriquet Li K'ung Mu, or "Hollow-eyed". It is generally supposed that he lived in the Yuan period, though tradition is vague about the time of his earthly existence. One account alleges that he was changed into a dragon, in which guise he ascended to heaven.

He felt no animosity at his pupil's lapse for he visited him in his home, and revived his mother whose funeral preparations were well advanced. This was the first occasion when the magic gourd came into play, for its contents were poured into the mouth of the old lady who left her bed in perfect health. Li disclosed himself to his disciple, and vanished in a sudden gust of wind. During his earthly visits he hung up the gourd on the wall at night, and leaped into it, emerging in the morning to continue his healing rounds. Several attempts at effecting the transmigration of mortals are recounted of him, notably that of the watchman Ch'ao Tu. Li proposed that this individual should follow him, like Shadrach, Meshak and Abednego, into a burning fiery furnace but Ch'ao, fearing to be accused of witchcraft, declined the invitation. The Immortal then proposed that he should step upon a floating leaf which would bear him, like a boat, across a turbulent stream. At a second refusal he declared that the cares of the world were evidently too heavy for him to attain immortality, so he himself embarked on the frail support, and disappeared. He had more success with his negligent disciple, for he returned after a couple of centuries, and taught him the way of everlasting life.

Li is sometimes represented standing on a crab, or accompanied by a deer. The gourd is always with him, and care is taken to indicate his deformity, by the iron staff with which he counteracts his lameness.

Chang Kuo Lao (張果老) belongs to the T'ang Dynasty, between the VII and VIII centuries of our era. He seems to have preferred the life of a hermit, and refused to leave his retreat on Chung T'iao Shan, in Shansi, in spite of persistent summonses to Court. At last, owing to the importunities of the Empress Wu (A.D. 684–705), he consented to present himself, but died of a stroke outside the Temple of the Jealous Woman. Though his body decomposed, he was seen again, alive and well, in the mountains of Heng Chou. His transportation was effected by means of a white mule which, when not in use could be folded up like a piece of paper and carried in the pocket. When required as a mount, Chang Kuo Lao had only to unfold it, and spurt water from his mouth upon the paper, which immediately was ready to carry him thousands of miles in one day. He usually rode the beast facing the tail, presumably steering by telepathy as he was an outstanding magician.

The Immortal is usually referred to as Chang Kuo Lao, the last character meaning venerable, a well-merited title if any credence is to be placed in his assertion that he was the re-incarnation of the Grand Minister to the Emperor Yao (2357–2255 B.C.) One story relates that in A.D. 735 he was summoned to the Palace at Loyang, where the Emperor Hsuan Tsung had him elected Chief of the Imperial Academy, as Very Perspicacious Teacher. At this time the well-known Taoist, Yeh Fa-shan was in high favour at Court and enjoyed the monarch's confidence. The Emperor asked him if he knew who Chang Kuo Lao really was, and received the reply that he was aware of his identity but if he revealed his knowledge he would fall instantly dead. He dared not speak unless the Emperor promised to go barefoot and bareheaded to Chang to ask his forgiveness. The Emperor thought the information worth the loss of dignity, so pressed the question. Fa-shan then said "Chang Kuo is a white spiritual bat, emerged from primeval chaos", after which revelation he dropped stone dead at his master's feet. The Emperor fulfilled his part of the bargain and tendered his apology for his indiscretion to Chang Kuo, who revived Fa-shan by sprinkling water on his face. Shortly after the disclosure of his identity Chang Kuo fell sick, and retired to the Heng Chou Mountain to die. When some time later his tomb was opened by his disciples, it was found to be empty.

Han Hsiaing-tzu　　　　　　　*Li T'en-kuai*

Among the feats of magic he performed whilst at Court were the drinking of aconite without ill effects, bringing down birds by pointing at them, and causing flowers to wilt. He could also render himself invisible at will. Although an ascetic during his lifetime, his image, riding on a mule or ass, is often hung in the chamber of a newly married couple. In his arms he carries a male descendant, with his usual attributes, the phoenix feather or the peach of immortality.

Han Hsiang-tzu (韓湘子) was born with a silver spoon in his mouth, and was brought up in the best circles of society. He was a nephew of Han Yu, a great statesman, who lived from A.D. 768 to 824. Besides reaching high official rank Han Yu was a noted scholar, poet and philosopher. The child was entrusted to his care, or was probably adopted by him, with the intention of supervising his education to bring him up to the standard of the triennial examination. The boy, however, soon outdistanced his master not only in learning, but in the performance of miraculous feats. Though the minister was no mean expert in Taoist arts, he was astounded when his nephew produced, from a handful of soil in a pot, an exotic plant on whose leaves were inscribed golden characters forming a poem.

"Mount Ch'in Ling is wreathed in mist.
"Where will you find a shelter for the night?
"In Lan Kuan the snowdrifts block the way,
"Your horse jibs wildly at his plight."

Han Yu asked the child the meaning of these verses, but had to be content with the reply that some day it would be made clear to him. Years later Han Yu fell from grace, and was sent in exile to the Prefecture of

Ch'ao Chou in Kwangtung. When he reached Lan Kuan, the Pass was blocked by a snowdrift so deep that his mount foundered. Whilst Han Yu was wondering where to take refuge from the blizzard, Han Hsiang Tzu appeared and cleared the path, recalling to his tutor's mind his childish prophecy. This encounter put heart into the old man, who had reconciled himself to dying in a damp, foggy land. On parting his nephew handed him a prescription, and assured him he would not only return in perfect health, but would be reinstated in all his honours.

Han Hsiang-tzu's exploits with growing plants have led to his association with horticulture, and he is occasionally depicted with a basket of flowers, or the peach of immortality. In the story of his association with his uncle, no mention is made of how he attained the status of immortal, and the explanation offered is that he performed his miracles after a fall from a tree which brought about his transformation. This account is elaborated by saying that he came under the patronage of Lu T'ung-pin and was carried off by the genii to the Heavenly Peach Tree, being translated to immortality when he slipped from its branches.

Han personifies youth among the Immortal Eight and, as he is an accomplished performer on the jade flute, has been adopted as the patron of musicians. The instrument is his normal means of identification in art.

Ts'ao Kuo-chiu (曹國舅) represents officialdom, and is shown with a tablet of admission to Court in his hand. He was related to the imperial family of the Sungs, being the younger brother of the Empress Ts'ao, wife of Jen Tsung (A.D. 1023-1064). Ashamed of the dissolute life of his elder brother, who ended by being condemned to death for murder, he withdrew to the mountains, resolved to expiate the family sins by a life of meditation. Mountains are frequented by the Immortals, so it was not surprising that, in the course of their wanderings, he was discovered by Han Chung-li and Lu T'ung-pin. They happened to have a vacancy in the establishment for, though seven grottoes in the Upper Sphere were tenanted, the eighth remained uninhabited. Finding Ts'ao in his retreat, with no clothing but wild plants, they inquired what he was doing. He replied that he was engaged in studing the Way. On being asked which Way he pointed to the sky. To the question "Where is the sky?" he gave the answer "In the heart," which decided his guests that he was worthy to be of their company. They left him a prescription for attaining perfection, and in a few days he qualified to occupy the empty grotto.

Another version of the story, obviously stemming from the same source, is so discreditable that it is a wonder the Seven Immortals admitted Ts'ao Kuo-chiu to their exclusive society. In this account he was an accomplice of the bad brother, whose crime is reminiscent of the biblical episode of David and Uriah the Hittite. The superfluous husband in this case was a graduate named Yuan Wen-cheng, of Ch'ao Chou Hsien, who was travelling with his wife to compete at the Imperial examinations. The younger brother, Ts'ao Ching-chih, was attracted by the lady and invited the pair to stay in his palace, where he disposed of the encumbrance by strangling the husband. As this means of wooing failed elicit a response from the widow, he had her confined in a loathsome dungeon, to force her to yield to his advances. The case came to the ears of the imperial

Censor, Pao Lao-yeh, probably through palace gossip, but according to the story, through the appearance of the soul of the murdered man. The elder brother, knowing that there was no means of hushing up the scandal once it was in the hands of this incorruptible official, counselled the culprit to destroy the evidence by throwing the woman down a well. The Star God T'ai Po Ching-hsing, in the guise of an old man, however, drew her up and connived at her escape from the palace.

When she gained the open road she met a procession which she mistook for that of the Censor, and presented herself at the sedan chair to make her complaint. The official unfortunately was the elder brother of the man she was accusing, who declared that she had acted disrespectfully towards him, and ordered her to be beaten to death. She was left for dead at the side of the road but, having a tough constitution, revived, and made her way to Pao Lao-yeh. As the result of her complaint Ts'ao Ching-hsiu was arrested for the assault and was exposed fettered in the cangue. The younger brother was confronted with the widow and condemned to death, for the murder of her husband. All the entreaties of the Emperor and Empress failed to save him from the scaffold, and his head was severed by the sword of the common executioner. His accomplice was released when, at the intercession of his aunt, the Emperor proclaimed a general amnesty. This narrow escape changed his nature, and he resolved to make amends by retiring from public life to a hermitage. There, through the exercise of abstinence and constant meditation, he came in touch with the Immortals who finally elected him to their company. He was apparently nominated because he had "the disposition of a genie," a characteristic he must have worked hard to acquire. Possibly it was felt that somebody of imperial birth would lend tone to the band, who were drawn from all walks of life, and represented every condition namely, poverty, wealth, aristocracy, plebeianism, age, youth, masculinity and femininity.

Ts'ao is depicted in court headdress and official robes, and carries a pair of castanets in one hand. He is the patron of the theatrical profession.

Nobody has yet determined the sex of Lan Ts'ai-ho (藍采和), but with their divinities this is a matter of small importance to the Chinese, as Gods and Bodhisatvas can assume any form which is most appropriate to their ministrations. In popular credence only one of the Immortals, Ho Hsien-ku, is purely feminine, Lan being represented as a youth of about sixteen carrying a basket of flowers. According to one account he is described as the Red-footed Great Genius Incarnate. The author of this version qualifies his statement by the limitation that, though he was a man, he could not understand how to be a man.

He, or she, is the mountebank among the Immortals, and usually plays a flute or clashes a pair of cymbals. Of unknown origin, his personal name is said to have been Yang Su. He lived in the T'ang dynasty, and roamed the country-side in a tattered blue gown, girt with a wooden belt. One foot was always bare, and a certain amount of eccentricity marked the selection of the clothing, as wadded underwear was donned in the heat of summer, whilst a couch of snow was preferred to the central heating of the winter k'ang.

Street singing provided a livelihood and, though generally regarded as a lunatic, the doggerel verse which Lan composed showed a strong moral tendency, denouncing the frivolities of life. When alms were bestowed the cash, with a square hole, were either strung on a cord and waved in time with the chant, or were scattered on the ground for the poor to collect.

In Chinese eyes this attitude to money, in one who had so little to spare, was a certain proof of insanity. The translation to immortality was quite in keeping with the rest of a disordered life, for Lan rose lightly to heaven on the fumes of the wine which was his earthly solace, dropping his shoe, belt, robe, and castanets, with the gesture of one who seeks to pluck the stars instead of the flowers of the field. In art, his musical attainments are overlooked as the flower-basket is his emblem, so he has been adopted as the patron saint of gardeners.

If there be any question as to the feminity of this irresponsible mountebank, none exists for the last of the band of Eight. Ho Hsien-ku (何仙姑) is undoubtedly the lady of the party, and her companions probably needed a softening influence. According to the oldest tradition she was a sort of Chinese Cinderella, who was rescued from a life of drudgery by Chung Li-ch'uan, who whisked her to paradise whilst she was stirring the kitchen pot. She had so little warning of her elevation that she left the earth with the ladle still in her hand, and early representations include it as her emblem. Later artists have transformed the curved object she carries into the lotus.

It is related that the flower of open-heartedness was given her later by Lu T'ung-pin (呂洞賓) as a symbol of identity, when she reached the mountain gorge where the Immortals dwell. She is sometimes depicted playing on the "sheng", or reed-organ, and she is credited with knowing a good cup of wine.

She was also said to be the daughter of Ho T'ai of

Ho Hsien-ku   *Lan Ts'ai-ho*

Tseng Ch'eng Hsien, in Kwangtung province, who lived in the days of usurping Empress Wu (A.D. 684–705) of the T'ang. At her birth six hairs were found growing on the crown of her head, and it is alleged that she never had more. This defect, however, has never been recorded in her pictures, and artistic licence has accorded her luxuriant tresses. This later story makes her out an ascetic by taste, who preferred the wild life of the mountains to the domestic duties of the home. She spent her time on Yunmu peak, about six miles from Tseng Ch'eng, where a stone bearing the name of the mountain was to be found. It resembled mother-of-pearl, and in a dream she saw a spirit who recommended her to take it in powdered form as an elixir of immortality. On waking she tried the recipe, at the same time vowing herself to a life of virginity. The charm took immediate effect and she acquired the art of levitation, floating from one peak to another in search of wild fruits, which she brought to her mother at nightfall. Gradually she found that it was no longer necessary for her to take nourishment, so she reduced the cost of living of the family to the great admiration of her neighbours. The story of the existence of such a paragon reached the ears of the Empress who issued a summons for her to appear at Court and lecture about her system. Whilst obeying the mandate, she disappeared from mortal gaze and joined the other genie. She is reputed to have been seen some fifty years later floating on an iridescent cloud at the temple of Ma Ku, the famous female Taoist magician, and later, in the VIII century, in the city of Canton.

The first biography probably enjoys the highest credence, as she is supposed to be of assistance in house management, a profession for which her independence of spirit, as later described, would seem singularly ill adapted. In fact she shone rather as a bread-winner, than in the role of a domestic drudge, and seems to have gone out of her way to avoid household duties. The only way of reconciling the two versions seems to be to subscribe to the doctrine of reincarnation, and that a dim recollection of her experiences as a scullion determined Ho Hsien-ku to shun any form of domesticity.

The Immortals, like the Chinese who invented them, have a prediliction for the hills rather than the sea as localities for rest and recreation. It is in wild romantic glens in the mountains that their grottoes are to be found, and where they are depicted and sung by the painters and the poets. There is, however, a legend of one voyage they made, to enlarge their knowledge of the wonders not to be found in the celestial sphere. Their usual mode of progression, sailing on cloud, was discarded at the suggestion of Lu T'ung-pin, who proposed that each should find his own means of locomotion for exploration of the novel element. Li T'ieh-kuai launched his iron crutch, which skimmed the tops of the billows like a canoe, while Chung Li-ch'uan's feather fan merely kissed the surface of the waves. Chang Kuo Lao rode his paper mule like a sea horse, and Ho Hsien-ku floated on her lotus leaf. Pictures of the expedition show most of these attributes changed into various sea monsters. The musical instrument of Lan Ts'ai-ho was observed by the son of the **Dragon King of the Eastern Sea**, who conceived the idea of stealing it and imprisoning its owner. The rest of the band came to Lan's assistence and declared war against the denizens of the deep, utterly defeating them. Innumerable other adventures are recounted in the saga, known as Pa Hsien kuo hai (八仙過海), the Eight Immortals crossing the sea.

The Star Gods

Primitive man, and for that matter many of his modern descendants, conceived himself to be the centre of the Universe, which revolved around him for his convenience. Sun and moon and all the heavenly firmament whirled around the Earth, on which he lived, in endless procession, completing their cycle within the twenty-four hours.

In China, the earth was conceived as a flat plate, with an inverted bowl, containing sun, moon and stars, above it. The Altar of Heaven was in the centre of the Middle Country, which was fringed with Lesser breeds without the Law. As even numbers were unpropitious, there were five points of the compass, North, South, East, West, and—the Middle. The division of the Celestial sphere into twenty-eight constellations was in accordance with the lunar, and not the solar, calendar, as in Western practice, and seven of these mansions were allotted to each of the four quadrants. Over each of these presides a supernatural creature. The Azure Dragon is Lord of the East, the Vermilion Phoenix of the South, whilst the West is represented by the White Tiger, and the North by the Black Warrior. This somewhat fanciful appellation designated the Tortoise which, in Chinese as well as Hindu mythology, symbolises the universe. Its dome-shaped back represents the vault of heaven, whilst its flat belly is the earth floating on the waters.

As our Western skies are peopled with the gods and heroes of Roman mythology, so the Chinese have translated their patron saints to dwellings in the stars. Their constellations do not correspond exactly to those accepted by the West, though they play a similar part in the determination of horoscopes. Some of the Star Gods are so important that they are honoured with a separate birthday, but all are included in a general thanksgiving on the 18th day of the First Moon. An altar is spread in the open courtyard, with three to five bowls of rice balls, cooked with sugar and flour, and one hundred and eight little lamps are lit before the table. The master of the house first worships the firmament as a whole, and then the particular star under which he was born. All the male members of the family then bow before their own patrons, each lighting three lamps, and taking the omens for the coming year by the length of time they take to burn out.

The three most important divinities are the Gods of Happiness, Longevity and Affluence. The last two, represented by the Shou Hsing and Lu Hsing respectively, are the Old Men of the Northern and Southern Measures, or Dippers. They are worshipped with a measure of rice decorated with stars, and surrounded by a pair of scales, a foot measure, shears and a mirror. An oil-lamp is lighted on the mound of rice, and the usual sticks of incense are burned, to ensure wealth, and the time to enjoy it.

The Great Bear is a highly important constellation as it is the home of Shang Ti, the Supreme divinity of the Taoist religion. Its seven stars, connected by straight white lines, may often be seen at the mastheads of junks dressed for a festival. This is less in honour of Shang Ti than of the Queen of Heaven, the sailors' protectress, who also dwells among the stars of the Northern Dipper.

The God of Joy, Chou Wang (紂王), was the disreputable representative of the Shang Dynasty. He was a sort of super-Nero, whose excesses led to his overthrow by some of his long-suffering vassals.

His successors were so delighted to be rid of him that they deified him, and assigned him a home on the planet Venus whence, from his earthly reputation as a Bluebeard, he is considered qualified to preside over marriages. Chou Wang is the nearest approach to eroticism in Chinese mythology, which is extremely puritanical, and allows no shrine or temple to be dedicated to its God of Love.

T'ai Sui, the Grand Marshal, is the spirit of the planet Jupiter, whose shrine may be found in the Temple of Jade Vacuity on Cheung Chau island. He is the head of the Ministry of Time, a Board consisting of one hundred and twenty officials, including the spirits of light and darkness, and the patrons of communications. He is also known as the God of the Year, and is supposed to change his residence annually, a notification of his new address being published in the almanac. The lucky line for the ensuing twelve months depends on this shifting meridian. At one time a belief existed that the fortunes of the Empire depended on the movements of the planet bearing his name, and the orbit of Jupiter was carefully studied as far back as 1000 B.C. The cult of its tenant, however, was not established until comparatively recently, when sacrifices were regularly made at the

opening of Spring. Though the Empire has passed, T'ai Sui is still venerated in private circles, as it is unwise to neglect a god who has the power of spreading pestilence and misfortune.

The Chinese considered the Pole Star, on account of its fixity, as the Purple Planet, and assigned it a place as the centre of the Universe. In it dwelt T'ai Yi (太乙), the Great Unity, or Supreme Spirit. This consequently was the emblem of the Emperor on Earth who stood for permanency, just as the Heavens revolved around the Pole.

The Pole seems to exercise a magnetic attraction on the Taoist pantheon as both Gods of Literature are located in Ursa Major. Their cult has probably diminished since the discovery was made that the study of the conversion table was more profitable than the ability to write an essay on the Analects. Wen Ch'ang has given his name to a constellation of six stars connected with the Great Bear, and was reputed to be a renowned scholar of the T'ang Dynasty, and a native of Szechuan. He is usually portrayed in a blue gown with a Ju Yi sceptre in his hand, mounted on a white horse with two attendants "Deaf as Heaven" (天聾), and "Dumb as Earth" (地啞), who are guardians of his secret in the disposal of intellectual talent.

The other denizen of the Bear is Kuei Hsing, a deformed figure with the visage of an imp. This dwarf, possessed of a brilliant intellect, passed first in the triennial examinations but, when he presented himself to receive the golden rose, his repulsive appearance caused the emperor to withhold the prize. The wretched scholar in despair attempted death by drowning, but was held up by a sea-monster, like Arian and the dolphin, and was carried to the heavens. To commemorate his achievement, the senior scholar in the examinations was allowed to mount the head of a bronze sea-monster in the palace, after the Imperial audience, and stand alone on the creature's head. The scholar's mount was one of two bronze tortoises which stand outside the T'ai Ho Tien, in the Forbidden City, with a pair of cranes symbolic of strength and longevity. They were furnished with dragons' heads, and were called Hao Heng. Their function was to exercise a restraining influence on official greed and rapacity.

The Star Gods are usually represented as putty-faced individuals with staring eyeballs. There is a fine collection of them in the annexe of a temple known as the Wan Shan Tien (萬善殿) on the eastern shore of the Winter Palace Lake, the Chung Hai, in Peking.

This building also houses the Ministry of Weather, with the twenty-four Dragon Kings who preside over the sun, moon, land, water, air, seas, rivers and lakes. The God of Thunder and the Goddess of Lightning are also represented in a hall which contains the twelve patron dragons of the Zodiac. The Star Gods are dressed in the robes of the Chou Dynasty, and wear hats with fringes adorned with beads, known as Mien Lu (Crown gems), a regal appurtenance of the period.

The main hall in the Temple was originally dedicated to the worship of the Great Bear, and was a rendezvous for Buddhist scholars. The black banner with the seven stars of the constellation is that of the dwarf, Kuei Hsing, and in the days of the Empire it was waved as soon as the candidates for the triennial examinations set to work. The banner was carried round the halls by two officials

Kuei Hsing as God of Literature

Ruan Kong as God of Literature

who, addressing the ghosts of former scholars, invited them to take their revenge on any candidate who had done them an injury. Failures usually attributed their lack of success to the acceptance of this invitation.

The Chinese, in their art, specialise in composite animals, like the dragon, phoenix and unicorn, so it is not surprising to find Kuei Hsing mounted on what strongly resembles a Pekingese dog, but is in fact their conception of a lion. He usually holds in his hand a seal with four characters. Though the early emperors, like their successors in modern times, received embarrassing presents of lions from tributary states, few Chinese artists had the opportunity of studying the anatomy of the beast, so the Palace dog was taken as the prototype. It is usually depicted with a collar and bells, playing with a worsted ball so as to preserve the milk which exudes from its claws. Nevertheless, it is a symbol of strength, and its effigy acted as a guard for temples and official residences.

The Hundred Gods

On 19th of the First Moon the streets in the Chinese quarters of town are congested with small processions of worshippers, bearing roast pigs on biers, and heralded with the sharp crack of fireworks. In front of certain shops people are gathered awaiting the share-out of the meat which, after being divided by a cleaver, is laid out

in portions on the pavement. The large temples, like that in Hollywood Road on Victoria Island, attract enormous crowds, and even small shrines have their quota of devotees. The offerings are laid out in front of the Patron Saint, whilst women, after making their obeisance, with a bunch of burning incense sticks in hand, ignite paper cartoons of the deities whose favours they seek, whilst small boys fling burning firecrackers under the feet of pedestrians to scare away evil influences.

Most of the celebrations take place the previous day, but the 19th of the First Moon has a deep significance in the family life of the native population, as it is the day on which newly-wed daughters may visit their parents, and it is known as the "Day of Meeting". In Heaven, it is the day when the gods gather together, to pay their respects to the Supreme Being, Yü Huang (玉皇), the Jade Emperor, and it is meet that mortals should follow their example. In fact they should facilitate the visit by food offerings to sustain them on their way, and bonfires of paper money for travelling expenses, as well as ladders to assist them in their ascent to Heaven.

The divinities in the Taoist pantheon are so numerous, and canonisation is so easy, that it would be impossible for any family altar to accommodate the images of those who might, in some emergency, prove useful, but it would be most unwise, according to Chinese ideas, to neglect them. They are consequently commemorated and propitiated *en masse* on this day of the year when, in the natural course of events, they have assembled together for their annual visit to the Lord of Heaven. A picture is therefore hung up on the family altar, with several tiers of representative divinities. In the upper row will be Kuan Yin (觀音), Goddess of Mercy, T'ien Hsien Niang Niang (天仙娘娘), the Heavenly Lady, with perhaps the sisters of "Good Sight" (慧眼) and "Many Children" (多子). The latter is the patroness of engaged couples, who sacrifice to her shrine at the Amah Rock above Bowen Road. On the tier below is depicted Kuan Ti (關帝), the God of War, Ts'ai Shen (財神), the God of Wealth, and the Patron of Medicine, three figures who enjoy the greatest popularity in the Taoist pantheon. A package of Chih Ma (紙禡), or cartoons of "All the Gods", is placed at the end of the altar, in order that there may be no Fairy Godmother who feels slighted at her omission and takes an appropriate revenge. The Chinese consider this precaution to be of the highest importance, and the cartoon may take the form of a single sheet with representations of a number of divinities, or a bundle portraying the most important gods separately. The single cartoon is a curious jumble of many-handed gods, borrowed from Hindu mythology, riding strange monsters, side by side with the early animistic symbols of the Chinese Nature cult. Figures of Heaven and Earth, the Dragon Kings, City Gods and the Fire Deity stand side by side with Confucius and his disciples, the Star Gods and the Ministers to the Weather. National heroes like Kuan Ti (關帝), Yueh Fei (岳飛), most famous of the City Gods, and Lu Pan (魯班), patron of carpenters, are included with the various divinities of trades and crafts. It is impossible to portray all gods under the sway of the Jade Emperor, as they number eight hundred, exclusive of Saints, whose name is legion.

Yü Huang, the Jade Emperor and Supreme Being according to the Taoists, has some claims to date back to Nature Worship as he has control over the rainfall and is in direct charge of the four Dragon Kings who supply the farmer with the necessary moisture for their crops. The Dragon of the East, assisted by the Dragon of the North, is the direct purveyor, but the Jade Emperor dictates the distribution. During the Ming Dynasty, the Eastern King was dismissed for dereliction of duty, and the Supreme Being appointed Hai Jui (海瑞) in his stead.

The Taoists adopted the Jade Emperor on what appear to be very slender grounds, except that the Buddhists had introduced him as an incarnation of Indra, and he enjoyed a popularity in the rival sect which could not be tolerated for financial reasons. According to some authorities he was an invention of one of the Sung emperors, who claimed to be in direct communication with the Supreme Being as late as A.D. 1000. The Taoist biography is so scanty as hardly to merit the exalted place Yü Huang (玉皇) holds in their pantheon. According to the legend, during his earthly span he was a normal sort of individual, noted for his kindness and charity. On the death of his father the Emperor, he abdicated, and led the life of a recluse without abandoning his good works. It seems a slender claim to such high promotion, and a logical explanation is that the Taoists, whose rivalry with the other organised religion was bitter for centuries, felt an urge to set up the Jade Emperor as an offset to the Lord Buddha. He, with the Law and the Priesthood, formed one Trinity, which the Taoists countered with the Way, "Tao" (道), the Classics, and their own Religious Orders. The peasantry consider the Jade Emperor as the impersonation of Shang Ti (上帝), or Heaven itself, and as such he has achieved immense popularity.

Monkey

Sun Hou-tze (孫猴子), the Imperial White Ape, to give him one of his many titles, is a highly popular divinity in the Taoist as well as the Buddhist pantheon. After a well-merited expulsion from the Taoist paradise, and prolonged incarceration, he retrieved his character by changing his religion and earning canonisation by the rival faith. In spite of his apostasy his reputation is probably higher amongst the adherents to his old religion, and his image is displayed in many Taoist temples. Though his official birthday falls on the 23rd of the Second Moon, it is always appropriate to worship him, and the sacrificial garments of red and gold, with the cloud-skipping sandals, are permanently in stock in the paper shops.

Innumerable legends have been recorded about the monkey from his birth to his elevation to sainthood under the title of Great Sage equal to Heaven (齊天大聖). Over the seas, in the kingdom of Ao-lai, is a mountain called Hua Kuo Shan, on whose precipitous slopes jutted out a rock on which an egg was formed. Fertilised by the breath of the southern breezes, from this was hatched a stone monkey, whose first act was to salute the four points of the horizon. The luminous beams from his eyes penetrated the palace of the Pole Star, and excited the admiration of the Jade Emperor at his latest creation. The beast's human intelligence soon

raised him to the kingship over all the monkeys, and this superiority engendered a craving for immortality. Through his association with P'u Ti Tsu-shih (普地祖師), who had already achieved this desirable status, he learned cloud-hopping with a leap of 36,000 miles, and could change his appearance into seventy-two different forms.

From the Dragon King of the Eastern Seas he obtained a weapon in the form of an iron bar, planted by the Jade Emperor as a tide gauge, and this made him irresistible, particularly as it could contract to the size of a needle, and be carried behind the ear. Armed with these powers he proceeded in true dictator fashion to organise the monkeys, and start a campaign of aggression against the four Sea Kings, at whose expense he furnished his realm. Yen Lo (閻羅), the Master of the Underworld, was obliged to note his misdeeds and, taking advantage of one of Monkey's drinking bouts, bound him and led him to the nether regions. On sobering up, Monkey played merry hell with the establishment and tore out the pages in the register of death bearing his own name and those of his subjects. As the grave no longer had power over him, he returned to earth triumphant, and the only way of mitigating the nuisance was to offer him employment in Heaven. The Jade Emperor accordingly nominated him as Grand Master of the Stables, but Monkey, discovering the derisory nature of the appointment, upset his master's throne, and broke out of the south gate to return to Hua Kuo Shan. A military expedition was then organised to bring him to reason, but Monkey proved so formidable an adversary that he had to be bought off with the appointment of Grand Superintendent of the Imperial Peach Gardens. These produce the fruit reserved for the banquet of the gods given on their ripening by the Queen of the Western Heaven but, as Monkey's name did not appear in the list of guests, he consumed the viands by himself and swallowed the Pills of Immortality compounded by Lao Chun (老君). He had now not only achieved double immortality but indestructibility as well and, on being brought to book for his misdeeds, defied all the efforts of the executioners.

The Taoist Pantheon, after failing to distil him in the Furnace of the Eight Trigrams to remove the elements of immortality, was obliged to admit defeat and invoke the aid of the leader of the rival sect. Buddha had no difficulty in convincing the culprit that there was no escape from his hand, and confined him in the mountains known as Wu Hsing Shan (五聖山). Here he remained for aeons until released by the intercession of Kuan Yin, to accompany the priest Hsüan Tsang (玄奘) on his pilgrimage to India in search of the authentic Buddhist scriptures. To limit his simian proclivities the Goddess imposed on him a golden fillet, which encircled his brow and tightened to produce an intolerable headache if he indulged in any of his monkey tricks. This still forms part of the sacrificial outfit when his worshippers present him with a new suit of clothes.

Hsüan Tsang, or Tripitaka, is a historical character of the T'ang Dynasty, who left a record of his pilgrimage and the incredible hardships he endured. At the time, the orthodoxy of the faith was being threatened by the Mahayanist schism, and a Council was assembled which ordered the engraving of the accepted doctrine on copper sheets which were buried under a stupa at Srinagar, in Kashmir. What modifications the Chinese introduced into the authorised version once it was in their hands is entirely their own affair, but they certainly revised the Indian conception of the Hells to suit the convenience of their ancestral spirits.

All Hsüan Tsang's human companions fell by the way, or turned back dispirited, one being frozen to death in the snow-bound passes of the Pamirs, but he achieved his object and returned by sea to his native country. His three strange companions, Monkey, Pigsy, and a man-eating monster embellished with a necklace of skulls, called Sha Ho-shang (沙和尚), may have been the allegorical embodiments of instability, avarice and lust, though the latter's role in the story is extremely nebulous. A whole cycle of legends, whose repetition invested them with authority, grew up from the 10th century onwards, and they were disseminated among the uncritical populace through the medium of the stage.

The guileless priest Hsüan Tsang is a pathetically helpless individual, whose weakness is redeemed by his singleness of purpose. He triumphs over every adversity by the valour and infinite ingenuity of Monkey who is equally at home confronting demons, monsters, or the priests of his discarded religion. Hsüan Tsang is merely a passenger in the hands of a highly efficient courier, who is the real hero of the saga compiled by Wu Ch'eng-en in the 15th century.

Monkey is highly popular with the humbler classes as a divinity who can render aid in all manner of circumstances, and point out a solution in any difficulty. His shrine occupies a niche in many temples, and his image in pottery is mass-produced in Hong Kong for worship in the home.

Occasionally, to entertain the pilgrims returning from a Boat People's festival, animistic dances, illustrating some episode in Monkey's career, are performed. Though devoid of make-up and properties, the uninitiated spectator is under no illusion as to the subject of the representation, so thoroughly does the actor enter into the spirit of his part. Drawing in his cheeks and contracting his fingers the performer sheds his human personality, and in a flash assumes simian guise. The deck hand, in black trousers and sleeveless singlet, is forgotten as Monkey triumphs over his enemies. Brandishing his invisible crowbar, and plucking out his hairs to turn them into legions of monkeys, demons and monsters are vanquished to the delight of the audience which knows each episode by heart.

According to the legend eighty difficulties were overcome on the outward journey, and one on the homeward, when the whole party suffered immersion in a broad river. The tales are as familiar to the Chinese as the plots of pantomimes to English schoolchildren.

The Queen of the Western Heaven

The first important religious festival in the Third Moon is the birthday of Hsi Wang Mu (西王母), Queen of the Western Heaven, and not to be confused with T'ien Hou (天后), the fishermen's Goddess whose anniversary is celebrated on the 23rd. The "Golden Mother of the Tortoise" was first mentioned by a metaphysician, Lieh Tzü (列子), who lived in the fifth and fourth centuries B.C. He was also the author of legends of the Islands of Immortals in the ocean, the Kingdom of Dwarfs and Giants, the Fruit of Immortality, and the Repairing of Heaven by Nu Kua Shih (有媧氏), with five-coloured stones. The conception of the idea that the Universe was supported on the back of a gigantic tortoise is also due to his fertile imagination. The Taoists were quick to take advantage of the potentialities of a popular female divinity, and wove endless legends round her personality to strengthen her hold on the adherents of their faith. Her family name is variously given as Hou, Yang and Ho, her own name being Hui, and first name Wan-chin. She had nine sons and twenty-four daughters. As Mu Kung, formed of the Eastern Atmosphere, is the principle of Male Air, and Sovereign of the East, so Hsi Wang Mu, born of the Western Air, is the passive, or female Yin (陰), and rules the West. The conjunction of the two principles engenders Heaven and Earth, and all life appertaining thereto. Hsi Wang Mu presides over all the genii dwelling in the K'un Lung Mountains (崑崙山), and on occasion condescends to communicate with favoured members of the Imperial family. In the Taoist hierarchy there are eight hundred divinities, and innumerable genii, or immortals. Three categories exist, Saints (Sheng-jen) (聖人), Heroes (Chen-jen) (真人) and Immortals (Hsien-jen) (仙人). According to the Taoist definition, the Immortals are recluses who dwell in the mountains. In the course of time illusory symptoms of death appear, but the body retains all the qualities of the living, and is merely a pupal stage in the cycle leading to perfection. Its occupant can travel at will throughout the universe, enjoy the pleasures of the table, and all the advantages of perfect health.

Hsi Wang Mu's Palace is above the snow line in the K'un Lung Mountains, now identified with the Hindu Kush, the legendary home of the Chinese race. The walls, constructed with pure gold, are three hundred and thirty miles in circumference, with crenelations of precious stones. Its inhabitants are divided into seven categories according to the colour of their clothes: red, blue, black, violet, yellow, green and nature-coloured. The Queen gives a periodic banquet, known as the P'an T'ao Hui (蟠桃會), at which the feature is the Peach Feast which ensures longevity and good fortune. Their ripening determines the date, for the orchard only puts forth leaves once every three thousand years, and it takes as much time again for the fruit to ripen. It was on one of these occasions that the Stone Monkey was evicted from Heaven suffering from a surfeit as he had consumed the entire dessert before the guests sat down to table. It proved impossible to devise an adequate punishment to fit the crime, as Monkey became indestructible, thanks to the peaches and copious doses of the pills of immortality. Only Buddha himself proved capable of controlling him, and henceforth he became an adherent to that faith, expiating his crime by bringing the scriptures to the Chinese Empire.

A replica of the palace exists in the north-east corner of the Pei Hai in Peking, once part of the Winter Palace, but now a public park. There is also near it a pile of rocks known as I Fang Shan (上房山), called after one of her supposed residences on a peak near Fang Shan Hsien in Hopei.

In paintings the Goddess is usually depicted dressed like a Chinese princess, attended by two handmaidens, one of whom carries a large fan and the other a basket of the famous peaches. She has further a retinue of five other girls, known as the Jade or Fairy maids attired in the colours associated with China. Her mount is usually a white crane, and a flock of blue-winged birds serve as her messengers. The Boat People of Hong Kong often treasure among their household gods a scroll of the Western Heaven, and it is on her crane that daughters who have died before reaching maturity are mounted in effigy.

Much research has been devoted to the origin of this divinity, and modern writers are inclined to the belief that the name Wang Mu was either a locality or some powerful sovereign in the West. Early missionaries identified her with Solomon's visitor, the Queen of Sheba, and Professor Giles with the Roman Goddess Minerva and the story of the Golden Apples. The association with the God of the East, an obvious after-thought, appears to be drawn from Hindu legends of their deity Indra. The K'un Lung Mountains are not only identified with the Hindu Kush, but also with Sumeru (Shun Mi 須彌) where Indra and his consort are reputed to reside.

According to the history of the Chou Dynasty, the Emperor Mu (穆王), in 985 B.C., was entertained by the Queen of the West at the Lake of Gems, and the Emperor Wu Ti (武帝), of the Han Dynasty, paid her a visit round about 100 B.C. Mu Wang (穆王), the first to make contact, was accompanied by his eight favourite horses, which have retained their popularity with artists and foreigners ever since.

Lu Pan

Carpenters, and the Building Trade in general, pin their faith on Lu Pan (魯班) whose birthday is kept on the thirteenth day of the Sixth Moon. He was a skilled craftsman, said to be a native of the State of Lu (魯). His name being Pan, he was canonised as Lu Pan. He seems to have been a sort of Leonardo da Vinci, for he is credited with producing a wooden kite, on which he rode high in the air.

Peking is full of legends of difficult constructional problems being solved by his aid. He is alleged to be responsible for the custom of putting gilt studs on the gate panels, as an emblem of security, as they represented the conch shell, whose occupant shuts himself in tightly at a touch. Lu Pan is credited with giving hints and assistance, in various guises, to Imperial contractors who were held up by some technical difficulty, or who had failed to hit off the right proportions in their planning. At Mahakala Miao, the Mongol Temple, for instance, the contractor designed the slope of the roof out of proportion, and, as it was an Imperial order, he decided to commit suicide. On the evening before he was to carry his resolution into effect, the cook employed for the workmen fell sick, and his substitute over-seasoned the dishes. When called upon to explain, all he would say was, Chia Chung Yen, which means, "I have put too much salt in." The contractor shrewdly saw that the phrase had a second meaning: "Add another set of eaves", and, acting on the hint, he achieved a highly successful novelty.

The wealthiest trade guild in Hong Kong is probably that of the Builders and Contractors which, since the War and influx of population owing to unsettled conditions on the Mainland, has been unable to keep pace with the demand for accommodation.

The guild has its private temple, which is not in the list of those under Government control, in Green Lotus Terrace about two hundred feet above sea-level in Kennedy Town. It is reached by a broad staircase, named Precious Dragon Terrace, less formidable than Ladder Street as the flights only consist of six steps with broad landings between each with shops on the left-hand side. The whole serves as a playground, immune from wheeled traffic, for innumerable lively children of the non-mendicant kind. Green Lotus Terrace is fifty feet wide, with well-grown trees shading the seaward wall, and the buildings are all substantial. The first is a school run by the guild, and next to it is the temple, solidly constructed of granite. It is comparatively new, having been built in 1928 to replace an eighty-year-old shrine, which either suffered from dilapidation, or was considered inadequate for worship of so popular a saint. It is essentially Taoist in style, with the roof ridge decorated with the two dragons and the lustrous pearl, whilst the facade over the door is filled in with frescoes illustrating famous poems. Below these are two square niches with porcelain figures, that on the left representing the Eight Immortals, and the one on the right, the life of Kuan Kung.

Above the lintel of the door is the dedicatory tablet, Lu Pan Hsien Shih Miao (魯班先師廟), the Temple of Lu Pan the Fundamental Teacher, and the posts are inscribed "Lu's architectural precepts hold good for ever" and "His method of measuring will last a thousand years".

Inside the ante-chapel is the usual shrine on the right, where those who have no problems to lay before the principal deity may acquire virtue at the cost of a stick of incense, and a stall for the purchase of the same commodity and sacrificial candles. There is also a fortune-teller on the premises, and on the other side a large tablet with the names of guild members.

The pillars supporting the roof are inscribed "He was so outstanding an architect as to qualify for canonisation" and "His tools and methods of construction were so brilliant that they can be used to cultivate peace". A large incense-burner was presented by the Contractors' Guild in 1928 in commemoration of the rebuilding of the shrine and is inscribed "Distribute your favours amongst us", a pious wish which must have been amply fulfilled.

Over the side doorways into the sanctuary are scenes from the "Three Kingdoms" taken from a Chinese novel. The main altar has a huge marble incense-burner, with two paintings of the Patron Saint, and an elaborately carved and gilded frontal, with hundreds of figures protected by a screen of wire mesh. According to the temple guardian they are simply decorative, and do not represent the Eight Immortals, or any particular scene from Chinese history.

The shrine itself is richly carved and gilded and contains two images of the patron, one of which is portable and is probably taken out on the birthday of the Saint, which is celebrated by a feast requiring all the resources of the Kam Ling Restaurant. This is held on the 13th of the Sixth Moon.

On Lu Pan's right is the altar of the God of Wealth, and on the left a tablet dedicated to Chang Tao-ling (張道陵), first Pope and founder of popular Taoism.

The tablet is in a frame surmounted by a red silk rosette and two pointed gilt talismans. It has the inscription "Bless all the Gods of Chang", and was erected on account of the assistance of the Master of Heaven (天師), when consultations were in progress as to what form the present building should take.

There are innumerable stories about Lu Pan and the way he came to the assistance of craftsmen in despair over the difficulties they were encountering. Naturally most of these miraculous interventions occurred in Peking, where the failure to execute Imperial commands might easily entail the execution of the defaulter. One monarch, a predecessor or successor of Kublai Khan, like him decreed a summer house whose design necessitated originality. The contractor was at his wits' end to discover some novelty, and his anxiety communicated itself to his staff. One day a poor workman in his employ dropped into a tea-house to refresh himself before his long trudge home to his aged father. At the table where he sat was a respectably dressed old man with an empty bird-cage of unusual design. The employee saw at once that it was exactly what his master was looking for, so he asked the price. The owner said that he would sell it for a thousand taels at which the workman was aghast, as he had not as many cash to bless himself with. He was forced to confess the state of his finances to the old gentleman, who told him not to worry as his master would be glad enough to pay the price. When he reached home he found the bird-cage on the table, and his father told him that it had been left by a man answering to the description of his tea-house acquaintance, who had put it down with a message to the effect that he would know what to do with it. Next morning he took it to the contractor, who was so delighted with the solution of the problem that he handed over the price without a murmur. The benefactor, of course, was Lu Pan.

During the Ming Dynasty, the famous pagoda Pai Ta-Ssü, outside the P'ing Tse Men gate of Peking, developed a dangerous crack and was in imminent peril of collapse. At this critical moment a strange workman appeared and started walking round the monument shouting "Mend the big thing" at the top of his voice. A few hours later it was seen that the fissure had been filled up and that the structure was once again sound. The people immediately attributed the miracle to Lu Pan, as nobody else could have made such a good job of it. The miracle is commemorated by a street song giving the credit where it was due, the last couplet being "A gaping crack upon its pedestal appeared, and by Lu Pan himself it was repaired".

A few feet below Green Lotus Terrace, and to the east, is a small temple dedicated to Kuan Yin, whose guardian is evidently in the Paper Shop business, as frames for the construction of various ritual objects and pots of paste in the lane outside the shrine testify to his activities. The north wall of the building is shaded by a sacred banyan tree at the foot of which is a good-sized cement altar. On the right side is a large granite tablet with three inscriptions. The centre line of characters assures the worshippers that the Stone from Mount T'ai Shan keeps off all demons, and encourages

Demon-dispelling altar

the belief that the pointed rock on its left was imported from Shantung. Such stones are found all over China with the inscription "The stone from T'ai Shan dares to oppose". The Chinese are aware that most of them are spurious, but consider the bare assertion of their origin is enough to impose on the ignorant devils.

The left-hand inscription refers to the "Old Banyan tree' (老榕樹), and the right-hand divinity is the local T'u Ti, or Earth God, who is roughly hewn in granite. The demon-dispelling divinities are completed by a clay tiger with green marble eyes, who has an incense burner to himself, and may be worshipped separately. Though off the beaten track, for only a narrow path leads up the hill, the shrine is evidently well patronised.

The God of Fire

It is diplomatic to worship the God of Fire on the 22nd of the Sixth Moon, as he can not only cause but also extinguish conflagrations. In Chinese towns fire precautions, and the means of combating an outbreak, were lamentably deficient, which rendered the good offices of the deity all the more important. In some districts he was worshipped for four days, beginning on the 17th of the Eighth Moon, when lanterns in his honour were hung in the streets. This was probably a Southern custom, which had the effect of killing two birds with one stone, as the lanterns are a feature of the Moon Festival, two days previously, and could be made to serve a double purpose.

Fire, like the weather, is divided into Celestial Ministries, with a President, Lo Hsuan, whose official honorific is Stellar Sovereign of Fire Virtue. Star Gods occupy the position of four of his subordinates, whilst the fifth is the "Heavenly Prince who receives fire".

All these worthies were, in their lifetime, members of the cabinet of the wicked Emperor Chou (紂王). Whilst fighting in support of the tyrant, Lo Hsuan was suddenly transformed into a giant with three heads and six arms, each wielding a magic weapon. Among them were a seal reflecting Heaven and Earth, a wheel with five fire-dragons, and a gourd containing ten thousand fire crows with various smoke-producing effects.

At the siege of the city of Hsi Ch'i this monster put in a gas attack to cover the launching of his fire birds who, with the effect of an atom bomb, set the place ablaze in a matter of moments. The whole town would have been consumed but for the intervention of Princess Lung Chi who shrouded it with a veil of mist and extinguished the conflagration with a heavy downpour of tropical rain. Her counter-measures deprived Lo Hsuan of the remainder of his magical powers, so he sought safety in flight. He failed, however, to effect his escape and was crushed by a pagoda hurled by Li Ching (李靖), Grand Marshal of the Skies, and Guardian of the Gate of Heaven. This divinity is always depicted with a golden pagoda in his hand, which he reserved as a threat for keeping his unruly son Na Ch'a (哪咤) in order.

The identity of the God of Fire is by no means fixed throughout the country, and a belief is widely current that he was originally a minister under the Yellow Emperor (黃帝), in 2689 B.C., described as the son of the legendary ruler Chuan Hsu (顓頊) who had sway over the elements of wood and fire. He governs the South under the name of Prince of those regions (南方君) or (南方赤帝). He is reputed to be extremely puritanical and easily shocked by indecency, so pictures liable to outrage his sense of fitness are pasted on the walls, especially the kitchen, the focal point of danger. It is considered most unlikely that he would risk offence by entering a place where such an exhibition was on view.

Another cheap insurance, often seen in Shanghai, is the display of the character for Water (水), his antagonistic element, on the spirit screen which protects the front gate of the compound from undesirable intruders of supernatural origin.

Legend records that Chu Jung (祝融), which was the personal name of the Ruler of the South, in his youth asked the Longevity Man to grant him immortality, but was told that he could not achieve it until he had reigned as Emperor and had chosen a site for his tomb on the southern slope of the sacred mountain of Heng Shan. He achieved Imperial status on the abdication of Hsien Yüan (軒轅), and taught his subjects the application of the purifying fire for welding and forging metal. Like St. Patrick he banished the snakes and venomous reptiles by encouraging the people to burn the undergrowth in the forests. He reigned two hundred years before achieving immortality, when he presumably had no use for the tomb he had constructed though the spot on which it is located still bears the name of Chu Jung Peak. His descendants, who migrated to the south, were the ancestors of the Directors of Fire.

He had a rival, in the shape of a celebrated magician named Hui Lu, who possessed a mysterious bird called Pi Fang and a hundred other fire birds which he kept caged in a gourd. By enlarging them he could start a blaze which would destroy the whole country-side. Huang Ti (黃帝) ordered his suppression, and Chu

Jung was entrusted with the task, which he performed by throwing a large bracelet of pure gold over his neck. This brought Hui Lu to the ground, and deprived him of all power. Having promised submission he was accepted as a disciple, and from that time always called himself the Disciple of the Master of Fire. In his subordinate capacity he achieved great popularity and in certain provinces he is worshipped to the exclusion of Chu Jung himself.

Public buildings and temples in Peking carry a fire insurance in the shape of a man riding on a hen among the roof animals (獸頭) on the ridge of the gable ends. This is popularly supposed to be a fire-raising demon who, after having been exorcised, was placed in a position from which he could not descend to resume his depredations. Another version of the story is that in the year 283 B.C. a particularly bloodthirsty tyrant, Prince Min of the State of Ch'i (齊), was overthrown by a coalition and was strung up to a roof ridge, without food or water, until he succumbed to the heat of the sun. As a perpetual memory of his crimes the liberated people placed his effigy, on the back of a hen, on the roofs of their houses. The bird, overweighted with its rider, could not fly down, and, to prevent its escape from the roof, a sort of dragon, known as a Ch'ih Wen (螭吻), was set up on the other end of the ridge. It was not until the Ming Dynasty that the other animals were added for decoration. A full set was assembled in the following order— hen, dragon, phoenix, lion, unicorn, celestial horse, Ch'ih Wen. In later days the conventional arrangement was abandoned and, in most cases, the only figures between the hen and the Ch'ih Wen are what foreigners call dogs, but are really lions.

Ti Tsang Pusa

The Festival of the Hungry Ghosts ends on the 30th day of the Seventh Moon, when the gates of Hell receive all spirits, neglected or well cared for, at the conclusion of their summer holiday. The date also coincides with the birthday of Ti Tsang Pusa (地藏菩薩), whom foreigners usually confuse with Yen Lo (閻羅) of the Lower regions. This error is fostered by the divinity's popular titles as "Lord of the Underworld", or "King of the Dark City", though he is not on the establishment of those houses of correction. He fulfils in fact the functions of a probation officer, with a right of entry to relieve the sufferings of the inmates. Ti Tsang, far from being identical with the King and Judge of Hell, who is himself one of the damned, is a blessed Pusa and glorious saviour-divinity who only visits the Infernal Regions occasionally on errands of mercy and love. His titles imply that he is the master and guide of those who seek to escape the torments of Hell, and that he is the Conqueror rather than the Ruler of the Inferno.

The Sanskrit name of this Bodhisatva is Kshitigarbha, meaning Earthwomb, or Earth Treasury, of which the chinese Ti Tsang is a translation. According to the theories of the Tantric Buddhists the world is six million miles thick, and its deepest and lowest layers are composed of diamond earth, which is absolutely indestructible. Even so is the inflexibility of the virtue and courage which animates the heart of Ti Tsang. He has registered a vow before the throne of the glorified Buddha that he will devote himself to the salvation of suffering mankind, and not relinquish his mission till all living beings are brought safely into the heaven of Buddhahood. He bears the name of Earth partly because his sympathy is, like that of Kuan Yin, all-embracing, and partly because his will to afford help to tortured souls is indomitable. The Chinese name for Hell is Ti Yu (地獄), or Earth prison, and the principal attribute of the Pusa is his ability to force its gates. He is generally represented holding a staff in his right hand and a precious jewel between finger and thumb in his left. When he touches the door with his crozier it instantly yields, and the radiant gem illuminates the darkness with celestial light. As the Bodhisatva moves on earth, metal rings on his staff jingle and give warning of his approach that no insect may be crushed underfoot.

Ti Tsang has his functions in this life as well as in the after-world for he is the supporter and comforter of the poor, hungry, sick and oppressed, the solace to the dying, and of individuals addicted to nightmares. The believer in this Pusa can ascend dangerous mountains, penetrate trackless deserts and forests and journey through bandit-infested regions, if with faith he repeats the sacred name, which assures the escort and protection of the gods of the locality. They, sharing the divinity's title, act as his retainers and form an invisible bodyguard for his worshippers. Even wild beasts and poisonous reptiles are rendered harmless by the spell.

In Japan, under the name of Jizo, an exact translation of Ti Tsang, the Saint holds one of the highest places in popular esteem. In essentials his cult varies little from the Chinese version to which it owes its origin, but one attribute has been added which greatly enhances the popularity of the divinity. He is regarded pre-eminently as the protector, comforter and loving friend of dead children. In Japanese art, the sturdy vanquisher of demons is depicted as children's tender playfellow.

This idea of a Redeemer and a descent to Hell is common to many religions, and such legends are to be found in the traditions of peoples as widely separated as the Greeks, Finns, West Africans, American Indians, and South Sea Islanders. A similar belief was associated with Mithraism, for Mithras was regarded as the divine friend of man, and a saviour from death and hell. Chinese Buddhism derives many of its doctrines from Hinduism. One of Krishna's most notable achievements was his invasion of the nether regions, where he overthrew Yama and rescued some of the souls suffering in purgatory. Similar feats are ascribed to Ravana, and the divine Vishnu. At the time Buddhist missionaries were spreading their faith to China, the religion in India was losing its characteristic features and was gradually absorbing the general trend of religious thought in the sub-continent. The result of the fusion of Buddhism and Brahminism produced what is now known as Hinduism, and is responsible for a great deal of duplication in the functions of the divinities. Practically all the attributes of Ti Tsang, for instance, are to be found in Kuan Yin, who is just as familiar a visitor to the underworld as her male counterpart. Wen Shu (文洙) and P'u Hsien (普賢) are worshipped for the same reason at Wu T'ai Shan and O Mei, it being the belief of the Mahayana mystics that all Buddhas and Bodhisatvas are ultimately an undifferentiated One, which constitutes the only reality.

Ti Tsang's main sanctuary is the lovely mountain of Chiu Hua, one of the principal objects of pilgrimage in old China, twenty miles from the southern bank of the Yangtze in Anhui Province, but his image holding his jingling staff is to be found in every Buddhist temple.

In Chinese pictures Ti Tsang is often represented accompanied by a dog, for whom he manifests a great affection. Its presence is accounted for by the fact that, on the death of his mother, he hastened to the underworld to comfort her and plead for favourable treatment. He sought her in vain, but his inquiries elicited the news that she had been reborn as a female dog whose identity he discovered on his return to earth. He at once adopted the animal which henceforth was his companion on his pilgrimages.

The Birthday of Confucius

Though the fall of the Empire signalled the cessation of the sacrifices at the Temple of Heaven, the cult of Confucius was confirmed, and even strengthened, by numerous Presidential edicts in the early days of the Republic. The President himself was to offer the sacrifices at the Temple of Literature, renamed the Temple of Confucius, in Peking, and the ceremonies were ordered to be repeated in the provinces by the officials and centres of education. A Decree of 18th January, 1915, laid down the ritual to be performed at the birthplace of the Sage at Ch'ü Fu in Shantung, and established his lineal descendant Duke K'ung, assisted by eight priests, to act as officiant at the sacrifices. A Ministerial Circular of 4th September, 1918, issued under the Presidency of Hsü Shih-ch'ang, prescribed the ceremonies for the observance of the birthday of Confucius:

1. All scholars should attend the Temple of Confucius to observe the usual rites and organise a torchlight procession, either by day or night.
2. All organised societies should attend, to show their respect.
3. All officials, members of public bodies and scholars should send representatives to the Confucian Temple, and honour the Sage by speeches.
4. The National flag will be flown, and illuminations organised by all public bodies and guilds as well as at educational establishments.
5. The day will be observed as a holiday in schools and official establishments.

There was a considerable revival of Confucianism during the struggles for power among the Republican elements in early 1920's in which the lead was taken by K'ang Yu-wei, the reformer who was exiled by the Empress Dowager after the unsuccessful attempt at a *coup d'état* in 1898. K'ang's ultimate aim was the restoration of the monarchy with the aid of the conservative literati who in the past held the reins of power, but vested interests were too firmly entrenched. With the withdrawal of the Nationalists from the Mainland, the young descendant of the Sage left his palace at Ch'ü Fu and took up his residence abroad, breaking the continuity of the annual sacrifices.

In Hong Kong there is always a celebration in Bonham Strand West, which is mainly occupied by Chinese banks and wholesale chemists, and the shops make a monthly contribution to their guilds, to be expended on this night by giving a free theatrical performance to the street.

The whole thoroughfare was illuminated on both sides by large orange silk lanterns and, though the actors might not have been of the first rank, the costumes and décor were of a very high order. Two stages were erected —one was for individual singers, whilst the other, further down the street, had a full theatrical performance with excellent new costumes. The stages were on the level of the heads of the crowd, which was dense. The lower classes predominated, with an occasional coolie still with his carrying pole. Children from three to nine were in great numbers, either on the shoulders of their parents or, like one small girl, naked but for a pair of red shorts, standing on stools they had brought to increase their stature. At eight o'clock a policeman occupied the stage, which was illuminated with three neon lights, and good-humouredly admonished the audience. The band, consisting of foreign-style fiddles, gong, drum and loud cymbals, played him off with the first bars of the overture, and a tall actor in white with dark blue facings emerged from the wings and declaimed in a stentorian voice. The crowd was highly appreciative, and infants were hoisted up to improve their field of vision. Behind a grille the mahjong tiles were continuously rattled by a party who seemed impervious to noise. After an oration lasting about ten minutes the young actor was joined by an elderly gentleman, gorgeous in coral-red robes, and later two maidens clothed in white samite appeared and sang their parts. The crowd, though dense, was not impassable, but it was easier to gain the main thoroughfare and inspect the second theatre by following a parallel street. Here the orchestra was re-inforced by a saxophone which blended harmoniously with Chinese music. A single invisible girl singer was attracting a slightly smaller audience than at the play further down, but her voice evidently had an appeal to the forces of Law and Order, for a policeman was sitting on the edge of the stage, with his legs dangling, jollying the onlookers. His professional services were in no demand, but he looked thoroughly contented with his assignment to the duty.

Just opposite the theatre was an open door, the office of the Guild of Wholesale Drug Exporters. The lintel was decorated with the usual triangular ornament surmounted by the Unicorn and Jade Book. The Unicorn is less common as a device in China than in England, where the Royal Arms have given him wide publicity. On the other hand, he is less shy about appearing in the flesh, and when he does he is welcomed as a creature of good omen, symbolising longevity, grandeur, felicity, illustrious offspring, and wise administration. He is reputed to be able to walk on water as easily as on land, and made his last appearance just before the birth of Confucius. Hence his connection with the Great Sage. Buddhists represent him as bearing on his back the Civilising Book of the Law. His predominant characteristics are somewhat complicated, as the male and female, though generically known as Ch'i Lin, are really Ch'i (麒) and Lin (麟), respectively. The female Lin exhibits perfect goodwill, gentleness and benevolence to all and sundry. The beast is endowed with the gift of knowledge of the time of appearance of good rulers. In form it resembles a large stag, but combines the body of a musk deer with the tail of an ox, the forehead of a wolf, and the hooves of a horse. Its coat is of the five colours of the races of the Empire—yellow, white, blue, red and black. It stands twelve cubits at the withers, and its voice is as the sound of musical instruments. The male only is provided with a horn, but the tip of it is fleshy and consequently unsuited as a weapon of offence.

It would appear to be a Buddhist rather than a Taoist conception, as it carefully avoids treading on any living thing or bruising the grass under its feet. When seen, it is always solitary, and only presents itself when a king of the greatest benevolence occupies the throne, or prior to the birth of a great sage.

Conceptions of the Ch'i Lin vary slightly with different authors, and the stone guardians of the Ming Tombs have the body of a horse garnished with large scales, and two horns bent backwards. Its age is reputed to be a thousand years but, as even terrestrial monarchs of unlimited virtue rarely exceed the allotted human span of life, so the greatest part of its existence must be spent in some celestial harbourage.

In the Taoist pantheon Confucius is addressed as the "Honoured One of Heaven, who causes literature to flourish, and the world to prosper". Since the adoption of the Western calendar there has been a dual observance of the birthday of the Sage, a fixed and a moving festival. The official date is the 27th August, but certain trades, goldsmiths, money changers, and dealers in medicine, cling to the old tradition of the 27th of the Eighth Moon.

The City Gods

The 25th of the Ninth Moon is the birthday of the most celebrated of the City Gods of China, whose cult arose in the Province of Anhui. These divinities, in all respects but one, may be compared with the Roman "urbani" as local protectors of various peoples. They are, however, of human origin, whereas the gods of the Mediterranean races were figments of the imagination.

The City Gods, Ch'eng Huang (城隍), as ascending humanity, and not descending divinity, form a convenient link between mankind and the higher gods who may be disinclined to lend an ear to the everyday trivialities of their clients. They act as spiritual go-betweens whose business it is to sift out the wheat from the chaff and pass it on to higher authority, if a solution is beyond their own competence.

Legend traces their origin back to the Perfect Emperor Yao (堯) when a deified "guardian of the dykes and ramparts" was the shadowy ancestor of the cult. This ruler, who ascended the throne in 2357 B.C., instituted the composite "Cha" (禙) sacrifices, of eight separate ceremonies, held as an autumn thanksgiving to celebrate the garnering of the harvest, which was completed by the Ninth Moon. The seventh sacrifice was in honour of the "Superintendents of Husbandry", whose duties comprised the maintenance of farm buildings and boundaries. They were gods of the land and locality, and were particularly charged with the Shui (水) and Yung (壅), irrigation and the upkeep of the mud-walls or dykes. In course of time the Yung was altered into Ch'eng (城), a city wall, and the Shui into Huang (隍), the moat, from whose spoil it has been raised. The Ch'eng Huang gradually abandoned the fields, and became associated entirely with cities.

Every walled town in China placed itself under their protection, just as every village had a shrine to the Earth God (土地) of the locality, and every household was supervised by the Prince of the Kitchen (竈王). Their popularity is due to the fact that all three are intimately connected with the affairs of the Underworld and the well-being of the Kuei Shen (鬼神), or souls of the dead.

The importance of the City Gods was greatly enhanced under the T'ang Dynasty, when their representative who guarded the capital, Si An Fu, was raised to the rank of Prince. This Imperial recognition spread their worship throughout the empire, but the seasons for the observances found no place in the Book of Religious Rites, and the Ch'eng Huang had to be content with an earth mound as an altar, or at the best a niche in the temple of some better established divinity. It was not until the early days of the Mings that the position was fully regularised. In the second year of Chu Yuan-chang (朱元璋) temples were generally established, and the plan on which they should be constructed was definitely laid down. It was decreed that these buildings should be in the form of official residences, and that the Spiritual Magistrates should be represented as officials judging evil-doers, and that they should hold ranks varying in degree with the importance of the city they represented.

All the Ch'eng Huangs together formed a Celestial Ministry of Justice subordinate to their chief, who was usually located in the capital. A prefecture had two City Gods, to correspond with the prefect and subprefect, whereas a Hsien city in charge of a simple magistrate only needed a single guardian. Ch'eng Huangs could be transferred from one town to another like any ordinary members of the administration, and they could be demoted for failing to give satisfaction. The Taoist Pope had power to unfrock a Ch'eng Huang on adequate grounds of complaint, and he could appoint a substitute by electing the spirit of some deceased official of outstanding virtue in his place.

The subjection of these divinities to the vicissitudes of an earthly official career seemed quite natural to the Chinese, as an outstanding public servant might always be canonised and continue his ministry in the Underworld. It was essential to have an efficient Ch'eng Huang in charge of a large city, because he was the sole protection against enemies and epidemics. His functions were manifold, for he reported on the actions of his parishioners for good or ill, much as the Kitchen God was the Celestial informer for the family. He had the right to suggest to the Lord of Heaven rewards for virtue, and to the King of Hell punishment for vice. Above all, the care of the dead rested in his hands, and his was the responsibility of detailing attendants to accompany the souls to the Courts of Punishment.

At the conclusion of the Feast of the Hungry Ghosts, when the spirits' month-long vacation is over, it is the Ch'eng Huang's duty to muster them and ensure that the full tally returns to the custody of the King of the Underworld. He also exercises some discretion in the selection of his subjects from among the living and, for this reason, he is provided with two attendants known as "instead of a boy" and "instead of a girl". If a child falls sick and is in danger of death its parents burn incense before the Ch'eng Huang, and beseech him to substitute one of these effigies, and not to claim the spirit of their offspring.

The usual Ch'eng Huang temple in a large city was the exact counterpart of the old official yamen, with flagstaffs at the gate and a hall containing a large figure of the deity dressed in a long robe and scholar's cap, with black satin boots with thick white soles. Numbered "arrows of command" were on the desk before him for his messengers to execute his orders. In two rows, to the right and the left, were his clerks, lictors and satellites with recording tablets or rods to carry out the prescribed punishments.

Three times a year at the feasts of the dead, the divinity was carried in a gilt sedan-chair round his parish to let loose or muster the spirits on their release from or re-incarceration in hell. On this last occasion the image passes the night in a house within the city walls, and not in his own temple, as his work is unfinished. Next morning he has to make the round of the southern suburbs escorted by the prefect or magistrate, to receive the congratulations and petitions of the populace.

Hong Kong, prior to the British occupation, possessed no city large enough a warrant a Ch'eng Huang temple. T'ang Lung-wen, one of the squires of Kam Tin, however, led such a saintly life and was so renowned for his generosity that he was adopted as the City Guardian in the Pok Lo district.

A Ch'eng Huang's Court may be seen in the T'ien Hou temple at Stanley at the east end of the sanctuary. The god is, however, only a guest as the images are in the keeping of the individual who farms the revenues of the shrine, and are stored in the building for convenience. His position is somewhat peculiar, for he is out of touch with his own clients and can hardly be expected to adopt the parishioners of the locality which affords him shelter. In fact, he is enjoying a prolonged holiday for, whilst there is usually a stick of incense smouldering at his altar to do him honour, he takes no part in the processions at the Hungry Ghost festival and no special attention is paid to him on that occasion.

The most famous of all the City Gods is the spiritual guardian of the dead in Hangchow, Yueh Fei (岳飛), whose loyalty rivals that of Kuan Kung himself. Yuan Shih-k'ai, in the brief space during which he arrogated to himself Imperial powers, decreed that he should be recognised as a God to preside over war and the destiny of Chinese military affairs, as a co-equal of Kuan Kung. A magnificent temple to the newly created deity was erected on the north shore of the Hangchow lake in the grounds which contain his tomb.

Yueh Fei was a Hunan man, whose birth was signaled by the appearance of a great bird which alighted on the roof of the house during the last days of the Sung Dynasty. His parents were renowned for their charity and upright character, and they went hungry to feed the poor. Their land was ever at the disposal of those who encroached to gain a subsistence. Their son was all that could be desired and grew into a high-spirited youth, whose courage was only eclipsed by his moral attributes. He was a noted archer and rose to the rank of general in the desperate days when the Sungs were struggling for existence against the Golden Tartars. His crowning victory routed a hundred thousand men commanded by the heir to the Mongol throne, but his very success was his undoing.

The Sung Prime Minister, Ch'in Kuei (秦檜), and his wife had both sold out to the Tartars, and they brought false charges against the successful general. Yueh Fei was thrown into prison, but escaped conviction when he tore off his jacket and revealed that his mother had tattooed on his back the characters Chin Chung Pao Kuo (盡忠報國), "Loyal and true to defend the country". On the production of this somewhat unconvincing documentary evidence he was acquitted, only to be re-arrested by his cowardly adversaries who caused him to be murdered in gaol in A.D. 1141.

After his death his merits were slowly recognised; so he was canonised, and restored to all his titles, whilst Ch'in Kuei was degraded and, with his treacherous wife, was doomed to everlasting infamy as the prototype of a traitor. Their images still serve as a spittoon outside the temple of their rival.

Lei Kung, the God of Thunder

The Ministry of Thunder comprises over eighty officials of whom the President is Lei Kung (雷公), but only six of its members are of sufficient importance to appear in effigy in a Chinese temple. Their worship in human form dates from the Han Dynasty, but the conception of the personality of the Thunder God underwent considerable modification with the introduction of Buddhism a thousand years later. Lei Kung was originally depicted as a strong man, holding a hammer and chisel, with a string of drums rumbling as he moved. His present birdlike form is probably derived from the Indian Garuda, a divinity half-man, half-bird who acted as messenger for the Hindu God Vishnu. It is his thunderbolt which causes the damage, for Tien Mu (電母), Mother of Lightning, merely flashes her mirror on the intended victim to ensure his aim. Thunder at unseasonable times is considered by the Chinese as a portent of political change and revolutions. In Hong Kong there is a belief that it is always absent when a typhoon is in the vicinity, and this assumption was responsible for heavy loss of life among the junk people in the great storm of 1906. Unburied coffins are credited with attracting the attention of Lei Kung, and have to be hidden from his gaze by covering them with a mound of grass or straw.

Lei Kung has made several appearances on earth, according to Taoist lore, so there is no doubt as to his identity. A youth named Yeh Chien-chao of Hsin Chou, in the course of his medical studies, was in the habit of searching the slopes of Chien-ch'ang Shan for fuel and healing herbs. One day he took shelter from a heavy shower under a tree and, after a violent thunder-clap, saw a winged creature with a blue face and bird's claws, held fast in a cleft in the trunk. He announced that he was Lei Kung and that in splitting the tree he had underestimated his stroke and had become wedged owing to the resilience of the wood. He offered a handsome reward for his liberation so the student enlarged the cleft by hammering in stones. Lei Kung thanked him and made an appointment at the same spot on the following day, when he presented his benefactor with a book. This was a guide to the production of thunder and rain, with a number of prescriptions for curing sickness and alleviating distress. The Thunder God informed him that he could summon him and his four brothers at will to his aid, but cautioned him to call on him sparingly as he had an uncertain temper. Yeh Chien-chao, with the aid of the precious volume, became a famous physician and cured all the ailments of those who applied to him, besides averting numerous famines by summoning timely rain. Only on one occasion did he summon Lei Kung himself to his aid, and this was when he was indicted for sleeping off a heavy debauch in the Monastery of Chi Chou Ssu. On the steps of the court he invoked Lei Kung who manifested himself with such a clap of thunder that the magistrate took refuge under the table and, on the passing of the storm, dismissed the case.

The Thunder God also appeared to punish an old harridan who was beating her daughter-in-law, but was baulked of his aim by her throwing a dish-cloth over his head. He was helpless till the rain washed it away enabling him to take off for heaven. As he gained height the neighbours saw that their divinity was furnished with a bird's head and talons, so they were able to fashion an improved likeness for the worship of future generations. Generally speaking he is a benevolent deity, who averts evil and, through his connection with the Rain Gods, assists in the production of good harvests. He discourages waste, and an individual who spills rice on the floor or treads it under foot risks being struck by lightning. The thunderbolt, Chien Shih (箭石), literally arrow stone, often depicted in Chinese art, is the emblem of the divine force of the Buddhist doctrine, which shatters false belief. The weapon, on account of the heat generated in its passage through the atmosphere, is reduced to its hardest metallic constituents, rendering it comparable with the most intractable of gems, the diamond. This gave rise to the Thunderbolt of the Gods, or the Diamond Mace, originally carried by Indra, the Warrior deity of the Hindu faith. Translated to China this deity figures as a subsidiary of Sakyamuni, under the name of Ti Shih (帝釋), or Yin To Lo (因陀羅).

Western liturgies include prayers for rain and for fine weather. The Chinese have realised also that a superabundance of moisture may become an embarrassment, and that it is desirable to have a means of turning off the tap when the needs of the crops are satisfied. They have consequently invented the Lady with the Broom, or Sao Ch'ing Niang Niang (掃晴娘娘), who can sweep away the clouds and restore the sun to his office of stimulating growth. She is the spirit of the Star San Shou, the Broom, whose paper images are cut out by farmers and are pasted behind doors to regulate the dispensations of Yu Shih (雨師), the Master of Rain. In the temples he occupies a position next to Lei Kung, and is dressed in yellow armour, as he is the reincarnation of a mortal who relieved a great drought in the reign of Shen Nung (2838–2698 B.C.). He is credited with the ability to pass through fire and water without singeing himself or getting wet, and he can also float through space, or change himself into a silkworm chrysalis. He is sometimes represented holding a plate with a small dragon on it in one hand, whilst he dispenses water with the other. He has a black-faced wife who carries a serpent in each hand and has others festooned about her ears, suggesting an Indian origin.

Patron Saints

In addition to the Essential Household Gods and the familiar T'u Ti, or Earth Spirits, each Guild, or Trade, has its Patron Saint, whose anniversary it celebrates. The Boat People put their faith in Tien Hou (天后), the Queen of Heaven, also known as the Holy Mother Ma Tsu P'o (媽祖婆), whose birthday they keep on the twenty-third day of the Third Moon. Her shrines are situated near the shore, all round the coast, and are visited on her fête by all the fishing and lighterage junks, bearing offerings, and a highly representative proportion of the floating population.

The Practitioners of Native Medicine worship Shen Nung (神農), the founder of Chinese Medicine and Divine Husbandman, who supposedly reigned between 2838 and 2698 B.C. He is one of the triumvirate in the Taoist Ministry of Medicine, as the successor of Fu Hsi, the leader and discoverer of the Eight Trigrams. As the father of agriculture, he taught the cultivation of the five grains, examined a hundred herbs, and wrote the Pen Ts'ao (本草) or "Essential herbs", the first treatise on the healing art.

He is a bit too remote for popular acceptance, and the Taoist Yao Wang, or Drug Prince, is the more beloved patron of the sick, and those who make a living by ministering to their needs. He was an eminent Taoist, named Sun En (孫恩), who lived at the beginning of the T'ang Dynasty.

He compiled a Medical Encyclopaedia in thirty volumes, which dealt not only with materia medica, but such branches of the art as acupuncture, massage, dieting, physical culture, and even love potions. His canonical name is Sun Chun-jen (孫存仁).

Money changers naturally put their trust in the God of Wealth, under the name of Chao Hsuan Tan (趙玄壇), who is worshipped on the fifteenth day of the Third Moon.

Blacksmiths cultivate the favours of Wai Ching-kung, a general who rendered valuable services to the founder of the T'ang Dynasty (A.D. 618–626), and also to his successors. He achieved his victories with a famous iron mace, with which he bludgeoned his enemies into submission. His birthday is celebrated on the tenth day of the Third Moon.

Restaurant keepers and wine merchants, having interests in common, share the patronage of Tu K'ang (杜康), an expert vintner in the Chou Dynasty (1122-247 B.C.). The exact period when he lived is unknown, but he is good for a drink on the thirteenth day of the Sixth Moon.

Tailors and slop-dealers combine with the makers of compasses and scientific instruments in honouring the Emperor Hsien Yuan (軒轅), to whom the invention of the mariner's compass is attributed. His consort taught the people the method of rearing silkworms and weaving their product. The lady's name was Lei Tzu (嫘祖), sometimes called Hsi Ling Shih (西陵氏).

The Patron Saint of Jewellers is Hu Ching, a Minister of Works in the Sung Dynasty (A.D. 960–1276). He achieved greatness by suggesting an ornament which concealed a disfigurement of the consort of one of the Emperors, who was so delighted by her improved appearance that he could deny nothing, even canonisation, to the favourite who designed the headdress.

Lu Yu, who died in A.D. 804, was the author of the tea classic (陸羽), a famous work on tea, and is worshipped by the trade as their tutelary deity. The plant is not indigenous to China, but was introduced from Northern India by Bodidharma, or Ta Mo (達摩), the Blue-eyed Brahmin, in A.D. 543.

Barbers worship Lu Tsu (呂祖) for no very evident reason. He is a rather low-class medicine man, to whom people pray for a prescription. They burn incense before his shrine, and draw a number out of a hat. The drug corresponding to the number is then taken from a shelf. The original panel practitioner was one Lu T'ung-pin (呂洞賓), one of the later Taoist patriarchs. Invested with magic formulae, and girded with a sword of supernatural power, he traversed the Empire, slaying monsters and vanquishing the powers of evil, during a period of four hundred years. In the 12th century temples were erected in his honour.

Kuan Ti (關帝), the God of War, is the patron of Pawnshops, Curio dealers and the late Manchu Dynasty. He was a General under the posterior Hans over two thousand years ago. Supporting Liu Pei, first Emperor of the later Hans, after suppressing three rebellions in Shantung, he was taken prisoner and executed in 220 B.C. He is worshipped in every house, and temples are dedicated to him all over the country, while his image is placed in the first hall of every Buddhist temple.

Paper-makers worship Ts'ai Lan, a scholar of the Second, or East Han, Dynasty, whilst the manufacturers of writing brushes put their faith in Meng T'ien (蒙田), a Commander-in-Chief in Inner Mongolia during the building of the Great Wall in Ch'in times. He made the first brush from the joint of a bamboo and the hair of a deer.

Ink and ink-slab makers, as befits a scholarly craft, have taken one of Confucius' seventy-two disciples as a patron. His name is Tze Lu (子路), and he has left a reputation for quick temper and an aggressive disposition. He always escorted his master on a journey, which can hardly have made for peaceful travel, though the sage probably got value for money.

The carvers of seals and stone tablets erect altars to Feng Chieh, and Wen Ch'ang (馮節、溫昶), inventor of the Chinese characters, while printers worship Feng Tao (馮道) and Pi Sen (畢昇).

Salt manufacturers and miners have Su Sa-tsu (蘇沙子), whilst distillers favour Tu K'ang (杜康), a scholar of the Ch'in Dynasty.

The patron of bean-curd makers is Liu An (劉安), and butchers have chosen Chang Fei (張飛) of the Han Dynasty to represent them. He was once a butcher himself, and was blood-brother to Kuan Kung after the famous "Oath in the Peach Orchard".

Professional cooks do not go further afield than the homely Kitchen God who presides over every family in the land. Dyers worship Kê Hung (葛洪) of the Ch'in Dynasty, whilst needle makers cultivate Liu Hai (劉海), whose only claim to fame seems to have been filial affection for his mother.

Shoemakers have taken Sun Pin (孫臏), a great strategist, and calligraphists have adopted Hsiao Ho (蕭和), a prime minister of the First Han Emperor, who acted as unofficial notary at the court.

Porcelain makers worship Lao Chün (老君) who

Kuan Kung, God of War

passed through the Tung Kuan and became a god, but the kiln operators have their own special patron in Kuo Kung (郭公).

Comb-makers have a patroness in the Green Goddess, Lu Hsien-nu (綠仙女), and jade carvers worship the white-robed spirit Pai Yih Shen (白衣神).

The paper shop people, who deal in religious furnishing appropriate for the various festivals, burn incense to Wu Tao-tze (吳道子).

Story-tellers have two patrons Liu Chin-tin (劉敬亭) and Tsui Tsung-yuan (崔振元).

Actors, and those connected with drama, worship T'ang Ming-Huang, fourth Emperor of the dynasty of that name. His wife, Yang Kuei-fei (楊貴妃), the famous Chinese heroine, was noted for her dancing and singing, and her husband formed his own orchestra for which he composed.

Restaurant keepers worship Kuan Kung (關公) or Kuan Yü (關羽) whilst fortune-tellers appeal to Kuei Ku-tze who was a hard worker, and dwelt in a cave before deification in the early Han Dynasty.

The manufacturers of firecrackers have adopted Ma Chün (馬君), whilst the paste-makers have oddly enough taken Lei Tze (雷子), the God of Thunder, who seems a queer representative for so quiet a profession. He is also the patron of sugar manufacturers who, as they waste a good deal of grain in their trade, worship him as an insurance against being struck by lightning as a punishment for prodigality.

Ma Wang (馬王) patron of horses is worshipped on the 23rd of the Sixth Moon, in those parts of the country where the animals are used for transport.

Temple Guardians

Contrary to Western belief, a sacred edifice in China enjoys no immunity from the powers of evil. Whereas the Devil is in mortal dread of Holy Water, according to Christian ideas, a Taoist or Buddhist temple and its vicinity is regarded as a club for all the disreputable spirits in the parish. Should a bridal red chair pass its portals a screen must be erected between it and the door to prevent evilly disposed ghosts abandoning their usual recreations for the greater attraction of a wedding feast.

To minimise the number of undesirable tenants both Taoist and Buddhist temples have guardian figures at the main entrance to exclude demonic influences. The selection of these janitors is odd, for neither set have the reputation of being outstandingly successful in this line of business. The Taoist representatives lived about 1122 B.C., at the time of the overthrow of the Shang by the Chou Dynasty. They were military men, both Marshals, named Chen Lung (鄭倫) and Ch'en Ch'i (陳西), respectively. One is familiarly known as the Snorter, and the other's nickname is the Blower, in Chinese Heng (哼) and Ha (哈). Heng was an acolyte of the famous Taoist magician Tu O, from whom he acquired a marvellous power of extruding a death ray of blinding white light when he snorted, which destroyed his enemies in this world and the next. He appears at first to have fought against the Chou for, on one of his off-days, he was overcome by their troops and was brought a captive to the general. The latter, realising the value of his unique powers, took him into his service and made him Master General of the Ordnance, with a concurrent command of five Army Corps. During one of the skirmishes he found himself confronted by the Blower, Ha, still in the service of the Shangs.

A battered image

This worthy had studied under the same master, and had acquired the trick of filling his lungs with deadly gas which he exhaled to the discomfiture of his enemies in whose ranks great swathes were mown by the noxious cloud.

These two when opposed appeared to be fairly well matched, until other legendary heroes joined the melée and the Blower was wounded in the shoulder by Na Cha (哪咤), being finished off with a spear thrust in the belly administered by Huang Fei Hu (黃飛虎), the Yellow Flying Tiger. The Snorter also failed to survive the battle for he succumbed to another supernatural being, known as Marshal Chin Ta Sheng (金大升), or Great Golden Pint. This individual stored in his entrails a mysterious substance called Niu Huang (牛黃), or Ox Yellow, and meeting the Snorter spat in his face, with a noise of thunder, a lump the size of a rice bowl. Struck on the nose and with his nostrils split, the impact felled him to the ground, and he was divided at the waist by the victor's sword.

After the final establishment of the Chou Dynasty, Chiang Tzu-ya canonised the pair, and conferred on them the guardianship of Taoist temples.

Their Buddhist counterparts, the Four Diamond (四大天王) or Heavenly Kings, the Kuvera of Brahminism, were four Indian brothers, and were said to have been introduced into China by Pu K'ung (不空), a Singalese Buddhist, in the eighth century A.D. According to Indian tradition they are supernatural beings who guard the slopes of paradise with a ghostly army. They were naturalised as Chinese citizens under the names of Mo Li Ch'ing (摩禮青), Mo Li Hai (摩禮海), Mo Li Hung (摩禮紅) and Mo Li Shou (摩禮壽).

The first brother is the Guardian of the East, has a fierce white countenance and a beard like copper wire. He carries a jade ring, a spear and a magic sword named Blue Cloud. On its blade are engraved the characters for Earth, Water, Fire and Wind. When he brandishes it a black wind springs up which produces myriads of spears, piercing men's bodies and turning them to dust. The storm is the herald of a conflagration which fills the air with golden fiery serpents. A thick fog also arises from the ground, blinding and choking all human beings who are enveloped.

Virupakshu, Sanskrit of Far Gazer, the Guardian of the West, is known as Mo Li Hai. He has a blue face and carries a four-stringed guitar, at the sound of which all men are enthralled to such an extent that the camps of his enemies catch fire whilst they are listening to his music.

Virudhaka, the Lord of Growth, has dominion in the South, as Mo Li Hung. His face is red and he holds the umbrella of Chaos, formed of pearls endowed with spiritual properties. When opened, universal darkness falls and when reversed it provokes violent earthquakes and thunderstorms.

The Guardian of the North, Vaisravana, has a perfect bag of tricks at his disposal, for he wields two whips and carries a panther-skin sack confining a creature known as Hua Hu Tiao (花虎貂). When in its home it resembles a white rat but, once at large, it takes the form of a winged white elephant of carnivorous habits. The god sometimes adds to his menagerie by the inclusion of a serpent, or other man-eater, which is always ready to carry out his orders. Black being associated with the North, Mo Li Shou, his Chinese pseudonym, is portrayed with a dark complexion.

Like their Taoist counterparts they lived in the Chou Dynasty, but were supporters of the House of Shang (商), for whom they raised an army of 100,000 celestial soldiers. Their exploits on earth are as disappointing as those of Heng and Ha, and they found themselves opposed by secret weapons more powerful than their own.

Unfortunately, on one occasion, after Mo Li Shou had let the rat out of the bag, the brute devoured Yang Chien (楊戩), a nephew of the Jade Emperor, who, being a magician himself, had no difficulty in cutting his way out. As he could transform his shape at will, he assumed the guise of his victim, and the owner put the wrong Hua Hu Tiao back into his sack. The four brothers celebrated their victory with a too generous allowance of liquor, and Yang Chien seized the opportunity to emerge from his bag with intent to deprive them of their weapons. He only succeeded, however, in carrying off the umbrella but, in a subsequent engagement, Na Cha, son of the God of Thunder, broke the ring of Mo Li Ch'ing. Huang T'ien Hua (黃天華), one of their adversaries, was armed with a spike, enclosed in a silk sheath, called the "Heart piercer", which emitted so strong a ray of light as to induce blindness. With this he overcame first Mo Li Ch'ing, and then two of his brethren. There only remained the owner of the Hua Hu Tiao who was still unaware of the transformation which had taken place in his sack. When he inserted his hand to loose his pet the beast bit it off at the wrist which rendered him an easy prey. So he died, and took his place with his brothers on each side at the entrance to Buddhist sanctuaries. As long as they keep on good terms with the Taoist hierarchy they are probably effective guardians against such spirits as beset their doors, but the Jade Emperor's family is certainly not to be trifled with.

Water Legends

Being an agricultural race the primitive Chinese naturally set great store on an adequate supply of water for the ripening of the crops, and those who lived south of the Yangtze supplemented their food with the fish which inhabited the great rivers and lakes. To ensure a constant ration they propitiated the gods of the waters in the form of dragons, probably suggested by the alligator which occurs in the central valley. The region suffers periodically from disastrous floods attributed, not to a too rapid melting of Tibetan snows, but to the uneasiness of the god whose watery residence happens to be in the district. He it is, or one of his clan, who provokes the rain, and, if there be an excess of moisture, it is to his authority that application for a mitigation must be addressed.

Some of the spirits now regarded as tutelaries of lakes and rivers are reincarnations of historical characters, such as Liu Yih, a graduate in the reign of Kao Tsung, of the T'ang Dynasty. The Taoist inventors of the legend connected with him place the date of his adventure between A.D. 676 and 679. The hero was returning home after an unsuccessful visit to Ch'ang An, where he failed in his licentiate's examination.

Whilst passing through Ching Yang Hsien he saw a young woman raggedly dressed, tending goats by the roadside. She somewhat taxed his credulity by claiming to be the daughter of the Dragon King of the Tung T'ing lake and divorced wife of the son of the God of the Ching river. She accosted the scholar as she had learned that he was journeying to the kingdom of Wu, a stone's throw from her native district, and wished him to appraise her father of her circumstances.

She told Liu Yih that he could deliver a letter if he went to an old orange tree, known as the "Protector of the soil", which grew on the northern bank of the Tung T'ing lake. If this were struck three times a janitor would appear. Liu took the missive and, as his sympathy had been aroused by the girl's story, he presented himself a few months later at the outpost of the Dragon King's domain. At his summons a warrior rose from the lake and inquired his business. Cleaving a path through the waters with his sword he led the way to the palace of Ling Hsu (靈虛宮), who immediately granted him an audience. The Dragon King was clad in violet robes, and carried a piece of jade in token of his office. Liu explained that they were neighbours, and recounted his adventure with the daughter with an expression of sorrow at her miserable condition. The Dragon King was much moved by the letter, and his whole court burst into loud lamentations. The King quelled the din, explaining that he was afraid that Ch'ien T'ang (錢塘) might hear. Liu Yih asked for an explanation and was told that the individual in question was the brother of the Dragon King, and was possessed of an ungovernable temper, quite capable of provoking a nine-year flood. At this moment the skies darkened, and a blood-red dragon a thousand feet long roared through the clouds with a sound like an underground train. It returned only a few moments later setting down the young woman last seen in her capacity as goat-herd. The Dragon King was delighted, and introduced his daughter to Liu, with the information that her husband was dead, and that her hand was at his disposal. Liu had a horrid suspicion that the husband had recently been liquidated to create a vacancy, so he excused himself, and went off to marry a mortal named Chang. She soon died, however, and a second union with a lady called Han was no more permanent. As the proximity to the lake seemed to have a deleterious effect on his matrimonial prospects, Liu moved to Nanking, and was approached to enter into an alliance with a lady from Fang Yang, in Hopei. Her father, one Hao, had been a Magistrate at Ch'ing Liu in Anhwei Province, but seemed to spend most of his time travelling. Liu agreed to marry the young woman, who, at the end of a year, produced him an heir. She then confessed that her travelling father was the Dragon King of Tung T'ing lake and that, when he saved her from her miserable life, she was determined to reward him with her hand. The pair were last heard of in A.D. 712 when they returned to the Lake district, but legend records nothing further of them for good or ill, except their apotheosis when Shang Ti (上帝) conferred on Liu the title Chin Lung Ta Wang (金龍大王), or Great Prince Golden Dragon, which was the utmost he could expect as a "failed B.A."

The old Mother of the Waters (Shui Mu Niang-Niang) (水母娘娘) is the legendary spirit of Ssu Chou, in Anhwei, who was allegedly responsible for the destruction of the

city by a disastrous flood in 1574. One authority states that she is the younger sister of the White Elephant which acts as door guardian at Buddha's gate. The beast in question is the "subtle principle of metamorphosed water" but the sister turned it into a veritable scourge. She inundated the city almost every year, so a report was sent to the Jade Emperor asking him to abate the nuisance. The witch, however, prevailed over the celestial armies and evaded every effort to curb her mischievous proclivities. One day she was seen near the city gate with two buckets of water, and Li Lao-chün suspected her of some fresh atrocity. He bought a donkey and, whilst she was engaged in bargaining, led it to the buckets to drink its fill. Unfortunately the capacity of the ass was unequal to the task, and a small quantity remained. The buckets in question contained the sources of the five great lakes, and the dregs were sufficient to cause a disastrous flood when Shui Mu Niang Niang overturned them with her foot. It was the end of Ssu Chou, which became the Hung Tze lake. Luckily it was the last mischievous act of the witch, for she was so hunted by Yü Huang's (玉皇) myrmidons that she fell a victim to a trick. Exhausted by the pursuit she was badly in need of food, so she patronised a vermicelli hawker who had set up her stall by the roadside. No sooner had she swallowed the first mouthful than the noodles turned to iron chains which wound themselves round her intestines. The end of the chain protruded from her mouth, and permitted her to be led by the Monkey God to a deep well at the foot of a mountain in Hsü I Hsien. The vermicelli seller was none other than Kuan Yin, who alone was a match for the cunning of the Old Mother of the Waters. In times of drought, when the springs are low, the end of Shui Mu's chain may be seen at the bottom of the well.

Tam Kung Temples

Though the image or tablet of Tam Kung (譚公) is to be found in many places of worship in Hong Kong, temples dedicated to this divinity are few in number. Tam Kung was not a native of Hong Kong but, like many other inhabitants of its hinterland, he made it his home and received enlightenment from the Nine Dragons of Kowloon. His attainments in magical lore gave him command over the elements, endearing him to the Boat People who place him only second to the Queen of Heaven in their affection.

The two main temples dedicated to him are at Shaukiwan and Wongneichong and there is a distinct connection between them. In many religions the reputation of a Saint rests largely on the unsubstantial evidence of dreams and visions and Tam Kung belongs to this order. Apart from the Water Folk his adherents are mostly to be found in the districts embracing Shaukiwan and Happy Valley. Whereas his fame as a weather controller evoked the prayers of those who earned their living on the sea, the landsmen were attracted by his skill as a medical practitioner who, contrary to the ethics of the profession, advertised his talents by influencing the subjective mind during the hours of sleep.

The inhabitants of the fishing centre gained the impression that their patron was in life a cowherd, who

184

after his translation had acquired the power of dispelling disease. The persistence of these dreams resulted in a drive for funds with the aid of which a temple was erected in his honour on the quayside. This shrine has always been famous for the efficacy of the prescriptions issued to worshippers by the highly unscientific method in vogue among the Chinese. On the high altar is a bamboo tube containing a number of slips of the same material, each bearing a numeral. The suppliant, after making an offering accompanied by prayer, kneels and shakes the receptacle from which one slip gradually rises above the others until it topples over and falls to the floor. The divining woods are then cast, and, if the answer is favourable, the numbered slip is taken to the temple attendant, who issues the corresponding prescription. As the balance between kills and cures appears to be favourable the shrine is very well supported, and its reputation is further enhanced by its fortune-telling successes.

Strange to say the patron of the establishment alone expressed his dissatisfaction with its location, and appeared to a boy in a dream complaining of the discomfort of his surroundings. When the story was circulated, a crowd of worshippers gathered, and the boy was bidden by the elders to walk in any direction he desired, until the spirit moved him to halt. He finally reached the lucky spot in Blue Pool Road, Happy Valley, which was dedicated as the site for the second temple. The villagers elected a committee of responsible members, to act as the managers, as soon as the building was completed. One of these made a fortune during his term of office, which confirmed the wisdom of founding a subsidiary shrine and stimulated competition for election to the board. As every resident offered himself as a candidate, a lottery was instituted, confined to the more substantial citizens, who were in a position to contribute ten dollars or over. This was sponsored by the K'ai Fongs' Association, winning tickets being inscribed with the two characters Tze Li (值理), Duty Member, which qualified the holders for a seat on the board.

It must not be supposed that the desire to serve on the committee sprang from the hope of enrichment through an illicit commission from the temple revenues, though doubtless it was recognised that the workman was worthy of his hire, and squeeze was taken for granted. The service of Tam Kung undoubtedly was attended by Luck and, in China, the old Roman and Greek Goddess of Fortune is the over-riding deity. Any action to court her favour is meritorious, and any deed which might offend her is to be eschewed. Hence the system of lucky days for every action of human life, from eating dog meat to vaccination against smallpox, from building a house to the disposal of the dead.

Tam Kung is a purely Taoist divinity, but such is the inextricable confusion of the two creeds practised in South China that it is not unusual to find him addressed with the addition of the character Fo (佛) signifiying Buddha.

A CHINESE BESTIARY

Of the four super-intelligent creatures which rule the points of the compass, the phoenix is allotted the southern quadrant, whilst the dragon and the tiger reign in the east and west, and the Black Warrior, or tortoise, has dominion in the north.

A Diversity of Dragons

English Heraldry is full of strange mythical beasts, the product of legend, or the improbable Travellers' tales recorded in the adventures of Sir John Mandeville. Dragons, phoenixes and unicorns are the common heritage of East and West, but their appearance and attributes differ widely in conception. The dragon in the West was a lineal descendant of prehistoric reptilian monsters of carnivorous habits, whereas in China he is a beneficent creature, symbolic of Imperial power. The Chinese artist depicts him as a composite animal with the head of a camel, the horns of a deer, eyes of a rabbit, ears of a cow, neck of a snake, belly of a frog, scales of a carp, claws of a hawk, and the palm of a tiger. His back is crested, with eighty-one projection. On each side of the mouth are whiskers, and the chin is decorated with a beard in which lies a brilliant pearl. The creature suffers from deafness, and people deprived of hearing are called "Lung" (聾), a play upon its name, for the dragon symbol is placed above the radical for the human ear. It breathes a sort of vapour, which may coagulate as rain or become incandescent, and its voice is as the sound of copper pans clashing like cymbals. This is the best kind of dragon, but there are lesser breeds: the Chinese recognise nine different forms of dragon each with its separate use and attribute. The Lung, which inhabits the sky, is infinitely the most important.

The Li (螭) is hornless, and is an ocean-dweller, while the Chiao (蛟), a scaly reptile, frequents marshes and mountain caves. It has a small hornless head, a crimson breast; its back is striped with green, and its sides are yellow. It has four legs, but in other respects resembles a thirteen-foot snake.

As regards the diet of the dragon, it appears to feed on swallows' flesh, and when people pray for rain they throw these birds on the water to ensure its assistance.

As the coat of arms of the British Royal Family has the lion and unicorn for supporters, so the Chinese Imperial coat, from the Han to the Ch'ing Dynasty, carried two dragons contesting for the "night-shining pearl". The Lung, or principal dragon, had numerous offspring, of which at least nine different species are used in decoration, on account of their individual peculiarities.

Bronze bells and gongs often have the P'u Lao (蒲牢) cast as a ring for suspension purposes, as this particular form of dragon cries out loudly when attacked by its principal enemy, the whale.

The Ch'iu Niu (囚牛) has musical tastes, and is carved as an embellishment for fiddle screws. The Pi Hsi (贔屭), being addicted to literature, is carved on the top of stone tablets, and is often used as a motif on the pedestal of tombstones. The Pa Hsia (霸下) was also a monumental ornament, as it was supposed to be able to cope with great weights. The Chao Feng (朝奉) had a predilection for dangerous situations, so was placed on the eaves of temples, whilst the Chih Wen (蚩吻), owing to its fondness for water, was carved on the road-bearers of bridges. It is sometimes represented as a fish with up-turned tail. The Suan Ni (狻猊), a restful creature, gives a reposeful attitude to Buddha's throne, whilst the Yai Tzu (睚眦), the sole bloodthirsty member of the group, adorns the sword hilt, as a guard.

Although one formidable member of the tribe, the Cha Yu, is addicted to human flesh, it only appears when the ruling sovereign is sufficiently lacking in virtue. This is just as well at the present juncture, as it is forty feet long, and adds the dragon's head to the body of a horse and the claws of a tiger. The Imperial Dragon was distinguished by having five claws, and the privilege of wearing it on the clothing was limited to the Emperor's sons and princes of the first and second rank. Those of the third and fourth had to be content with a four-clawed emblem, and those of the fifth and certain officials were only entitled to a five-clawed serpent.

The lower portion of China, from the Yangtze Valley southward, abounds in great lakes and rivers, the monster's natural habitat, and lends itself better to aquatic sports than the droughty North. The dragon is consequently more honoured in this region than in those other parts of the Celestial territory where he is only invoked in the case of shortage of rain. Dances in his honour are held in various central and southern provinces, and the Dragon Boat Races on the Double Fifth are exclusively a feature of the South.

In Kwangtung Province two villages, Ho Lung and Lotus Pond in the Chung Shan district, have for centuries been in keen competition to stage the more elaborate performance, and the ritual has reached a high stage of perfection with teams of twenty-three men to operate a dragon one hundred and seventy feet long. In other provinces there are variants of the dance which savour of pure buffoonery, and evidently stem from the same origin as the Lion dance, mounted to amuse a rustic population. Historically the tradition dates from the Sung Dynasty, when the image was made of straw covered with black material. It had some connection with the Lantern festival on the 15th of the First Moon which takes place during a period when all self-respecting dragons are in hibernation. The stuffed monster was merely used emblematically as a lantern bearer to lend tone to the proceedings.

In Szechuan a paper representation is used with Chinese lanterns as an illuminant, and its appearance was greeted with shouts of "Look at the great dragon firecracker". As the procession passed crackers and rockets were fired, some aimed directly at the unfortunate beast whilst the crowd performed a war dance to the accompaniment of drum and clarinet. The entertainment ended when the dragon was consumed by fire. It is possible that this was a rain-making ceremony, the idea being that if the dragon were made sufficiently uncomfortable he would produce the moisture requisite to extinguish the flames. As a last resort, in the North, the Dragon's tablet was exposed to the rays of the summer sun by Imperial decree to induce him to furnish the antidote. Operating this form of dragon must be an arduous, and at times dangerous, duty, so the actors are recommended to hold an olive in their mouths as a prophylactic against heat and fumes.

In the Yangtze Valley the image is made of reeds or bamboo for the framework, covered with white material and blue scales. The body is illuminated with candle lanterns, and is supported by seven or eight operators armed with long poles. The movements of the beast are dictated by a man in front carrying a large red ball, representing the sun, or the night-shining pearl, and the dance is carried out to the accompaniment of crackers. This performance corresponds to the English mummers who hope to benefit by the generosity of the well-to-do, and seems to have no religious significance.

In Hunan the dragon is again made of paper, with a patterned material for the scales. Its complement only consists of three men for head, body and tail, with a leader for the pearl in front. Twelve others precede the parade with banners, and musicians follow behind. The cortège then makes the round of the village, and is welcomed by the heads of families, burning incense, and letting off firecrackers. The dragon's head is then decorated with a strip of white cloth three feet long by an inch wide, for which modest emolument it performs the dance.

In Hupei the dragon's fertilising powers are evidently regarded as applicable to the human race as well as the soil. The image is much longer than the Hunan variety, and it is made of paper illuminated with lanterns. It is received by all families in the village with incense and candles. Should there be a male heir, the head of the monster is decorated with a red cloth, but, if a son is lacking, sacrifices of beef, pork and mutton must be prepared for its consumption. The dragon, being the essence of the Yang (陽), or male principle, is regarded in this province as the obvious source of supply where sons are needed to carry on the family name.

Kweichow sports a dragon with an open mouth showing teeth and tongue, each joint of the body being lit with a lantern. The man operating the tail must be a clown, to raise a laugh. Each family visited provides itself with suitable fireworks, so that the dragon goes through its evolutions in a cloud of smoke and flame. The Chinese are so casual with explosives that a seat in the audience would seem preferable to the role of a performer, were it not for the fact that an onlooker is quite capable of dropping a cigarette in the magazine. A glorious detonation was provided in this way in Singapore for the Silver Jubilee, which put a premature end to a Japanese fireworks display.

Several districts in Fukien specialise in Dragon dances, but the effigies are smaller than the Cantonese variety, and there is considerable difference in the movements performed. In the old capital of Szechuan, Ch'eng Tu, three kinds of properties are used, namely, a dancing variety, a double dragon, and a fire dragon illuminated for night performances. A red ball representing the sun is substituted for the night-shining pearl, with a paper ingot of silver wrapped in red silk.

The Phoenix

The Feng Huang (鳳凰) like the dragon is a composite conception, combining all that is beautiful in the ornithological kingdom. The derivation of its name implies that it is the emperor of birds, just as the unicorn surpasses every animal on earth. It is an imperial emblem, symbol of the Empress. One author, whose imagination must have outrun his scientific approach, described it as resembling a wild swan in front, and a unicorn behind. He gave it the throat of a swallow, the bill of a chicken, the neck of a serpent, and the tail of a fish. In this it had twelve feathers, but an extra one grew in an intercalary year. The forehead is that of a Manchurian crane, but it is crested like the mandarin drake and, whilst it is striped like the tiger, its back has the dome shaped appearance of the tortoise.

Unlike the Arabian phoenix, which from its curved beak is obviously a member of the birds of prey, the Chinese creature is gallinaceous, and it is probably to the pheasant family that one must look for its origin. The golden and silver pheasants occur in the southern provinces, and both were embroidered as badges of rank on the robes of civil officials in Imperial days. Reeves' pheasant, with tail feathers sometimes six feet long, decorated with black bars, is found in the northern mountains, and the Amherst in the foothills of Szechuan.

As at least twenty varieties of the family are listed in China there was ample scope to combine their characteristics, and embroider the result even more lavishly than the designs on the mandarin's patches. As Williams says "the drawing does not correspond very closely with the description given above, from which it would appear that the artist has taken the Argus pheasant as his pattern, making such modifications as suited its divine character." Naturally, as an emblem of royalty, the bird exhibits all the symbolism embodied in Chinese religious tradition. The feathers of the tail are of the five colours, named after

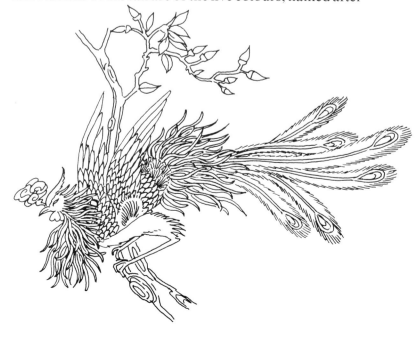

Phoenix

187

the five cardinal virtues, and it is five cubits in height. The tail is graduated like Pandean pipes, and its song resembles the music of that instrument, having five modulations. Like the unicorn it only appears when order reigns in the kingdom, and never more than one is seen, though this is invariably accompanied by a flock of lesser fowl. To satisfy the susceptibilities of the Buddhists it will not peck at, or injure, insects or bruise the grass by its tread. It alights only on the Wu T'ung tree, feeds only on the seeds of bamboo, and quenches its thirst only at the sweet fountains. It might be classed as an occasional migrant, for its home is in the Vermilion Hills, where it awaits the times of peace and good government.

It was seen at the birth of Confucius, and Chinese drawings commemorate the occasion with the phoenix flying in the skies, whilst the unicorn wanders on the hillside. The mother of the Sage is depicted in the foreground.

The tree which it has selected as its resting place, the Wu T'ung (梧桐), or drysandra, is a very rapid grower, and is an ornamental species with a bellshaped blossom, white on the outside, and reddish-brown within. The seeds are often used as a flavouring for the filling of Moon cakes for the mid-autumn festival.

The pheonix ranks second among the four super-intelligent creatures and, presiding over the south, symbolises the warmth of the sun and the summer harvest. Like the Arabian bird it is generated by fire, and is often depicted rising from the flames, or on the sun's disc. As this is "yang", or male in principle, its influence in the production of children is considerable. For this reason, though it typified the Empress, just as the dragon was identified with her consort as the highest in the land, it figured at the weddings of the poorest of their subjects, stamped in gold with the "Double Hsi" of marital happiness, on lucky money envelopes and the paraphernalia of the marriage rites.

As a decorative motive in ceremonial costume, it was formerly employed by the Empresses of China in the centre of the frame of the black headdress affected by Manchu women. After the last Emperor's abdication it was only used on the most formal occasions such as his birthday. Its restricted use must have been of some consolation to the wearer, as the headdress with its jade tassels weighed six pounds, and had to be worn from dawn to dusk. Were it not for the honour conferred by wearing the imperial symbol, it would be regarded by most mortals as an infliction which could well be dispensed with.

In Chinese art the pheasant, on account of its beauty, is sometimes employed instead of the phoenix. The designation "Feng" comprises two varieties, an archaic form which resembles the Argus, used as a motif on antique bronzes, and a later version derived from the characteristics of the pheasant and the peacock. Even the name of the phoenix, like that of the unicorn, is composite, for the "Feng" is the male, and the "Huang" the female, of the species. The combination might be rendered "Crested love pheasants". Though they never appear together, on earth at any rate, Chinese poetic licence refers to their fellowship as inseparable, and use it as a symbol for matrimonial pairing. Their eggs form the food of the fairies, which possibly accounts for their scarcity.

Its first recorded appearance was in the reign of Huang Ti, about 2600 B.C., an era of great tranquillity, as it returned and actually nested in the palace of the Emperor Yao in 2350 B.C. The period is so shadowy that historians may be forgiven recording this lapse in its solitary habits. It was only in the Han dynasty that it was elevated to the rank of an object of worship. Later, its visits to the Empire became commonplace, and sightings were recorded to round off a successful reign or flatter an impressionable monarch. Chinese history is rather short of native dynasties, so it is not surprising that its last appearance was at Feng Huang in Anhwei, where it was discovered scratching at the tomb of Hung Wu's father, hailing the advent of the Mings. Its visitation was of considerable commercial importance to the town, which exported huge quantities of pictures of the bird to all parts of the country.

Paper Tigers

The feast of Excited Insects (驚蟄), which falls a fortnight before the Vernal Equinox, is usually marked by the appearance of the first swallow, testifying to the accuracy of the Farmers' Calendar. The day is also noteworthy for a rash of Paper Tigers, and women returning from their marketing may often be seen with this mascot perched on top of their bundles. In Stanley there is a rock shrine facing the sea a couple of hundred yards short of the T'ien Hou (天后) temple, whose altar carries a pointed stone on a flat base. This is the emblem of the Soil, source of all fertility, both animal and vegetable. It must not be confused with the Earth divinity whose symbol is a cylindrical jade core, squared on the outside. On the vigil of the feast a number of Paper Tigers are placed on the altar by their purchasers and incense is burned before them, after which they are left for twenty-four hours to acquire potency from association with the Nature divinity. At dusk they are taken home and their lips are smeared with fat pork to attach them to the house, much as butter is applied to the feet of a new cat in England. They are a cheap insurance against demons and disease as they only cost ten cents. Yellow paper is pasted over an oval frame of bamboo slips, whilst fore and aft two hoops, like wagon raves, arch the back and furnish the legs. Black lines drawn with the brush in ink indicate the stripes, and the head gives a creditable impression of the beast it is intended to represent.

The Chinese have always been familiar with the tiger which is still found in Manchuria, and is common in the southern provinces. It is the ambition of every Chinese artist to paint a tiger, which symbolises bravery to such an extent that the soldiers of the empire wore tiger uniforms to strike terror into their foes. The head was painted on the shield, or the portholes of men-o'-war and on the bows of revenue cutters to overawe smugglers. Virtues were ascribed to the ashes of the bones and many parts of the beast in the treatment of disease, whilst the whiskers are a specific deterrent against tooth-ache.

The tiger in China, and not the lion, is the king of land beasts, just as the dragon rules over the denizens of the water; and it is one of the creatures of superior endowment which are of paramount importance in the practice of Feng Shui. The White Tiger (白虎) rules the western quarter after reaching the age of five hundred years when he changes to that colour. The title White Tiger was originally bestowed on a canonised general in the service of the last emperor of the Yin Dynasty. His side chapel may be seen in the temple of Pei Ti (北帝) at Cheung Chau (長州).

His birthday is observed on the Feast of Excited Insects at the beginning of the Second Moon, and is very popular with the Cantonese who worship him to avert gossip and quarrels during the coming year. Offerings of eggs and slices of fat pork are laid before his shrine. In temples which have an effigy of the Tiger it is put out in front of the building to give more space for people to do it honour. It is also propitiated to keep the house free from snakes and rats, though the co-existence of the two is incompatible.

Man-eating tigers are credited with great intelligence in partitioning the country round their lairs and visiting each section according to a fixed system, based on the Chinese calendar. Their victims are alleged to become devils after digestion, but the scent of dog flesh has an intoxicating effect on them, and it is believed that burnt horn is a prophylactic, whilst a hedgehog is an efficient guard against their depredations. According to Chinese belief, the man-eating habit is dictated, not by increasing age which renders futile the pursuit of normal game, but at the instigation of the spirits of those who have already been devoured. According to K'ang Hsi's great dictionary, if a tiger destroys a man, his spirit has no courage to seek another asylum, but he serves the beast as his slave. Normally, those who die a violent death may return to the world if they can find a substitute. This accounts for the belief that it is dangerous to go to the rescue of a drowning man, as he is being dragged down by a spirit seeking another to take his place.

According to the astrologers the star Alpha of the Great Bear gave birth to the first tiger, which represents the masculine principle in nature. His kingship over the other beasts is recognisable by the character Wang (王), or Prince, in the four stripes on his forehead. He is seven feet in length, as that number is male, and his period of gestation is seven months.

The Chinese think he has no equal as a demon-dispeller, and his image is painted on the walls of houses and temples to keep evil spirits at a distance. Small bronze images of the beast were used as sleeve weights in tombs for the same purpose, and his effigies have their own altars in temples in districts where the tiger is plentiful in nature. Though Hong Kong lays no claims to infestation, tigers occasionally drift into the New Territories, and one was shot on the Island during the Japanese occupation, so it is not surprising that certain temples display him among the deities who stave off disaster. To be on the safe side, however, it is not unreasonable to expend a penny to have a six-inch warden in the home, and in March a roaring trade is done in Paper Tigers.

In astrology the Tiger is associated with the autumn when it descends from the hills and becomes a nuisance round the villages. It is personified by the constellation Orion, which is most conspicuous at this time of year. Being the campaigning season, when the farmers could exchange hoes for swords, and the dividends were highest, the legend gained credence that Huang Ti (黃帝),

the Yellow Emperor, had trained tigers as troops, which accounts for their military connection down to the last century.

Père Wieger, in his research through the stories of man-eating tigers, states that it is very rare to find the enslaved spirit taking vengeance on his master by assisting in his destruction. He only came across one instance which is alleged to have occurred as far back as A.D. 755. Usually the demons enthusiastically assist the tiger to make a fresh kill so that a new spirit may act as his guide, whilst the old one qualifies for reincarnation. If the master is killed, its demon is in a frenzy of grief, for it is homeless and has lost all hope of redemption, and has no alternative to becoming a hungry ghost.

One typical story of a tiger and his attendant is attributed to a famous hunter who lived at Sung Yang (松陽) in Kwanghsi Province. When he discovered the track used by a beast, he set a spring gun with a trip wire, and the tiger usually succumbed to a bolt from his cross-bow. One day he set his trap in a well-worn track but, on visiting the place in the morning, found that it had been sprung without the quarry being touched. This occurred again and again, so he decided to set a watch and one night climbed a tree close to his weapon. Near midnight he saw a child, dressed in black, coming cautiously along the path, examining every inch of the track. He found the trip wire, followed it to the cross-bow where he removed the quarry, released the trigger and went on down the path. Then came the tiger who stepped out as if he had not an enemy in the world. The hunter came down from his tree and reset his trap but, on the return journey, the child again rendered it harmless. The man after his discovery was too quick for him and, jumping from his hideout, he promptly placed another bolt in his bow. This time there was a considerable interval before the tiger followed his scout, and when he did he took the shaft straight in the heart, and fell dead without a struggle. Not long afterwards the child came back along the path and evinced signs of grief at his master's fate, after which he vanished into thin air.

In Peking, prior to the Japanese war, children might often be seen wearing tiger clothing to protect them against harmful influences. The jacket was made of special yellow cloth patterned with appropriate stripes, and the cap had furry ears. Even tiger shoes were provided, with whiskered heads on the toes, and tails at the heels. These were usually made in the home, but an inferior quality could be bought at the Lung Fu Ssü (隆福寺), a fair which was held three times a month.

It is believed that the best protection against a tiger if a meeting cannot be avoided is an umbrella opened in his face. Examples of the success of this method are occasionally seen in works of art.

The Tortoise

The Tortoise is one of the four intelligent creatures. He is sacred to China, and is the symbol of longevity, strength and endurance. When P'an Ku was at work as architect of the universe, a task which occupied eighteen thousand years, these four creatures were his companions, and were the progenitors of the animal kingdom. Under the name of the Black Warrior (玄武), the Tortoise presides over the Northern quadrant, and is the symbol of winter. Both Hindus and Chinese regard it as representative of the universe, as its dome-shaped back typifies the vault of heaven, its belly the earth floating on the waters, and its longevity is a particular recommendation to a race which so ardently desires old age. It combines the Yang and Yin principles in nature, as its back is marked like the constellations in the heavens, and its body has lines corresponding to the earth. From the markings on its back are said to be derived the Eight Trigrams (八卦) attributed to the discovery of the mythical Emperor Fu Hsi, who left them as a legacy to mankind. These are combinations of the continuous line, which represents the male principle, and the broken stroke, which denotes the female. They are said to be the basis of mathematics, and each has its attributes from power to submission, besides being connected with an animal and a specific point of the compass. Plaques with the symbol of creation in the centre, surrounded by the eight trigrams, are considered protection from misfortune, and are frequently set up in Hong Kong, when the Feng Shui of the locality has been pronounced unfavourable. They are sometimes painted on mirrors, which have the power of deflecting evil influences, and double the value of the charm.

On account of the connection with the diagrams, the tortoise-shell is employed for divination. There are numerous forms of the creature, one combining the qualities of the dragon with its own nature, while another is the river god, to whom enormous strength is attributed. Hence he is frequently carved as a plinth to funeral tablets. A similar idea prevails in India, where a Hindu legend makes the tortoise a supporter of an elephant, which bears the globe on its back. The "Record of Science" (格物志) limits the age of the tortoise to 1,000 years, but Wang Ch'ung (王充), in his Lun Heng (論衡), states that when it has reached three hundred it is no bigger than a coin, and may still be supported by a lotus leaf. Even at 3,000, when its colour is blue with green rims, it is only one foot two inches in length.

One of the Chinese explanations of the Creation is that the world came into existence through the union of a tortoise and a snake. This belief is perpetuated in Hong Kong by the sale, at festivals, of representations of the pair intertwined. They are made of some sort of paste, attractively coloured, but have a short life as ornaments, as their composition is highly attractive to cockroaches, who render them unrecognisable after a night's exposure to their attentions.

The tortoise, however, has a most unenviable position in the Chinese vocabulary. To call a man a tortoise is the most deadly insult which can be offered. It casts reflexions on his parentage for the beast is supposed to have forgotten the eight characters which denote the moment of his birth. An alternative rendering is that he has forgotten the Eight Laws of politeness. In the North a tortoise drawn on a wall is the usual warning to "Commit no nuisance". It is the only creature who knows when it is going to rain, so speculations as to the weather are apt to be dangerous, and in North China to ask a man if he thinks a shower is imminent is an insult. The same idea can be conveyed by putting a hand on his head, as the tortoise is supposed to turn warm at the approach of rain. Sir Walter Hillier, in the *Chinese Language, and How to Learn It,* gives as an example of abusive language the epithet "Devil's daughter suckled scabby-headed tortoise" but it does not come so smoothly off the tongue as Wang Pa Tan (Turtle's Egg), a common term of endearment among muleteers and camel drivers.

Unicorn

The Chinese unicorn has none of the pugnacious spirit of his British counterpart, and would not dream of disputing the crown with any member of the cat tribe. He is essentially a mild beast, and prefers the society of scholars to that of warrior princes. On his first appearance, he emerged from the Yellow River and presented the legendary Emperor Fu Hsi with a document, from which the Chinese language is said to have been evolved. He heralded the birth of the author of the Analects, but only his stone effigies, guarding Imperial tombs, have been seen since.

Lion

Chinese artists, when familiar with their subject, draw extremely faithful representations of all living creatures, and impart to them life and movement rare in Western art. Every one of them aspires to paint the tiger, the symbol of strength, and the result is usually very convincing. The lion, on the other hand, is not indigenous to the country, so he has become a stereotyped replica of the original artists' conceptions, obtained from specimens sent as presents or tribute to the early emperors. Later representations of the King of Beasts have taken the Pekingese dog as a model. The Lion did not occur in early Chinese art, but owes its origin to the introduction of Buddhism, as the defender of law and protector of sacred buildings. It is always depicted sèjant, squatting on its hind quarters, with a cub or worsted ball under one of its forepaws. Chinese lions suckle their young through their claws and, the milk having mystic properties, the male is provided with a toy to collect it. Hollow balls were placed in the hills by some country people, in the hopes that lions, who cannot resist a game, would leave behind some of the precious liquid.

In the Lion Dance, which may sometimes be seen after a religious festival, two men manipulate the cloth or paper lion, whilst a third operates the ball in front.

Being the emblem of strength it is lucky to touch the paws of sculptured lions, and the guardians of the Hong Kong Bank, both in Hong Kong and in Shanghai, show bright patches from the friction of countless hands.

Dogs

The Chinese attitude to dogs is entirely different to

190

that of Europeans. Possibly the thousands of years of civilisation which separated them from the hunting and pastoral stages of man's development partly accounts for this. The hunter in pursuit of game, and the shepherd tending his flock, are dependent on the sagacity of the four-footed assistant, which creates a bond of companionship. It is in the man's interest to cultivate good relations and attach the animal to his person, so he not only sees that it has an adequate supply of food and water, but takes it for exercise when not actually employed in the chase. The Chinese, on the other hand, regard the dog purely as a burglar alarm, and it is not a member of the family but a wretched cur chained to to a kennel in the yard. Even the rich, who purchase pedigree foreign dogs hardly ever take them for a walk, but entrust their exercise to a coolie. This individual rarely has a passion for walking, so he takes his charge to some shady spot off his master's regular beat, and sits down for the stipulated time to converse with the passers-by.

The exception to this rule was to be found in the palace, where the ruling house was so often an invader, a nomad from the plains of Mongolia or a hunter from the forests of the North. The Manchu, like William the Norman, was obsessed by the chase, and the innumerable ladies of the court were bored by the seclusion of the harem. The Emperor cherished his hounds, whilst his concubines sought distraction in the breeding of lap dogs. Their hobby was catered for by the horde of eunuchs in the Forbidden City, who established various strains, and sought to ingratiate themselves with the Court ladies by presents of particularly fine specimens. After the fall of the Manchus and before the expulsion of the last Emperor from the palace, the small dogs were exclusively the province of the eunuchs. No stud book was kept, and the mating was rather haphazard. This Emperor himself abhorred them, on account of the mess they made, and was only too ready to give them as presents to any foreign lady who obtained an audience, and wished to be the possessor of a real palace dog.

It is significant that the Mings, the only true Chinese dynasty since the Hans, banished the dogs, and lavished their affections on cats, to the great discontent of the eunuchs, who had made handsome profits out of supplying pets to rich officials. One of them, incensed at the loss of his perquisites, uttered a protest, complaining that the cats were so noisy that they caused the Imperial children to sicken and die. He proposed their confinement to special quarters, and hinted that the sovereigns who encouraged the interest in cats and pigeons, with no other society than women and eunuchs, might fail to realise the importance of raising children.

The peak of the breeding of Pekingese was reached in the XIX Century, when the Empress Dowager was in power. In the main, colour and its distribution were considered of more importance than make and shape. To the Chinese, every colour has its value, laid down by the immutable laws of geomancy which permeate their lives. The ancient "Book of the Five Elements" prescribes that "Should a man breed a black dog with white ears, he shall become rich and noble. His family will prosper if he produces a white animal with a yellow head. A yellow dog with a white tail will ensure officials in every generation, whilst a black dog with white forelegs portends the birth of many male children in the family.

A yellow dog with white forelegs merely brings good luck, but a white with a black head adds riches to good fortune. Finally, a white dog with a black tail will cause the family through all generations to ride in chariots." A pure white dog, being the colour of mourning, was not an asset, as the Chinese hate to be reminded of death,

If there was no systematic stud book, a very good record of the palace dogs was kept in the dog books of each occupant of the throne, in which outstanding specimens or particular favourites were depicted by the court painters. From these drawings the current fashion of breeding at any given period can be deduced.

The origin of the Pekingese is a matter of speculation, but the Chinese became interested in lions, which were not indigenous, during the T'ang dynasty when Hsuan Tsang made his famous pilgrimage to India to bring back the Buddhist scriptures. Sakyamuni is recorded to have overcome a herd of intoxicated elephants by stretching out his hand and releasing five lions from his finger tips, whilst Manjusri was accompanied by a small dog which turned into a lion when he was in need of a mount. The spirit and valour of these small dogs, who do not hesitate to attack an animal many times their size, and the paucity of living models of the King of Beasts probably accounts for the same metamorphosis in Chinese art.

When the Roman Empire transferred its headquarters to Byzantium, Maltese dogs became pets for the fashionable ladies, as this island was assigned to the eastern ruler in the partition. A prosperous trade route overland connected China with Constantinople until it was interrupted by the wars of Islam. As monarchs often included dogs among the presents sent to foreign courts, it is quite possible that the vogue for the small palace dog arose in this way. They are described by Chinese writers as being imported from Fu Lin, or Fo Lin, but there is no record of their similarity to lions before the time of Kublai Khan. Fu Lin has been identified with Constantinople, and a pair of its dogs was sent as an Imperial present to one of the Chinese rulers. To this day in the Capital they are never called Pekingese in native parlance, but simply hsiao kou (小狗) or small dogs. The breeders paid more attention to the shape of the head than anything else. This is attributed to the fact that strong and well-developed body points are the rule rather than the exception, and the chief weakness is in the degeneration of the head. The Chinese distinguish between two head forms, the abacus-ball or "suan pan tze'erh", and the apple-shaped head or "ping kou". Both are held in equal esteem. The characteristics of the former are shortness between the face and the back of the head, combined with a broad dome, giving it a rectangular appearance.

In this type, the ideal aimed at is to have the eyes far apart, and the tip of the nose and forehead so much in the same plane that a silver dollar will lie flat on the plane of the nostrils without obscuring the vision of either eye. The face should be as rectangular as possible, and not long or oval shaped.

The "apple-head" is broad from the face to the back of the cranium, has a domed forehead, the front of the skull being protuberant, and the eyes are closer together. The most sought after colours are the tortoise-shell face which simulates laughter; the three-flower face, black round the eyes, yellow on the forehead, and white round the mouth; and the head black with the body of another colour.

In addition to the long-haired Pekingese, whose mantle, due to the shortness of his legs, often sweeps the ground, there is the Chinese pug, whose origin defies investigation. The existence of short-mouthed dogs used for the chase is recorded as far back as the times of Confucius, but there is no evidence, or probability for that matter, that they had any connection with the modern pet. The Chinese name for the breed is "Lotze", and as the characters are the same as those formerly used to denote Russia there is a possibility that their ancestors were imported. Efforts to trace their origin to Lochiang in Szechuan, famous for dogs in the 8th to 11th centuries, came up against a blank wall for the name is forgotten in those parts, where the breed is called Ching Kou (京狗) or dogs from the capital. They differ from the Pekingese by being short-coated and very elastic in the skin. The point which most appeals to the Chinese is the Prince character (王) formed by three wrinkles on the forehead split by a vertical bar, like the stripes on the skull of the tiger. The other traits of conformation are similar to those of the Pekingese.

The third of the small dogs popular in the capital is the Tibetan, always referred to as the "Lion," or shih-tze kou (獅子狗). The country of its origin had no written records before the seventh century A.D. when Srong-tsangampo introduced Buddhism, and founded a monarchy at Lhasa. The religion at this period had been enriched by a strong infusion of Hinduism, with a goodly company of Gods and Demons, whose number was swelled by the inclusion of the supernatural phenomena already domiciled in a barbarous and rugged country. One of the beliefs current then was that if a man laid his hand on a fledgling eagle it would be transformed into a small dog. This gave rise to the name "Lags K'yi" or hand dogs.

St. Mark's lion surmounts a column outside his cathedral in the square in Venice, and the Tibetans bred their lion dogs in honour of Manjusri, finding this

Lion Dog hua yah "Flowery Duck"

method of obtaining them easier than taking them from the eerie. China's relations with the country have often been stormy, and they invaded it and burned the palace as early as 633 A.D. When peace was re-established a Tibetan king, Khri-srong-Ide-tsan, who was an ardent supporter of Buddhism, was favourably disposed to the stronger power as his mother was an Imperial princess. It is quite possible that the small dogs formed part of, or accompanied the tribute sent to Si An, then the Chinese capital. It is not until the Ch'ing dynasty that they came into vogue, for the Manchus, who had practised Shamanism in their forest-clad homes, favoured Lamaism, rather than the more orthodox forms of Buddhism. The Tibetans, anxious to ingratiate themselves, played on the similarity of the word Manchu with their famous dog-loving divinity Manjusri, and the emperor was flattered to have the small beasts following him like the attendant of the Saint. Dogs were sent to all the Ch'ing monarchs down to the time of the Empress Dowager in 1908, when she was visited by the Dalai Lama who presented her with several specimens.

Some of these shih-tze kou are as small as the Pekingese, but generally speaking they are larger. They have occasionally been interbred to reduce the size. They are longer-nosed than the flat-faced Pekingese, and are long-coated with wavy hair, and squarer in the body, not being waisted like the Pekingese. In fact, when full-coated it is hard to tell whether they are coming or going. The forepaws are strongly developed, and well adapted for digging, a pastime in which they freely indulge. To protect them against the stony nature of their country of origin they have been provided with a lavish growth of hair between the toes, which is apt to become matted like felt if they are transferred to regions with civilised communications, and the lumps must be removed with sharp scissors. Their courage is phenomenal and they will attack a large dog with a suddenness and fury which so discomposes the adversary that they are usually victorious. As pets, they have a great deal of dignity and rather resent being treated as lap dogs. They are devoted

Chinese pug or ha pa

to their masters, but slightly distrustful of strangers. They may be of any colour, but must be strong in bone, short-legged and large-eyed.

In Sir John Jordan's day dogs were excluded from the British Legation in Peking for fear of rabies, but an exception was made for the Military Attache whose Tibetan, by an act of special favour, was rated as a cat.

For reasons already advanced, there are few types of sporting dogs in China. With the fall of the Manchus those kept for the chase have disappeared, and it is only on the fringes of the empire that animals as accessories to the hunter have survived. In Mongolia there is a huge and powerful breed which serves the dual purpose of minding the flocks and warding off the depredation of wolves, and in Tibet some of the Grand Lamas kept sporting dogs, though their religion forbade the taking of life.

A Chinese variety of greyhound, known as the hsi yang min-tzu, comes from the Muslim districts of Kansu and Shensi where it is used for the pursuit of hares and foxes. It is smaller than its British relation and nearer in size to the whippet.

In South China the Chow has proved a great asset to the professional bird shooter in putting up game, for his sturdy build and bustling methods enable him to flush the francolin and pheasant from the jungly thickets in which they seek refuge.

There are at least three distinct forms of Chow in the South, as there are both short and long haired animals with the black mouth and tongue, and the ordinary village dog which does not possess this characteristic. All are supposed to be descended from the wolf rather than the jackal, which makes them one-man dogs, suspicious of all but their master. Gilbert White, famous as the author of the Natural History of Selborne and an acute observer, described a pair in 1802. As they were fresh from the country of origin, undeveloped to modern show standards, the characteristics of the animals he saw would be very similar to those of the Chinese Chow today. He wrote "they are about the size of a spaniel; of a pale yellow colour, with coarse bristling hair on their backs. Sharp, upright ears, and peaked heads, which give them a very fox-like appearance. Their hind legs are unusually straight, without any bend at the hock, or ham, to such a degree as to give them an awkward gait when they trot. When they are in motion their tails are curved high over their backs. Their eyes are jet black, small and piercing: the inside of the lips and mouths of the same colour, and their tongue blue. These dogs bark much, in a short thick manner, like foxes, and have a surly, savage demeanour, like their ancestors, which are not domesticated but tied up in sties, where they are fed for the table on rice-meal and other farinaceous food. They did not relish flesh when they came to England."

The origin of the name 'chow' is a matter of pure guesswork. The first traders were more interested in making a fortune than in the intricacies of a foreign language, particularly one so curiously accentuated as Cantonese. For communication a barbarous form of pidgin English was evolved, keeping the Chinese construction, and adding a double "ee" to the end of each substantive. With the spread of literacy and social contacts with foreigners, this has become virtually a dead language. There is a suggestion that the name was derived from the Portuguese pronunciation of the

Chinese "chih" (喫) to eat. Preserved ginger, an important article of trade, went under the name of chow-chow. In the north, the foreigner's name for the watch dog was a "Wonk". It is a contemptuous term, as the animal's lack of courage did not commend itself to the English. It is not like the "Pi" of India, merely an abbreviation of the word pariah, but rather is a corruption of the Chinese "huang kou" (黃狗) or yellow dog. The Contonese pronunciation of the word to eat is "chuk", and they call a dog "gow" to rhyme with "how". One derivation is as probable as the other. Chow, however, is the foreigner's idea of the Chinese word for food, and, as the dog was an article of diet in Canton, he may have acquired the name on account of his culinary properties.

Many Chinese are revolted at the idea of eating dog flesh, but proof of the wideness of the practice is furnished by the Calendar, which lays down the days on which it should not be consumed.

The Book of Rites according to a Chinese commentator classified the canine race as hunting-dogs, watch-dogs and those commonly known as the edible variety, which were bred for the pot. Their food value was assessed by colour, and a black animal was thought to be the most nutritious. Flowery dogs, of mixed colour were deemed the most palatable, yellow and white being in a lower grade. The puppies were fattened on rice, reaching culinary maturity at nine months. The Chinese attribute all sorts of consequences to partaking of a particular diet, and a dish of dog meat was credited with the power of reducing fatigue due to lack of sleep. It was accordingly prescribed for students competing in the provincial and national examinations in Imperial days, on account of the strain and protracted nature of the tests.

The public marketing of dogs' flesh was prohibited by the Republic in 1915, but like the multitude of organic laws, drafted to give some occupation to the underlings of the Minister of Justice, it probably found its way into a pigeon-hole as a monument to their industry.

The northern watch dogs seem to have derived from the shepherd, but have the tail curled over the back. The predominant colour is black, or black and tan. One variety, which is much esteemed, has tan eyebrows which has earned it the name of the "four-eyed" dog. This peculiarity is believed to double their vision, and enable them to see in the dark. Their bark is far worse than their bite, and generally speaking they are spiritless animals who, away from the homestead, can be put to flight by a small Pekingese or Tibetan. Rabies, at any rate till the present Government thinned out the roving scavengers in the cities, was very common, and the Chinese had some peculiar ideas on the danger of the malady.

According to their beliefs, the colour of the animal and the time of the infliction of the wound were of material importance. In Tibet, where the animals feed on carrion, a regular scale was laid down for the danger to be apprehended. The poison of a white rabid dog with a red, flushed nose was mortal at all times. That of a red dog increased in potency at midday, midnight, or sunrise. A multi-coloured brute was most dangerous from 8 a.m. till an hour after noon, whilst spotted dogs were to be avoided at twilight, or 9 p.m. The bite of a yellow cur was certain to produce fatal results if inflicted at dusk, or 9 a.m. The disease would pronounce itself in man seven days after the bite of a white dog, but a month must elapse for the diagnosis of hydrophobia if the animal were black. Sixteen days was the period of incubation for a multi-coloured dog, twenty-six for an ash-grey one and from one month to seven and a half months if the beast were red. A blackish-yellow dog infects man three to seven months after the bite, but it needs a year and fifteen days for a spotted dog to pass on the virus. A bluish-black or tiger-coloured dog has the longest period, namely a year and eight months, but it is difficult to cure if the poison were injected at 7 p.m. or dusk, or in the case of a black dog, at dawn. On the other hand, if a blue dog bites at midday, a red one at midnight, a spotted one at dawn, or a white dog early in the morning, a cure is easily effected.

The dog plays an important part in Chinese mythology for the T'ien Kou (天狗) or Heavenly Hound, outshines his master Erh Lang (二郎), as the sun does the moon. In all the stories of the deeds of the pair, the dog is the hero and its owner is merely approached for the loan of his services. The one exception is purely local, for Erh Lang is credited with saving Peking from an inundation by driving off the dragon who had failed to regulate the water supply. A temple, the oldest in the city, was erected as a thank-offering for this meritorious feat, but it is the dog and not the master who attracts the congregation. Dog owners sacrifice to this King of all dogs when their pets are sick, and his altar is covered with small canine effigies in recognition of cures effected. Otherwise the Hound of Heaven enjoys small popularity, for he roams the skies on evil bent. His attempts to swallow sun and moon are the causes of eclipses, and the peasantry turn out to a man to frustrate his efforts to deprive them of light. As the dog is averse to noise, all the kitchen utensils are brought out and clashed together to produce a din which beggars description and can be heard for miles. Though the court mathematicians have been able to predict eclipses for centuries, the common people, having seen the object of their solicitude re-emerge from the shadow unscathed, see no reason for altering the methods adopted for its protection.

The dog presides over certain years and hours as one of the twelve animals in the horary cycle. It dominates the watch which falls between 7 p.m. and 9 p.m. Women born at this time are in danger of losing their children, which are snatched from their homes by the Heavenly Dog, and can only protect them by procuring a portrait of Chang Hsien (張仙) which is hung in the bedchamber. The Immortal is shown with his bow bent towards the skies in which is a likeness of a winged dog, flying below the clouds.

The power of the dog at the time of eclipses was demonstrated in Imperial days, when the Emperors went to worship the sun outside the east wall of the capital. They took care not to pass in front of the Dog Temple, making a detour to avoid it rather than offend the giver of light by recognising the enemy which obscured it.

Cats

Though the cat is regarded as a minor deity in China it by no means occupies the position it has claimed for itself in the English household. The view of the Kentish labourer that it would not be a home without a cat is not shared by the Chinese peasant whose outlook is strictly utilitarian. He keeps no cat which does not justify its existence as a mouser, and the idea of regarding Puss as a fireside pet has simply never occurred to him. The cat often wears a collar and leash by day to prevent it straying, and it is let loose at night to pursue its amours or the local vermin as the spirit moves it, for even a Chinese has little control over its independence.

The earliest historic cat was domiciled in Egypt, then the granary of the civilised world which centred in the Mediterranean. Its economic importance as a protector of the crops made it an object of worship as the God Pasht, from which, according to some feline devotees, our diminutive Puss is derived. The Chinese cat also wars upon rats and mice and, as the latter destroy silkworm larvae and cocoons, the animal has been appointed their Patron Saint. Pictures of cats are hung up on the walls of rooms devoted to the breeding of caterpillars which, till quite recently, was exclusively a cottage industry.

The Chinese attitude to domestic pets is quite different to that which obtains in the West. Neither dog nor cat is treated as a companion. Rather, the old-fashioned Chinese lavished their attention on pets whose vocal activities gave them pleasure, and concentrated on birds, crickets and grasshoppers. Breeding to certain accepted standards was reserved for goldfish and pigeons, and except in the Palace, where Pekingese and Tibetans (or Lion Dogs) amused the Court ladies, the role of the dog was purely as guardian of the house. The cat never even won a place among the six domestic animals which give their names to the horary cycle denoting the twelve watches of the day and night. The dog was just included after the more important members of the farm-yard, namely the horse, sheep, boar, ox and cock, on whose co-operation agriculture depended.

China possesses a wild and a domestic cat whose voice earned it the onomatopoeic name of Mao. Biology not being a strong subject with the ancients, the hare is also called a wild, or hill, cat (山貓). The composition of the character represents an animal which catches rats in grain, and it has been referred to in the classics as the domestic fox. In the North, where the winters are bitterly cold, catskin caps with ear flaps are popular to such an extent that those who wish to retain their mousers vandyke bits of fur out of their coats to spoil their market value. These cats are larger and longer-haired than the Southern variety, which evidently has inherited a strain from Malaya and Siam. This is noticeable in the kinky or short tail which is found throughout South East Asia. According to the Malays a legendary princess was bathing and, seeking a place to dispose of her rings, slipped them over a cat's tail, and secured them by tying it into a knot. When she retrieved her jewellery the kink persisted, and has remained hereditary ever since.

The Chinese are particular in selecting a cat, and consider those with yellow eyes and numerous ridges in the roof of the mouth the best. When choosing they open the mouth and count the rugae with a pair of chopsticks. Two in a litter of kittens is the ideal number as more are considered to be weakly. A kitten with large ears is rejected, on the somewhat surprising grounds that it will not listen when it is addressed, and generally pays no attention to the expressed wishes of its owner. This complaint against the feline race is not confined to the

Chinese, as the cat's independence is proverbial, though the size of its ears is not usually connected with its neglect to obey orders. As Buddhistic teaching inhibits the taking of life, superfluous kittens are not disposed of at birth, but are abandoned in some bushes when weaned, in hopes that their appeals for food will attract the compassionate. If they try to gate-crash a house they are anything but welcome, as the advent of a cat betokens approaching poverty. A power of divination is one of the cat's attributes, and it is supposed to be able to foresee a rich harvest of rats and mice owing to the dilapidations resulting in a fall of income. Another ill omen is to have a cat stolen from a house, whilst a cat washing its face portends the arrival of a stranger. This latter belief exists also in Russia.

A "butterfly" cat is considered very lucky. This is a tabby with blotched, instead of striped, markings, usually symmetrical, and roughly in the shape of the insect's wings. The combination of cat and butterfly denotes longevity from seventy to ninety years which probably accounts for its popularity. Strictly speaking, a dead cat should not be buried but should be hung on a tree. Fortunately in Hong Kong the Sanitary coolies have no such inhibitions, and corpses quickly disappear from sight.

Cats are credited, probably because of their affinity to the tiger, with the power of scaring off evil spirits. The dog keeps human marauders from breaking in, whilst the cat performs the function of expelling any lurking malignants who have entered unperceived. Its powers of seeing in the dark enhance its efficacy as a night watchman.

According to one Chinese author it is possible to tell the time of day by observing a cat's eye. At midnight, noon, sunrise and sunset, the pupil is like a thread. At 4 and 10 o'clock, morning and evening, it is round like the full moon, but at 2 and 8 o'clock it is elliptical. The end of the nose is always cold except on the day of the summer solstice, when it becomes warm.

Cats are occasionally fattened for food among the poorer classes in Canton, and are sold in the shops specialising in dog meat. Rice forms a considerable part of their diet with the immature fish which have little other marketable value.

Horses

The Manchus won all their victories with their cavalry, and such was their respect for the animal which contributed to their conquests that they perpetuated its memory in the dress of their officials. The sleeves of the administrators' robes ended in a cuff shaped like a horse's hoof which completely concealed the hands, and the queue which they imposed on the conquered races is said by some to be derived from the tail. At the Revolution, the first sign of an emancipated Cantonese was its abolition, in spite of the unsightly effect of the hair standing up straight on the previously shaven forehead. In Peking, however, the tonsorial order was more honoured in the breach than in the observance, and police action was required to enforce it. The Mongols still adhered to the custom, at any rate up to the Japanese invasion, as did old "Jumbo", sacristan of the British

Embassy chapel in Peking, to the day of his death.

The Mongolian pony is the best-known Chinese breed, though a distinct race exists in Szechuan. Foreigners are more familiar with the former as they were exclusively used for racing in the Treaty Ports. The Mongol dealers were very jealous of their monopoly and would never part with a mare unless proved to be barren, so the competition was practically confined to geldings. Until the first Great War handicapping presented no difficulties but, after the Kolchak campaign in Siberia, the Mongol ponies in the Hailar district were interbred with Russian stock which produced a larger and faster animal.

Some marvellous misinformation as to the history and uses of the horse is recorded in the Pen Ts'ao (本草), or Chinese Materia Medica of 1596. The most useful kind to the doctor are the pure white, but those found in the south and east of the country are small and weak. If a horse is fed on rice he will become heavy-footed, and rat's dung will make him herring-gutted. He can be prevented from eating or put off his feed by rubbing the teeth with dead silkworms, or black plums, and the same effect is produced by hanging a rat or wolfskin in his manger. He will contract disease if fed from the pigs' trough, but if he has a monkey as stable companion he can be kept in good health.

The "chestnuts" above the knees, generally considered as the rudimentary thumb, are the horse's night eyes which enable him to travel in the dark, a belief also current in Finland. Medicinally, they are useful for tooth-ache. If a man suffers from insomnia and it is desirable to administer a sleeping draught, the ashes of a horse's skull mingled with water should be given to him, and he should have a skull as a pillow.

The points of a horse are given in the Ma Ching (馬經), written early in the 17th century, which informs its students that the eye should be spherical like a banner bell, with a bean-shaped pupil with white streaks, and the iris of five colours. If the nose bears marks like the characters Kung (公) and Huo (火) he will live to see forty springs. The ears should be shaped like a willow leaf, the neck like a phoenix or crowing cock. His tongue should resemble a two-edged sword, and, if his gums are not black, he should enjoy a long life. He should be well boned but lean in flesh, not shying at sight or sound. The breast and shoulders should be broad, projecting slightly forward. Incidentally this characteristic makes China ponies very heavy in the forehand, and inclined to stumble and, as they are very short in the rein, the rider not infrequently finds himself on his head.

The head should be inclined and the neck arched with three small protrusions on the crown. The bones of the leg small, terminating in light hooves.

The Mongolian pony, living under its natural conditions on a plateau 6,000 feet above sea-level, with a scalding wind and winter temperature well below zero, must be constitutionally extremely hardy. The breeders allege that it loses its speed when stall-fed and transported to the plains. Wolves are a menace, but the ponies adopt a regular formation to minimise their attacks. The mares make a ring, heels out, around the foals, and the stallions cruise about outside to break up the pack by offensive tactics.

In Chinese art the horse is the symbol of speed and

perseverance, and a nimble-witted boy earns the nick-name of a "thousand li colt" (千里駒). Tourists are always attracted by the Eight Horses (Pa Chun 八駿) which are carved in various materials. The set must be complete, or it has no value in Chinese eyes. They commemorate the eight chargers of Mu Wang (穆王), 1001–746 B.C., the fifth ruler of the Chou Dynasty. This emperor was extremely attached to his team, and made all his royal progresses throughout his realm behind them in a chariot driven by his henchman, Tsao Fu (造父). The animals, each of which had his distinctive name, were finally pensioned off for faithful service, and turned out to graze. One of the set is always shown rolling on his back to indicate his liberation from harness. They are produced in porcelain, crystal, jade or ivory, embroidery and painting, and are sometimes cast in bronze.

The God of Horses celebrates his birthday on the 23rd of the Sixth Moon, and is worshipped particularly in the North, where the animal supplies the chief means of transportation. His image is furnished with three eyes and four hands holding various offensive weapons. Originally he had a triple incarnation as the Ancestor of the species to whom the spring sacrifices were offered. In summer he was honoured as the First Breeder, and in winter propitiated as the Celestial Horse-breaker, who also dispensed or withheld the diseases which afflict the equine race.

A relic of these attributes is to be found in the pictures of the divinity, which represent him with three faces, though on the sacred posters he is often shown as an enthroned king with a retinue of three attendants, to whom he presumably delegates his seasonal functions. Sometimes he appears as the Celestial charger, the mount of the Dragon, or star Kang (元), a group of stars in the feet of the constellation Virgo.

The worship of the Horse God was part of the Imperial ritual and was celebrated in the stables by spreading a table of offerings between the hours of eight and ten in the morning. The example was followed in every farm-yard, where a paper image was burned to ensure the prosperity of the equine members of the establishment. In Peking, during the reign of the Mings, a temple called the Ma Shen Miao (馬神廟), or Horse Spirit shrine, stood within the precincts of the royal stables, on the site now occupied by the National University. As the Chinese are intensely conservative in nomenclature the seat of learning is still referred to by its equine association.

The Pool of the White Geese

When a big river flows into the sea, forming an estuary of a certain shape, it is not unusual to encounter rough water when the rising tide meets the downflow of the stream. The bores in Hangchow Bay on the China Coast, and in the Severn at the apex of the Bristol Channel attract many spectators. The stretch of water leading to the port of Canton had an evil reputation for storms. For two hundred years all overseas trade with the Chinese Empire was conducted through the great southern emporium, and the foreign factories were based on the Portuguese settlement in Macao. The establishments in Canton were only manned during the

Casting a net

trading season, after which the personnel were withdrawn to the colony at the mouth of the Pearl River. The stretch of water between it and the factories was known to the merchants and shipmasters as the Macao passage, but the Chinese called it the Pool of the White Geese, and it had a sinister reputation for a rough journey.

This was attributed, not to any natural phenomena but to the mischievous activities of a couple of celestial geese who, dissatisfied with their heavenly provender, descended in search of what the earth might offer. Their owner was no less a person than Wang Hsi-chih (王羲之) a renowned scholar and statesman of the Chin dynasty (321–370 A.D.) He is generally acknowledged as the greatest exponent of the flowing form of Chinese calligraphy known as the "grass character". His outstanding merits earned him early canonisation and, as he continued to practise his penmanship in the after life, his scrolls were highly prized by his fellow-immortals. He complimented a Taoist of San Yin with a copy of a well-known passage from the scriptures (道德經), and received a pair of white geese as the reward for his services. Wang, like many men of brilliant intellect, was too preoccupied by his art to devote much attention to animal management and, though he liked to have the birds round him when pursuing his studies, the only nourishment he dispensed to them was the remains of the ink of his palette. Though it was celestial pigment it could hardly have sufficed their needs.

One day, when their master had been invited to a festive gathering, the birds were left to mind the house, and decided that a change of diet would be welcome. Their daily routine of watching old Wang wielding his brush, until their turn arrived to clean his ink slab, was as monotonous as the Victorian conception of "casting down golden crowns beside a glassy sea", so they welcomed the opportunity to escape. They set course for the Pearl River, at the head of which Canton was rising to eminence as a trading port, and there was already considerable junk traffic in the approaches. After a sedentary life, the idea of action appealed to the birds, and they amused themselves by ravaging the river, upsetting the vessels with the storms they raised, and snatching the lives of the seamen to convert them into wandering spirits. Their capture was beyond the powers of man, and their appearance spread terror into the maritime population. As there was no getting rid of them, propitiation was the only remedy, and each ship approaching or leaving the port was enjoined to offer sacrifices, as an insurance against molestation. The passage then came by the name of the Pool of the White Geese (Pai Yen T'an 白雁潭), and it was dominated by the harpies for many centuries.

In the reign of the famous Ming Emperor Yung Lo (1403–1424 A.D.) the great sorceress Tang, having fallen out with the Royal House whose patronage she had failed to enlist, set out on a pilgrimage of the Empire, looking for a sensitive spot in which to foment an insurrection. As she approached Canton, she was surprised to find her junk-master preparing the usual sacrifices to buy a favourable passage. The witch, who wished to advertise her powers to gain the adherence of any disaffected subjects, persuaded the boatmen to withhold their offerings, guaranteeing them security against assault. The two geese flew in to meet the vessel, expecting their regular tariff and, when they were disappointed, raised such a storm that the junk nearly capsized in the waves. The sorceress, however, was ready with her charms and stilled the waters, to the fury of the birds who flew on to the deck to close with their adversary. There they were subdued and captured. Tang's first idea was to destroy them but, when she learned of their identity, she spared their lives in the hope that they would be useful to her in promoting her anti-dynastic schemes. She took them into her service, and found a tool to head the rebellion in Huang Hsiao-yang, whom she persuaded into believing that he was the predestined ruler of the Empire. He succeeded in capturing Canton, and the geese assisted in the operation by raising storms which prevented relief by the government navy. They were proof against ordinary arrows, and effectually sealed the river, till Yung Lo enlisted the services of a renowned marksman who was world famous as the "Divine Archer."

This Robin Hood felled one of the geese with a shot through the eye, the only vulnerable spot, and was taking aim at the second, when his hand was stayed. The commotion on earth had attracted the attention of Wang Hsi-chih, who had just woken up to the absence of his pets and connected them with the disturbance. He revived the fallen bird and, gathering up a goose under each arm, went off to justify his action to the commanding general.

As the abatement of the nuisance was the only concern of this official, it was a matter of no moment whether they attained immortality through death or translation, and he gratefully accepted the solution. The rebellion was eventually suppressed, Huang and his instigator being removed from the scene, but the memory of the white geese is preserved to this day in the Chinese name of the Macao Passage.

The wild goose is said to be peculiarly the bird of the Yang (陽鳥) or principle of light and masculinity in nature. It always flies in pairs, and hence is used as an emblem of the married state. In the ritual of the Chou dynasty it was enumerated among the betrothal presents, the bird being dyed red for the occasion. There is a Chinese belief that the bird never mates a second time, and a libation is poured out to the geese on the occasion of the bridegroom fetching his bride from her father's house.

A wild goose is depicted on the Chinese postal flag, and on the dollar values of the last issues of the Manchu Empire stamps in honour of Su Wu (蘇武) of the 2nd Century B.C. who, captured by the Hsiung Nu, or Turkic tribes, contrived to inform his master of his whereabouts by affixing a letter to the leg of a goose. The bird was subsequently brought down by an arrow in the Imperial Hunting Park, and an expeditionary force was despatched to rescue the sender.

The Rats' Wedding

The celebration of the Rats' Wedding Day is annually observed on the 19th of the First Moon. Everyone goes to bed early, so as not to disturb the revels of their four-footed tenants. As a wedding without a banquet would be a Barmecide's Feast, at which the rats would be certain to take umbrage, a collation is spread, and placed within the reach of these exalted visitors. The offering is made to induce the more benevolent rodents to exercise restraint over the more unruly of their tribe, to moderate their appetites during the year or, at any rate, divert their depredations from the household of their benefactor.

The reverence for rats, though probably arising from a desire to counteract the damage done to crops, seems to have its origin in a Northern legend. About five hundred years ago a large and handsome member of the species took up its abode in a cavern in the hills north of Peking to escape the great heat of the summer after the fashion of many other residents of the capital. The change was so beneficial that it was finally metamorphosed into a beautiful woman. One day some charcoal burners erected their shelter close to her lair, and one man was left behind to prepare the food, whilst the rest gathered the wood as raw material for their craft. As he was busy sorting out the ingredients for meat dumplings, he heard a knock at the door and on opening it found a woman outside. He was much gratified when she offered to cook supper but, on watching her knead the dough, he was horrified to see a claw mark in the stiffening paste. Looking closely at her hand he noticed for the first time that it was similar to the foot of a rat. Assured that she was an evil spirit, he seized his axe for self-defence, and struck off one of the offending hands, whereupon she vanished in a sheet of flame. On the return of his companions a search party was organised, which traced the drops of blood to the cavern on the hillside but, on entering, it was found untenanted. On this slender evidence they were certain that the rat was not only capable of assuming human form, but that after such cavalier treatment it had achieved immortality. Its flitting is still commemorated by women in the North who, on this day, provide a treat to induce it to use its influence to safeguard their larders from marauders of its tribe.

If a very large rat, with a paunch of aldermanic proportions, takes up its residence in a house, it is treated as an honoured guest, for this is the Money Rat (錢耗子) whose arrival indicates the advent of affluence, more than compensating for his board and lodging. The rat is not the only money-spinner in the

Peking home, and other creatures are cherished for their affinity to wealth. A red spider must on no account be destroyed and one form of centipede is highly esteemed as a lodger. It is not the variety found in the South, which figures among the five poisonous creatures, but is higher on the leg, and is a useful member of the household in keeping down the flies. Its construction adapts it admirably for dealing with these pests for, as it catches its prey, it passes it down its legs like a conveyor belt to the larder near the tail, accumulating a stock without interfering with the chase. The legs are put into reverse when the money-centipede feels inclined for a meal. A snake which enters a house is never killed for the serpent is a guardian of treasure. Finally, a kitten of a peculiar golden shade is welcomed in a litter as it is a "Money cat" who will improve the financial status of the family.

The Three-Legged Toad

Stretching from the frozen North to well into the tropics, China has many species of toads and frogs, but the batrachia have evoked so little interest that one name, Ha Ma (蛤蟆), practically covers the lot. The frog-hunting expeditions, indulged in by the literati in Peking in celebration of the Dragon Boat Festival, for which facilities for racing were lacking, had as quarry the Chinese toad, *Bufo asiaticus*. This creature, if held firmly in one hand, whilst a wart-like swelling behind the eye was touched with a hot iron, yielded a white juice whose medicinal properties were akin to digitalis. The liquid was collected on a glass plate and, after evaporation, was used in powder form as a heart stimulant. The toad is known in folk-lore as one of the Five Poisonous Creatures, and it is sometimes differentiated from the frog by the prefix lai (癞), meaning virulent.

Though indifferent to natural science, the Chinese are second to none in gastronomy, and the edible frog (*rana esculans*) is distinguished by the special name of T'ien Chi (天雞), Heavenly Chicken. The origin of the appellation is that the spawn was supposed to fall with the dew from heaven, but the great majority of people who lack the benefits of a classical education, and are uninterested anyway in etymology, substitute the T'ien (田) of field for the similar-sounding character denoting the sky.

Though natural history among the Chinese is usually devoid of scientific basis, their mythology is probably the richest in the world, and the language has adapted itself to its requirements. The Chinese do not see a Man in the Moon, so familiar to Western children, but a toad, the reincarnation of Heng O (恒娥), who stole, and swallowed, her husband's elixir of life and fled from his wrath to the satellite.

A whole series of legends have been woven about this Chan (蟾), as it is called, many of which are hard to reconcile. Some believe that it periodically tries to swallow, not only the pill of immortality, but the planet on which it resides, causing an eclipse.

Another story credits the Chan as being the property of a 10th-century Minister of State named Liu Hai (劉海), who was a proficient student of Taoist magic.

He employed it as a charger to carry him instantaneously from place to place. The creature was not entirely reconciled to this mode of life, and occasionally escaped by diving down the nearest well. Its passion for the gleam of gold, however, invariably led to its recapture, when its master dangled a string of cash before its eyes. He is popularly represented with one foot on the toad's head, holding in his hand a ribbon, or fillet, on which are strung five golden coins. The design is known as "Liu Hai sporting with the toad" (劉海戲蟾), and is regarded as highly auspicious and conducive to good fortune. Another version of the story, inconsistent with the last or the moon theory, is that the reptile lived in a deep pool which exuded a vapour poisonous to the neighbourhood, and that it was thus hooked and destroyed by Liu Hai, exemplifying the fatal attraction of money to lure men to their ruin.

The providence of the old Taoist in always having money in his pocket against the contingency of losing his pet has caused his adoption as one of the many Gods of Wealth, though he is usually depicted, not as the staid Minister, but as a boy, the symbol of prosperous posterity.

In this character he is sometimes shown playing with the Ho Ho (和和) twins, the trio acting as acolytes to the more conventional Gods of Wealth for, in the pursuit of affluence, worshippers dare not neglect any divinity possessing the power to distribute riches. There is no very satisfactory origin of the Harmonious Pair, who can be recognised in effigy by their symbols of a lotus and a box. If found among the wedding presents they signify the wish for connubial bliss, and the give and take between partners which makes for happiness. The Ho means harmony, or unison, and the character for water lily also signifies to sustain. The legend associated with the pair makes them brothers, born of different fathers, who entered into a business partnership and made a fortune. Then discord arose which made them bitter enemies. Seven generations passed before the feud was resolved through the intervention of some supernatural agency. The partnership was re-created on the understanding that co-operation was more profitable than rivalry, and the Ho Ho immortals were adopted as the patrons of merchants who recognise the value of union and peaceful harmony in business.

Though the implication of their attributes may suffice for merchants with a modicum of education, most of the coloured representations of the Heavenly Pair are furnished with suggestive titles for the unlettered, who like to get their money's worth, and to know what to expect from the divinities they patronise. The Ho Ho formula is consequently always expressed in terms of money. "Harmony and Union bearing wealth", "Harmony and Union offering valuables, piling them up, and helping to grow rich" are some of the superscriptions. The box is often shown uncovered, revealing gold and silver ingots, coins and jade, and, as wealth is supposed to bring contentment, occasionally a peach and a bat are thrown in to foretell a care-free old age.

Chinese Fish Stories

Fish stories are suspect the whole world over, and China is not behind-hand in testing one's credulity.

The bibulous angler of *Punch* addressing a scarecrow with extended arm: "You're a qualified liar. There never was a fish that size!" bluntly expressed what the laws of politeness forbid to be uttered in the Celestial Republic. There is a fish on the market in Hong Kong, which is sold as Sang (Sheng) Yü. Yü, of course, is fish, and the Sang means raw. It is a denizen of fresh water, and belongs to the Snakehead Group, its scientific name being *Ophiocephalus maculatus*.

Usually when offered for sale it is about as thick as a man's wrist, but its purchase is a very tricky affair. No one would dream of buying a dead specimen, and the greatest caution must be exercised before becoming the possessor of a live one. The fact is that a perfectly edible-looking fish may be a Dragon-unicorn in disguise, in which case it is a most deadly poison. The fishmonger, accordingly, when the price is agreed on, dashes the fish violently on the stone floor, and beats it with a stick. If this ungentle treatment causes it to extrude a pair of forelegs, it is a Dragon-unicorn all right, and the customer is at liberty to rescind the bargain. He is still not quite safe, however, as a very tough, obstinate Dragon-unicorn may resist the walloping, and refuse to betray itself in the normal manner. The purchaser must, therefore, still take precautions to safeguard himself and his family by introducing into the stew, of which the fish forms part, a catty of lean pork. It must on no account be fat and, when the dish is ready, the cook must take the omens by the state of the meat. If it remains a solid lump, and retains its shape, the fish is a Sang Yü but, if the pork disintegrates, the thing was a Dragon-unicorn after all. The only course then to pursue is to throw away the dish, no matter how expensive were the ingredients. This is a Cantonese story, which every Southerner in Hong Kong knows, but it is not current in the North, where the fish, being tropical, would not survive the winter. The family has a wide range from India to China and, on account of the tenacity with which it clings to life out of its natural element, is held in superstitious awe by its captors. Of *Ophiocephalus melasoma* a naturalist said in 1822 that "in the lower parts of Bengal the persons dedicated to religion, from some ancient prejudice, considered it unlucky to say if it were good, or bad", and it was discovered in 1878 that some of the Karens of Burma regard these fish with horror and refrain from eating them. They have a legend that they were formerly men, changed into fish for their sins, and "if people eat them, they will be transformed into lions".

In art, fish is employed as an emblem of wealth on account of the similarity of its name with the pronunciation of the Yü (裕), of abundance, or superfluity. The waters of China have never been lacking in members of the finny tribe, and it is a staple of the native's daily food, though not to the same extent as in Japan. Its reproductive powers are immense, so it is also a symbol of regeneration and, as it is perfectly content in its element, it has come to be a sign of connubial bliss. It is one of the charms to avert evil, and is among the auspicious signs in the Footprint of Buddha. In this connection it signifies freedom from all restraints as it moves where it will, and Buddhahood fully emancipated knows no restrictions.

The Carp, whose overlapping scales resemble medieval armour, is regarded as the symbol of martial prowess, and is admired for its persistence in battling with the currents. The Yellow River sturgeon, who sometimes gets confused with the carp, is said to ascend the stream in the Third Moon of each year, and those who make their way through the rapids of Lung Men (龍門) (the Dragon Gate) actually become dragons. The arduous toil put in to achieve this happy result has made the carp, not the sturgeon, the symbol of literary eminence after surmounting the grinding mill of the Examination Board. Various legends exist of letters being found in the stomachs of carp, when the cook was cleaning the fish for the table, so it is also the emblem of correspondence. From 1898 to 1913 it figured on the stamps of the Empire and Republic for the values 16 cents to 50 cents.

The Chinese have a story similar to that of Arion who was rescued from drowning by a dolphin, in the shape of Kuei Hsing, the deformed God of Literature. Having been refused the Golden Rose which he had gained at the examinations, owing to the emperor's revulsion at his hideous appearance, he threw himself into the sea in an effort to end his blighted career. A sea monster of unspecified aspect rose from under him and bore him up to be transported to the star over which he now presides.

The Chinese regard the elephant as one of the four animal-representatives of strength, the others being the lion, leopard, and tiger. Its form was familiar to sculptors and artists as, though it gradually receded under the impact of civilisation to the southern regions· of Yunnan, tributary states sent presents of elephants to the Court at Peking, and the Students' Quarters in the British Embassy actually occupied the site of the Empress Dowager's stables. The animal is sacred to Buddhism, but, in this connection, Chinese art depicts a variety with a human eye and a loose skin. This is known as the Royal Elephant.

In Hindu legends, the elephant is connected with the birth of Buddha, and the Siamese believe that their sacred white variety is a reincarnation of some future divinity. In the avenue approaching the Ming tombs are numerous huge stone carvings of beasts and warriors, among whom are four elephants. A belief persists that if a woman can lodge a stone on the back of one of these she is assured of male progeny.

A purely mythical conception is the T'ao T'ieh (饕餮) or Beast of Greed. It is depicted on the inner side of the spirit screen, which protects doorways from evil influences. The noxious emanations can only travel in straight lines, hence they can be deflected by a screen overlapping the gate, or turned back by a mirror, particularly if reinforced with the Eight Trigrams. The T'ao T'ieh image was probably erected as a curb to the rapacity of magistrates, who could not avoid facing it every time they left the office. It is usually represented with enormous eyes and a mouth garnished with tusks. Its appearance on earth coincided with the reign of the Emperor Yao, but his successor Shun issued a decree of banishment. An ogre called T'ao T'ieh, with a huge belly and emaciated face, is found on ancient bronzes as a deterrent to gluttony. For some mysterious reason, the hilts of officers' swords in the Chinese Navy carry this motif, though their opportunities for prize money have been few and far between.

The fox, on account of his slyness, is an object of

veneration and small shrines, similar to those of the Earth Gods, are erected to him in various parts of the country. He is credited with the power of metamorphosis into the likeness of a beautiful maiden, so it is always good policy to be polite to him lest he assume the form of a sister-in-law, or even wife. In a Shantung shrine, tiny women's shoes are left as offerings to assist the transformation, in the pious hope of immunity from his attentions by the donors. It is always considered good policy to propitiate the King of the Rats, or Locusts, so that he may divert the attention of his minions to the crops of less charitable neighbours. The fact that foxes often make their earths in old tombs, and are seen emerging from them, accounts for the belief that they are transmigrated souls looking for a new lodging. At the age of fifty he can take the form of a beautiful woman, or, if a misogynist, he can turn into a wizard, with all the power of magic at his command. When he reaches the millennium, he is admitted to heaven, as the Celestial Fox. His colour changes to gold, and he has nine tails, serving the sun and moon, and versed in all the secrets of nature. This entitles him to worship, and he is invoked for the cure of disease, and also acts as a subsidiary God of Wealth.

Clay images of the fox in wayside shrines represent him as a well-dressed official with a sly cast of countenance, accompanied by a comely wife. In some parts of China it was customary for the officials to keep their seals of office in a fox chamber (狐仙樓), but the character for fox was never written, as it was extremely offensive to the animal. A similar-sounding Hu (胡) was substituted meaning "How", and even this was split into its component parts (古) and (月) to avoid the least affront. The fox was also regarded as a sort of custodian of documents and, should difficulty arise in locating a particular file, a stick of incense was burned, with an appropriate prayer to the divinity. Doors and windows were then shut, and the room was left untenanted for a while. On the worshipper's return he hoped to find the missing document jutting out beyond the others.

The deer is credited with long life, and is one of the symbols of longevity, as it is depicted as the mount of the Star God Canopus, in the constellation of Argo. This benevolent ancient is invariably shown with a peach, and has an immensely high forehead, with white hair and eye-brows. The peach is the P'an T'ao which blossoms every three thousand years, and only yields its fruit three thousand years later. In many Chinese households, he is the central figure of a carved wooden set consisting of the Eight Immortals and two children riding on water buffaloes. He is produced on birthdays, with his peach of life, having been summoned to the celebration by the despatch of the children "over the hills".

The deer is said to be the only animal able to find the sacred fungus of Immortality, or Plant of Long Life, whose seeds are reputed by the Taoists to form the food of the Immortals. It is sometimes limned in the mouth of the animal, and also forms the design for the shape of the Ju-Yi sceptre.

The Queen's Beasts

It was very appropriate that the Lion and the Dragon, symbolic of the two races responsible for converting a small fishing base into one of the greatest emporia of the world, should figure in the demonstration of loyalty on the Coronation of Her Majesty, in the Colony of Hong Kong.

Both performed their traditional dances before His Excellency the Governor, who received their homage as Her Majesty's representative. Both are mythical beasts, unknown to zoologists, and are more akin to the wyverns and basilisks of heraldry than to Western conceptions of the creatures which bear their nomenclature. The lion was never indigenous to China and, though specimens must have reached the capital as tribute, or embarrassing gifts from Eastern potentates, the animal portrayed in modern art bears little resemblance to the original. It is nearly always depicted sèjant, with a trifid tail, instead of the long, tufted appendage, and both sexes wear the curly mane. The forehead is domed, and the eyes are large and bulging. In fact the Tibetan dog (known as the Lion Dog) (獅子狗) has supplied the model, and the popularity of the motif is coincident with the introduction of Buddhism. The Lion is the protector of their temples, and, according to one legend, the Master on his journeys was accompanied by a pack of these small dogs who turned into lions to clear the path when his progress was obstructed by wild elephants. In China their carved images are placed outside temples and important buildings to guard the entrance.

Chinese lions

The Lion dancers are probably the descendants of wandering troops of mountebanks and Indian animal trainers, who roved through the countryside picking up a living much as the gipsy bear-leaders wandered through central Europe giving entertainment to the rustics. Their season was the autumn, when the harvest was garnered and the work in the fields was at a minimum. Lions are supposed to suckle their young through their claws, and to be fond of playing with a ball, so a sphere is one of the properties of the act. The lion is made of cloth with two or three men under the skin, one carrying the cardboard head, and another manipulating the hind quarters. The dances, named Shua Shih-tze (耍獅子), or "exercising the lion", were originally designed for exorcising demons, as the animal is the Protector of religion. In Hong Kong some of the less reputable street societies adopted the dance as part of the ritual and, as "long bearded" lions, if they met the "short bearded" variety, had to fight, the performance was made subject to a certain degree of control. When dances are given in Hong Kong, there is usually a wealthy sponsor who has coins on the "money tree", and the lion strives to get his share, his successful efforts being known as "picking the green".

Chinese heroes of antiquity did not kill the dragon, they cherished him. In fact laws were passed for his convenience, as it was forbidden to build an ordinary house of more than one storey for fear of impeding his flight. The Chinese dragon was the essence of the male principle, producer of rain, and hence the fecundating element in nature. He was the symbol of the emperor, and his image decorated the royal standard, the postage stamps, and the coin of the realm. Nothing like him had ever been seen, so he had to be imagined, and the result was a composite picture like the Great Beast of the Apocalypse. He has the head of a camel, horns of a deer, rabbit eyes, and ears like a cow. His neck is serpentine, whilst he has the belly of a frog, scales of a carp, hawk-like talons, and the palm as the pad of a tiger. On each side of his mouth are whiskers, and a beard hangs under his chin partly masking a brilliant pearl.

The Lion dance has no special significance, and may be performed on any occasion, but such an event as the Coronation renders the appearance of a dragon indispensable as, being one of the four fabulous creatures of good omen (the others are the phoenix, unicorn and tortoise), it has been representative of the auspicious prediction of the supernatural divinity of a long line of Imperial rulers. A gold dragon is therefore a *sine qua non* of the procession sponsored by the Chinese community. Its head is constructed of gauze of the Five Colours, ornamented with velvet spheres of the same. The jaws are of seven variegated lengths of silk, and the body is constructed of pink and green Chinese pongee. On this are sewn scales of gilt aluminium. The spine, with eighty-one vertebrae, is of stiff velvet with gilded plates. Its total length is over one hundred and fifty feet, and its accessories comprise a phoenix, the Imperial consort's emblem, two carp, a tablet, and effigies of the sun and moon.

Before its appearance in the Coronation ceremony the dragon had to repair to a temple to have the spirit breathed into it. Till then it could not bend, or perform any of the evolutions necessary for the dance. Thence it had to proceed to the waterfront to gaze upon its natural element, after its eyes had been opened by a high official of the Government, who anointed them with blood obtained from pricking the comb of a cock. The sponsors were the members of the Fruit and Vegetable Merchants' Guild, and their employees formed the motive power. On Victoria Island the dragon paraded in front of the Hongkong and Shanghai Bank, and in Kowloon before the Shamrock Hotel.

The dragon dance, performed as the principal feature of the Chinese Coronation procession, has been a tradition in Sun Wei district of Kwangtung for over three hundred years. Descendants of immigrants to Hong Kong, versed in the complicated technique, operated the monster after six weeks' training under an expert in the ritual. The full performance comprises no less than fifteen figures, and takes four hours to com-

plete. Time, in the old days, was not a matter of consideration to the Chinese, but modern life with its continual accent on acceleration has necessitated drastic cuts in the programme. The actual dance before His Excellency occupied only ten minutes, and the figures were chosen from the following:

First: Moon over a golden plate. Second: The reverse of the Chinese character "chih" (之). Third: The double carp. Two red carp on poles are carried by performers, and the dragon sports with them in the water. It is an allusion to the belief that if a carp can force his way through the rapids at the Tung Kuan on the Yellow River he becomes a dragon. The fish was consequently adopted by scholars, competing at the official examination, as an example of success achieved through hard struggles. Fourth: Double golden coins. Fifth: Two flying butterflies. Sixth: One carp swimming through the golden gates. Seventh: Two carp passing the gate. Eighth: Coiled Dragons. Ninth: Dragon twisting round a pagoda. Tenth: The Dragon dances in a whirl. Eleventh: A straight Dragon. Twelfth: A lively Dragon playing with the precious pearl. Thirteenth: The Dragon stands on a bridge playing with the water. Fourteenth: The Dragon becomes air-borne, and, Fifteenth, returns to his lair.

All these movements are performed at the double, and the work is very exhausting, particularly in hot weather, smothered with the dragon's skin. The operating team numbers twenty-three. One bears the head, which weighs forty pounds, another the tail, and twenty men support the sections of the body. The tempo is taken from the 23rd, the carrier of the Precious Pearl, in pursuit of which the monster performs his evolutions. The head is over seven feet from the tips of the yellow stag horns to the white beard which fringes the chin. At night the eyes are illuminated with electric lamps. Each man carries his section on what looks like a maul for driving in pickets, but for the solid head four hoops of bamboo are substituted for lightness. By raising or lowering the bearers, an undulating motion can be imparted to the dragon, but all has to be done in time, and intense drilling is necessary to give a convincing effect. The actual steps are learned with a skeleton apparatus consisting of twenty-two bearers lashed together with lengths of cord to keep the proper interval. The head, being the most important part, is weighted so that the leader from the first is manipulating the same burden as at the actual performance. Later, his followers don a mock-up skin, but it may not be furnished with a head, as it would offend the real dragon. No trouble was spared to make the Coronation dragon as magnificent as possible. The head, particularly, was a work of art, with glaring eyes and open jaws, revealing a long red, pointed tongue. The hide, in variegated silk, was sewn with small silver bells which jingled as the beast moved, and the sunlight caught the hundreds of golden scales attached to fabric. These were oblong in shape, and about three inches long. A dragon was embossed on each, with an inscription in Chinese characters "In commemoration of the Coronation of the English Empress". Later they were sold as good-luck charms.

Two phoenixes, emblematic of the Dragon's consorts, accompanied him in the procession, which was led by the bearer of the magic pearl. This is mounted on gymbals at the end of a five-foot stave and, to a large extent, determines the monster's movements. As the actual dance is so exhausting, about five relays of bearers have to be trained, making a hundred in all. In their village the whole population takes part in the Dragon festivities as in the case of the Passion Play at Oberammergau. Even the children join the parade, carrying lanterns, until they are old enough to be enrolled in one of the principal parts. The body is naturally the easiest to work, as it only exacts perfect timing of movement. The senior operators gradually work up to the head, and finally graduate to carrying the pearl, which is the role of the star performer. He moves ahead of the dragon which follows his movements and takes the time accordingly. The band, which follows behind, consists of a conch-shell horn, three gongs and a treble drum.

The autumnal recreations of the rural population of China were catered for by travelling bands of mountebanks among whom the Lion dancers and stilt walkers were the most popular. Earlier the latter were got up as historical, or legendary, characters, and masqueraded with painted faces and false beards singing humorous ditties for the entertainment of the villagers who proffered hospitality. Men dressed as women, and women as men, to produce a lively parody of life in general. The fisherman, begging priest, shrewish beldame, and woodcutter were mimicked in a manner in keeping with the intelligence of the audience. In Kansu, small girls standing on a wooden platform surmounting a long pole were carried by men performing a sort of cake-walk. This was the origin of the "Yang Ko" (秧歌), the "Yang" (秧) meaning to raise, and was a survival of an old "No" procession mounted to ward off pestilence. Even Confucius gave it his blessing, and attended the performances to identify himself with the life of the countryside.

CHARMS & TALISMANS

The Chinese have probably retained more of their primitive beliefs than any other civilised race. Relics of the days when early man peopled stones, trees and brooks with kindly or malevolent spirits exist in all nations. The new moon receives a bow, and money is turned in the pocket in many parts of the British Isles. Primitive man probably connected the moon with silver, and her consort with gold, so it was silver which had to be turned over. Wishing-wells and Blarney stones still hold the imagination of the populace, and horseshoes, though becoming a comparative rarity, are never allowed to lie by the lucky finder. In China, "Deliver us from evil" is the watchword of nearly every section of the population, and a roaring trade in talismans is done, particularly by the Taoist clergy. In fact popular Taoism derives a large part of its revenues from this source. As an abstract religion it had little general appeal, as the average man had not leisure to devote to his own perfection and ultimate immortality. Chang Tao-ling, the original "Master of Heaven", and first Taoist Pope, brought the religion to the common people by the invention of charms, originally incised on bamboo slips, but now always printed on paper, or written on a scrap of silk. These ward off all evil influences, and keep at bay malevolent spirits, visible and invisible.

Children, being the most precious heritage of the Chinese, need special protection and, at birth, charms are obtained from the Temple, and are held in readiness against the delivery. They are immediately fastened round the neck or body of the infant, and sometimes a sprig of cypress is added to ensure its longevity. A piece of raw ginger is hung up at the street door to ward off evil spirits and strangers. The latter are always suspect as, should their birthday coincide with that of the newborn, their presence may cause its death.

A piece of fern is hung up to discourage evil spirits, but this is done on other occasions as well, whereas the ginger is confined to childbirth. A favourite way of cheating the spirits is to dress the treasured boy in female clothes, and to place bangles round his wrists and ankles so that he may be mistaken for a girl. A daughter leaves the clan on marriage, and takes money out for a dowry. Her duties are to the ancestors of the family into which she marries, so her relative importance compared with her brothers is small. A dog-collar round the neck also deceives the demons into passing over a boy, who may be mistaken for something as worthless as a hound.

There is a whole string of luck charms in silver to hang round a child's neck, but these are getting hard to find. He should have a silver lock to fasten him to life, and a chicken's leg in order that he may be able to scratch a good living. That he may have no fear of dogs, a scrap of the fur of one of these animals is sometimes thrown in. Red threads are tied round the wrists of little boys, to ensure long life and fortify the memory. One of the most potent charms is a bracelet or anklet of silver, beaten round a coffin nail. In certain places in South China, paper dolls are made or bought to represent each member of the family. These are kept together in a basket to symbolise the fact that the family should remain united. The mother occasionally removes them one by one, with the request that each may take upon it the evil due to fall upon its corresponding personality. Finally the dolls are burned in the presence of the relatives, and a drink, whose main components are sulphur and cinnabar dissolved in wine, is served as a further protection against the evil influences. It is somewhat reminiscent of the brimstone and treacle of Victorian days, and probably just as efficacious. The leavings are smeared over the lips and ears of the children to counteract pimples and eruptions, or are sprinkled about the house to dispel cockroaches and the Five Poisonous Animals.

The Five Poisonous Animals are the viper, scorpion, centipede, toad and spider. Sometimes images of them are procured, and are worshipped by families to whom only one son has been vouchsafed. Pictures of them are often made in black silk, on red cloth pockets, worn by children for the first time on one of the first five days of the Fifth Month. This is a sovereign remedy against colic, which prevails at the time of year. Their effigies are often found on certain brass castings, used as charms against evil spirits. A popular medal is the image of Chang T'ien Shih (the Master of Heaven) riding a tiger, and brandishing his demon-vanquishing sword. It was with this that he conquered the pests, and embodied their poison in his famous Elixir of Life. Each creature gave up its essence to form the true Dragon-Tiger Elixir.

The sword is a powerful antidote to demons, so in some villages miniature weapons of willow are made as a defence against the supernatural. Bunches of mugwort (artemesia vulgaris), flag, sprigs of garlic, and other aromatic plants are hung over doorways. The flag, or wild iris, has leaves shaped like a sword. The virtues of mugwort as a dispeller of troublesome ghosts dates to the earliest times, and magistrates acting as coroners always stepped over a burning pile to prevent the spirit of the deceased following them home.

A number of old brass or copper cash are sometimes strung together, with an iron core down the centre to stiffen the whole into the semblance of a sword. They are hung at the heads of beds, so that the Emperors, whose reigns are commemorated by the coins, may keep away evil spirits by their august presence. They are infallible in houses where persons have committed suicide, or have met an unnatural death, and are also of use to the sick in aiding their recovery.

The "Hundred family lock" to clasp a child to life is made by the father going round among his friends and obtaining a small donation from each. Adding his own luck penny, he buys the lock and hangs it round the child's neck, thus co-opting a hundred guarantors for his son's attainment of longevity.

Mirrors have a discouraging effect on demons, so the bride is always furnished with one in her wedding-chair. They may be seen in Hong Kong on the walls or windows of houses which face in a dangerous direction, in relation to the Feng Shui of the locality. They can be reinforced by adding the eight trigrams. The Ku T'ung-ching, or Ancient Brass Mirror, is credited with the virtue of immediately healing any who have lost their reason at the sight of a ghost. It is kept in the chief apartments of the rich to guard against such an eventuality, on the principle that prevention is better than cure.

The "Tiger's Claw" (Hu chao) wards off sudden fright, besides endowing the wearer with the courage of the animal.

The Peach, besides being the emblem of longevity, has a good influence on demons. Amulets of its wood, or stones, are hung round children's necks to prevent them being stolen and used as foundations for new buildings to give them solidity. Only a devil would think of using such unsubstantial material, as a kidnapper would certainly turn his catch to more profitable account. Padlocks are made from flat peach stones and are fastened by the mother to her children's feet. The Hundred Family Lock has its counterpart in the Hundred Family Tassel, which is hung on the dress of an infant. In this case the parent begs a bit of thread from each of his acquaintances, and the talisman is made from the various contributions.

Spells are formed either by the union of several characters, or by the use of Sanskrit or Tibetan words. They may be for personal wear in the form of amulets, or be used as posters, on doors or walls. Those used for the cure of the sick may be burned to ashes and swallowed, or may be written on leaves, and infused in a potion. The Triangular spell is written on paper, and folded in triangular form. It is then fastened to the child's dress to keep off evil spirits and sickness.

All classes of society attribute protective properties to jade, and the mineral is carried on the person by practically every Chinese. It is believed to ward off misfortune in life, and to safeguard the body after death. Jade bangles or anklets are sent to babies when a month old as auspicious presents for their preservation. These are changed as the child grows out of them. Every girl in Hong Kong wears a jade bracelet, and married women sometimes two, the second being on behalf of her husband. If a bangle is broken by a blow it is considered that the jade has absorbed a shock which would otherwise have resulted in a broken wrist.

In a family where infant mortality has been high, and elder sons have died, it is customary to protect a younger survivor by inserting a jade ring in one of his ears. Should he fall desperately ill, and be in danger of death, the jade is attributed with the power of calling the spirit back to re-enter the body by the orifice.

The mineral is also credited with the power of preventing the dissolution of the body, and is placed in a coffin before burial.

According to a very ancient Chinese belief every woman is represented by a tree in the spirit world. If the ghostly counterpart of herself blossoms, children will be born to her. On the law of opposites, red blooms signify girls, with white for boys, whilst bare branches portend an empty cradle. Should such a disaster befall her, a child may be adopted with the certainty that it will inherit the family characteristics. As in agriculture one tree is grafted onto another, an apple on a crab, to improve the fruit, so the child is regarded as a graft to renew the barren stock.

The willow is regarded as the emblem of light and enemy of darkness, a belief which casts it for a talisman against the spirits of evil, who lurk in the shades. The third emperor of the T'ang Dynasty, Kao Tsung (高宗), ordered his court to wear willow wreaths on their heads to guard them against the venom of scorpions, and other well-known characters carried amulets of the wood to ward off sickness. The Ch'ing Ming Festival, which falls about our Easter time, sees the tree fully in leaf. In Kiangsu, women going out to sweep the graves, stick sprigs in their hair to avert evil spirits, and in other provinces sprouts called "willow dogs" are worn all day. To omit this precaution entails rebirth as a yellow dog in the next re-incarnation, no pleasurable prospect in China.

The Five Elements

The Chinese have a great affection for the number five, which crops up in all sorts of unexpected places, usually stemming from the same source. The Five elements (五行) are the constituent essences of manifested nature, namely Metal, Earth, Fire, Water and Wood. They are specified in China's oldest philosophical document, the Great Plan, and have ever since been considered to be the fundamental forms of matter. The T'ai Chi (太極), or Great Ultimate, is divided into the Yang and the Yin, from which spring the Five elements but, according to Chu Hsi, they are not identical with the objects whose names they bear, but are subtle essences whose nature is best defined by them. They are identified with the five planets, Mercury corresponding to Water, Venus to Metal, Mars to Fire, Jupiter to Wood and Saturn to Earth.

A complete scheme of affinities has been worked out, ranging from their influence on parts of the human frame to their connection with musical notes, with rank and quality.

In human beings the parent elements run, Metal, Earth, Wood, Water, Fire, whilst the corresponding child elements are Wood, Water, Earth, Fire and Metal. As time is denoted by a combination of the Celestial stems, derived from the elements, with the twelve terrestrial branches of the animals of the horary cycle, the hour of birth of a child is of supreme importance in determining its future career. Thus, on the exchange of the "Eight characters" prior to the ratification of a contract of marriage, the elements of the pair must harmonise or the engagement will be broken off. Water produces Wood, but extinguishes Fire. Fire produces Earth, but melts Metal, whilst the Wood kindles the Fire, and destroys Earth. Metal is friendly to Water, and inimical to Wood. Earth is the source of Metal, but soaks up Water. When negotiations are in progress for a marriage and the girl's element is destructive to that of a boy, it is considered that she will dominate the partnership, so another bride is sought.

From the operation of the five elements proceed the five atmospheric conditions, the five grains, five colours and five tastes. As an agricultural country the grain crops were of supreme importance to China, but their identity varies with the latitude. The south, up to the

Yangtze, is the most favourable area for the cultivation of rice, and a wheat belt exists in the valley of the Yellow River. In the north different kinds of millet form the staple crop. The five Grains (Wu Ku 五穀) are generally identified as hemp, millet, rice, wheat and beans.

The five colours, which were incorporated in bars on the first national flag adopted by the Chinese Republic, also represented the nations making up the old Empire. Red for the Manchus, Yellow for the Chinese, Blue for the Mongols, White for the Moslems, and Black for the Tibetans. Their corresponding elements are Fire, Earth, Wood, Metal, and Water.

The tastes are salt, pungent, bitter, sour, and sweet. The parts of the human body dominated by the same influences are the spleen, lungs, heart, liver and stomach.

Odd numbers belong to the Yang, or male category, and are therefore luckier than even, so the Chinese have added the centre to the normal four points of the compass. The North is governed by Water, the West by Metal, South by Fire, East by Wood, and the Centre belongs to Earth. The order of society and its affairs are also affiliated; the Prince, or ruler belonging to Earth, the subject to Wood, the minister to Metal, whilst affairs and things are in the province of Fire, and Water. The corresponding qualities are loyalty, love, righteousness, worship, and knowledge.

Connected again are the "Five Rulers", Wu Ti (五帝), who are identified with the five sacred mountains of Taoism. The Yellow Emperor of the Centre is incarnate in the peak of Sung Shan in Hunan, and his authority extends over the forests and waterways. The Red Monarch of the South who inhabits Heng Shan in Hunan, assumes responsibility for ordering the stars in their courses, and for the good conduct of all marine monsters, including the dragon himself. The White Emperor of the West specialises in ornithology and mining, and the spirit of the second Heng Shan, in Hopei, is in charge of the four great rivers and the animal kingdom. The destinies of mankind, in this world and the next, are in the hands of the Azure Emperor, in the most revered of all mountains, T'ai Shan of Shantung.

Their cult persists, particularly in South China, where Canton is under their special protection. Its title, the City of Rams, dates from their visit, clad in their appropriate colours, and descending from the heavens mounted on sheep. In the hand of each divinity was an ear of corn. As they alighted in the market-place the rams turned to stone, and have remained in that condition ever since. The spirits of the Genii ingratiated themselves with the inhabitants by prophesying that the city would never be visited by famine, before they vanished into thin air. As the rams had lost their locomotive power, they were left behind, either because their metamorphosis had depreciated their value to their owners, or as an earnest of their promise. One of the largest temples in the city is dedicated to the five, and the petrified rams are still its main attraction.

The Five Emperors, though their promise concerned famine and not freedom from disease, are credited with the ability to avert disease as well. Cholera is thought to be their speciality so, instead of purifying the water supply, the local populace would parade their images in sedan chairs through the streets of Canton, in an intercessary procession complete with drums and banners.

It is not always easy to trace the implications of the number "five" to the origin of the elements, though they usually lead back indirectly to this source. For instance, the Fifth is known as the Dangerous Moon, as the sun's rays are then strong enough to incubate the germs of disease, and the monsoon rains are not yet strong enough to wash away the accumulated garbage of the gutters in which they breed. Red threads are tied to the wrists of little boys, to protect their lives, or five coloured ones symbolic of the Five Poisonous Creatures. These are the viper, scorpion, centipede, toad and spider, a team powerful enough to neutralise any pernicious influence. Alternatively, pictures of them are worn by the child in black thread on red pockets on one of the first five days of the month. The talisman is removed after noon, which is called throwing away evil.

The Buddhists, not to be outdone by their rivals in the possession of sacred hills, selected four to correspond with the earthly elements of their creed. Air for Wu T'ai, Fire for O Mei, Water for P'u T'o, and Earth for Chiu Hua, strictly in accordance with Chinese beliefs. The elements were assigned because of the geographical peculiarities of each locality, and their location sprang from the desire to place a physical monument of the religion in each of the four points of the compass. Though Chiu Hua is nearer the centre of China as it is today, at the time of its selection nearly all the territory on the right bank of the Yangtse lay to the south of the "orthodox" states of the Chou (周) Empire. The four mountains are the legendary seats of the four Bodhisatvas, or Pusas, so prominent in the mythological and symbolic system of the Mahayana. Wu Tai is sacred to Wen Shu, O Mei to P'u Hsien, Chiu Hua to Ti Tsang, whilst Kuan Yin is enthroned on the Fairy Island of P'u T'o.

Finally, five is the number of the classic family in China. Three boys and two girls. Here there is no obvious connection with the elements unless, with the theory of their descent from the primeval forces of nature, it is to ensure the predominance of the male element over the feminine complement.

The Meaning of Presents

Symbolism plays a large part in the selection of gifts which are not only useful, but convey good wishes for health and happiness in a graceful form. There is no question of sending an unwearable tie, or a box of unsmokeable cigars to a crusty old bachelor. At a birthday party for one of riper years, especially long noodles will be provided, which express the desire that longevity may bless the recipient. Long life, affluence, happiness, and posterity to comfort the soul after death are the main desiderata of every Chinese, and their art has been largely devoted to symbolising the blessings which every family craves. The Chinese language is monosyllabic, and possesses a very limited number of sounds. To remedy this defect, and for the sake of clarity of expression, four tones in Mandarin, and seven to nine in the Cantonese dialect, considerably expand it, but even so some of the sounds have over a hundred and thirty different meanings. Only by the context may it be possible to know whether the reference is to a chicken or a mirror, and Chinese when conversing are frequently obliged to outline the character on their palm with the forefinger to indicate the object of discussion. This similarity of sound forms the basis of much of their symbolism in art, and they are quite willing to sacrifice a tone to drag in a decorative object to convey their good wishes for happiness or prosperity.

Every Chinese carries a piece of jade for his protection, and many of these fragments of precious stone are carved in symbolic designs. For the wealthy, these carvings took the form of belt buckles, or what were called "finger jades". They often served as a counter-weight to the tobacco pouch which was passed on a silk cord through the girdle. A favourite design is the butterfly and cat. It is a natural combination, for no cat can resist the fluttering insect if it ventures within reasonable range. To the Chinese, however, it symbolises longevity, for the word tieh (蝶) for butterfly expresses the wish that the recipient reach the age of seventy to eighty (耋), while the mao (貓) of cat prolongs his life to ninety (耄). The squirrel and grapes also denote longevity, as in Chinese literature the trailing tendrils of the vine are likened to eternity or, at any rate, ten thousand years, which is almost perpetual lease of life. The design is very ancient, and is often found on bronze mirrors.

The deer (鹿) nearly always accompanies the God of the Southern Measure who has the power of conferring old age. When used symbolically as a pun, it also suggests a comfortable income (祿). It has its uses in after life as, with the crane, it escorts the soul to immortality. For this reason it is often seen, clipped out of cypress twigs, in funeral processions. The Boat People of the Canton delta, practically alone among the Chinese, accord spirits to those who have died before marriage, and images are made to commemorate them, the boys being mounted on lions, and the girls on cranes.

In the Palace of the Hsi Wang Mu (西王母) (Royal Western Mother), situated in the K'un Lung Mountains of Central Asia, grows a peach tree whose fruit ripens only once in three thousand years. It has the property of conferring longevity on all who eat it. On its ripening the Eight Immortals and the Shou Hsing (Longevity Star God) join in the feast to renew their youth. For a birthday feast, therefore, images of the Immortals and the Star God are placed on the table, in the hope that some of the properties of the fruit which he holds in his hand will be conferred on the individual who is being honoured.

"Buddha's hand", the fruit of a citrus tree, known as Fo Shou (佛手) is near enough to the sound of Fu (福) (happiness) and Shou (壽) (Longevity) for it to represent these desirable conditions. The tree is therefore often sent as a present about New Year in Peking, and the fruit is often carved in jade or ivory. It is a favourite gift of the Chinese servants to their European employers, though few of the recipients are aware of its significance.

In China, one magpie does not stand for sorrow and two for mirth, but it is a question of the more the merrier. One such bird is Hsi (喜), and so (囍) is happiness. Double the character and you have matrimonial felicity. Five magpies make a well-balanced design, and increase the luck according to their abundance.

The desire for affluence in pre-Republican China was usually dependent on the acquisition of an official post as, if wealth were accumulated in any other way, the tax-collector was the beneficiary. Every family therefore desired to enjoy the protection of a member in the Mandarinate, and to share with him the spoils of office. Scholarship was the sole road to the Civil Service, so numerous gifts conveyed the wish for success in the examinations. A delicate hint to the candidate to exert his energies was the effigy of the carp who strove to mount the rapids to become a dragon. To the Western mind such a metamorphosis might suggest the conversion of a harmless, if unpalatable, fish to a rapacious monster, to which indeed the old-time mandarin was often compared, but the Chinese conception of the dragon was widely different, and his benevolent qualities offset his awe-inspiring appearance. The peony, often seen on porcelain and in paintings, is symbolic of riches and nobility. If depicted with a White-capped Chat, a bird of the warbler family, it expresses the wish that good fortune and honour may last till the hair turns white.

The cock, with his crown, depicts literary success, and, shown above the flower known as cock's-comb, the design expresses the hope of official promotion. It is the usual Chinese play upon words where the Kuan of "comb" (冠) changes to the Kuan (官) of "official".

From the above few instances it will be seen that a gift from a Chinese nearly always has some implication and, as it is the worst of crimes to hurt the feelings of anyone, the wish accompanying the gift will invariably be kindly. There is consequently no risk in finding out the intention, which will add to the value of the souvenir.

Thus, in making gifts the Chinese nearly always select an object which symbolically conveys a wish for the wealth, contentment or longevity of the recipient. A vase, through the play on words of its name, brings peace and tranquillity into the home. The obsession of keeping the whole family under one roof, like a hen with a brood of chicks, might entail endless friction were it not for the spirit of tolerance which is one of the strongest characteristics of the race. It naturally follows that Chinese artists have devoted their skill into fashioning articles, or embellishing them with designs, reminiscent of the blessings of life which all desire to attain.

Symbolism in Chinese Art

Health, Wealth, and Happiness are accepted good wishes for a European, and, to judge by the frequency of their representation, the Chinese equivalents are the Gods of Longevity and Wealth; Happiness being a good third in the form of the bat. Wishes for long life are conveyed in numerous forms of the Chinese character for longevity, sometimes highly conventionalised, the peach, gourd, cicada, and ling chih (靈芝), the mushroom which bestows immortality.

Prior to the introduction of the Mexican dollar through contact with the West, ingots of gold and silver were used for currency, the only coinage being the cash, which had a square hole in the centre for the convenience of stringing. Representations of four cash, each with four Chinese characters, are a frequent decoration on porcelain.

The use of the bat is far more subtle, and arises from the Chinese love of punning, or taking a concrete emblem with a similar sound to represent an abstract idea. The character "fu" (蝠), for bat, is similarly pronounced but differently written from the one which stands for Happiness. The design of the Five Bats is a pictorial rebus standing for the Five Blessings (福), namely old age, wealth, health, love of virtue, and a natural death.

Visitors to the temple festivals will see toy halberds on the stalls where fairings are sold, and may wonder at the popularity of such a weapon in a land where the soldier ranks between the barber and the actor, at the lower end of the scale of society. The word chi (戟) for halberd, however, is similarly pronounced to that meaning auspicious.

Floral designs are much in vogue, and the "Three Graceful Plants" or "3 Friends" are the Plum, Pine and Bamboo. The Pine, being evergreen, is regarded as an emblem of longevity, and is used metaphorically for friends who remain constant in adversity. The founder of the Taoist sect, Lao Tze, is said to have been born under a plum tree. It is symbolical of Winter in the Four Seasons, the peony representing Spring, the lotus, Summer, and the chrysanthemum, Autumn. On account of the durability of the bamboo it also portends old age.

Possibly the favourite flower of the Chinese, who illuminate it at night in Peking to enjoy it longer, is the peony, which is a symbol for riches and nobility. It is depicted on some of the early postage-stamps of the Imperial regime (1894).

The symbolical meaning of the lotus is derived from its connection with Buddhism. The seed-pod, blossom and bud represent the past, present and future. Its leaves and roots signify progeny and steadfastness in the family, two essential requisites in a land where the clan is of primary importance.

The ripe fruit of a pomegranate, usually depicted as half-open, betokens fecundity, and is taken to mean Many Noble Sons, while the Chrysanthemum typifies endurance.

Other symbols for the literati, once the all-important class in China, are the pearl of fulfilled wishes, a stone chime for blessings, clouds of good luck, books and scrolls, artemesia leaves, a tripod, and a pen brush and chessboard.

The most universal of the line ornaments is the Pa Kua, or Eight Diagrams. These diagrams are arranged in a circle, and each consists of three broken, or unbroken, lines. The unbroken represent Yang, the male, light, creative power, and the broken Yin, the female, dark, and receptive element. A light and dark figure, the T'ai Chi, may form the centre, representing the mingling of the two forces, or symbol of creation.

Old Chinese rugs are now practically unobtainable, and foreign firms operating in Peking and Tientsin before the war often supplied their own designs. In general, however, the native ones were far more beautiful and, with the craftsman's horror of a vacuum, they were highly decorated with symbolical figures. The borders are usually the key pattern, or meander, and, in the case of temple rugs, the Buddhist emblems, (卍) or (萬字), are freely used. The meander consists of squares within squares, resembling the character Hui, to revolve, and symbolises reincarnation. The Swastika stands for infinity. The Eight Buddhist symbols are: the Jar, Umbrella, Lotus, Fish, Conch-Shell, Canopy, Wheel of the Law, and the Mystic Knot. The Eight Treasures:

Dragon Pearl, Lozenge, Stone Chime, Rhinoceros' Horn, Golden Coin, Mirror, Books and Artemesia Leaf. They are generally entwined with fillets of ribbon.

The emblems of the Taoist Eight Immortals consist of the Sword, Fan, Flowerbasket, Lotus, Flute, Gourd, Castanets, and Musical Tube.

These motifs constantly recur in Chinese Art, and the above is a most inadequate sketch of what may be encountered with the thousands of legends connected with their folk lore. A whole book has been devoted to the White Monkey alone, and a visit to a Taoist temple will leave the foreigner bewildered.

Since the fall of the Empire, the Dragon has become less important in design. In the early Treaty Port days he was ubiquitous and in great demand by foreigners. The five-toed dragon was the Imperial prerogative, Princes having the four-toed variety. He is usually represented endeavouring to catch the sun or a flaming pearl, or contending with a mate for the same prize. The Chinese Phoenix, the badge of the Empress, must have been suggested by the Argus pheasant, though, in the matter of colouring, art has far transcended nature. Its five hues are compared with the human virtues: Uprightness, Decorum, Wisdom, Humanity, and Sincerity. When portrayed with the Dragon, it signifies perfect marriage.

The Tortoise is often used as a plinth for a memorial tablet, and is venerated for its age and durability.

The Red Hare is a supernatural beast which once inhabited the moon. According to Taoist tradition it is still there, occupied in compounding the Elixir of Life on the head of a toad. The toad is credited with a futile attempt to swallow the satellite, and is therefore an emblem of the unattainable. Should he be depicted with the Immortal Liu Hai, who holds a string with five cash, the intention conveyed is most auspicious, and conducive to money-making

No race as artistic as the Chinese could have overlooked the butterfly, and none have surpassed them in its treatment. The Western butterfly is invariably figured in an unnatural "set" position, while the Celestial insect is nearly always on the move, and full of life. Its name, Tieh (蝶), signifies the wish that the recipient should attain the age of seventy.

Longevity

The author of the lines "Man wants but little here below, nor wants that little long" evidently had not the Chinese in mind when he penned the sentence. In the spacious Georgian days of large houses, adequately staffed, and when money had real purchasing power, the only worry of the upper classes was the punctuality of the meals. Three meals a day, and a fire blazing in the grate were taken for granted, and there was no need for the master of the house to exert himself in any way to procure the necessities of life. Want may mean need, or desire and, in the first sense of the word the Chinese peasant lacks every amenity which the writer would have considered as his birthright. He or his family may spend hours scavenging for the few sticks and rubbish to put under the pot, whilst wondering if there is enough rice in the bin to fill it. Possessions he has none, and he must toil from dawn to dusk to keep body and soul together. Yet, he wants to enjoy this state of misery for as long as possible and longevity is the highest ambition. The worship of old age, which is far more honourable in China than in any other country, permeates the whole race, and no precaution is omitted from birth to beyond the grave to ensure the prolongation of life.

The process starts as soon as the child sees the light for, at that moment it becomes a year old. An infant born a minute before midnight on New Year's Eve is two, on the first stroke of twelve. This is because he has lived in two years of the sixty-year cycle. The method of reckoning would be most unfair in western countries where age limits are fixed to decide whether a child shall receive higher education or be relegated to the primary school, but the Chinese recognised no limits, and even octogenarians sat for the examinations for official posts.

Even after death a man may add to his years, for his descendants, to honour his memory, often inscribe his ancestral tablet with a credit balance in his favour. Clothing or underwear discarded by old people is in great demand. No matter how tattered or perished is the fabric, it is never used for cleaning rags, but young mothers compete for it to wrap round their infants in order that the virtue acquired by contact with longevity may be transferred to them.

Children's birthdays are not generally observed but, once they reach maturer years, the anniversaries are occasions of great importance. The highlight of the celebration is a feast, with chicken if it can be afforded, and invariably "Long life noodles". A bowl of these inordinately long strips of vermicelli, swimming in clear soup, presents an embarrassing problem for the uninitiated. Though a certain number may be subdued, and induced to coil in manageable proportions round the chopsticks, one or two dripping whiskers will prove recalcitrant, and threaten disaster to the clothing and table-cloth. They must be consumed, for the rite is equivalent to drinking the health of the host, and the only way to dispose of them is to abandon all foreign ideas of propriety in eating, and lift the bowl to the mouth.

When China's currency was based on a silver standard, the main medium of exchange for a vast proportion of the population was the copper cash with a square hole in the centre for the convenience of stringing the coins together. When given as "Lucky money" on birthdays, the pieces were tied together with red cord for luck and longevity.

Large quantities of fungi are eaten in every province as they are supposed to possess valuable tonic and dietetic properties. The Ling Chih (靈芝草) or Plant of Immortality, grows at the roots of trees. When dried it is very durable, and has been taken by the Chinese as an emblem of longevity.

Large speciments, or imitations in gilded wood, are often part of the decoration of Taoist temples, and the fungus frequently adorns pictures of the Eight Immortals, as its spores form part of their diet. It is a capricious grower, as it only appears during the reign of virtuous monarchs, sharing in this respect the habits of the phoenix and the unicorn. Some authorities claim that the Ju-Yih (如意), often given as a present conveying the wish "May it be in accordance with your heart's desire", derived its shape from the sacred fungus, and

was thus an emblem of longevity, but the Buddhists hold that the lotus was taken as the model, and this flower is usually carved on the upper end.

The symbols as a reminder of long life are innumerable, the character Shou (壽) being stylised in every conceivable form. In the animal kindom the deer is taken as the emblem, and the God of Longevity is often depicted riding on its back. The stag is credited with a span of a thousand years before its coat turns grey, and it takes another five hundred to become pure white. At two thousand its horns turn black, and it achieves immortality. During the Han dynasty, the dove or pigeon, supposed to be the messenger of Hsi Wang Wu (西王母), Queen of the Western Heavens, was adopted as a symbol, and its image crowning a jadehandled staff was bestowed on a person's eightieth birthday.

The Manchurian crane is credited with an almost endless span of life, eventually becoming the mode of transport of the Eight Immortals. At funerals its image crowns the banner with the deceased's name and titles, and the rites performed to assist the soul in its quest for paradise are accompanied by many reminders of long life in the future state. The ancestral tablet of the dead is decorated by the priest with sprigs of evergreen, cypress or pine, signifying a sturdy old age. In the final stage of the commitment of the body to the ground large effigies of auspicious animals were carried in the procession. These were constructed of cypress twigs and gave the impression of being fine specimens of the topiarist's art.

As a mode of address the word "old" was a mark of respect and anyone of superior class was referred to as Lao Yeh (老爺). Yeh literally means sire, or grandfather and the term might loosely be translated as Old Master. It had none of the slightly disparaging significance of the expression "Old man" in English, inferring that an individual was past his prime, but more nearly approached the sailor's nickname for the master of the ship to whose experience in navigation he owed his safety. With the disappearance of the literati at the time of the revolution, the appelation fell into disuse, and the expression Hsien Shen (先生) or "Before born" was substituted.

The term Lao Yeh was applied to those of rank regardless of seniority. When the old Empress Dowager returned from exile after the Boxer Rising, she forced herself to admit that the foreigners had come to stay, and that she would have to make some concessions, by receiving the wives of diplomats. In order to inform herself of what might be expected of her and to be briefed on the peculiarities of these ladies, whose misfortune it was to have been outside the pale of Chinese civilisation, she summoned two daughters of an ex-ambassador, who had been brought up abroad, to serve as her informants. One of the girls was only fifteen and, by Court etiquette, had not reached the age of putting up her hair in the Manchu style. When her mother pointed this out, and objected that if her hair were dressed in the Chinese fashion she would be mistaken for one of the servants, the old Empress ordered her to wear boy's clothes. Years after the Empire had fallen, and she was a middle-aged married woman, former palace servants, who met her in the street, greeted her as "Lao Yeh".

The God of Longevity, Shou Hsing (壽星), was originally a stellar divinity, situated in the first two of the star groups Chiao (角) and K'ang (亢). On account of this precedence, seniority was implied. When the star is bright, the nation will enjoy peace, but its dimming indicates an unsettled period. In the reign of Ch'in Shih Huang-ti in B.C. 246, the Emperor first offered it sacrifices, but for the common people a less nebulous personality was evolved, and Old Longevity descended to earth in human form. He is represented as an ancient with a high, dome-shaped forehead, armed with a rugged staff, and bearing in the other hand a peach from the tree of immortality. That nothing may be wanting to ensure that the years he bestows may be accompanied with all the blessings of life, he is often surrounded by other auspicious emblems. The deer he rides not only reinforces his power to prolong existence but promises that it will be accompanied by official emoluments. The bat circling his head is a harbinger of happiness, and the Manchurian crane brings long life to enjoy it.

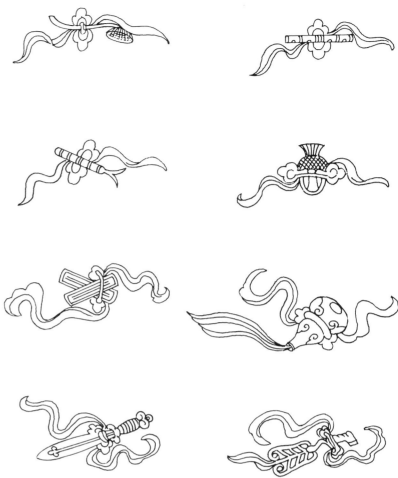

Emblems of the Eight Immortals

Emblems of longevity

Religious Symbolism

In its original form the Taoist religion set as its goal the status of immortality through abstraction from mundane things. Though this aim proved impracticable in a competitive society, its traces remain in the ardent desire for longevity, whose divinity Shou Lao (壽老) resides in the star Canopus. Old fashioned families possessed a set of the Eight Immortals, the Pa Hsien (八仙), which decorated the banquet table on anniversaries, with two children on the backs of water-buffaloes, whom they had despatched to fetch the God from beyond the hills. His symbol is the peach from the fabulous tree, P'an T'ao (蟠桃), which blossoms every three thousand years, and bears fruit after three more milleniums.

The Immortals themselves do not appear in art till the XII Century, and it was not until the Ming and Ch'ing dynasties that they attained their popularity in

decoration and jade carving. Each of them has an emblem, which is often substituted for the whole figure.

The fan, with which he is credited with the power to resuscitate the dead, is carried by Chung Li-ch'uan (鍾離權) though it is occasionally replaced by a fly-whisk.

Lu T'ung-pin (呂洞賓) is armed with the demon-dispelling Chien (劍) or sword.

The beloved beggar Li T'ieh-kuai (李鐵柺) on account of his infirmity is never far from his iron crutch, whilst his symbol is the Pilgrim's Gourd, Hu Lu (葫蘆), the source of magical spells.

A pair of castanets (Pan 鈸) is in the hands of Ts'ao Kuo-chiu (曹國舅), whilst Lan Ts'ai-ho (藍采和) has a flower basket on her arm, and is sometimes portrayed with a gardener's spade.

Chang Kuo Lao (張果老) holds a bamboo tube and rods (Yu Ku 魚鼓) a form of drum, whilst Han Hsiang-tzu (韓湘子) entertains himself with the music of a flute (笛).

Finally, the female member of the troop Ho Hsien-ku (何仙姑) is associated with a lotus flower, a later development of the ladle which she still held in her hand when rescued from a Cinderella-like existence as a kitchen maid.

It is important to memorise these attributes, for the Chinese artist, with his passion for oblique references, is apt to substitute them for their owners, whilst still conveying the idea of their connection with the wish for long life and eventual immortality. They are generally displayed with the embellishment of ribbons, or fillets

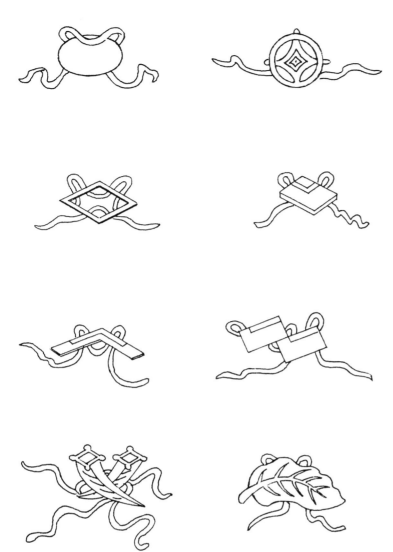

The Stone chime (磬) is an instrument of percussion consisting of a T-square plate made of jade, or sometimes of bronze. As one of the treasures it was occasionally carved on the ends of rafters, when it represents a word of similar sound—ch'ing (慶) meaning felicity.

A pair of Rhinoceros' Horns (犀角) symbolises happiness. They are sometimes found very elaborately carved for ornamental purposes, and were used as drinking vessels in the olden days, as they were credited with the power of revealing the presence of poison, by sweating.

Coins for warding off evil are called Pi Hsieh Ch'ien (避邪錢). To acquire this virtue they are sometimes strung round the neck of the local City God (城隍) and are then added to a child's necklace of amulets. The square hole in the middle was for the convenience of carrying them on a string.

Ancient mirrors were credited with the magic power to protect their owners against evil, Hu Hsin Ching (護心鏡), making concealed spirits visible, and revealing the secrets of the future. They were also the symbol of unbroken conjugal happiness. Many house entrances in Hong Kong, particularly if the building is approached by a straight road, along which malign influences can move, are protected by a looking-glass.

Books are the badge of the scholar from whose ranks the ruling class in China was exclusively drawn. Litera-

The Eight Tresures

which indicate their sanctity. Pieces of red cloth attached to anything are believed to possess the efficacy of a charm, and represent its rays or aura, much as the halo distinguishes the Saint. They are often used for the decoration of porcelain, and in embroidery.

The Pa Pao (八寶) or Eight Treasures, are also similarly represented, and, consist of the Pearl, Lozenge, Stone Chime, Rhinoceros' Horns, Coin, Mirror, Books and Leaf. They are sometimes referred to as the Eight Ordinary Symbols.

The term Chu (珠) or Pearl is generically employed to a variety of spherical objects, particularly the pearl for which the Chinese dragon shows so strong a partiality. On the roof-ridge of Taoist temples a pair of the saurians are usually depicted, contending for its possession, and in the dragon dances it is used as a lure to stimulate the antics of the beast. In Buddhism, the Wonder-working pearl (如意珠) is also one of the Seven Treasures, which represent the regalia of a Chakravartti, or universal sovereign.

The Lozenge, called Fang Sheng (方勝), occasionally has a compartment in the upper side, and is sometimes shown in pairs with the ends interlocked like an ancient jade musical instrument. It is said to be an emblem of victory.

The eight Buddhist emblems

210

ture, therefore, was greatly venerated and the two books formed a conventional sign of good augury. Some of the great Chinese classics, such as the Book of Changes (易經), were believed to be endowed with the property of averting evil spirits if placed under the pillow at night, or if the bedroom were adjacent to the library where they were kept.

The mugwort, or artemisia, is used in many countries as a means to ward off sickness. In China bunches of its leaves are hung on the lintels of doors during the Fifth Moon, the season of epidemics. Magistrates, after dealing with a case of suicide, were wont to step over burning artemisia to prevent the spirit of the deceased haunting them. Each of the Eight Treasures thus has some talismanic property which appeals to the credulous.

The symbols peculiar to the Buddhist religion long antedate the invention of the Eight Immortals, and are derived from the Eight auspicious signs on the Master's foot. They comprise the Wheel of the Law, Conch Shell, the Canopy, Umbrella, Lotus, Jar, Fish, and Mystic Knot. They are made of wood or clay, and stand on the altars of the temples, or are worked into architectural designs.

The Wheel of the Law is also known by various names such as the Wheel of Truth, the Holy Wheel, or the Indestructible Wheel of the Cosmos. It exemplifies the crushing effect of the Master's teaching on error and superstition.

The Conch Shell is one of the attributes of royalty, and the emblem of a prosperous voyage. Its tone, when blown, typifies the voice of Buddha expounding his doctrine.

The Canopy is a symbolic representation of the lungs of the divinity, whilst the Umbrella is the emblem of the spleen.

The Lotus in the Oriental religion bears almost the same significance as the Cross in Christianity, as it is the emblem of redemption. Though rooted in the foulest mire, the blossom rises unsullied above the water; so the meanest soul will eventually reach Nirvana. The manifestations of Buddha are always represented on the lotus throne, and from this eminence the Master surveys with compassion the sorrows of the world.

The Jar is a vase with a lid, such as would be used for the storage of sacred relics of the Saints, or an urn for cremated ashes. It sometimes symbolically represents the stomach of the Buddha.

The Fish is an old Christian symbol, and the Chinese make use of the design emblematically for a variety of reasons. The name resembles the sound of the word abundance, or superfluity (餘), whilst owing to its reproductive powers it suggests regeneration. It is content with its surroundings, so typifies connubial bliss. It is also a charm to avert evil and, among the Buddhist symbols, signifies freedom from restraint as it moves easily in any direction. Even so, the Buddha state knows no trammels, but enjoys complete emancipation.

The Mystic Knot probably owes its origin to the talismanic sign worn on the breast by Vishnu, but it has been adopted by Buddhist lore to represent the intestines of the founder of the faith. It is a sign of longevity, as it has no end, and it is also a reminder of the eight Buddhist warnings.

Although appertaining strictly to the imported religion, orthodoxy is so much at a discount in Hong Kong,

and borrowing so general, that it is not unusual to find the Buddhist symbols used for decorative purposes in a Taoist temple. The wooden processional staves carried by children at the principal festivals are often crowned with a pair of symbols, one an attribute of the Lord Buddha and the other of one of the Eight Immortals. Similarly the robes of the priesthood are embroidered with circular patches, the centre of the design being the Taoist Trigram, whilst the border bears the Buddhist signs.

Another of the auspicious signs on the foot of Buddha is the Swastika, which figures in various forms in Chinese art. It may have been introduced with the religion or be merely a variant of the meander used in Diaper Patterns. It is used to decorate the stomach or chest of images in temples, is to be found on the eaves of houses, on embroidery and porcelain. The symbol is of very ancient origin, and is not confined to India where the Buddhists appropriated it from the monogram of Vishnu and Siva, for in Scandinavian inscriptions it figured as the battleaxe of Thor, and in South America the Peruvians held it in great respect. The Chinese emblem has the crampons pointing to the right, whereas in the Nazi badge they turned to the left.

The term Swastika is derived from the Sanscrit Su "well", and As "To be", meaning "so be it", and denoting renunciation of will. The Chinese sometimes use it in place of the character Wan (萬) meaning ten thousand, the highest figure which they could conceive. Of heavenly origin, it is described as "the accumulation of lucky signs, possessing ten thousand virtues". This property accounts for it being placed over the heart of images of Sakyamuni Buddha as a seal (佛心印), as it embodies the whole mind of the divinity.

According to some authorities the Swastika represents the birth of fire, or its cradle, the pith of the tinder from which in ancient days fire was derived by inserting a stick at the intersection, and whirling it round to create a draught. On the other hand it may simply signify the turning motion when producing fire, or symbolically represent the course of the sun in its apparent orbit.

The Red Swastika Society performs many of the functions of the Red Cross in China. It was founded in 1917 in the province of Shantung by an Army Colonel Liu Shao-chi and the District Magistrate Wu Fu-sun. Gathering together a few interested friends they formulated a new religion embodying the best elements of Confucianism, Taoism, Buddhism, Islam and Christianity. The doctrine of life beyond the grave strongly appealed to them, and they sought communication with departed spirits by means of the sand tray (沙盤木筆) and wooden pen. This urge to get in touch with lost loved ones was undoubtedly stimulated by the heavy casualties in the first World War, and manifested itself in England by the activities of such national figures as Sir Arthur Conan Doyle and Sir Oliver Lodge.

Originally called the Tao Yuan (道園) or Garden of the Way, the new religion spread like wildfire throughout China and by 1928 counted two hundred branches. Ten years later this figure rose to five hundred, and overseas lodges were founded in Malaya and Japan. Under the title of the World Red Swastika Society (世界紅卐字會) its aims were the rejuvenation of its members, and the concentration on acts of benevolence. The society practises three forms of service to mankind, educational, medical, and relief work, in the form of charity. Most of the lodges maintain a school for poor children, and a clinic for those who cannot afford medical fees and drugs. In accordance with the reverence shown by all Chinese to the sacred mountain T'ai Shan (泰山) the mother temple was erected at Tsinan Fu, the capital of the province, and services were held on the Hill of a Thousand Buddhas itself.

There is a flourishing branch in Hong Kong, with headquarters in Golden Dragon Terrace.

The Eight Diagrams

The Eight Diagrams (八卦), or Trigrams as they are sometimes called, are supposed to have been derived from the markings on the shell of a tortoise discovered by the legendary Emperor Fu Hsi (伏羲). They are represented by certain mystic signs, arranged in a circle, forming the combinations of continuous and broken straight lines. The former is the Yang Yih (陽儀), symbol of the male, and the latter the Yin Yih (陰儀) emblematic of the female principle. According to Chinese belief, they form the basis of mathematics, and figuratively denote the evolution of nature, and its cyclical changes.

An abstruse but highly revered work, known as the "Canon of Changes" (易經), which was compiled by Wen Wang (文王) (B.C. 1231–1135) and his son Chou Kung (周公), has served as a basis for the philosophy of divination and geomancy. Each symbol has a name, represents some object, has individual attributes and is connected with some animal and some point of the compass. The first, Ch'ien (乾), has three unbroken lines, and represents Heaven, tireless strength, the horse, and the south. The second, a broken line above two unbroken, is Tui (兌), and represents still water, pleasure or complacent satisfaction, the goat, and the south-east. The third, Li (離), has the broken bar between two continuous lines and corresponds with fire, as in lightning, or the sun. It stands for brightness and elegance, the pheasant, and the eastern quarter. The fourth, Chen (震), has two interrupted lines above one continuous line, and symbolises thunder, or moving power. It is connected with the dragon and the north-east.

Sun (巽), the fifth, has two continuous straight lines above, with a broken one below. It is connected with wood, and the wind, and symbolises flexibility and penetration. The fowl and the south-west quarter are associated with it.

The sixth is Kan (坎), a continuous line between two interrupted lines whose attributes are water, in rain, clouds, springs and streams—in motion, not stagnant— and the moon. It rules the west, and signifies difficulty or danger. The pig is the animal.

The seventh trigram is composed of a single unbroken line above, with two interrupted lines below. Its name is Ken (艮) and it represents hills and mountains, resting or the act of halting. It is associated with the dog, and the north-west.

The final symbol, K'un (坤) consists of three broken lines and, being all feminine, is the Earth as opposed to Heaven. Its qualities are capaciousness, and submission. The Ox and the North complete the cycle.

The number of combinations and permutations were increased by Fu Hsi, or one of his successors by doubling the number of strokes to six, which increases the forms by the square of eight, namely sixty-four. A six-fold multiplication of these again takes the varieties to 384, which completes the number to which the diagrams are practically carried. In the design of the stamps commemorating the Empress Dowager's sixtieth birthday, every sort of felicitous symbol was employed, and the trigrams were used as corner ornaments in the 3 cents and 6 cents. At the same period, the double trigram was issued as a postmark to cancel the stamps on mail to sixty-four towns, the capital, Peking, naturally being allotted the all-male symbol.

Though most effective as a cancellation, for it practically obliterated the design of the stamp, it conveyed little information to the recipient as to where the missive was posted. There was no time and date and, should the wielder of the chop inadvertently hold it upside down, the office of origin was automatically changed by the different sequence of the breaks and continuous lines.

The T'ai Chi (太極), symbol of creation, is a circle divided by a curved line into two equal parts, one dark and one light. A favourite amulet made in copper, silver or jade, with this emblem surrounded by the Eight Diagrams, is believed to preserve the wearer from misfortune, and to foster his prosperity. Octagonal frames with the trigrams, and a mirror in the centre, may often be seen outside houses in Hong Kong as a protection against evil spirits. If an access road runs straight towards the building, and space precludes the erection of a spirit screen the symbol is affixed over the door to turn them back.

Ancient mirrors are supposed to be endowed with the power to protect their owners from evil, and were called Hu Hsin Ching (護心鏡), as they were believed to make malignant influences visible, and to reveal the secrets of futurity. At marriages the sun's rays are occasionally flashed upon the bride to bring her luck, and a small looking glass, flat or concave but always round, is frequently hung on the bed curtains. This again is a protective measure to avert the approach of evil. The devils, as would be imagined, are anything but pleasant to look upon and when they see themselves reflected

Tai chi and trigrams

they immediately take flight, and turn their backs to eclipse the image.

The association of the diagrams with looking-glasses is very ancient. Bronze mirrors of the T'ang dynasty, cast over a thousand years ago, often include them in the elaborate decoration on the back. The centre of the design may be the circle of the T'ai Chi, or Great Ultimate, surrounded by the four super-intelligent creatures, the Dragon, Phoenix, Tiger and Tortoise. Then come the diagrams inside a ring of the twelve terrestrial branch animals. Some of these mirrors have the property of reflecting the back design in a more or less shadowy pattern if the sunlight is cast upon a wall, or flat surface. This phenomenon results from wavy irregularities in the surface produced by polishing, consequent on uneven pressure on the back. The property of being able to project the magic symbols would naturally enhance the value of the mirror in the eyes of all.

One of the most powerful of all China's secret societies was the Pa Kua (八卦), or Eight Diagrams fraternity. It was founded, like the Triads, at the end of the Ming or beginning of the Manchu dynasty. Its originator was a poor labourer to whom one of the Immortals, in the guise of a mendicant monk, presented a revelation of the Great First Cause as Wu Sheng (無生), or "Unbegotten", or the "Unbegotten Venerable Mother" (無生老母), guardianship or province being the leading idea. The founder Li Hsien T'ien (李先天) is believed to have been the incarnation of the "Unbegotten" and he elaborated his doctrine on the basis of the diagrams, appointing that number of disciples to spread the religion.

The sect allied itself with the Manchus in the reign of K'ang Hsi, and assisted in suppressing the Mahommedan revolt in Kashgaria. Li refused all rewards for his services, and merely asked for the toleration of his religion.

The organisation of the Society was simple, the Eight branches being divided into four Military and four Civil. It had three grades of officers, who alone could admit fresh members. Meetings were always held at the equinoxes and solstices and at other fixed times. Religious exercises consisted mostly of deep-breathing, and the recitation of charms followed by a spiritualistic séance. The medium, known as Ming Yen (明眼), or the Clear-eyed one, was often a woman, or a girl, whose main duty was to scrutinise the members' hearts and minds for signs of lack of sincerity.

It is certain that, in course of time the society's leaders became anti-dynastic, though many of the rank and file were unaware of the fact, and continued to regard it as a purely religious organisation.

Purveyor to the Gods

The Chinese simply call it the Paper Shop, but this does not imply the stationer and newsagent, from whom one orders one's Times, Daily Mail, or Herald, according to one's shade of political opinion. It is true that the articles displayed are manufactured largely from paper, but it is a disembodied spirit who is thereby gratified. The Emporium contains all the requisites for Chinese religious worship, and a few of the indispensables for

conveying gifts at festivals in a befitting manner. It would be crude to present "Lucky Money" naked in the form of a very worn dollar bill, but, when enclosed in a red envelope with good wishes embossed in gold, the value of the gift is enhanced and, if the amount is small, the donor's face is saved, at any rate for the moment. A small note can be placed in a large envelope, or an important contribution in a small, so that the recipient is always open to surprise.

Carefully hung on the wall of the shop at the entrance are several thick wax candles, dyed red, with hand-moulded dragons in gold in high relief. These are used in all forms of religious functions from the family ancestor worship, marriages, and funerals to the temple, where two candlesticks flank the central vessel of the Wu Kung on the altar. Sticks of incense, varying in thickness from three-inch to a wax vesta, are ranged along the western wall. On the opposite wall are pigeon-holes, containing bundles of Bank-notes issued by the HELL BANK, for use of departed spirits in the next world. The Taoist conception of the after-world is a realm organised much on the lines of ancient Chinese jurisprudence, with a king instead of a magistrate, with his attendant yamen runners, and lictors. Those spirits who have led fairly blameless lives may be re-incarnated and, where the balance of an evil past only slightly outweighs the good, they may be let off with a caution, or only a slight sentence, accompanied by minor punishment. The more guilty, including those convicted of unfilial conduct, and people who allowed their animals to become a public nuisance, are passed on to distinct, and separate infernos, according to the merits of their case, where something lingering, with boiling oil or molten copper, awaits them. The Buddhists are even more lavish in their conception of the hereafter, and have a hundred and twenty-eight hot hells under the earth, eight cold hells, and 84,000 miscellaneous ones scattered about the universe.

Judging by the variety of specie stocked by the Paper Shop—ingots of gold and silver, cardboard dollars covered with tin foil, and bank-notes of various denominations—the spirit of venality cannot be absent from the attendants of these Internal Courts of Justice, and a judicious douceur may considerably ameliorate the condition of the departed.

Perhaps the most interesting line of stock is the collection of charms, and talismans in the form of coloured scrolls, which are either burned before the appropriate deity, or are hung to avert evil influences. The outline of each picture is impressed on the paper by woodblock, after which the colour is applied by hand. They vary in quality from those designed to meet the needs of the poorest, at thirty cents, to real works of art for the houses of the well-to-do. The robes of the divinities are usually lavishly adorned with gold.

Every Chinese town had a printing-press for these scrolls, and a full packet was burned at the New Year Festival, to honour the "Hundred Deities". They are termed "Chih Ma" (紙馬), or paper horses, though they rarely contain a representation of the animal in question. There is evidence that, in their early history, human and animal sacrifices accompanied the burial rites of heroes and persons of importance, and that horses, for the use of the spirit in the hereafter, were invariably included. As economy, and common-sense,

The White Monkey – "Great Sage Equal to Heaven"

children. The rat is an emblem of wealth, so that its acquisition would be an endowment for the large family hanging on to his skirts.

One of the most popular effigies is Kuan Ti, the God of War, who was the Patron Saint of the Manchu Dynasty. He was a historical character, named Kuan Yu (關羽), and was a native of Hsieh Chou, in Shantung, becoming a General under the late Han Dynasty. After brilliant exploits he was captured, and executed in 220 B.C. Even after his death he is supposed to have exerted a powerful influence for the benefit of his country, and in recognition of his meritorious services he received the posthumous awards of a dukedom in the 12th Century. In 1128 he was raised to the rank of Prince, and in 1594 he was finally awarded the title of Emperor. He is worshipped in every house, and his image is placed in the first hall of the Buddhist monasteries, besides being the tutelary deity of money-making enterprises.

In pictures he is always portrayed with a red face, usually attended by a black-faced man with a halberd, and pink-visaged youth with a money bag. The scroll is always hung with the edge of the halberd towards the direction of suspected danger from evil influence. In the North the attendant with the halberd is always placed behind the left shoulder of Kuan Ti, but in Hong Kong they are taking no chances, and the two attendants are transposed in one version of the picture so that, hung on either side of the door, with a spirit screen in front, perfect security is guaranteed.

Black faces are the terror of demons, who are also allergic to tigers, so a black-visaged man, armed with a magic sword and mounted on the Royal beast, is one of the most powerful deterrents. In his left hand he holds a coin for warding off evil, known to the Chinese as Pi Hsieh Ch'ien (Flee depravity money). As the coin bore the Emperor's reign title it was considered a potent charm against evil.

A female Flower Fairy who delivered her Imperial Consort besieged in a city, by obtaining the magic sword from her mother, is depicted brandishing the blade over her head, and, with her shoulders adorned with four yellow and scarlet banners, is bought by a mother for the protection of a new bride.

One powerful and locally popular talisman was not in stock, presumably having been sold out at the Festival of Tam Kung, as these charms are highly seasonal. It portrays a very wideawake individual, mounted on a Pekingese dog, with a seal or tablet in his hand. This bears the inscription "Tzu Hsing Cheng Chao" (紫星正照), which, being literally interpreted, means the "Purple Planet looks straight", or "has his eye on you". The Purple Planet is the Pole Star, connected with the Spirit of T'ai Yi (太乙), the Great Unity, or Absolute. On account of its fixity in the Heavens, it stands for permanency. The Chinese may be forgiven for confusing a star with a planet when it is remembered that Venus is referred to in the West as the Morning or Evening Star. This talisman always has a column behind the mounted figure, and occasionally the magic sword is included.

On their birthdays, it is customary to present the divinity to be honoured with a new suit of clothes. The appropriate outfit for Tam Kung was the official hat of the Chou Dynasty, robes, and Manchu riding-boots. Small red boots are provided for the female deities, as

prevailed over superstition, stuffed effigies replaced the actual flesh and blood until, in the T'ang Dynasty, paper horses were substituted. The only trace of the noble animal which now survives is the name.

The "White Monkey", whose adventures take a whole book to record, is a popular item. His superscription in Chinese is "Great Sage, equal to Heaven". He was first worshipped in return for some supposed services rendered to the individual sent to India, by special command of one of the T'ang Emperors, to obtain books on the Buddhist religion. The same Emperor conferred on him the title by which he is generally known. The birthday of 'His Excellency, the Holy King' is believed to occur on the 23rd day of the second lunar month, when he is specially worshipped by Chinese of all classes. By virtue of his mischievous nature he is supposed to be in control of all imps, and hobgoblins, and things that go bump in the night, so his kind offices are solicited in keeping them at a respectful distance from mankind.

There is an amusing gentleman named "Chang Hsien" (張仙), who is depicted drawing an arrowless bow at a black rat, with scarlet wings, perched on a cloud. Clinging to his red robe are five children, while a brace of red cats, each endowed with two tails, are rubbing against his legs. He is probably identifiable with Chang Kuo, the Immortal, who had a state for sport, and is connected with marital happiness and the birth of

Chang Hsien, guardian of children

cally confined to the Celestial Empire. Silk from China was known to the Romans, whose appreciation of the new textile was so great that its source, Serica, was named after that product in the same way that the English refer to porcelain by the country of its origin. Tea was not popularised in Europe till the East India Company extended its trade to Canton, and, though its export probably preceded China's other monopolies, jade is practically unknown to all but specialists in Chinese art. Even among the cultured classes the belief exists that all jade is green.

The Chinese have three names for jade: first, Yü (玉), of which they recognise nine kinds—(1) fen (珺), the colour of clear water; (2) pi (璋), indigo blue; (3) pi (碧), moss green; (4) fu (琂), the colour of kingfisher feathers; (5) kan (玵), yellow; (6) chiung (瓗), cinnabar red; (7) men (瑞), blood red; (8) hsieh (璽), lacquer black; and (9) cha (瑳), opaque white. These are all nephrites from the Khotan-Yarkand region of south-western Turkestan.

Pi Yü, a dark green rather opaque nephrite, is found near Lake Baikal, and in the form of jadeite in Yünnan. The emerald green is mined in Burma, has a different chemical constituent, and is called Kingfisher chrysoprase (fei ts'ui) (翡翠) by the Chinese. The dealer's name is Jewel jade, and the stone is more akin to the emerald, being jadeite instead of nephrite.

The Chinese have always attributed magical properties to the stone, and practically every man or woman carries a piece on the person. It is supposed to have medicinal qualities and acts as a talisman against disease and accident. Women nearly all wear a bangle and, should it be shattered by a blow, are convinced that it has saved them a broken wrist. The sonorousness of jade has always appealed to the Chinese ear, and the emperor used to summon his attendants by striking a gong consisting of a thin slab of the mineral. Humbler men wore a string of small jade discs suspended from the top button of their gowns, whose tinkling as they moved provided them, like the lady of Banbury Cross, with music wherever they went.

The commonest form of finger jade, so called because it could be constantly handled, was used as a pendant and counterweight to the purse or tobacco pouch carried at the belt. The Japanese copied the idea in the Netsuke, usually of ivory, on whose embellishment some of the greatest artists displayed their talent. But where they turned their ingenuity to depicting a conjuror with empty hands, whose tame rat has slipped out of sight behind his shoulder, the Chinese relied on their old motifs for the symbolism, whereby the precious stone conveyed a wish for longevity, happiness or advancement.

The sacred peach stood for longevity, and the pomegranate for the continuity of the clan; the butterfly, a life span from 70 to 80 years, and the cat added yet another decade. A horse lying down with a monkey climbing on its back, whilst a butterfly settled on its flank, wished the recipient advancement to the rank of marquis, and a long life to enjoy his honours. The squirrel and the grape vine is a very old design found on early bronze mirrors, the tendrils indicating a clinging to life.

Different designs are characteristic of various dynasties. Han jade was simple, and Sung is exemplified by the boldness of the carving. Ch'ien Lung work is marked

they are credited with the adoption of the practice of foot-binding. Even the "White Monkey" is catered for on his natal day, a gilt and paper crown, red jacket, and yellow cloak being provided. The kit includes a tiny pair of white shoes, for cloud-hopping, and two red cardboard buckets slung at the ends of a carrying pole. His birthday occurs on the twenty-third day of the Second Moon, but it is appropriate to worship him at any time.

The Chinese are practical businessmen, and move with the times. A cardboard motor-car has now taken the place of the Peking cart and mule which was consigned to the flames at an important funeral to facilitate the departure of the deceased. The glass case which contains the scarlet and gold lucky money envelopes also displays air mail stationery, and fairyland merges into materialism. For this is a Paper Shop.

Finger Jades

Jade is a mineral of remarkably limited distribution, and its exploitation, like that of silk and tea, was practi-

by its high finish. As a general rule the older the object the poorer is the quality of the stone. Improved transportation has made it easier to select the better quality at the distant source. Up till the Christian era jade pebbles were quarried in Shensi and Honan, and, after the supply ran out, the Khotan district was opened. The antique jade is full of flaws, but the Chinese look upon these imperfections with indulgence. They say that their beloved stone is like a friend, never perfect, but not to be criticised on that account.

It is only by practice that a foreigner can distinguish good from bad jade. Jewel jade is even harder, for it is only by comparison that the merits of two stones can be judged. It is, however, relatively simple to determine if the object is jade or glass, the substance which most nearly resembles it. Jade cannot be scratched with a sharp pointed steel implement and, if a drop of water is applied on the end of a match, it will stand out like a bead on jade, whereas on glass it at once begins to spread.

Three cities in China specialised in the carving, Canton, Suchow, and above all Peking, where the craft was entirely in the hands of the Mohammedans. Canton first obtained its supplies from Yünnan, but the natives of that province discovered the Burmese mines to the west of Myitkyina in the 13th century, and from then till the sea route was opened the raw material travelled overland. Green jade is consequently much more in evidence in South China than in the North. Merchants differentiate between what is known in the trade as "old" and "new" Fei Ts'ui. The former is the jade mined before the practice of blasting was adopted. The shattering effect of modern methods produces infinitesimal cracks, which do not affect the stability of the stone, but detract from its appearance in the eyes of those who know what they are looking for. A dealer will always call his customer's attention to the fact that the object he is offering is "old" jade, but will refrain from comment if the jewel is of recent origin.

Small dealers of carved jades in Hong Kong are less familiar with comparative values of colours and workmanship prized by the Northerner than their Peking fellow traders, and bargains are still to be picked up. The collection of finger jades is a fascinating hobby as so much individuality in carving is to be found. There is no such thing as mass production, for the shaping of the piece is effected entirely by abrasives, and the same craftsman would never produce an exact replica. Prices vary from a couple of dollars to anything a foolish individual is prepared to pay for a specimen he feels he must possess.

It is impossible to define in words what constitutes good or bad jade. With two identical colours one may appear dull and lustreless, whilst the other is glowing with life. Worn next to the skin jade often recovers, and the change is as striking as the difference between tarnished silver and that in daily use. Bad cracks should be sufficient to reject a piece, but a judgment of quality only comes by long practice.

Up to the Sino-Japanese War the standard of carving in Peking was very good, and delightful specimens of modern workmanship could be obtained for a few dollars. The quality of the stone was probably better than in the antiques, as only such material as was worth working was sent from the mines. A very high finish

was obtained reminiscent of the famous work in the Ch'ien Lung era. The line, however, was not so fluent as in the old carving, unless an antique design was copied. Since the new regime was established, an ever-increasing amount of modern work has been seen in Hong Kong, and what has appeared bears distinct marks of foreign influence in design. It cannot be said to be an improvement on native craftsmanship, and will make little appeal to true lovers of things Chinese.

Westerners have little or no conception of the immense variety of gradations and shades which are to be found in Chinese jade. The nine classical colours may be taken to correspond with the seven colours of the solar spectrum as seen in the rainbow, but between them exists an infinite variety of derivatives, labelled by the Chinese by their resemblance to some natural object. An artist's palette has Chinese and ivory white, chrome yellow and aureolin, prussian blue and cobalt, vandyke brown and burnt sienna, and the nomenclature of jade is not a whit behind in variety. Chicken bone, mutton fat, egg, ivory, duck bone, antelope, fish belly, shrimp, kingfisher, nightingale and cow hair are a few of the names taken from the animal kingdom. Rose madder, chrysanthemum, cassia flower, betel nut, date skin, rice, chestnut, sandalwood, and spinach are some of the vegetable shades. Pure white with a stain of orange is highly esteemed and is known as orange peel. In the reign of Ch'ien Lung a private seal of this material was cut to commemorate the Emperor Kao Tsung's seventieth birthday, the orange peel decorating the head of the lion which surmounted it. Chalk, coal, lime, emerald and coral also figure in the colour spectrum, whilst semi-transparent jade is known as water, morning dew, and sky after the rain. Candle red, rouge, baby-face pink, wine, blood red, and ink black are also recognised. Good Chinese jade is silky in texture and the surface has an oily appearance, whereas the Burmese stone more nearly resembles glass. In fact, the greater the resemblance the better the jade.

With the passing of the Manchus the respect for the dead has greatly diminished, and many objects of jade from rifled tombs have come on the market.

Before the Sino-Japanese War much scientific excavation took place round Loyang, one of the early capitals of the race, and the results were collected into museums, but there were many enthusiastic amateurs whose motive was pure cupidity and the Peking curio-dealers were stocked from their ghoulish activities. The early Chinese, who never practised embalming, believed that jade prevented corruption after death, so they closed the nine orifices of the corpse with plugs of that mineral. The mouthpiece was often in the form of a cicada, which, as it spends many years underground in the larval stage, is symbolic of the resurrection. A jade fish, emblematic of watchfulness, closed the eyes, whilst the sleeves were weighted down with tigers to warn off the evil spirits.

These are known as Han jades, but scholars are still divided as to whether the word is the character for the dynasty during which the custom arose, or whether it is han (琀) which means to place gems in the mouth of a corpse. Very old specimens often come on the market from tombs, and these are usually roughened by the action of minerals in the soil.

Small stylised representations of the Ancestor Weng Chung (翁仲) were included in the objects enclosed in

216

Weng Chung—"The Ancestor"

itself, but sometimes it can be revived by friction with the human body, and the Chinese will put themselves to infinite trouble to recondition it. Their belief in the possibilities of resuscitation is recorded in the posthumous papers of Ch'en Hsing, an idolator as far as the precious stone was concerned but, in the light of modern science, a perfect mine of inaccurate information. According to him jade taken from the ground where it has lain since the 3rd century B.C. should not be worked at once, as its structure is loose. It must be treated by rolling between the palms, or nourished by being kept next to the heart for a year or more, when a revival will take place. It is then known as wax flesh bone, and further treatment for a year or two will bring it to the point called wax flesh skin. If the process be persevered with, the structure of the stone will revert to normal, and it will harden stratum by stratum, the colours becoming gradually widespread over the surface. This renewal cannot be hurried but must be proceeded

the coffin. These figures, often only an inch high, represent a bearded man with his hands hidden by his long sleeves. His features are indicated merely by slits for eyes and mouth, and his circular headdress is cut away on the crown to leave the back standing up. White and brown jade predominate in examples dating back to the Chou Dynasty, but the name derives from third century B.C. when Ch'in Shih Huang (秦始皇) honoured the famous warrior Yuen Weng Chung by the erection of a statue.

Another product of the tomb is the "Chicken's heart", the gift from a husband to his wife to ensure fertility. The heart-shaped object is always surmounted by a hornless dragon, whose tail protrudes through an elliptical hole in the centre of the plaque. The heart is usually decorated with conventional clouds symbolic of the rain in the stimulation of the crops. It was worn as a chest protector much as pendants were fashionable at the beginning of the present century, though modesty would always have prevented its use as an ornament. It accompanied its owner to the grave where it protected her from the attentions of undesirable spirits seeking reincarnation.

Jade long buried loses its lustre and becomes dead

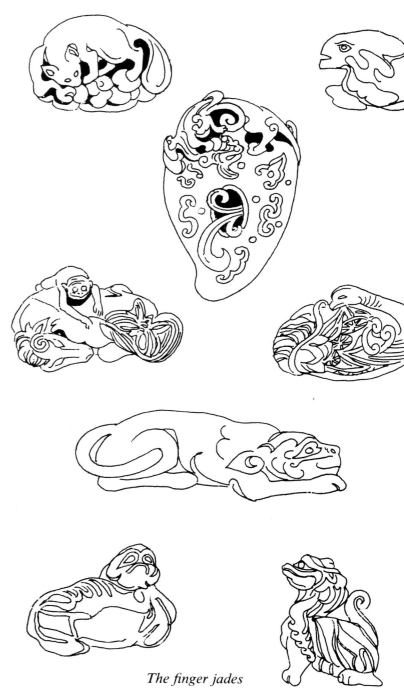

The finger jades

217

with gradually over a period of at least ten years. Until it is completed the substance has gone from the stone, and only the spirit is left. Though jades may lie buried in the ground for three thousand years they can always be nurtured by human heat.

These measures are admitted by the author as heroic, and he suggests a system of beliefs by different wearers to achieve the desired end. His beliefs are widely shared, and there is no doubt that a dull piece of jade can regain its surface polish by the treatment he recommends.

THE MEASUREMENT OF TIME

Until comparatively recently both the Chinese and the Japanese, who copied from them the system of measurement, were unconscious of the time factor which plays so important a part in Western civilisation. The boatman or rickshaw coolie looked for his reward according to the distance travelled rather than the proportion of his day consumed in the accomplishment of a journey. Short periods were described as the time taken to drink a cup of hot tea, consume a bowl of rice, or for an incense stick to burn. Punctuality was the exception rather than the rule, and tomorrow meant some date in the indefinite future. The most important person enjoyed the right to arrive last at a dinner-party, and the entertainment might be disastrously delayed by two guests of equal rank waiting upon one another's departure from home in order to ensure the coveted distinction.

Though the clock regulates the hours of work in a factory and the movement of rail and river communication, the vital events of life, such as the moment of birth and death, are still governed by the old system. No Chinese marriage can be arranged without the exchange of the data which enables an astrologer to determine the compatibility of the parties involved, and the disclosure of the time of birth is essential when consulting a fortune-teller.

The day is divided into twelve watches of two hours, each presided over by a beast who may be mythical, wild or domestic. The system is very ancient, and, though its attribution to the Yellow Emperor in 2637 B.C. may be taken with a grain of salt, it precedes the Han Dynasty.

The twelve in order are Rat, Ox, Tiger, Hare, Dragon, Snake, Horse, Sheep, Monkey, Fowl, Dog and Pig.

For the purposes of astrology they are accorded male or female attributes. The odd numbers are naturally masculine and the even feminine in character. Though the point is of little interest to any but professional fortune-tellers, there is a sort of *aide-memoire* by which the sex can be determined. The ox has a cloven hoof, and so do the sheep and boar, producing an even number as opposed to the club-like foot of the tiger and horse. The hare has a split lip, and the snake a forked tongue. The dragon, symbol of the emperor, has five claws, whilst rat, tiger, monkey and dog have an odd number of toes on the forefoot.

Unlike our system of watch-keeping at sea the Chinese dog-watches of two hours start at the odd, and not the even, numbers, the first being from 7 p.m. to 9 p.m. It is marked by a single stroke on a wooden block, or hollow bamboo tube. Watchmen, in towns in the interior, were maintained by subscription collected from householders in the ward, through which they perambulated all night striking the hour. At the end of each period they collected at some central point whence they restarted, or dismissed, with a tattoo on drum and clarinet, which began with a slow and measured beat, gradually increasing in time till it ended in a brisk rattle. In Peking, the Drum Tower, in the northern part of the Tartar City, set the time by a clepsydra for the

neighbouring wards, and the change of beat quickly spread to the adjacent districts. Long after the Republic had been established the watchman continued to make his rounds throughout the night, maintained by voluntary subscription of those who felt that his presence added tone to the locality.

The twelve animals who preside over the watches of the day are known as the Earthly Branches, or Ti Chi (地支), and the year is denoted by combining them with the ten Celestial Stems, T'ien Kan (天干).

These are the Five Elements, Wood, Fire, Earth, Gold and Water, to each of which is allotted a pair of characters neither of which is the one in ordinary use, but is a symbol reserved for divination. The cycle begins with the combination Chia Tzu (甲子), or Wood Rat, for the first year, continuing with I Ch'ou (乙丑), Wood Ox, for the second. As the least common multiple of ten and twelve is sixty, the cycle is completed in that year, all combinations having been exhausted. A Chinese will often give his age by stating the animal which ruled the year of his birth, which is unhelpful as the creature occurs five times in the cycle.

Sixty years is a short span in the history of China, and it would be impossible to determine a date were not the reign period specified in addition to the "Fire Tiger", or "Water Dragon". Most of the emperors were considerate enough to die or abdicate before they started a second round, though the rule of K'ang Hsi (1662–1723) just over-stepped the mark.

The age of a Chinese has nothing to do with the number of years which have elapsed since his birth, but with the number in which he has been in existence. If a baby be born on the last day of the Twelfth Moon he is reckoned as two years old on the following morning, although not a whole day may have elapsed since his birth, for he has lived during two years. This method of reckoning might have entailed unfairness in competitive examinations for scholarships had any age limit been imposed but, as unsuccessful candidates continued to present themselves until they were octogenarians, no hardship was involved.

The desire to live to a ripe old age is so inherent in the race that it is not surprising to find the sixtieth birthday celebrated with unprecedented honour. It means that an individual has completed the cycle in all its combinations, a matter deserving the warmest congratulations. When the Empress Dowager, Tsu Hsi (慈禧), achieved this happy status in 1894 a special commemorative set of stamps, embodying all the symbols for longevity and felicity, was issued to mark the event.

With the lunar calendar the year was never constant. A common year consisted of 354 or 355 days, whilst an intercalary could not have less than 383, or more than 385. Even so, there was another kind of legal year which determined sentences, such as banishment. This was assessed at three hundred and sixty days, so that in common years the deficiency from short months had to be added, whilst in intercalary years the days in excess were remitted.

The time of mourning, a question of paramount importance, was fixed at three, five, nine, twelve or twenty-seven months, according to the degree of relationship. It was computed from the date of decease, or from the time the notification was received. The days in default for short months were not supplied, and, if an intercalary month occurred, it was not counted either.

China never had a Statute of Limitations, and an obligation remains no matter when it was incurred. English Law takes the commonsense view that if the payment of a debt has not been demanded for six years, the creditor has evinced so little interest in the matter as to deprive him of pressing his claim. In Chinese Law there is no cancellation of such an obligation and, if proof is produced of a debt it must be liquidated, if necessary by the descendants of the man concerned in the transaction.

When Sir Reginald Johnston was a magistrate at Wei Hai Wei, a man produced an old document which acknowledged a loan of a tiao (弔) or string of cash incurred in the year 1783. The defendants in the case had not the slightest intention of repudiating it, but wanted a decision as to the proportioning of responsibility according to relationship among the clan whose great grandsire had borrowed the money. Another complainant at the same court pleaded that his neighbours were cultivating his land. He explained that he had just returned to Shantung from Manchuria and intended to farm his property, but found it in occupation by others. It turned out that his forebears also had emigrated towards the end of the XVIII century, and had not been near their native village since. With him, time stood still and he expected the few acres to be in the same condition as when abandoned, all ready for the plough when the family returned.

These instances came before a British Court, where the law in such matters was administered according to Chinese custom, so decisions were given in agreement with their tradition. A similar incident occurred in the case of a Catholic Mission, which was forced to abandon its property during one of the periods of persecution. Before the Fathers left their buildings, they concealed the red title deeds in the coping of a well, and reported their action to the Vatican. Over a century later their report came to light, and orders were sent for a search to be instituted. The well was still in use and the title deeds were recovered from their hiding place. They were recognised without question by the authorities, and the property was restored to the Church.

Government offices appear to have been as tenacious of their records as private individuals. There never seems to have been a clearing out of dead issues, and every paper was kept, apparently for an indefinite period. During the reign of Tao Kuang (道光), early in the 1830's, two French missionaries, Abbés Huc and Gabet, made an extensive tour in Mongolia and Tibet, and their observations were recorded in vivid style. So entertaining was the work, and so little was then known of the Celestial Empire, that it was read as fiction forty years later. The journey took place during a period of tension between Chinese and foreigners, and the missions in the interior were, to say the least of it, unpopular. Events were working up for a rupture of relations which exploded in the so-called Opium War, and doubtless there were accusations of espionage. Abbé Huc mentions the trial and execution of the French Bishop of Szechuan at Cheng Tu but when he and his companion left Tibet, their passage through China was expedited by the officials in such a way as to preclude all investigation.

Eightly years passed before the outbreak of the 1914–18 War, when the British Consul at Cheung Tu was transferred to another post. As he was packing for his departure he was interrupted by a farewell visit from the head of the foreign affairs department in the provincial capital. This individual was quite excited by a discovery made by his underlings in classifying old documents. He invited the Consul to visit his office, and there laid before him the whole proceedings of the trial of the bishop, together with all his personal effects, including his pectoral cross.

Perhaps the most flagrant disregard for the time factor marked the military operations of those Warlords who carved out their satrapies after the end of the First World War. Many of these leaders had graduated from banditry, and nearly all were grossly superstitious. The handling of large bodies of men, whom they raised by conscription, and the co-ordination of their movements, was entirely beyond their capacity. Most of them included in their staff a professional astrologer, and on his predictions the timing of military movements depended. The proximity of the enemy and the concentration or dispersion of one's own forces were of minor importance. When the geomancer had read the omens and rendered his report, the odds were that the Commander kept the information to himself, and failed to communicate it to his subordinates or to any but the personal staff who accompanied him. The confusion which resulted often beggared description but, as the adversaries employed the same methods, the system eliminated pitched battles and bloodshed. Propitious hours for movement were usually around 2 a.m. and, as foreign advisers and observers were never informed, they were invariably left behind, to follow the army as best they could.

The Chinese Calendar

China has always been a conservative country with a population 85% agricultural, which held to the belief that what was good for their forefathers, and had been tested by countless generations, was sacrilege to tamper with. Although the Republic with its new broom introduced the Western calendar, neither the Nationalists nor Communists have succeeded in weaning the people from their old hardy annual, with its predictions for the harvest, fortune-telling, talismans, and lucky days for the normal activities of life. Though most of the printing presses on the Mainland, located in every market town, which produced coloured representations of the gods, have been fully occupied churning out anti-American propaganda, the Government has been obliged to issue a limited edition of the Kitchen God who presides over every hearth, and whose presence acts as a check on the behaviour of the family. In the South, this divinity is usually indicated by the two characters Ts'ao Chun (竈君) (Stove Prince), but the North of China favours his portrait which is renewed every New Year's Eve, when he returns from his annual visit to the Jade Emperor (玉皇) to whom he renders a report on the general moral tone of his hosts.

The colour scheme of the Communist Kitchen God is not unpleasing, and he is depicted seated behind an altar with his wife on his right hand. Two attendants are at either end of the table which bears the usual five vessels, and in front are the Gods of Happiness and Longevity holding the characters of Fu (福) and Shou (壽). Above the heads of the principals is a red inscription "Make your best effort to produce more" (努力生產), and there is a border of the Eight Immortals (八仙), four on either side. The opportunity to slip in a little further propaganda has not been missed, for, flanking the heads of the divinities, are two labels "Anti-America, Aid Korea" (抗美援朝) and "Defend the country, protect the home" (衛國保家).

The poster is surmounted by a brace of blue dragons, trimmed with red, contesting for the lustrous pearl, and under it is a calendar showing the dates of the breaths and joints* of the year to aid the farmers in their planting. The date gives 1954 and not, as might be expected, the number of the year since the foundation of the "Central Flowery People's Harmonious Country".

Every family who can afford it buys a copy of the Farmers' Calendar for, according to its predictions, each individual Chinese directs his most trivial action. The calendar dates back to the Emperor Yao (堯) who in 2254 B.C. ordered his astrologers to determine the solstices and equinoxes, and fix the seasons so that the farmer might know when to plant his crops. A special board of mathematicians, headed by a Minister of State, annually prepared the document which was submitted to successive emperors before distribution.

The more expensive edition is a perfect mine of information on subjects ranging from fortune-telling to a simple method of acquiring proficiency in the Malay language.

The first twelve pages are invariably printed in red, and start with a crude woodcut of a boy bearing a branch and leading the Spring Ox (春牛). This is a symbol of the Li Ch'un (立春) festival, which falls close to our 4th February and inaugurates the farming year. Originally connected with the worship of the Gods of the Soil (土地) the ceremonies included the slaughter of an ox but, in the course of time, a clay, straw, and finally (by Imperial rescript) a paper effigy was substituted for the living sacrifice. Fukien, one of the last provinces to accept Chinese civilisation in its entirety, persisted until quite recently in immolating a real buffalo, whose carcass was distributed among the various officials taking part in the spring procession. The effigies now carried are fashioned in accordance with the prescriptions of the calendar, and by this means the public can estimate the prospects for the harvest in the coming year. If the head of the ox is painted yellow, great heat is foretold for the summer season. If green, there will be much sickness in the spring. Red brings drought, and black a superabundance of rain. The Meng Shen (芒神), or Spirit Driver, by his position and attire also gives valuable indications of things to come. His dress is purposely misleading as he is credited with behaviour which is precisely opposite to that of a normal individual and wears warm clothing to indicate the prospects of a scorching temperature. If he is in mourning, a bumper

crop may be expected, whilst a red belt foretells much sickness and high mortality.

The text prescribes the size and dress of this effigy. Meng Shen, the herdsman, in 1954 was armed with a mulberry branch whereas in the preceding year he carried a willow switch. The image in both cases was three feet six inches in height, but the dress was entirely different. In 1954 he wore a white jacket and scarlet belt, with his hair in two tufts and his lower limbs covered with trousers, socks and shoes. The latter indicate heavy rain and were not far wrong in their predictions, for Central China was visited with the most disastrous floods for many years, and at least five provinces including the "rice bowl" in Hunan were inundated.

The compilers of the calendar, however, seem to have ignored the warning and preferred to say acceptable things, for they softened the blow by declaring that the Earth Mother (土母) had predicted "Let no one be alarmed. All grain will do well and produce a bumper harvest, and all farmland will have at least one good crop. In Central China (Szechuan, Hupei, Hunan and Anhwei—the area in fact devastated by floods) there will be gales with hail, and wells will run dry. Silkworm keepers will be scouring the country for mulberry leaves, but the caterpillars will be doing their duty, so what more is necessary?" The events of the year were predicted by a poem, which, in spite of the colour of the ox, suggested that it had been inspired by the wishful thinking of the Ministry of Agriculture.

"What more can be desired than the full harvest which awaits the coming year? Do not worry, but enjoy life. The elders lean on their ploughs and contemplate the sprouting grain. Farmers sigh with content, for they have rain at the right season. It is confidently expected that the grain will fill thousands of sacks, and this dream will come true in the end. There will be a good yield of silk, so to conclude we say, this will be a bumper year."

The site of a grave is an all-important subject with the Chinese, though they have no compunction in desecrating the cemeteries of their enemies or fallen dynasties. The locality is chosen by the astrologer in accordance with the rules of Feng Shui as it affects the individual concerned. A diagram of lucky directions is also published annually in the farmers' calendar, accompanied by a few guiding principles. In 1954 the East and West directions were lucky, but the North was disastrous as the Divinities who preside over death and ill fortune reside in that quarter. People should avoid attending the funerals of friends born in the year of the Rabbit, Rat, Cock and Horse. As a funeral is a social event of the first order, which, if sufficiently noisy and expensive, gives face to the survivors, a little subterfuge in concealing the age of the deceased seems justifiable.

On page 12 of the calendar are given the lucky days for travelling in the First Moon. These are the 3rd, 5th, 6th and 10th for all but those born under the sign of the Pig, Rat, Ox and Snake.

For good fortune and wealth the 5th, 8th, 15th and 17th are lucky except for Rabbit, Dog and Rat folk. If not born under the sign of Rat, Rabbit, Dragon or Cock a profitable business can be opened on the 5th, 8th, 9th or 14th of the months.

Asking gods for blessings can best be accomplished, with a good hope of success, on the 3rd, 8th and 15th,

---

* the fortnightly periods of the solar year.   221

but this does not apply to Dog, Rat or Rabbit people.

Each year has a different Patron Saint, who watches over the farmers' interests. The Grand Marshal T'ai Sui (太歲) is the spirit of the planet Jupiter, who presides over the Ministry of Time with the aid of one hundred and twenty minor officials. He is supposed to change his dwelling every year and the location of his abode is determined by the almanac, the lucky line for the twelve months depending on its position. The function of the annual patron is to protect livestock from sickness and ward off floods.

T'ai Sui came to be looked upon with awe, as it was believed that the fortunes of the Empire depended upon the movements of his planet, whose orbit took twelve years to complete. His worship dates back to 1000 B.C. but the god was not promoted to Imperial sacrifices until the late Ming or early Manchu Dynasties. Though his official rites were discontinued with the advent of the Republic, he still has a large private following, more from fear than from love, as he can invoke disease and misfortune and must be placated before embarking upon any enterprise.

His heredity might well give cause for some apprehension for he is popularly believed to have been the son of Queen Chiang, consort of the infamous Emperor Chou, last of the Yin Dynasty. When he was born, he looked like a formless lump of flesh, so repulsive that the favourite concubine Ta Chi (妲己) poisoned his father's mind by alleging that a monster had been born in the palace. The over-credulous monarch at once gave orders that the infant should be abandoned outside the city walls, but a passer-by, Shen Chen-jen, recognised it as an immortal, and carried it to his cave where he led a hermit's existence. Being on terms of intimacy with the Immortal Eight, he entrusted the child to Ho Hsien-ku, who acted as his nurse and brought him up. During his boyhood he was known as Yin Chiao (殷周), or Yin Deserted of the Suburb. When he reached the age of understanding his parentage was revealed to him, and he was further informed that his mother had been killed, like Jezebel, by being thrown from an upper window. Yin Chiao, though still of tender years, approached his rescuer and begged him to allow him to avenge his mother's death. The Goddess T'ien Fei (太妃) armed him with two magic weapons, a battle-axe and a club, both of gold. When the Shang army suffered defeat at Mu Yeh, Yin broke into the tower where the infamous concubine, Ta Chi, had taken refuge, and brought her before the conquering King Wu who gave him leave to pole-axe her with either of his weapons. In spite of their magical properties, however, she escaped for she was in the same line of business herself, and was either a fairy vixen or pheasant, so she transformed herself into a cloud of smoke and dissipated into thin air. To reward Yin Chiao for his filial piety in his not too successful contest with a demon, the Jade Emperor canonised him with the title of T'ai Sui, Marshal Yin.

As T'ai Sui he can do injury to houses and palaces, to people at home as well as to travellers on the highroad. He has, however, a peculiarity in that he never operates in the district in which he himself resides, but always in regions adjoining it. Thus, if some constructive work is to be undertaken in his temporary parish, the inhabitants of neighbouring areas take precautions against his evil influence by hanging out the appropriate talisman. An elaborate diagram is necessary to determine his location at any given moment. This consists of a representation of the twelve terrestrial branches and ten celestial stems, indicating the cardinal points and their intermediates. The four cardinal points are further verified with the aid of the Five Elements, Five Colours, and the Eight Trigrams. By using this device T'ai Sui's residence for the year can be located and the position of threatened districts determined.

After the predictions for the abundance, or otherwise, for the harvest, comes a pictorial adaptation of the Eight Trigrams for the ensuring year. The compass is divided into four quadrants bounded by North-East, South-East, North and South-West in which are inscribed predictions for fortune-tellers and practitioners of Feng Shui. Generally speaking North and South are lucky for everybody, whilst East is distinctly unfavourable. Directions are also given for seeking out lucky sites for tombs. During the second, fourth, sixth, seventh, eighth and eleventh moons sites for graves in either the North or the North-Easterly direction are unfavourable down to East-South-East. From South-East to South-South-East the influence is good.

A page gives the terrestrial branches and the information that this year (1954) is that of Water and the Snake. There is also a concordance of the Western year with the Chinese. Fortune-telling by the animals of the Zodiac and the planets occupies the rest of the red pages except the twelfth which records the lucky days for travel, investments, opening business, worship, starting school and thanksgiving services.

The rest of the book is in ordinary black type, starting with a page giving four woodcuts of Huang Ti (黃帝), or Hsien Yüan (軒轅), whose body is variously partitioned by characters for the four seasons and the twelve animal signs, by which an individual can consult the omens associated with the time of birth. On the whole it is luckier to be placed above than below the belt.

The 14th page gives the twenty-four solar joints and breaths of the year at which the fortnightly changes in the weather occur. It also serves as a Nautical Almanac for Kwangtung Province by giving the times of the tides.

Page 15 carries a woodcut of Chang Tao-ling (張道陵), the first Taoist Master of Heaven and inventor of charms and talismans. Examples of his cabalistic signs for all occasions, and directions for their use, are furnished for those who prefer to copy them by hand rather than employ a professional. Some are to be pasted on the door to scare off wild animals, and others are designed to be carried on the person. In all, thirteen specimens are provided, with instructions for getting into a reverent state of mind before putting pen to paper. Even shoes and articles of clothing may harbour lurking demons, so the first talisman protects the wearer against their entry. The second dispels malignant spirits from the furniture, and the third is a general charm against all disasters. Mosquito-nets and bedding are protected by the fourth, and the kitchen has a talisman of its own.

Domestic animals of the farm and household are immunised from disease, and can be prevented from straying or entering the living quarters. A special charm also protects the poultry run, and keeps the chickens out of the house. Clothing is protected from damage by birds, not only of the domestic order, but from a bombing raid by a flock of migrant starlings. An all-risk policy for travel by land and sea is effected by the ninth hieroglyphic, and the tenth covers the potential dangers from birds of the night. The owl, an impious bird, reputed to devour its mother if not sufficiently fed when a nestling, is specially mentioned, but there is also a nine-headed fowl, the very sight of which is a harbinger of disaster.

The final charm is probably the most potent in the catalogue, for it ensures against all the bogies and hobgoblins not specifically mentioned in the preceding list.

Charms should be written after tapping the front teeth three times, and filling the mouth with clear water. The calligraphist should then face the East, spit out the water and utter the following dedicatory incantation:

"Almighty Yin Yang (陰陽), the sun rises in the East. I inscribe these charms with reverence, which should banish all ill-luck and sweep away every disaster. The water is holy, and the eyes rival the sun in brightness. To all the Heavenly Host of Warriors and Heroes, your task is to fight against evil, and to slay demons, turning bad into good. This is a command to execute my orders without delay."

Having provided a deterrent for all evil influences which may affect the person and his immediate environment, the almanac gives a table of suitable or unpropitious days for weddings and travel. Though this information may be obtained from day to day, in the end of the book there is a separate index by which a lucky one can be rapidly determined. Dates to be avoided at all costs are the 3rd, 7th, 13th, 18th, 22nd and 28th of each month.

The Chinese attach far more importance than Westerners to the days on which a visit to the barber is permissible. To get a shampoo on the 1st of any moon shortens one's expectations of life. On the 2nd and 3rd a haircut is lucky, but on the 4th the hair will fade. Even worse befalls on the following day, as the hair will fall out. The 6th produces blemishes of the skin, but good luck will attend a clip on the 7th. The 8th prolongs life, whilst the 9th foretells a wedding, 10th promotion, and the 11th brightens the eyes. A haircut on the 12th betokens trouble, but the 13th is accompanied by the gift of sons. A windfall of money follows the barber's ministrations on the 14th, and good news on the succeeding day. It is very bad luck to have one's hair touched on the 16th, and a shampoo on the 17th darkens the skin. The 18th attracts burglars, 19th bad luck, and the 20th induces poverty. Illness is brought by the 21st, but good fortune attends the 22nd and 23rd. The 25th means damage to eyesight, but nothing good or bad eventuates from the 27th. Fights and quarrels may be expected from the 28th, but the 29th is a lucky day. The 30th is not a day to choose as it brings ghosts.

Having detailed the rewards and penalties for visiting the barber on any specified day of the month, the calendar devotes an equal amount of space to the lucky and unpropitious days for cutting out dresses. If this operation is performed on the 1st, friends and relations will call, and their entertainment will doubless interfere with a whole-hearted attention to detail. A frock cut out on the 2nd will beget more dresses, whilst to choose the third renders the home liable to a visit from a housebreaker. Damage will be incurred if material is cut on the 4th, but the 5th will bring a windfall of money.

Food and good luck attend the next two days, but the 8th is to be avoided as it brings sickness in its train. More pay or a windfall is the reward for cutting a dress on the 9th, and an armed robbery is the penalty for desecrating the 10th.

Water trouble will be experienced if tailoring is undertaken on the 11th, but the next two days are rewarded with the acquisition of something very precious or money. A dress cut out on the 14th brings long life, without specifying whether it is the garment or the individual who is so blessed, but probably the latter. The five days from the 16th to the 20th are all disastrous; fire, trouble, gossip, loss, and a heart-breaking farewell attend dress-making on these occasions. Both the 21st and 22nd bring good luck, as does the 24th, but the 23rd is an unpropitious date. Money comes after cutting out on the 25th, whilst a garment made on the 26th will wear for a long time. The 27th is neither good, nor bad, but something good to eat will reward the woman who takes her shears in hand on the 28th.

Page 17 of the calendar gives the days when it is lucky to set a bed. The Chinese bed in the North accommodates the whole family, and the guests for that matter. It is an earthern platform running the whole width of the room against one wall, and usually contains a furnace underneath to provide central heating in the winter. Its construction is quite a feat of engineering, and setting the bed by no means implies merely the removal of a truckle couch from one position to another.

Page 18 contains a mass of miscellaneous information. It gives the days suitable for paying visits, and the manner of presenting oneself. Suitable days for cutting the baby's hair are also indicated. The following page gives the place, month and day when the God of Fertility pays his visit.

The dangerous periods for children are given on the next page, the Chinese word used being "Kuan" (關), or mountain pass. Unpropitious times to be born are given as between 11 p.m. and 1 a.m., 3 a.m. and 7 a.m., as well as from 11 a.m. to 1 p.m. in the 7th, 8th, 9th and 12th Moon.

On pages 21 and 22 are to be found instructions for protecting the unborn baby, with two appropriate charms, which should be copied, and directions for their use.

Just as Westerners connect a burning ear with the idea that someone is thinking of them so the calendar interprets certain symptoms such as eye twitching, palpitation, sneezing, seeing magpies and dreams. Fortune-telling by the stars, and their influence on babies, is given on two pages, and another is devoted to Patron Saints whose festivals coincide with the birthday. Two pages are devoted to lucky directions and another three to the import of special days of the year.

Fortune-telling according to the Five Elements comes next, followed by the twenty-four "Kuans", or Dangerous Passes, for children born at specified hours. These are illustrated by woodcuts showing the particular peril to which they are susceptible. Children born during a certain watch in a given month must avoid wells, as they will be in danger of falling in to their destruction. Measles threatens those born at no less than three periods, and they fall into the hands of a stocky little devil, clad only, like our primitive ancestors, in a collar and apron of fig leaves. The "Heavenly Dog Pass" indicates danger from the canine race, and faith should be put in Chang Hsien (張仙), the immortal who protects children from the thievish tricks of the heavenly hound by defending them with bow and arrow. The danger of measles is portrayed by a seated child to whom a python, coiled round a tree, is making seductive advances. Anyone born in the second or third month during a certain watch is in peril of fire and water, and is shown waist-deep in a fast-flowing stream unable to emerge owing to a conflagration on an overhanging cliff. The fifteenth Pass is that of the God of Thunder chasing a boy with a battle-axe. The enraged deity is shown with his tongue protruding, and his thunderbolt at the ready in his left hand. There is a "Five Devils Pass" (五鬼關), which carries the inhibition to avoid priests and all in clerical orders of the Taoist sect. In another illustration those born at the appropriate hour should keep clear of temples.

On the whole the second month appears to be that from which the largest number of misfortunes may be expected. "Built amid fragrant trees and flowers, an icy winter blast shrivels the garden", meaning that misfortune will shatter promising plans.

A great deal of space in the Chinese Year Book is devoted to fortune-telling. Western nations have evolved numerous methods of looking into the future, from palmistry to the pattern formed by sodden leaves at the bottom·of a tea cup, but they must concede the prize to the Chinese for their ingenuity in selecting their means of divination. Three pages are devoted to the finger-joint and date method. The date of birth is all-important to every Chinese, as it must be produced before entering into a matrimonial alliance. The Eight Characters are those representing the hour, day, month and year of birth, and, before the engagement is valid, the data for both parties must be submitted to an astrologer for a verdict as to their compatibility.

Instructions are given to farmers for their planting, and examples of two talismans to assist the germination of the seed and protect it against insect pests. This is followed by fortunes assessed according to the weight of the day, and then there is a reconciliation table between the Chinese and Western calendar. In the Celestial Empire time was reckoned in cycles of sixty years, each of which was designated by the combination of a heavenly "stem" with an earthly "branch". The stems were made up of the five elements, and the five cardinal points, and the branches of the twelve animal signs of the zodiac. A historical date is given by its cyclical combination in the reign of some particular emperor. For the purpose of dating any work of art on which the maker has inscribed the reign, and Chinese year, Father Peter Hoang, of the Nanking Mission, produced a concordance with the European calendar in 1904. He states that, if a date is wanted before the Christian era, 2 must be added to the figure of the year. If the sum is less than 60, subtract it from that number, and the difference gives the cyclical year. If the sum exceeds 59, divide by 60, and subtract the remainder from 60. The difference then gives the cyclical sign. 43 B.C., for instance, with the addition of 2 would be 45 which, subtracted from 60, leaves 15, or the fifteenth year (Wu Yin) of the Chinese calendar. 202 B.C. with the addition of 2 equals 204 or 3 × 60 plus 24. Subtracting the remainder from 60 gives 36, the Chinese year whose

characters are Chi Hai.

If the year is in the Christian era, 3 must be subtracted from the number of the year and, if the difference is less than 60, it gives the cyclical sign. If it is greater than 59 divide by 60 and the remainder will give the sign. If there is no remainder the 60th sign is the answer. Thus for A.D. 221 subtract 3, getting 218, divide by 60 leaving a remainder of 38, and it is the 38th, or Hsin Ch'ou, year of the Chinese calendar.

After the reconciliation statement the calendar reverts to fortune-telling and devotes ten pages to the implications of physiognomy. Eight pages are alloted to charts of the face and hands, and two to amplification of the data marked thereon. Chicken, snake or rat eyes, for instance, denote excessive fondness for the opposite sex, whilst large round eyes with a shifty glance reveal a cruel nature, whose owner will turn out a trouble-maker, even risking imprisonment at the dangerous age of 35 to 39. A man with a pendulous nose will be a Court official, but an eagle beak masks a murderous disposition no matter how friendly the outward appearance may be. Despite education and position the individual remains mean, cruel and corrupt. A man with a sheep's mouth disappoints his friends and acquaintances, as he squanders his money on feasting and drink and has nothing left for household expenses. A monkey mouth indicates a childless condition and, if one be born with this characteristic, the father will die.

Moles and blemishes on the face have special significance. If a girl has a mole above or below the lip she will be so forthcoming with her favours as to be in no need of a matchmaker. In a man, however, a mole above the upper lip indicates that he will always enjoy good wine and food which he does not have to pay for. Good luck is illusory if the mark is at either corner of the mouth, and a mole on the bridge of the nose is a bad omen for the happiness of a man's wife and son.

A plump face indicates great riches, whilst a bony countenance foretells a short life not extending beyond thirty years. Freckles show that fate is overshadowed, whilst a moon face, combined with an arrogant nature and clear aura, foretells a rise to high rank and, in the case of a woman, selection as a princess or queen.

The Chinese divide the face into three parts, the forehead representing Heaven, the chin Earth, and the nose the human inhabitants. The forehead should be wide, and the rounder the better as it means a happy childhood and early distinction. The chin should be wide and square for longevity, but fame will be achieved only later in life. The nose should be straight and central, nostrils not too small, as on this feature depends the worldly prosperity of the owner.

The next ten pages of the calendar are also devoted to fortune-telling by dates, five coins, and the twenty-eight constellations respectively. The divination by coins is a game of pitch and toss, the coins being arranged in a vertical row of heads and tails, and the fates for thirty-two combinations are printed on the left of each illustration, ranging from all heads to all tails.

The Chinese recognise eight planets, including the sun and moon, and twenty-eight constellations, whose grouping differs from that conventional in the West. A number of bamboo slips, with their names engraved, are shaken up in a cylindrical receptacle, and a short poem, corresponding with the one which falls out, gives the fortune of the manipulator.

A list is given of the Hundred Names (百家姓) under which practically all Chinese families are classified. These originally corresponded with the hsien, or counties, and in each district everyone had the same clan name. The system corresponded somewhat to that which obtains in Scotland, where the head of the clan is known by the name of his estate. Even when the names did not correspond, it was customary to address a man by what is equivalent to his Christian names tacking on the name of the town as a patronymic. Thus, Wang Tso-ming of T'ai Yuan Chun would be T'ai Yuan Tso-ming. This title was always used in official documents such as marriage certificates as a respectful ending.

A couple of pages are devoted to a long ballad dating from the 14th century, shortly after the Mings overthrew the Mongols. It was written by the Prime Minister, concurrently Chief of Staff, of the First Emperor of the Chinese Ming Dynasty, Chu Yuan-chang (朱元璋). Chu himself was born a peasant and, as his soldier associates had little pretensions to literary attainments, it is not surprising that the style commands small respect from scholars. It has, however, enjoyed a wide popularity among all classes as it purports to predict the fate of the empire for a thousand years. It is entitled the Shao Pin Ko (燒餅歌), or the ballad of the Buckwheat Cakes, and some of its predictions have been so literally fulfilled that it is reverenced by many highly educated people. The end of the Mings was foretold with great accuracy in the words "The thousandth offspring steps up, the Ancestors in embroidered robes climb higher to the Ancestral Hill".

North of the Forbidden City in Peking stands Coal Hill, behind which was situated the mortuary chapel of emperors awaiting burial. The last Ming Emperor, Chung Chen (崇禎), driven from his palace by the approach of the rebels, climbed the hill and hanged himself on a sophora at the east end. It is fashionable to decry the Manchus, but they possessed many amiable traits and, alone of all Chinese dynasties, respected the tombs of their predecessors. The guilty tree was placed by them in chains as accessory to the death of an emperor.

The fate of the luckless Kuang Hsu is predicted in the words, "when the byre is on fire the oxen can be saved, but a tiger caught in a morass can never get clear". The prophecy continues, "add a cross and a mouth to a lady with a double cross" (吉 plus 廿 = 禧). This gives the clue to the characters for the famous Dowager Tsu Hsi (慈禧) described as "holding the baby in her arms, and making the decisions herself". She reigned during two minorities, and finally deposed her nephew to rule the empire until their deaths which occurred almost at the same hour. Even well-educated Chinese are enormously influenced by these predictions as a belief in prophecy is inherent in the race. The ballad ends with the coming in five hundred years of an emperor who would strengthen the realm.

The poem is followed by "twenty-four stories of filial piety", after which is described another method of telling fortunes by hour, date and month of birth, each having a corresponding weight. A table of totals added together casts the horoscope. A couple of pages are devoted to the story of Confucius' encounter with a child prodigy, where the sage was snubbed by a brat who declined to play, as all time not devoted to the acquisition of learning was wasted. He refused to become a disciple of the Master as he had parents to whom he owed a duty, brothers in whose companionship he delighted, and a good tutor from whom he wanted to learn everything possible. This edifying story of the perfect prig precedes instructions for telling fortunes by the twenty-eight constellations, after which is described Mr. Tang Kung's (董公) method of picking out lucky days for people born under certain stars.

Some moral precepts are then offered such as "Once married, try to save, to bring your children up well", and these are mixed with commonsense advice to "Beware of pickpockets", and keep out of street fights which do not concern one. Everyday hints like "Early to bed, early to rise", "Eat regularly" and "Dress for comfort, not display", are sandwiched in with rules for the care of children, medical recipes and elementary sanitation. Proverbs include such truisms as "Though every hair on a tiger's head can be limned by an artist, he cannot penetrate the mask of a human countenance". Fortune-telling might almost be classed as an obsession, for it recurs persistently throughout the book, and directions are again given describing the effect of moles on the face or body, shape of eyebrows, wrinkles, and palmistry.

Examples are given of modes of address and the working of invitations for formal occasions, weddings and banquets. Then comes a sort of perpetual calendar giving the "joints and breaths", or fortnightly periods of the solar year, from 1890 to 1962. Good and bad days for certain activities, such as making a hen-coop, accepting a cat, buying a horse, starting breast-feeding, and building a shrine for the Patroness of Silkworms, occupy five pages. Ten more detail the misfortunes which may befall an individual born in a certain moon. For instance, if a stove is built in his house he may be attacked by sickness or rheumatism. He will escape these inflictions, however, if he cuts out the appropriate charm, which is illustrated, and hangs it up, or burns it and swallows the ashes. Each moon has an evil spirit, which must be conjured by saying "You devil, hurry away, by Order!"

Seven pages are designed for professional fortune-tellers to enable them to select lucky days, but these are couched in terms incomprehensible to laymen. The complete calendar includes also the telegraphic code, where the characters are arranged in the order of the radicals, and each is given a four-figure number, and lessons in the Malay language for Overseas Chinese.

Cheaper editions omit these refinements which are inapplicable to the vast majority of the purchasers of the book. Almost at the end is the most sought-after information on which practically every Chinese bases his daily actions. This is the day-to-day summary of what is unlucky, or lucky, to do. The penalties for transgression are often horrible to contemplate, though many of them are deferred to the next world, where one's relative may catch the blast. Filial piety demands consideration for their comfort, so the calendar is followed with the closest attention.

The book ends as it began, but the Spring Ox for the following year is printed in black, instead of red. Directions for wooing luck, wealth and longevity complete the volume.

THE CREATION

The origin of the Chinese race has baffled anthropologists, for it has left no traces of primitive culture, such as stone implements, in the land it now inhabits. The accepted theory is that tribes which had reached an agricultural stage of civilisation, descended from the mid-Asian highlands and established themselves in the valley of the Yellow River, bringing with them a mythology they had acquired in other lands. They traced their descent to P'an Ku Shih (盤古氏) sometimes called the Chinese Adam, but more nearly corresponding to the Grand Architect of the Universe, for man was the last and least of his productions. He owed his existence to cosmogonical evolution, when the Great Monad separated into the male and female principles (Yang 陽 and Yin 陰). By a similar process these were subdivided into the Greater and Lesser, and from the interaction of the four agencies P'an Ku was produced. P'an is a basin, synonymous with the shell of an egg, and Ku means secure or solid, indicating that he was hatched from chaos and materialised into the shape of the powers which produced him.

His mission, during his existence, was to shape the universe as it is now known, and he is usually represented holding a chisel and fashioning great masses of rock, floating in space. Sun, moon and stars, constructed before he turned his attention to earth, are depicted in the gaps he has hewn out of the granite, and his companions are the four superintelligent creatures, dragon, tiger, phoenix and tortoise. These are the progenitors of the animal kingdom. His labours continued for eighteen thousand years, and, to cope with his gigantic task, he increased in stature six feet every day.

When his task was completed, he died for the benefit of his creation, animating the whole universe. His head was transmuted into mountains, and his breath formed the winds and clouds, whilst his voice may still be heard in the rumblings of thunder. His left eye shines in the sun, whilst the moon owes its light to his right. His beard was transformed into the stars, and his four limbs into the four quarters of the globe. The outlying portions of his anatomy were converted into the five sacred mountains, and his blood provided the irrigation for the rivers. Veins and muscles were the stratification of the earth, and his flesh the soil. Skin sprouted as vegetation and forests, teeth and bones formed minerals, and marrow the pearls and gems. Sweat descended as beneficial rain to produce the crops, and man sprang from the parasites which had accumulated on his body after eighteen milleniums of unremitting toil. It is hardly an attractive explanation of the origin of the human race, and seems to have been invented in the fourth century A.D. by a Taoist recluse, author of the Biographies of the Gods. The theory of the negative and positive principles of universal life, or the First Cause, was probably accepted by the Chinese at the dawn of their civilisation, when more active minds began speculations on the nature of their surroundings, but it needed centuries, and Taoist imagination to embellish the story of evolution into a myth which found general acceptance.

Other records divorce P'an Ku from human form, and give him the head of a dragon and the body of a serpent, the opening of whose eyes produced light, breathing, wind, and utterance, thunder. In the "Elucidation of Historical Records" (史記索隱), Sau Ma Chen (司馬真), writing in 720 A.D., puts the number of years between the creation and the birth of Confucius as 3,276,000.

The disintegration of P'an Ku was followed by an era of giants, materialising as the Heavenly, Terrestrial and Human sovereigns. Their reign lasted eighteen thousand years, conferring many benefits on mankind, for, during this period they learned to eat and sleep, good government was introduced and the relations between the sexes were established. Their successors, Yu Ch'ao Shih (有巢氏) and Sui Jen Shih (燧人氏), advanced the civilisation of mankind by the introduction of housing, fire, and its application in the cooking of food.

Yu Ch'ao Shih's housing programme was, in fact, nothing more advanced than the construction of nests in trees as a protection against wild beasts, and the erection of dwellings on the ground was introduced by Huang Ti (黃締).

Legendary history reaches somewhat firmer ground with the advent of Fu Hsi (伏羲) the first of the Five Emperors who reigned between 2953 and 2838 B.C. Said to have been miraculously born after a gestation period of twelve years at Ch'eng chi, in Shensi, Fu Hsi taught his people to hunt, fish, and tend flocks. He invented implements to split wood, and introduced music by revealing how to twist silken threads into cords. From the patterns on tortoise shell he constructed the Eight Diagrams (Pa Kua 八卦) from which was developed a whole system of philosophy. These are represented by a series of signs consisting of the combination of straight lines arranged in a circle. Created from two primary forms Liang Yih (兩儀), one continuous Yang Yih (陽儀) and one broken in the centre Yin Yih (陰儀), they represent the male and female principles, and figuratively denote the evolution of nature and its cyclical changes.

Wen Wang (文王), founder of the Chou dynasty, devoted himself to a study of these diagrams, appending an explanation to each, which he embodied in an abstruse work, known as I Ching (易經), the Canon of Changes. Its obscurity makes it the most venerated and least understood of all the Chinese classics, so it forms the basis for the philosophy of divination and geomancy, which the layman leaves to professionals.

Fu Hsi is credited with instituting marriage laws to succeed promiscuity, and with extending the boundaries of his Empire to the Eastern seas. His capital was in the province of Honan, but the seat of government was moved to Shantung by his successor Shen Nung (神農). As the patron of Agriculture, this Perfect Emperor was worshipped at a special altar west of the Temple of Heaven in Peking in the Third Moon, when the ceremony of Imperial ploughing was performed.

Fu Hsi and his six successors are alleged to have

covered a period of 596 years, the most distinguished reign being that of Huang Ti (黄締), the Yellow Emperor, who divided his territory on the decimal system. Ten towns made up a district, and ten districts a department. Ten of these went to the province, of which there were ten in the empire. Weights and measures were fixed on the same principle, and he originated the calendar cycle of sixty years. He opened up his empire with communications, building roads and bridges, and constructing ships to carry goods by sea and on the inland waterways. The Yellow Emperor is regarded as the founder of the Chinese State, as his territory extended from the Gulf of Peichihli in the north to the Yangtze in the south, and from the sea to Shensi in the west. Fu Hsi, Shen Nung and Huang Ti have been chosen by the Taoists to preside over their Ministry of Medicine.

Four reigns, covering two hundred and forty-one years intervened between Huang Ti and the great semi-historical characters, the Emperors Yao (堯), Shen, and Yü (禹). Confucius and Mencius never tired of holding them up as shining examples of the Golden Age. It was during this period that China experienced the flood, probably caused by the overflowing of the Yellow River changing its course in the lower reaches. Years of unremitting toil and energy were expended remedying the disaster, and countless lives were sacrificed.

Yü (禹), the third of the Perfect Emperors, founded the Hsia (夏) dynasty (B.C. 2205–1766) and from this period the throne became hereditary, instead of elective as it had previously been.

The Legendary Period

During the decline of the Shang Dynasty (商紀) which covered a period of six hundred years to 1154 B.C. China was rent with civil wars, in which Gods and Immortals were alleged to have participated. The accounts of the struggle are important, less for their historical accuracy, than for their appeal to artists of all subsequent ages. Written in the concise classical style admired by scholars, with what might be termed portmanteau phrases, sinologues in their translations have been apt to cling to the original text so closely that the English meaning is obscure to the ordinary reader. The stories have a parallel in the Nibelungs' Ring so beloved by the Teutons, and a wealth of imagination has been lavished in creating the monsters and giants who contended, lending their assistance impartially first to one side and then to the other. Although the events recorded took place five hundred years before the introduction of organised religion, Taoist Heroes and Immortals figure freely in the narrative. For instance, in the final struggle of the dynasty for survival, one of these, Chun T'i, was summoned to take one of the contestants to the abode of the blest, as he had attained the necessary degree of perfection. The theatre of operations was the middle reaches of the Yellow River in the north of what is now Honan province, where K'ung Hsuan was defending the Chin-chi-ling pass against the troops of Chiang Tzu-ya. As Heaven favoured the cause of the attackers, the removal of the opposing commander was calculated to demoralise the defence, and any scruples of the general about deserting his troop were likely to be overcome by the attractions of immortality. K'ung Hsuan, however, offered strong resistance to the project, and Chun T'i found himself whirled aloft in a luminous rainbow. His magic nevertheless prevailed and he reappeared in a cloud of fire, equipped with eighteen arms and twenty-four heads. Throwing a silken cord round his adversary's neck, he extended his wand and turned him into a one-eyed red peacock. Mounting on the back of his reluctant steed, he crossed the skies to the Western Paradise, leaving a trail of multicoloured clouds.

With the removal of the commander the defence lost heart and the pass was quickly forced. The assault parties were then faced with the key of the position, the village of Chieh-p'ai Kuan, which was held by a host of genii and Immortals led by a powerful Taoist, T'ung T'ien Chiao-chu (通天主教). It was a formidable stronghold, and the attackers were forced to call on the assistance of Lao Tze himself, who descended from the heavens to organise the assault. Like all primitive Chinese towns walled for defence, the place had four gates at the cardinal points of the compass and, as there were only three commanders, Chun T'i had to be recalled after his successful mission. All previous attempts at effecting an entry had failed with heavy losses, for immediately a soldier crossed the threshold a clap of thunder resounded, and a mysterious sword which flashed lightning descended on his neck. Chun T'i was in the van of his assault column and would have suffered a similar fate had he lacked the protection of his Seven Precious branches, which he carried as an umbrella.

As soon as the lightning heralded the descent of the sword the branches blossomed into myriads of lotus blooms, which formed an impenetrable shield. The other gates being forced simultaneously, a grand attack was launched on the citadel of the place. T'ung T'ien Chiao-chu with the remnants of his army stood at bay, facing his celestial foes. He made an onslaught on the most lightly armed, Chieh Yin Tao-jen, who carried nothing more formidable than a fly whisk. His sword stroke was parried by a five-coloured lotus, which sprouted from this innocent looking implement, and he had not recovered from his astonishment when he was set upon by Lao Tze with his staff, and Yuan Shih T'ien-tsun with his jade mace. Chun T'i, also intervened in the melee by materialising one of his spiritual peacocks, who took the form of a giant with twenty-four heads and eighteen arms. This imposing array of strength completely disconcerted Tung T'ien Chiao-chu who fled in a whirlwind of dust. With the departure of its leader the defence collapsed, and Yuan Shih T'ien-tsun was left master of the field.

The discomfited T'ung T'ien however was loath to admit defeat, and was determined on his revenge. He evoked the spirits of the Twenty-eight constellations, and again took the field. His adversary was Wu Wang (武王) a feudatory prince of the state of Chou, who eventually founded the dynasty of that name (周紀). Chun T'i again lent his assistance to the adversaries of the Shangs. When they closed for battle, he disarmed both the Immortal Wu Yun and T'ung T'ien Chiao-chu himself. The former wielded a magic sword with which he attacked Chun-T'i, but all his blows were parried by a blue lotus flower, which was handled with great dexterity. Finally, the sword was shattered when it fell upon a magic wand, and when the useless weapon was exchanged for a club, no better success was achieved. Chun T'i, having disarmed him, decided to break off the duel, and summoned a disciple who carried a long bamboo pole like a fishing rod. At the tip was a line furnished with a large hook, from which dangled a golden-bearded turtle. This was none other than Wu Yun himself, whose defeat had forced him to assume his original form as the Great Spiritual Tortoise. In this guise he was despatched in charge of the disciple to the Western Heavens, where he was admonished to leave mundane affairs alone in the future. Having disposed of celestial opposition, Chun T'i was now free to deal with the earthly commander T'ung T'ien Chiao-chu, who, finding no means of coping with his Immortal adversary, left the field and was never heard of again. One of his subordinates, P'i Lu Hsien, seeing his master defeated on two successive occasions, was so impressed that he followed his conqueror to the Western Heavens, where he attained Buddhahood. He is known as P'i Lu Fo, and ranks high in the hierarchy of the religion.

Chun T'i's festival is celebrated on the sixth day of the Third Moon, and his effigy usually carries eight arms and three faces, one of which is that of a pig.

FAMILY LORE

Chinese Family Names

Chinese names are always a stumbling-block for foreigners who, without instruction, are doubtful which of the three characters is the surname, and which correspond to given or personal names.

The Chinese are far more lavish than the Westerner in their appelations for, though an individual keeps his surname for life (unless criminally known to the police), at every memorable event of his career, such as entering school or getting married, he adds to his stock. Thus he gradually acquires a variety of names by which he is known to different sections of society from his school friends to his business acquaintances, or fellow artists.

The surnames recorded in the Pai Chia Hsing (百家姓), or the "Hundred Family names", total four hundred and eight single, and thirty double, clan names of which the commonest are Wang, Chang and Li. It is one of the first tasks of a child entering school to commit them to memory. As in our telephone directory the surname comes first, and the names which distinguish a particular member of the family follow.

About a month after a boy's birth a feast is given, and he is endowed with his "Milk name" (乳名), which entitles him for the first time to recognition in society. The event corresponds to a christening when a child is received into the Church. The name sticks to him for life, as do all his later names, but is usually reserved for use in the family by relatives and neighbours who have known him from infancy. It can be used in official matters if he has no "Book name". It generally consists of a single syllable but, for euphony, south of the Yangtze the honorific prefix "Ah" (阿) is usually appended, whilst in the north "Hsiao" (小), or "Little", is substituted.

On entry into school, a great event still in the lives of the Chinese, the occasion is marked by the bestowal of a new name called the Book (Shu 書名) or School name (學名) which consists usually of two characters reflecting on his condition, prospects, studies, or some other event connected with him. He is addressed by this title by his teacher and schoolfellows, in official matters and in anything concerned with literature.

On marriage a youth adds two more names to his collection, his "Style" or "Great Name" (Tzu 字), which his parents and relatives use, as well as his Milk name, and for acquaintances and friends outside the family circle another style is adopted called the "Hao" (號). These follow the surname but, since the Revolution, Chinese much in contact with foreigners sometimes reverse the order, and adopt the Western practice of converting the Hao into initials. Well-known examples are T. V. Soong, C. T. Wang and the late V. K. Ting. Occasionally, like Wellington Koo, Minister of Foreign Affairs and Ambassador, the "Wei Lin" of the Hao has been converted into a similarly sounding Christian name.

In addition to these, every scholar, in the old days at any rate, assumed one or more "Studio names" (Pieh Hao 別號), and officials on taking a degree, or entering into Government service, added an "Official name" (Kuan Ming 官名) to their other means of identification.

After death a man was known by a posthumous name (Shih Hao 諡號), inscribed on his tablet in the Hall of the Ancestors. The Imperial Family dead were provided with a Temple name (Miao Hao 廟號), and it is by these that past emperors are always referred to. The ruler's name during his lifetime was completely taboo, and only the reign title, which had nothing to do with the individual occupying the throne, described the period of his control. These Temple names can usually be translated as the "Lofty", "Virtuous", or "Exalted" Ancestor. The Sovereign's personal name was regarded as so sacred that no one was permitted to utter, write, or make use of a phrase which vaguely resembled it as long as the same family remained on the throne, even after the death of the monarch who bore it. To prevent a subject from being indicted for the offence of *lèse majesté* the characters composing the name were altered by changing or adding to their components. This taboo was carried even further for it is not considered proper for a child to use his own parents' personal names which implies disrespect.

As might be expected where large families are the rule rather than the exception, children are often simply numbered off and, though "junior" is on the debarred list, "Primus", "Secundus" and "Tertius" up to "Duodecima" are common appelations. To avert the attention of evil spirits who may wish to deprive a man of his only son, the boy may be called by some name calculated to discourage further investigation such as "Puppy", or his head may be shaved and he may answer to the nickname "Buddhist priest". Nicknames are universal, and usually reflect on a man's physical peculiarities. Dwarfy, Fatty, Flat-nose are some of the terms of address, whilst the visitation of smallpox sticks to an individual long after he has recovered from the disease. It is difficult to find out what the Chinese call foreigners but, in Tientsin, a long-legged jockey was always referred to as Hou Ch'i Yang (猴騎羊), or Monkey riding a sheep. Another gentleman in a well-known firm, whose name was a household word for dog condition powders, was first called "Dog Drugs" and later, as his popularity decreased, "Beneath the notice of a dog", or Kou Pu Li (狗不利).

The nomenclature of girls is much more simple than that of their brothers as they are reduced to a Milk name, a marriage name, and nicknames. After her wedding a girl retains her maiden surname, and is only addressed by that of her husband through courtesy. In official documents her two surnames are given, the combination serving to identify her. Thus if her maiden surname were Chang, and she married into the Li clan, she would be designated Li Chang Shih (李張氏), the last character corresponding to née Chang, as that was her first name. A well-born Chinese woman will never divulge her personal name, even in court. Strangers have to be content with the combination cited above of the two surnames, for she labours under the apprehension that, were it revealed, some mannerless lout would address her by it. The wives of the lower classes do not suffer from this inhibition, and will tell their names freely in most places, though in certain districts a woman will only give the husband's name (not surname) followed by the word sister, aunt, or mother, according to the age of the person in question.

The Chun Ming (郡名), or territorial appellation, is hardly ever used except for girls on their marriage documents. A list of these geographical names corresponding to the clans is given in *Giles' Dictionary*.

A further complication is introduced by the use in some case of T'ang Ming (堂名) or Family Hall names. These are arbitrary, and are chosen in connection with some event in the family's history. The characters are generally inscribed in one of the principal rooms of the mansion, and are used on tombstones and in legal deeds. A man of means, in possession of an estate, is sure to have one of these, which he has probably inherited from his family unless he is a self-made man, in which case he has to invent one. It represents himself, and also his family. On his death, his sons (if they continue together in the same compound, as is usually the case) retain the name, and use it either together or separately. If brothers separate, and set up individual establishments, they add certain characters to the T'ang Name, indicating cadet branches numbered according to seniority.

The T'ang name is often used in business, some partners using it whilst others are registered under their normal cognomens. The practice leads to endless difficulty in fixing responsibility in the case of bankruptcy proceedings.

The choice of personal names for children is in the hands of the parents, though, in selecting the style, in some districts the recipients are consulted. It is very general to find the first character constant throughout a generation of brothers and cousins, the clan selecting from a word in some poem which has been adopted by the family. The system was extended in the case of the Imperial family where all collaterals of the same generation bore the same initial character. Thus the generation of the Emperor who reigned under the title of Kuang Hsu (光緒) was Ts'ai whilst his successor's was P'u. The succeeding generation is Yu.

It is a common mistake of Westerners to refer to an emperor by his reign title, and to write about Lord Macartney's embassy to Ch'ien Lung. Samuel Pepys might just as well have entered in his famous diary when summoned to Court that he had had an interview with the "Restoration", or Evelyn when criticising Oliver Cromwell have called him the Commonwealth. The only admissible name for the greatest and best known of the Manchu emperors, when his personality is in question, is Kao Tsung (高宗), or the "Lofty Ancestor".

The multiplicity of names describing any individual is undoubtedly confusing to the foreigner but, in his relations with his Chinese friends, only their clan or surnames are of importance for direct intercourse. Should an acquaintance or public figure crop up in conversation he must be referred to by his surname and the style he has adopted for identification outside his own family circle.

Children in China

In the days of Queen Victoria, the average Englishman's knowledge of the manners and customs of the Chinese was confined to the contents of a missionary sermon, and the sensational literature typified by Dr. Fu Manchu. From the former he learned that the heathen were addicted, not only to black idolatry, but to such reprehensible practices as foot-binding, and female infanticide. An uncritical mind accepted all these statements without reserve but, should the monstrous assertion that the whole of the female population was murdered be investigated, it invariably turned out that its author could furnish only hearsay evidence. Though the preacher himself had never come across an actual case in his parish, he knew of districts in which it had occurred. In any case it made excellent propaganda, and the mission received corresponding support. It was known that the Chinese practised polygamy, but it never occurred to anyone to query their source of surplus women. The Church inveighed against female slavery in the form of the Mui Tsai system, but failed to explain the source of supply, and how it could be reconciled with wholesale extermination. Dyer Ball, who injects a good deal of prejudice into what he says about the Chinese, in writing on this subject says, "The longer one lives in China the more one feels the necessity for caution in saying what does, and what does not, exist here. Some authors have been egregious sinners in thus writing about a small part of China in which they have resided: they have judged the whole of this vast empire, with its diverse inhabitants, manners and customs, from a small part of it, reversing the mathematical axiom that the whole contains its parts, into 'one small part contains the whole'."

From a commonsense point of view, there is no reason to believe that in China female births are greatly in excess of male. To satisfy the needs of ancestral worship an heir must be produced, so each boy must find a wife at eighteen. Should she be sterile, he may take a second to ensure the succession. There is, consequently, a definite need for a superfluity of the weaker sex on religious grounds alone. What probably appeals quite as much to the poorer classes is that a girl has a marketable value and, should the worst come to the worst, and starvation prevent her being reared, a home can always be found for her. The Mui Tsai system probably differs little from the old custom of apprenticeship in the Middle Ages in which a child was bound for a certain number of years. The employers have definite obligations towards their bondmaids, who are nurtured in a gentler atmosphere than that obtaining in the hovels which witnessed their birth. Their labour is probably much lighter than in the rice-fields, and they must be liberated, and married at the age of eighteen.

Even in Hong Kong, children are readily marketable and girls are bought for companionship by childless wives. Should a boy be purchased, he is regularly enrolled in the clan, and is entitled to his share out of property on the decease of his adoptive father. A young mother, although her primary object in life is to ensure the male succession, often welcomes a girl as the first-born, as she acts as unpaid nurse for the younger children, besides being a help with the household chores. In the case of failure to produce the desired heir, adoption is frequent. If possible, a relative with a superfluity of boys is approached to make over one of them to undertake the responsibilities of ancestral worship for his kinsman. Failing such an arrangement, recourse is had to purchase. The Chinese adoption of agnates is not a matter of choice, but of compulsion. The brother, when living, may demand a nephew, and, when dead, a nephew is given to him unasked. It is not only in his interest, but in that of the whole family, that the succession should be continued.

There is absolutely no distinction between such an adopted child, and a natural son. He cannot be disinherited, at least for any reason not applicable to a natural son, and he pays the respects due to his dead adoptive father as a son, and to his natural father as a nephew.

Should a man die, over the age of sixteen, without heirs to carry out the ancestral worship, a child may be adopted by his family and recognised as his son, and lawful successor. Probably about five per cent of Chinese families adopt children, seventy per cent of them being males. In some provinces the custom of adopting the children of strangers is prevalent, and the merchants of Amoy have a custom of adopting sons to act for them as agents overseas. In this case, the acquisition of the child is usually by purchase, though the demand has also stimulated a source of supply from kidnappers.

The myth of wholesale infanticide was probably engendered by the burial customs of the Chinese, which deny the right of sepulchure to children of tender age. It is considered unlucky to bury a child of under three, for fear of death striking at another member of the family. Consequently the tiny bodies are often left exposed, sometimes near a public cemetery, and sometimes on the seashore, or consigned to the current of a river. One of the protagonists of infanticide states that in the Northern cities baby towers are provided, perhaps for unwanted children, though they are principally used for receiving the dead bodies of infants. In discussing infant mortality in Hong Kong fifty years ago, Dyer Ball asserts that only 72 per thousand survived their first year, so in rural areas where Chinese medicine held sway the problem of the disposal of corpses must have assumed an alarming aspect. The Boat People alone recognise the child to possess a soul which is commemorated after death, and make images of their deceased children, the boys mounted on lions, and the girls on white cranes.

Generally speaking the Chinese are devoted to their offspring, and take the greatest pride in their accomplishments. They are never corrected for risking their lives in a last-minute dash in front of a motorcar, but are picked up and congratulated for putting life and limb in peril. This is because a close shave by another individual cuts off one's bad luck, and transfers it to the individual who has crossed one's path. Should the adventure end in a fatality, the chauffeur is invariably held to blame in a native Court of Law, on the grounds that as a car goes faster than a child its driver must be in the wrong. Chinese jurisprudence takes no account of accident, and is only concerned in fixing responsibility. The delectable game of "last across" can also be played with junks, who shave under the bows of an oncoming steamer, on the principle that the narrower the escape

the more completely are their besetting devils cut off. As steam must give way to sail, their manoeuvres engender a good deal of hard swearing from the bridge.

Chinese children are far less quarrelsome than European, and they seem to lack the competitive and possessive spirit which is the cause of so many infantile squabbles. The small girls mother the brood, and carry their young brothers on their backs without attempting to compete with them for the possession of the plaything of the moment. The English child cannot see another engaged with a toy without feeling the impulse to do something better with it. Disputes then arise ending in violence and tears. This never seems to occur in a Chinese family, where the child certainly possesses more self-control. A girl will pick up a new toy after her brothers have abandoned it, but will never prefer a claim for "fair shares for all" when it first makes its appearance. The motive is certainly tolerance rather than apathy, and a spirit of sweet reasonableness pervades all childish games. Girls, when they grow up, are a dead loss to the family for, on marriage (always an expensive affair to the parents), they leave the clan, and move to that of the husband. The value set on children may be gauged from the number wearing amulets in the streets of Hong Kong. A boy is often dressed as a girl to make evil spirits believe he is not worth claiming. Protective amulets of all sorts are worn, a favourite one including a silver dog-collar, to ensure his being passed over as something worthless. There is a regular assortment of silver charms, always comprising a lock, a chicken's leg, and a bell. Jade or silver anklets are worn, again to give the illusion that the infant is of the other sex and, lest the child should be afraid of dogs, a scrap of fur is sometimes included in the assortment. On festivals the children accompany their parents everywhere, and are not regarded as extras. The Chinese fail to comprehend that they occupy space and, if it is a question of reckoning numbers for land, or water transport, conveniently count them out. They feel most indignant should fares be required, or charges of overloading be levelled on account of the family.

The paying of attentions to Chinese children is usually a sure way to the parents' hearts. A recognised method of slipping a bribe to an official in the days before the Communists' clean-up was to send a gaudy picture-book to the son and heir, inadvertently forgetting a note of high denomination left between the leaves.

There are no inhibitions about late hours, and the children on holidays stay up with the elders to all hours of the night. On the other hand, like dogs and cats, they seem capable of taking a nap at any time, and curl up no matter where they are set down. Ideas of comfort are very primitive, if indeed they exist at all. The labourer will go to sleep, with his hoe for a pillow, to ensure that it is not stolen, in the middle of the highway, and the children are just as indifferent to the hardness of their resting places.

The Babies' First Run

The Confucian, or scholarly, interpretation of religion was intensely conservative, and clung to the primeval conceptions of the Chinese race which still form the core of its various forms of worship. The oldest, and holiest books of the Empire lay down that the universe consists of twin souls or breaths, the Yang (陽) and the Yin (陰). The former represents light, warmth, productivity and life, and the heaven from which they proceed, whilst the Yin holds sway over darkness, death, and the earth. The Yang harbours a multitude of Shen (聖), or Saints, to do its bidding, whilst the Yin's myrmidons are the Kuei (鬼), including demons which beset the path of man. Both are equally worthy of worship, the Saints for the restraining influence they may exercise on the devils, and the Kuei to induce them to transfer their attentions to those who are more lax in placating them.

Even man's soul is composed of these two elements: his "hun" (魂) emanating from heaven constitutes his finer qualities of intellect and virtues, whilst the earthy "p'o" (魄) represents his passions and vices. The first returns to heaven on his demise, whilst the second accompanies him to the tomb. The Yang and Yin together compose the Tao (道), or order of the universe. It never occurred to the imagination of the inventors of this animistic conception that some force must have brought it into being, and that a Supreme Power, or Creator, was worthy of worship.

The Confucian literati who governed the country were always bitterly opposed to any innovations, and the organised religions of Buddhism and Taoism were frequently persecuted as heresies dangerous to the welfare of the State. Both were obliged to admit the primitive conceptions to their liturgy, and accept its divinities in their pantheon. Competition for congregations also led to an interchange of saints.

In the Christian church a child is brought as soon as possible to the sacred edifice for baptism, by which it is received into the community. In China a baby's existence is officially ignored until it is a month old. Then a reception is held in its honour, and it is duly presented to the world.

Its religious life also starts simultaneously, for it is taken to the temple to acquaint the gods of its fathers with its existence. If a young mother is blessed with twins of different sexes it is considered highly auspicious if the boy makes his appearance into the world first, for then a dragon and a phoenix are born. As soon as they are a month old both are wrapped in red robes to be carried in the arms, and not on the back, to the temple. The mother takes charge of the son, whilst her mother-in-law follows with the daughter. An amah leads the procession carrying a tray with the sacrifices of chicken and eggs. On arrival at the shrine three candles are lighted in the incense burner before the Queen of Heaven, and a stick of incense is placed in the receptacles before each divinity, that none may feel neglected. Only four, however, are invoked to protect the children, and to attract their attention a "Call spirit flag" (招魂旛) is planted in each of their incense burners. The first to be honoured is the Patron of the Temple T'ien Hou, and, after her spirit has been invoked, Kuan Yin, whose shrine is always near at hand. The Hsuan T'an (玄壇), or Dark Altar, accommodates nine separate protective divinities, presided over by a tiger, who are sworn enemies of every sort of demon or adverse influence, so an introduction here is indispensable. Finally the City Gods, or Ch'eng Huang (城隍), who are responsible for all departed spirits in the parish, must be invoked.

The sacrifices are laid by the amah before the main altar, and the mother takes her stand facing it with her son in her arms. She presents him by raising her hands to the level of her chin, and then bowing three times till the infant is just above the knee. This dedication is repeated, kneeling. The mother-in-law hands over the girl, who is presented in like fashion. No priest is involved in the ceremony, but the fortune-teller, who combines the parts, lays out his paraphernalia on a table behind the altar which carries the five vessels, in hopes of patronage. In this case he is disappointed for the service ends with an ear-splitting detonation of a bunch of firecrackers, set off by the amah in the central court. These explosions are supposed to clear the way of the returning procession from any lurking demons.

A local belief, almost incomprehensible to Western mentality, is that if a child falls into water, and is in danger of drowning, no parent or relative may rescue it or it will surely die. Considering the gambling instinct which is so prevalent in the race, it would be thought that the barest chance of survival would be preferable to the certainty of destruction for the want of a saving hand.

The Care of Children

The ensurance of a healthy posterity to fulfil ancestral observances and care for the souls of the departed is of such paramount importance in Chinese family-life that it causes no surprise to find numerous divinities specially charged with children's welfare. Even before marriage the Seventh or Tzu Sun Niang Niang (子孫娘娘) is approached at the Amah Rock by engaged couples who invoke her blessing on a fruitful union, and at the wedding feast special cakes, called Tzu Sun Po Po (子孫婆婆), are eaten in her honour by the bridal couple as they sit side by side after the ceremony.

Births are announced to the T'u Ti, or God of the Locality, who may serve a household, compound, or the whole village, and acts as registrar of its increase or decline. He is immediately informed of any sickness in the family, and the cures he effects are commemorated by votive offerings of rags, or an inscription to decorate his shrine. Tree spirits have always been credited with healing properties and every village in Hong Kong has one or more banyan which acts in the capacity of its physician.

Although Western medicine may be said to be fairly established, and most women trust themselves to maternity hospitals rather than witch doctors, belief in the efficacy of the gods is by no means extinguished, and they are usually called in to assist in the cure. Quite recently an earth-coolie woman sent her sick child to hospital where a kidney complaint was diagnosed. She promptly repaired to the T'ien Hou temple and burned incense before the presiding goddess. In her prayer she offered a chicken, pork, fruit, paper clothing and crackers for divine assistance in the recovery of her child. She then cast the divining woods, but three times in succession they fell adversely, and it was evident that her terms had not been accepted. However, she was a resourceful woman. She apologised to the Deity for promising so much, as she felt that the sacrifice might be regarded as too ostentatious for one of her low degree, and made a fresh vow more in keeping with her means. Four oranges, a personal gift of two gilt talismans mounted on red paper, a catty of oil for altar lamps and the usual clothing and crackers were substituted for the more lavish sacrifice. Recourse to the dice immediately elicited a favourable reply and, as the hospital discharged the child in perfect health, she saved herself ten dollars on the transaction. As far as this suppliant is concerned Ma Ku's (麻姑) curative capacity is firmly established as, like the confessor in Gilbert's ballad of Gentle Alice Brown, "she does these little things for her so singularly cheap".

The Queen of Heaven, as a matter of fact, is less of a child specialist than a general practitioner. She has been vested by the Taoists with many of the attributes of her Buddhist rival Kuan Yin, and hears all petitions with a sympathetic ear. In her capacity as the Mother of the Measure (斗母), a Star Goddess, she holds the books of life and death.

Probably the most efficacious divinity in this particular temple is the Ch'eng Huang (城隍), or City God, who sits with his court at the east end of the sanctuary. He has among his attendants two children, "instead of a boy" and "instead of a girl", and petitions to substitute one or the other for an ailing child are often made by his worshippers. In this case, however, he is only a guest, a refugee from the Mainland awaiting the day when a more tolerant administration will restore him to his parishioners.

Children have no lack of protectors, for their prenatal care is entrusted to Chang Hsien (張仙), whose portrait, bow in hand, hangs in the sleeping apartment. With his arrow he is prepared to shoot down the Heavenly Dog who roams the skies seeking to devour the young and innocent. Chang is the patron of pregnant women and, during the Sung Dynasty, was worshipped by those desirous of offspring. Another version of the origin of this deity also dates from the Sungs, whose Emperor Jen Tsung dreamed of a handsome youth with a white skin and black hair, who carried a bow. He informed the ruler that the Star T'ien Kou (the Heavenly Dog) (天狗) was in the sky threatening the sun and moon, whilst on earth it devoured little children. Only his presence kept it at bay. On waking, the Emperor ordered a portrait of the young man to be prepared from his description and put on exhibition. From the date it was made public, childless families adopted the habit of writing the name Chang Hsien on tablets which they worshipped. As a stellar deity Chang presides over the culinary department of the gods, and orders the banquets.

A picturesque relic of old China makes the round of the villages on the island, announcing his presence with a handbell. He wears a floppy straw-hat and long grey gown to his ankles, and carries on his back a chest of drugs surmounted by a live monkey. Painted on the box is the inscription, Liu Jih-huai (劉日輝) of Lo Fu Shan (羅浮山). This is a famous monastery in Kwangtung, where the monks are believed to impart, not only a thorough knowledge of medicine, but the appropriate spells which double its efficacy. A graduate of Lo Fu Shan consequently acquires a prestige which exalts him over his fellow practitioners as would a Harley Street address among Panel doctors.

His qualifications are painted under his name and state that he is a children's specialist with sovereign remedies for flatulence and constipation. There is something mediaeval about his make-up, which conjures up visions of the Leech of Folkestone, with a stuffed crocodile somewhere in the background. One wonders if the monkey is merely an advertisement, or if he acts as dispenser. From the casual way in which Chinese select their remedies by casting lots in a temple, it is not beyond the bounds of possibility that he combines the parts. Every fortune-teller and quack in Hong Kong claims to be a graduate of Lo Fu Shan, but the old doctor's pantomime is so convincing that he deserves the benefit of the doubt.

Children's doctor

Birthdays

Foreigners are often surprised to find that Chinese conventions are the exact opposite of their own, and form the opinion that they have dropped into a topsy-turvy world. There is, however, no right and wrong in such matters though there is sometimes a logical reason for adhering to one habit rather than another. The rule of the road, for instance, dates from the days when only the quality were mounted, and the hazards of travel were such that cavaliers preferred to pass a stranger sword hand to sword hand. When the methods of roadmaking advanced to such a stage that wheeled traffic was possible, the driver was placed on the right of the vehicle so that the lash of his whip would not incommode the passengers behind him. Europeans, with close communications and considerable intercourse for the purposes of trade, had many opportunities of observing one another's mode of life and adopted foreign conventions if they found them more practical than their own. China, on the other hand, was surrounded by civilisations inferior to her own, and most of her neighbours were barbarians from whom she had nothing to learn. Thus traffic kept to the left, until the influx of American cars altered an age-old tradition.

Birthdays in Europe are the highlight of a child's existence, while grown up people tend to dislike being reminded of their age, but in China the reverence for seniority causes children to be ignored and adults to be congratulated on having passed another milestone on the road to longevity. Very little notice is taken of a child though, in the Shun Tak district of Kwangtung province, a mother will give her offspring a steamed egg for breakfast as the yolk, with the Chinese indifference to colour values, is deemed to be red. Its consumption will redden the heart of the child (Hung Hsin 紅心) and make it enthusiastic or diligent. A few parents also give presents or toys in the same district, but this mark of attention is the exception rather than the rule throughout the country.

The red letter day in a child's life is when it has survived for a month, before which date it is not regarded as a member of society, and the first anniversary of its birth is also observed. Infant mortality in China was abnormally high and, to ensure the favour of the Gods, children are brought to the local temple as soon as they are fit to be taken out, though the Boat People usually wait till they are about a year old to include them in the annual pilgrimage to the Queen of Heaven or Tam Kung's festivals. On these occasions another junk may be sent on ahead very early in the morning to keep a berth in front of the building, and the presentation is marked with a tremendous firework display. As the string of crackers burns upwards, wooden discs open like oysters, each displaying a Chinese character of auspicious omen. Presents consist mainly of food, but on the first anniversary different articles are placed before the child to determine the path of life in which he is most likely to succeed. Pens and paper indicate a scholarly bent, whilst an abacus portends a business career. Tools of a trade are also offered, and the choice displayed by the infant is taken as an omen for his future.

Afterwards, no notice is taken of a birthday till a youth or maiden comes of age, and marriage is contemplated. This is when the boy reaches sixteen, though girls often wed at fourteen. Birthdays then assume much more importance, and the parents-in-law send presents of food and clothing, but whether the lad's own father and mother mark the occasion with gifts is at their own discretion. Generally speaking, it is not considered proper for those closely related to make presents, as there is no ceremony between those nearly akin, and the bearing of offerings partakes of outward form.

All sons and daughter have to prostrate themselves before their parents on their birthdays and at the New Year, in old-fashioned families, and wish them a long life. This practice was universally observed, except by the dregs of society, and was called Pai Shou (拜壽). In certain disticts of Kwang Tung the young children used to club together and buy sweetmeats, such as dried fruit, which were boiled in water, the liquid being presented to their parents to drink. When grown up, the occasion was marked with a wine party given by the younger member of the household, to which relatives on both sides of the family were invited. Chicken and long-life noodles were an essential part of the feast.

The most important anniversaries for a man were the years 21, 31, and so on, when he entered a fresh decade. The odd numbers, pertaining to the Yang (陽) or male principle, were especially appropriate to his sex, and in Canton province at least, the distaff side was differentiated by observing the 20th, 30th year, where even numbers prevail.

New Year is everybody's birthday, as it is from that date that age is reckoned, regardless of the actual day the individual first saw the light. Once that morning dawns every man, woman, and child is a year older. Part of the celebrations of the festival consist in firing crackers in honour of the domestic animals and grains, on which man depends for subsistence. The first of the year is the birthday of the chickens, the second of the dogs, third pigs, fourth ducks, fifth oxen, sixth horses, whilst on the seventh there is a universal birthday of mankind. Cereals follow the livestock, with rice on the eighth, fruit and vegetables of the ninth, and wheat and barley on the tenth. Various rites must be performed to secure the best returns, and the pigs' festival entails a sacrifice to the God of Wealth. On the Ducks' Day the public bath-houses reopen, and priests are employed to ensure an auspicious result. A chicken has to be provided, whose blood is sprayed on the doorposts of the establishment to guarantee that nobody is drowned or asphyxiated in the steam. It is lucky to visit relations on the Horses' birthday, but on the universal day of mankind one should stay at home and eat red beans, to the number of seven for a man and fourteen for a woman. This is a prophylactic against sickness valid for a year.

All the divinities in the Buddhist and Taoist pantheon have their birthdays, which correspond to the Saints Days in the western calendar. The Gods are visited with offerings by those who have found their intervention in their affairs successful, and each temple reaps its annual harvest from the donations at the festival of its patron saint.

Etiquette

China, prior to her contact with European traders, had enjoyed milleniums of isolation, surrounded by nomadic tribes who contributed nothing to her culture. Her civilisation was already set by the time the race was established in the upper reaches of the Yellow River, for there is no evidence of a Stone Age in the history of the Chinese, though palaeolithic and neolithic implements, fashioned by aborigines, have been found in the soil of the empire she conquered.

As each successive dynasty decayed and became effete, waves of more virile barbarians invaded China and seized power, but all, without exception, eventually succumbed to the superior civilisation of the conquered country, and were absorbed until indistinguishable from the native. The last emperor of the Manchus, though a fine Chinese scholar, whose poems were accepted and printed anonymously by Republican publishers, could not speak a word of his own language. Outside competition was so negligible, and the strength of the empire so over-whelming, that the Chinese assumed that they had nothing to learn from distant savages until they were forced to admit their superior military technique. The soldier has never enjoyed a high reputation in the Middle Kingdom, where compromise was always preferred to bloodshed, and a face-saving line of retreat was invariably left open to an adversary.

One of the main difficulties of foreign intercourse was the refusal of the Western representatives to comply with Chinese etiquette, and accord to the Emperor the customary salute. The Chinese ruler was entitled to divine honours, and the neglect of the kow-tow to the great Kao Tsung was as insulting as Ribbentrop's Nazi salute to His Majesty King George V. The prostration, when performed in the long robes of a Chinese official, is a graceful gesture, no more objectionable than the Court courtsey of a debutante at a presentation, though the attitude is ridiculous in Western diplomatic uniform.

Many Chinese customs are the direct opposite of those adopted in the West. The principal guest is seated on the left instead of the right, and a horse is mounted on the off side. Women wear trousers, and men the long gown. Instead of shaking hands with an acquaintance as earnest that a weapon will not be used against him, the Chinese clasps his own hands before him and moves them up and down several times, To a superior they are raised as high as the forehead, and the gesture is accompanied by a profound bow. Ladies should take the left sleeve in the right hand, and imitate the motion. In beckoning, the finger was held down rather than up.

Both hands are used to pass an object, and it indicates slovenliness to employ only one. Similarly, the recipient should use both in accepting a cup of tea or anything that is offered.

Chinese entertaining is done at restaurants, and among the old-fashioned a stranger is never invited into the home for a meal. An eating house with a large clientele has ingredients and flavourings beyond the capacity of anything but a palace, so more honour can be done to the guest. According to old custom men and women eat separately, even husband and wife, and younger members of the family wait till their elders are seated before joining the circle. After the meal it is customary to wipe the face and hands with a towel wrung out in boiling water. These are brought round by the servants at a restaurant, but in the family each member will leave the table to perform his ablutions.

The host must see his guest to the door, the latter begging him to restrain his footsteps to which the answer is that politeness demands the attention.

It is the host's business to see that the wine circulates, and it should never be poured out by servants.

Communications are woefully inadequate in a country so highly cultivated as China, where every parcel of land is exploited. No such thing as a right of way exists, and the farmer has a perfect right to plough up a footpath crossing his field. Similarly his neighbour has equal justification in walking through the crops to take his produce to market. As a result a compromise is effected by leaving a single-file track, cultivated to the very verge. Custom accords the right of way to the man with a burden regardless of rank, and the unencumbered individual steps aside to let him pass.

One of the principal causes of friction between the Chinese and the Westerner has always been the time factor which, until the Communists placed themselves under Russian tuition, never occurred to the Oriental. That time was money was simply incomprehensible to a population who had oceans of time and very little cash. Bargaining for an article was part of the day's entertainment, and the vendor felt cheated if his first price were accepted. An important deal necessitated adjournment to a back room where endless cups of tea were consumed, and every possible subject was exhausted before business was discussed. When a deal is in progress, the results of which neither side is anxious to disclose to the world at large, the two principles close and place their hands inside each other's sleeve. The bargaining is carried out by applying pressure to each other's wrist, one raising his bid, and the other reducing his original demand until the sale is effected or the would-be purchaser cries off.

Politeness and the small rules of etiquette were so ingrained in every Chinese that he despised those who were ignorant of his normal conventions. The usual term of abuse was the epithet describing the tortoise, the creature which has forgotten the eight laws of politeness, abbreviated to "Forgotten eight", or the spawn of such a reptile. Inability to conform to Chinese ideals in ceremony, as well as in more important matters, is partly responsible for their superiority complex towards races who, they think, will not or cannot be made to understand propriety.

Chinese Dress

Though the Chinese office-worker has to a great extent adopted the fashions of the West, the conservative peasantry still clings closely to the old traditions and turns its back on mass production. One of the main winter occupations of the women, once the harvest is gathered, is the fabrication of clothing for the family, and its needs are few. The basic conception is a loose pair of trousers for both sexes, and an almost equally loose-fitting coat. With these two essentials a Chinese is completely dressed, and the embellishments are not necessities but luxuries. Other articles are added, owing to the weather, or the length of the owner's purse, but are merely, with the exception of footwear and headgear, an elaboration of the basic idea. In the North, where the winters are bitter, and the sumer sun sends the thermometer above 100 degrees Fahrenheit, extra layers are added with each drop of the autumn temperature till the Great Cold in January, after which they are shed progressively with the return of spring. In May, the children have got down to their birthday suits, their bodies appearing tallowy white, whilst their faces, with exposure to the sun and wind, are as brown as berries.

Though the scholar and house-boy may affect the long robe, there is no difference in the cut, and it is still the jacket which comes to the ankles instead of ending at the base of the spine. The waistcoat is built the same way, and simply lacks the sleeves. In the North, women's jackets are longer than the men's, reaching well towards the knees, a trait noticeable in the dress of Hakkas of Hong Kong who originated in the province of Shantung, and their sleeves are wider.

The collar usually fits tight to the neck. The décolleté of European women on their first contacts with the Chinese must have been little short of scandalous, as modesty is an agelong tradition. Old ivories are distinguishable by the fact that the drapery of female figures invariably comes up to the neck, whilst the arms, and sometimes the hands, are similarly concealed. In dressmaking, the fitting of the collar is really the one difficult operation, and there seems to be no rule of thumb by which the art can be acquired.

The trousers are as adaptable as the jacket. In the South they are worn loose, and rolled up to the knee

Raincoats

for work in the rice fields, but in the North draughts are excluded by tucking them into white socks and securing them with a black band round the ankle. They are kept up by a girdle at the waist, where there is unlimited fullness, as no attempt is made to shape them to the human anatomy. The fact that the waist is smaller than the hips has no more occurred to the Chinese than it did to the London tailors till the end of the first decade of the present century.

In purely native dress nothing in the form of a vest or shirt is worn, though the habit has spread owing to the example of foreigners and the flooding of the country with cheap Japanese and locally made underwear. The women's innermost garment is of close-fitting thin material, tightly buttoned up the front but, above this, the usual piling up of jackets takes place should the weather warrant it.

Cotton is the universal wear as the Chinese have reserved their wool for the manufacture of rugs and carpets or felt for the soles of slippers and sleeping pads. The introduction of woollens seems to have exercised a deleterious effect on the eyesight, engendering complete colour blindness for, whereas with their silks and cottons their matching sense was impeccable, they commit the greatest atrocities in the combinations of knitted accessories.

Shoes, in the North, are made at home, and are more like bedroom slippers than anything else. The uppers are of cloth and the soles of rags endlessly stitched together with hemp twine, until they are virtually of the consistency of rope. In the winter, if the wearer could afford it, felt soles were used as a protection against the cold.

In the South, wooden clogs with a leather strap are often worn by the lower classes, but the labourers mostly go barefoot in the fields.

The round, paneled satin cap with a cord button is disappearing, but it was the general between-season wear for men in the North. In the summer most men go bare-headed, using a fan to shade the eyes. In Hong

Head-dresses of different races

236

Kong, the different races are distinguishable by their woven basket-work hats. The Cantonese wear the conical shape, associated with the pantomime Aladdin, whilst the Boat People affect the mushroom style which is not so cumbersome with the rigging, and presents less opportunity for the caprices of the wind. The Hakka woman is recognisable by the valance of cloth, and the absence of crown, whilst the Hoklo wears a flat-brimmed hat with a hemispherical crown.

These hats serve as a protection against the rain as well as the sun, and obviate the use of an umbrella. As a waterproof the peasants adopt a sort of cloak and skirt made of superimposed palm leaves reminiscent of the goat-skins of Robinson Crusoe. They give better protection than those of plastic, are cooler, and last longer, but they are more expensive.

From the Yangtze to the south a very popular summer material is the shiny black silk impregnated with a sort of lacquer which makes it waterproof. The price is high and it is purgatory to wear in a hot sun.

Fans

The fan is purely an oriental product of civilisation, whose introduction is due to the dictates of climate, and the prevalence of flies which high temperatures

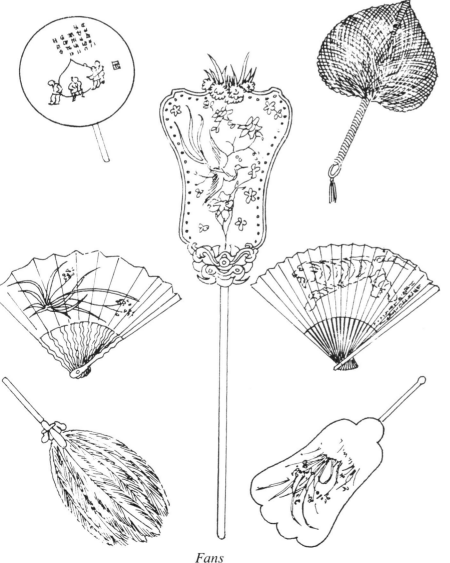

Fans

engender. Early paintings testify to their use in religious ceremonies in Egypt as far back as 3000 B.C. and an instrument called a flabellum, to keep insects off the sacred vessels, was part of the church furnishings in Europe in the Middle Ages. The appearance there of fans as a personal accessory, however, only dates from the opening of Portuguese trade with the Orient, when they achieved instant popularity with the ladies. They solved the problem of what to do with the hands, aided flirtations and, if necessary, concealed the blushes.

The beautifully decorated specimens brought from China found a ready market, and the idea was quickly adopted and copied all over the continent. Implements of feathers to create a draught had long been in use for winnowing, but presumably ill-fitting windows and doors had hitherto provided all the ventilation necessary for the human frame. In China, on the contrary, the chaff is separated from the grain by throwing sieves-full of corn into the air, and allowing the wind to carry away the lighter particles.

Fans have been used in China from remote antiquity, and the circular form was very popular in the T'ang dynasty, when the Cantonese had become reconciled to considering themselves an integral part of the Empire. The folding form was a Japanese invention, introduced during the tenth or eleventh century, through Korea. As a medium of art they are unsurpassed, for they lend themselves to every form of decoration, and an immense variety of materials can be employed in their fabrication. Rigid fans are made of silk, paper, feathers, and from the leaves of the P'u K'uei (蒲葵), Livistonia chinensis, a palm found in low lying districts of the southern provinces. Folding fans are stretched on an immense variety of frames, bamboo, ivory, horn, bone and sandalwood, often elaborately carved. The highest prices are asked for ornamental work in mother of pearl, lacquer and tortoise-shell.

As the Chinese adopted them for personal use, and not for agricultural purposes, it is not surprising that men carry them as well as women. When not in use they are usually tucked into the sleeve or sash, and may even be pushed down the collar behind the neck. In addition to their cooling propensities they also come in handy to emphasise points of speech, or trace characters in the air, when there is an ambiguity about the spoken word. The language has comparatively few sounds and each one is susceptible to an enormous number of interpretations. Thus, when two acquaintances are involved in a conversation which transcends the price of pigs and the backwardness of the crops, they must have recourse to the written word. Characters are traced on the palm with the forefinger to indicate which word is intended, or with the folded fan on the tea table.

On the arrival of the bride at the bridegroom's house, which is to be her future home, her spouse receives her as she descends from the red chair and, after giving her a tap on the head with his fan, uses it to lift her veil and behold her face for the first time.

When an individual was presented to the Emperor, or some high official, and performed the nine-fold K'o T'ou, the closing of the fan with a snap was the signal for him to arise from his prostration, and the only acknowledgement of his salute.

Custom dictates that women's fans and men's are not identical, and the difference is principally in the number of ribs in the frame. A man's fan may contain nine, sixteen, twenty or twenty-four, the last two being favoured, whilst a woman's fan may not have less than thirty. In the decoration the female figure may only be depicted on those used by ladies, and they are quite out of place for employment by an adult male. Different kinds of fans are carried at different seasons by all who can afford to follow the fashion, and to produce one too early or too late in the year provokes ridicule.

As the Chinese appreciate calligraphy as much as painting, many fans are decorated with poems by those who are of a literary turn, and presents of verses are exchanged between acquaintances of the old scholarly class. So popular was the practice, that the lines were sometimes referred to as the "fan language".

In the temples large fans of embroidered material, mounted on poles, accompany the portable image of the divinity for processional purposes, as an adjunct to the ceremonial umbrella. In legend, the fan is the emblem of Chung-li Ch'uan, the Senior of the Eight Immortals, and with it he is credited with reviving the souls of the dead. According to a famous story he came across a widow fanning her husband's grave, as it would be unseemly to remarry till the earth was dry. Chung took the fan from her and with one stroke accomplished her desire. She hastened off to her lover, leaving him the fan as a memento. On his return home his wife was intrigued at his carrying a woman's fan, and he told her the story as an amusing instance of the fickleness of the sex. She professed to be outraged, and protested that no decent woman would be guilty of such a crime. The old magician, to test her constancy, feigned death and was duly encoffined. Shortly after, he reappeared in the guise of a young student who claimed to have been a disciple of her late husband. The widow fell in love, and acceded to his suggestion that they should make a powerful elixir from the brain of the deceased. When the coffin was opened for this foul purpose, the lover resumed his natural form, and upbraided his wife for her inconstancy. The wretched woman was so overcome with shame that she hanged herself, whilst Chung-li Ch'uan severed his connection with mortals by setting fire to his cottage, and establishing himself in a mountain retreat with the fan, and a book of spells.

Many of the famous artists of the Sung and later dynasties, specialised in painting landscapes and floral designs on fans, and the frames were also decorated with painting or carving. It was a general practice to paint one side of the surface, whilst the other side was reserved for inscriptions. The two arts being complementary, the fan provided an admirable medium for the display of both.

The Chinese Cuisine

It would not be an overstatement to maintain that the Chinese are the best cooks in the world. With them eating is a matter of supreme importance. No Chinese pays a visit empty-handed, and in nine cases out of ten the present is food. His normal greeting takes the form of an inquiry as to whether his acquaintance has eaten, and the intimation that one has not dined is ample excuse for breaking off an embarrassing interview.

All Chinese consider that our tastes and table manners are deplorable. Their food comes from the kitchen in edible form, and does not entail a surgical operation and the knowledge of anatomy of fur and feather on the part of the host before the guests can begin to ply knife and fork. Kitchen routine is scrupulously clean, and all food is manipulated with chopsticks instead of fingers. Flavouring has been brought to a fine art, and the Chinese have a far wider knowledge of herbs than the Europeans. After all, the basis of Worcester Sauce is soy, which has seasoned the coolie's meal for countless generations. As a rule, the foreigner in China does not appreciate Chinese food. The diplomats, who are bound to exchange hospitality, thoroughly enjoy an invitation, but the merchant, either from indolence or conservatism, usually affects a positive dislike to accepting the hospitality of his business acquaintances.

Chinese never invite guests to their houses, where only members of the family are entertained. All dinner-parties are given in restaurants, and it is not unusual for a wealthy man to make a present in this form. The system resembles the book-token. Many restaurants issue tickets for varying amounts, which entitles the holder to a feast on any day convenient to him. The recognised number is ten, and it is usual to give the proprietor a day's notice in advance. It is not essential that the donor should be asked, and the choice of guests is left entirely to the recipient of the ticket. When the Manchu Emperor's English tutor was appointed Governor of Wei Hai Wei, his pupil sent him a ticket on the "Loyal Heart Restaurant", kept by the late palace cook, and on this occasion the Chinese Imperial tutors and a few army officers were invited. As with all Chinese dinners the party broke up early, and, when the old scholars were asked how they proposed to spend the rest of the evening, they replied that they were about to engage in a competition in writing poetry.

Chinese dishes can be reckoned in the thousands, and every province and even town has its speciality in the preparation of certain comestibles. Peking, as the capital, and centre of the Civil Service examination system, was justly renowned for its restaurants, and, as students from every province competed for official posts, their gastronomic needs were catered for in the style to which they were accustomed. There were well over a thousand eating-houses in the city.

Taking it by and large there are four different styles of cooking which are outstanding: Peking, Shantung, Canton and Szechuan. China has many Mahommedans, particularly in the North-west, and, while pork is the staple food of the rest of the population, "Mutton Houses" in the Turkestan style cater for the faithful. The south is well off for sugar, whereas north of the Yangtze it is imported, so the sweets in the Canton cuisine are infinitely better than those in the Shantung. The food is also more highly seasoned with spices and chillies. Peking dusk is rarely found south of Tientsin, but Birds' nests and Sharks' fins are transported all over the country as invariable adjuncts for a high-class feast. The nests are only found in the Indonesian archipelago, and are the gelatinous product of a small swift, or sea swallow. They resemble isinglas, of a white colour with a tinge of red. In soup they impact a flavour which is considered particularly delicate.

Sharks' fins produce a thick, turtle-like, brown soup,

in which the laminated flippers take a certain amount of negotiating with chopsticks. Another soup is made of sea-slugs, or bèche-de-mer, which resembles the rind of pork, both in appearance and taste. There is no end io the soup repertoire, and one particularly good clear variety has poached pigeons' eggs floating on top, which show no tendency to co-operate with the luckless foreigner's chopsticks, and far more inclination to emulate Humpty-Dumpty on their way to his mouth.

For a large dinner-party the restaurateur usually provides a private room, with a partition forming an ante-room in which the guests assemble. Here they drink cups of tea, and crack melon seeds, when the foreigner would be drinking cocktails. On the announcement of dinner, the host takes up the wine-pot and conducts the guest of honour to his place, amid loud and insincere protestations of unworthiness. Age counts before honesty, and the old gentleman is finally urged into his backless seat, and his wine is poured out. The next senior is then led in, placed on his left, and duly wined. The chair on the right is then filled up, and so on alternately, till only the host's place at the foot of the round table is vacant. The principal guest should then totter round, and seize the wine-pot to serve the donor of the feast. Wine is drunk hot, poured from a pewter pot, which has a water-jacket to keep its contents warm. The best is made in Shao Shing (紹興) in Chekiang province, and the taste resembles dry sherry. The alcoholic content is very low, and it is drunk from tiny receptacles, about the size of an egg-cup without the stem. The colour is brownish yellow, but foreigners should beware of the colourless variety known as Pai Ka'rh (白乾), which is sixty per cent alcohol. Each place is laid with the implements for eating, consisting of a pair of ivory chopsticks, whose Chinese name is the "Nimble brothers", a small bowl and porcelain spoon for the liquids, and a saucer on which to place the discards. Small bones, prawn skins and unwanted bits of gristle are thus disposed of. The chopsticks must never be laid down across the rice bowl, which is a breach of good manners. In the North a bowl of rice is served almost immediately, but in Canton it comes in about half-way through the meal. Not to finish the rice is an insult to the host, since it has acquired an almost sacred significance as the staff of life.

The table is already laid with the eight cold dishes, which correspond to hors d'oeuvres—cold steamed chicken in strips with some kind of small green beans, shrimps and vegetables, black eggs whose antiquity is a Western legend. As a matter of fact they are simply ducks' eggs, pickled in lime. Their keeping qualities being superior to fresh eggs, they sometimes command a slightly better price, but not enough to warrant the assumption that they have been locked up as capital for a period of years. Ham, and bamboo shoots, which are nice and crunchy, usually figure in the hors d'oeuvres. The host toasts his principal guest, giving the warning "drink at ease", and picks up his chopsticks as the signal to begin. Drink as you please is the alternative to no heel-taps, which comes later in the evening. Then the wine-cup must be exhibited bottom up, as an earnest that the glass has been emptied, and drinks are the forfeits for the loser at a game of "fingers out". This is a sort of game, where one contestant holds out a certain number of fingers, and his opponent has to display the right complement, or empty an extra glass.

The meal proper begins with the eight hot dishes, often heralded by the famous birds' nest soup. This is drunk with the porcelain spoon from the small bowl, the host serving certain favoured guests. It is a great compliment to receive from his chopsticks some particularly succulent morsel from one of the dishes though, as Chinese taste differs from European, the guest may feel some embarrassment in disposing of a lump of fat pork, or a generous bouquet of garlic. Before the soup has been removed a plate of chickens' livers is on the table. These are utterly unlike the degenerate piece of india-rubber tucked under the bird's left wing, which was the perquisite of the dowager in a country house in pre-war days. They are rolled in flour, and cooked for a few moments in lard or oil in a hot pan. This treatment swells them out, and they melt in the mouth. A dish of mushrooms in thick brown sauce follows close on their heels, and the empty tureen of soup is removed to clear the decks.

There is a murmur of approval as the head waiter puts down the bowl of sharks' fins, as this sets the seal on the lavishness of the feast. It and the birds' nests are just as necessary to a banquet as a turkey to a Christmas dinner. The whiskery fin is not easy to manipulate gracefully, but the soup is first-rate. Very little goes out when the tureen is removed to make way for a bowl of mushrooms and prawns fried in their shells. These should be chewed whole, as the most savoury part lies in the integument. It can be soon reduced to manageable proportions for the reception of which the discard saucer is always handy. A couple of sweets follow, a great favourite being lotus seeds in syrup. They are believed to possess some aphrodisiac properties, which recommend them to a race with whom posterity and longevity are prime considerations.

The foreigner is now beginning to sense the end, but he is to be disappointed, for the clearing away of the sweets heralds the arrival of the most enormous baked fish he has ever seen on a dinner-table. The host delicately turns back the skin with his chopsticks, and it is passed round for each to help himself. There is no getting away from it, and a refusal entails being saddled with a larger portion than would voluntarily have been taken. Rice has now been supplied to all guests, and it is easier to eat when the fish and its sauce have caused it to coagulate.

Drink as you please has long been abandoned, and the host has started a round of no heel-taps. Every guest toasts his neighbour, and the boys are busy replenishing the wine-pots. Glasses should be filled by the host, or guests, and not by the attendants. Two more dishes are brought in, and the host presses the merits of some savoury meat balls, or a bowl of frogs' legs, known as Field Chickens. When it becomes certain that all can eat no more, the waiters hand round towels wrung out in boiling water, with which the guests wipe their perspiring faces and hands. Before rising, it is usual for each guest to rinse his mouth, as it would be an insult to good tea to approach it after a heavy meal. The guests then adjourn to the ante-room, where they find a generous supply of fruit awaiting them. There is, however, not much variety, and dessert consists mainly of oranges and bananas. The end comes swiftly, and there are no long sittings. In about ten minutes the principal guest takes his leave, and the party breaks up. Every scullion in the restaurant emerges with loud shouts to speed the parting guest, just as he welcomed his entry. The host sees off the last, and turns back to settle the bill and give instructions as to the disposal of the remains of the feast. This will keep him going at home for a couple of days, for what he has paid for is his, and the Chinese are a thrifty race.

In Hong Kong and the old Treaty Ports many foreign customs have been adopted, and, though a business dinner would consist entirely of men, a convivial party for some celebration would include the ladies, and children, for that matter. There is always a tendency for the women to sit together, a relic of the old taboo, though foreign customs are followed at diplomatic official parties. It is quite unnecessary to go to a restaurant for a good meal, as, with very short notice, any establishment will supply from one dish to a whole feast at the customer's own home, with service complete. Chinese families all supplement their dinner-parties with at least one restaurant speciality, the final touches to the cooking being completed in the house.

The Cantonese are singled out from the rest of the Chinese race by their partiality for dogs and cats on the menu. These animals, antagonistic in life, carry on the feud in the after life, for it is believed that death will ensue if they are eaten at the wrong period of their existence. The cat must be at least two years old, whereas a fat puppy is most esteemed as a table delicacy.

A famous Cantonese dish is known by the euphemistic name of the "Meeting of the Dragon and the Tiger," but it is only obtainable in the autumn months when the snakes go into hibernation. They are then at their fattest, as they have accumulated in the summer a supply of food to last them to the spring. The serpent plays the part of the Dragon, whilst the cat has the Tiger's role. Should chicken be included in the ragout, it impersonates the Phoenix. Thus the consumer partakes of three of the four superintelligent creatures, those who guard the East, South and West quarters of the horizon.

After-Dinner Entertainment

Any tourist passing through Hong Kong or Singapore, attracted by the brilliant lighting effects in the shopping quarter, would have no difficulty in deducing how the Chinese spend their time after the evening meal. The traveller would see crowds pouring out of the cinemas at the end of each performance, and would hear the rattle of mahjong tiles from almost every house in the side streets. Both these forms of entertainment are comparatively new, for Dyer Ball, writing "Things Chinese" half a century ago, does not mention the game among the various forms of gambling in which the Chinese indulge. As to the cinema, fifty years ago moving pictures were merely a novelty, thrown on the screen in the interval of a concert or variety show. The scope was limited to outdoor scenes, such as a train arriving at a railway station, or a procession like the Lord Mayor's Show taken in what appeared to be a downpour of rain. Five minutes was about all the audience could endure without the affliction of a blinding headache.

The Chinese anticipated the Cinema by the Ying Hsi (影戲) or Shadow Play. This consisted of an illuminated screen behind which the operator, singing the dialogue, manipulated puppets made of donkey skin. Arms, heads and legs were articulated and a very lively sense of motion was imparted to the figures. The plays enacted were all traditional, and animals were introduced as well as men and women. The performer worked his characters from behind the screen, with assistants to hand him a new figure as required. Originally the puppets were made of paper and, as all the plays depicted acts of violence, the performers believed that they gradually became Mei (魅), or possessed by malevolent spirits. Hence, they had to be frequently destroyed to prevent their becoming harmful to their owners.

This procedure was most uneconomical, entailing the constant preparation of new sets, so a fresh model of transparent donkey-skin was evolved. As the puppets were liable to the same infestation, they were immersed in water after each performance to drown the malignants.

The profession was highly specialised, and the artists hailed from Luan Hsien (灤縣), a market town on the Luan river flowing from Jehol into the Gulf of Peichihli. The cinema, however, soon put the shadow play out of business and, at the beginning of the war with Japan, only two troops were performing in Peking. There is a chance of revival, as the new Government in China is doing its best to encourage native arts, to foster the spirit of national pride, and the Luan Hsien Ying Hsi (灤縣影戲) may still have a future before it.

The Chinese, above all other races, are connoisseurs of food, and their banquets are devoted to its discussion rather than the promotion of social intercourse. When the last dish has been removed, tea and fruit are served in the anteroom, as a signal for the break up of the party, and only a few minutes are allowed for polite farewells and congratulation to the host. There is no lingering over port and cigars before joining the ladies for an hour or two of conversation in the drawing room. The night is still young, so it may be wondered how the guests dispose of their time before retiring for sleep. The question was posed to the senior Imperial Tutor after a feast in honour of the return of one of his colleagues from abroad, and he replied that he was a member of a small club of scholars, who met together in the evening for literary discussions. Each composed a poem on a theme set by the scholars in rotation, and the works were adjudged in order of merit by a concensus of opinion.

Among the merchant class story-telling was a popular form of entertainment, and a plot with an ingenious swindle was certain to appeal to the audience. Confidence tricks are usually dependent on the successful arousing of cupidity in the victim, and a suspicion of illegality often enhances the attractiveness of the proposal. One such story relates the downfall of a money-changer who sought to take advantage of a customer's ignorance.

In Imperial days China's currency seems to have been devised to cause the greatest inconvenience to everybody. Paper notes were in use in the T'ang dynasty, but the ordinary peasant carried out his transactions in copper cash, a string of a thousand of which were nominally worth an ounce of silver. As this metal varied in value from day to day, there were constant fluctuations in the rate of exchange. For more important deals the silver was cast in ingots, roughly the shape of a woman's shoe, and stamped with a seal guaranteeing quality. Sycee shears were used to subdivide the blocks, some of which were of considerable size, and more weighing was necessary to detach the required amount. The silver dollar, Spanish or Mexican, was introduced by foreign traders to liquidate their accounts, but it was not until the reign of Kuang Hsu (光緒) that this form of coinage was minted in the country.

A confidence trick was worked on one of the Peking change shops by an individual who came in with a silver bangle to sell. Whilst the proprietor was weighing it and appraising the value, a second man appeared and accosted the customer. He said he had been to his house to deliver a letter and a parcel, and that the servants had informed him about their master's movements. The man took delivery of the packet, and the messenger departed. The recipient pleaded illiteracy, and asked the shop proprietor to read the letter for him. It purported to be from his brother who had emigrated overseas, and said that as his business had prospered he was sending a remittance of ten taels, and hoped soon to make a further contribution to the family expenses. On hearing the good news the man said that he would not sell the bracelet, as it had a sentimental value, but would dispose of the package of silver which had so opportunely arrived. The shopman put the parcel on the scales, and found that it weighed eleven rather than ten ounces. Thinking to take advantage of the client's ignorance, he promptly paid up at the rate stated in the letter. Shortly after his customer had left, a third man came in and told him he had been duped by a notorious swindler, and that the silver was counterfeit. He hastened to open the packet, and cut one ingot in two with the sycee shears, only to discover that it was pewter. As the man seemed well-informed he asked if there was any chance of tracing the thief, and on payment of a dollar he was led to a low teahouse, where he found his late client drinking with a table of boon companions. The place was, in fact, a resort of gamblers and gangsters. However, when accused of a swindle, the man was perfectly polite. He said he knew no more than the money-changer about the contents of the parcel and that, if the silver were bad, he was perfectly ready to make restitution. He got an admission that he had been paid for ten taels, but to safeguard himself demanded that the consignment brought should be verified on the scales of the teashop manager. When the weight registered at eleven ounces, he became most indignant, and accused the money-changer of substituting another bundle to swindle him. The roughs in the teashop, having followed the argument with interest, took the part of the gangster and adopted a threatening attitude, so the merchant was forced to withdraw before worse befell.

The Home Physician

Chinese native medicine is based on a mixture of empiricism and faith-healing, little removed from the alchemy of the Middle Ages, and, in fact, as petrified as the written language. Whereas, in Europe, the science has been raised by research and experiment to a remarkable degree of exactness, and not only the cause, but the remedy, for most diseases is known, the Chinese doctor continues to put his patient on a light diet of duck for no better reason than that the bird floats on water. A remarkably high degree of civilisation was achieved thousands of years ago, and it would be natural to suppose that centuries of trial and error would have brought some advance in medical knowledge, each discovery adding to the wisdom of previous generations. The curative properties of many substances are undoubtedly known, but the methods of administering them are open to the gravest objections. For pulmonary complaints, a cooling drink composed of herbs is recommended, but this is alleged to possess no virtue unless matured in a sealed bamboo tube, stored in a cesspit which, if possible, should be one frequented by gentlemen only! Phlegm can be cleared by grinding a dried fish, known as a "sea sparrow" (海雀), to powder, which is then blown into the patient's larynx through a tube. The drug shops in Hong Kong also sell dessicated sea horses as a remedy for cancer. Calcium is essential for bone-building, but it is hardly necessary to obtain it from the bones of fossilised prehistoric monsters which alone, according to Chinese medical science, can impart the essential virtue.

Fortunately for the survival of the race, the indifference of the communications rendered access to a professional doctor difficult, and it was vital to have someone in the family with a knowledge of home-nursing and first-aid. Before the advent of Western ideas, the splitting of the family was regarded as a primary disaster, and all the members of each social unit lived in one compound, building fresh accommodation as the births and marriages outnumbered the deaths. One of the female members of this group nearly always had a taste for nursing, and to her was passed on the store of medical knowledge acquired through countless generations. In most cases, and certainly in the peasant classes, the recipes were never recorded in writing, but were handed down verbally to an understudy who acted as dresser to the wise woman. She, herself, probably added to her store of knowledge from discussions with neighbours, and on marriage would disseminate her prescriptions among the clan of her adoption. These old ladies were no mean herbalists, and the West has not been slow to acknowledge the value of medicinal rhubarb, one of their panaceas. Ginseng (人參) is probably the most famous of Chinese drugs, and it was formerly reserved for the use of the Emperor and his household, though he conferred it on high officials suffering from a break-down in health. Its scientific name is Panax ginseng, and it is found wild in the forests of Manchuria and Korea. It is a most potent tonic in cases of debility, but only the wild variety appears to retain its full strength, and the cultivated root is not highly esteemed.

The Chinese never discovered the cause of diseases carried by parasites such as the flea and mosquito. They did, however, find out that the slough of a domestic spider affords the same relief as quinine when the fever is coming on. Discarded spiders' skins are usually available about the house, and, powdered and disguised with other food, produce the desired result. Even Western-trained doctors admit that the remedy works.

Small-pox is so endemic in the country that little notice is taken of it, and it is not unusual in the North to see children in the streets with running sores. To accelerate the eruption of the spots, after which apparently the crisis is considered past, fragrant weed

241

(Hsiang ch'un) (香椿) is used. The fact that the brat is then at the most infectious stage as a carrier, is nobody's business. The French proverb that "other people's misfortunes are easy to bear" is heartily subscribed to in China.

The rash produced by measles can also be accelerated by the use of the same herb, or by the exposure of the body to red light. No kind of meat, fish, or sea food should be served to the patient. Fried food should be avoided, and everything should be steamed or boiled. Complications and after-effects on the eyes are recognised, so there should be no exposure to sunlight, and the windows should be screened with red drapery or paper. Throat trouble is to be anticipated if anything salty is given before the lapse of three weeks. Ginger and onion chopped small will alleviate the irritation, and stop scratching.

In cases of fever, fatty foods should be avoided, and chicken is poison if the bird be a cock. The Chinese are very particular about the sex of a chicken, and even Western-trained physicians are inclined to respect the taboo.

Some people are allergic to crustaceans, but the Chinese believe that the shell of a lobster, crab, or prawn, reduced to ashes, will act as a corrective. In the case of a surfeit of noodles, the water in which they have been boiled will bring relief. There is a good deal of the "Hair of the dog" in their antidotes. Crabs should be eaten with ginger, and washed down with a powerful spirit distilled from Sorghum, known as "Pai ka'rh", about the nearest thing to pure alcohol invented. After the meal, hot sugared water should be drunk.

In cases of headache, a shelled hard-boiled egg, in which a silver coin has been inserted, should be applied to the temple. This will draw out the poison, and the coin will blacken whilst the yolk of the egg becomes striated. Fresh mushrooms will bring out fever but, if accompanied by a rash, the irritation will be increased.

Bleeding from the nose can be arrested by raising the hand above the head. The right hand should be used if the haemorrhage is from the left nostril, and vice versa. Cold water or a lump of ice, applied to the nape of the neck, takes the place of the door-key used as a Western first-aid. A plug of cotton-wool, impregnated with Chinese ink (the older the better), should be placed in the affected nostril. A finger lightly pressed against the septum, where it connects with the upper lip, has a beneficial effect.

Certain foods are antagonistic, so persimmons and crab should not be eaten at the same meal. Peanuts have a deleterious effect on cucumber, and onions with honey are to be avoided.

To arouse a person from a faint, pinching of the upper lip below the nose is recommended. It is certainly a sensitive spot, and the method may be preferable to a bucket of cold water. Mental cases are said to yield to treatment by employing the gall-stone from a horse, or the woody substance which forms round an obstruction in the intestine. Solid matter found in the yak will cure any illness accompanied by a high temperature. A grain of salt should be administered with these last three prescriptions.

During pregnancy water chestnuts should not be eaten, especially before the third month. Even the scent of a musk deer is dangerous, though the likelihood of an encounter with the animal must be an infinitesimal risk. Rabbit meat is forbidden lest the child develop a hare-lip.

As contraceptives, lotus leaves burned to ashes and eaten are a sovereign remedy against pregnancy. On the other hand, the seeds are esteemed as an aphrodisiac. The nursing mother should drink hot water, in which sugar has been dissolved, for at least thirty days after her delivery, and it is desirable that this treatment should be continued for a hundred days.

Dropsy may be cured by burning water-melons to ashes, and consuming the residue. Should a cure be effected, the patient must then abstain from melons for life. If there is a recurrence of the malady, the charm will not work a second time, and the disease is pronounced incurable.

If a child suffers from nervous shock after a fright, it is held that the spirit has deserted the body, and must be recalled. Otherwise there is grave danger of a warlock taking possession of an unoccupied body. As a fox fairy is a most undesirable relative at any time, and the Chinese have no desire to introduce some wandering alien into the clan, the child's dress must be taken to the spot where the accident occurred, with the invocation "Come back! Come back!", on which the soul returns to its proper habitation.

Whooping-cough is cured by taking the skin inside a hen's egg for a hundred days. This is known as the "Phoenix dress". Chicken liver, dried and ground to powder, is good for the baby's stomach. The preparation probably destroys those vitamins which have recently been discovered by Western science in liver, but no exception can be taken to the idea which has most likely been handed down since Aesculapius practised medicine.

For asthma, a small gourd known as Huang Ching Kua is considered efficacious, and eye trouble may be alleviated by pig's liver, steamed with chrysanthemums. This treatment, at any rate, is less open to objection than that practised by the professional medicine man, who uses substances positively deleterious to so delicate an organ.

An infusion of dried mulberries, or a salted lemon, is infinitely preferable, as a cough cure, to a powdered sea sparrow puffed down the throat by an individual whose lungs are not above suspicion of infection from tuberculosis.

Western-trained physicians can hold their own with any in the world, and a hundred years of Medical Missions have done much to spread the practice of enlightened treatment, but one glance at the native drug stores will prove that old methods are still popular. China is intensely conservative, and foolish patients often prefer to take the advice of some old crony in the selection of a quack to patronising a physician of established repute. Elementary precautions against the spread of infection are neglected, and epidemics are attributed rather to the wrath of God than the ignorance of man. The race survives in spite of, rather than on account of, its doctors, and the home physicians must be largely responsible.

National Health Insurance

Centuries before Mr. Asquith's Liberal Government brought in its first health insurance scheme, usually

242

attributed to Lloyd George under the "ninepence for fourpence" slogan, the Chinese who was unlucky enough to need the services of a doctor applied to his gods to protect him and grant him a happy issue out of his misfortune. Most medical treatment was inextricably mixed up with religion, and the ashes of charms played an important part in what can only be described as a faith-cure. In spite of the growing popularity of Western medicine, a belief still lingers that without divine intervention the treatment will be inefficacious.

The prospective patient accordingly makes arrangements, before committing himself to the tender mercies of the doctor, for a service to be held which will guarantee no slips on the part of the practitioner, and will facilitate his own recovery. The officiant is usually a wise woman who combines the part of amateur priestess with that of a clairvoyant. Her visible means of subsistence may be the profession of a pig tender, or a hawker. In any case, the community always knows how to lay hands on her when her services as go-between with the gods are required.

In one case, the officiant lived in a squatter's hut ten feet square, with a door in three of the walls, and a window in the other. The place had a little garden and blue convolvulus covering the roof. The furniture was designed to take up as little space as possible and consisted of a couple of cane chairs, a stool and a very narrow settee. The altar was a bamboo table, in the centre of which was a bowl acting as incense burner, a vase of paper gladioli and three or four plates containing fruit. Oranges, pears and a plate of bananas, as her Patron Saint likes their scent, formed the sacrifice, with about a catty of roast pork.

In the centre of the table was a bowl containing red paper for wrapping up lucky money, and on the top lay a silver talisman on a thin chain. This was inscribed with the name of Buddha and four characters (長命富貴), for long life, riches and honour. The inscription was stamped in the metal, and not engraved. As a reredos to the altar a red paper had been pasted on the wall, with a eulogistic description of the family. The central column of characters read "All ancestors of Tan from first to last", whilst on the right "They planted the heart's farm and put in good seed" and on the left "Their descendants enjoy the harvest and continue the good work". The patient himself wrote down the name of the divinity to whom he was entrusting his cure and her address: "The Cassia Mountain Moon-flower cave". The lady is known as the Third Daughter-in-law (三娘), and Fifth Princess (五宮主), under which he subscribed "In the very presence" (顯聖).

Before the altar a straw kneeling-mat was arranged and the priestess stood to the right, whilst the patient took up his position in front of the altar.

Four candles were then lighted on the altar, but the draught from the three doors made them flare to such an extent that the paper gladioli caught fire, and the vase had to be passed out hastily to the gaping children outside. The youth then lighted three thick yellow sticks of incense, whilst the officiant recited the prayers for his protection. He knelt on the mat and performed the three-fold prostration touching the floor with his forehead. Still kneeling he removed his tie, opened the shirt and was invested with the amulet which was placed round his neck by the priestess. She then brought him three packets of paper clothing and money, which she lighted before handing them over. Each was waved up and down before the altar in token of offering, and was then handed out to be consumed in the open air.

The ceremony ended by the priestess pouring out a libation of wine on the floor. The patient, now ready to face the medical profession, buttoned his shirt and readjusted the tie.

Sacrificial offerings are treated in the same way as ordinary presents, and it is not good form for the priestess to accept the whole, on the grounds that the donor has been too generous. She consequently makes the round of her contributors, and returns a couple of oranges, and a piece of the red paper which lay on the altar with twenty cents "lucky money".

The identity of the Protective Divinity is obscure, to say the least of it, and her address is equally fictitious.

Charms in China are all beneficent, protecting against evil spirits, and there seems to be no such thing as an ill-luck talisman to bewitch an enemy. Possibly such things exist among the primitive aboriginals in Kueichow and Yünnan, but presumably the more cultivated consider that the atmosphere is already so charged with devils seeking whom they may molest that it is superfluous to add to their number. Care is taken, however, not to offend Taoist priests who are credited with the power of invoking misfortune on those who cross them. There is usually a good deal of criticism about their rapacity, but no open accusations are made for fear of provoking reprisals.

SOCIETIES & MARTIAL ARTS

Secret Societies

All authorities are agreed on dividing China's Secret Societies into four categories, political, religious, a combination of the two, and those established for personal reasons. As an example of the first, the Red Eyebrow Society, Ch'ih Mei Hui (赤眉會), started in a revolt about the beginning of the Christian era, under one Wang Mang, whose adherents dyed their eyebrows. The Elder Brother Society, Ko Lao Hui (哥老會), in its present form dates from the establishment of the Manchu rule, and was anti-dynastic. Of religious sects there are the Vegetarians, bound to a life-long abstinence from meat to gain happiness now, and a reincarnation in a wealthy family. It was founded in the T'ang dynasty, and showed a certain amount of intolerance of non-adherents to its rule by massacring a missionary establishment in Fukien in 1895. The best-known of the politico-religious societies is the Triad, divided into a Red and Green "Pan", the former being strongest in Szechuan, and the latter in the Yangtze Valley and Kwangtung Province. An example of the fourth group is the Golden Orchid, whose girl members are sworn never to marry.

As with the fundamentals of all religions, there is a close resemblance the world over of secret societies and, no matter for what purpose they were originally founded, there is a tendency for their power of combination to be misused for political ends, or the enrichment of the individual. Freemasonry, though it retained its ideals in England, at once assumed a political character when transplanted to the Continent, and the Triad Society, which was ostensibly formed for the restoration of the Mings, had completely lost sight of its goal when the revolution broke out in 1911. With such a practical race as the Chinese, this urge to band together was almost invariably due to oppression and misrule rather than chivalrous attachment to a fallen dynasty.

A number of the religious societies owed their origin to the persecution of a sect, which went underground, and may either have retained its doctrines, or modified them with the addition of fresh blood. Thus religious societies may have become political, or large societies may have split up, and the parts have developed separately. The history of the movements is thus impossible to follow, for societies overlap, and change their names and principles. Most of their records were in manuscript, which often had to be hurriedly destroyed lest it should be produced as evidence by a government which harshly suppressed any subversive element. This attitude was quite comprehensible, as costly politico-religious wars took place in the 17th and 19th centuries, when the White Lily Society rebelled in Hupei, and more than 20,000 members were executed in four months. The revolt, aimed at the overthrow of the Manchus, spread through six provinces and assumed the proportions of a civil war.

The Boxer rising in Shantung had its origin in the revival of an association which had long existed in the province and whose smouldering embers had never quite been extinguished. It burst into flame as a political movement with the German seizure of Kiaochow, and what had long been under a ban was recognised by the Government, who accepted as volunteers individuals against whom it was loath to use force. Once started, and officially encouraged, the organisation spread like wildfire when indoctrinated with ideas of invulnerability and xenophobia. For the former belief the Red Lamp Soceity was responsible. This was founded by a woman, and young girls, wearing red trousers and girdles, joined it to act as priestesses for the initiation of the Boxer Braves. Spiritual hosts descended to reinforce the rebel bands who had been hypnotised into the belief of their invincibility. The chief aim of the movement was the extermination of the foreigners, and its motto was "Protect the Country, and Expel the Foreigner". There were, however, various internal factions ready to make use of the association. The revolutionaries were trying to discredit the Manchus, whilst dynastic and clan factions saw their interests threatened by the Reform movement of 1898, and wished to replace the Emperor by P'u Tsum (溥春), son of Prince Tuan. Yuan Shih K'ai, the Provincial Governor, never lost his head, and disproved the invulnerability claim with his own revolver, after which he cleared the sect from his satrapy into Chihli.

The best-known secret society in Central and South China is undoubtedly the Triad, or Three Harmonies Society (三和會). It started life as anti-dynastic, and owed its origin to three monks, who made their escape from a monastery burned by Manchu troops during the conquest of the country. Its motto was "Fan Ch'ing Fu Ming" (反清復明) or "Overthrow the Manchus and Restore the Mings". The virtues on which the society was founded were fraternity, filial piety, and religion. In one of their rings of silver gilt, with the seal of the characters of longevity and good fortune (福壽), was a cartouche bearing the inscription "The Temple's teaching is the Three Great Principles" (寺文○三大艮). The order in which the characters were inscribed made the sentence meaningless except to the initiated. In its words of exhortation it is written "If people insult you, injure, revile or abuse you, how should you take it?" "You should bear it, suffer, endure and forgive it." This seems inconsistent with a rebellion of the dimensions of the T'aip'ings, were it not condoned by the fact that every Chinese is, in duty bound, to revolt against bad government.

Each Lodge in the Society is governed by a President, two Vice-Presidents, one Master, two Introducers, one Fiscal (for disciplinary purposes), thirteen Councillors, among whom is a Treasurer and a Receiver. There are also agents and minor officials, while some of the brethren are appointed as recruiting agents. The officials are appointed by the whole vote of the Lodge. Contributions of varying amounts are made at Chinese festivals.

The Triad does not share the Freemason's diffidence about proselytising. If a desirable recruit does not react favourably to persuasion, he is brought along to the Lodge in a sack. As in every Chinese undertaking, the novice has to have a sponsor who guarantees him. The candidates are suitably impressed before they reach the Hung Gate, which is guarded by two Generals, who are sent to obtain the Master's permission for them to enter. They are then brought to the Hall of Fidelity and Loyalty, where two more Generals demand their credentials, and the candidates kneel four times. Here, they are instructed in the objects of the Society, and are exhorted to be faithful and loyal to the League. The oppression of the Tartar dominion is emphasised, and promises of protection are extended to those who serve faithfully, and dire threats are pronounced against those who have the temerity to refuse to join. The last Hall before the Lodge is the Circle of Heaven and Earth, and the Triad is considered "within the circle" as a Mason is "on the square". After passing through, the candidates arrive at the East Gate of the City of Willows, guarded by Han P'ang. Here they kneel twice before entering the Council Room.

Here a catechism of 333 questions is asked and replied to, some verses being repeated as a proof. They have reference to the objects of the Society, its tools, banners and parts of the Lodge, and an outline of its history. After the examination to the satisfaction of the Master, the initiation proper takes place. Before the revolution, the cutting-off of the queue as a symbol of rebellion against the Manchu rule and the braiding of the hair in Ming style were the outward manifestations of anti-dynastic motives. As the absence of the pigtail openly marked a revolutionary, a false one was worn attached to the usual round cap. The candidates are then clothed in sackcloth and ashes in mourning for the Mings. Faces are washed to symbolise cleansing of hearts, after which the outer garments are removed and replaced with long white robes, with a red handkerchief as a headdress. Later a pair of straw mourning sandals ane put on, and the candidates are led before the altar on which is a white porcelain censer. The whole company present nine blades of grass to pledge fidelity in memory of the original vow by the dispossessed monks. After a service in which Taoist and Buddhist divinities are honoured, as well as the national heroes and nature spirits, the oath of fidelity is read to the candidates, who remain kneeling during the recital of its thirty-six articles. These enjoin the practice of equity and justice among members, and the shielding of brethren and their families in troubled times. After reading the oath, fingers are pricked, and blood mixed with the ceremonial wine in the chalice, and a white cock is sacrificed to make it the more binding, as those who break the vow deserve to perish like the victim. The burning of the oath in the presence of the neophytes ensures that the gods have assumed the responsibility of punishing the backsliders.

The President then presents the entered apprentices with their certificates, on the back of which their names are written in a secret form, unintelligible to the minions of the law. Triad inscriptions are often groups of eight characters of which, to make sense, the outer pair must first be read, then the next two combined and finally the centre pair. In the case of the ring, the top two characters had to be coupled, and the remaining three read in a triangle. The Society has its own Court of Law and Code and deals with all cases affecting relations between brethren, which are kept out of the hands of the civil power.

Members have various recognition signs, such as the way of sitting down when introducing themselves to the brethren, and they can be tested by the tea-cup method. Tea is served with an odd number of cups, three, five or seven, and, according to the way they are filled and distributed, the degree of the newcomer can be determined. When a conference is desired, the senior member sits down, and his place at once becomes the head of the table. Other members take rank according to their standing in the society, and fill up the board on his left and right alternately. The place immediately opposite the leader must be left vacant, that nothing may be in the line of treasure coming to him. This consideration is probably the key to the whole matter for, at the time of the Revolution, nothing whatever was done to promote the Ming interests, and the abdication of the Manchus was the signal for a scramble for power and self-advancement. Yet there was a direct descendant of the last of the Mings and, ironically enough, his poverty was alleviated, not by the Republic, but from the Privy Purse of the Manchu Emperor who, until driven out of his palace by the Christian General, received him annually on the day his pension was due.

The Triad Society of today occupies much the same position as Tammany Hall in New York in the time of Boss Croker. One section of Shanghai was virtually run by it, and the administration was so permeated that the new Chief of Police, who was appointed to cleanse the Augean stables, soon discovered that his chauffeur was a member, and was paid to stage a breakdown and telephone a warning to any establishment which it was proposed to raid. After the Japanese occupation, the Society was valuable in the Resistance Movement, and almost daily assassinations of puppet employees may be laid to its door. Prior to the Sino-Japanese War, piracy on the coast was very highly organised on a scale far too ambitious for the simple fisherfolk of Bias Bay.

First-class tickets would be booked for the gang at the agency of a foreign shipping company, and the pirates would emerge on the second day, and take charge, diverting the vessel to the well-known haunt just outside Hong Kong territorial waters. It would be rash to assert that patriotism alone was the motive for the anti-Wang Ching-wei crusade in Shanghai, for the puppets, with the able assistance of the Japanese Special Service Branch, were competing seriously in the rackets which had hitherto been a monopoly. Very few Japanese fell to the assassin's gun though, to give them the benefit of the doubt, they did shoot the official vaccinator in the execution of his duty.

Most writers are uncomplimentary about the activities of the Society, and one sums it up by saying that it is a combination to carry out private quarrels, and uphold the interests of the members in spite of law, and lastly to raise money by subscription, or by levying fees on brothels and gaming-houses.

Chinese Shadow-Boxing

Foreigners, passing through some secluded spot immune from wheeled traffic, are sometimes intrigued by encountering a solitary Chinese performing rhythmic

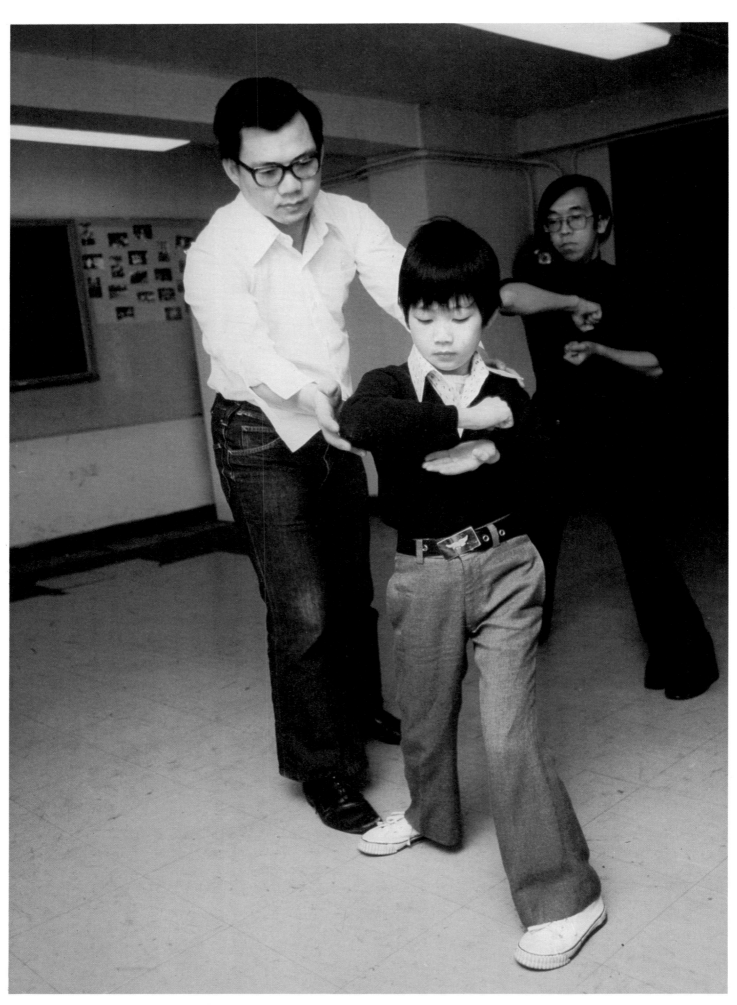

A martial arts class . . . a mental stimulant as well

motions in a state of complete absorption which renders him oblivious to their presence. Occasionally there is a diminutive acolyte, in the shape of a small boy, who stands a few paces behind the performer, copying his every motion. The odds are that he has no connection whatsoever with the principal, but has seized the opportunity of getting a little free instruction in a science difficult to acquire. It is, in fact, a system of exercises designed to give the practitioner complete balance and muscular control, firstly for the improvement of health, and in later stages for self-defence. The Japanese who, before they turned their eyes westward after their illusions were shattered by the invasion of Perry's black ships, borrowed much of their culture from China, probably stole the secrets and developed it along their own lines into what is now known as judo, or jiu-jitsu.

The Chinese call the science the "Great Ultimate Fist", or T'ai Chi Ch'uan (太極拳). The symbol for T'ai Chi is the circle divided by a symmetrical curve into two equal parts, one dark and one light, representing the yolk and white of an egg, the complementary forces which form the motive force of the universe. Legend attributes its origin to one Hsu Hsien-p'ing (許宣平) of the T'ang Dynasty, and it was still practised during the brief Mongol invasion. Chang San-feng (張三峯) at the age of 67 set up a school at Chung Nan Shan, which was infested with tigers, one of his pupils being Wang Chung-ô (王宗岳). Another disciple, Kang Feng-ch'i, introduced modifications to the system and formed a southern school, but this failed to survive the death of its originator, whereas the primitive methods have been handed down through various families to the present day. The secrets were jealously guarded as the property of that closely knit and exclusive unit, the Chinese family, so that practice was not widely diffused throughout the country.

Chinese custom always demands a story to account for the origin of any practice, and these fables are usually mediaeval rather than primitive. In this case Chang San-feng, who practised the art in the Tiger's Den, is said to have conceived the theory after witnessing a combat between a bird and a snake. The bird flew down from a tree and made a vigorous onslaught on the serpent who evaded the attack time and again, by coiling itself so as to present no vital target to the lance-like beak. Finally the attacker tired, and made an unbalanced movement, whereupon the snake struck like lightning.

All movements in the exercises are performed slowly with perfect balance, and there is always a withdrawal before an advance. In all there are thirteen movements: eight of the arms, and five of the legs. Turns are made to the eight points of the compass, the cardinals and those immediately between them. The movements, all depending on circular motion, have most fascinating names such as "Returning to the mountain, carrying a tiger", "Finding a needle at the bottom of the sea", or "A girl at her loom".

Not only is every muscle of the body brought into play, but the exercises act as a mental stimulant as well. The heart is tranquillised, promoting longevity, and the brain is used to activate the members, so that there is no limit to the strength exerted, which is proportionate to the will.

To achieve the best results one should be an early riser, for it is recommended to start before sunrise, facing east to absorb the strength from the fountain of all energy. The ordinary person takes up the study largely for health reasons as a cure for headaches, digestive troubles and rheumatism. The exercises are sufficiently mild to be suitable for all ages to keep fit and as a relaxation from mental strain.

The advanced course is a method of self-defence against an adversary, and two partners spar with one another much as the Japanese teach judo in their elementary schools. The defence in eight directions is said to be derived from the Pa Kua (八卦), or Eight Trigrams, which figuratively denote the evolution of nature, and its cyclical changes. They are combinations of three straight lines, arranged in a circle, said to have been evolved from the markings on a tortoise-shell by the legendary Emperor Fu Hsi (伏羲). The continuous line represents the Yang, or male element, and the broken the Yin, or female complement. The principle is to retire before an enemy's attack, and only to counter when he has overreached himself. The defender's movements, like his model the serpent, are unceasing, puzzling the adversary, and denying an opening for a decisive blow.

Hong Kong has a great expert in the art in Mr. Tung, a Northerner, who taught the system in the Pearl River estuary for twenty years prior to its "liberation". He attended a nation-wide rally at Nanking in Nationalist days, and was one of the twenty-six out of four hundred who lost no points in the competition.

Although a knowledge of Japanese jiu-jitsu has penetrated to every country in the world, Chinese shadow-boxing seems to have been entirely neglected by foreign authors. In Hong Kong Mr. Tung Yin-cheih has published in Chinese a comprehensive manual on the subject, entitled the *Definition of Great Ultimate Boxing* (printed by the Commercial Press) and containing a large number of diagrams and photographs. The book opens with a foreword and testimonials from friends and pupils, and then tells the story of the bird and the snake. This is illustrated by a line drawing of a bearded man looking out of a window, and watching the contest in his front garden on the lawn between a stone pine and a banana tree. Then follows a manuscript in the author's calligraphy, and his autobiography. Eight diagrams of the T'ai Chi (great ultimate) and the Pa Kua (八卦) trigrams precede an illustrated explanation of the health-improving qualities of the exercises. This seems to be no exaggeration, as those who have taken up the practices thoroughly endorse the claims advanced in their favour.

The art of self-defence is described, with eighty-one leads and counters being illustrated. Full details of the correct position of readiness are given, followed by eight different ways of "catching the peacock's tail". The attacking gesture of "how to use the whip" is demonstrated by three examples, evidently provoking retaliation, as instructions follow for the defence of the head. The "white crane" has two methods of "spreading its wings", and then the left knee is employed to ward off an attack. "Playing the guitar" is the expression used to counter an assault on the left arm, and it is repeated in another form by using both right and left arms. There is a counter with the left knee, followed by a lead "as if slinging a heavy iron ball". This provocation calls for a defence "as if shutting a door", and after it the exponent expands and contracts his arms in a cruciform manner

A strenuous course in self-defence

before seizing his opponent as if he were "carrying a tiger to its mountain lair". The victim naturally struggles, so five illustrations are given of how to peep out from under one's arms before he escapes one's clutch, when, after this reconnaissance for a safe exit, one should break and jump away "like a monkey". Having got clear, attack in a dive.

A moment of relaxation follows this strenuous encounter, and it is recommended to raise the hands as if to start again, before stretching the arms "like a white crane". The adversary, somewhat resentful at the attempt to carry him off bodily, now retaliates, so a counter with the left knee is necessary to keep him off before attacking from below as if "picking up a needle from the sea bed". The arm should then be raised as if to "dig a mine in a mountain", and the waist should be threatened as if "swinging the iron sphere". The practitioner then retreats, still dragging his ball and chain, and then steps forward to try to "catch the peacock's tail". An assault with the whip then follows, before waving the hands as if to "make clouds" to baffle the opponent. Things now get a bit mixed for, after using the whip, dizziness is likely to supervene and it is recommended to stretch out the hands to discover the whereabouts of the opponent. Having located him he should be attacked with the feet, first the right, and then the left. The next movement is to turn about on one leg, and ward off the adversary with the left and right knee before advancing, pushing the invisible "iron ball".

This provokes an attack which should be avoided by stepping aside to defend with both hands, before turning sideways to deliver a kick. The surprise evoked by this gesture should be taken advantage of to attack as if "struggling with a tiger". A method of breaking away is then recommended with a parting kick for good measure. Before the adversary can retaliate his head

The golden cock stands on one leg

should be attacked with both hands, "as swiftly as the wind".

This completes forty of the eighty-one exercises detailed in the manual for self-defence. The Chinese attach far more importance to the tranquillising effect of the system on mind and body than they do for its value in overcoming an opponent. It keeps the muscles under perfect control and occupies the mind to the exclusion of everyday worries. There are none of the dangerous locks and throws which the Japanese have introduced into jiu-jitsu.

Tung Yin-chieh's book ends with a chapter on the "Great Ultimate sword play" in which there are fifty-one movements. The fencer first lunges as if to "pierce three rings", and then gives a stab "as quickly as a meteor travels". The next movement should be made as lightly as a "swallow skimming the water", after which a lunge is made to the right and left before pointing at the heart. Then attack "like a cat after a rat", before resting the sword "as a dragon droops its head". The weapon should be lowered "like a bee returning to its hive", before lunging to either side like a "phoenix spreading its wings".

The next movement must be made as quickly "as a shooting star", and then the left arm should be extended "like a phoenix wing" whilst the swordsman waits as if "to hook a fish". This is only a prelude to a double-sided attack like "a pair of dragons diving to the depths of the sea", after which exertion a rest, like "birds going to roost", is prescribed. The sword should then be used like a "black dragon shaking his head", a "green dragon putting out to sea", and a "gale which sweeps the lotus leaves". A lunge is made as if a "lion were shaking his

Swinging the ironball

head", before a recovery like a "tiger nursing his mask in his paws". A horse is the next simile and the attack is delivered like a "white stallion leaping a stream", but is stopped as if "pulling up a runaway".

It is now recommended to take stock of the position and study the adversary, brandishing the sword as if "dispelling a gale of wind" before attacking "like a typhoon". Some quick thrusts follow, like a "meteor chasing the moon", and a "heavenly horse streaking across the sky", after which a swipe is delivered from below, "like pulling up a blind". Both sides are next assaulted like "two running wheels", after which there is a withdrawal like a "swallow carrying mud to her nest". After imitating "a falcon unfolding its wings", the lower limbs are attacked as if trying to "pick up the reflection of the moon from a pool of water". The sword should then be recovered as if "holding the moon in one's arms", prior to a quick lunge as if "a warrior were diving into the sea". Next the torso is the target, as if a "water buffalo were gazing at the moon", after which an attack is put in as if "wild geese were being shot with bow and arrow". Other similes are "a dragon squirming up a pillar", and "picking up flowers like the Jade Lady weaving". If the swordsman gets bewildered he is recommended to move as if "directed by Gods".

A fully qualified boxer requires three years' instruction. The most important point is to relax and not to try too much, being content to learn one or two, and certainly not more than three, movements a day. The whole course can be accomplished in three months, with a further three for revision and correction interspersed with some gymnastic exercises. The third three months should be devoted to the theory and fundamental rules of the Great Ultimate, before completing the year with a similar period in learning its application to self-defence.

During the second year six months should be given to cultivate balance rather than the use of force. During the seventh month there should be daily practice with an opponent. Then a month should be given to jumping exercises, turns and swings. For the ninth month, muscle development is important, and the year is completed with a combination of physical exercises with jumping, turning and skipping.

The sword-training occupies half of the third year, and the last six months should be devoted to revision and perfection of all movements, by which time the student should be fully qualified.

AGRICULTURE

Until the impact of the West opened up its communications China was purely an agricultural land, and the importance of the cultivator was recognised by the fact that the farmer ranked in the order of society next to the official governing class. The raising of grain was considered so vital to the country's economy that the Emperor used to set the example to his subjects each spring by a ceremonial ploughing (躬耕) at the Temple of Agriculture in the capital. Special plots of ground were set aside for the purpose, and that used by the ruler was kept apart, and left untouched if some unavoidable circumstance precluded his attendance. Rice and four species of millet constituted the grain to be sown, the former being reserved for the Head of the State. All the implements used in the ceremony were yellow, as were the oxen which drew the plough. The Emperor's task was to trace eight furrows, from east to west, accompanied by the Minister of Finance on his right, holding a whip and the Viceroy of the metropolitan province on his left with a box of seed. A third high official sowed the grain. The Princes and other officials ploughed eighteen furrows of their own, attended by a number of ancient peasants to straighten up the job. When the grain was reaped in the autumn it was stored in a special barn, and was used exclusively for sacrificial purposes.

The ceremony was repeated in the Provinces by the viceroys acting on behalf of the sovereign. The official and his retinue first repaired to the Temple of Shen Nung (神農), the father of agriculture, where they worshipped the patron and the spirits of earth and grain, and then performed the symbolic breaking of the soil.

Newcomers to China are always amazed at the primitive nature of the farm implements, and at the results achieved with such a paucity of equipment. The plough's design has not been modified since the country was young, as it is without coulter or wheel, and is merely a sharp point set in a very rough piece of bent wood. When the last furrow of the day has been turned it is carried home on the peasant's shoulder. When the iron shoe becomes worn out the remains are sometimes suspended on the outside of the farmer's clothing, or he wears it in a red bag to dispel evil spirits who go in dread of sharp metal. The furrow cut is only about five inches deep. In the rice fields the harrow used is equally primitive in design, often consisting merely of a heavy stick armed with a single row of stout wooden teeth. A broad hoe is used in dry fields and soft land, and the fields are remarkably clean. This is not surprising as the whole family assist in the weeding and, in the North at any rate, these products of nature have a market value as camel feed. Grass and any other rubbish is also collected for fuel, as firewood is extremely scarce. The spade is comparatively rarely used. Rakes are made of bamboo, and the reaping is done with sickles. A flail is used to thrash grain from the stalk, and winnowing is mostly performed by throwing up sieves-full of the residue, and letting the wind carry off the chaff.

Unlike the nomadic tribes inhabiting their north-west borders, who have religious scruples about breaking the earth, the Chinese depend for their sustenance on the products of the soil; and grass, which is essential for livestock, would be an inadmissible luxury. Little opportunity is left for cattle raising, and such beasts as are found on the farm form the tractive force. In some parts of the country there is a distinct prejudice against eating beef, as the slaughter of the ox who draws the plough is regarded as a poor reward for his services. Sheep are seldom found, so wool was of no consideration for clothing, and its place was taken by cotton, hemp and, for the well-to-do, silk. Except for pork, eggs and fish, the products of the chase played a far more important part in the diet of the race than the flesh of domestic animals. The Chinese character for a home is a pig under a roof. An old Manchu official whose hobby in his declining years was research into the origin of his native script, advanced the theory that at the time the language was formed houses were built on piles, the animals occupying the basement. In many places the same roof covers the whole family.

Many of the symbols connected with agriculture are graphic representations of primitive ways of farming. Irrigation was all important, and the well (井) was the centre of the village community. The character consists of two vertical lines, crossed by two horizontal strokes, like the sign for sharp in musical notation. The water supply was in the central enclosure, whilst eight families cultivated the outer squares. The central space was tilled by community labour to provide the tribute grain to satisfy the tax-collector. Cottages were not built on the arable, but together on some less productive land to form a village for mutual protection. The Imperial Government fostered initiative assessing taxation according to the productivity of the land. The reclamation of fields on river banks or on the seashore was encouraged by the remission of all dues for five years, to enable the farmer to recoup himself for the outlay.

Methods of watering the crops vary all over the country. In the south, where rice is the staple crop, mountain streams are diverted and canalised into a network of gutters leading to every part of the property. Wheels with buckets attached raise water from stagnant ponds to higher levels, or a pail with a couple of ropes attached is swung endlessly by two men to scoop up the contents of a brook. The carrying pole is the universal means of transportation, and men may be seen walking between the vegetable rows irrigating both sides at once with a pair of watering cans.

Except in Manchuria, which was only recently colonised by the Chinese, there were few large farms, and the holdings were mostly in the hands of peasant proprietors. In Kwangtung a mu (畝), or one sixth of an acre, would support a single person. The owner of two acres of good land, with a family of five, could live without work on the produce of his property. Seven acres put the landlord in the wealthy class, and very few owned as much as a hundred.

The answer to the success of the Chinese in maintaining such a vast population is sheer hard work and extreme attention to detail, rather than the application of scientific methods. Fertilising material is collected from every available source, and thus the productivity of the soil is conserved. Every inch of cultivatable earth is utilised, and the hill-sides are terraced on a most elaborate system. Work goes on from before dawn until after dark in the growing season, and the continuous manuring of plants at this period seems to obviate the necessity for the rotation of crops practised elsewhere.

Man is essentially the worker, and the character for "male" (男) is a combination of "field" (田) and Li (力), "strength". In many parts of the country, however, the women share his burden, and plenty may be seen in Hong Kong, planting rice and carrying buckets of pig feed. In some districts, however, they are not employed in the fields at all, but confine their energies to the care of the poultry, rearing of children, and making clothing for the family.

A great deal of Chinese mythology is connected with the divinities who assure good harvests, and the farmers are careful to propitiate them. The rain-producing dragon, and the sun-loving phoenix, the spirits of land and grain, and the God of the Locality (土神), all have their altars in the fields. Special paper charms, Hu Shen Fu (護身符), of no significance to the town-dweller, are bought to keep evil spirits off the cultivated land and protect the pigs and chickens. The superior kind are crude, coloured cartoons depicting the tutelary deities, but cheaper mascots are available where their names are simply written on paper.

SOME HONG KONG TEMPLES & MONASTERIES

The Castle Peak Monastery

Though everyone may have heard of the Buddhist Monastery at Castle Peak, few foreigners have visited it, owing to the fact that it is off the beaten track. Its imagined inaccessibility has conferred on what must be one of Hong Kong's oldest foundations a comparative immunity from the tourist traffic, though the difficulties are more apparent than real. It cannot be reached by car, and a visit entails a short sampan trip across the bay, and a walk of a mile and a half rising gradually to the height of four hundred and fifty feet.

There is no difficulty in finding a boat for the crossing as, if a car stops, its passengers are immediately accosted by sampan girls, only too anxious to ferry them across. A couple of girls take the oars, rowing facing forwards with the looms crossed and one foot braced against a transom across the decking. A landing is effected at some stone steps in a fishing village, about half a mile from the concreted path leading up to the temple. At the base of the hill is a small cluster of houses with a factory for making beancurd, of which the monks are the chief patrons. Like all monasteries, their principal source of income is the restaurant, where vegetarian food is served to the guests in return for a donation, though there are no fixed charges. Another product of the industry is Fu P'i (腐皮), or the skin of the curd, which is made in circular vats to the number of fifteen in a separate kitchen. Each container simmers over a slow fire, and as the skin forms on top of the liquid it is bisected with a sharp knife and is hung, after being

rolled up, on a wooden peg so that the drips fall into the pot. All Buddhist establishments are renowned for these two products, so there is much competition for their custom.

The path now leaves the cultivated plain and mounts the hill through a pine wood interspersed with an outcrop of granite boulders. Most of the large trees were felled for firewood during the Japanese occupation, but the slope has been replanted, and a few old gnarled specimens are a reminder of what the grove must have been. The monastery grounds are entered through an honorific arch of granite, decorated on top with the Taoist emblems of the dragons contesting for the lustrous pearl, and bearing the inscription "Hsiang Hai Ming Shan" (香海名山), Hong Kong Sea Illustrious Mountain. On the reverse side the corresponding panel reads "Hui T'ou Shih An" (回頭是岸), "the shore is just behind." This is a Buddhist proverb meaning that if one has fallen into sin, one can be drawn safe to land by amending one's ways. The motto was contributed by T'ieh Tan (鐵禪), a famous abbot of Canton, when the arch was erected in 1929. The names of twenty Chinese benefactors who defrayed the cost are inscribed on the upright panels.

The monastery occupies several terraces, on the first of which is a small brick building with a shrine to one of the Bodhisatvas. Suspended from the roof is a large bronze bell, gilded over and provided with a striker in the form of a battering ram. This is slung level with the rim, and can be activated by a strip of cloth within reach of the worshipper. As each passage of a sutra is read, the suppliant gives a pull at the bellrope, causing

Pei Tu shrine, Castle Peak Monastery

253

Po Lin Monastery

the wooden striker to impinge on the bell to attract the attention of the divinity and punctuate the sentence.

A flight of broad steps leads up from this court to the principal shrines through a solid gatehouse. A pavilion surmounted by a peaked roof houses Wei T'o, the guardian of Monastery, in full armour and with his gilded sword resting its point on the ground. He faces inwards towards the main temple. In a corresponding position on the outward side of the pavilion is a statue of the Buddhist Messiah, Mi Lei Fo (彌勒佛), the Indian Maitreya.

The principal building is locked but the interior is visible through the wooden screen which protects the front. The altar stands before the three usual images, with Amita in the centre, flanked by Kuan Yin and T'ai Shih-chih. The building itself is of more interest than its furnishings, for it is mainly Taoist, the roof ridge being surmounted with two elaborate dragons with the pearl between them, though Buddhistic lions squat on the corner eaves. The explanation is simple, for the monastery fell into decay some time in the reign of Tao Kuang (1821–1850) and the rival religion took over the site. The new establishment was called Ch'ing Yun Kuan (青雲觀) or "Blue Cloud Monastery", and many buildings were added. It received considerable support from the laiety at first, but its remoteness probably caused the congregations to fall off, and the monks found more lucrative employment nearer the centre of activity of the rising port. In any case the site became deserted till 1918, when the Buddhists resumed control and the first priest who took up residence became the abbot.

Taoist influence in religious matters has by no means been exorcised for, with the usual spirit of tolerance displayed by the Chinese, there is a temple to the Mother of the Measure in a court, on the right of the Buddhist shrine. The Buddhists worship her under the name of Maritchi (摩利支) and she is represented with eight arms, which are holding various weapons or religious insignia, and she is reputed to dwell among the stars which form the Dipper or the constellation Ursa Major. The Taoists also identify her with their rival to the Goddess of Mercy, T'ien Hou (天后) or the Queen of Heaven.

In a corresponding hall on the left are three racks, each holding a large number of ancestral tablets, whose worship is entrusted to the monks. All are more heavily gilded than those in the Fanling retreat, and the framework of the shelves is finely carved in high relief. One has a motif of Manchurian cranes and bamboo.

Another sight of the monastery is a garden with an arbour known as Hai Yueh T'ing (海月亭), the Sea Moon pavilion, which was erected as it afforded the best view of the moonlight on the bay. There is also a tomb for fish, as the Buddhists deprecate the taking of life, and acquire merit from ransoming the soul of animals by purchasing them from their captors. If still alive the fish are released into their native element, but if the spirit has fled they are interred to prevent them being eaten as food.

Above the buildings is a small recess in the rocks, where the granite has disintegrated forming a hole which can hardly be dignified by the name of a cave. This formerly contained the bones of a whale, who is alleged to have perished in an attempt to crush the mountain. It was probably stranded in the shallows of the bay, but

Stone image of Pei Tu

that does not make so good a story. Presumably its legendary strength made its relics the object of the acquisitive zeal of visitors, for the skeleton vanished piecemeal until only such unportable objects as the ribs remained to confirm the tale.

Above the main temple is another terrace, on which stands an empty pavilion known as the Hall of the Law (法亭). On the northern side is a grotto with a stone altar to the God of Fertility, represented by the usual conical stone. Above it, in a dark recess, reached by a flight of steep granite steps, is a plainly carved stone effigy of Pooi To (Pei Tu) (杯渡) the first abbot of the monastery. The characters denoting his name are puzzling to a foreigner, for their translation is "cup ferry". The Chinese are extremely fond of such nicknames, and would probably be equally non-plussed if they found a reference to Oliver Cromwell's son, who succeeded him as Protector, as "Tumble-down Dick". The fact is that the old monk's worldly possessions included a wooden bowl, which he used as a sampan to cross unfordable streams. As he had travelled widely he acquired the nickname, which is fortunate, for he had no other.

The date given for the selection of the name, Pei Tu Shan (杯渡山), is A.D. 428, when the Cup Ferry monk became abbot of the monastery. Five hundred years later, in A.D. 954, a military officer called Ch'en Hsun (陳巡) paid a stone mason to carve the figure of the saint which is now in the grotto on the highest terrace of the temple. A fort was erected, and a garrison installed on the hill for the control of piracy about a hundred years later, and though all trace of the buildings have disappeared the present name, Castle Peak, probably derives from its existence.

The first trace of Pei Tu in legend or history places him on the borders of Shantung and Hopei provinces, where he started his vagabond career. He was in fact a professional tramp, without any pretensions to culture, and of disreputable appearance. He was about forty when he paid a visit to the capital, then at Chien K'ang (健康), where his unsavoury appearance was the subject of considerable comment. His jacket was a mass of holes, and a frayed rope served as a belt. He alternated between fits of silence and loquacity, and rolled himself in the snow to show his contempt for the comforts of

The monastery on Lantau where One Thousand Buddhas bless you . . .

life. He was not a vegetarian but, though this trait may lower him in the estimation of the orthodox, it must be remembered that he lived a hundred years before the advent of Ta Mo, the first Chinese patriarch, and that as the religion was not codified till Hsuan Tsang's pilgrimage, another century on, he may be excused an imperfect acquaintance with the rule.

He travelled light, as his only worldly goods consisted of a rice basket and his famous wooden cup. This is first mentioned after his visit to a monastery named "Yen Hsien Ssu" (延賢寺) whose abbot gave him a room. Whilst in residence he wished to cross the Kua Pu Chiang (瓜步江) but the ferryman, who judged his clients by appearances, thought him a bad risk, and refused him as a passenger. Pei Tu just launched his cup, steeped in and floated merrily across. Miraculous transportation by water is not unknown in western hagiography, where saints have been recorded as putting to sea on altar stones, lighting fires with icicles, and turning bandits into wolves.

Pei Tu's vagabond career seems to have blunted his sense of moral values as far as the ownership of property is concerned, for he left one house with a golden Buddhist image taken without the owner's consent. When pursued on foot and on horseback, he could not be overtaken, though he appeared never to be pressing his step. At last he reached the bank of the Meng T'ien river (孟津) which, the deprived owner hoped, would prove an impassable obstacle. The Saint, however, still had his wooden cup in reserve and, tossing it into the flood, escaped with his ill-gotten gains.

The basket, his other piece of luggage, also had miraculous properties for, on one occasion, nine men could not lift it. When the interior was examined, however, it was found to contain nothing more than a pair of worn-out shoes and the wooden cup.

Whilst on a prolonged visit to a man named Lei, the saint one day asked his host to make him a new coat, as he needed it by noon. When the mid-day hour struck it was still not ready, so Pei Tu announced his intention of going for a stroll promising to return in the evening. When dusk fell he had not come back, but the house was pervaded with an uncanny sweetness. Tracing the scent to its origin, Pei Tu was discovered lying dead in a cave. He was lying naked with his ragged coat under him, and water-lilies growing at his head and feet. Lei, as his host, felt responsibility for giving him a decent burial, so returned next morning with a coffin. By then the lilies had wilted, and were as dead as Pei Tu. The corpse was duly interred but, after a few days, a man from North China visited Lei and told him he had seen Pei Tu walking with his rice basket near the town of P'eng Ch'eng (彭城). To prove him wrong Lei undertook an exhumation, but found nothing in the coffin save a pair of worn-out shoes.

The Saint showed every evidence of vitality during his sojourn in P'eng Ch'eng, where he billeted himself on a scholar who was as poor as the proverbial church mouse. This individual, whose name was Huang Hsin (黃欣), was ashamed at the miserable entertainment he could offer, and apologised for the food, only to be told that it was the best in the world. One day the saint demanded thirty-six rice baskets, but the establishment only ran to ten. Pei Tu ordered a further search in all the odd corners, where the full tally was unearthed. Most of them were old and broken but when Huang was told to inspect them more closely he found they were quite new. Pei Tu took the baskets one by one, and wrapped them up carefully, and when his host came to open them he found them full of coins. This made his fortune, and left something over for distribution to needy neighbours.

It was the parting gift of Pei Tu, for a month later he appeared on the seashore of eastern Shantung. There he encountered an old fisherman from whom he begged one of his catch. The man was a surly individual, and formed the poorest impression of the saint. At first he refused to comply with his request and then, to rid himself of the importunate beggar, he flung him a specimen which was not only dead but no longer fresh. Pei Tu took up his prize and looked at it lovingly, then he gently threw it into the sea, where it swam away. The next fisherman he accosted treated him even more churlishly, and refused any assistance, so he dropped a couple of small stones in the man's net. In a flash two water buffaloes took their place and started a battle. The net was soon torn to shreds, and then the beasts vanished. When the fisherman turned to pin the responsibility on Pei Tu, he too had disappeared into thin air.

In the ninth month of the third year of Yuan Chia (元嘉) of the Liu Sung dynasty (劉宋), A.D. 426, the old saint, after many more adventures, visited a lake named Chih Shan Hu (赤山湖) where he again died and was buried not far from Nanking. This, however, did not prevent his reappearing two years later to a friend, with whom he had lived earlier as physician to his wife. This time he merely came to say goodbye as he announced that he was migrating to Chiao Kuang (交廣) (the two southern provinces including Annam) and was not returning. He made the journey by sea, in his usual craft, accompanied by a priest, and settled in as abbot of Castle Peak monastery.

Unfortunately, at the very moment he became connected with the neighborhood the records cease. Even his image, carved four hundred years after his death, must be somewhat apocryphal, and the sculptor's sense of fitness has provided him with garments which, though blackened with the smoke of incense, show no signs of wear and tear.

The image is locally known as the Happy Monk, and it is believed that he can transfer his contentment to those who touch his heart and then place their hand on their own. Many pilgrims climb the steep steps to the dark hole in which his shrine stands, in the search of happiness so easily acquired.

At present there are only ten monks resident in the monastery, though five more come over periodically from Tsun Wan. There is a large new restaurant for sightseers, capable of accommodating a couple of hundred, and the gardens are well laid out, with a wealth of flowering shrubs and fruit trees. Every form of citrus is represented, and enough bananas to feed the monastery. Camellias and sweet-scented cassia abound, and there are numerous rose beds. Around the buildings the old trees were spared during the depredations of the Japanese occupation, among them many fine banyans and eucalyptus. At the summit of Castle Peak is a large granite boulder on which are carved the characters Kao Shan Ti Yih (高山第一). "The finest high mountain". The inscription is attributed to Han Yu (韓愈), a famous

Tin Hau Temple, Stanley

258

scholar of the T'ang dynasty, who lived from A.D. 768–824. The Chinese call the hill Ch'ing Shan (青山) or the green mountain, as the grass always keeps its colour even in the dry season, when the surrounding country is brown and bare.

Affiliated to the Buddhist Monastery at Castle Peak is a second religious house, situated on Fo Yung Shan just to the north of Tsun Wan village. It is easier of access than the older establishment as a concrete motor road, serving a weaving factory, gives access to the main gate. At the entrance of the path to the granite steps, several water colour posters inform the visitor that the precincts are a sanctuary for birds and fishes whose lives, in Buddhist eyes, are not a whit less sacred than those of human beings. The monastery, entitled Chu Lin (竹林), Bamboo Grove, is entered by a square court in which stands a large shrine to the Earth God, Guardian of the hill (土地山鎮).

The monks evidently grow all their own vegetables, for extensive gardens have been laid out full of lettuces and broccoli. In odd corners are small basins, hexagonal or oval, full of goldfish, and usually decorated by the figure of one of the Eighteen Lohans, mounted on a tiger or a dragon. Water is evidently piped from a spring on the hillside, as several of these little ponds have a rockery with a fountain in the centre.

The main building is L-shaped, with two storeys, the upper one serving as dormitories for the monks. It stands on a terrace with a large, square, uncultivated space in front, bearing the marks of the burning pits used for the Magnolia festival. The temple, in the centre of the principal block, bears the inscription Chu Lin Chan Yuan (竹林禪院), Bamboo Grove Hall of Contemplation.

The altar, in front of the Three Manifestations of Buddha, is furnished with a very fine set of the traditional five vessels in pewter, with the central incense burner surmounted by a gilded lion. Their mint condition evidences their newness, for the Wu Kung are rarely seen undented. Between the altar and the shrine is a wooden pagoda, reaching nearly to the roof, filled with images of Buddha and decorated with brass lotuses alternately used as oil lamps and as containers for artificial flowers. Wei T'o, Guardian of the temple, is represented twice. He stands leaning on his sword facing the high altar, with a second smaller image in a corner. In the south-west corner opposite him is a shrine to Kuan Kung, purely a Taoist divinity, but so popular with every section of the community as to explain his inclusion in the Buddhist pantheon. Sir Reginald Johnston advances two reasons for this admission. In the first place as "God of War" he is regarded as a valuable champion to enlist on the side of true religion; in the second place he was a tutelary deity of the Manchu dynasty. He speculated as to whether the image would tend to disappear with the advent of the Republic, but it seems its other claims have favoured its retention.

The two side walls of the temple are decorated with highly coloured frescoes of Buddha in various forms, Kuan Yin, and the Lohans with their characteristic animal mounts. The Eighteen, also called Arahats, "Destroyers of the passions", or "Worthies", are the personal disciples of Buddha, patrons and guardians of his system and its adherents, both lay and clerical. Sixteen were of Indian origin, and two are native pro-

ducts. One story to account for their inclusion was that the reigning emperor ordered their likenesses to be painted and that the artist miscounted, so that identities had to be found for his superfluity. Each is posed in an unvarying attitude with his distinctive badge or symbol, like those of the apostles and evangelists in the Christian church, the key of St. Peter, and the lion of St. Mark. The diversity of Chinese candidates for the apostolic succession lends colour to the supposition that their inclusion was the result of a clerical error. In many temples the seventeenth and eighteenth places are accorded to Nandimitra and Pindola, but sometimes the Imperial Buddhist patron Wu Ti (武帝), A.D. 502, first ruler of the Liang dynasty, is substituted. Kumarajiva, the great translator in the early fifth century, sometimes takes his place, or Dharmatrata, a scholar who lived in the first century, is preferred in certain monasteries. The patron of tobacco-sellers, Pu Tai Ho Shang (布袋和尚) or the Calico-bag monk, is portrayed seated, holding the open end of a sack which he carries on his back. Alternatively he is sitting inside the bag, with three or six young thieves, representing the deadly sins, playing round him.

Samantabhadra and Lohan

A much later attribution is that of Chi Kung (濟公) who lived at T'ien T'ai in Chekiang, and was well-versed in Buddhist doctrines. As a youth he was brilliant and, on entering a monastery after three years' mourning for his parents when he was orphaned at eighteen, he was employed by the Prime Minister Chin (秦) to deputise for him at Buddhist services. As a monk his precept was better than his practice for he indulged in wine, and scorned the disciplinary rule. He posed as an eccentric, an attitude always rewarded with indulgence in China, and revelled in worldly affairs. His uncanny intelligence in setting law-suits, curing illness, and consequently vanquishing demons, was so outstanding as

259

to earn him the title of the Mad Healer (濟顛).

It is believed that when the Buddhist Messiah, Maitreya (彌勒佛), returns to earth, the Lohans will collect all the relics of Sakyamuni, and will erect over them a magnificent stupa, before being consumed in a fiery ecstasy. Their ashes will be absorbed in the fast dissolving Nirvana or, to put it more tersely, they will vanish in smoke.

Arahatship implies the possession of certain supernatural powers and the attainment of Nirvana, though the Saint in question is not eligible for Buddhahood. The Chinese have extended the title beyond the circle of the eighteen disciples who are appointed to certain stations in various parts of the world, to include their subordinates, who run into legions. A temple in Canton boasts of five hundred Lohans, and a Peking collection includes the traveller Marco Polo. Most of the pictures and images are derived from the work of T'ang dynasty artists, based on descriptions from Buddhist records. The two Chinese representatives are distinguishable by the dragon and the tiger, and are called Hsiang Lung (降龍) "vanquishing the dragon", and Fu Hu (俘虎) "subduing the tiger", respectively.

The lower storey of the wing of the main building contains the refectory in the centre of which is a seat for the lector, raised on a dais before the altar of Buddha. There are four long, solid tables, set with bowls and chopsticks for thirty-four monks and lay brethren. Leading out of the dining hall on the south side is the guest reception room, where an excellent vegetarian meal may be obtained. The walls are decorated with scrolls, and specimens of calligraphy executed by the fraternity, and there is a large portrait of a deceased abbot. The brother who entertains guests is a recent refugee from China.

A path on the left of the monastery leads up the hill to the abbot's lodge on a wide terrace cultivated as a vegetable garden. The house is guarded by yet another statue of Wei T'o in a pavilion surmounted by a pointed roof. The guardian is himself protected by a glass case, and is surmounted by the inscription Hu Ch'ih Fo Fa (護治佛法), "Maintain and guard the Law of Buddha."

A corresponding path to the east of the main block contours the hill at a gentle slope and then rises steeply, where it has been surfaced with concrete, in hairpin bends, to the shrine of the Goddess of Mercy. The last fifty yards are decorated with lotus flowers traced in the cement. A group of granite rocks, capping a spur on the southern slop of Tai Mo Shan (大帽山), is topped by a cubical boulder and a natural cave has been formed by the erosion of the less stable stone. Kuan Yin has probably replaced some far older primitive divinity in so obvious a setting. In front of the cave is a flagged terrace with the lotus in the centre, and a small pavilion for refreshment on the eastern side. Steps lead down to the living quarters of the guardian, who provides tea for pilgrims. There is only a small porcelain image of the divinity, also in a glass case, but the view from an unaccustomed angle is well worth the ascent. The caretaker wears his hair long, but otherwise exhibits none of the characteristics of the hermit. His hospitality is limited to tea and peanuts, but he is a good host and a fluent conversationalist. According to his account the shrine, in its present condition, was only built about twenty years back and its appearance confirms the asser-

tion. The whole establishment lacks the atmosphere of antiquity which marks the temple of Castle Peak, but its situation and comparative accessibility redeem this shortcoming. The track up to the monastery branches off the new military road about two hundred yards from Tsun Wan, and is marked by the inevitable bean curd factory which is the concomitant of every vegetarian community.

Redecorating the Temple

The religious establishments at Fanling show every sign of vitality for the Taoist temple on the hillside above the railway station has been recently remodelled, whilst the Contemplative Retreat for Old Ladies on the edge of the rice cultivation, not only laid out a pleasure garden, complete with ornamental pavilions, just above the rival establishment, but also entirely renovated its own place of worship.

To celebrate the event, services lasting three days were held, and open house was kept for all friends and well-wishers. A continuous stream of visitors, mostly bearing gifts of food, descended from every train. Many joined in the worship, and it was not unusual to see a girl in modern slit gown kneeling beside a shaven-headed nun in brown vestments. Others explored the gardens, bright with chrysanthemums and dahlias and scented with the flowers of cassia. In Hong Kong the commonest tree of this species flowers in the autumn, with clusters of yellow blooms which look, at a distance, like laburnum or golden chain. The variety most esteemed by the Chinese has small waxen blossoms which fill a whole room with a delicate perfume. It is believed to flourish in groves in the moon, and under its shade the Jade Rabbit sits compounding the elixir of life. In Peking it blossoms about the time of the Moon Festival,

Buddhist priest and acolite

260

Obeisance at Taoist temple on Cheung Chau

and small specimens in pots are sent to friends as a seasonable gift.

Though the residents of the Retreat are strictly Buddhist, the gate giving on the rice fields is guarded by the shrine of T'u Ti (土地), the God of the Locality, on whose miniature altar incense burns, and a libation of wine stands in a cup. This particular Earth God has a long white beard and, clad in a red waistcoat and blue official robes, he bears a strong resemblance to Father Christmas.

T'u Ti was an institution with the Chinese long before the advent of the organised religions and, as they declined to dispense with his services as registrar of births, deaths and marriages, both Buddhists and Taoists were obliged to add him to their pantheon. He probably obtained his new coat at the time the more orthodox images were regilded. All had a lavish application of gold leaf, and new drapery had been provided in the principal shrine. The curtains screening the three main images, with Amita in the centre flanked by Kuan Yin and T'ai Shih-chih (太勢至), were red with a floral design. The altar before the door into the courtyard was furnished with an orange silk frontal bearing the full invocation to the principal divinity "Namah Amitaba" (Hear us Amitaba Buddha). In Peking, Buddhists are very strict on the question of colour and, in choosing their silks the Tibetan sect will only accept the pure golden yellow reserved for Imperial use, and reject any material with a suspicion of red or orange. In the recess at the right of the high altar, Ti Tsang Pusa (地藏菩薩) was resplendent with burnished gold and many offerings lay on his altar. He can always be identified by his warning staff with its loop and jingling rings, and by the lustrous jewel he holds between finger and thumb of the left hand.

Several newly painted fish-head drums were disposed about the sanctuary, all gleaming with scarlet and gold. One, which lay on a board below the great bell which summons the faithful to prayer, was about thirty inches in diameter.

The high altar was dressed with vases of chrysanthemums and pyramids of oranges and apples. A pummelo with an orange on top, giving it the aspect of the gourd so beloved by the Chinese, occupied a position on most of the shrines. A large pile of red packets contained tea, which is distributed to all visitors on leaving, as it possesses medicinal properties.

Each parting guest was also furnished with a "Lucky money" envelope endorsed "Buddha's strong and skilful hand", as a memento of the occasion. These gestures are in return for the contributions of sympathisers in the shape of gifts for the temple, ranging from oil for the altar lamps to silk for the draperies, with fruit and food for its servitors. One woman brought a stack of carboard boxes, with no less than four hundred white dumplings stamped with a red design. Another produced tins of Ovaltine, whilst grapes, oranges and pummeloes filled up every available space on the altars.

Until recently the temple was served by a priest from the Hsi Lin (西林) Monastery at Shatin, which has a dormitory for refugees from the mainland, who are supernumerary to the ordinary establishment. Now the residents of the nunnery have given a home to a septuagenarian, exiled from his temple in Canton, who ministers to their religious needs. The vital force behind the community is probably "Auntie", who, after devoting her life to organising the households and happiness of senior Service officers, retired to embrace religion with unabated fervour. She rises for the first service at 3 a.m. and declares that she has never felt more energetic in her life. Certainly her appearance does not belie the assertion.

During the festival the services were almost continuous, one hour in three being spent in prayer. The congregation knelt in a row before the altar with the orange frontal, and the officiating priest with a server stood at a lectern before the image of Amita. On the right of the worshippers was the drummer, with a silver bell suspended over the percussion instrument. When the full prostration was made at particularly solemn parts of the service, the worshippers opened their hands as they struck their foreheads against the ground.

After the benediction the congregation formed single file and circled the temple twenty one times, intoning the name of Amitaba. Then everyone adjourned for a meal, the foreigners in a private room, and the Chinese guests in the refectory. Enormous quantities and variety of excellent vegetarian food were consumed, ending up with fruit and tea though "Auntie", acquainted with the peculiarities of foreigners, produced strong coffee to wash down the lunch. Buddhist establishments are renowned for their bean curd, or Tou Fu, of which the Chinese are connoisseurs. They always lay in a stock in the villages in preference to the town, for they state that in a small community everybody knows who makes it, whereas if bought in a large centre its origin is anonymous. In the first case the maker can be quickly brought to book if his product is below standard, whereas in the second, his identity being concealed, he escapes censure.

Most of the people who have stored their ancestral tablets in the temple, to derive the benefit of the inmates' care and their prayers and sacrifices, take the opportunity of making a pilgrimage to perform their personal act of worship. The altar before the seventy odd green and gold memorials was loaded with grapes and oranges, whilst innumerable sticks of incense smouldered in the censer. Wei T'o, guarding the back door, was a striking figure resplendent with gold leaf. As a rule his weapon, though at hand for use, is not carried in a threatening manner. The divine thunderbolt is cradled in the crook of the arms with the hands raised in prayer, or the point of the sword is resting on the ground. In this case, however, the gilded halberd is stretched out as if ready to strike, and the flowing garments make the figure full of action.

These Old Ladies' Homes, of which there are a number in Hong Kong, are an admirable conception. Some, for the poor, are charitable organisations, others which cater for those who have laid by some savings charge an entrance fee. In both cases any visitor must be struck with the atmosphere of happiness which reigns there. The pensioners look as if they have not a care in the world, which is indeed a fact. Once accepted they need take no thought for their bodily wants until they close their eyes for the last time. They enjoy congenial society and can work as little or as much as they please, whilst their own room ensures their privacy. Those whose aspirations soar beyond the grave have the consolation of religion, and can dedicate their declining years to ensure a favourable reception in after life. In actual fact the healthy occupation of mind and body which is imposed by the regime, tends to promote abnormal

Ngong Ping Monastery, Lantau

longevity, the ambition of every son and daughter of Han. It would seem that they have discovered the elixir of life sought by their Taoist confrères, which invests them with the cloak of immortality.

In any case it is a privilege to visit them, for the warmth of their welcome is a heartening experience. Every guest is presented with a packet of the health-assuring tea and an envelope of lucky money, whilst those who have brought gifts are laden with food and peanuts in addition. The Chinese are a hospitable race, and eagerly seize any occasion for a party, so a festival is a golden opportunity. As far as the hostesses are concerned the event will form the topic of conversation for weeks, and the subject will be dissected from every angle. Having less resources from reading, the spoken word assumes a greater importance, and discussions are pushed to a length incomprehensible to a westerner.

Temples at Stanley

Several rocks with small shrines in front of them indicate the primitive religion of the fishing population which must for centuries have based its operations on the two bays divided by Stanley peninsula. The temple of the Queen of Heaven, however, evidently owes its origin to the prosperity of the Chinese village which caters for the wants, not only of the Boat People, but of the cultivators who have exploited every available square inch of arable land. The square building stands in a gently sloping valley, between two streams which cut their way through the sand at the northern end of the bay. A concrete path, passing an old rock shrine just beyond the hotel, gives access to the building and serves the valley for the marketing of its vegetable produce.

The main door of the temple is guarded by two stone lions simply carved in the Southern style, and just before the entrance stands a large cast-iron incense-burner, dedicated to the "Saint of the Eastern Sea", and presented by the Householders Association of the village.

On crossing the threshold one finds oneself in a sort of ante-chamber in one corner of which is a shrine to the God of Good Luck and Virtue, who, according to the inscription, hands out the yellow metal to those who are pure in heart. Judging by the patronage he receives, the streets of Stanley should be paved with gold. The main portion of the temple accommodates a perfect pantheon of divinities, each a specialist in his own line, but this Gate God is a general practitioner, attending to any form of request, and is readily accessible to all. A veritable forest of incense sticks smoulders before him as evidence of his popularity. In a small chamber at the east end of the hall is a professional fortune-teller whose services are in great demand. A screen separates the ante-room from a central court, open to the sky, in the middle of which is a large, square basin dry at the moment, but which would greatly add to the picturesqueness of the chamber were it planted with lotus. Against the northern wall is an altar dating from 1800 whose frontal is decorated with coloured carvings of the Eight Immortals.

The sanctuary beyond contains an amazing assortment of gods, mostly ranged on a broad shelf against the north wall and flanking the principal shrine of the Queen of Heaven. This divinity is duplicated, as for everyday use

she is portrayed enthroned between her traditional attendants, whilst curtains conceal a much larger image behind her, only unveiled for her annual festival. Numerous votive offerings decorate the shrine including a junk, balanced by a vase of flowers, and a toilet case with mirror and small drawers containing make-up and hair ornaments. There is an interesting seven-branched candlestick, provided with small saucers for a wick in oil.

At the east end of the sanctuary is a section devoted to a miscellaneous collection of divinities, whose names and attributes are recorded in green and red on a poster behind them. This is known as the Dark Altar, or the "disaster killing" shrine, and it offers an example of the charm guaranteed to achieve the desired result. A wooden tiger, about to spring, is a notorious enemy of evil spirits, and it is reinforced by a skin of the real beast hanging on the wall, whose resistance to moths has not been commensurate with his influence over the powers of darkness. This was the gift of an individual who attributed his escape from demoniac possession to the intervention of the image.

The other members of the anti-disaster group are the Demonslaying Boy, His Imperial Majesty the White Ape, Field Marshal Yin (殷), a sort of lightning conductor, and the "Most observant pundit in astrology and geography".

The local God of Wealth may be worshipped here also, in the form of the Wu Ch'ang Kuei (無常鬼), or "Unpredictable Ghost", whose headdress bears the inscription "One glance brings fortune". He was trans-

The unpredictable ghost Wu-ch'ang Kuei

264

Shing Wong Temple (Buddhist)

lated from his shrine in the Feng Hsin Ku (馮仙姑) temple at Causeway Bay when it was demolished for building development. There is a rather battered clay image of the Celestial Dog (天狗), companion of Erh Lang (二郎), who was instrumental in the capture of Monkey when he made Heaven too hot to hold him. Those so inclined may worship the "Five Ghost Boys", and the "Door-hanging Ghost" or the two "Pacifying Lads".

On the left of the Dark Altar is a gilt image of Hsüan Tsang (玄奘), carrying the Warning staff with its jingling rings, who might be mistaken for Ti Tsang Pusa, were it not for the fact that his left hand is open and unprovided with the pearl which is one of his attributes. This divinity is also a newcomer who migrated in the late autumn of 1954 with the Unpredictable Ghost from the other side of the island.

The Imperial White Ape, better known as the "Great Sage equal to Heaven" (齊天大聖), is depicted in an unusual attitude, for he is carved walking on his hands. He forms part of a trio consisting of the Water God, Shui Shu Huang Ti (水屬皇帝), holding aloft a boat, and Tam Kung (譚公), Hong Kong's local Saint, whose influence over the weather endears him to the fisher-folk. He does not enjoy a separate festival here, but is amenable to petitions at all times of the year.

The shrine of the Queen of Heaven is flanked by two male figures, the left being Wen Ch'ang (溫昶), one of the Gods of Literature, and the right Chiang Wang Yeh, whose speciality is picking lucky days. Then comes a canopied shrine for Kuan Yin (觀音), whose left supporter is Pao Ch'en, a virtuous magistrate of the Sung

The Dragon Mother of Yueh Ch'eng

Dynasty, and a red paper poster on the wall to the Patron Saints of the temple. In the north-east corner are three Saints, Kuan Kung (關公), Pei Ti (北帝), and Lung Mu (龍母), the Dragon Mother. The Taoist temple in Hollywood Road is dedicated to her, but her place of origin is Yueh Ch'eng (悦城) on the West River not far from the Kwanghsi border. Prior to the War a regular boat pilgrimage, lasting several days, took place in the Fifth Moon. Against the east wall of the sanctuary is a shrine containing the Ch'eng Huang (城隍), or City God, surrounded by his officials and lictors. As a rule, a town has to be of considerable importance to support a Ch'eng Huang, and old Kowloon City never achieved that status. The Stanley divinity is merely a guest god transplanted from the Mainland by the lessee of the temple revenues, and stored within its walls for convenience.

A curious relic has been preserved at the west end of the sanctuary in the shape of the bell and drum belonging to the famous pirate, Chang Pao-tzü (張保仔), who captured Hong Kong and Lantau in 1770. The bell, surmounted by the usual dragon, bears the date of casting, the 32nd of the reign of Ch'ien Lung (乾隆), or 1768. It was given to the temple by a member of the congregation. A red label, pasted on the bell, gives a transcription of the lettering and states that it is a hundred and eighty-eight years old.

The drum is painted navy blue, with peonies in gold on the barrel. This motif was carried out on the skin, but long use has obliterated much of the design. Gold lettering announces that it was made by Teh Wu Sheng Chih in Canton City, Ta Hsin Road, and that the materials were selected by the Hua Cheng Shop. It was presented to the T'ien Hou (天后), Mother Saint of Chik Chu (赤柱), by her devoted disciple Weng Yüeh-hua.

God of the Water, Shu Huang Ti

266

Pirates' bell and drum, Stanley

Behind the figure of Hsüan Tsang is another inscription, on red paper posted on the wall, to the Patron Saint of the Year, and the Matron, Patron Saint of children.

Consecrating a Temple

Pei Ti's little rock temple in the west bay at Stanley has been derelict since the Japanese occupation, when the inhabitants of the village, desperate for fuel, unroofed the shrine and appropriated the rafters. On a petition from the local elders, the building and its surroundings were reconditioned by the Secretariat for Chinese Affairs and the management was leased to the Stanley K'ai Fongs. The temple is approached by a narrow path along the cliffs, which renders access by processions precarious, and it can be reached from the beach, after negotiating the rocks, by a flight of granite steps. The spirits which serve Hong Kong evidently

have a predilection for rocks, and an even greater affinity for caves and grottoes formed by their disintegration. In this case the brick structure has been built round one of these niches in the cliff, whilst outside some local Earth God has taken up his residence in another cleft, where he is further protected from the elements by the addition of a concrete screen. Broad granite steps lead down from the land approach, shaded by an ancient banyan whose trunk forms an arch, with its sprawling roots in the hillside, and a lopped off branch resting on the balustrade. This guard rail is carried on round the building, culminating in a semi-circular balcony before the main entrance. It provides a very necessary protection to the worshippers from a sheer drop of thirty feet onto the rocks. Decorated with glazed tiles, it adds to the picturesqueness of the tiny temple in which the accommodation for the congregation is only fourteen feet square. From landward it is impossible to get a comprehensive view of the complex, except at so great a distance as to eclipse the detail, and it is only from the sea that the shrine detaches itself from the cliffs and its leafy screen.

Before the days of a piped water supply it was probably much frequented by the fisher-folk, as a few feet above high water mark there is a well, locally supposed to have medicinal qualities. The presence of a constant flow, independent of water restrictions, determined one of the Tanka to provide his family with a shore base, in the shape of a two-roomed shack, the temple being used as a hen run and a playground for the children.

The interior decoration of the reconditioned shrine was the responsibility of the village elders, and a house to house collection provided funds for the opening celebration. Various people donated furniture, and craftsmen gave their services free, to construct incense burners and a carved screen to frame the images of the Deity. This was painted scarlet and gold, with the name and the title of the God, and the decorations consisted of tree peonies and two lucky bats.

As it was highly desirable that the patron should start his new ministry with a favourable impression of his congregation, and as the unfortunate episode of his previous eviction had to be obliterated, a puppet show was engaged to perform for two days and three nights for his entertainment. Workmen were already busy with the erection of a gigantic matshed for the theatricals which form part of the T'ien Hou (天后) festival on the 23rd of the Third Moon, so it was a matter of a few hours' diversion from their task to run up a theatre and a Royal Box for the divinity, fifty yards in front of the footlights. The whole affair was elaborately wired, and was a blaze of lights during the evening performances.

A lucky day was first determined for the inauguration of Pak Tai (北帝), and the puppet show started on the eve of the consecration. The God's box was occupied by a scarlet scroll setting forth his name and titles illuminated by a red lamp. Half the village crowded on to the beach for a performance lasting four hours, and there was a constant coming and going, till the finale of clashing cymbals and clanging gongs brought down the curtain.

Images of the deities are supposed to be unconscious of their surroundings until their eyes have been opened with the touch of blood drawn from the comb of a cock. Two representations of Pak Tai, one permanent and one portable, had been ordered from the carvers in Yaumati and these, wrapped in red paper, were installed on the altar of the temple on the first day. The lucky hour for the vitalising ceremony was declared to be in the afternoon of the 24th of the Second Moon. As the shrine had been abandoned for so long at the mercy of the elements and the desecration of domestic fowls, a cleansing ceremony was indicated, before the eyes of the God were opened to his surroundings.

The temple was first hung with innumerable paper talismans, candles and incense were lit, and an exorcist performed the office. His brows were encircled with a red ribbon as a fillet, and round his waist was an apron skirt in three panels. First he performed a ritual dance and then, arming himself with two musical instruments, he made a spirited onslaught on the intruders. A buffalo horn was taken in one hand, whilst the other grasped a piece of metal shaped like a spear head, its ends furnished with a loop garnished with rings. It is an abbreviated form of the warning staff always carried by Ti Tsang Pusa (地藏菩薩) to obviate the destruction of creatures who crawl underfoot. The horn was blown sideways, and the staff jangled in all directions to expel the evil influences, whilst the exorcist, assisted by three priests and the village elders, burned demon-diffusing talismans and scattered the ashes to the four winds of heaven. Silent spectators of the ritual were the paper images of the Red Horseman and one of the Judges of the Underworld.

When the temple had been thoroughly cleansed, the priests put on their vestments, and the village elders produced a struggling cock. Its comb having been pricked the officiating priest dipped a Chinese brush in the blood, and annointed the eyes of the two images.

A gesture was then made of sprinkling drops of blood on all the temple furnishings, including the inanimate onlookers. The Red Horseman after being blooded was committed to the flames, his ashes dropping sheer into the sea, sped on his way to his element with a volley of crackers.

The service ended, the smaller image was carried in procession to the beach for installation at the puppet show, and his appearance caused instant panic among the audience who fled incontinent. As a matter of fact an injunction had been issued to certain age groups, that they might not cast their eyes on the divinity before he had taken his seat for the play, but the crowd was taking no chances of courting ill luck, and all thought it preferable to be on the safe side.

The age groups are determined by casting lots in the temple, but there is a certain elasticity about them, and the figures can be juggled so as to include other categories. Thus, if 62 is a banned number, by reversing it people of 26 might conceivably be affected. By adding the two digits, children of eight might be included as susceptible to the evil eye.

All minor ailments in the village for several days after the installation of the God were attributed to the lèse majesté of looking at his image when eyes should have been averted, and there was a constant procession to his temple, with incense and offerings, to apologise for the slight.

A fresh scroll setting out his titles was first affixed as a reredos, and an immensely thick stick of incense was ignited before the figure. The usual shooting for luck on beach then took place under his patronage, after which the audience adjourned for the evening meal. As soon as darkness fell the puppet troupe gave a gala performance.

Most of the important images for temples in Hong Kong were carved in Sheklung, prior to the change of régime in China but, as materialism has superseded religion, there is at present little demand for the services of these artisans on the mainland. Some moved from Fat Shan to Hong Kong, and certain craftsmen, who specialise in the Buddhistic pantheon, transferred their business from Shanghai.

Pak Tai should be represented as holding a furled-up banner in his hand, his right foot supported by a serpent and his left by a tortoise. The union of these two creatures is usually symbolic of the formation of the universe, but their presence in this connection has nothing to do with the legend of the creation.

Village Shrines

Quite apart from the many temples of organised religion in Hong Kong, every village possesses numerous places of worship, presided over by a tree or gigantic rock, at which most primitive rites are practised. Most of these sanctuaries are credited with being inhabited by a local spirit whose function is to dispel sickness and promote procreation. Unless worship is actually being performed, or the sacred places are decorated for New Year, these village shrines are apt to be overlooked even by an observant visitor, for they are inconspicuous, and often camouflaged by a hawker's stall, which distracts the eye.

The organised temples are well maintained, for this is the responsibility of the Government which farms out the revenue to private individuals and, after keeping the fabric in good repair, devotes the surplus to charity. Certain hospitals, such as the Tung Wah, have several temples as part of their endowment. Many village shrines, however, receive no monetary offerings, and, in a large number of cases, have no structure to maintain. Sometimes a small brick shelter is erected with some handy shack for an ancient who has no other visible means of subsistence and so becomes a self-appointed guardian of the mysteries. The offerings usually amount to about five cents a head, which nobody grudges to the enterprising exploiter of the deity.

Prior to the erection of the large T'ien Hou temple at Stanley, it is probable that the fishermen frequented a small shrine on the rock point in the centre of the West Bay, which is the obvious landing place for their catch. It consists of a brick structure with the usual tiled roof on the top of a rough mound on the promontory with an altar on the north side. The object of worship is a wooden tablet in a carved frame mounted on a rectangular base, and bearing two inscriptions in tarnished gold characters. The left-hand column reads "The shrine of the Ancient Water Immortal, Defender of the realm, and Protector of its people", whilst the other assures the faithful that the "Almighty God of Wealth brings riches to all worshippers at his altar". At the winter solstice a grey porcelain burner was full of smouldering incense-sticks, interspersed with Chao Hun Fan (招魂旛), or Spirit-calling flags. These consist of stiff oblong pieces of paper crudely stamped with the effigy of some unidentifiable god in green and red. They are mounted on sticks, and the top of each banner is decorated with a tab of scarlet paper. On the altar in front of the tablet stood a libation of black liquid, probably soy, in a cheap china cup. Three pointed stones of granite flanked the tablet, votive offerings suggestive of the phallic origin of the worship. One was a water-worn boulder, shaped like a neolithic axe, which might have been the contribution of a Stone Age ancestor of the aboriginal Boat People whose ancient beliefs persist into the twentieth century.

Adjacent to the Stanley Hotel is a huge granite rock against which a small open-fronted shrine has been erected. Steps lead up the altar, on which stands a single pyramidal stone. Built in connection with this is a two-roomed cottage to house the guardian of the shrine, to whom it has evidently brought a certain degree of affluence. In fact he has extended the business by increasing his pantheon to include three divinities in his bedroom. Against the north wall is an altar with a wooden shrine containing a gilt image of Hung Hsing (洪聖), one of Hong Kong's most popular gods. The worshippers are assured that "His favours are like sunshine illuminating the world", and that "His virtues are showered like a flood on all inhabitants of the earth". Two tablets to Tam Kung and the Queen of Heaven flank the central shrine on the altar. On the west wall of the temple, whose name is the "Palace of the Great Prince" (大王宮), is a list of subscribers to its repair and unkeep. To a foreigner the conglomeration of buildings looks like an ordinary cottage, for the front is hidden by a creeper-covered trellis, and only two characters over the arch inform the natives that the spot is sacred ground (聖地). The camouflage is increased by the fact that the rock shrine is masked by the stall of a soft-drinks hawker, who has even adorned the lintels of the shrine with the advertisement of his wares.

There is a very big pig-farm at the foot of the valley, with an enterprising owner who improves his breed with imported boars. These modern ideas do not prevent him acquiring a monkey, to "keep the pigs happy" as a local resident explained. It is difficult to see what form of entertainment the ape provides, as he is confined to the farmhouse where he has little opportunity of contact with the "gentlemen who pay the rent". The only possible origin of the belief seems to be the association of the divine White Monkey with Pigsy in their pilgrimage to India in search of the Buddhist scriptures. On this occasion, famous in Chinese folklore, Monkey, as the dominant partner, was largely responsible for the success of Tripitaka's mission, and was canonised for his services. The Pig, on account of the fact that he had not lost his appetite, and lacked refinement and appearance, was only appointed official scavenger to all Buddhist altars throughout the world. It is reasonable to suppose that his descendants benefit by the unconsumed portion of the rations offered at Monkey's shrine, the surest means of contributing to their happiness.

Local Worthies

Some of the divinities in the Taoist pantheon enjoy a purely local popularity, and have little appeal to those sections of the community for whose special interests they do not cater. Thus T'ien Hou (天后), the maritime goddess, though invented to offset the Buddhist Kuan Yin, has few shrines or adherents among the cultivators of the interior, or the landsmen of the North. Allegedly a native of Fukien, that province is naturally her stronghold, but her territorial claims are rivalled by those of her profession, as she was a fisherman's daughter. There are over two dozen temples dedicated to her in Hong Kong, and her shrine is to be found in the port cabin of every Boat-family's junk. As the perils of the sea are ever present, and the elementary precaution of learning to swim has never occurred to these simple-minded water-folk, they pin their faith on the protection of the deity who rescued her parents from a nameless grave. Death without a known place of burial is the worst fate which can befall a Chinese, so Ma Chu's act of filial piety in drawing their junk safe to land by will power alone, during a raging typhoon, ensured her canonisation.

A much less widely known saint is the Dragon Mother of Yueh Ch'eng (悅城龍母), to whom a temple in Hollywood Road is dedicated. Her effigy is also worshipped in the T'ien Hou temples at Stanley, Aberdeen and Yeo Kuk Street, and the Tam Kung (譚公) shrines in Wongneichong and Shaukiwan.

Yueh Ch'eng is a town on the West River, about two-thirds of the distance between Canton and Wuchow, on whose site an old woman once earned her livelihood by catching fish. In searching for firewood she came across a gigantic egg, which she carried home, and incubated. From it was hatched a strange creature whose assistance proved most beneficial to her fishing activities. By accident, however, she cut off a portion of the creature's tail, upon which it left her mourning her loss as there was a noticeable deterioration in her catch. Some years later the creature returned so gorgeously changed that she recognised it for a dragon. The story filtered through to the Emperor who issued a summons to the old lady to present herself at court, and give an account of her method of raising Imperial beasts. She only performed half the journey when she was overcome by homesickness and turned back. There was no need for her to walk, as the dragon at once appeared, and deposited her instantaneously on the banks of the West River. Her story created a great sensation, and was passed on from generation to generation among the fisherfolk, who all hankered after a summons to court and free transportation by Dragon Express. Eventually, as she was the only one to benefit by the experience, she was canonised as the patroness of navigators of the stream. Prior to the closing of the frontier there was an annual pilgrimage to her shrine by boat from Hong Kong.

The story lacks conviction, for one is left wondering at the reactions of the Emperor whose summons was unheeded, and who, in those days, possessed the sole right to confer the honour of canonisation. The critical faculty, however, is not strongly developed among her worshippers, and the legend probably grew from the habit of giving thanks to some great rock in the West River Gorge, after a successful passage of the narrows.

A purely local worthy is Tam Kung who, though a native of Wei Yang, received enlightenment and performed his miracles within Hong Kong, his instructors being the Nine Dragons of Kowloon.

His control over the weather endears him to the Boat People, who observe his festival, on the 8th of the Fourth Moon, with the same ceremonies as those accorded to the Queen of Heaven a fortnight previously. The main festival is at Shaukiwan, and other temples are dedicated to the Saint at Aberdeen and Wongneichong, and there is an image of him in the T'ien Hou temple at Stanley. His spirit tablet is also to be found on the altar of a small temple to the north of the village, dedicated to another popular sea divinity, Hung Hsing (洪聖).

There are at least nine temples to this elusive deity about whose antecedents little or nothing is known to his worshippers, who rest content in the belief that he is potent in seafaring lore. Even the guardians of the shrines differ widely in their details of his biography. One considers him reincarnated as the Dragon King who rules the southern seas, and suppresses all monsters and phantoms inimical to those whose business is dependent on their waters. The most general view is that he was a virtuous official, who was canonised for his services to the people. According to one version his name was Hung Hsi and, during the T'ang Dynasty, he was a third-degree graduate and Governor of Kuan Li. During his tenure of office he encouraged the study of astronomy, geography and mathematics, establishing an observatory whose accurate predictions were of the greatest value to traders and fishermen. Unfortunately he sacrificed his health by overwork in the interests of his people, and died on the 13th of the Second Moon. A memorial was sent to the reigning Emperor who declared him worthy of worship under the posthumous title of "Kuang Li Hung Hsing Ta Wang" (廣利洪聖大王). The gentry, in various places around the coast, erected temples to his memory.

Another account makes him die at a ripe old age as an honoured official who curbed the violent, and protected the defenceless. His spirit carried on his life's work, and saved many from typhoons and local disasters. Canonisation followed and the first temple was erected to him under the name of Po Lo (波羅), in Luk Po Si. His full title is "Nan Hai Kuang Li Hung Hsing Ta Wang" (南海廣利洪聖大王).

It is preferable to discard the sea monster legend, and think of Hung Hsing as the precursor of the Jesuit fathers, who for eighty years issued warnings to mariners from the Siccawei observatory thereby mitigating the dangers of navigation for the craft of all nations. By devoting their lives to the broad humanitarian principle of bringing safety to every seaman on the China coast regardless of race or creed, they compare favourably with the protagonists of the Marxian doctrine who have decreed that the divulgence of such information constitutes a capital offence.

A single temple, situated at Quarry Bay, is dedicated to the "Second Uncle", in Cantonese: Yee Pak Kung (二伯公). It is said to be over sixty years old, and was erected in honour of a certain Ho Chen (和珍), or Shih Lou (石樓), who lived in the reign of Ch'ien Lung (1736–96). Being a second son, the affectionate honorific of Second Uncle was posthumously bestowed on him. He was an extremely intelligent lad but, though he perfected himself in the classics at a tender age, he never had the luck to qualify at the Imperial examinations. One day he encountered a Taoist who had mastered the mysteries of his creed and could perform miracles. Under his able tuition Ho Chen became an adept, and gained popularity in his lifetime by his willingness to help others who applied to him in distress. His death was universally mourned, and many beside his own family worshipped at his tomb. It was then found his good influence had outlived him, and occasionally miracles were performed through the invocation of his spirit.

Towards the end of Ch'ien Lung's reign the district in which his native place lay, Fu T'ang in Chang Lou (長樂) county, was overrun by the Mao Shan sect, an anti-dynastic secret society. This was one of the names of the White Lotus Society which was formed in the reign of the Mongol Emperor Wu Tsung as a protest against persistent misrule. It was given a religious complex by Han Shan-t'ung (韓山童), grandson of the founder, who declared that the advent of Maitreya, the Redeemer, was at hand.

Han's position was strengthened by the allegation that he was a descendant of the Sung Dynasty which had fallen before the Mongol invasion, but he was captured and executed early in the rebellion. His son carried on the revolt and was actually proclaimed Emperor, but died in Nanking in 1367, and the prize fell to his friend Chu Yuan-chang who seized the throne as the first of the Mings. The society reappeared with the break-up of that dynasty, and joined forces with a rebel leader, who was defeated and killed in action. Chinese secret societies frequently go underground with a change of name, when repressive measures threaten their security, and it was as the Mao Shan Chiao (茅山教) that the White Lotus raised its head in 1794 in the last years of Ch'ien Lung. The rebellion was at its worst in Hupei and West China where the old technique was followed in producing an alleged descendant of the Mings as a leader. The rising lasted ten years, and in the first four months twenty thousand adherents of the sect were beheaded. Even these drastic reprisals were unavailing, for the movement spread over six provinces. The whole of Chang Lou county was ravaged, and the birthplace of Ho Chen was threatened. The inhabitants accordingly held a service at the tomb, offering through a child prayers for protection. The "Uncle" was responsive and, speaking in the voice of the petitioner, said: "Fear not! Plant as many banners as possible around the village and the sandbanks which fringe the river. I will order the hosts of Heaven to intervene on your behalf."

The legendary period during which supernatural interventionists were most active was just prior to the accession of the Chou Dynasty in 1122 B.C. when, during the civil wars, a multitude of demi-Gods, Buddhas and Immortals took part on one side or the other, some favouring the old and some the new administration. Not only could they change shape at will, become invisible, or multiply their limbs, but they also exploited every sort of unconventional weapon from poison gas and germ warfare to atom bombs in the shape of thunderbolts.

The Second Uncle, however, was not so spectacular in his form of assistance for he caused a thick fog to descend upon the delta which frustrated the rebel operations until a relieving force of Imperial troops forced their withdrawal. The escape of the town was of course attributed to divine intervention, and the county magistrate forwarded a petition to the throne for the canonisation of Ho Chen, and started collecting funds for the erection of a temple to his memory. In his lifetime he

Buddhist monks at prayer at Ngong Ping monastery

earned universal respect as an honest, upright man and has always been held in reverence as a powerful divinity. His shrine is esteemed on account of the excellence of the prescriptions for remedies, obtainable after going through the usual preliminaries of casting lots to determine the appropriate medicine, so he is most in vogue as a God of Healing. His festival coincides with that of Tam Kung, the local fishermen's divinity, being celebrated on the 8th of the Fourth Moon.

A secondary image in this temple is that of the Sleeping Buddha to whom petitions are offered for the fulfilment of desires which do not involve medical treatment. This is another instance, of which there are plenty in Hong Kong, where the two religions flourish under the same roof. Though in the past each has suffered persecution at the hands of the other, who happened to enjoy Court patronage at the time, and both have been anathema to the rigid Confucian as heretical, it is a combination of the two, superimposed on Ancestor worship, which forms the basic faith of China.

One of the big temples in Kowloon is dedicated to Hou Wang (侯王), the Prince Marquis, who is an historical character, named Yang Liang Chieh (楊亮節). When the last emperor of the Southern Sung Dynasty, Ti Ping, was finally driven out by the victorious Mongols about A.D. 1280, he fled by sea with his court, and landed at Kowloon. The commander of his personal bodyguard was Yang who, on landing, was pronounced physically unfit to endure the hardships of further campaigning. He was, accordingly, left behind to organise the defence works in case of pursuit. There he died of the complaint which had incapacitated him, and he was buried in the West City. A posthumous title of marquis was conferred upon him for his bravery, loyalty and upright character which endeared him, not only to his fallen sovereign, but to the local inhabitants as well.

As their protector against the Mongol hordes they erected a temple in his memory in the eighth year of Yung Ch'eng (A.D. 1731). It has been renovated in the reigns of Ch'ien Lung, Tao Kuang, Hsien Feng, and Kuang Hsü. In 1918 a further restoration took place by the Residents' Association of Kowloon City headed by Chan Pak To and Tam Fa, who was a third-degree literary graduate under the Manchus. These K'ai Fongs, or Street and House Societies, play an important part in social welfare, and membership imposes almost closer ties than blood relationship. Inscriptions in various temples bear witness to their participation in the religious life of the community they serve.

Hou Wang's birthday is celebrated on the "Double Sixth", or sixth day of the Sixth Moon, and, besides the original temple in Kowloon City, shrines are dedicated to him at Tai O and Tung Chung. The latter is said to have been in existence for over a hundred years.

Though Yang's loyal exertions undoubtedly shortened his career, they did not qualify him for the crown of martyrdom which was accorded to three virgins commemorated in the shrine of Feng Hsin Ku (馮仙姑), in T'ien Hou Temple Road. In the reign of Ch'ien Lung, about two hundred years ago, three maidens, named Feng, Cheung and Ho, took the vows of chastity and sisterhood and pledged themselves to live and die together. They probably entered a nunnery and devoted themselves to good works, for there is no record of their forming an anti-marriage secret society like the Golden

Orchids. Unfortunately their beauty attracted the attentions of the famous pirate Chang Pao-tzü (張保仔) who, about 1770, captured the Island and Lantau. As they repulsed his advances and were determined to preserve their chastity, death was the only alternative. To commemorate their resistance movement, a temple was erected in Causeway Bay early in the present century.

Though he can hardly be classed as a local worthy, any boy would rather find a pirate in his family tree than a saint and, after all, Chang Pao-tzü's relics are preserved in a temple. He made his base at Stanley, where his main fleet was concentrated in Chik Chu Wan. The small promontory in the centre of the bay was used as a look-out and signal station, from which he kept in communication with his ships by bell and drum. These instruments are still on view in the Temple of the Queen of Heaven, labelled with their owner's name. In the south of the bay, local inhabitants point out a sort of Tarpaean rock, from which he precipitated his enemies or prisoners whose ransoms failed to meet his expectations. His depredations extended to the Pearl River, where he maintained an advanced post in a fort mentioned in Hunter's *Fan Kwae in Canton*. After his death the business was successfully carried on by his wife, who proved not a whit less efficient in extracting tribute than her spouse.

When the English were forced by the hostility of the authorities in Canton to seek a place where they could careen their ships undisturbed, and settled on Hong Kong, the first landings were made on the south side of the island, near Aberdeen, and a camp was established on the neck of Stanley peninsula now occupied by St. Stephen's School. The Boat People were the first to make friends, but the arrival of the troops was less popular with the cultivators. Old men still remember stories of poisoning the wells, which sound uncommonly like modern atrocity propaganda. There may, however, be some sub-stratum of truth in the allegation, for any outbreak of an unfamiliar disease would certainly have been attributed to design and not accident. With the best will in the world the introduction of an alien element into an isolated population may have disastrous results. The inhabitants of Tierra del Fuego were practically exterminated by measles, contracted from traders and missionaries who brought in a complaint for which the local people had no immunity, and up to the beginning of the present century typhoid had claimed fifteen times as many victims as battle casualties in the campaigns of every nation.

The few shallow wells in Stanley were probably contaminated and the sparse civilian population, which drew its water from the same source, shared in the disaster which overtook the troops. Early records prove that health conditions were lamentable, though malaria was probably the chief cause for complaint, and there were thus recriminations on both sides, but it is odd that the well-poisoning story should have survived a century of occupation.

In 1894 Hong Kong was visited by a severe epidemic of bubonic plague, introduced from Canton. The highest mortality occurred in a congested Chinese area then known as Taipingshan near the present situation of Cat Street where there were 70 to 80 daily deaths, during the summer months. People fleeing from the infected district undoubtedly carried the plague to Cheung Chau

Initiation ceremonies at the Buddhist monastery of Ngong Ping

The sword of the spirit of the north Cheung Chau

where the inhabitants, thoroughly alarmed, sought the assistance of the God. A stranger from the Chao Chow district, locally referred to as "Crane brother", who joined in the petitions every day, suddenly announced that the Spirit of the North God had entered into him, and that he could abate the epidemic. He ordered the congregation to get ready a decorated chair for him to visit the houses where the sickness raged, and he would effect a cure with his blessings. The Chinese are always suspicious of outsiders, and prophets are more likely to be successful in their own village than elsewhere, contradicting the accepted theory, so they scorned him as an impostor. Without attempting argument, he simply settled down in the temple and remained for days sitting like a drunkard or a half-wit, mumbling inaudibly the whole time. The villagers finally decided that he was indeed possessed, and agreed, after a consultation of the elders, to give him a trial. A collection was taken up and the man was paraded round the parish in a sedan preceded by a band, without the slightest effect on the incidence of the sickness. He returned to his meditations in the temple and, after several days, announced that he was the Emperor of the North, that the people had sinned grievously but that he would cure them if they built a chair of knives for him to ride in. The people by now were fully convinced, and a chair was constructed with knife blades for seat, arms and foot-rest. A great crowd of spectators accompanied it to the temple, where the Crane Brother staggered out bare-footed as if intoxicated, and took his seat without evincing the slightest discomfort. Eight villagers acted as bearers and started a parade, preceded by the band, and followed by the temple officials and parties carrying offerings. The whole circuit of the island was made before returning to the

temple, where the man alighted without a scratch on his body. This time his progress was successful, as the plague stopped as suddenly as it had begun.

There was a recurrence, however, a couple of years later by which time the incarnation of the Emperor of the North was no longer available. A local fisherman was accordingly called upon to enact the role. This he performed with equal success and emerged unscathed from the chair. Plague has been unknown in the island ever since.

The Temple sword's connection with the dissipation of disease was revived by an incident which took place during the Japanese occupation. With their usual mania for security, the Japanese military authorities confiscated the weapon when they took over the island. Shortly afterwards an epidemic of influenza in a mild form broke out and the village elders sent a deputation to the Commandant, attributing the disease to the sacrilege which had been committed. They evidently made out their case, for the sword was returned to the altar by the Commandant himself at the head of a large procession in which the military were well represented. As the sickness was already on the wane, the restoration of the weapon probably had little effect on its disappearance but, as far as the inhabitants are concerned, its efficacy is now unchallenged.

The temple also takes pride in a second, and complementary, relic in the shape of a sawfish's snout of considerable size. Grateful petitioners often leave votive offerings of small replicas, of local origin, which are placed on the side altars with an inscription identifying the donor.

The Patriarch of Cheung Chau

The sheltered harbour of Cheung Chau, only open to the west, where it is screened by the bulk of Lantau, must have been a natural fishing base from prehistoric times. To this day about a third of the population of thirty thousand are fishermen, aborigines of the Canton delta who probably are descended from a race which earned its living upon the waters long before agriculture was introduced, and Chinese civilisation spread to the Mon-Kmer tribes now occupying the southern provinces. It is not surprising that primitive religious beliefs persist in the island despite the counter-attractions of organised religion.

At the north end of the village is the rich Taoist temple called Yü Hsü Kung (玉虛宮), the Palace of Jade Vacuity, which makes large annual contributions to the charities of Hong Kong. Its high altar is dedicated to the Dark Spirit of the North (玄天上帝), who was reincarnated in the Crane Man to stay the plague there sixty years ago. According to the temple manager, the iron chair with knife-edged supports, in which the embodiment was carried on his healing mission, was removed by Government orders and was sent to the British Museum. The only relic of the episode is the long, demon-expelling sword, which is still shown to visitors. Before the altar stand two figures facing inward. These are Ch'ao Kung-ming (趙公明), one of the manifestations of the God of Wealth, and the woman adversary who caused his death. She is known as T'ao Hua Nu

Sign of the times ... Wong Tai Sin Temple with a high rise building in the background

275

(桃花女), or the Peach-blossom girl, for Ch'ao, who was immune to the wounds inflicted by ordinary cold steel, succumbed when she pierced his effigy with peach-wood arrows.

On the outer wall of the temple, to the south of the main entrance, are pasted sheets of red paper setting forth the contributions of various guilds to the annual festival, which takes place early in the Fourth Moon. The whole village is thus made aware that such a society or individual has promised a floral screen, two set pieces of fireworks, material for the dragon, one lantern, two thousand crackers, a silver plate, and a further contribution towards the tail of the dragon or lion. The catalogue ends with the expression of the hope that an adequate return may be made for the expenditure. This savours of commercialised religion but is not a whit less mercenary than the motive recorded in one of our Hymns Ancient and Modern, where an extortionate rate of interest is confidently expected.

At the southern end of the village is a platform mounted by a few granite steps, on which is a receptacle for burning paper. On the east side is the gigantic hole of a banyan tree, distorted by pollarding, whose corrugated bark offers little hold for the red paper cutouts of children, pasted to its uneven surface as votive offerings. A penthouse arrangement in the form of a tent protects the shrine from the weather and offers shade to all the gossips in the neighbourhood. Before the altar is a granite incense-burner, about four feet long, bearing the inscription "The Patriarch of Cheung Chau", whilst the shrine itself is called the altar of the Grand Tutelary Deity. A large Chinese lantern also bears this inscription. There are four shrines to children whom the tree was powerless to save. Successes seem to outweigh failures, and it is recorded that, in the year of the Sheep, Hsieh Ying was cured and the parents sent a laudatory poem,

to the effect that every trouble had melted away like the morning mist, and their prayer was granted. Besides the official incense-burner, the back of the shrine is packed with pots and jars containing individual contributions. Practically all worship is done early in the morning, when the old lady, the self-appointed or hereditary guardian of the tree, waits for the receipt of custom. Her takings are not large, as each worshipper contributes a token amount only. Business is slack during the rest of the day, when a young girl assumes charge of the takings. There is another sacred tree about a hundred yards east of the main street towards its northerly end. This is surrounded by a concrete platform with a pointed stone set at the base of the trunk. A building, like a lean-to stable, provides shelter for the proprietor, its outside walls being covered with felicitous inscriptions on red paper. One of these intimates the hope that patrons will be generous but, as all knocking failed to attract attention, there was no opportunity for a display of lavishness.

Altar with the Five Vessals, Cheung Chau

The Earth Gods are well catered for in Cheung Chau, and many shops display their unpretentious shrines. A communal altar is to be seen at a cross-roads, whose central feature is a rough pointed stone with a tablet to the Earth Gods of the Five Directions. Above are the three characters for Virtue, Longevity and Happiness, between two plaster scrolls with edifying sentiments. The right-hand inscription reads "The longer life the more virtue and felicity", and the left "A heart of gold brings longevity and virtue".

The altar is approached by three steps, and there is a large hole in front for burning paper clothing and money.

The sacred trees in South China are usually banyans (*ficus retusa*), and are admirably adapted by nature for the purpose as the timber has no commercial value. The wood entails prodigious labour in the splitting and does not repay the trouble as it burns badly and produces a volume of choking smoke. They give good shade, however, and provide excellent meeting places for the village elders, when not promoted to the rank of grandfather to the community.

Details of the decoration in temple at Cheung Chau

276

SOME LOCAL LORE

Giant Strides

One of the most attractive spots in the New Territories is the stretch between the two Tai Pos on the southern shore of Tolo Harbour. The road from Shatin, after wriggling its way to contour the three out-lying spurs of Tai Mao Shan, straightens out to cross the railway, and, with a right-angled turn, is carried along a causeway with water on both sides. A halt at the corner is always profitable. On the right is Island House, surely one of the finest sites in Hong Kong, and the causeway itself is ever a scene of animation. It forms a shelter from the sea for a large number of fishing junks, afloat at high tide and stranded on the mud at the ebb, revealing to the visitor the social habits of the Boat People. Hakka women, with their distinctive hats, bring vegetable produce to barter for fish, but they are camera-shy, and without an introduction turn their faces from the photographer.

The original Mandarin name for Tai Po (大埔) was Ta Pu (大步) or "Giant strides" for, many centuries ago, it was on the outskirts of a dense forest, the lair of every sort of wild beast. If the collection of firewood necessitated an entry into its gloomy recesses, the villagers were warned to take long steps, lest the tigers and snakes caught up with them.

There is still evidence that the district was once heavily wooded, for the roots of gigantic trees were grubbed up when the foundations of the road were being engineered and, until quite recently, a hill known as Kam Shan (禁山) was thickly wooded. This spur is now called the Embroidered Mountain but, before it was cleared for building, it was the Forbidden Hill and its forests were spared in deference to its significance in the local geomancy. A substratum of truth about the wild beasts still clings to the place as it is the market for such fauna as now inhabit Hong Kong despite the encroachments of man. Civet cats are usually available, and wild boar still roam the wooded slopes of Tai Mao Shan. Comparatively recently an officer of the garrison was badly gashed from knee to ankle by a wounded boar, when armed with nothing more effective than a butterfly net.

The oyster fisheries of Hong Kong are mostly on the Castle Peak side of the Territories, but quite a profitable industry is centred in Tolo Habour, and investigations into the possibility of producing cultured pearls are being carried out. Should they be successful, a very ancient local occupation will be revived, for in the fourth year of K'ai Yuan (A.D. 716) natural pearls were discovered in nearby waters. The method of fishing was crude in the extreme, and great loss of life was entailed. A diver weighted with a stone was simply lowered over the side of a sampan with a rope round him, and he was hauled up when his companions thought fit. So heavy was the mortality, that a compassionate official named Yang Fan-ch'en (楊範臣) sent in a petition of protest, and temporarily put a stop to the practice. The fisheries were reopened on a more ambitious scale during the Southern Han dynasty, when the provinces of Kwangtung and Kwanghsi were united to form a knigdom separated from the rest of China. In A.D. 964 Tai Po became a military post with a garrison of 8,000 for fishery protection. A large quantity of tortoiseshell was also collected for the decoration of the Emperor's palace in Canton. Two years later, however, the Sung dynasty revoked the order, and turned the guards into a local constabulary.

The Mongols again revived the fisheries, and organised 700 families of Boat People as collectors, appointing three very highly paid government officials to supervise their efforts. There was, however, no improvement in method, and the mortality was as high as ever, provoking a most violent protest on the grounds of humanity from a local elder, Chang Wei-yin (張惟寅). An Imperial order closed the industry down, but it lingered on sporadically till the Mings in 1374, when it was realised that the beds were worked out and fresh sources of supply near Lei Chou (雷州) were tapped.

Curiously enough the Buddhists claim credit for being the first to put a stop to this hazardous industry. According to the legend, the Emperor Wen Tsung, of the T'ang Dynasty, was inordinately fond of oysters, and the fishermen were forced to furnish the palace with enormous supplies of the delicacy without payment. One day, an oyster of exceptional size was served at the Imperial table, and his Majesty anticipated an unprecedented gastronomic treat. All efforts to open the shell were, however unavailing.

The disappointed monarch was about to discard it in disgust when the shell opened of its own accord, disclosing a perfectly formed mother-of-pearl image of the Goddess of Mercy. The Emperor was so overcome with awe at the apparition that he gave orders for it to be preserved in a gold-inlaid sandalwood box, and he consulted the local oracle, the Buddhist monk, Wei Cheng. The sage interpreted the miracle in the following words. "This matter is not devoid of significance. The Pusa Kuan Yin has chosen this means of inclining your majesty's mind to benevolence and clemency and of filling your heart with pity for your oppressed people." The Emperor's reaction was to abolish the forced levy of oysters and to issue an edict that the image of Kuan Yin was to be admitted to every Buddhist temple throughout the kingdom.

The original market at Tai Po was erected on land bought by members of the T'ang family, near a temple which has now disappeared. This shrine was dedicated to an individual named T'ang Shih-meng (鄧師孟) who volunteered as a substitute for his father when the old gentlemen was held to ransom by the pirate Lin Feng (林鳳). As he discovered that a corsair's career was contrary to the precepts of Confucius, he threw himself overboard and his body was washed ashore at Tai Po. The surrounding land was owned by the T'angs and the temple was maintained from part of the market revenues, from 1672 onwards. Early in the XIXth Century a man named Wen Yuan-che (文元著) tried to break the monopoly, and erect places of business near the market.

After a long lawsuit he was only permitted to build dwelling houses and it was finally settled in 1892 that only the T'ang family had the right to trade. A violent typhoon in 1872 destroyed the whole village of Wen Wu (文屋村) so, after the failure of the lawsuit its inhabitants combined with those of Fanling, Lam Tsun and Ch'uan Wan (船灣) to open a new shopping centre. This was euphemistically named T'ai Ho Shih (太和市) the 'Utmost Harmony Market', and it was a success from the first. All trade deserted old Tai Po, which is now a very poor and dilapidated village.

The Walled Villages

Before the War Hong Kong supported an excellent publication, the *Hong Kong Naturalist*, which, like the English *Field*, contained something of interest to everybody. Unfortunately, practically all copies were lost during the occupation, and complete sets must be exceedingly rare. In the 1930's several articles under the title of "Legends of the New Territories" were published by Mr. Sung Hok-p'ang (宋學鵬) who devoted much space to the "walled villages of Kam Tin". The defences, consisting of a brick wall and ditch, are believed to have been erected in the reign of K'ang Hsi (1662–1721) when the new Manchu Dynasty had only a tenuous hold on the southern coast line, as they possessed no navy, and were threatened by the famous pirate Cheng Ch'eng-kung (鄭成功), better known as Koxinga (國姓爺), who had inherited his father's business, and a formidable fleet. To prevent him effecting a lodgement on the coast the new ruler adopted a scorched-earth policy and withdrew all the inhabitants sixteen miles inland, leaving the fields uncultivated. Interlopers from time to time crept back and annexed unoccupied ground, granting wholly unauthorised squatters' rights to their successors. Land titles consequently were in a state of unutterable confusion when the Territories came under British administration.

The most popular village with tourists is Kat Hing Wai which boasts a pair of handsome wrought-iron gates, removed by one Governor, and restored by another. On the leasing of the New Territories in 1898 the villagers, seeing a body of soldiers approaching, closed the gates and put themselves in the normal state of defence adopted on the appearance of their own military, between whom and bandits they drew no distinction. The gates were forced, and, the peaceable nature of the inhabitants having been determined, they were persuaded to keep open door by removing the gates. In 1925 a petition to the Governor, Sir Edward Stubbs, resulted in the restoration of the gates, and a tablet with a long inscription commemorates the incident.

Kam Tin, though its present appearance makes it hard to believe, was formerly the seat of an extremely powerful clan which owned the whole of Hong Kong island, then known as Chik Chu Shan (Red Pillar Hill) (赤柱山), preserved in the Chinese name for Stanley. When the Sung Dynasty was in desperate straits, and was driven out of its capital K'aifeng by the Mongols, the Emperor Hui Tsung and the next in succession were captured, as were the mother and wife of K'ang Wang, the Commander-in-Chief. His ten-year-old daughter,

however, was spirited away by the ladies of the court who fled southward into Kiangsi Province. Here, one of the T'ang family occupied the post as District Officer of Kung Yuan where he raised a militia in support of the Sungs. The fleeing princess, seeing the royalist flag, put herself under T'ang's protection (A.D. 1129). On his return to Kam Tin she accompanied him, and her identify was disguised by the fact that her household had merely given out that she was the daughter of a high official. She settled down contentedly in the security of family life and, when she reached marriageable age, wedded Tzu-ming (白明), son of her protector. On a truce being signed between the Mongols and K'ang Wang (康王), the latter succeeded to the throne, and his posthumous title is Kao Tsung (高宗). He at once instituted inquiries for his daughter. The posting of an official notice caused much alarm and despondency in the T'ang family at having entered into a matrimonial alliance without the Emperor's consent, but the princess insisted on their making a clean breast of it, as she owed her life to the clan of which now she was a happy member. A petition was sent by the District Magistrate to the capital and Kao Tsung issued a summons for the couple to appear at Court. After a year's residence the princess pined for Kam Tin and begged to be allowed to return to her home. The Emperor endowed her with many wharves in the district for "face powder expenses", and a large area of hill and forest for pin money. As soon as she returned the princess manifested her charity by opening her estates to the public, and allowed burial sites to be appropriated on the hillsides. In the 51st year of K'ang Hsi (1712) her dowry was still being used by the peasants for free cemeteries. Some of the wharves she bestowed on the monastery of Tzu Fu Ssu, including one near Shek Lung, which still exists.

The princess is known in the T'ang family as Huang Ku (the Emperor's Aunt) (皇姑) though in literature she is referred to as Sung Tsung-chi (宋宗姬). She practised virtue and humility all her life, and had no ambitions. When her end approached a site for her grave was selected by an eminent Feng Shui man named Li Pai-shao who decided upon Lion Hill near Shek Lung. When the lady was asked whether she preferred to lie at the beast's head or tail, she inquired what difference it would make, and was told that if she chose the head her descendants would all be distinguished men, but if on the tail they would be more humble people. She replied that she did not want her descendants to be great, but that they should enjoy red rice and herrings, the farmers' diet, which should content them.

A curious legend connected with the grave concerns a prophecy by the Feng Shui man who inserted a tablet inscribed with the words: "Three hundred years hence, an ignorant youth named Su (蘇), who knows nothing of astrology, will want to alter the way this grave faces. If he is given his way, not only will trouble descend on the T'ang family, but he will be cursed with ill luck himself." When the time was up the family was in distress, and had an idea that something was wrong with the siting of the princess' tomb, so employed a man named Su to effect the alterations. It was only on the opening of the grave that the tablet was discovered, and it effectually put an end to the project.

Later generations of the T'ang family seem to have been remarkably poor judges of astrologers, for the

Feng Shui men they consulted not only ran them into needless expense but their advice disastrously affected their descendants. The clan reached the height of prosperity, as regards numbers, in 1850, though inbreeding had probably sapped its virility. However, genetics in those days had not attained their present importance, and quantity made a greater appeal than quality, so a Feng Shui man was consulted to increase the stock which then stood at the peak of eighteen hundred living males. The geomancer, who seems to have been something of a landscape gardener, recommended the demolition of a pagoda, the alteration in the course of the stream to make three ponds, and the erection of a school to hide the river from the village. From the moment the work was completed the clan began to decrease, probably from malaria owing to the proximity of stagnant water, and births did not exceed deaths for another eighty years. In 1930 the banks of the stream were repaired which got rid of the marshes, and a group of houses known as Ch'ang Ch'un Li (長春里), Eternal Spring residence, was erected on the site of the destroyed pagoda.

Another indifferent sorcerer was commissioned, in the closing days of the Ming Dynasty, to select a lucky day for the erection of an ancestral hall to house the tablet of the eleventh ancestor. The central beam, however, was probably not seasoned for it began to put out green shoots shortly after it had been secured. Another Feng Shui man was called in, who declared that his rival had picked a propitious day for boat building and not for house construction. As the Dragon Boat festival was approaching the villagers took him at his word, pulled down the beam, and converted it into one of those craft. As soon as it was launched it rose out of the water, and quantities of gold and silver rained down from the skies to fill it to the gunwales. On being loaded it again took the water till emptied by the clan. The manoeuvre was repeated several times until the T'ang family was in affluence. They waited, however, several years for another lucky day to erect the substitute beam for their ancestral shrine which was named the Lai Ch'eng T'ang (來成堂). This still stands in Shui T'ou village where it is known as the Small Ancestral Hall.

At least one of the family was canonised by popular acclaim though it is doubtful if his elevation received Imperial confirmation. This was T'ang Hsi-shui (鄧喜瑞), who was born in 1788 and whose charitable deeds are still remembered. When he was twenty-eight, he had already made a fortune as a farmer and employed over a hundred hands. He was a peace-loving individual who detested all signs of strife or quarrel, a characteristic which was swiftly exploited by his good-for-nothing relatives. All the rascals in the parish bled him unmercifully, as he could never resist composing a dispute. The usual procedure was to start a mock fight outside his door and, when the disturbance had aroused him, to declare that one of the contending parties owed money to the other. This invariably brought the response "Cousins, do not quarrel over money" after which the imaginary debt was discharged, and the proceeds of the robbery were divided between the actors. The racket was so notorious that some of his relatives took him to task for his gullibility, but failed completely to convince him. It was his way of sharing his fortune with impoverished clansmen.

A more admirable trait in his character than this compounding of felonies was his habit of making a periodical tour of the market and buying up the unsold stock of his distant kinsmen. When they delivered this at his house they were bidden to a feast, after which they were reimbursed for what they had consumed. Their host apologised for not having been able to invite their families, and asked them to use the money to provide a similar entertainment for their dependents.

Hsi-shui died at the age of fifty-six and two years later a pedlar from the Pok Lo (博羅) district announced that, when they had opened the temple of their City God sometime previously, the character T'ang Lung-wen (鄧龍文) had been found inscribed on the hem of the robe of the divinity. Thinking that it was a practical joke they had tried to erase the lettering, but the harder they rubbed the clearer the characters stood out. Lung-wen (龍文), "the Literary Dragon", happened to be the friendship name of T'ang Hsi-shui, and further inquiries elicited the fact that the discovery coincided with the date of his death. It was thus evident that his spirit had been selected to look after the interests of the dead in a neighbouring county. To strengthen the conviction an extraordinary incident occurred at the reburial of the Saint, for it was discovered that the heart was intact and had suffered no decay. Whilst the villagers were gaping at the miracle, a dog suddenly leaped into the grave and snatched it up, disappearing in a cloud of dust and violent gusts of wind.

Chinese Ch'eng Huang (城隍), or City Gods, are invariably selected from historical characters who have made a name for virtue on earth and are in an ascending scale of humanity, thus serving as a link between the higher divinities and the people's petitions. They act as spiritual intermediaries, accessible to popular prayers and petty concerns with which it would be unseemly to disturb their more important superiors.

The Hakkas

With the advent of the industrial era and factory-made garments national costume, with its charming individuality, was doomed to disappear. Instead of the pride of achievement in the display of some particularly effective variation of the local tradition, or a masterpiece of embroidery whose execution had brightened the long winter evenings, cheap substitutes were adopted whose manufacture gave no pleasure to their creators and which afforded their wearers no personal satisfaction.

Visitors to Hong Kong, making their first tour of the New Territories, are always impressed by the Hakka women, with their longer jackets and picturesque head-dress with its pleated valance, whom they see working in the fields. They are always to be met with on the causeway skirting Tolo Harbour to the entrance of Tai Po Market. Tourists usually alight at this fascinating spot, where the small fishing junks find a convenient shelter, screened from the weather by the breakwater of the road embankment, but those anxious for a photographic souvenir soon find that the Hakka ladies are not very co-operative. Seeing them in proximity to the junks a false impression is gained that they and the Boat People lead a common existence, but this is far from the truth, as it is to the land, rather than the water that they look for a livelihood.

The Hakkas are quite distinct from the Cantonese, who form the bulk of the population, in language, dress, and manners. Those found in the South of China were not originally of that region; their family genealogies indicate that they came from the North, being the last wave of an immigration from colder climes.

Where they originated is a matter of contention, but it is generally supposed that they inhabited the Yellow River Valley region when its course ran from west to east, along what is now the line of the Lung-Hai Railway. They are supposed to have emigrated from northern Hunan in the IV and again in the IX century. Some found their way to Chekiang and Fukien, and others to Kiangsi province. Those who settled amid a civilisation not dissimilar to their own doubtless were assimilated, but others who entered broken and mountainous regions, where the valleys were already taken up, were forced onto the more rugged slopes, and maintained their individuality of language and customs. In the Sung and Mongol dynasties there were further migrations, and many settled in Kwangtung province, where they can trace their genealogies back for twenty generations.

In some districts they have monopolised the whole countryside, as in the prefecture of Chia Ying in Kwangtung province, which is entirely peopled by them, whilst in others they form a half, a third, or less, of the population. Yet again, there are regions where they cultivate the rougher hillsides, leaving the lower alluvial slopes to the pen ti (本地) or original inhabitants. This is generally the case in Hong Kong, for the Hakkas are not afraid of work, and have a perfect genius for rearing pigs. Seeing them carrying their burdens over the rocky trails on the hillsides, has created a false impression that they are China's highlanders, but this is only a regional phenomen where they were late comers in the distribution of land. In other places they are spread over the plains as well as any cultivatable spot in their neighbourhood.

They have a distinctive language of their own, which is more akin to the northern dialect than to Cantonese, and some authorities consider that it is probably the original speech of the race, Mandarin having been modified by successive invasions from the North.

The sexes are not so strictly separated in the home as in the case of the Chinese, and the women were never subjected to foot-binding, which presumably only came into fashion after the southerly migration. Although there are some very rich members of the race, in general they have to work hard for their living, and the fact that the women do a high proportion of the manual labour in the fields could be advanced as a practical reason against their adopting a custom which would be so great a handicap.

They are a simple people, but very contentious and their disputes occupy a good deal of time in the Courts of Law. Those who have abandoned agriculture for town life have mainly found employment as barbers, stonemasons, and foreign ladies' tailors. The word Hakka means strangers (K'o Chia 客家), implying that they are foreign to the soil. In the Straits they are known as Khek or Kehs, from the Fukien pronunciation of the Cantonese Hak.

From the records of Chinese history they suffered a bloody persecution under the Ch'in dynasty (249–209 B.C.) which provoked their first migration to Anhwei and Kiangsi, where some changed their names, and they were left alone to prosper by their industry. In A.D. 419 the Chinese turned on them once more, and the programme ended in a general stampede, which scattered them into the mountainous regions in the south-east of Kiangsi on the borders of Fukien Province. Again in the T'ang dynasty they were uprooted, the majority taking refuge in the mountains of Fukien, whilst a smaller number settled in the higher peaks which separate Kiangsi and Kwangtung.

Under the Sungs, many took up arms in defence of the last prince of that dynasty, and thousands of them laid down their lives in the final stand against the Mongols, west of Macao. Their first appearance in Kwangtung dates from the short-lived Yuan dynasty, but they did not settle down and become permanently established until it was displaced by the Mings (A.D. 1368).

Fresh differences with their Fukien hosts then caused a further migration, in which the Hakkas had the best of it, for they came in such numbers that they drove everything before them in the Ka-yin-chü prefecture, which has remained their stronghold ever since.

Changes of dynasties, with the disturbed conditions which accompanied them, seem always to have effected their migration, for after the Manchus seized power, they spread to the west and south-west of Canton.

They were somewhat more receptive to the teaching of Christian missionaries than the Cantonese, and took their conversion very seriously. In one instance the adoption of the new religion produced disastrous results for, after conversion by an American Missionary named Roberts in Canton, a Hakka named Hung Hsiu-ch'uan (洪秀全) convinced himself that he was a full brother to the founder of Christianity, and that he was entrusted with a Messianic mission. It was certainly not one of peace, for he and his followers carried fire and sword throughout the Empire, destroying everything which came in their path. He might have been excused as an iconoclast for burning the palace of the Taoist Pope, in the Dragon-Tiger Mountains, but there was little excuse for his rapine in the Yangtze Valley, where he shattered the porcelain kilns, and many historic monuments.

On arrival at the old capital, Nanking, his followers proclaimed him Emperor under the title of T'aip'ing (太平), or Great Peace, but the legitimate occupants of the throne always referred to his rabble as Ch'ang Mao Sei (長毛賊), or long-haired bandits, which was probably an apter description.

There was so much evil and corruption in the rebel ranks, thanks to their affiliation with the Triad Society, that it is certain that their rule would have been in no way preferable to that to the Manchus, for the mass of the followers of the King of the Heavenly Realm of Universal Peace were only bent on murder, rapine and loot. The mania of this ephemeral monarch increased with power, and he developed into a visionary, haunted with the strangest hallucinations. Like Hitler, he issued his biography claiming his divine origin and containing, in the eyes of the church which nurtured him, many other blasphemies. After an unsuccessful march to Peking, for which only one division was detached, dissension arose in the ranks of the insurgents and one of his lieutenants, the Eastern King, with twenty thou-

Hakka ceremonial apron and riband

The third ribbon secures the apron across the loins, but nowadays a piece of tape has been found to be equally efficient, and what the eye does not see the heart does not grieve for. A plain black apron is always worn for everyday use.

In full dress the Hakka women wore a black apron with a triangle of embroidery on the bib, and a triple zig-zag braid across the garment just below. This might be of any colour according to individual taste. The top was held close to the breast by a silver chain round the neck which hooked to a pair of ornaments sewn on to the bib. These took the form of the peony of abundance, above the bat of happiness, and the chain ended with peony bosses. The belt which held the apron at the waist had butterfly clasps, one of the emblems of long life, and consisted of triple chains strung at intervals with six silver coins. These were usually old twenty-cent pieces when the metal was still the standard currency. The butterflies are provided with a hook which engages in a cotton loop sewn on either side of the apron at the level of the waist.

This outfit is one of the wedding presents given by her mother to a daughter on her leaving home, and she wears it for the first time when she returns to visit her parents after the marriage. Later, it is worn whenever she wishes to acquire face at a party, or for receiving some guest whom it is desirable to impress. Hakka women may be seen bringing a basket of chickens to market wearing their jade bangles and all their jewellery, but their gala attire is usually reserved for non-working days. For carrying pig feed, or hoeing a vegetable patch, a length of tape serves the same purpose as a variegated ribbon, and costs much less, so there is little market for these traditional accessories. Very few women are skilled

sand of his followers, was beheaded. The rebellion was finally stamped out by an able loyal general, Tseng Kuo-fan (曾國藩), with the assistance in the Lower Yangtze of Charles Gordon's "Ever-victorious Army".

Hakkas are the most conservative race in clinging to their characteristic dress, but the more decorative accessories are fast disappearing, and can only be found in the more remote villages of the New Territories. Prior to the War their woven ribbons were easy to obtain, but they were never cheap as the material was entirely silk, and their construction might easily occupy a whole day's work. There is nothing repetitive about the pattern, and the art of weaving was passed from mother to daughter, for no directions were ever written down. The design often changes continually throughout the same band and each ends in a tassel composed of the different coloured strands of silk used in its composition.

The Hakka hat, to which the women cling in spite of the inconvenience of the valance in windy weather, is far more expensive than the headdresses of the Cantonese, Boat People and Hoklos, on account of the pleated material which differentiates it from the unadorned article. It is put on over a head-covering of black crepe, rectangular in form, and measuring about a yard by eighteen inches. This is secured by one of the three woven ribbons, and in cold or wet weather it is sometimes worn without the hat, particularly by old-fashioned women. Another of the ribbons is used to keep the hat from blowing away, a contingency which, owing to the vast area exposed, must be a constant threat to the wearer.

Hakka woman weaving riband

in the art of weaving the bands, and those who still practise it only find in it a part-time job. Good examples are still to be had in Hakka villages off the beaten track, such as Sai Kung, but in others the products lack the firmness of texture which appeals to the connoisseur. The loom is primitive in the extreme, the warp being tied to a flat piece of wood which can be attached to the wall, or, if the operator prefers to work in the open, to a tree. The vertical threads vary in number according to the width of ribbon to be made. The other end of the warp is secured to a second strip of wood hooked on to the woman's waist and, by applying the tension of her body, the threads are kept straight. The weft is made by passing shuttles with various coloured silks, as if darning a stocking, and the pattern is formed by the number of vertical strands crossed or missed as the thread traverses them. The whole is tightened up with a thin stick, like a paper knife. When the requisite length has been attained the ends are decorated with a large bunch of silk threads which form a tassel. The general ground colour varies, from red for a bride, to white for a widow.

Dyer Ball, in *Things Chinese*, states that Hakka women often wear tassels for earrings, but he must have confused them for the ornaments at the ends of the ribbon which secures the hat. Young women wear small earrings, but the older ones have very elaborate ones in the form of a silver basket.

Hakka Funeral Customs

When a Hakka is on the point of death, the body is lifted out of the bed and is placed on the floor, which has previously been strewn with dry grass covered by a mat. If the deceased has reached a ripe old age, a matter of supreme importance in China, several years are added to the actual span to increase his or her importance in the underworld. As the Chinese always add one or two at birth, the determination of how long a subject has actually lived would be beyond the power of any biographer.

When the coffin is brought, the body is carried out of the death chamber, and the grass is thrown away. A pail of fresh water, infused with pummelo leaves for the ritual ablution, is brought and left to stand where death occurred, draped with a new pair of trousers with a blue waist band. The Hakka word for trousers "fu" is a homonym for the sound of "luck".

A new earthenware cooking pot containing rice and water, a salt fish and a dried octopus, with some grass for fuel and the means of ignition, are placed on the high road, and the deceased is informed that, owing to the distance, he will have, in future, to cook for himself. This ceremony is repeated at the graveside, and marks the severance of the ties with the everyday life of the family. It is the farewell gesture of the kitchen staff, but the injunction can hardly be taken seriously, as the deceased is furnished with ample money to obtain culinary assistance in the next world.

Prior to the closing of the coffin, relatives and friends pay their last tribute to the body. The officiating priest is then consulted to determine whether the soul will return, the answer being obtained by casting the divining

woods. The Hakkas call them cups (pei) and if both fall with the flat side up the reply is propitious. One round and one flat is also lucky, but if both curved surfaces are showing a negative response has been received. One throw is not considered conclusive, and confirmation is required. The method of counting differs from that of the Cantonese, where one flat and one round is negative. Should the spirit indicate an intention of coming back, an immediate alarm is raised, for its purpose may be to entice some other soul to the shades. Every sort of talisman is accordingly packed into the coffin, to obviate such a disaster. Finally, if a woman is buried, the next of kin places a white flower in her hair before covering the face, and breaks a comb, letting one portion fall inside the coffin and the other half on the ground outside. This is symbolic of the severance of all ties.

The Hakkas and Cantonese have not adopted the custom, in the North, of breaking a saucer or bowl on the coffin by a junior member of the family. The receptacle is for drinking in Hell all the water wasted on earth and, to mitigate the punishment a hole is drilled in the bottom to let most of the liquid run off before consumption.

The coffin is not closed until just before the cortège is formed for the journey to the cemetery, and the face of the corpse is left uncovered. This is a precaution against foul play, so that the relatives on the side of the family to which the deceased belonged may satisfy themselves that death was due to natural causes. It is a high honour to nail down the lid, so this last duty must be performed by the next of kin, some important member of the other side of the family being invited to assist him.

Prior to the moving-off of the procession, a meal is served to the family and mourners who have attended out of respect for the dead. This is strictly vegetarian, and no comment whatsoever may be made about its quality. It follows the rules of the Buddhist monasteries, where travelling monks are entertained indefinitely on the understanding that they do not criticise the cuisine. Guests are also provided with two or three pounds of sweets to take away with them. These must be of good quality and be wrapped in white paper. The covering is thrown away immediately after leaving the house of sorrow to symbolise the casting-off of mourning, whilst the mouth is filled with sweetness.

A similar antidote is administered, after the funeral has taken place, to sympathisers who call to offer condolences during the period of mourning. On departure they are presented with lucky money, wrapped up in white paper. This should be stripped off and thrown away immediately after leaving the house of bereavement, and the money should be spent on sweets before returning home.

The Hakkas, like other Chinese, subscribe to the somewhat Irish doctrine that "the most important thing in life is to be buried well," and to this end the most sumptuous coffin that finances allow is often purchased in anticipation of the event. In some cases over twenty years elapse before it fulfils its purpose of honouring the deceased. This somewhat gruesome reminder of mortality is rarely kept in the house, but is stored in readiness by the undertaker, who also has a repository for occupied products of his trade, until a fortunate day for their interment can be determined by the astrologer.

There is no doubt that some of the rites performed at

the interment are very ancient, and stem from the fear that the spirit, bewildered in its new environment, will be reluctant to leave its familiar surroundings. If it hangs around the house its presence is undesirable, and the enforced inactivity may tempt it to commit mischievous or baneful acts. Its journey to Purgatory occupies forty-nine days, its passage being guided and made smooth by services held usually on days which are odd multiples of seven. It is essential, however, to get it started. Hence the breaking of the comb by the nearest relative as an intimation of an irrevocable parting from even the nearest and dearest. The hint to be gone is conveyed by placing the pot of food at the cross roads, well away from the homestead, and the repetition of the gesture at the graveside. Precautions are taken to determine if the spirit has the intention of returning by consulting the omens, and talismans are placed in the coffin to neutralise any evil if a positive response be obtained. During the forty-nine days of wandering in search of its final resting place the spirit has no fixed address, so it is impossible to communicate with it through a medium. Once duly installed in the Ancestral tablet, at the culmination of the days of mourning, it is accessible to petitions and has a legitimate status in the family.

The Boat People

Since the War there has been an amazing change in the physique of the Southern element of Hong Kong's population and, whereas in the old days a Northerner was conspicuous, now there is little to differentiate him from the Cantonese. Enormous interest is evinced in every form of sports, and in games, previously the sole province of the Westerner, the Chinese are now in the international class. The Boat People have not been unaffected by modern trends, and the younger generation ceases to regard itself as a race apart, or admit any difference between its customs and ways of thought from that of the shore population. The Old Man, however, never forgets his origin, and prefaces every remark "We Water Folk do this, or do that". He is shrewd enough, all the same, to take advantage of those benefits of civilisation such as the health services which are an obvious advance on the old tribal practice. All the boat children now see the light in a maternity ward, whereas he personally delivered his own brood. He has complete faith in foreign-trained doctors, and despatches his family to consultations armed with the estimated fee. Unfortunately many of the patients do not share his enlightened views, and get diverted to some arrant quack on the recommendation of a chance-met gossip. When they do finally get bedded down in a clinic it is usually selected near some port of call of the family, and a deputation literally squats on the doorstep for moral support and comfort of the patient. Boatwomen must be the despair of doctors, for their relatives supply them with anything they fancy in the way of food, regardless of what diet may be prescribed. There is an affinity between them and the gypsies in the customs appertaining to childbirth, as the woman is considered unclean for a month after parturition. She may not touch any boat which is not her own home, so if she gives birth ashore she must re-embark from alongside the quay.

Hygiene on board seems to be excellent as the junks are kept scrupulously clean. Paid hands mess on the fo'c'stle and the owners on the poop, squatting in a circle round the dishes on the deck. This is invariably washed down after each meal. The kitchen is on the port side aft, with the water tank handy alongside it.

There is no doubt as to who is Master on board, for if a brat emerges from the cabins with a dirty nose it is promptly sent back for cleaning up, and the mother is admonished. Living at such close quarters engenders habits of tidiness, and even the sampan girls keep their minute craft as bright as a new pin. Everything has its place to which it is returned immediately after use.

Compared to the land dwellers, there is very little sickness, and tuberculosis seems to be unknown in the family. Open-air life and constant exercise has bred a hardy race. An infant, missing in the morning, was found peacefully asleep among the bales in the hold, after a roll of about fifteen feet which never evoked a cry. Small girls develop a magnificent carriage from carrying their infant brothers on their backs, and like doing it. For a boy to carry a baby is infra dig, but they will submit to it as a condition for being included in an outing.

The Boat People are probably the most law-abiding section of the population and do not give much work in the courts beyond infraction of the rules for carrying too many passengers. Where human beings are concerned, though not in money matters, Chinese ideas of figures are elastic. A family counts as two, no matter the number of children. A four-seater car can easily have a coefficient of expansion undreamed of by its designers, and the foreigner never fails to be dumbfounded when he sees it disgorge its contents. Noah, in packing his ark, was an amateur compared with the Chinese *mater familias*, whose offspring pour out like bees from an overturned hive.

Accidents will occur, but litigation is rare, and all disputes are referred to the Harbour Master, a shrewd judge and a sympathetic arbitrator. A junk may be unloading, moored to the quay, when a dumb lighter

Master

cast off too late by a launch crashes into its side and several planks are stove in. The owner rushes straight to the Harbour Office and reports the accident. He is given a form to fill in, whilst the parties complained of are summoned. They are told to attend next morning, which gives the injured party time to get in touch with the builder for an estimate of the cost of repairs. The principals appear at the appointed time, accompanied by a contingent from their families, who swarm into the passage. The decision only takes a few minutes to give. The unloading junk was obviously blameless, and the fault lies with the tug master for excessive speed of approach, and the dumb lighter for not dropping its anchor in time to check the weight. The claim for damage is the actual repair bill, loss of earnings whilst the junk is idle, and pay of the hands outside the family who must be kept during the period of inactivity. The Harbour Master finds against the launch and lighter, agrees that the damage claim is reasonable and sends the disputants into the passage to settle the compensation. He is well advised to take this course, for the Chinese arrange these matters to their own satisfaction in a way incomprehensible to Western ideas of equity. In this case they divide the total bill into three, each bearing his share of the costs.

The aggrieved party gets his repair bill for nothing, but foregoes compensation for wages, and loss of earning. Everyone is satisfied, and no ill-feeling is left.

Junk mistress

Like fishermen the world over who deal with such an unpredictable element as the sea, the Boat People are strongly religious. The shrine of their Patron Saint, the Queen of Heaven (天后), occupies an honoured position against the junk's side in the port cabin and a light burns before it. Vows made on special occasions are fulfilled at the annual festival of the deity on the 23rd of the Third Moon, when a pilgrimage is made to the Tai Miao, Joss House Bay. Women will promise a hundred eggs for the gift of a male child or recovery from sickness. Families join together to defray the expenses of the feast and the launch which tows the decorated junk to its destination. Each child born during the past year is introduced to its patroness by the gift of a lantern on these occasions. Priests do not take part in the worship, and offerings are made direct by the head of the family. Their services are requisitioned, however, for the festival of the Hungry Ghosts and Thanksgiving services on the recovery of a member of the family from sickness and, of course, for funerals. The family always appears to patronise the same band of spiritual guides.

Each junk has its own religious pictures, such as the Eight Immortals, or the Western Heaven, and these are brought out for combined services which affect the whole family. If two junks are concerned one altar for each will be set up at the ends of the well deck, the officiating priest serving each in turn. It can hardly be said that the congregation displays much devotion or religious zeal, such as manifest at revivalist meetings, and it rests content in the knowledge of having performed a good deed in subsidising the professionals to perform the appropriate service. People drift in and out as curiosity moves them but the counter-attraction of a puppet play leaves the church singularly bare. The women, as in most religions, seem the most devout but, as a rule, they have definite duties to perform, either attending to the candles and incense, burning paper clothing, or launching boats or lanterns on the waters of the harbour. The men are responsible for the shrines, which constitute the luck of the year, and its guardian is determined by casting lots. This is done by dropping two wooden objects, rounded on one side and flat on the other. If both fall the same way up, the luck is good, but if a round and flat surface is exposed it is cancelled out. Each young man has ten throws, kneeling, after making his prayer to the divinity, and the one with the greatest number of successes keeps the shrine in his cabin for the year. This entails early rising to burn incense before it, so luck carries its obligations.

The Boat People never pay a visit without bringing a present in their hands, which usually consists of a couple of tins of cigarettes, and a box of food from one of the most famous Kowloon restaurants. The Patriarch is very jealous of the reputation of his family, and those members who do not conform to his standard of liberality are forbidden to visit his foreign acquaintances. One notorious screw's curiosity got the better of her, and she slipped away for a reconnaissance without the knowledge of the family. Unfortunately for her she was unable to restrain her tongue, and soon found herself having an uncomfortable interview with the enraged Master. Not only had she disobeyed his injunction, but he was convinced that she had let the family down. "And what did you take?" he roared. "A bunch of bananas, I suppose!" shaking his fingers at her to imply that she had gone empty-handed and had made good use of her digits to help herself.

This ritual of "exchanging gifts", so often referred to in the Chinese calendar, must be rigidly observed by foreigners accepted as friends by the Boat People, and all birthdays are duly commemorated by presents and an invitation to a dinner party. Orders are issued to accept no contracts for the day in question and, if some misunderstanding has taken place, the junk will work a night shift to fulfil the obligation.

Hong Kong can justly lay claim to the possession of one of the most beautiful harbours in the world, and its animation during the hours of daylight is probably unsurpassed. For a tourist, the countless junks on every conceivable course and with an endless variety of colour in their sails are a constant source of fascination. Nearly all are single-masted but beyond that there is no uniformity. Every shade of brown and ochre dots the harbour. Some sails are indigo, a fashion very prevalent since the War, and some are fantastically patched with contrasting material, or so full of rents and gaps as to give the impression of being unable to hold the wind. An occasional big three-master may cross the line of vision setting out on, or returning from, a fishing expendition. Sampans and small junks fill up the open spaces cutting it fine across the bows of a ferry or incoming freighter, thereby leaving ill luck and parasitic devils to the inheritance of the larger craft. As a tourist liner warps out, several sampans filled with beggars crowd up to the stern in quest of the small change still encumbering the passengers' trouser-pockets. An old crone with a net directs operations of a couple of diving boys who act more as a bait than anything else, for her proficiency is such that there is little necessity for them to go overside. The sense of frustration she engenders leads our "fact-finding" visitors to condemn the whole race of Boat People by its least worthy representatives, for, like the racketeers of Chicago, they achieve the widest publicity. It is libellous to state that the Boat People are filthy in their habits, and create a foul miasma which not only obscures the harbour but penetrates several streets into the city. Yet this was the verdict of a recent factfinder. He omitted to say that Hong Kong provides the quickest turn-round in the world, and that the race he maligned formed nearly onetenth of its population.

The Boat People are not Chinese, but aborigines, the original inhabitants of the delta who have never changed their primitive habits of fishing, and getting their living upon the waters. The Cantonese, who inherited the soil, belonged to the Mon-Kmer Empire of Indo-China, and were an agricultural race with little regard for the rights of those whom they dispossessed. Laws were framed forbidding the Boat People to settle ashore, to intermarry, or to sit for the examinations which alone qualified an individual for advancement. In the reign of K'ang Hsi the ban on shore residence was relaxed to the extent of being allowed to build a shack on the water-front, but education and intermarriage were still forbidden. The Boat People still adhered to their fishing, and provided services in the form of water transport, but they were despised and ridiculed by the nick-name of Tan Kar, or Egg family. They intensely dislike the term and refer to themselves as Shui Jen, or the Water Folk. They are to be found all over the Canton delta but do not stretch so far up the coast as Swatow, where there is another aboriginal tribe known as the Hoklo.

Most estimates put the numbers of Hong Kong Boat People at 200,000 of whom 140,000 are fishermen. Their methods are primitive, and most uneconomic according to Western standards, for they take about eight pounds of fish a day, compared to 360 for a North Sea fisherman. If the Boat People were uninterested in agriculture, the Cantonese saw no profit in organising the fishing industry, and no company would put up the capital for modernisation, which has been left to Government to initiate. The fisherman's capital is in his vessel and gear, but it is also the home of his family, which, on a large vessel, may be up to eighty souls. This circumscribes his activities and militates against the education of his children. He cannot sell what is his home and invest in a more economical ship specialised for his trade without sacrificing the mode of life to which generations of his ancestors have been accustomed. Often out of a twenty-four-hour fishing expedition fifteen hours are consumed in reaching the grounds and in the return voyage under sail, and few have the educational qualifications to act as engineers on a power-driven craft. A Chinese village has for centuries been organised on definite lines with elected elders responsible to some higher authority for the households within their jurisdiction, but the Boat People work on a purely family basis and, if a spokesman is necessary for several units, the chances are that he is selected by lots cast before the deity of a temple near their anchorage. If the matter is of minor importance anyone with an errand which takes him in the vicinity of the official concerned will be deputed to act for the community.

Though extremely conservative, where their interests are concerned the Boat People are quite receptive of new ideas. Government has already provided a supply of ice for the better preservation of fish in transit, and installed methods of drying the catch artificially. The suggestion is that the old sailing junks should remain as houseboats for the superfluous members of the family, moored within reasonable distance of some educational facilities for the children, and that power craft should gradually be introduced for actual fishing operations.

At present the biggest junks are long-liners which visit distant grounds and fish from sampans. Purse-seiners are much smaller vessels, working in pairs owned by the same or allied families. They fish at night and lower a sampan with a bright light to attract the shoals. The seine is paid out astern of the sampan, and gradually is brought in a circle round the fish. Just before it closes the light is doused, and the sampan slips out before the purse string is drawn.

The Water Folk are largely a self-contained community, dependent for their services on other members of their race. Most of the small craft are operated by women whose husbands find employment as paid hands in the lighterage trade. There are floating shops, restaurants, and even those devoted to the oldest profession in the world. Food is mostly bought ashore in the open market, and drinking-water is stored in a square wooden tank alongside the cooking galley. The latter is taken on from a water-boat which plies its trade in the night anchorage.

The aristocracy of the harbour Boat People are the owners of the one-masted lighters which load and discharge cargo from ships lying at the buoys. They are classified by the sort of goods they handle, and a collier will never accept general cargo, or vice versa. During the Japanese occupation the lightermen were the wealthiest section of the population for, until bombing emptied the harbour, their services were in constant demand and, by the aid of false bottoms, they exacted a high price for their labours. They waged their own private war against the invaders, and booty was considerable. Coal and unmarketable goods were thrown overboard, but food and disposable objects were pooled, and scrupulously shared out among the community. Friends ashore partook of their hospitality and great risks were run in delivering the goods, which, had their origin been suspected, would have formed the subject of a capital charge. Practically everyone else was on the verge of starvation, and many owed their survival to their generosity.

During this period the Boat People made their first contacts with foreign civilisation, for they alone could patronise the restaurants of the big hotels. Chairs were unknown to them, as meals on board are always taken squatting on the poop. The waiters at the Peninsula and Gripps were none too flattered in being obliged to serve birthday parties where all perched round the table with their feet on the seats.

Wartime friendships were strengthened with the return of "Our" Government, as the Boat People call it, and their curiosity about foreign customs and modes of life led to a constant interchange of visits. Such foreign inventions as proved their usefulness were adopted, and small stools were shipped for entertainment in the Chinese style. After many a family council a shore establishment was sanctioned for the business manager of the junk as it facilitated the search for contracts. It was a sore break with tradition but the whole family shared in the benefit, for it gave a rallying point for children attending school until their proper home returned from work, and tied up for the night. Finally the Senior Lady abdicated her control of the second junk in favour of her eldest son and became matron of the shore base.

The family consists of the Old Man and his three consorts. No. 1 Lady has borne him three married sons, a brace of daughters who have contracted alliances, and a much younger boy of about ten. At this age among the Boat People he is already rated as an able-bodied seaman. No. 2 Lady is good-natured and feckless and her sole contribution to the stock was a daughter. No. 3 was an after-thought, the fruit of post-war prosperity, whose previous professional experience was darkly hinted at by the distaff side of the family. Attempts were made to dislodge her by the concealment of various articles and the insinuation that she was responsible for their disappearance, but the Old Man silenced all gossip by declaring that if they could prove their allegations he would put the culprit in a pig basket and throw her in the harbour, but if not he wanted to hear no more about it. Being childless, the lady brought with her a daughter, near marriageable age, and a son both acquired by purchase. The latter is a necessity for carrying on the ancestral worship. Both are accepted as full members of the family entered by marriage. The daughter has already been provided with a dowry, far in excess of the natural children wedded in less prosperous times, and

Turning the red cakes to change the luck

the son is regularly enrolled in the clan which entitles him to an equal share in the property on the death of the patriarch.

The eldest son, now master of the consort junk, has three sons and a couple of daughters. He previously shared the command with No. 1 Lady, though by virtue of the relationship her word was law. In China the older generation is always right, and the older it becomes the more infallible. The brain of the family is concentrated in the second son, the business manager, who lives in a Kowloon flat and is responsible for the contracts. He married a good-looking young woman whose offspring are entirely female. This is disastrous anywhere in China but, among the Water Folk, the customs of succession make it imperative to produce a male heir. On the death of the head of the family all property is shared equally among the male descendants. Thus the first son, in this case, would get four shares, one for himself and another for each of his sons, whilst the second would inherit only his own portion. As the lady seemed incapable of doing her duty a second wife was taken. She too was afflicted with the daughter complex, so a family conclave was held in which it was decided that the third son, who has almost a superfluity of males, should make over one of them to his less fortunate brother. He, however, was loath to admit defeat, and for some time refused the

Boat children

offer. The child, if transferred, will belong to his senior wife, as would the eldest son produced by a concubine. This is the only way of ensuring that the ancestral rites of a woman who has no direct male heir are observed after her death.

When a baby is born, day and hour are noted for the "Eight characters" and are submitted to an astrologer for a horoscope. About four years ago the seer's report was wholly unpropitious, and he stated that the boy would bring no credit to the family, and had better be given away. The Old Man received the verdict from his womenfolk and thought the matter over for a couple of days when he announced that it was a nice baby anyway, and should be kept regardless of its possible influences on the family fortunes.

A Junk-Warming

The family capital is all sunk in their lighters, and these have a comparatively short life. Heavy cargo being constantly dropped on deck gradually opens the seams, and salt water engenders claims for damage which cuts into profits. The old junk is usually disposed of for about half the purchase price, and savings are withdrawn to make up to about 75 per cent of the cost. The balance is obtained by borrowing from allied families' hoards. The Boat People are always ready to help one another out on these occasions, as the money is safe, and it does not matter in whose stocking it temporarily rests. It is usually paid back within three to six months, and saves the ruinous interest charged in the usury shops.

The family with whom we are concerned owned two

junks and a small lighter and, as the latter was letting in water badly, it was decided to order a new, large vessel, which would be worthy of carrying the First Prize Shrine at the next Tam Kung Festival. At the scramble at Shaukiwan, on the Feast of the Patron Saint, the junk won the honour of providing the biggest and best shrine at next year's celebrations and, as business was booming, something had to be done to uphold the family's prestige. About six months ago a launch for towing was purchased, which paid for itself in half that time. Though sail costs nothing, time is valuable, and much is wasted tacking about the harbour against an adverse wind. The launch is the solution and, when not needed by the owner, it pays handsome dividends by towing other cargoes to their destination. The new junk was built to order, and all relations and friends were invited to the ceremony.

The new vessel was dressed with signal flags from prow to stern, including the house flag which was white, with a wavy border and the owner's cypher in the centre. Above the staff was a small bunch of evergreen to wish a long life, and under the overhanging bow was fixed a Taoist talisman decked with two red silk ribbons. This was surrounded by a piece of fat pork, symbolic of many feasts, a pummelo leaf, and a spike of cactus. The pummelo is always the ingredient of the ritual bath taken by the bride before the wedding, so may be taken as evincing the desire that the clan may never grow less. The cactus evidently means good luck, and is probably the usual play upon words in which the Chinese take their delight.

Everything in the ship, down to the bamboo pole which was held by two young women as a hand-rail for embarking passengers, was brand new. A carpenter was still busy fixing the accommodation ladders. The owner was fussing round, checking everything, and pointing out any slovenly work to the contractor. An unevenness in the planking of the fo'c'stle demanded an immediate remedy. It then transpired that there was a double deck, for, to prevent heavy weights damaging the beautifully finished roof to the crew's quarters, a skin of pine planking absorbed the shocks. These twelve-inch planks were fastened below by battens two inches deep, forming protective squares like a chessboard. The great mast of Oregon pine was stayed with four wire guys, and the yard was raised by a winch, instead of by hand as in the smaller lighters. The welldeck, three feet below the level of the fo'c'stle, was twenty feet by twenty-four with bulwarks of teak. At the aft end was a shelf four feet six from the well-deck, and four feet broad, running the whole beam of the ship. This gave access to the cabins. The owner's stateroom was on the starboard side, half the space being occupied by a bed which would accommodate a good proportion of the family. The floor was covered with oil-cloth, and the walls with mirrors. Locker space for the accommodation of personal belongings was all built in under the shelf which forms the promenade deck outside for the infants. Communicating with the large cabin, but with a separate entrance from the deck, was another of equal size which housed the carved shrine for the Queen of Heaven, the Patroness of the craft. Both cabins had chests of drawers as well as the lockers, and both communicated at bed level, with two smaller cabins over the stern. Some bright pictures, gifts of friends for the occasion, had already been hung, and several more were stacked against the port bulwarks on the main deck. Above the cabins, on the poop, and right aft was the kitchen to port, and general storeroom to starboard. The lavatory was on the starboard side, hard up against the stern post. Water is usually carried in oil drums, on the port side, handy to the kitchen, but this was also provided with a large, wood-covered cistern amidships on the poop. Across the well-deck aft was a red silk banner with the inscription "Peace and Tranquillity on Sea and Land", the gift of the Hong Kong and Shanghai Lightermen's Guild. Red paper scrolls were pasted to the cabin, with inscriptions such as: "May the ship's business yield advantage".

When all the guests had assembled, and every inch of the ship had been explored, orders were given to cast off, and the owner let off two packets of crackers as the junk warped out from the Praya. The huge tiller was shipped, the tackles were roved and manned by two of the younger women, who took their orders from the "Old Man" for'ard. A tow line was passed to the launch, and the junk's bows were swung for her home anchorage at Yaumati. The celebrations were to take the form of a dinner for a hundred people, all furnished by one of the best Kowloon restaurants. The tow was slipped about half-way up the typhoon anchorage, in the centre of which a whole village of big lighters stood out silhouetted back against a glorious sunset. The big junk nosed in to the quay as darkness fell, and made fast alongside her consort, which was illuminated by the glare of the kitchen fires as the professional cooks put a last touch to the feast. As she made fast, crowds of friends and relatives came aboard, children, in their best clothes, swarmed everywhere, and more and more congratulatory presents were thrust into the hands of the proud owners. There were enough pictures and complimentary scrolls to cover every inch of wall spaces. Birds were a very favourite motif, and there was one mirror decorated with a peacock and a peony, to such an extent as to render its use as a looking-glass completely illusory. As a devil deterrent, however, it was both useful and ornamental, for both bird and blossom were convincingly portrayed.

A table was finally rigged aft of the well-deck to display the gifts, prominent among which were two large porcelain vases containing gladioli and evergreens. The gift of a jar signifies the donor's good wishes for peace, the word being the same as that for a vase. These were tied together with a red silk cord, which was evidently part of the offering. Tins of cigarettes, and a couple of cases of "Green Spot", were among the consumables.

Though the big junks in the typhoon anchorage moor in the centre of the shelter, and can only be reached by sampan, the quay walls are the home of the smaller craft, and a haze of smoke hung over them as they prepared the evening meal. They are just as self-contained as the larger craft, and even the water taxis adorn the mat roofing with their family photographs and small personal belongings. Over the stern of one was a hencoop, with feeding trough outside and egg-rack handy to the kitchen.

As soon as the junk was fast, the crew rigged four petrol pressure lamps from the corners of the awning for illumination, and four round tables on collapsible trestles were placed in the four corners of the welldeck for the principal guests. Other tables were set up on the fo'c'stle. Chopsticks and bowls were dealt round as if by magic, while the owner circulated, receiving congratulations until dinner was served. He ignited two long strings of crackers which detonated at the prow with deafening effect. Forty sat down to the main feast, wine being served by the married daughters of the family. In China no servant should serve the drinks, which duty is an obligation of the host. The first dish was an excellent chicken soup, followed by mushrooms, and a dish of chicken and walnuts. Then came abalone soup, sweet-sour pork, fat pork, duck, and more chicken.

The foreigner's method of carving at table, the last served inheriting a tepid portion, has always struck them as barbarous, and they strive to present their viands in a form which can be readily dealt with. There are exceptions to every rule, however, and the fowls of the air usually contain inedible fragments of splinters, possibly on the assumption that the nearer the bone the sweeter the meat.

The "Old Man" went round, glass in hand, toasting his guests and receiving congratulations. Among the Boat People, and fishermen generally, "No heeltaps" is taboo, as there is a superstition that bottoms dry means casting ashore, and no one wants to see a vessel out of her element. The children perched like swallows on a telegraph wire along the bulwarks, and bowls of a delicious mixture of all the dishes were handed to them by their parents. Near the end of the meal, a huge fish was served, with a superlative brown sauce which was greatly in demand for flavouring the rice. As the tables emptied of the principal guests, a relay of younger relatives took their places. One of the young boatmen spoke good English, and explained the construction of the ship. The bulk of the wood came from Lungchow, and the cabins were constructed of a form of camphor wood, which accounted for the aromatic scent. The Boat People do themselves well, and everything they buy is of the best quality. Both the Master and the Mistress of the new vessel saw all their guests off, and the foreigners were accompanied ashore by one of the sons of the house. It was a first-rate party, and even the lack of the means of communication failed to damp the sense of cordiality which prevailed.

On such an occasion, mahjong is the principal distraction after dinner and it is probable that the game originated among the sea-faring folk, tiles being substituted for cards which proved unmanageable in a stiff breeze. Both sexes play but, if a party is given, the women abstain to devote their whole time to the entertainment of their guests.

Thanksgiving Day

No one can accuse the Boat People of ingratitude towards their deities for favours received, though there is a tendency on the part of Western nations to lay more stress on personal petitions than on the General Thanksgiving, which usually wipes off all scores between the beggar and the Deity. For some months the No. 3 Lady had been prostrated with a mysterious illness, and was constrained to vow a handsome recompense to the gods for her recovery. During her slow convalescence she made gradual preparations for fulfilling her obligations, and

Thanksgiving sacrifices

the manifestation of her gratitude was made an occasion for public rejoicing. The junk was moored at Yaumati quayside, near its normal anchorage, and the fo'c'stle was adorned with four paper scrolls affixed to the well-deck awning. The outer pair were red, and the inner red, white and green. The Master ran up a new house flag for the occasion. At the for'ard end of the well-deck amidships were two tables. The one nearest the fo'c'stle was arranged as an altar, with a paper reredos depicting the Southern Gate of Heaven. Nine cardboard figures on wooden stands might have represented the Eight Immortals, if they had been accompanied by their traditional symbols, but only one had the peach, which is inseparable from the Star God of Longevity who frequents their company. The Nine Niang Niang of healing were ruled out, as the figures were obviously of the male sex. The Boat People accepted them as the Immortals and, as it was their festival, there was no need to cavil. Three "joss sticks" of incense were burning in a censer, and seven little porcelain saucers with oil and wick were prepared to be lit at the appropriate moment. In the centre was a wooden tub of rice, flanked by two dishes of oranges, both large and small. One plate of pink dumplings lay on the left of the altar, whilst the rest of the space was occupied by five platters of barley sugar, the conventional gift of friends who have been invited to the celebration. A second square table formed an extension to the altar, and on the left tide was the sacrificial roast pig, with blue paper rosette on nose and tail, and a cleaver planted between its shoulders. On its right was a dish with a roast chicken, complete with head, curved like the spout of a coffee-pot. The rest of the space was occupied with six dishes of barley sugar and a plate of oranges, and piled on top were two cardboard boxes such as good pastrycooks use to send out presentation moon cakes. Behind this table was a round stool, bearing a tray for ceremonial purposes, and on it were arranged incense sticks, two lumps of barley sugar with small paper banners, a wine cup and an oil saucer.

The second altar in front of the poop had a paper reredos with ten figures depicted on it, the top row masked by a red paper scroll. There was a red and gold frontal, of no very patent design, but spangled with small stars. On the altar were two candles, two incense burners, a wine pot and mixed dishes of pastry, oranges and sugar. The service began at this altar. Two Taoist priests put on their robes to the accompaniment of the band of cymbals and clarinet and, seating themselves on either side, chanted the office, whilst one of the daughters-in-law of the house burned large cocked hats of paper in a bucket at the bows. A meal to all on board was then served, the viands having first been presented at the altar. The priests disrobed, and took their repast between the two altars, whilst the boat family and their guests ate either on the poop or fo'c'stle.

After this, the band gave the signal for the main service, and candles were lit at the for'ard altar. Three very thick sticks of incense were ignited and placed in front of the reredos. The clergy robed, and the officiating priest, who had not hitherto taken part, kowtowed to the "South Gate of Heaven", and then turned about to read his office at the other altar. Between the chants, he knelt and prostrated himself to the corners of the altar. The youngest son of the "Old Man" was on in this act,

Junk Thanksgiving services

and was by no means a willing acolyte. It was his duty to kneel upright behind the celebrant, holding an incense burner shaped like a small frying-pan. Evidently the Litany was too much for his endurance, or his knees had not been sufficiently hardened to the deck, for, after a few contortions, he rolled over on one side, and ignited the priest's robe with his smouldering incense.

There is a delightful informality about all these rites, for the audience makes no attempt to join in the service, but treats the whole affair as a theatrical performance. Children swarm everywhere, and nobody stops attending to his, or her business. The "Old Man", who is paying for the entertainment, might be running a cocktail party, for he is assiduous in making the rounds with a tin of cigarettes, and basks in the knowledge that he is the author and giver of a feast which has been becomingly displayed.

The officiating priest concluded his service at the aft altar, for which he had removed his shoes, displaying a pair of what strongly resembled "socks:—silver-grey" of army pattern. He turned round to the "South Gate of Heaven" and chanted, standing. He then sat cross-legged, tailor fashion, and pushed his acolyte into a similar position facing the altar. At 12.20 p.m., things were evidently approaching a crisis, for the band started up, and the main burning of offerings, punctuated with crackers, took place. The priest rose and saluted both altars. Taking a taper and a stick of incense, he ignited the seven lamps on the for'ard altar, and then put on his shoes. He removed a tray of tea leaves from the altar, and scattered over it the ashes of the incense. The card-board figures of the Immortals were removed, one by one, and placed on the other altar.

The No. 3 Lady, who was the beneficiary of the Mercy of the Gods, then came on, for the first and last time, and prostrated herself before both altars. The priest now sat in front of the "South Gate of Heaven" altar, with the "frying-pan" incense burner, and gave the benediction, after lighting two small oil-lamps on the round stool, and placing his amulet in the tray. He then squatted with his amulet and a list of the contributors to the feast, and gave the signal for the final burning of the paper offerings. With these, packets of money and tea were also sacrificed. The list of contributors was then read out, the amulet (of two half-moon shaped pieces of wood, strung together) was dropped, after each name, to tell their fortune. During this interval, one of the young boatwomen anointed the sacrificial fowl with the wine with her fingers. The small stool with the tray was then taken midway between the two altars, and the priest walked round it. His acolyte then picked up the tray and, stepping over a piece of brown paper, which had been ignited for the purpose, carried it into the cabin, amid a final burst of crackers.

The reason for the two altars was that the family owns two junks, and the reredos scrolls had been removed from their normal sanctuaries for the occasion. These had to go back to their everyday use, accompanied by the priests who reconsecrated them. The cardboard figures were the property of the religious authorities, and were moved to give both altars a share in their patronage.

The priests' fees for the service are considerable, and include certain perquisites from the feast which, however, they do not attend. There is usually some slight dispute as to their entitlement, and they are shrewed bargainers.

Fishermen at Stanley

Stanley village, consisting of a flagged Main Street, with its seaward houses standing on stilts, forms an admirable base for a fleet of about fifty small junks. Chik Chu Wan, or Stanley Bay, is almost landlocked, being exposed only to the south-west and, when the summer monsoon sets in, the fishermen transfer their operations to T'ai Tam Bay on the other side of the isthmus, which is only four hundred yards distant from their shopping centre. The catch is mostly marketed locally, but Chik Chu Wan is also used as a shelter for the larger junks who fish in more distant waters, and use it as an anchorage after landing their catch at Aberdeen.

The local junks are all purse-seiners, and use a net whose meshes are evidently designed to let nothing escape, for fry, the size of skipper sardines, find a ready market in the village. The seine is worked from the fore part of the ship, as the space behind the mast is taken up with the living accommodation. This consists of three compartments each protected from the weather by a semi-cylindrical awning with sliding curtains which can be pulled down to exclude the rain. The for'ard space is the owner's living room, aft of which a smaller space forms the sleeping quarters. If the family consists of three generations the old people have the larger compartment, and the rising family is allotted the bedroom. Beyond it is a still smaller space for the kitchen, aft of which is just enough clear space on the poop for the helmsman. The bedroom awning can be dismantled amidships to use the sweeps, possibly the most usual mode of progression. When all the awnings are in place, during rainy weather, it is impossible to stand up, and a journey to the kitchen must be performed on hands and knees. Any hired men, needed for the working of the nets, sleep in the hold, the deck of the living cabins being practically flush with the gunwale.

The Boat People share the Chinese predilection for a crowd as no less than fifteen form the complement of these tiny craft. The children attend the local school, and the sampan which ferries them to and fro carries nine or ten, whereas three Europeans find themselves cramped in the same space.

All the fishing is done at night, just after dusk and before dawn, as the feeding habits of the quarry resemble those of the moths whose nocturnal flights occur at the same periods. The junks work in pairs and the fish are attracted by strong lights operated from a sampan. A poorer class of fisherman, who cannot afford such a vessel, makes a livelihood by skirting the shore only a few yards out with a lamp in the bows of his sampan and a hand net over each side. Fish appear to be attracted by the beating of a drum, or any percussion instrument such as a wooden box tapped rhythmically with a stick. These primitive methods certainly achieve results, as

A purse seiner

290

quite large fish can be seen to be dipped out a couple of feet beyond the breaking surf.

The massacre of the innocents, however, is to be deprecated, in the interests of the fishermen themselves, as the destruction of the fry, which have enough natural enemies to contend with anyway, can only result in a gradual depletion of the stock and lean years ahead. Part of the work of the Fisheries Research Unit will be to persuade the Boat People that an increase in the size of the mesh will result in heavier catches in the years to come. Dynamite, again, is no respecter of size, or persons for that matter, as too many accidents are connected with its use. This more exciting method of obtaining fish is usually practised off the rocks, very early in the morning, before the forces of law and order are upon the scene. The operators are not the only ones to benefit, for sampans converge from all directions to join in the scramble for the spoil.

The purse-seiners are jaunty little craft usually about twenty feet overall and fifteen on the water line. The smaller type carries one mast only, but a few have a foresail, shipped where one would normally expect to find a bowsprit. The beam is not more than seven to nine feet and the vessels only draw three feet of water. The freeboard, when fully loaded, cannot be more than two feet three inches. Regularly they are beached, for burning the bottoms or scraping the hull and oiling. They are drawn up stern foremost at spring tide and rest upright upon their flat bottoms. It is surprising what comes out of them, not only the human element, but the clutter of clothing and miscellaneous stores. Yet if one boards them on a working day, everything is tidy and everything has its place. When ashore the children play on the beach, whilst their elders are engaged in mending nets and sorting gear.

As regards religion, the majority are Taoists who worship the Queen of Heaven at a large and well-kept temple about a quarter of a mile from the shore. A few have embraced Christianity and are ardent Pentecostals, even abjuring tobacco as part of their discipline. They are most friendly to foreigners, and it is always easy to arrange a fishing expedition in the late afternoon before they start the serious operations of the evening. On these occasions a line and sinker is used over the rocks which skirt the bay, and an immense variety of fish are hooked if sufficient dexterity in striking is acquired. As far as the novice is concerned the fish are well able to take care of themselves and can remove the bait without revealing their presence nine times out of ten.

The poorer fishing families, and the Hoklos who can be distinguished by their long, open boats, scrape a livelihood by this method, obtaining their bait from the purse-seiners as they return with the catch in the early morning.

The most important job of the day is the drying of the nets which are brought ashore in a sampan immediately the boats return. As a large proportion of the catch is dried at the same time the proximity and nature of the beach is of high importance to the industry. The nets are spread out at full length in the sand, and are examined for damage, after which the catch is distributed on the sound portions of the mesh. The children are brought ashore, either to attend school or to play and get sufficient exercise for their physical development.

Later in the afternoon the nets and fish, now dried, are gathered in, the former carefully folded so as to pay out properly for the night's work, and the men return to their junks by sampan. When the nets are stowed on board the evening meal is taken, and all is set to move off to the fishing grounds as dusk falls.

Nets and sails have to be mended periodically, and dyed. The former operation is performed by the men on the beach used for the daily drying, but for the dyeing the junks move to a small cove in the west of the bay where there are pits and a steaming vat, the property of a landsman. Rope and string has also to be made, usually a man's job, whilst drinking-water and firewood must be collected by their spouses. The women have to cook and keep the boat clean, besides making all the clothes and seeing to their repair.

Every month, at the new and full moon, special worship is rendered to the ancestral tablets and the shrine at the prow. At New Year the junks remain at their moorings for several days and only resume operations when a lucky day has been fixed by casting lots in the temple, and sufficient crackers have been discharged to banish adverse influences.

APPENDIX I

The twenty-four Solar "joints and breaths" of the year.

Approximate date in Western calendar

Feb. 5th Li Ch'ün	立春	Beginning of Spring	Aug. 8th Li Chiu	立秋	Autumn begins
Feb. 19th Yü Shui	雨水	Spring rains	Aug. 23rd Ch'u Shu	處暑	End of heat
Mar. 6th Ching Chë	驚蟄	Feast of excited insects	Sept. 8th Pai Lu	白露	White dews
Mar. 20th Ching Fen	春分	Vernal equinox	Sept. 23rd Ch'iu Fen	秋分	Autumnal equinox
April 5th Ch'ing Ming	清明	Clear and bright	Oct. 8th Han Lu	寒露	Cold dews
April 20th Ku Yü	穀雨	Grain rain	Oct. 23rd Shuang Chiang	霜降	Hoar frost falls
May 5th Li Hsia	立夏	Beginning of Summer	Nov. 7th Li Tung	立冬	Beginning of winter
May 21st Hsiao Man	小滿	Grain fills	Nov. 22nd Hsiao Hsüeh	小雪	Early snow
June 6th Mang Chun	芒種	Grain in ear	Dec. 7th Ta Hsüeh	大雪	Great snow
June 21st Hsia Chih	夏至	Summer solstice	Dec. 21st Tung Chih	冬至	Winter solstice
July 7th Hsiao Shu	小暑	Slight heat	Jan. 6th Hsiao Han	小寒	Slight cold
July 23rd Ta Shu	大暑	Great heat	Jan. 21st Ta Han	大寒	Great cold

APPENDIX II

The Ten Celestial Stems (天干)

Stems		Five elements			Five cardinal points		
1. Chia 甲 } 2. Yi 乙 }		Mu	木	Wood	Tung	東	East
3. Ping 丙 } 4. Ting 丁 }		Huo	火	Fire	Nan	南	South
5. Wu 戊 } 6. Chi 己 }		T'u	土	Earth	Chung	中	Middle
7. Keng 庚 } 8. Hsin 辛 }		Chin	金	Metal	Hsi	西	West
9. Jen 壬 } 10. Kuei 癸 }		Shui	水	Water	Pei	北	North

Twelve Earthly Branches (地支)

Branches		Animals			Branches	Five Elements			Branches	Eight Points of Compass		
1. Tsu	子	Shu	鼠	rat	寅 卯 }	Mu	木	Wood	卯	Tung 東 East		
2. Ch'ou	丑	Niu	牛	ox					酉	Hsi 西 West		
3. Yin	寅	Hu	虎	tiger	巳 午 }	Huo	火	Fire	午	Nan 南 South		
4. Mao	卯	T'u	兔	hare					子	Pei 北 North		
5. Ch'en	辰	Lung	龍	dragon	申 酉 }	Chin		Metal	丑 寅 }	Tung-pei North-east	東北	
6. Ssu	巳	She	蛇	snake								
7. Wu	午	Ma	馬	horse	亥 子 }	Shui		Water	辰 巳 }	Tung-nan South-east	東南	
8. Wei	未	Yang	羊	sheep								
9. Shen	申	Hou	猴	monkey					未 申 }	Hsi-nan South-west	西南	
10. Yu	酉	Chi	鷄	fowl	丑 未 辰 戌 }	T'u		Earth	戌 亥 }	Hsi-pei North-west	西北	
11. Siu	戌	Ch'uan	犬	dog								
12. Hai	亥	Chu	豬	pig								

List of Temples administered by Government, exclusive of private places of worship belonging to clans or guilds
CHINESE TEMPLES*

Name of temple	Locality	God(s) worshipped	Date founded
Che Kung 車公	Shatin.	CHE KUNG— 車公	Said to be over 120 years old.
Chuk Neung 祝娘	Sai Tau Village, Kowloon City.	CHUK SHU SAM NEUNG— 祝 氏 三 娘	
Fung Sin Ku 馮仙姑	22, Tin Hau Temple Road.	FUNG SIN KU—Chu Sin Ku, 馮 仙 姑 祝 仙 姑 Ho Sin Ku and 何 仙 姑 Tong Sam Chong. 唐 三 藏	Between 30–40 years ago.
Fook Tak Che 福德祠	Shaukiwan.	TO TEI—Ng Tung, Kwun Yum, 土 地 五 通 觀 音 Kam Fa and 金 花 Chai Tin Tai Sing. 齊天大聖	Rebuilt 48 years ago.
Hung Shing 洪聖	Apleichau.	HUNG SHING—Pau Kung. 洪 聖 包 公	Said to be over 100 years old.
Hung Shing 洪聖	129–131, Queen's Road, East.	HUNG SHING— 洪聖	
Hau Wong 侯王	Kowloon City.	HAU WONG—Sik Ka Fat. 侯 王 釋 迦 佛	
Hau Wong 侯王	Tai O.	HAU WONG— 侯王	Said to be in existence for over 200 years.
Hung Shing & Pak Tai 洪 聖 北 帝	Shek Suen, Lantau Island.	HUNG SHING & PAK TAI— 洪 聖 北 帝	
Hung Shing 洪聖	Southern shore of Siu Ah Chau.	HUNG SHING— 洪聖	
Hung Shing 洪聖	On the shore at Shek Suen, Lantau Island	HUNG SHING— 洪聖	
Hung Shing 洪聖	Shek Po Tsai, Tai O.	HUNG SHING— 洪聖	
Hung Shing 洪聖	Fuk Tsun Street, Taikoktsui.	HUNG SHING— 洪聖	
Hung Shing 洪聖	Cheung Chau Island.	HUNG SHING— 洪聖	
Hau Wong 侯王	Tung Chung.	HAU WONG— 侯王	Said to be in existence be- tween 100–200 years.
Hung Shing 洪聖	Lantau Island.	HUNG SHING— 洪聖	
Kwun Yum 觀音	Apleichau	KWUN YUM— 觀音	
Kwun Yum 觀音	Rear of Li Po Lung Terrace.	KWUN YUM— 觀音	
Kwun Yum 觀音	4, Pound Lane.	KWUN YUM— 觀音	
Kwun Yum 觀音	36, Tai Ping Shan Street.	KWUN YUM—Tai Sui 觀 音 太 歲	Said to be over 100 years old.
Kwong Fook Che 光 福 祠	40, Tai Ping Shan Street.	TO TEI— 土地	
Kwun Yum 觀 音	Hunghom.	KWUN YUM—Pau Kung, 觀 音 包 公 Tai Sui, Kam Fa 太 歲 金 花 and Kwan Tai. 關 帝	Rebuilt 64 years age.
Kwan Tai 關帝	Kat Hing Street, Tai O.	KWAN TAI— 關帝	
Kwun Yum 觀音	Kowloon City- Shatin Pass.	KWUN YUM— 觀音	

Name of temple	Locality	God(s) worshipped	Date founded
Kwun Yum 觀音	Shantung Street.	KWUN YUM—Kam Fa, Tai Sui, 觀　音　金　花　太　歲 Pau Kung and 包　公 Kan Kung Fat. 簡　公　佛	Said to be in existence for over 70 years.
Lin Fa Kung 蓮花宮	Tai Hang I.L. 1351.	KWUN YUM— 觀音	
Mo Tai 武帝	Hoi Tan Street.	KWAN TAI—Lung Mo, Kam Fa, 關　帝　龍　母　金　花 Kwan Yum and Tai Sui. 觀　音　太　歲	Rebuilt 62 years ago.
Man Mo 文武	128–130, Hollywood Road.	KWAN TAI & MAN CHEONG— 關　帝　文　昌	Said to be over 100 years old.
Pak Tai 北帝	Lung On Street, Wanchai.	PAK TAI—Kwun Yum, 北　帝　觀　音 Sam Po Fat and Tai Sui. 三　寶　佛　太　歲	Said to be over 100 years old.
Pak Tai 北帝	Round the western corner of Stanley Bay.	PAK TAI— 北帝	
Pak Tai 北帝	Hok Un Kok, Hunghom.	PAK TAI—Wah Kwong, and 北　帝　華　光 Tsoi Pak Shing Kwan. 財　帛　星　君	Rebuilt 20 years ago.
Pak Tai 北帝	196, Yu Chow Street.	PAK TAI—Pau Kung, Wong Tai Sin, 北　帝　包　公　黃　大　仙 Kwun Yum and Tai Sui. 觀　音　太　歲	Said to be over 67 years old.
Pak Tai 北帝	Corner of Leven Road & Shung Yan Road.	PAK TAI— 北帝	
Pak Tai 北帝	Cheung Chau Island.	PAK TAI— 北帝	
Sui Tsing Pak and Tin Hau 綏靖伯	Tai Ping Shan Street.	SUI TSING PAK & TIN HAU— 綏　靖　伯　天　后	
Sui Tsing Pak 綏靖伯	12, Tik Lung Lane.	SUI TSING PAK— 綏　靖　伯	Established about 70–80 years ago.
Sam Tai Tsz 三帝子	198, Yu Chow Street.	SAM TAI TSZ—Pau Kung, 三　帝　子　包　公 Cheung Mo Fat 張　母　佛 and To Tei. 土地	Over 100 years & rebuilt 50 years ago.
Sheung Tai 商帝	Ma Tau Chung.	SHEUNG TAI— 商帝	
Sam Shan Kwok Wong 三山 國王	Ngau Chi Wan.	SAM SHAN KWOK WONG— 三　山　國　王	
Tin Hau 天后	Stanley.	TIN HAU—Tam Kung, Pak Tai, 天　后　譚　公　北　帝 Kwun Yum, Kwan Tai, 觀　音　關　帝 Lung Mo and Hong Kung. 龍　母　康　公	Said to be over 180 years old.
Tin Hau 天后	Tsun Wan, N.T.	TIN HAU— 天后	Said to be over 81 years old.
Tin Hau 天后	53, Main Street, Shaukiwan.	TIN HAU—Kwun Yum, 天　后　觀　音 Pau Kung, Kwan Tai, 包　公	

Name of temple		Locality	God(s) worshipped	Date founded
Tam Kung	譚公	Wongneichong	Tsai Tin Tai Shing and 齊 天 大 聖 Hoi Sum Fat. 開 心 佛 TAM KUNG—Pak Tai, 譚 公 北帝 Yin Tang Fat, 延 登 佛 Lung Mo, Wong Tai 龍 母 黃 大 Shin and Lui Cho. 仙 呂 祖	Said to be over 52 years old.
Tin Hau	天后	Wongneichong	TIN HAU—Kwun Yum. 天后 觀音	
Tam Kung	譚公	Shaukiwan.	TAM KUNG—Lung Mo, 譚 公 龍 母 Ng Tung and 五 通 Ngok Wong. 岳 王	Said to be over 50 years old.
To Tei	土地	Shaukiwan.	TO TEI— 土地	
Tin Hau	天后	Aberdeen.	TIN HAU—Wa To, Lung Mo and 天 后 華陀 龍母 Tsoi Pak Sing Kwan. 財帛 星 君	Said to be over 110 years old.
To Tei	土地	4, Lan Kwai Fong.	TO TEI— 土地	
Tin Hau	天后	Shek Tong Tsui.	TIN HAU—Sam Po Fat, 天 后 三 寶 佛 Pau Kung and Tai Sui. 包 公 太 歲	Said to be over 59 years old.
Tin Hau	天后	Tung Lo Wan.	TIN HAU— 天后	
Tam Kung Sin Shing 譚 公 先 聖		Aberdeen, A.I.L. 72.	TAM KUNG— 譚公	
Tin Hau	天后	Tai Tam.	TIN HAU— 天后	
To Tei	土地	Stanley (Pak Yeuk).	TO TEI— 土地	
Tai Wong	大王	Apleichau.	HUNG SHING— 洪聖	
Tin Hau	天后	49, Ha Heung Road.	TIN HAU—Yu Loi Fat, Tai Sui and 天 后 如 來 佛 太 歲 To Fa Sin Nui. 桃 花 仙 女	Said to be over 68 years old.
Tin Hau	天后	Ping Chau Island.	TIN HAU— 天后	
Tin Hau	天后	Fat Tong Mun (Joss House Bay).	TIN HAU— 天后	
Tin Hau	天后	Tai O.	TIN HAU— 天后	
Tin Hau	天后	On northern shore of Tai Ah Chau.	TIN HAU— 天后	
Tin Hau	天后	Tsing Yee Island.	TIN HAU— 天后	
Tin Hau	天后	S.D. 1 Lot No. 7118 & 7119.	TIN HAU— 天后	
Tin Hau 天后 and Hip Tin Kung 協天宮		Sai Kung.	TIN HAU & KWAN TAI— 天 后 關 帝	
Tin Hau	天后	Cha Kwo Ling.	TIN HAU— 天后	
Tin Hau	天后	Lantau Island.	TIN HAU— 天后	
Tin Hau	天后	S.D. 1 Lot No. 5316.	TIN HAU— 天后	
Tin Hau	天后	On the northern shore of Sha Lo Wan Bay.	TIN HAU— 天后	
Tin Hau	天后	180–184, Yee Kuk Street.	TIN HAU—Kwun Yum, To Tei, 天 后 觀 音 土地 Tai Sui, Tsai Kung Fat 太 歲 濟 公 佛	Rebuilt about 39 years ago.

Name of temple	Locality	God(s) worshipped	Date founded
		and Lung Mo. 龍 母	
Tin Hau　　天后 Tung Shan　　銅山 Tin Hau　　天后	Temple Street S.D. 2 Lot No. 1101. To Kwa Wan Island.	TIN HAU— 天后 Unknown. TIN HAU—Lung Mo and Kwun Yum. 天　后　龍　母　　觀　音	Rebuilt in 1951.
Tin Hau　　天后 Three Precious Buddhas 三　寶　佛 Wong Tai Sin 黃大仙	Lyemun. Shatin. Chuk Yuen Village, 　Kowloon City.	TIN HAU— 天后 SAM PO FAT— 三寶佛 WONG TAI SIN— 黃大仙	
Yuk Wong Kung Tin 玉　王　宮　殿 Yee Pak Kung 二伯公	Ah Kung Ngam, 　Shaukiwan. Quarry Bay, M.L. 　No. 1.	YUK WONG TAI TAI— 玉王大帝 NGAI SHEK LAU YEE PAK KUNG. 危　石　樓　二　伯　公	Said to be over 34 years old. Said to be over 60 years old.

B33　　*as in 1953/54.
　　　Names of gods are
　　　given in Cantonese.

INDEX

Adoption, 84, 86, 88, 91, 230, 231, 286, 287.
Agriculture, 10, 12, 13, 16, 70, 74, 183, 194, 220, 221, 251, 252, 280.
All Souls' Day, *see* Cheung Yeung.
Almanac, *see* Calendars.
Amah Rock (Yin Yang Shih), 83, 84, 140, 171, 232.
Amulets, 86, 137, 203, 204, 210, 231, 243.
Ancestor Worship, 1, 4–8, 16, 17, 42, 57, 69, 70, 71, 74, 84–91, 98, 103–105, 108–113, 118–124, 129, 132, 140–146, 150, 152, 157–160, 203, 207, 213, 229–232, 255, 262, 279, 286, 287.
Ancestral Tablets, 7, 57, 59, 82, 85, 86, 89, 96, 100, 101, 108, 116, 119, 142, 150, 152, 157, 190, 207, 208, 255, 262, 270, 279, 283, 291.
Animals, the Twelve, 80, 81, 219, 222.
Ape, the White (Monkey), 1, 12, 16, 27, 28, 142, 172, 173, 184, 207, 214, 215, 264, 266, 269.
Arahats, 259, 260.
Artemisia, 203, 207, 211.
Astrology, *see* Fortune-Telling.
Avalokitsvara, 13, 142.

Bank of Hell, 47, 59, 85, 120, 213.
Banyan Trees, 146, 160, 175, 232, 257, 267, 276.
Bats, 65, 86, 100, 114, 163, 166, 198, 206, 207, 209, 267, 281.
Boat People, 1, 3, 4, 8, 18–21, 25, 28, 37, 42, 50–53, 57, 68, 74, 87, 88, 92, 116, 139, 152, 173, 174, 181, 184, 206, 231, 235, 237, 264, 269–272, 277, 279, 283–291.
Bodhisatva, 13, 57, 142, 168, 176, 177, 205, 253.
Bodidharma (Ta Mo), 5, 72, 181, 257.
Branches, the Earthly (Ti Chi), 219, 222.
Breaths, the Solar, 10, 221, 222, 225.
Brides, 41, 74, 80–92, 203, 204, 212, 214, 232, 237.
Buddha, 2, 12, 16, 30, 39, 40, 48, 53, 57–59, 66, 101, 142, 155, 172, 173, 177, 184–186, 199, 211, 242, 255, 259–262, 272.
Buddha's Hand, 47, 206.
Bun Festival, 1, 3, 25–29.
Butterfly, 13, 16, 59, 62, 66, 83, 195, 205, 207, 215, 281.

Calendars, lunar and solar, 1, 7, 10, 13, 16, 75, 137–139, 169, 170, 189, 193, 219, 220–225, 227–285.
Calico Bag Monk (Pu Tai Ho Shang), 259.
Carp, 8, 62, 199, 201, 206.
Castle Peak (Ch'ing Shan), 253–260
Cat, 114, 191, 194, 198, 206, 214, 215, 240.
Celestial Weaver, 4, 41, 74.
Chan, *see* Three-legged Toad.
Chang Hsien (Protector of Children), 194, 214, 224, 233; *see also* Chang Kuo Lao.
Chang Kuo Lao (Taoist Immortal), 163, 166, 167, 169, 209, 214; *see also* Eight Immortals.
Chang Pao-tzŭ (pirate), 266, 272.
Chang Tao-ling (first Taoist Pope), 59, 80, 117, 140, 149, 175, 203, 222.
Chang T'ien Shih (title, Taoist Pope), 23, 73, 117, 128, 149, 150, 179, 203, 280.
Chao Hsuan-tan (a God of Wealth), 181; *see also* Ch'ao Kung-ming.
Chao Hun Fan (Spirit Calling Flags), 84, 105, 232, 268.
Ch'ao Hsiang T'i (an exorcist), 133.
Ch'ao Kung-ming (a God of Wealth), 7, 8, 23, 181, 274–276.
Charms, 55, 111, 117, 136, 137, 140, 149, 203–214, 222, 243, 252, 264.
Chen Lung, Marshal (the Snorter), 182, 183.

Ch'en Ch'i, Marshal (the Blower), 182, 183.
Cheng Ch'eng-kung (Koxinga: pirate), 61, 278.
Ch'eng Huang (City Gods), 5, 11, 70, 76, 136, 171, 178–180, 210, 232, 233, 266, 279.
Cheung Chau, 1, 3, 25–29, 36, 170, 189, 272–276, 293.
Cheung Yeung (Autumn Festival of the Dead), 5, 69, 70, 71, 72, 109, 140, 179.
Chi Kung (Mad Healer), 259–260.
Ch'i (Breath of Nature), 111, 112.
Ch'i Lin, *see* Unicorn.
Chiang (Empress), 222.
Chiang Tzu-ya (a Chou Dynasty commander), 183, 227.
Chiang Wang Yeh (Lucky Day God), 266.
Chickens, 74, 112, 176, 212, 219, 234, 292.
Chicken's Bride (proxy), 84, 85.
Chicken's Heart (amulet), 217.
Chieh Chih T'ui (of Ch'ing Ming fame), 17.
Chieh Yin Tao-jen (a celestial warrior), 227.
Ch'ien Lung (Reign title), 116, 215, 216, 230, 266, 270, 272.
Ch'ien Tang (Dragon King's brother), 184.
Chih Ma (cartoon of the Hundred Gods), 171, 213.
Chik Chu Wan, 51, 160, 266, 272, 290, 291; *see also* Stanley.
Chin Dynasty, 16, 81, 196.
Chin Ta Sheng (Celestial Marshal), 183.
Chin T'a, *see* Urns.
Ch'in Dynasty, 86, 181, 280.
Ch'in Kuei (a Sung Prime Minister), 180.
Ch'in Shih Huang Ti (Emperor), 67, 209, 217.
Ch'in Shu-pao (a Gate God), 78.
Ching Chë (Feast of Excited Insects), 1, 13.
Ch'ing Dynasty, 39, 186, 192, 209.
Ch'ing Hsu (Lenient Magistrate), 42, 50, 53, 55, 130.
Ch'ing Ming (Spring Festival of the Dead), 1, 16, 17, 70, 98, 109, 140, 179, 204.
Chiu Hua Shan (Buddhist Sacred Mountain), 177, 205; *see also* Four Sacred Mountains.
Chou (Wicked Emperor, Yin Dynasty), 176, 222.
Chou Dynasty, 20, 22, 150, 170, 174, 181–183, 196, 197, 214, 217, 226, 227, 270.
Chou Wang (Wicked Emperor, Shang Dynasty), 8, 80, 170; *see also* God of Joy.
Chrysanthemums, 69, 207, 260, 262.
Chu Hsi (Codifier of Feng Shui), 111, 204.
Chu Jung (a Fire God), 39, 176; *see also* Gods, Fire.
Chu Yuan-chang (Emperor), 179, 225, 270.
Ch'ü Fu (birthplace of Confucius), 177.
Ch'u Yuan (of Dragon Boat fame), 3, 36–38, 116.
Chuan Hsu (a legendary Emperor), 39, 176.
Chun T'i (a Taoist hero), 227, 228.
Ch'un Tsu (Dragon Boat Cakes), 37, 38.
Chung Chen (Emperor), 225.
Chung Kuei (Protector against Evil Spirits), 117.
Chung Li-ch'uan (Taoist Immortal), 3, 33, 163, 165, 168, 169, 209, 238; *see also* Eight Immortals.
Cicada, 96, 206, 216.
Clairvoyance, *see* Spiritualism.
Cock, 9, 12, 81, 84, 98, 100, 114, 117, 152, 194, 201, 206, 241, 245, 267, 268.
Coffin, 70, 71, 87, 96–100, 109, 111, 114, 118, 121, 130, 180, 203, 204, 282.
Comb, Broken, 135, 182, 282, 283.
Compass, 111, 112, 114, 181.
Conch Shell, 174, 202, 207, 211.
Confucius, 7, 11, 39, 40, 66, 71, 73, 87, 104, 123, 140, 143,

150, 153, 171, 177, 178, 181, 188, 192, 202, 211, 225–227, 232, 272, 277.
Constellations, 67, 68, 112, 117, 138, 169, 189, 224, 227.
Cowherd, 4, 41, 74.
Crane, 104, 105, 139, 152, 170, 174, 206, 208, 209, 231, 255.
Crane Brother, 274.
Cypress, 7, 9, 37, 98, 108, 203, 206, 208.
Cup Ferry Monk, *see* Poooi To.

Dark Altar (Hsuan T'an), 50, 135, 232, 264, 266.
Deer, 8, 139, 164, 166, 178, 200, 206, 208, 209.
Demons, Devils, 31, 37, 50, 51, 101, 104, 110, 116–118, 130–136, 146, 149, 173, 175, 176, 188, 189, 192, 200, 203, 204, 212, 214, 232, 243, 259, 264, 268, 288.
Demon King (Mo Wang), 22.
Diamond Kings, the Four, 183.
Divination (casting lots), 1, 8, 20, 21, 25, 32, 39, 45, 146, 185, 190, 212, 219, 224, 226, 232, 233, 268, 272, 282–285, 290, 291.
Divorce, 87, 92–95.
Dogs, 10, 12, 16, 62, 81, 112–114, 116, 120, 122, 137, 139, 176, 177, 189–194, 200, 203, 204, 212, 219, 231, 234, 240, 279.
Donkey, 130, 133, 134, 167, 184, 240.
Dragon, 1, 9, 13, 36, 39, 55, 62, 81, 82, 101, 111–113, 139, 163, 169–171, 174, 176, 180, 183, 184, 186–188, 190, 194, 196, 199, 200–203, 206, 207, 210, 212, 213, 217, 219, 221, 226, 232, 240, 252–255, 259, 260, 266, 269.
Dragon Boat Festival, 3, 36–38, 76, 116, 186, 198, 279.
Dragon Dance, 186, 200–202, 210.
Dragon Kings, 4, 11, 169, 170–172, 184, 270.
Dragon Mother (Lung Mu), 266, 269.
Dragons, the Nine, 31, 112, 113, 184, 269.
Dragon Prince (Lung Wang), 4, 39, 40.
Dragon-Tiger Mountains, Palace, 59, 73, 117, 149, 150, 280.
Dragon-Unicorn, 199.
Drum, Fish-head, 45, 52, 57, 103, 262.

Eagle, 139, 192.
Eclipses, 62, 194, 198.
Eight Buddhist Symbols, 53, 207.
Eight Characters, 81, 85, 104, 112, 136, 190, 204, 224, 287.
Eight Horses (Pa Chun), 174, 196.
Eight Immortals (Pa Hsien), 31, 33, 44, 153, 163–169, 173, 200, 206–209, 211, 213, 221, 222, 227, 238, 264, 284, 289, 290.
Eight Laws of Politeness, 39, 190, 235.
Eight Taoist Emblems, 53, 207.
Eight Treasures, 40, 101, 207, 210, 211.
Eight Trigrams (Diagrams), 108, 112, 113, 117, 172, 181, 190, 199, 204, 207, 211–213, 222, 226, 247.
Elephants, 183, 184, 191, 199, 200.
Elixir of Life, 33, 65, 66, 149, 165, 198, 203, 207, 260, 264; *see also* Pill of Immortality.
Empress Dowager (Tsu Hsi), 40, 71, 130, 150, 177, 191, 192, 199, 205, 208, 212, 219.
Epidemics, 5, 23, 70, 72, 117, 136, 179, 272–274.
Equinox, 67, 74, 75, 213, 221.
Erh Lang, 12, 194, 266.
Exhumation, 109.
Exorcism, 117–118, 133, 135, 136, 140, 268, 274.

Fan (Yu Mao Shan), 33, 163, 169, 207, 209, 238.
Fanling, 40, 57–59, 165, 255, 260–264.
Feng Hsin Ku (a Hong Kong temple), 266, 272.
Feng Huang (Phoenix), 81, 82, 101, 139, 167, 169, 171, 176, 186–188, 201, 207, 208, 213, 226, 232, 240, 252.
Feng Shui (Geomancy), 96, 98, 100, 109, 111–114, 119, 155, 189–191, 204, 219–222, 226, 278, 279; *see also* Fortune-Telling.
Five Cardinal Points, 44, 72, 118, 169, 205.
Five Colours, 44, 72, 138, 187, 201, 204, 205, 222.
Five Elements, 72, 138, 204, 205, 219, 222, 223.
Five Grains, 181, 204, 205.

Five Poisonous Creatures, 149, 198, 203, 205.
Five Rulers (Wu Ti), 5, 8, 44, 72, 73, 205.
Five Sacred Mountains, 5, 44, 72, 160, 205, 226.
Five Seasons, 72, 138.
Five Seers (Wu Sheng), 8, 133.
Five Tastes, 138, 204, 205.
Five Vessels (Wu Kung), 7, 16, 44, 68, 96, 157, 213, 232, 259.
Five Virtues, 188, 205, 207.
Flute, 41, 164, 167, 168, 207, 209.
Fly-whisk, 33, 163, 165, 209.
Fortune-telling (Astrology), 42, 65, 67, 70, 81, 85, 88, 89, 96, 104, 119, 137–139, 146, 174, 185, 189, 219–224, 226, 232, 262, 278, 282; *see also* Divination, Feng Shui.
Fox Fairies, 80, 125–129, 242.
Foxes, 125–129, 199, 200.
Four Bodhisatvas, 177, 205.
Four Elements, 73, 183.
Four Sacred Mountains, 73, 160, 205.
Fu Hsi (Legendary Emperor), 39, 80, 181, 190, 212, 226, 227, 247.
Funerals, 70, 87, 96–109, 111, 114, 133, 146, 213, 215, 221, 282–284.

Geese, Two White, 196–197.
Geomancy, *see* Feng Shui.
Ginger (emblem), 25, 31, 132, 203.
Ginseng, 241.
God of Agriculture, 11.
Gods, City (Ch'eng Huang), 5, 11, 70, 76, 136, 171, 178–180, 210, 232, 233, 266, 279.
Gods, Door, 8, 74, 119, 157.
God, Earth (T'u Ti), 5, 9, 12, 13, 21–23, 66, 74, 77, 78, 95, 108, 135, 140, 142, 146, 157–159, 175, 178–179, 181, 188, 200, 232, 251, 252, 259, 262, 267, 276.
Gods, Family, 7, 82, 152.
Gods, Farm, 1, 13.
Gods of Fertility, *see* Gods, Soil.
Gods, Fire, 4, 39, 171, 175, 176.
Gods, Gate, 8, 74, 78, 157, 264.
Gods of Grain, 251, 252.
God of Harvests, 13, 252.
God of Healing, *see* Second Uncle.
God of Horses (Ma Wang), 4, 182, 196.
Gods, the Household, 8, 9, 11, 100, 108, 157, 158, 160, 181.
Gods, the Hundred, 1, 11, 171–172, 213.
God of Joy (Chou Wang), 80, 169, 170, 221.
God, Kitchen (Tsao Wang), 5–9, 41, 63, 64, 76–78, 119, 140, 157, 158, 179, 181, 220, 221.
Gods of Literature (Kuei Hsing, Wen Ch'ang), 68, 170, 171, 181, 199, 266.
Gods of Locality, *see* God, Earth.
God of Locusts (Marshal Liu Men), 13, 200.
God of Longevity (Shou Hsing; Star God), 67, 68, 163, 169, 200, 206, 208, 209, 221, 289.
Gods of the Measure (Lu Hsing, Shou Hsing), 67, 68, 206.
Gods, the Nine, 146.
Gods, Soil (Gods of Fertility), 5, 10, 13, 67, 74, 135, 188, 221, 223, 251, 252, 255.
Gods, Star, 1, 10, 11, 41, 42, 67, 68, 113, 163, 168–171, 175, 200, 206, 208, 233, 289.
God of Thieves, 68.
God of Thunder (Lei Kung), 71, 96, 170, 180, 181, 224.
Gods of War (Kuan Kung, Kuan Ti), 78, 122, 171, 174, 179, 181, 182, 214, 259, 266.
Gods of Wealth, Affluence, 1, 7, 8, 22, 23, 67, 68, 78, 169, 171, 181, 198, 200, 206, 234, 264, 268, 274.
God of the Year, 170, *see also* T'ai Sui.
Goddess of Lightning, 71, 170, 180.
Goddess of Mercy, *see* Kuan Yin.
Goose, 164, 165, 176, 206, 207, 209, 262.
Guilds, 20, 23, 28, 31, 32, 61, 70, 143, 174, 177, 178, 201, 288.

Hakka, 21, 79, 86, 92–95, 98, 101, 106, 124, 136, 158, 160, 236, 237, 277, 279–283.
Halberds (emblem), 18, 27, 32, 78, 207, 214, 262; *see also* Swords.
Han jades, 216, 218.
Han Chung-li, *see* Chung Li-ch'uan.
Han Dynasty, 16, 66, 69–71, 149, 165, 174, 180–182, 186, 188, 191, 208, 214–216, 219, 277.
Han Hsiang-tzu (Taoist Immortal), 164, 167, 209; *see also* Eight Immortals.
Han Yu (9th Century Scholar), 164, 167, 257.
Happy Monk, *see* Poooi To.
Heavenly Hound (T'ien Kou), 12, 62, 194, 223, 224, 233, 266.
Hedgehogs, 8, 133, 189.
Heng O (Moon Lady), 62, 64, 198.
Heng Shan (Taoist Sacred Mountains), 72, 176, 205; *see also* Five Sacred Mountains.
Ho Ho (the Harmonious Pair), 198.
Ho Hsien-ku (Taoist Immortal), 40, 164, 168, 169, 209, 222; *see also* Eight Immortals.
Hoklo, 21, 92–95, 124, 237, 285, 291.
Horoscopes, 81, 85, 98, 139, 169.
Horses, 4, 10, 81, 111, 112, 139, 152, 174, 176, 178, 182, 186, 194–196, 212, 215, 219, 234.
Hou Wang (a Hong Kong divinity), 272.
Hou Yih (famous archer), 64.
Hsi Lin Monastery, 40, 262.
Hsi Shen, *see* Chou Wang.
Hsi Wang Mu (Queen of the Western Heaven), 12, 39, 64, 163, 164, 166, 172–174, 206, 208.
Hsia Dynasty, 22, 227.
Hsien Yuan (Emperor), 176, 181, 222.
Hsu Hsien-p'ing (Founder of T'ai Chi Ch'uan), 247.
Hsuan T'ieh Shang Ti, *see* Pei Ti.
Hsuan Tsang (Tripitaka), 12, 27, 28, 57, 172, 173, 191, 214, 257, 267, 269.
Hsuan Tsung (Emperor), 166.
Hu Yin-lin (a Ming scholar), 14.
Hua Kuo Shan (Monkey's birthplace), 172.
Hua Shan (Taoist Sacred Mountain), 72, 134, 164, 166; *see also* Five Sacred Mountains.
Huang Ku (the Emperor's Aunt), 278.
Huang Ti (Yellow Emperor), 39, 72, 176, 188, 189, 205, 219, 222, 226, 227.
Hui Lu (Disciple to the Fire God), 39, 176.
Hui Tsung (Emperor), 165, 278.
Hun (the Superior Soul), 132, 133, 153, 232.
Hun Tun (Winter solstice cakes), 74.
Hundred Names (Pai Chia Hsing), 225, 229.
Hung Hsing (a Hong Kong Divinity), 10, 28, 269, 270.
Hung Hsiu-ch'uan (founder of T'aip'ing Society), 280.
Hungry ghosts, 98, 100, 109, 116, 142, 150, 166, 189.
Hungry Ghosts, Festival of, 4, 42–61, 70, 103, 110, 129, 136, 140, 146, 176, 179, 289; *see also* Magnolia Festival.
Huo Sheng (a Fire God), 4.

I Ching (Book of Changes), 211, 212, 226.
Immortals, the Eight, 31, 33, 44, 153, 163–169, 173, 200, 206–209, 211, 213, 221, 222, 227, 238, 264, 284, 289, 290.
Indra, 172, 174, 180; *see also* Jade Emperor.

Jade, 71, 96, 101, 105, 109, 119, 128, 163–165, 167, 178, 182–184, 188, 196, 204, 206, 209, 210, 212, 215–218, 231, 281.
Jade Emperor (Yü Huang), 8, 14, 16, 22, 50, 77, 149, 171, 172, 183, 184, 221; *see also* Shang Ti.
Jade Lady, *see* T'ien Hsien Niang Niang.
Jade Rabbit, *see* Moon Rabbit.
Jade Vacuity, Temple of (Yü Hsü Kung), 1, 23, 25, 28, 170, 274–276.
Jen Tsung (Emperor), 167, 233.
Jizo (Japanese Ti Tsang Pusa), 177.

Johnston, Sir Reginald, 220, 238, 240, 259.
Joints, the Solar, 10, 221, 222, 225.
Joss House Bay, *see* Tai Miao.
Jupiter, *see* T'ai Sui.
Ju Yi (sceptre), 170, 200, 208.

K'ai Fong (Residents' Association), 50, 185, 267, 272.
K'ai Tzu-chu (first ancestral tablet), 150.
Kam Tin, 179, 278.
K'ang Hsi (Emperor), 139, 189, 213, 219, 278, 285.
K'ang Yu-wei (leader of Restoration Movement), 71, 177.
Kao Tsung (Emperor), 16, 39, 116, 183, 204, 216, 230, 235, 278.
Kat Hing Wai, 278.
Kitchen God (Stove Prince), 5–9, 41, 63, 64, 76–78, 119, 140, 157, 158, 179, 181, 220, 221.
Kites, 70, 174.
Koxinga (pirate), *see* Cheng Ch'eng-kung.
Krishna, 177.
Kshitigarbha, 176.
Kuan Kung (God of War), 1, 8, 11, 120, 122, 174, 179, 181, 182, 259, 266.
Kuan Ti (God of Wealth, of War), 3, 78, 171, 181, 214.
Kuan Yin (Goddess of Mercy), 1, 3, 14, 16, 18, 28, 34, 48, 50, 55, 57, 75, 79, 96, 101, 103, 105, 106, 128, 136, 142, 146, 171, 172, 175, 177, 184, 205, 232, 233, 255, 259, 260, 262, 266, 269, 277.
Kuang Hsu (Emperor), 150, 225, 230, 241, 272.
Kuei Ch'ai (death harbingers), 132.
Kuei Hsing (a God of Literature), 68, 170, 171, 199.
Kuei Shen (souls of the dead), 179.
Kuei Tang Ch'iang (Wall-building Ghost), 130.
Kuei T'i Tou (Barber's Ghost), 132.
K'un Lung Mountains (home of Hsi Wang Mu), 173, 206.

Lan Ts'ai-ho (Taoist Immortal), 164, 168, 169, 209; *see also* Eight Immortals.
Lantern Festival, 1, 4, 10, 62–66, 175, 186.
Lao Chun (preparer of Pills of Immortality), 172, 181–182.
Lao Tze (founder of the Tao), 50, 149, 163, 164, 166, 204, 227.
Lei Kung, *see* God of Thunder.
Lenient Magistrate, *see* Ch'ing Hsu.
Li Ching (Grand Marshal of the Skies), 176.
Li Ch'un (Beginning of Spring), 1, 10, 11, 75, 221.
Li K'ung Mu, *see* Li T'ieh-kuai.
Li T'ai Po (poet), 65.
Li T'ieh-kuai (Taoist Immortal), 33, 153, 164, 166, 169, 209; *see also* Eight Immortals.
Liang Dynasty, 72, 259.
Ling Chih (Long Life Mushroom), 67, 200, 206, 208.
Lion Dance, 1, 3, 20–22, 28, 32, 52, 53, 86, 121, 186, 190, 200, 202.
Lions, 50, 139, 171, 176, 188, 190, 191, 199, 200, 206, 231, 255, 259.
Liu Hai (a God of Wealth), 181, 198, 207.
Lo Hsuan (a Fire God), 175, 176.
Lohans, 259, 260.
Longevity, Emblems of, 7, 8, 50, 66, 67, 69, 86, 100, 104, 105, 108, 113, 149, 158, 163–165, 170, 176, 178, 195, 198, 200, 203–209, 215, 219, 225, 234, 239, 244, 247, 262, 276, 281.
Lotus, 4, 39, 40, 55, 57, 63, 65, 68, 86, 164, 198, 207–209, 211, 227, 259, 260.
Lu Hsing (a God of Wealth, Star God), 7, 67, 68, 169, 206.
Lu Pan (Master Builder), 1, 4, 11, 39, 171, 174.
Lu T'ung-pin (Taoist Immortal), 3, 33, 163–165, 167–169, 181, 209; *see also* Eight Immortals.
Lu Yu (author of the tea classic), 181.
Lucky Money, 5, 8, 76, 79, 82, 89, 91, 104, 105, 108, 188, 208, 213, 243, 262, 264, 282.
Lung Mu, *see* Dragon Mother.
Lung Wang, *see* Dragon Prince.

Ma Chu, *see* Kuan Yin.
Ma Ku, *see* T'ien Hou.
Ma Wang, *see* God of Horses.
Macao, 61, 112, 196, 197, 280.
Mad Healer, *see* Chi Kung.
Magnolia Festival, 4, 29, 42, 57–59, 259.
Mahjong, 21, 30–32, 89, 92, 114, 178, 240, 288.
Maitreya (Mi Lei Fo), 57, 255, 260, 270.
Malaria, 112, 132, 272, 279.
Manchu Dynasty, 8, 61, 70, 71, 81, 85, 98, 114, 123, 133, 143, 155, 181, 188, 191–193, 195, 197, 205, 208, 213, 214, 216, 222, 225, 235, 244, 245, 251, 259, 278, 280.
Manjusri, 191, 192.
Mao Shan Chiao (White Lotus Sect), 270.
Marco Polo, 64, 260.
Maritchi (Buddhist Mother of the Measure), 18, 255.
Master of Heaven, *see* Chang T'ien Shih, Chang Tao-ling.
Master of Rain (Yu Shih), 180.
Measure, Matron of the (Tou Mu), 18, 68, 233, 255; *see also* T'ien Hou.
Measure, the Northern (the Great Bear), 67, 68, 169, 189; *see also* Lu Hsing.
Measure, the Southern (Canopus), 67, 169, 206; *see also* Shou Hsing.
Medicine, 116, 136, 181, 184, 232, 241, 242.
Mei-jen (match-makers), 81, 85, 89.
Mencius, 227.
Meng Shen (Spirit Driver), 11, 221.
Mi Lei Fo (Buddhist Messiah), *see* Maitreya.
Min (Prince), 176.
Ming Dynasty, 8, 12, 14, 34, 41, 61, 67, 77, 101, 114, 155, 172, 175, 176, 178, 179, 188, 191, 196, 197, 199, 209, 213, 222, 225, 244, 245, 270, 277, 279, 280.
Ming Huang (Emperor), 117, 182.
Ministry of Exorcisms, 117.
Ministry of Fire, 175.
Ministry of Justice, 179.
Ministry of Medicine, 181, 227.
Ministry of Thunder, 180.
Ministry of Time, 122, 170.
Ministry of the Weather, 170, 171, 175.
Mirrors, *see* Spirit Mirrors.
Mo Wang, *see* Demon King.
Mon-kmer tribes, 274, 285.
Money Animals, 197, 198.
Mongol (Yuan) Dynasty, 64, 68, 179, 180, 225, 247, 270, 272, 277, 278, 280.
Monkey (the White Ape, Great Sage), 1, 12, 16, 27, 28, 142, 172, 173, 184, 207, 214, 215, 264, 266, 269.
Monkeys, 81, 215, 219, 269.
Moon Cakes (Yueh Ping), 4, 62–65, 121, 188.
Moon Festival, 1, 4, 10, 12, 62–67, 76, 78, 98, 121–123, 175, 188, 260.
Moon Hare/Rabbit, 64–66, 207, 260.
Moon Lady, *see* Heng O.
Mother Earth, 133, 221.
Mother of Lightning (T'ien Mu), 180.
Mother of the Measure, Buddhist, *see* Maritchi, Taoist (Tou Mu), *see* T'ien Hou.
Mother of the Western Heaven, *see* Hsi Wang Mu.
Mountebanks, 34, 66, 121, 168, 200, 202.
Mounting the Heights (Teng Kao), 5, 20, 35, 69, 70, 116.
Mu Kung (Counterpart of Hsi Wang Mu), 173.
Mu Wang (Emperor), 174, 196.
Mui Tsai (adoption through purchase), 84, 88, 230, 231, 286; *see also* Adoption.
Musical Instruments, 21, 31, 45–47, 51–57, 65, 70, 96, 103, 105, 117, 178, 186, 202, 268.

Nephrite, 215–218.
Netsuke, 215.

New Year Period, 1, 5, 7–10, 12, 66, 75–79, 85, 136, 146, 152, 157–160, 206, 213, 220, 235, 268, 291.
Nirvana, 211, 260.
North, Spirit of the, *see* Pei Ti.
Nuns, 57–59, 85, 100–106, 150.

O Mei Shan (Buddhist Sacred Mountain), 73, 177, 205; *see also* Four Sacred Mountains.
Ox of Spring, 1, 11, 221, 225.
Oxen, 10, 11, 41, 75, 112, 139, 178, 194, 212, 219, 234, 251.
Oysters, 9, 25–28, 277.

Pa Hsien, *see* Eight Immortals.
Pa Kua, *see* Eight Trigrams.
Pa Li Chuang Pagoda, 114, 155.
Pagodas, 53, 57, 109, 114, 155, 175, 176, 278.
Pai Chia Hsing, *see* Hundred Names.
Pak Tai, *see* Pei Ti.
P'an Ku (Architect of the Universe), 12, 189, 226.
P'an Kuan (Guardian of the Living), 117.
P'an Tao, *see* Peaches of Heaven.
P'an Tao Hui (Peach Banquet), 173.
Paper Money and Offerings, 1, 4, 5, 7, 10, 12, 16–20, 23, 25, 31, 32, 41, 47–61, 65, 68, 71, 72, 84–86, 88, 89, 98, 100–108, 110, 120–122, 124, 133, 135, 143, 146, 203, 213, 232, 243, 284, 288–290.
Paper Shops, 4, 23, 55, 62, 65, 77, 100, 136, 140, 172, 175, 213–215.
Patron Saints (Tzu She), 1, 4, 11, 13, 30, 33, 39, 41, 68, 78, 88, 120, 121, 157, 164, 165, 167, 168, 171, 174, 177, 178, 181, 182, 194, 198, 259.
Peach Blossom Maiden, 23, 274–276.
Peaches of Heaven (emblen of longevity), 8, 12, 33, 65, 67, 79, 104, 108, 163–165, 167, 172–174, 181, 198, 200, 204, 206, 209, 215, 289.
Peachwood, 7, 23, 78, 117, 118, 204.
Pearl, 8, 96, 174, 183, 186, 187, 200–202, 207, 210, 221, 253, 255, 266, 277.
Pearl River, 79, 196, 197, 272.
Pei Ti (Pak Tai, Spirit of the North), 1, 22, 23, 25, 28, 189, 266, 268, 274.
Pei Tu, *see* Poooi To.
Peking, 8, 12, 26, 33, 35, 39, 40, 70, 71, 75, 76, 81, 82, 87, 114, 128–131, 135, 153–157, 160, 170, 173–177, 189, 193–199, 206, 207, 212, 215, 216, 219, 226, 238, 241, 260, 262.
Pekingese Dogs, 113, 171, 190–194, 214.
Pen Ts'ao (Book of Essential Herbs), 181, 195.
Peony, 33, 101, 206, 207, 266, 267, 281, 288.
Perfect Emperors, *see* Shen Nung, Yao, Yu.
Pheasant, 80, 112, 187, 188, 207, 212.
Phoenix, *see* Feng Huang.
Pi Fang (Fire Bird), 176.
Pi Hsieh Ch'ien (Warding-off Evil Coins), 210, 214.
Pi Kan (Civil God of Wealth), 8.
Pig, 10, 74, 112, 139, 194, 212, 219, 228, 234, 251, 269.
Pigsy (Tripitaka's companion), 27, 173.
Pill of Immortality, 33, 62, 64, 66, 149, 165, 172, 198, 207, 260; *see also* Elixir of Life.
Pine (evergreen), 8, 9, 37, 66, 76, 104, 207, 208.
Plum (prunus), 33, 40, 75, 79, 207.
P'o (inferior soul), 131, 132, 153, 232.
Poooi To (Pei Tu, Cup Ferry Monk), 255–257.
Pomegranate, 40, 65, 207, 215.
Puppet Shows, 4, 31, 39, 44, 48, 52, 240, 267, 268, 284.
Pu Tai Ho Shang, *see* Calico Bag Monk.
P'u Hsien (Bodhisatra), 16, 177, 205.
P'u T'o Shan (Buddhist Sacred Mountain), 73, 142, 205; *see also* Four Sacred Mountains.
Purple Planet (Pole Star), 113, 170, 172, 214.
Purgatory, 4, 53, 101, 108–110, 140, 150, 152, 283; *see also* Underworld.

Queen of Heaven (T'ien Hou), 1, 3, 8, 10, 16, 18–21, 25, 26, 28, 30, 32, 37, 41, 50, 52–55, 68, 88, 105, 136, 142, 146, 152, 169, 170, 173, 179, 181, 188, 232, 233, 235, 255, 264–272, 284, 291.
Queen of the Western Heaven (Hsi Wang Mu), 12, 39, 64, 163, 164, 166, 172–174, 206, 208.

Rabbit, see Moon Rabbit.
Rabies, 193, 194.
Rams, 5, 8, 72, 112, 205.
Rats, 1, 11, 13, 81, 104, 114, 183, 189, 197, 200, 214, 219.

Sacred Rocks, 5, 51, 74, 83, 84, 140, 142, 146, 150, 157, 160, 171, 232, 264, 269.
Sacred Trees, 5, 51, 74, 77, 136, 140, 142, 146, 150, 157, 160, 232, 268.
Sacred Wells, 77, 158, 160.
Sakyamuni (Buddha), 3, 30, 180, 191, 211, 260.
San Kuan (Taoist Trinity), 9, 13, 61.
Sao Ch'ing Niang Niang (Lady with the Broom), 39, 180.
Séances, 4, 62, 118–125, 211, 213.
Second Uncle (Yee Pak Kung), 270, 272.
Secret Societies, 85, 213, 244, 245, 270, 272, 280.
Shamanism, 123, 192.
Shang Dynasty, 8, 22, 80, 123, 170, 182, 183, 227.
Shang Ti (Supreme Taoist Divinity), 169, 170, 172, 184.
Shao Lin Monastery, 72.
Sheep, 81, 122, 123, 194, 219, 251, 292.
Shen Nung (Father of Agriculture), 149, 180, 181, 226, 227, 251.
Shen Tsung (Emperor), 114, 155.
Sheung Sau Pu (Book of Life and Death), 130.
Shou Hsing (God of Longevity, Star God), 67, 68, 163, 169, 200, 206, 208, 209, 221, 289.
Shui Jen, see Boat People.
Shui Kuan (of the Taoist Trinity), 9, 13, 61.
Shui Mu Niang Niang (Mother of the Waters), 184.
Shui Shu Huang Ti (Water God), 266.
Snake, 1, 13, 22, 23, 39, 80, 81, 110, 133, 139, 176, 180, 183, 186, 189, 190, 219, 221, 226, 240, 247, 268, 277.
Solstice, 5, 36, 74, 75, 136, 138, 146, 213, 221, 268.
Spirits, Souls, 4, 17, 25, 29, 36, 42–61, 70, 71, 82, 96, 98, 100, 101, 112, 123–125, 129–132, 143, 146, 150, 153, 155, 179, 189, 203, 204, 206, 209, 210, 213–231, 242, 267, 282, 283.
Spirit Screen, 17, 78, 113, 176, 194, 212, 214.
Spirit Mirrors, 112, 113, 190, 199, 203, 204, 210, 212, 213, 288.
Spirit Calling Flags, see Chao Hun Fan.
Spiritualism, 4, 62, 118–125, 130, 135–137, 211, 213.
Spring, 1, 10, 11, 16, 75, 196, 251.
Stanley, 23, 25, 36, 50, 179, 188, 264–272, 278, 290, 291.
Star Gods, see Gods, Star.
Stems, Ten Celestial (T'ien Kau), 204, 219, 222.
Stove Prince, see Kitchen God.
Sui Jen Shih (a legendary sovereign, 226.
Sun Hou-tze, see Monkey.
Sun Worship, 1, 11–13, 65, 69, 74.
Sung Dynasty, 13, 14, 16, 34, 111, 152, 164, 167, 172, 179–181, 186, 215, 233, 237, 266, 270, 272, 277, 278, 280.
Sung Shan (Taoist Sacred Mountain, 72, 205; see also Five Sacred Mountains.
Swastika, 121, 146, 207, 211.
Sword (Chan-yao Kuei), 33, 164, 165, 207, 209.
Sword (for dispelling demons), 32, 37, 59, 117, 118, 132, 149, 203, 214, 274; see also Halberds.

Ta Ching (Reign title), 116.
Ta Han (Great Cold), 10, 75, 138, 236.
Ta Mo, see Bodidharma.
Tai Miao (at Joss House Bay), 1, 3, 18, 20, 72, 284.
Tai Mao Shan (New Territories), 277.
Tai Po, 40, 158, 277–279.

T'ai Chi (Buddhist Yin Yang symbol), 44, 84, 204, 207, 212, 213, 247, 249, 250.
T'ai Chi Ch'uan, 247–250.
T'aip'ing Rebellion, 71, 128, 150, 155, 244, 280.
T'ai Po Ching-hsing (Star God), 168.
T'ai Shan (Taoist Sacred Mountain), 34, 72, 73, 129, 175, 205, 212; see also Five Sacred Mountains.
T'ai Shih-chih (Mahasthama), 57, 255, 262.
T'ai Sui (Marshal Yin, Jupiter), 170, 204, 222.
T'ai Tsung (Emperor), 78.
T'ai Yi, see Purple Planet.
Talismans, 2, 9, 18, 44, 76, 77, 84, 88, 91, 111, 113, 117, 132, 135, 136, 140, 146, 149, 175, 203–218, 220, 222, 233, 243, 268, 282, 283, 287.
Tam Kung, 3, 8, 10, 30, 32, 36, 37, 146, 184, 185, 214, 235, 266, 269, 270, 272, 287.
T'ang Dynasty, 13, 16, 67, 68, 71, 75, 78, 80, 134, 142, 166, 168–170, 172, 179, 181–183, 191, 204, 213, 214, 237, 240, 244, 245, 259, 260, 270, 277, 278, 280.
T'ang Family, 277–279.
T'ang Lung-wen (a Hong Kong City God), 179, 279.
T'ang Ming Huang, see Ming Huang.
Tao (order of the Universe), 232.
Tao Chun (of the Three Pure Ones), 50.
Tao Kung (Reign title), 220, 255, 272.
Tao Yüan (Red Swastika Society), 121, 143, 146, 211.
Taoism, 8, 59, 61, 67, 68, 73, 77, 78, 80, 84, 96, 100, 105–108, 117–119, 134, 136, 139–150, 153, 158, 160, 165–167, 169–175, 180–185, 203–207, 209–228, 232–234, 243, 245, 253, 255, 260–262, 266, 269–274, 287, 289, 291.
Taoist Trinity, see San Kuan.
T'ao Hua Nu, see Peach Blossom Maiden.
T'ao T'ieh (mythical beast), 199.
Tea Plant (origin of), 72, 181.
Teng Kao, see Mounting the Heights.
Three-legged Moon Toad, 62, 64–66, 198, 207.
Three Pure Ones (Taoist Divinities), 44, 50, 55, 117.
Ti Chi, see Branches, the Earthly.
Ti Kuan (of the Taoist Trinity), 9, 13, 61.
Ti Mo (Black Patch Ghosts), 130.
Ti Ping (Emperor), 272.
Ti Shih, see Indra.
Ti Tsang Pusa, 57, 176, 177, 205, 262, 266, 268.
Ti Yu (Hell), 110, 177; see also Underworld.
Tibet, 44, 45, 55, 158, 183, 192, 193, 200, 204, 205, 220, 262.
T'ien Hon (Queen of Heaven), 1, 3, 8, 10, 16, 18–21, 25, 26, 28, 30, 32, 37, 41, 50, 52–55, 68, 88, 105, 136, 142, 146, 152, 169, 170, 173, 179, 181, 188, 232, 233, 235, 255, 264–272, 284, 291.
T'ien Hsien Niang Niang (Heavenly Lady), 34, 171.
T'ien Kan, see Stems, Ten Celestial.
T'ien Kou, see Heavenly Hound.
T'ien Kuan (of the Taoist Trinity), 9, 13, 61, 108.
T'ien Mu, see Mother of Lightning.
Tiger, 1, 7, 8, 13, 14, 51, 55, 59, 78, 81, 112, 113, 123, 133, 134, 139, 146, 149, 152, 169, 175, 183, 186, 188, 189, 195, 199, 203, 204, 213, 214, 216, 219, 226, 240, 247, 259, 260, 264, 277.
Tortoise, 22, 23, 39, 169, 170, 173, 186, 189, 190, 201, 207, 212, 213, 226, 228, 235, 268.
Trance, 18, 120, 133, 153.
Triad Society, 213, 244, 245, 280.
Trigrams (Pa Kua), 108, 112, 113, 117, 172, 181, 190, 199, 204, 207, 211–213, 222, 226, 247.
Tripitaka (Hsuan Tsang), 12, 27, 28, 57, 172, 173, 191, 214, 257, 267, 269.
Ts'ai Shen, see Gods of Wealth.
Tsao Wang, see Kitchen God.
Ts'ao Hon (Empress), 164, 167.
Ts'ao Kuo-chiu (Taoist Immortal), 164, 167, 209; see also Eight Immortals.
Tsu Hsi, see Empress Dowager.

Tsun Wan, 257, 259.
T'u Ti (Earth God, God of the Locality), 5, 9, 12, 13, 21–23, 66, 74, 77, 78, 95, 108, 135, 140, 142, 146, 157–159, 175, 178, 179, 181, 188, 200, 232, 251, 252, 259, 262, 267, 276.
Tung Chih (Winter solstice period), 74, 75.
Tung T'ien Chiao-chu (Taoist Commander), 227, 228.
T'ung T'ing Lake, 3, 36, 184.
Tzu Sun Niang Niang, 35, 80, 84, 140, 171, 232.
Tzu Sun Po Po (Bridal cakes), 80, 82, 84, 92, 232.

Underworld (Hell, the Shades), 4, 14, 22, 42, 47–61, 98, 100, 106, 110, 130, 140, 142, 150–153, 172, 173, 176, 177, 179, 213, 282, 283.
Unicorn, 28, 171, 176, 178, 186, 188, 190, 201, 208.
Unpredictable Ghost (Wu Ch'ang Kuei), 42, 50, 132, 264, 266.
Urns, 108, 109, 136.

Vampires, 130, 131, 133, 153.
Vegetarian Food, 4, 5, 9, 25, 47, 50, 59, 253, 257, 260, 262, 282.
Vishnu, 40, 155, 177, 180, 211.

Wan Li (Reign title), see Shen Tsung.
Wang Hsi-chih (famous calligrapher), 196–197.
Weasels, 8, 133.
Weaving Maid, see Celestial Weaver.
Weddings, 74, 80–95, 212, 213, 232, 234.
Wei Shen (Protectress of Flowers), 33, 40.
Wei T'o (Protector of Books), 57, 131, 255, 259, 260, 262.
Wells, 9, 41, 77, 96, 123, 124, 130, 158, 160, 251, 267, 272.
Wen Ch'ang (a God of Literature), 68, 170, 181, 266.
Wen Shu (Bodhisatva), 16, 177, 205.
Wen Tsung (Emperor), 277.
Wen Wang (Compiler of I Ching), 212, 226.
Weng Chung (the Ancestor), 216, 217.
Western Heaven (the Western Paradise), 64, 96, 98, 174, 227, 228, 284.
Willow, 11, 13, 16, 79, 117, 203, 204, 221.
Wolves, 133, 178, 193, 195.
Wu (Empress), 164, 166, 169.
Wu Ch'ang Kuei, see Unpredictable Ghost.
Wu Ch'eng-en (15th Century author), 173.
Wu Hsing Shan (Monkey's Prison), 172.
Wu Kung, see Five Vessels.
Wu Sheng, see Five Seers.
Wu T'ai Shan (Buddhist Sacred Mountain), 73, 177, 205; see also Four Sacred Mountains.
Wu Ti (Moon-viewing Emperor), 65, 72, 77, 174.
Wu Ti, see Five Rulers.
Wu Tsung (Emperor), 270.
Wu T'ung (Phoenix tree), 188.
Wu Yueh Chieh (Double Fifth), 36; see also Dragon Boat Festival.

Yang (male principle), 33, 50, 69, 75, 84, 111, 112, 173, 186, 188, 190, 197, 201, 204, 205, 207, 212, 219, 226, 232, 235, 247.
Yang Ko (Grain Dance), 67, 140, 202.
Yang Kuei-fei (famous concubine), 182.
Yao (legendary Perfect Emperor), 64, 138, 149, 166, 178, 188, 199, 221, 227.
Yao Wang (Drug Prince), 3, 181.
Yee Pak Kung, see Second Uncle.
Yeh Fa-shan (famous Taoist scholar), 166.
Yellow Emperor, see Huang Ti.
Yen Kuan Niang Niang (a healing divinity), 34.
Yen Lo (King of the Underworld), 4, 14, 42, 45, 48, 50, 57, 172, 176, 179, 213.
Yin (female principle), 50, 63, 69, 84, 111, 112, 173, 190, 204, 205, 207, 212, 219, 226, 232, 235, 247.
Yin Dynasty, 189, 222.
Yin, Marshal, see T'ai Sui.
Yin To Lo, see Indra.

Yin Yang Shih, see Amah Rock.
Ying Hsi (shadow puppets), 240.
Yo Shih Fo (the Healing Buddha), 57, 59.
Yü (legendary Perfect Emperor), 149, 227.
Yu Ch'ao Shih (a legendary sovereign), 226.
Yu Ch'ih Ching-te (a Gate God), 8, 78.
Yü Hsu Kung, see Jade Vacuity, Temple of.
Yü Huang, see Jade Emperor.
Yu Shih, see Master of Rain.
Yuan Chia (Emperor), 257.
Yuan Dynasty, see Mongol Dynasty.
Yuan Shih K'ai (Warlord), 179, 244.
Yuan Shih T'ien (Taoist Primeval Deity), 22, 227.
Yuan T'ien Shang Ti, see Pei Ti.
Yueh Ch'eng (home of Dragon Mother), 266, 269.
Yueh Fei (a City God), 1, 11, 171, 179.
Yueh Lao-yeh (Old Man in the Moon), 65, 80.
Yueh Ping, see Moon Cakes.
Yung Ch'eng (Emperor), 272.
Yung Lo (Emperor), 155, 197.